Brave New Hungary

Brave New Hungary

Mapping the "System of National Cooperation"

Edited by
János Mátyás Kovács and Balázs Trencsényi

LEXINGTON BOOKS
Lanham • Boulder • New York • London

Published by Lexington Books
An imprint of The Rowman & Littlefield Publishing Group, Inc.
4501 Forbes Boulevard, Suite 200, Lanham, Maryland 20706
www.rowman.com

6 Tinworth Street, London SE11 5AL, United Kingdom

Copyright © 2020 The Rowman & Littlefield Publishing Group, Inc.

British Library Cataloguing in Publication Information Available

Library of Congress Cataloging-in-Publication Data Is Available

ISBN 978-1-4985-4366-8 (cloth)
ISBN 978-1-4985-4368-2 (pbk)
ISBN 978-1-4985-4367-5 (electronic)

Contents

Acknowledgments   ix

Introduction: Historicizing an Anti-Liberal Turn   1
János Mátyás Kovács and Balázs Trencsényi

PART I: THE EMERGENCE OF THE REGIME:
IDEOLOGIES, SYMBOLS, AND VALUES   7

1 Reinventing Hungary with Revolutionary Fervor:
   The Declaration of National Cooperation as a Readers'
   Guide to the Fundamental Law of 2011   9
   Renáta Uitz

2 Totalitarianism without Perpetrators? Politics of History
   in the "System of National Cooperation"   29
   Ferenc Laczó

3 Civil Society in an Illiberal Democracy: Government-
   Friendly NGOs, "Foreign Agents," and Uncivil Publics   51
   Virág Molnár

4 Beyond Electioneering: Minority Hungarians and the
   Vision of National Unification   73
   Gábor Egry

5 The Role of Religion in the Illiberal Hungarian
   Constitutional System   95
   Gábor Halmai

6   The Right Hand Thinks: On the Sources of
      György Matolcsy's Economic Vision   111
      János Mátyás Kovács

**PART II: FACES OF SOCIAL ENGINEERING:
EXCLUSION, CO-OPTATION, AND REDISTRIBUTION**   **137**

7   Toward a "Work-Based Society"?   139
      János Köllő

8   The Fear of Population Replacement   159
      Attila Melegh

9   Votes, Ideology, and Self-Enrichment: The Campaign of
      Renationalization after 2010   185
      Péter Mihályi

10 Viktor Orbán's Propaganda State   211
      Miklós Haraszti

11 Ideology or Pragmatism? Interpreting Social Policy
      Change under the "System of National Cooperation"   225
      Dorottya Szikra

12 The Central European University in the Trenches   243
      Zsolt Enyedi

**PART III: HUNGARIAN *SONDERWEG* OR
REGIONAL BACKSLIDING?**   **267**

13 The Post-Communist Mafia State as a Criminal State   269
      Bálint Magyar

14 Democracy for Losers: Comment on Bálint Magyar   291
      Stephen Holmes

15 Nothing But a Mafia State?   303
      Balázs Váradi

16 What, If Anything, Can the EU Do?   311
      Jan-Werner Müller

17 Supply Side Revolution: The Consequences of the
      2015 Polish Elections   331
      Radosław Markowski

18 Regime, Parties, and Patronage in Contemporary Romania   357
      Silvia Marton

Conclusion: Hungary—Brave and New? Dissecting
a Realistic Dystopia 379
János Mátyás Kovács and Balázs Trencsényi

Index 433

About the Editors and Contributors 445

Acknowledgments

We wish to express our gratitude to the Central European University, Budapest, and the Institute for Human Sciences, Vienna, for supporting our research. Thanks are due especially to Mónika Nagy, Luise Wascher, and Christian Rogler for coordinating our research activities, to Stefan Gužvica for formatting the manuscript and preparing the index, and to Cody James Inglis for double-checking some of the texts. Last but not least, we are very grateful to Tom Bass for the linguistic editing of the contributions.

Introduction

Historicizing an Anti-Liberal Turn

János Mátyás Kovács and Balázs Trencsényi

Dystopia has acquired a new name. What was laughed at as "*Puszta-Putinism*" yesterday is called "Orbanism" today, reinforced by three consecutive election victories of Viktor Orbán and his Fidesz party (the Alliance of Young Democrats). It is described, with outright fear or defiant sympathy, as a regime that represents an alternative to modern liberal democracy in Europe and beyond. The Hungarian prime minister who, after proclaiming his "System of National Cooperation" (SNC) in 2010, was ridiculed as an epigone of Jörg Haider or Silvio Berlusconi, has become a role model in his own right, hailed as "Trump before Trump."

Currently, a substantial number of analysts put Hungary under the heading of "illiberal democracy," next to Turkey, Singapore, and Russia, or among "hybrid regimes" like Kazakhstan and Azerbaijan. Likewise, "Orbanization" (Orbanistan, Viktatorship, and so on) started serving as buzzwords for radical populism and nationalism as well as the decline of republicanism, the rule of law, and the welfare state. By erecting a fence along the Hungarian–Serbian border in order to block a stream of refugees in 2015–2016, Orbán became a populist icon, a gifted international troublemaker whose political influence may greatly exceed his country's actual power.

While the SNC has been expanding with breath-taking speed during the past nine years, social scientists focusing on Hungary were rather slow to catch up with new developments and seldom offered a sober and comprehensive understanding of the new regime. A good part of the literature revolves around Orbán's personality as well as spectacular metaphors to describe the regime while (a) neglecting a thorough empirical study of the nuts and bolts of the SNC, (b) ignoring their historical and comparative contexts, and (c) disregarding the ideational sources of the undertaking in particular. A fair amount of recent political science research has discussed the "stumbling" and "backsliding" of emerging capitalist democracies both in Eastern Europe and in the global South.[1] However, although Hungary features prominently in public discussions about the rise of authoritarianism,[2] in-depth book-length analyses of the Orbán regime are hard to find.[3]

During the 1990s, Hungary was used as a textbook example of consolidated liberal democracy. Today, scholarly literature often refers to our country as a model of an "inverse transition." How could these alarming changes materialize in the twenty-first century, two decades after the 1989 revolutions and a few years after the country joined the EU? In seeking to answer this question, our research group first examined the analytical vocabulary that has been used to describe the SNC in recent years. Do terms such as "illiberal democracy," "liberal autocracy," "post-communist mafia state," "mutant fascism," "electoral authoritarianism," to name some of the most popular labels, cover Orbán's regime appropriately? Why does it slip out of our hands, resisting definition? Are its amorphousness, incomplete nature, and variability the reason for that? Could the analysts become more successful if—rather than making snapshots—they would focus on the whole film of Orbanization? To be sure, capturing a multifaceted process of evolution that originates in numerous sources by freezing one, albeit controversial, still image such as "illiberal democracy" or "electoral authoritarianism" may create the impression of stability, matureness, and even authenticity, thereby reinforcing the regime's own apologetic discourse. Is the SNC a veritable system (writ large) or rather a calculated—almost systematic—move toward becoming a system? Undoubtedly, this large-scale attempt at social engineering is based on a *bricolage* of elements that once seemed to be incompatible. Does this fact guarantee the originality of the experiment? Finally, what role does Viktor Orbán play in constructing the regime carrying his name? Did he have a master plan of leaving liberal democracy behind and has he managed to collect absolute power under the new regime? How can he harmonize being a spiritual chief of a missionary movement and a strong-handed cynical architect of "national cooperation?"

Our volume goes beyond the initial shocks of (and lamentations on) "How could all this happen?" We wanted to avoid using emotional language in defense of the key values of liberal thought under attack. The authors set out to (a) explore, in their particular fields, the role of core ideas in constructing the regime; (b) trace its evolution and assess the (in)coherence of its emerging parts; (c) identify the precedents of the SNC in the Hungarian past and its counterparts in other Eastern and Central European countries; and finally (d) examine whether or not the regime constitutes an original type of emerging capitalism.

Brave New Hungary brings together leading representatives of various disciplines, generations, and persuasions inside and outside Hungary. The volume grew from a joint research project initiated in 2014 by *Pasts, Inc., Center for Historical Studies* at Central European University, Budapest, and the *Institute for Human Sciences* (IWM), Vienna, which led to an international conference in Vienna in June 2015 and a number of smaller meetings. The research process did not end there: over the past years, the participants have engaged in additional inquiries and new research partners joined the group.

The book consists of three main parts. Part I presents the historical and ideological roots of the System of National Cooperation, and the ways in which values, political doctrines, and symbols shaped its evolution in fields like the constitutional coup resulting in a new "fundamental law," the rediscovery of "mythic nationalism," or the invention of "unorthodox" principles in economics. Part II includes studies on the main socio-economic and cultural pillars of the regime, ranging from renationalization to workfare, social exclusion, and conquering the mass media. In Part III, the authors discuss the SNC in a comparative context, subjecting the thesis of the regime's uniqueness to critical scrutiny. The volume ends with the editors' conclusions, linking the research findings of the contributors to a broader discussion on the rise of anti-liberalism in Eastern and Central Europe and beyond.

NOTES

1. See, e.g., Collier and Levitsky 1997; Linz 2000; Carothers 2002; Fish 2005; Rupnik et al. 2007; Bunce, Stoner-Weiss, and McFaul 2009; Levitz and Pop-Eleches 2010; Levitsky and Way 2010; Cameron and Orenstein 2012; Innes 2013; Bermeo 2016.
2. See Müller 2013, 2018; see also the chapter on Hungary in Kirchick 2017, 40–70; as well as Scheppele 2013, 559–62; Levitsky and Ziblatt 2018; Krastev and Holmes 2018.
3. As regards Hungarian language publications, the only exceptions are a collection of essays edited by Bálint Magyar and Júlia Vásárhelyi 2014, 2015; Jakab and Urbán 2017; and Debreczeni 2017. Besides a political biography of Viktor Orbán written by Paul Lendvai (2017) as well as Bálint Magyar's analysis of the Hungarian "mafia state" (Magyar 2016, Magyar and Vásárhelyi 2017, Magyar 2019), the only existing volumes published in English on the SNC to date are a collection of essays edited by Péter Krasztev and Jon van Til (2015), which focuses on the lack of "domestic democratic agency," Paul Lendvai's (2012) book that ends with the advent of Orbán's regime, and András L. Pap's (2017) monograph, which examines the constitutional aspects of "national cooperation."

BIBLIOGRAPHY

Bermeo, Nancy. 2016. "On Democratic Backsliding." *Journal of Democracy* 27 (1): 5–19.

Bunce, Valerie, Kathryn Stoner-Weiss, and Michael McFaul, eds. 2009. *Democracy and Authoritarianism in the Postcommunist World*. Cambridge: Cambridge University Press.

Cameron, David R., and Mitchell A. Orenstein. 2012. "Post-Soviet Authoritarianism: The Influence of Russia in Its 'Near Abroad.'" *Post-Soviet Affairs* 28 (1): 1–44.

Carothers, Thomas. 2002. "The End of the Transition Paradigm." *Journal of Democracy* 13 (1): 5–21.

Collier, David, and Steven Levitsky. 1997. "Democracy with Adjectives: Conceptual Innovation in Comparative Research." *World Politics* 49 (3): 430–51.

Debreczeni, József. 2017. *Az Orbán-rezsim 2010–201?* Budapest: DE.HUKÖNYV Kft.

Fish, M. Steven. 2005. *Democracy Derailed in Russia: The Failure of Open Politics*. Cambridge: Cambridge University Press.

Innes, Abby. 2013. "The Political Economy of State Capture in Central Europe." *Journal of Common Market Studies* 52 (1): 88–104.

Jakab, András, and László Urbán, eds. 2017. *Hegymenet. Társadalmi és politikai kihívások Magyarországon*. Budapest: Osiris.

Kirchick, James. 2017. *The End of Europe: Dictators, Demagogues, and the Coming Dark Age*. New Haven, CT: Yale University Press.

Krastev, Ivan, and Stephen Holmes. 2018. "Explaining Eastern Europe: Imitation and Its Discontents." *Journal of Democracy* 29 (3): 117–28.

Krasztev, Péter, and Jon Van Til, eds. 2015. *The Hungarian Patient: Social Opposition to an Illiberal Democracy*. Budapest: CEU Press.

Lendvai, Paul. 2012. *Hungary: Between Democracy and Authoritarianism*. New York: Columbia University Press.

———. 2017. *Orbán: Hungary's Strongman*. Oxford: Oxford University Press.

Levitsky, Steven, and Lucan A. Way. 2010. *Competitive Authoritarianism: Hybrid Regimes after the Cold War*. Cambridge: Cambridge University Press.

Levitsky, Steven, and Daniel Ziblatt. 2018. *How Democracies Die: What History Tells Us about Our Future*. New York: Crown.

Levitz, Philip, and Grigore Pop-Eleches. 2010. "Why No Backsliding? The European Union's Impact on Democracy and Governance before and after Accession." *Comparative Political Studies* 43 (4): 457–85.

Linz, Juan J. 2000. *Totalitarian and Authoritarian Regimes*. Boulder, CO: Lynne Rienner.

Magyar, Bálint. 2016. *Post-Communist Mafia State. The Case of Hungary*. Budapest: CEU Press.

———, ed. 2019. *Stubborn Structures. Reconceptualizing Post-Communist Regimes*. Budapest: CEU Press.

———, and Júlia Vásárhelyi, eds. 2014 and 2015. *A magyar polip*, Volumes I and II. Budapest: Noran Libro.

———, and Júlia Vásárhelyi, eds. 2017. *Twenty-Five Sides of a Post-Communist Mafia State*. Budapest: Central European University Press.

Müller, Jan-Werner. 2013. *Wo Europa endet. Ungarn, Brüssel und das Schicksal der liberalen Demokratie*. Berlin: Suhrkamp.

————. 2018. "Homo Orbanicus." *The New York Review of Books*, April 5, 2018.

Pap, András László. 2017. *Democratic Decline in Hungary: Law and Society in an Illiberal Democracy*. Abingdon: Routledge.

Rupnik, Jacques, Martin Butora, Bela Greskovits, Ivan Krastev, Alina Mungiu-Pippidi, Krzysztof Jasiewicz, and Vladimir Tismaneanu. 2007. "Is East-Central Europe Backsliding?" *Journal of Democracy* 18 (4): 5–64.

Scheppele, Kim Lane. 2013. "The Rule of Law and the Frankenstate: Why Governance Checklists Do Not Work." *Governance* 26 (4): 559–62.

Part I

THE EMERGENCE OF THE REGIME

IDEOLOGIES, SYMBOLS, AND VALUES

Chapter 1

Reinventing Hungary with Revolutionary Fervor

The Declaration of National Cooperation as a Readers' Guide to the Fundamental Law of 2011

Renáta Uitz

In the general elections of 2010, the Christian conservative coalition of Fidesz (Alliance of Young Democrats) and KDNP (Christian Democratic People's Party) led by Viktor Orbán won 52.73 percent of the vote. Due to the distortions of the election system, Fidesz's electoral victory translated into a two-thirds majority in parliament. This permitted the winners to write a new constitution for Hungary, titled the Fundamental Law.[1] The president of the republic signed it on April 25, 2011, during the Easter weekend.

The Fundamental Law instantly attracted criticism (especially Bánkuti, Halmai, and Scheppele 2012; Halmai 2012; Tóth 2012) and was received with reservations by European constitutional actors, such as the Council of Europe's expert panel on democracy (the Venice Commission), the European Commission, the European Parliament, and also the European Court of Human Rights. Critics argued that the Fundamental Law is a product of an anti-democratic, illiberal, or populist turn in Hungarian politics and highlighted the threats it presents to the rule of law. Hungarian and foreign scholars routinely noted its faults such as its rushed adoption in parliament without the involvement of the parliamentary opposition or broader public participation, its zeal to incapacitate the Constitutional Court, its numerous subsequent amendments adopted in defiance of the Constitutional Court and European constitutional actors, its systemic removal of institutional constraints on the exercise of raw political power (checks and balances) – and the list goes on.

Admittedly, the Fundamental Law preserved Hungary's parliamentary form of government, complete with an indirectly elected president, and also left the Constitutional Court in place (with strategic alterations). The most significant structural changes affected the architecture of the judiciary, including the creation of a powerful president for the National Office for the Judiciary. Independent institutions (such as the National Bank, the State Audit Office, and the ombudsman) were also preserved but with altered powers. Key constitutional actors, such as the chief justice of the Supreme Court (*Kúria*), the prosecutor general, and the president of the National Office of the Judiciary, are elected for a nine-year term, while the justices of the Constitutional Court and the president of the State Audit Office are elected for 12 years by a two-thirds majority in parliament. Such lengthy terms of appointment enable the current parliamentary majority to staff key constitutional offices with friendly appointees, thus undermining the ability of these bodies to serve as checks on the political majority of the day – and also imposing uncomfortable constraints on future majorities with different political colors.

After its Fourth Amendment most Hungarian constitutional scholars appear to agree that the Fundamental Law has departed from the minimum standards of European constitutionalism (Sonnevend, Jakab, and Csink 2015), but less wary observers (Küpper 2012) and the Hungarian government often point out that similar rules exist in other constitutions. Admittedly, the parliamentary form of government is the perfect setup to empower a prime minister backed by a disciplined parliamentary majority. The rest is a matter of politics not constitutional design. As for politics, the architect of the Fundamental Law appears to be committed to a form of managed democratic rule, willingly submitting to national elections, organized according to the regular constitutional calendar, so long as they return an overwhelming majority for the ruling party. The election rules fundamentally redesigned in 2013 did just that, giving Fidesz a two-thirds majority in parliament in 2014 and 2018.[2]

Attempting to draw attention to the constitutional crisis in Hungary, scholars and commentators invariably called it populist, illiberal, an "unconstitutional constitution" (e.g., Scheppele 2014), and, even more dramatically, a "constitutional coup" (Scheppele 2014; Vörös 2017), a "Frankenstate" (Scheppele 2014), and populist authoritarianism (Müller 2018). More broadly, Hungary is viewed as being symptomatic of a global democratic backslide or authoritarian backlash. The debate on the proper labeling of the Hungarian constitutional regime was put to rest in the summer of 2014 when Prime Minister Orbán proclaimed that he intended to build an illiberal democracy in the heart of Europe.[3] Although a political actor's own words can hardly replace scholarly analysis, in light of this statement it is time to begin the quest to find the right label for the Fundamental Law among the global family of constitutions and investigate what difference it makes if scholars settle on it as a "sham" (after Law and Versteeg 2013) or an "abusive" constitution (after

Landau 2013). In brief, time has come to inquire into *what a constitution does* (or at least is expected to do) exactly *for a self-proclaimed illiberal regime* in twenty-first century Europe.

To do so, the adoption and subsequent tweaking of the Fundamental Law needs to be discussed in the broader political and discursive context where it was created. Just before the constitution-making project was launched, in June 2010 the newly seated Hungarian Parliament adopted the Declaration of National Cooperation,[4] a document that can serve as a handy readers' guide about the Fundamental Law's constitutional reality. The terms of the Declaration of National Cooperation reveal how strategic constitutional engineering was used to reclaim "Hungary for the Hungarians" in a pseudo-revolutionary fervor. In this quest the Fundamental Law is one building block among many legal and constitutional measures adopted over the course of several years among elements such as a media law reform, an election reform, a judiciary reform, to name a few. As a calculated side-effect, the same legal measures also serve more pragmatic purposes like political self-perpetuation and a profound redistribution of wealth (patronage).

The Declaration of National Cooperation does not establish a coherent grand ideological frame for constitutional transformation. Instead, it provides an elastic web of references to explain a long-term political project (Enyedi 2015, 230). The point of meticulous constitutionalization and legalization of key moves is not about seeking legitimation by manufacturing compromise or consensus. Rather, legalization serves as a way of documenting measures taken in the name of the people (but without the participation of their representatives) to mark the boundaries of the regime and to scare off all those who do not belong. Thus, legalization has little to do with adherence to the rule of law; it is about formalizing the product of the naked exercise of political powers via the most public display of governmental will: the *Official Gazette* (*Magyar Közlöny*).

PRELUDE: CONSTITUTIONS AND CONSTITUTION-MAKING IN ILLIBERAL REGIMES

Prime Minister Orbán's illiberal regime and its constitution are hardly unique: the constitutions of democracies are outnumbered by the constitutions of other types of regimes around the world (Elkins, Ginsburg, and Melton 2014, 145–46). Nonetheless, as far as their texts are concerned, even clearly authoritarian constitutions differ way too little from democratic ones (Elkins, Ginsburg, and Melton 2014, 141–64). Detectable differences appear in the absence of safeguards for judicial independence and weaker constraints on the executive (Elkins, Ginsburg, and Melton 2014, 152, 155–56). Yet, the scope and nature of executive powers in the black letters of authoritarian constitutions do not offer an obvious script for the unconstrained and arbitrary exercise of powers as witnessed in the political practice of such regimes. In fact, a narrow focus on technical constitutional details easily hides key features of a regime, as it draws away attention from patterns that characterize the exercise of political powers under a constitution. Such patterns are revealed only when the analysis focuses on the rationale for the adoption or amendment of particular constitutional provisions.

Although constitution-making in 2010 was a surprise in Hungary (as it was not on Fidesz's election program), even the adoption of the Fundamental Law has been a gradual process. The process commenced in parliament in June 2010 with the appointment of a drafting committee.[5] On July 5, 2010, parliament amended the 1989 Constitution to eliminate the most important obstacle to making a new constitution with a two-thirds majority by removing the requirement that called for a four-fifths majority to introduce the detailed rules on making a new constitution (Article 24(5)) (see Arató 2010). With the same amendment, the ruling majority also altered the manner of election of Constitutional Court justices, signaling that the Constitutional Court was not beyond the reach of its ambitions. By the time the Fundamental Law was adopted, the 1989 Constitution had been amended several times, and this wave of adjustments did not cease even after the completion of the Fundamental Law in the spring of 2011.

The parliamentary committee's initial draft was downgraded to a concept note after a debate on the protection of fetal life made the project so precarious that Prime Minister Orbán personally intervened in the preparations. Drafting was then transferred to a committee of three Hungarian expert politicians who made their product famous for drafting it on an iPad (Simon 2011). The draft constitution was made public on March 14, 2011. Parliament adopted the Fundamental Law on April 18, 2011, solely by the votes of the governing coalition, without votes from the opposition.

The adoption of the Fundamental Law was meant to be a major landmark in Hungary's constitutional transformation, and it was to be implemented by a series of statutes adopted by Parliament (many of these, the so-called cardinal laws, requiring two-thirds majorities). Except that in the frenzy of transformative lawmaking, by June 14, 2016, the Fundamental Law was amended six times (not including transitional provisions that were invalidated by the Constitutional Court in December 2012).[6] Enthusiasm for amendments cooled but did not cease altogether, when Fidesz lost its constitution-making majority in parliament shortly after the 2014 elections.[7] As soon as Fidesz returned with a confident two-thirds majority in 2018, the Fundamental Law was adjusted to daily political needs with the Seventh Amendment that enables the defense of Hungarian constitutional identity against Europe, imposes restrictions on seeking asylum, and also enables the creation of new administrative courts.

PLACING THE FUNDAMENTAL LAW IN THE SYSTEM OF NATIONAL COOPERATION: THE CONTEXT OF ITS CREATION AND ITS CONSEQUENCES

The opening passages of the "first unified Fundamental Law of Hungary" declare it to be "the basis of our legal order: it shall be an alliance among Hungarians of the past, present, and future. It is a living framework expressing the nation's will and the form in which we wish to live," adding that "We, the citizens of Hungary, are ready to found the order of our country upon the cooperation of the nation."

When reinserted into the context of its inception, the opening passages of the Fundamental Law outline an ambitious political project. Once he was requested to form a cabinet, on May 14, 2010, prime minister-elect Viktor Orbán recalled to the freshly convened parliament what conservative Prime Minister József Antall (1990–1993) used to say in the early years of the transition to democracy when deputies complained about the slow pace of the reforms. Antall's response was, "You should have made a revolution instead." In 2010, Orbán continued by acclaiming that "And now we did just that. So let us recognize the revolution that took place in the polling booth and take responsibility for building a system of national cooperation founded by Hungarians" (Orbán 2010). At the time Orbán's appeal to a revolutionary mandate sounded like sheer pathos, without practical consequences. Then the newly elected parliament passed a political declaration, announcing the System of National Cooperation (*Nemzeti Együttműködés Rendszere*). This preceded the establishment of the constitutional drafting committee by two weeks.

According to the Declaration of National Cooperation the elections of 2010 amounted to a new social contract. The declaration describes the new order as one based on a constitutional revolution (*alkotmányos keretek között megvívott forradalom*), stemming from democratic popular will (*demokratikus népakarat alapján létrejött*) and rejecting compromises (*megalkuvást nem tűrve*). To honor the revolution that was discovered after the fact, the government passed a resolution on the requirements for the proper display of the Declaration on the System of National Cooperation in government buildings.[8] Specifically, the display was expected to be in color, at least 50 centimeters by 70 centimeters in size, mounted in a dignified manner. The resolution provides for maintaining the proper condition of the display as well as its replacement, when necessary. In response, the Office of the President László Sólyom, the Constitutional Court, and the judiciary under the direction of the National Judiciary Council refused to display the declaration.[9] This was the first major instance of open constitutional conflict between the ruling political majority and those governmental actors that by design were meant to impose constraints on the newly elected government and its overwhelming majority in parliament. In the months and years to come the judiciary was taught a lesson about their proper place in the new constitutional regime via means (for instance, multiple constitutional amendments, court packing, removal from office, and tweaking of jurisdiction) that were sharply criticized by European constitutional actors. These measures were all adopted in the spirit of national cooperation, as formulated by the declaration.

The spirit of national cooperation was invoked shortly after the elections of 2010 (and before the adoption of the Declaration of National Cooperation by Parliament) in a widely cited study by *Századvég,* the think tank tied with numerous personal and financial ties to Fidesz. The study explained the System of National Cooperation as a regime free of abstract ideologies and as a system characterized by pragmatic daily decisions (G. Fodor, Fűrész, and Giró-Szász 2010). This was meant to be in contrast to the ideology-laden transition to democracy. Note that the problem with transition or reform was not so much that it suggested slow, peaceful transformation (as opposed to violent rupture) but that the notion of transition has become associated with transition to (constitutional) democracy since 1989.

As promised in the Declaration of National Cooperation, the Fundamental Law has served as a legal tool for gradually reinventing the political community as "Hungary for the Hungarians," in line with the revolutionary sentiment expressed in the polling booth. At first glance, the preamble of the Fundamental Law, the creatively titled National Avowal, and Article U, added by the Fourth Amendment, suggest that the Fundamental Law is a symbolic constitutional identity project. Indeed, many have observed that the Fundamental Law's symbolic proclamations point in competing directions. It seeks to situate itself in the Hungarian constitutional canon with an appeal to the "achievements of the historical constitution" (Article R(3)) and also with marking Hungary's contributions to Europe's struggles and successes. The National Avowal expresses that "We are proud that our king Saint Stephen built the Hungarian State on solid ground and made our country a part of Christian Europe one thousand years ago" and also reminds readers that "our people has over the centuries defended Europe in a series of struggles and enriched Europe's common values with its talent and diligence." Article U denounces communism at length, and the National Avowal proclaims the invalidity of the 1949 Stalinist constitution, saying that "[w]e do not recognize the communist constitution of 1949, since it was the basis for tyrannical rule; therefore we proclaim it to be invalid."

In legal circles the discontinuity clause is cause for a major legal headache: the Fundamental Law was adopted in compliance with the 1949 Constitution, profoundly revised in 1989 and with subsequent amendments. In order to overcome this obvious legal challenge, constitutional lawyers suggest treating the National Avowal's discontinuity clause as an instance of "mere political rhetoric" that does not affect formal constitutional continuity (Sonnevend, Jakab, and Csink 2015, 67). (In practice the argument of constitutional discontinuity has not been raised seriously, as the wiping out of an entire legal system overnight would result in insurmountable legal and practical problems.)

Although the symbolic layer of the Fundamental Law is convoluted, a deeper engagement with constitutional and legal developments on the ground suggests that it has enabled the creation of a new Hungary on the pragmatic political and legal level along the lines envisioned in the Declaration of National Cooperation. Note at the outset that the Fundamental Law was meant to be a historic founding gesture for a new Hungary. Still, the Fundamental Law did not end up constraining its creators, as a constitution in the spirit of constitutionalism would be expected to do. Rather, it was adjusted in order to enable the legalization of such political moves that were justified with reference to ideas and commitments expressed in the Declaration of National Cooperation. In practice, the Declaration of National Cooperation serves not so much as a political manifesto but also as a loose web of references in which future political measures could be fitted and justified creatively and on the fly – exactly as explained by the *Századvég* study in 2010.

The result is that the constitutional reality of the Fundamental Law is difficult to capture through legal analysis alone: when the maze of legal measures and piecemeal adjustments are recorded, legal analysis alone cannot show the practical effect of these changes on the ground. At the same time, social science analysis often falls short of making sense of practical developments in earnest, as the ideology connecting the dots is too flexible and malleable to hold up to a methodology insisting on unveiling a clearly defined ideology (e.g., a populism of a certain kind) on account of practical measures (against the odds, see Enyedi 2015; Bátory 2016). A context-sensitive analysis would need to acknowledge that instead of executing a strict ideological agenda, the Hungarian government keeps adopting political and economic measures in the form of legal rules that are justified by terms enshrined in the Declaration of National Cooperation.

THE DECLARATION OF NATIONAL COOPERATION AS A READERS' GUIDE: RECLAIMING HUNGARY FOR THE HUNGARIANS

Reclaiming Hungary for the Hungarians requires defining both who is and is not Hungarian. As such, it is not a mere rhetorical exercise in political symbolism but a political program carried out in practice.

Hungarians have been understood by the government to include all persons of Hungarian descent, irrespective of their physical location. This is a departure from the 1989 Constitution that placed the locus of sovereignty in the people living inside the geographical boundaries of the Republic of Hungary (Article 2(2)). The Fundamental Law guarantees Hungarian citizenship by birth, on account of being born to Hungarian parents (Article G(1)). With the electoral reform of 2013, Hungarian citizens living abroad became eligible to vote in the national elections even without a registered address in Hungary. With this extension the Orbán government sought the votes of Hungarian minorities living in neighboring countries that were cast by a postal ballot. At the same time, Hungarian citizens living abroad who maintained a registered Hungarian residence were required to vote in person at embassies and consulates (but not by mail). The distinction is not accidental: while Hungarian minorities in neighboring countries are expected to be conservative, Hungarians living abroad who have a registered Hungarian address are suspected of being dissenters, who left in search of a better life after the 2010 elections.

The Fundamental Law's anthropological presuppositions about a proper Hungarian are clear: she is a God-fearing (preferably Christian) married individual who is willing to make sacrifices for family (also in the form of supporting her elderly parents, see Article XVI(4)) and country: the National Avowal proclaims that "individual freedom can only unfold through cooperation with others." This is a departure from a constitutional regime that posits the protection of individual liberty as its cornerstone. Unlike its predecessor, the Fundamental Law explicitly protects fetal life (Article II) and privileges family based on heterosexual marriage "as the basis of the survival of the nation" (Article L(1)). In light of this, it is hardly an accident that discrimination based on sexual orientation or gender identity is not prohibited expressly by the Fundamental Law (Article XV(2)). In practice such nuances depend on the implementing legislation and, ultimately, on the Constitutional Court.

According to the Declaration of National Cooperation "[w]ork, home, family, health and order will be the pillars of our shared future." These key elements are traceable in the regular functioning of the political process under the Fundamental Law, and the Hungarian government seems unconcerned that the protection of marriage-based families (especially after the Fourth Amendment) does not resonate with demographic data on Hungarian families (who increasingly tend to share households without being married) or that privileging similarly situated married couples over unmarried ones without objective reasons runs counter to European human rights standards.

In June 2015 the prime minister emphasized that, as a result of deep structural renewal, Hungary was "not a welfare society, it's a labor-based or work-fare society."[10] This resulted in the overhauling of the social welfare system to a public works regime in which even people with disabilities were included. The basis for these measures was established in the Fundamental Law, providing in Article XIX(3) that the "nature and extent of social measures may be determined by an Act also *in accordance with the usefulness to the community of the beneficiary's activities*" (emphasis added). The European Court of Human Rights found that despite such systemic aims and the need to rationalize government spending, stopping the disability pension of an applicant retroactively, by the force of law, violates European human rights standards.[11]

The project of reclaiming Hungary for the Hungarians builds on a continuously reinforced us vs. them dichotomy. The concept of the demonized "other" is rather flexible, and it ranges from generic foreigners, "Europe" and its supporters, to refugees and migrants, to Roma, George Soros, and to literally anyone who has the capacity or dares to dissent.

Since the Charlie Hebdo attack in Paris in early 2015, Prime Minister Orbán has taken an outspoken stance against immigration in Europe. This anti-immigrant rhetoric is fueled not so much by the increased visibility of refugees or migrants in Hungary but by the rise in the popularity of the far-right wing party, Jobbik, which has grown to be the largest opposition party since the spring of 2015. Insisting on labeling refugees as "economic migrants" and emphasizing the pressure they place on the Hungarian economy, the Hungarian government became (in)famous in Europe for its inhumane treatment of refugees during the peak of the crisis in 2015, building a fence on its southern border and engaging in hate-filled propaganda against refugees.

Coinciding with the marginalization of the parliamentary opposition, nongovernmental organizations (NGOs) became more prominent in the public debate (to the extent the Hungarian media space permits), seeking to remind the public about constitutional minimums and human rights standards. Many also use freedom of information requests to ensure at least a minimal level of transparency about governmental operations. As a result of limitations on meaningful public debates on the national level, European monitoring and control mechanisms have become crucial for voicing dissent against domestic developments. Hungary's leading civil rights NGOs have been successful public interest litigators before European courts for years. In the era of the Fundamental Law, their efforts target key pieces of the government's constitutional reform project (Bátory 2014; Uitz 2014; Uitz 2017a).

In response, the government chose a multifaceted strategy to neutralize NGOs: in addition to founding and funding its own NGO-like entities (quangos), it decided to put the funding of independent NGOs under closer scrutiny, in the form of harassment through tax audits and transparency rules. As a complementary measure, the government found it necessary to install restrictions on the operation of private universities accredited abroad, targeting the Central European University (see further Uitz 2017b). As the *coup de grâce*, in early 2018, the government tabled a second bill, further stigmatizing foreign-funded NGOs with a bill officially titled "Stop Soros."[12] The aim of this measure is to impose a special tax on organizations support-ing or sponsoring illegal migration with foreign funding. By the time the Stop Soros package was adopted after the 2018 elections, it was complete, along with a measure criminalizing the assistance of illegal migration and any sort of alleged public or media support for migration.[13] The president of the Venice Commission pleaded with the Hungarian Foreign Minister to no avail for halting the parliamentary vote on the bill before the Venice Commis-sion renders its advisory opinion.[14] While the bill was pending in parliament, government-friendly media kept themselves engaged with printing hastily combined lists with names of "Soros mercenaries," including prominent scholars, journalists, human rights lawyers, and civil society activists.[15]

The "other" is a malleable concept, prone to be defined by the momen-tary needs of the political majority. In the heat of the election campaign in the spring of 2018 Prime Minister Orbán departed from his usual migrant-mongering and presented the people of Miskolc with the image of a familiar threat: the settler with a different culture. For a change the prime minister referred not to refugees but to Roma and other poor families who moved to the city after 2005 – with the assistance of a governmental social housing program.

THE REVOLUTIONARY MANDATE
AND ITS MANY USES

The Declaration of National Cooperation presents the political project of reclaiming Hungary for Hungarians as a revolutionary undertaking, and the Fundamental Law has been routinely explained by Prime Minister Orbán as an important achievement of this process.[16]

In the imagination of constitutional scholars, revolution is a cradle of constitutions; its mention creates the ultimate sense of *tabula rasa*. What a constitutional revolution does is much less clear, but it certainly permits the creation of new institutions and the abolition of old ones. When a certain institution (such as parliament or a constitutional court) is retained, the revo-lutionary sentiment justifies the radical resetting of its foundations.

When viewed from a revolutionary perspective, the renaming of the Supreme Court to *Kúria* (its historic name) and the removal of its serving chief justice, the closing of the office of the ombudsman and its renaming to Commissioner for Fundamental Rights, the replacement of the data protec-tion ombudsman with a Hungarian National Authority for Data Protection and Freedom of Information, the profound reorganization of the administration of the judiciary, and the resizing and recrafting of the Constitutional Court appear to be moderate measures. With a revolutionary logic it is normal that civil servants can be dismissed without justification and with immediate effect (revolutions have done worse to servants of predecessor regimes), that (as mentioned) previously paid civil service severance pay is taxed retroactively with 98 percent income tax, that judges are forced into early retirement, and that persons with disability pensions are redirected to be active and useful members of the workforce. Revolutionary fervor also explains the manner in which these changes were carried out: often in haste, without proper parliamentary deliberation, without transitional rules, and without access to domestic remedies (a standard avenue typically available in constitutional democracies when one's fundamental constitutional right are at stake), and at times with retroactive effect.

While formally Hungary remains a constitutional republic, the government introduced political institutions and practices that increasingly erode or replace the structures of representative democracy. The perfect replacement for actual public participation in decision-making is national consultation. In order to tap into the will of the people, it is sufficient for the government to consult the people informally, and an actual referendum is better not risked. Between 2010 and 2017 the government organized seven such informal polls via direct mail called national consultations.[17] By now altogether eight million such questionnaires have been mailed to registered voters directly, and billboards soaked in government propaganda remind the audience to send in the right answer. In the National Consultation on the "Soros Plan," the government received a record number of 2.35 million responses according to its own account.[18]

Likewise, the consultation on the Fundamental Law in February 2011 clearly was meant to replace any formal popular affirmation of the final product.[19] The national consultations on social-welfare issues – "Stop Brussels" and the (non-existent) "Soros Plan" – are clear instances of propaganda campaigns to reinforce the government's policy positions on matters of public concern. In practice, very little is known about how a national consultation is prepared or how the responses on questionnaires are processed by the government. The national consultation of May 2015 on illegal migration and terror threats reportedly received a little over one million responses.[20] In response to a freedom of information request, the Prime Minister's Office clarified that the documents related to the preparation of the national consultation do not constitute public interest data.[21] As a national consultation is not an official poll, getting access to the responses received and processed by the government is a challenge: MPs who sought to see the responses of the consultation on the Soros Plan and suggested that the government reported an inflated response rate were placed under investigation for criminal libel upon the government's request.

The dangers of asking the actual people were well demonstrated in October 2016 when the government put the following question on a referendum: "Do you want the European Union to impose the mandatory settlement of non-Hungarian citizens in Hungary without the support of the Hungarian Parliament?" That the question was a constitutional non-starter both under Hungarian law and EU law goes without saying. The point was to create yet another opportunity for the government to engage in active propaganda against refugees, with a strong anti-EU flair. The referendum was unsuccessful, as almost 60 percent of the voters abstained, cast invalid votes, or went against the proposal.[22] This result was due to the highly creative campaign run by civil society and satirical party (the Two-tailed Dog Party) that the government could not silence despite serious efforts to this effect.

The prime minister was not discouraged easily: he sought to validate the will of 3.4 million voters (i.e., the 40.3 percent of the votes cast in favor of the proposal) through proposing a constitutional amendment to protect Hungary's "national and constitutional identity" from European invasion (Trócsányi 2016). This first attempt at passing a Seventh Amendment fell two votes short of the required two-thirds majority in parliament in November 2016 (Uitz 2016b). The government did not have to wait long for a victory: on December 5, 2016, the Constitutional Court interpreted the Europe clause of the Fundamental Law (Article E(2)) in the spirit of the rejected constitutional amendment, authorizing the government to continue its fight against Brussels in defense of national constitutional identity (22/2016 (XII. 5) AB decision)[23] (Halmai 2017). As soon as the government regained its two-thirds majority in parliament in 2018, the clause was passed as part of a much more extensive Seventh Amendment.

From this incident the government learnt not to take unnecessary risk with turning to the people for affirmation. The government spent much of 2016 on developing a bid for the 2024 Olympics, a clear object of national pride that was also a convenient project on which to spend public funds. Unexpectedly, in the spring of 2017 a newly formed political movement, Momentum, succeeded in gathering 266,000 signatures (exceeding the 138,000 minimum required) to question the wisdom of bidding for the summer Olympics at a municipal referendum in Budapest. Before the actual referendum could take place, the city withdrew the Olympic bid in agreement with the government and the National Olympics Committee. Not being dissuaded from a "120-year-old Hungarian dream" by a few thousand Budapest residents, the project leader announced that Hungary nevertheless would build all venues in quick succession as foreseen in the Olympic bid. Such infrastructure projects remain an important form of excessive patronage (corruption), literally cementing loyalty to the regime.

The constitutional regime of the Fundamental Law is built on the elimination of opportunities for dissent. Replacing referenda with national consultations is only a small instrument in a larger toolkit. Measures range from the takeover of the ownership of electronic and printed media[24] (including the advertising market[25]) to curbing press freedom and aggressive litigation to protect the reputation of the majority parties and their faces. Techniques for eliminating dissent and silencing the opposition also include electoral engineering, cutting down on the parliament's sessions, and using procedures of urgency and the excessive use of the disciplinary powers of the speaker in the remaining parliamentary sessions.[26]

Finally, the revolutionary mandate is a perfect disciplining tool. In addition to a highly visible law enforcement presence, the regime tends to keep its enemies at bay with a rapidly changing legal environment and the unceasing threat of selective prosecution at the hands of a loyal prosecution service. When such prosecution lingers for years, it might be little consolation if charges are dropped or thrown out of court as unfounded. It is also noteworthy that some celebrity defendants and witnesses, such as Klára Dobrev, the wife of former prime minister Ferenc Gyurcsány, learnt about being subpoenaed as a witness in a tax fraud case involving companies under her management not from the mailman but from the government-friendly press.

The revolutionary terminology suited the high spirits of the spring of 2010, although the formula of revolution in the polling booth was strained from the start. Initially it may have been a rhetorical reaction to calls for "consolidation." Yet it has quickly become a convenient shorthand to justify a wide range of unexpected measures taken in the name of the people without their actual participation. With the re-election of Fidesz in 2014, the revolutionary rhetoric ran its course, so Prime Minister Orbán explained in an address in June 2015 that instead of the term "reform" or even "structural reform" he prefers to talk about "renewal of the country."[27] In the spirit of the Declaration of National Cooperation, the Hungarian government is famous for its defiance of compromises and constraints. This is technically made possible by its overwhelming parliamentary majority. Although the defiant tone sounds odd on the European scene, it is easy to explain by the revolutionary mandate that makes the Orbán government stand up against foreign enemies and demand the proper respect that is allegedly due to Hungary. To be sure, potential foreign enemies are many and actual specimens are chosen as the opportunities present themselves: the list is led by the European Commission and the European Court of Human Rights, although Mr. Soros (as a global enemy) and lately the UN also have entered the roster.

CONCLUDING REMARKS: WHY BOTHER
ABOUT UNDERSTANDING THE
FUNDAMENTAL LAW BETTER?

Until 2010 Hungary was the poster-child of the literature on transition to democracy. This literature routinely assumed that a robust constitutional court keeping the political branches at bay and protecting fundamental rights was central to a successful transition to democracy, while a flexible (easy to amend) constitution would not be a major shortcoming. The news that a flexible constitution may be used to undermine a robust constitutional court comes at the time when processes of internationally supported democratization record highly visible failures, and scholarship on the rule of law has come to admit that its very subject may have transformed beyond recognition (Krygier 2014). It is time to ask whether assumptions made about the success of the Hungarian transition to democracy have caused certain premises about the transition to democracy and democratic consolidation to solidify into poisonous uncontested assumptions in scholarship.

The search for labels takes authors writing and researching non-democratic regimes hostage because labels and metaphors matter. Labels and metaphors can unduly sensationalize, exaggerate, or banalize, undermining the otherwise valid analytic point one is seeking to make. The search for the right term exposes the dilemma at the core of the quest for finding the right measure to size up trouble (i.e., the constitutional crisis at hand). Is there a problem – or rather – what is the problem when there are no tanks on the streets, no curfew, and no systematic arrests (as in a proper coup)? The problem is that the current labels do not acknowledge adequately that Hungary's Orbán or Poland's Kaczyński regimes do not wish to (and do not need to) turn into full-blown oppressive apparatuses with arrests, routinized torture, and mass disappearances. Just the right amount of oppression, with fixed yet regular elections, a well-disciplined press and the semblance of smoothly operating government will do just fine (Müller 2018). Taken together, these features permit constitutionally sanctioned power maximization, so long as those regular elections are guaranteed to return the parliament with the rulers' preferred composition.

The lesson from the Hungarian case is not only that a national actor can take pride in calling himself illiberal, a term regarded as derogatory in Western academia, but also that the vernacular matters in its explanatory potential for better understanding and further comparison. The revolutionary terminology in the vocabulary of National Cooperation served not simply as a justification for profound changes but also as a counterpoint to the language of regime change or transition. Apart from wanting to find a new name for a new era starting with 2010 (to distinguish it from the venerated days of 1988–1989), it was also an attempt to deter attention from the memorable appearance of Viktor Orbán of Fidesz calling for constitutional democracy at the most important non-event of the era, the reburial of former Prime Minister Imre Nagy (Rév 2005). When read in this light, it is not such a surprise that after the 2018 elections, Prime Minister Orbán announced on the radio that the time had come to turn Hungary's illiberal democracy into a Christian one.[28]

Thus, a second lesson is that when studying a national constitution in its political context, it is not helpful to search for an ideology on the ground that is consistent to the degree social scientists ideally would prefer. Illiberal and populist leaders often care more about delivering on pragmatic outcomes than on ideological consistency. Instead, scholarship needs to account for the consequences of the inconsistencies of the prevailing ideological frame.

Third, the gradual nature of Hungary's constitutional transformation is easily lost on observers who are in search of one, and only one, formative gesture. It appears that illiberal rules do not need to be in a rush to make radical changes, so long as they expect to get reelected with a solid majority in regular elections. This can be relatively easily achieved by careful electoral reform and well-managed elections, a logistical challenge. It is worth recalling that the OSCE's electoral observation mission in Hungary's 2014 general elections concluded: "[while] the elections were efficiently administered and offered voters a diverse choice [. . .] the main governing party enjoyed an undue advantage because of restrictive campaign regulations, biased media coverage, and campaign activities that blurred the separation between political party and the state."[29] Once the machinery of the new constitution is in place, several constitutional actors are at the ready to produce palatable outcomes across a longer period of time. If the constitutional machinery is built well, such actors do not need to be coerced to perform their duties as expected: the genius of the design and the impression it makes on its servants takes care of the rest.

Finally, an equally important lesson is being open to understanding local events for what they mean for local constitutional and political actors. Observers of Hungary continue to be fascinated by the extent to which the Orbán government insists on constitutionalizing and legalizing its operation. One way to see this behavior is to simply (or maybe cynically) mimicking the formalities of the rule of law in an attempt to satisfy European constitutional actors. Another way is to admit that every regime has to find a solution to its coordination problems, and printed legal rules are a conventional way to handle these.

Such instrumental explanations aside, it is clear from the outset that this extreme legalization has nothing to do with a genuine aspiration to adopt legal rules through reasoned debate while adhering to certain preset rules for settling disagreement or reaching compromises in the spirit of constitutionalism and the rule of law. Since 2010 essentially all such ideals were ridiculed at some point.

The appeal of the legal form appears to be that it is instantly recognized as black letter evidence on the will of the government. Thus, the legal form is the perfect way to document promises and demands, to issue directions and credible threats in a public and widely recognized form, neatly printed in the *Official Gazette*. Such rules are not meant to endure. They simply record an ever-shifting *status quo* till further notice. Until then the boundaries of the political community are reinforced by highly credible threats of persecution (via prosecution, if needed) and not by open repression. As a beneficial side-effect, the legal form helps because it is familiar. International observers and makers of democracy and rule of law indices find the terms for which they are looking. On the domestic scene legal rules ensure civil servants that they have a respectable job (as opposed to being cogs in the machinery of arbitrary rule packaged in the fading pages of law reports).

Misunderstanding the point of extreme legalization in the midst of such profound legal change runs the risk of attributing such significance to constitutional and legal rules which their very authors did not intend. As Prime Minister Orbán reminded us right before his impending reelection, the Fundamental Law is an important building block of the System of National Cooperation – and not more than that.

NOTES

1. Since the Fundamental Law does not appear to constrain the powers of the ruling majority, several Hungarian scholars question its constitutional nature. Those who treat it as a constitution note that it was adopted in compliance with formal procedural rules on constitutional amendment, as prescribed by the (amended) old 1989 Constitution.

2. The electoral reform was justified by reducing the size of parliament to almost half (386 to 199 MPs). It included redrawing electoral districts, altering campaign finance rules, changing campaign rules on making it more difficult for the opposition to draw attention to itself, enfranchising Hungarian minorities living abroad, and even awarding compensation to the overall winner for votes that would have been lost if a seat went to an opponent.

3. Full text of Viktor Orbán's speech at Băile Tuşnad (Tusnádfürdő): Orbán 2014.

4. 1/2010 (VI. 16) OGY resolution.

5. 47/2010 (VI. 29) OGY resolution establishing a drafting committee.

6. 45/2012 (XII. 29) AB decision, available in English translation on the website of the Constitutional Court. Available online: http://www.mkab.hu/letoltesek/en_00 45_2012.pdf. The text of the Transitional Provisions among other articles were then adopted as the Fourth Amendment to the Fundamental Law in the spring of 2013.

7. When it did not have a constitution-making majority, the government caved for the sake of passing the Sixth Amendment: the rules as adopted were a far cry from

the version preferred by the government. Initially the government sought the power to declare an emergency with reference to a threat of terror of its own (Uitz 2016a). The Sixth Amendment requires prior authorization to do so by a two-thirds majority in parliament. Lacking such a majority in parliament the government has to settle for imposing a state of intense monitoring (*fokozott ellenőrzés*) "to prevent, investigate and interrupt illegal acts" throughout Hungary as a policing measure. This is not a constitutional state of emergency, yet police are able to stop, ID, and search (frisk) anyone at their discretion.

8. 1140/2010 (VII. 2) government resolution.

9. For a collection of clippings from the Hungarian national news agency, please see Galamus 2010. Later in the month the public prosecutors also refused to display the Declaration.

10. GLOBSEC 2015, see at 1:03:04.

11. *Nagy Béláné v. Hungary*, [GC] Application No. 53080/13, Judgment of December 12, 2016.

12. "Magyarország kormányának javaslata," http://www.kormany.hu/download /c/9a/41000/STOP%20SOROS%20T%C3%96RV%C3%89NYCSOMAG.pdf, accessed June 25, 2019.

13. Act No. 6 of 2018 on the Amendment of Certain Acts in Connection with Measures against Illegal Migration.

14. Council of Europe 2018.

15. For example: Gorondi 2018.

16. See Orbán's speech of March 5, 2018: Orbán 2018.

17. Three were held on diverse social-welfare measures in September 2010, in May 2011 and September 2012, the one on the Fundamental Law in February 2011, one on migration and terror threats in May 2015, one to Stop Brussels in April 2017, and one on the Soros Plan in October 2017.

18. "A családok védelméről," https://nemzetikonzultacio.kormany.hu/, accessed June 25, 2019.

19. Referendum is not required as a condition for amending the Hungarian Constitution or passing a new one. Commentators were calling for a referendum to repair the lack of inclusivity of the constitution-making process.

20. "Nemzeti konzultáció a bevándorlásról," https://www.kormany.hu/downloa d/4/d3/c0000/Bev%20konzultáció%20eredményei.pdf, accessed June 25, 2019.

21. "Közérdekű adatigénylés," https://kimittud.atlatszo.hu/request/4544/response /7532/attach/4/SMiBiz224%20K15051113341.pdf, accessed June 25, 2019.

22. "Népszavazás 2016," http://www.valasztas.hu/20, accessed June 25, 2019.

23. "Decision 22/2016," https://hunconcourt.hu/uploads/sites/3/2017/11/en_ 22_2016.pdf, accessed June 25, 2019.

24. For reporting from a Hungarian transparency NGO, atlatszo.hu on this see atlatszo 2018a.

25. atlatszo 2018b.

26. The Grand Chamber of the European Court of Human Rights found the latter to violate freedom of expression in *Karácsony and others v. Hungary*, [GC] Application Nos. 42461/13 – 44357/13, Judgment of May 17, 2016.

27. GLOBSEC 2015, see at 1:02:19–24.
28. Reuters 2018.
29. OSCE 2014.

BIBLIOGRAPHY

Arató, Andrew. 2010. "Post-Sovereign Constitution-making in Hungary: After Success, Partial Failure, and Now What?" *South African Journal of Human Rights* 26 (1): 19–44.

atlatszo. 2018a. "Infographic: Explore the Media Empire Friendly to the Hungarian Government," January 16, 2018. https://english.atlatszo.hu/2018/01/16/infographic -explore-the-media-empire-friendly-to-the-hungarian-government/.

———. 2018b. "This is How Politics Distorts the advertising Market in Hungary: Threats, Blackmail and Corruption," August 2, 2018. https://english.atlatszo.hu/20 18/08/02/this-is-how-politics-distorts-the-advertising-market-in-hungary-threats -blackmail-and-corruption/.

Bánkuti, Miklós, Gábor Halmai, and Kim-Lane Scheppele. 2012. "Disabling the Fundamental Law." *Journal of Democracy* 23 (3): 138–46.

Bátory, Ágnes. 2014. "Uploading as Political Strategy: The European Parliament and the Hungarian Media Law Debate." *East European Politics* 30 (2): 230–45.

———. 2016. "Populists in Government? Hungary's "System of National Cooperation." *Democratization* 23 (2): 283–303.

Elkins, Zachary, Tom Ginsburg, and James Melton. 2014. "The Content of Authoritarian Constitutions." In *Constitutions in Authoritarian Regimes*, edited by Tom Ginsburg and Alberto Simpser, 141–64. Cambridge: Cambridge University Press.

Enyedi, Zsolt. 2015. "Plebeians, Citoyens and Aristocrats or Where is the Bottom of the Bottom? The Case of Hungary." In *Populism in the Shadow of the Great Recession*, edited by Hanspeter Kriesi and Takis Pappas, 229–44. Colchester: ECPR Press.

Fodor, Gábor G., Gábor Fűrész, and András Giró-Szász. 2010. "Az ideológiák vége." *Magyar Nemzet*, May 18. https://mno.hu/migr_1834/az_ideologiak_vege-237670.

Galamus. 2010. http://www.galamus.hu/index.php?option=com_content&view=arti cle&id=17883:nemzeti-egyuettmkoedesrl-szolo-nyilatkozat-kifueggesztese-2010 -julius-6-ai-leltar-17537&catid=79&Itemid=164, accessed June 25, 2019.

Halmai, Gábor. 2012. "From the 'Rule of Law Revolution' to the Constitutional Counter-Revolution in Hungary." *European Yearbook of Human Rights*: 367–84.

———. 2017. "The Hungarian Constitutional Court and Constitutional Identity." January 10, 2017. https://verfassungsblog.de/the-hungarian-constitutional-cour t-and-constitutional-identity/.

Krygier, Martin. 2014. "Transformations of the Rule of Law: Legal, Liberal and Neo." Paper presented at KJuris at Dickson Poon School of Law, KCL, October 1, 2014.

Küpper, Herbert. 2012. "Ungarns neues Grundgesetz von 2011: Kein Grund zum Jubel, aber auch noch nicht das Ende der Demokratie." [Hungary's New Constitutional Law of 2011: No Reason for Exaltation, But Not the End of Democracy Either]. *Suedosteuropa-Mitteilungen* 52 (3): 80–101.
Landau, David. 2013. "Abusive Constitutionalism." *University of California Davis Law Review* 47 (1): 189–260.
Law, David and Mila Versteeg. 2013. "Sham Constitutions." *California Law Review* 101 (4): 863–956.
Müller, Jan-Werner. 2013. "Defending Democracy within the EU." *Journal of Democracy* 24 (2): 138–49.
———. 2015. "Should the EU Protect Democracy and the Rule of Law inside Member States?" *European Law Journal* 21 (2): 141–60.
———. 2018. "Homo Orbanicus." *New York Review of Books*. April 5, 2018.
Orbán, Viktor. 2010. "Orbán Viktor beszéde," May 14, 2010. http://2010-201 4.kormany.hu/hu/miniszterelnokseg/miniszterelnok/beszedek-publikaciok-inter juk/orban-viktor-beszede-a-magyar-orszaggyules-alakulo-ulesen-2010-majus-14, accessed June 25, 2019.
———. 2014. "Full text of Viktor Orbán's Speech at Băile Tuşnad (Tusnádfürdő) of 26 July 2014." https://budapestbeacon.com/full-text-of-viktor-orbans-speech-at-b aile-tusnad-tusnadfurdo-of-26-july-2014/, accessed June 25, 2019.
———. 2018. "Orbán Viktor beszéde az Igazságügyi Zsebtörvénytár bemutatásán." http://www.miniszterelnok.hu/orban-viktor-beszede-az-igazsagugyi-zsebtorven ytar-bemutatasan/, accessed June 25, 2019.
OSCE. 2014. "OSCE/ODIHR Final Report." https://www.osce.org/odihr/elections/ hungary/121375, accessed June 25, 2019.
Reuters. 2018. "PM Orban Vows to Preserve Hungary's Christian Culture." https:// uk.reuters.com/article/uk-hungary-orban/pm-orban-vows-to-preserve-hungarys-ch ristian-culture-idUKKBN1I80PB, accessed June 25, 2019.
Rév, István. 2005. *Retroactive Justice: The Pre-history of Post-Communism*. Stanford, CA: Stanford University Press.
Scheppele, Kim Lane. 2014. "Hungary and the End of Politics How Victor Orbán Launched a Constitutional Coup and Created a One-party State." May 6, 2014. https://www.thenation.com/article/hungary-and-end-politics/.
Simon, Zoltán. 2011. "Hungary First to Write a Constitution on an IPad, Lawmaker Says." March 4, 2011. http://www.bloomberg.com/news/2011-03-04/hungary-f irst-to-write-a-constitution-on-ipad-lawmaker-says.html.
Sonnevend, Pál, András Jakab, and Lóránt Csink. 2015. "The Constitution as an Instrument of Everyday Party Politics: The Basic Law of Hungary." In *Constitutional Crisis in the European Constitutional Area, Theory, Law and Politics in Hungary and Romania*, edited by Armin von Bogdandy and Pál Sonnevend, 46–123. Oxford – Portland, OR: C. H. Beck – Hart – Nomos.
Tóth, Gábor Attila, ed. 2012. *Constitution for a Disunited Nation. On Hungary's 2011 Fundamental Law*. Budapest: Central European University Press.
Trencsényi, Balázs. 2013. "From Goulash Communism to Goulash Authoritarianism." http://www.iwm.at/read-listen-watch/transit-online/from-goulash-commun ism-to-goulash-authoritarianism/, accessed June 25, 2019.

Uitz, Renáta. 2014. "Expelling Dissent: On Account of the ECtHR Judgment in *Baka v Hungary*." June 3, 2014. https://verfassungsblog.de/expelling-dissent-account-ec thr-judgment-baka-v-hungary-2/.

———. 2016a. "Hungary's Attempt to Manage Threats of Terror through a Consti- tutional Amendment." April 28, 2016. http://www.constitutionnet.org/news/hung arys-attempt-manage-threats-terror-through-constitutional-amendment.

———. 2016b. "National Constitutional Identity in the European Constitutional Project: A Recipe for Exposing Cover ups and Masquerades." November 11, 2016. https://verfassungsblog.de/national-constitutional-identity-in-the-european -constitutional-project-a-recipe-for-exposing-cover-ups-and-masquerades/.

———. 2017a. "The Return of the Sovereign: A Look at the Rule of Law in Hungary – and in Europe." April 5, 2017. https://verfassungsblog.de/the-return-of-the-sover eign-a-look-at-the-rule-of-law-in-hungary-and-in-europe/.

———. 2017b. "Academic Freedom in an Illiberal Democracy: From the Rule of Law Through Rule by Law to Rule by Men in Hungary." October 15, 2017. https:// iacl-aidc-blog.org/2017/10/15/academic-freedom-in-an-illiberal-democracy-from -the-rule-of-law-through-rule-by-law-to-rule-by-men-in-hungary/.

Vörös, Imre. 2017. "A 'Constitutional Coup' in Hungary between 2010–2014. On Some Aspects of the Exclusive Systemic Exercise of State Power with Regard to Constitutional Law, International Law, and European Law." In *Twenty-Five Sides of a Post-Communist Mafia State*, edited by Bálint Magyar and Júlia Vásárhelyi, 41–68. Budapest: Central European University Press.

Chapter 2

Totalitarianism without Perpetrators?

Politics of History in the "System of National Cooperation"

Ferenc Laczó

Claiming to represent a new political generation that would overcome the country's obsolete but still acute divisions, Fidesz has tended to act as a "memory warrior" (Kubik and Bernhard 2014) concerning matters of culture and history. Around the turn of the millennium, the party's declared agenda of recreating national unity became intertwined with the exclusivist idea of "national" versus "non-national" sides. The first Fidesz government between 1998 and 2002 may not have attempted to implement profound changes in the landscape of Hungary's institutions devoted to the study of recent history, but it did make some suggestive symbolic interventions, especially during the celebration of a millennium of Hungarian statehood in 2000. More consequentially, during its reelection campaign in 2002 the first Orbán government inaugurated the House of Terror to be headed by Mária Schmidt, the crucial memory activist of the Hungarian Right.[1]

The manner in which the permanent exhibition of the House of Terror has represented recent history is noteworthy for at least two reasons. The crimes of the recent past may have been referenced abundantly in its visually powerful rooms, but the origins of both of the two subsequent "totalitarian" periods in Hungary were depicted as largely external to Hungarian society. The exhibition also raised grave suspicions about the genealogy of Fidesz's chief political opponent at the time, the Magyar Szocialista Párt (Hungarian Socialist Party or MSZP). Moreover, the nationalistic adaptation of the theory of totalitarianism ignored the credentials of the democratic opposition out of whose circles political liberalism developed. The stakes of the discourse on recent Hungarian history were thereby clearly raised.

By the early twenty-first century Fidesz politicians repeatedly suggested that anti-communists battling post-communists was at the heart of the profound political division of the country (Mark 2010). In this rendition the former appeared as righteous victims still seeking appropriate recognition, while the latter were directly linked to local communist perpetrators who have not been made to account for their crimes. In the fall of 2006, when the 50th anniversary commemoration of the 1956 Revolution included radical rightist attempts at symbolic reenactment (von Klimó 2006), the new anti-communist plot was further radicalized as it drew an analogy between the worst communist-era crimes and interventions by riot police under the then ruling MSZP. This radical right-wing narrative received widespread endorsement as the legitimacy of the second Ferenc Gyurcsány-led government (2006–2009) gravely eroded.

INSTITUTIONAL INNOVATIONS

Upon their return to power with a supermajority in 2010, the leaders of Fidesz decided to drastically reshape the institutional setting of the study of recent history and, more generally, the discourse around the national-historical community (Boda and Körösényi 2013). Several new centers such as the Committee of National Remembrance, the Research Institute and Archives for the History of Hungarian Regime Change, and the Veritas Research Institute for History were launched. At the same time, several long-standing institutes, such as the Institute for the Study of 1956 Hungarian Revolution and the Institute of Political History, lost most of their state support – the former even lost its independence before it got effectively abolished through a forced 2019 merger with Veritas. The aforementioned new historical institutes constitute the pillars of a state-endorsed project to build a new canon of historical interpretation that includes copious references to Hungarian society's experiences with the dictatorial rule and violent methods of communists. Such references and research agendas, however, are not coupled with political support for unhindered archival access to key documents from the communist period such as the files of the state security apparatus (Ungváry 2017).

The Veritas Institute was established in October 2013 and currently lists 26 employees, with right-wing military historian Sándor Szakály acting as its director.[2] The aim of the Veritas Institute is to deal with "underexplored aspects" of Hungarian history from the last 150 years. The new institute offers an alternative to the scholarly work of the Institute of History of the Hungarian Academy of Sciences with its more than hundred researchers. (At the time of writing, the autonomy of the latter is being consciously undermined, just like that of the Hungarian Academy as a whole.) The scholarly core of Veritas consists of three chronologically organized research groups, which respectively deal with the era of the Dual Monarchy,[3] the Horthy era,[4] and the post-1945 period.[5] Tellingly, the president of the advisory board is no other than former Prime Minister (1993–1994) and minister of the interior (1990–1993) Péter Boross, while vice-director of research Endre Marinovich used to serve as the chief of staff of the first Prime Minister after the regime change, the conservative József Antall. Importantly, neither of them are trained historians.

After a rather slow start marred by several rounds of controversy, Veritas launched its book, yearbook, and research papers series in 2015. Whereas its first yearbook of 2014 contains sixteen studies on rather diverse topics, the first three books the Institute released all concern the life and times of Antall (Bába 2015; Sáringer 2015; Tóth 2015). This is a remarkable choice not only because of the involvement of the aforementioned high-profile political personalities but also because it reveals a substantial overlap with the agenda of the Research Institute and Archives for the History of Hungarian Regime Change, an institution that has been operating under the supervision of the Prime Minister's Office since its simultaneous creation in 2013.

The Research Institute and Archives for the History of Hungarian Regime Change is directed by Zoltán Bíró, with Sándor M. Kiss – whose main research expertise concerns the history of 1956 and subsequent repressions – acting as head of research. The website of the institute currently lists altogether 36 employees, including a director and two vice-directors, one senior research fellow, one further research fellow, and nine assistant research fellows.[6] Unlike the gradualist beginnings of Veritas, the Research Institute and Archives for the History of Hungarian Regime Change released nineteen publications within the first three years of its existence. These nineteen volumes are truly diverse – they include single- and co-authored monographs, edited and documentary volumes, memoirs, and thematic journal issues – and of rather mixed scholarly value. The topics covered range from communist memory politics, cultural policy during late communism, the reburial of Imre Nagy and his associates in the summer of 1989, to Hungarian-American relations around 1989, in addition to protests and strikes between 1988 and 2013, the blockade of taxi drivers in 1990, and the integration of the post-communist MSZP into the democratic political system. Arguably, this wide scope corresponds to the generic goal of "comprehensive exploration and documentation" of the system change that the Institute's website promises.[7] Somewhat predictably in light of the leadership's profile, the clearest thematic thread consists of laudatory works on the history of the agrarian populist (*népi*) movement.

The Committee of National Remembrance may be viewed as the third major new pillar of state-endorsed history writing. Created in accordance with a stipulation of the Fundamental Law adopted in 2011 and eventually established in 2013 with individual mandates of no less than nine years, the committee consists of five members, three of whom were elected by the Hungarian Parliament, one appointed by the Minister for Justice, and one by the Academy of Sciences. It is headed by Réka Földváryné Kiss, who is no other than the daughter of the aforementioned Sándor M. Kiss. The agenda of the committee consists of uncovering the operation of the communist dictatorship, preserving its memory on the level of the Hungarian state, honoring its victims, and contributing to the persecution of crimes to which the statute of limitation does not apply.

The elaborate report the committee submitted about its 2014 activities to the Hungarian parliament provides a detailed sense of its various pursuits.[8] Based on this document, the Committee aims to conduct prominent research into the history of the Ministry of Interior and the operation of the state security apparatus but also is interested in exploring the foreign policy and the economic, military, cultural, and legal history of communist-ruled Hungary. While it remains to be seen how and to what extent these wide-ranging ambitions shall be fulfilled, similarly to the above-described two institutions, the Committee also has established its own series of publications with the first six volumes made available in 2015 (Borvendég 2015; Csatári 2015a, 2015b; Cserényi-Zsitnyányi 2015; Halmy 2015b; Sáringer 2015; Szilágyi and Bottoni 2015).

Thanks to its support of such newly endowed contemporary historical institutes, compounded by allocating substantial amounts to some previous initiatives, Hungary's current leadership devotes more resources to endeavors in historical studies than under any other post-1990 government. Due to the aforementioned top-down intervention, today's political rulers also have achieved significantly higher levels of centralization and created new opportunities to discipline professional discourses. It remains unclear what exact shape political influence over historians' discussions shall take beyond all the welcoming remarks and prefaces by leading politicians. The ambition to exert such influence, however, was articulated clearly in the preamble of the new Fundamental Law where the alleged dates of the loss and regaining of Hungarian sovereignty were controversially specified as March 19, 1944 (the day the German occupation of Hungary began) and May 2, 1990 (the day the first democratically elected post-communist parliament opened).

NATIONAL SELF-HISTORICIZATION

Several scholars have explored how some of the recently institutionalized interpretations of history, especially those related to the new-old commemorations of Trianon, had their origins in staunchly nationalistic segments of

Hungarian civil society (Feischmidt 2014). Various observers also have noted that the new official discourse in fact endorses a familiar independentist narrative of unrecognized Hungarian sacrifices, the major difference being that in earlier epochs the role of foreign oppressors was reserved for the Ottomans and the Habsburgs, whereas the updated version assigns such roles to Nazi German and Soviet imperialism.[9] While I consider the correlations between such national victim narratives and contemporary mobilization of resentment to be strong, I would not wish to focus my present argument on the normative advantages of self-critical historical cultures.

My aim below is not so much to discuss why the substance of this new agenda might be considered controversial, since this has already been done by several highly qualified experts, but rather to show what some of the local and transnational roots of this agenda are. I shall thereby also aim to suggest an explanation why this agenda has managed to fit into broader regional and all-European frameworks without its controversial aspects being noticed at first. Second, I will provide a case study of the official manner of commemorating the Holocaust, a crucial transnational historical topic of the early twenty-first century. More concretely, I will focus on the 2014 commemorations of the 70th anniversary of the Holocaust in Hungary to demonstrate the concrete implications of depicting totalitarianism without local perpetrators. Last but not least, I will aim to show that the difficult balancing act of focusing on victims while ignoring perpetrators only resulted in further societal polarization regarding the recent past.

Before attempting to place the current Hungarian situation in comparative and transnational contexts, a brief exercise in historicization is needed. After the fall of communism and the end of the Cold War, a "minimal liberal consensus" emerged in the West as well as the new democracies of East Central Europe being integrated into it. By talking of such a consensus, I do not mean to suggest that liberals acquired a dominant political position in East Central Europe. I merely wish to indicate that in the years immediately following 1989 they succeeded in shaping intellectual discussions and the horizons of expectations more than any other political-ideological force (Szacki 1995).

By arguing that the recent European past had been defined by illiberal extremes, broadly liberal forces could claim to possess a privileged viewpoint to draw its lessons. Even if there were alternative currents in the politics of history of a more illiberal or even anti-liberal kind in the 1990s, representatives of this dominant stream employed totalitarianism as a counter concept to liberal democracy. They thereby presented a most influential interpretation of the new dictatorships of the twentieth century as constituting dire warnings against democratic ambitions without the institutional guarantees of liberalism.

In spite of their moment of intellectual dominance, Hungarian liberals proved unsuccessful at transforming the country's historical culture. In retrospect, we may identify several reasons behind this failure such as being strongly identified with a neoliberal reform agenda, their rising levels of corruption, and their conspicuous inability to meaningfully involve members of younger generations. As Zoltán Gábor Szűcs's excellent monograph on the early years of political democracy after 1989 notes, Hungarian liberals in fact found little use for more elaborate discussions of history: they tended to view history as a domain prone to be dominated by nationalistic views and of secondary political importance anyway (Szűcs 2010). Moreover, right after the fall of the communist regime, Hungarian liberals identified a much graver form of anti-democratic culture to exist on the right. Consequently, they were more likely to critique forms of Hungarian nationalism than institutional and personal continuities between the communist and post-communist times.

While their premonitions about the moderateness, even reasonableness of the post-communist left, and the potential radicalization of the right have proven justified, the political conclusions liberals drew from their diagnosis arguably still amounted to a strategic mistake. Their resulting anti-anti-communism soon brought them into a coalition with the post-communist MSZP, which in turn would make their stance on questions of recent history appear somewhat hypocritical. They continued to make some of the same demands while silently accepting that they would not be met. This in turn created preconditions for a right-wing campaign opposing both post-communism and liberalism employing, among others, the politics of history. The governing alliance of post-communists and liberals established in 1994 coincided with the emergence of Fidesz's new, activist, if not downright revolutionary conception of conservative politics, the polarized reception of which yielded a veritable *Kulturkampf* by the turn of the millennium – or, as some have preferred to call it, a Hungarian "cold civil war" (Szilágyi 2010).

As it became all too evident toward the end of the first decade of the twenty-first century, the influence of liberal interpretations had been countered effectively. The attempt to explain the liberal agenda's declining popularity in Hungary would have to include – besides the above-mentioned shortcomings of liberal representatives – the loss of credibility of a vision built around notions of Westernization and Europeanization. Since the early shocks of the transition, East Central Europe may have experienced a period of economic development but did so without any real convergence with the most developed parts of Europe (Greskovits and Bohle 2012; Valuch 2015). One may argue that as structural inequalities within Europe were increasingly attributed to the very project of Europeanization, nationalistic resentment grew stronger. The cultural and political forms of such resentment need to be critiqued, but the socio-economic context of the rise of nationalism, i.e., very real frustrations resulting from inequalities in larger European frameworks, should not be underestimated. In retrospect, a significant loss of trust among members of the political elite in the key projects of post-communist times of "joining the West" and "integrating into Europe" appears to be a rather logical consequence of the institutional completion of the integration process which, however, failed to deliver the promised benefits – even as support for the European project remains far more widespread among members of Hungarian society than the critical and increasingly hostile discourses of the dominant party might make one suppose.

The already grave political situation of liberal forces was compounded by the fact that no new and attractive liberal vision of the future was developed in the early twenty-first century. The resulting absence of a normative future horizon created new possibilities for rightists. Whereas influential agrarian populist (or *népi*) intellectuals of the transition years, such as Sándor Csoóri or István Csurka, tended to draw on transnational discourses in a rather anachronistic manner, self-declared conservatives of the younger generations adapted revived transnational discourses to present critical takes on modernity in the name of tradition and common sense. They articulated fierce attacks on intellectual and progressive politics to legitimize a much more flexible exercise of political will.[10]

WIDER EUROPEAN SHIFTS

Recent shifts in the overall interpretation of twentieth-century European history have in several respects aided such revisionist local agendas. When the recent past is discussed, the symbolic center of the continent is no longer a provincial West German town called Bonn where, out of a laudable self-critical impetus, any attempt to compare Nazism and Stalinism was often depicted as problematic even during the second half of the 1980s. The epochal changes associated with 1989 exerted an immense impact on how Europe remembers its age of catastrophe, too. One of the major historiographic consequences of 1989 has been an eastward shift of focus to a once multicultural zone of multiple catastrophes. If the center of twentieth-century European history was indeed the bloodlands as identified by Snyder (2010), then the thesis of two comparable ("totalitarian") regimes clearly made much more sense. However, as Mark (2010) has noted, in much of Central and Eastern Europe, the decades since 1989 not only brought about the meteoric rise of references to twin totalitarianisms but actually saw such anti-totalitarian discourses increasingly prioritize the transnational experience of communism.

Considered in a broader context of radicalizing anti-communism in Central and Eastern Europe, with a heavy recourse to national traditions and identity, the Hungarian story has several features that make it comparable to the cases of Croatia, Romania, and Slovakia. Perhaps the most important is that whereas the communist regimes conformed more closely to basic characteristics of the totalitarian model than the preceding right-wing regimes, the latter were responsible for graver crimes, including active involvement in genocide against their own (by this time legally gravely discriminated) citizens during the Second World War (Vági, Csősz, and Kádár 2013). This means that the crimes of communism in Hungary could be seen as practically equaling those of right-wing authoritarianism only after the frame of comparison was enlarged. A somewhat ironic consequence is that the current governing side, all its conspicuous nationalism notwithstanding, has a vested interest in internationalizing discussions of twentieth-century history and doing so in a very specific manner.

To grasp better why international reactions to the politics of history of the current Hungarian government have long been rather muted, it seems crucial to reflect on what the wave of European Union enlargement in 2004–2007 meant in terms of historical perspectives being integrated and excluded. One of the key facts of the last decade has been the rise of Poland to middle power status, which has increasingly enabled its representatives to assume the role of spokespersons for East Central Europe as a whole, especially in German forums. The mainstream Polish perspective on the joint Nazi-Soviet responsibility for the beginning of the Second World War in 1939 and on partly simultaneous, partly consecutive foreign occupations by totalitarian powers thus exerted a notable impact on the European discourses of recent history. The basic tenets of this Polish perspective were shared in influential East Central European circles outside Poland, including Hungary with its often idealized image of Polish nationalism and manifold links to the Polish Right. This gradually yielded a seemingly regional ambition to depict Nazism and communism as evil twins and East Central European countries as the victims of the most vicious imperial projects.

Before we prematurely would maintain that the recent European declaration of August 23 as the European Day of Remembrance for Victims of Stalinism and Nazism amounted to a recognition of the historical experience of the new EU member states in East Central Europe as such, we ought to recall that a substantial number of these countries, including Hungary, were not directly impacted by the Molotov-Ribbentrop Pact of 1939 (Kaminsky, Müller, and Troebst 2011).[11] The frequently reiterated basic formula of treating the histories of the two halves of the continent – which may be summarized all too succinctly as successful democratization, economic development, and increasing integration after the terrible crimes of the Second World War in the West and double occupation by totalitarian imperialists in the East – actually effaces basic features of the histories of countries such as Hungary but also its neighbors Croatia, Slovakia, and Romania, which may have had Soviet-type regimes as a consequence of the Second World War but which actually played relatively autonomous roles on the side of Nazi Germany during the war years. In other words, one may argue that Hungary's by now semi-official narrative concerning totalitarian regimes as a result of double foreign occupation closely resembles the mainstream Polish version, the major difference being between the actual historical roles the two countries played during the war. Somewhat polemically, it seems that the European integration of East Central European countries and the accompanying ambition of a minimal regional as well as Europe-wide consensus have made right-wing reinterpretations of recent history south of Poland appear much less controversial than it would have been otherwise.

Within its interpretative scheme defined by a nationalistic form of anti-totalitarianism, contemporary Hungarian politics of history makes copious references to the history of the Holocaust. However, as the 70th anniversary commemorations of 2014 have shown, Holocaust commemoration can reveal with particular force the peculiar official ambition to create a vision of history with totalitarian crimes at its symbolic center, which are meant to remain vaguely explored and largely unspecified. Such a nationalistic manner of Holocaust commemoration is dependent on an innovative adoption of the double occupation thesis to the case of Hungary.

Prior to covering key commemorative efforts of 2014 more concretely, their transnational prehistory deserves some attention. An appropriate place to start might be that the power and symbolic position of Germany in Europe began to improve since 1989, while our understanding of the scope of Holocaust perpetrators has also evolved. For decades, mainstream depictions of Nazi perpetrators tended to focus on a relatively small group of German political leaders. Since the 1990s several waves of revelations have pointed to the widespread involvement of German institutions and ordinary German citizens in the crimes of the Third Reich (Browning 1998). This novel acknowledgement of the deep social roots, and even the shocking popularity, of the Nazi agenda has been increasingly accompanied by a Europeanization of the image of the Holocaust, including its perpetrators. The almost exclusive focus on German perpetrators known from previous decades has been complemented by an emphasis on the direct criminal responsibility of large numbers of non-Germans across the continent (Stone 2010; Grabowski 2013).

Around the turn of the millennium, when commemorating the Holocaust emerged as a kind of historical cultural entry ticket to the European Union, the broader conception of perpetrator groups made confronting local responsibility an international pattern from France to Poland. Admittedly, in several East Central European countries, such as Romania, Slovakia, or – to a somewhat lesser extent at the time – Hungary, this was accompanied by attempts to rehabilitate anti-Semitic leaders of Nazi-allied states. How much an earnest confrontation with societal involvement in the Holocaust was locally desired and effectively fostered in fact greatly varied.

Back in 2000, prior to its full inclusion into European Union structures, Hungary was among the countries that dedicated themselves to participating in international efforts at furthering Holocaust remembrance. As part of the new commitment assumed under its first Fidesz-led government, the country introduced a Holocaust Remembrance Day on April 16 (the day the first ghettos and so-called relocation camps were established in the country in 1944). It is highly improbable that decision-makers around the turn of the millennium saw any reason to consider that in the spring of 2014 the commemorations of the Holocaust's 70th anniversary would therefore coincide with the electoral campaign.[12] In the early years of the new century when Hungary was among the most consensually supported candidates heading for European Union membership, hardly any prominent politician would have been concerned that by 2014 extensive critical scrutiny could be directed toward the country's recent political evolution (Müller 2012) and, more specifically, toward its nationalistic politics of history.

In the meantime, however, the growing strength of local ethnic nationalism (Feischmidt 2014) and authoritarian tendencies under the second premiership of Viktor Orbán turned the country into one of the most controversial member states of the European Union. As part of Hungary's rightward shift in the early twenty-first century, anti-Semitism strengthened in certain layers of society (Kovács 2011). How widespread Hungarian anti-Semitism truly is and how significant a danger it might pose have become contested questions again. Especially since Fidesz returned to power with a supermajority in 2010, varied international forums have raised concerns regarding how Hungarian society has reflected on the role the country played during the Second World War and how it has dealt with its co-responsibility for the Holocaust.

DUAL AGENDA

In relation to the Holocaust, three key questions appear to have divided Hungarian public opinion since the end of the Second World War: the relative responsibility of Hungarians and Germans, the ideological explicability of Hungarian involvement focused on the questions of fascism and anti-Semitism, and the way the victims ought to be categorized and remembered. Starting prior to 1989 but taking on much greater force afterwards, ideological explanations focused on Hungarian fascism largely were discredited, the Hungarian role in the implementation of the Holocaust came to be discussed more openly (Kovács 2015), and the Jewishness of the victims would finally be acknowledged openly and officially emphasized (Fritz 2012).

However, nearly three decades after the end of the communist regime, it looks like the transformation of Hungarian historical culture has proven to be incomplete. Regarding the Holocaust, the aforementioned self-critical reassessments have given way to mixed blessings in the midterm. Increasingly powerful reactions to the aforementioned trends in the early twenty-first century were manifested in outright rejection of Hungarian responsibility, softer forms of historiographical revisionism, and novel practices of symbolic exclusion that have all gone more public since the global economic crisis hit Hungary in 2008–2009 (Kovács 2011; Laczó 2018).

As emphasized above, since the Fidesz-dominated state's ambition to institutionalize a new vision of the country's recent past has been in evidence for years without the exact weight and specific interpretation of the Holocaust in the emerging canon being sufficiently defined, the 70th anniversary of the Holocaust in Hungary took place at a time when discussions over the prevalent and most appropriate forms of Holocaust commemoration began to turn polemical (Shapiro 2013).[13] In late 2013, partly in direct response to such polemics, the government led by Viktor Orbán announced its intention to counter "forgetting and indifference" and declared 2014 a Year of Holocaust Commemoration (*Magyar Holokauszt Emlékév*).[14] The founding document of the Year of Commemoration described the Holocaust as a crime against law, humanity, nature, and equality and called it "the tragedy of the entire Hungarian nation."[15]

As a major component of the official initiative to commemorate the 70th anniversary of the Holocaust, the Hungarian government decided to establish a *Civil Alap* (Civil Fund).[16] The intention behind the Civil Fund, as announced by László L. Simon, president of the parliamentary Culture and Press Committee at the time and former secretary of state for culture (2012–2013), was to familiarize society "with the aims of the year of commemoration through involving the Jewish communities of Hungary," support "processes of dealing with history" (*szembenézés a történelemmel* in the original), and help "the activities of the civil sphere."[17] Remembrance was meant to be fostered primarily through programs that directly dealt with the Hungarian Holocaust (*magyar holokauszt*) and also through ones that would discuss "Jewish traditions" while tackling "the losses suffered by local communities" – both within Hungary and in Hungarian minority communities abroad (Ablonczy 2011; Simon 2014; Fedinec 2015).[18] Its broad agenda also enabled the Fund to support scholarly research and publications as well as the creation of artistic works and their exhibition.[19] A rather generous sum of around HUF 1.5 billion (approximately EUR 5 million) was to be allocated for these purposes.

By the deadline for submissions in late 2013, the *Civil Alap* received 1,073 valid applications. According to the official communiqué of the Fund on January 8, 2014, more than 400 applicants were meant to receive financial support totaling HUF 1.8 billion (or around EUR 6 million).[20] For reasons to be addressed below, by May 26, 18 of the winning applicants resigned from accepting government funding.[21] Some of those who eventually refused to cooperate with the *Civil Alap* launched the alternative platform *Memento 70 – Tisztán emlékezünk* (Memento 70 – We Remember with Honor) on April 17, 2014. This independent movement of Holocaust commemoration included a host of crucial Hungarian Jewish institutions, such as the *Magyarországi Zsidó Hitközségek Szövetsége*, the main umbrella organization of Hungarian Jews, the *Magyar Zsidó Kulturális Egyesület*, one of the leading Jewish cultural associations, the Budapest University of Jewish Studies, the Hungarian Jewish Museum, the Hungarian Jewish Archive, and the Hungarian Zionist Alliance.[22] However, according to the website of *Memento 70*, their campaign of fundraising largely failed to generate the desired amount.[23]

The controversy surrounding the year of commemoration was triggered by the perception of an official ambition to picture the Holocaust in Hungary as the genocide Nazi Germany committed against the Jews of Hungary and thereby downplay Hungarian co-responsibility. The topic of Hungarian rescue has certainly emerged as one of the main focuses of official initiatives. Next to high-profile events, such as "Get to Know and Recognize – The Message of Hungarian Rescuers for the Twenty-first Century" organized by the Tom Lantos Institute and the Institute of Foreign Affairs and Trade,[24] an international symposium dealt with the topic at the Hungarian Parliament under the title "Rescuers – 'God Announces His Arrival through Them'." The explicit aim of devoting such attention to the exceptional and exceptionally uplifting examples of rescuers has been to contribute to moral education. However, as various observers did not fail to point out, the strong focus on rescuers at the expense of sufficient attention on Hungarian perpetrators may suggest an apologist agenda. In accordance with the emphasis on the German occupation of Hungary in March 1944, national resistance emerged as another though less prominent focus of conferences and new research.

The ambition to downplay the Hungarian share of responsibility arguably was manifested already in these topical priorities, but it was widely perceived to define two new state-endorsed projects: the decision to open a new museum dedicated to the victims of the Holocaust and to erect a statue commemorating the victims of the German occupation in the center of Budapest. In 2000, upon Hungary making the above-mentioned commitment to furthering Holocaust remembrance, the Holocaust Documentation Center and Memorial Collection Public Foundation was established to serve as the successor of the Hungarian Auschwitz Foundation. Under its aegis, a Holocaust Memorial Center – the first of its kind in post-communist East Central Europe – was inaugurated on Páva Street in Budapest in 2004, with its permanent exhibition opening its doors to visitors in 2006. However, in a number of respects the center fell short of expectations as its visitor numbers remained low and several rounds of infighting hampered its functioning. When Fidesz returned to power with a supermajority in 2010, the leadership of the Center was exchanged with Szabolcs Szita, a noted Holocaust historian and former employee, being reappointed to serve as director. In 2014, Szita was removed, to be temporarily replaced by György Haraszti, who until then fulfilled the function of chairman of the public foundation's board. As a result of intractable developments, György Haraszti in turn was removed in the summer of 2015 when Szita returned again to head the institution.

The latter change of personnel already took place in the context of more encompassing changes that raised anxieties regarding the future of the Holocaust Memorial Center. The idea to open another Holocaust Museum may have been originally raised by Szabolcs Szita himself, but by 2013–2014 it was no other than House of Terror director Mária Schmidt who was appointed to head the alternative project to be called the House of Fates. With the controversial reference to the notion of fate, a key expression of Jenő Lévai – the doyen of early postwar researchers dealing with the Holocaust in Hungary – was revived, in implicit opposition to Imre Kertész's later conception of fatelessness. (Ironically, this happened shortly prior to the establishment of the Imre Kertész Institute in Budapest, which is meant to cultivate the memory and legacy of the sole Hungarian writer who has been awarded the Nobel Prize and which is operated by the same public foundation as the House of Terror.) However, neither did much information regarding the rationale behind the new museum and its exact plan filter through to the public, nor was it sufficiently clarified what its opening would mean in terms of the independence, future contents, and exact function of the already existing Holocaust Memorial Center. Practically the only announcement with regard to the future contents of the House of Fates concerned how the new museum shall be devoted to one of the most shocking elements of the Holocaust, the Nazi murder of over one million children.

The increasingly transparent dualistic agenda of the year of commemoration, combined with the skepticism many of those concerned felt toward Schmidt's competence and intentions, soon led to sharp criticisms of the museum plans.[25] The main worry of the critics has been that the new museum might potentially ignore the Hungarian perpetrator side of the Holocaust. The largely unspecified though already controversial plans also generated alternative proposals to establish a museum devoted to Hungarian-Jewish coexistence (Szántó 2015). Following little evidence of progress on the House of Fates (except its planned building, the former train station of Józsefváros), and the resignation of several crucial members of the advisory board, a basic concept was eventually sketched by András Gerő, who aimed to position himself as the intellectual mastermind behind the project.

In an extended essay, Gerő (2014) introduced the future museum as an attempt to convey "the symbolic and spiritual" meaning of the Holocaust. He explained that the permanent exhibition would refrain from a more conventional historical presentation. It would rather aim at offering a cathartic experience to its visitors, which would hopefully result in "outraged rejection" and "mobilize their hatred of hatred." However, if infighting weakened the Holocaust Memorial Center and, according to Gerő, its relative lack of public success legitimized launching the House of Fates, further infighting in Fidesz elite circles, combined with the continued opposition of Hungarian Jewish representatives, seems to have condemned this controversial initiative to at least momentary failure. By 2019, the realization of a second Holocaust museum in Budapest still appears uncertain – even though unexpected twists have become an integral part of its far from fateful plot by now.

The second controversial official initiative concerned the statue commemorating the German occupation of Hungary. This initiative proved even more divisive and led to an extended and emotionally charged polemic. The controversy surrounding the planned monument repeatedly entered the international media, and the acclaim the Hungarian government might have received for generously endowing the Year of Commemoration thus appeared irreparably wasted. Focusing on the history of the Holocaust and highlighting Hungarian co-responsibility, critics of the statue saw in the initiative a blunt attempt to visually represent the thesis of the preamble of the new Hungarian Fundamental Law, whereby Hungarian sovereignty was supposed to have ended on March 19, 1944, i.e., prior to the mass deportation of most members of the Hungarian Jewish community.

Whereas critics of the plan focused on the occupation statue as a glaring example of wanting to separate commemoration from the question of historical responsibility, apologists of the government stressed the official devotion to national commemoration. The tiny minority of the statue's intellectual defenders aimed to interpret the statue as dedicated to all Hungarian victims of the catastrophic final year of the Second World War, which may not devote exclusive attention to Jewish victims but was by all means meant to include them, too – an argument that revealed with special clarity the dualistic official agenda of the year of commemoration, that of honoring the victims without casting doubts on nationalistic visions of history. Moreover, polemics in favor of the controversial statue plan opened a space for cruder claims, according to which the debate opposed those interested in an encompassing recognition of victims to those who aimed at the privileged recognition of their own particular group of victims. In other words, the response to the critics of the occupation statue also included a dose of what scholars have labeled secondary anti-Semitism: the thinly veiled suggestion was that Hungarian Jews were using and abusing the memory of their previous suffering.

Public voices tended to be critical toward both the idea of the statue and the concrete plan of its realization. However, opinion polls conducted at the height of the controversy have shown that the proposal divided Hungarian society more than anything else. The increasingly open clash between the ambition to build a new national canon and the traumatic personal and family memories of members of Hungarian society thus further polarized interpretations of the recent past. The 70th anniversary of the Holocaust in Hungary ultimately only reinforced the bitter divisions it was meant to help overcome.

Aiming to take this increasingly embarrassing issue off the agenda without resigning from its original plan, the government eventually decided to erect the monument at night and refrained from inaugurating it – even though the German occupation statue, if anything, provided the opponents of government policies with a new symbol (Horváth 2015). In other words, the regime persevered in its dualistic agenda for the Year of Commemoration but ultimately failed to find a convincing balance between its nationalistic focus on victimhood and sincere attention to the actual history of the Holocaust in Hungary.

CONCLUSION

From the point of view of the Fidesz government led by Viktor Orbán, the pragmatic challenge related to the 70th anniversary of the Holocaust in Hungary appears to have consisted of how to continue framing the recent past in a nationalistic key while improving its much damaged reputation by fulfilling international expectations toward its politics of history. What this challenge resulted in was a dualistic agenda of commemorating the Holocaust: an attempt was made to paint an image of totalitarianism without perpetrators, i.e., commemorating victims without foregrounding historical responsibility.

As I have argued above, the transnational preoccupation with totalitarianisms and the double occupation of Eastern European countries upon their entry into the EU in the early twenty-first century at first made Fidesz's agenda in the politics of history internationally less controversial than it would otherwise have been. The prominent international functions of Mária Schmidt, the leading memory activist of the Hungarian Right, in connection to Germany (until recently, she was on the curatorium of the Ettersberg Stiftung and received the German-Hungarian Friendship Prize from the German Business Club Hungary in 2017) but also on the European level (Schmidt is also on the Academic Committee of the House of European History, for instance), may serve to illustrate a wider pattern. However, the regime's agenda of Holocaust commemoration in 2014 clearly indicated that its local ambitions diverged from international expectations. No matter how seemingly generous in fostering remembrance, Hungary's new official politics of history has been contested as insufficient and even as inappropriate both locally and internationally.

Through the power games it has played with the historical profession in recent years, the current Hungarian regime may seem to be aiming at a revolution in the perception of history. However, based on the contents of its politics of history, what Fidesz offers is rather a working experiment of merging varied and often incongruous discourses. Many constitutive elements of the historical vision the regime has propagated since 2010 are all too familiar from earlier epochs (independentism, the myth of resistance, the generalized suffering of Hungarian society, and so on) or anything but unique to Hungary in the present (such as, most importantly, the theory of a dual occupation by totalitarian powers). The lack of innovation and indeed the lack of coherence of this historical vision of totalitarianisms without local roots and perpetrators might indeed be two of its most comforting aspects. Even so, the ultimate question has to remain open: will the national counterrevolution in the name of overcoming post-communism devour more nuanced interpretations of the recent past?

NOTES

1. In more recent years, Schmidt has been responsible for a host of major commemorative series, such as the centenary of the First World War, the 70th anniversary of the Holocaust in Hungary, and the 60th anniversary of 1956.

2. See https://www.veritasintezet.hu, accessed June 25, 2019.

3. Based on the website of the Institute, the agenda of this group consists of researching the events leading up to the start of the First World War, which is potentially of significant interest to international audiences, as well as two more narrowly Hungarian topics, the significance of the Wekerle Administration (1906–1910) and the life of István Tisza.

4. The research group on the Horthy era has a rather broad agenda with several key components relating to the controversial histories of the "Jewish question" and German-Hungarian relations.

5. The group on the post-1945 period intends to deal with reprisals and resistance to the communist regime, the role and perception of the Red Army in Hungary, and what Veritas calls "Moscow-type arrangements" in the country. Second, the group shall research the trials related to war crimes and other mass crimes (with the potential intention of starting rehabilitation procedures). Last but not least, its members shall devote their attention to the activities of the Antall and Boross administrations.

6. See http://www.retorki.hu/rovat/vezetok-es-munkatarsak, accessed June 25, 2019.

7. See http://www.retorki.hu, accessed June 25, 2019.

8. The report also reveals how the 70th anniversary of 1945 became a major preoccupation. The report of the Committee is available at http://www.parlament.hu/i rom40/04325/04325.pdf, accessed June 25, 2019.

9. Note that in Hungarian, just as in German, incidentally, the words for victim and sacrifice are the same (*áldozat, Opfer*).

10. Without being an explicitly or exclusively conservative forum, the bimonthly *Kommentár* has emerged as perhaps the most prestigious venue for younger conservative intellectual opinion. Beyond print media, blogs such as *Mandiner, Konzervatórium*, and to a lesser extent, *Jobbklikk* have played notable roles in publicizing younger conservative views, too. Whereas some authors with recurrent appearances in these venues have distanced themselves from Fidesz, others have received important appointments since 2010.

11. The idea of such a European Day of Remembrance was proposed during the Slovene and Czech EU presidencies, two countries not directly impacted by the agreement between Hitler and Stalin. The reasons behind supporting such commemorations thus would have been to be explained through references to ideological visions rather than to the specific historical experiences supposedly shared by Eastern Europeans.

12. The general elections of 2014 were eventually held a mere ten days before the date of the main anniversary.

13. It may be seen as indicative of how serious international concerns have gotten that Paul A. Shapiro, back then the Director of the Mandel Center for Advanced Holocaust Studies of the United States Holocaust Memorial Museum, repeatedly critiqued developments in Hungary already prior to the 2014 "year of commemoration." See, for instance, the testimony Shapiro gave at "The Trajectory of Democracy: Why Hungary Matters" session of the U.S. Commission on Security and Cooperation in Europe in March 2013.

14. See http://holokausztemlekev2014.kormany.hu/, the site is not available any longer. The website of *Infopoly Alapítvány* https://infopoly.info/h-2014/, accessed June 25, 2019, features a database documenting the Year of Holocaust Commemoration.

15. "Az emlékév szellemi alapvetései." http://holokausztemlekev2014.korman y.hu/az-emlekev-szellemi-alapvetesei. The document expresses that "the Hungarian Holocaust cut out our own Jewish part since in our coexistence, even if controversially, we became part of each other" (translation by author).

16. See http://holokausztemlekev2014.kormany.hu/civil-alap-2014.

17. See http://holokausztemlekev2014.kormany.hu/civil-alap-2014.

18. A slight majority of the victims of the Holocaust in Hungary were not from the post-war territory of Hungary – upon 1945, Hungary was to lose again the territories it reacquired between 1938 and 1941. On the history of three of these four "re-annexations" in Hungarian, see Ablonczy 2011; Simon 2014; Fedinec 2015.

19. I ought to clarify that Osiris Kiadó also applied and received financial support to publish my book manuscript *Felvilágosult vallás és modern katasztrófa közt. Magyar zsidó gondolkodás a Horthy-korban.*

20. The list of the winning entries can be found under "Civil Alap – támogatott pályázatok," at http://holokausztemlekev2014.kormany.hu/civil-alap-2014. Since neither the applications nor the list of those applicants who were not supported is publicly available, no substantial analysis of what kinds of projects were preferred could be conducted.

21. The resources they were originally meant to receive, amounting to over HUF 60 million, were soon reassigned to another nineteen applicants.

22. The broad Hungarian Jewish coalition behind the initiative reveals that the governmental strategy of building new alliances with local Jewish organizations was narrowly based and achieved only moderate successes.

23. On June 2, 2015, www.memento70.hu informed its readers that only six percent of the desired amount of donations was collected.

24. This particular event took place on October 30. The Tom Lantos Institute "was established in Hungary in May 2011 by the decision of the Hungarian Government and the U.S. Senate" and "core funding of the organization is provided by the Ministry of Foreign Affairs and Trade through the Centre for Democracy Public Foundation."

25. While Schmidt was among the few who conducted scholarly research into the history of the Holocaust in Hungary before 1989, she started to articulate national-apologetic standpoints regarding the Horthy regime afterwards and soon began to downplay the significance of the Holocaust.

BIBLIOGRAPHY

Ablonczy, Balázs. 2011. *A visszatért Erdély, 1940–1944*. Budapest: Jaffa.
"Az emlékév szellemi alapvetései." http://holokausztemlekev2014.kormany.hu/az-emlekev-szellemi-alapvetesei.
Bába, Iván. 2015. *Rendszerváltoztatás Magyarországon*. Budapest: Veritas.
Boda, Zsolt and András Körösényi, eds. 2013. *Van irány? Trendek a magyar politikában*. Budapest: Új Mandátum.
Borvendég, Zsuzsanna. 2015. *Újságírásnak álcázva*. Budapest: NEB.
Browning, Christopher. 1998. *Ordinary Men: Reserve Police Battalion 101 and the Final Solution in Poland*. New York: Harper Perennial.
"Civil Alap – támogatott pályázatok." http://holokausztemlekev2014.kormany.hu/civil-alap-2014.
Csatári, Bence. 2015a. *A Tájékoztatási Hivatal története. Szirmai István elnöksége alatt*. Budapest: NEB.
Csatári, Bence. 2015b. *Jampecek a pagodában. A Magyar Rádió könnyűzenei politikája a Kádár-rendszerben*. Budapest: NEB.
Cserényi-Zsitnyányi, Ildikó. 2015. *A politizált gazdasági rendőrség*. Budapest: NEB.
Fedinec, Csilla. 2015. *"A Magyar Szent Koronához visszatért Kárpátalja, 1938–1944*. Budapest: Jaffa.
Feischmidt, Margit et al. 2014. *Nemzet a mindennapokban. Az újnacionalizmus populáris kultúrája*. Budapest: L'Harmattan.

Fricz, Tamás, Kund Halmy, and Tímea Orosz. 2014. *A politikai túlélés művészete. Az MSZMP/MSZP hatalomátmentésének természetrajza: érvelés és gyakorlat (1988–2010).* Lakitelek: Antológia Kiadó.

Fritz, Regina. 2012. *Nach Krieg und Judenmord. Ungarns Geschichtspolitik seit 1944.* Göttingen: Wallstein.

Gerő, András. 2014. *Magyar másik. Értelmezések és reprezentációk.* Budapest: Habsburg Történeti Intézet – Közép- és Kelet-európai Történelem és Társadalom Kutatásáért Közalapítvány.

Grabowski, Jan. 2013. *Hunt for the Jews: Betrayal and Murder in German-Occupied Poland.* Bloomington: Indiana University Press.

Greskovits, Béla and Dorothee Bohle. 2012. *Capitalist Diversity on Europe's Periphery.* Ithaca, NY: Cornell University Press.

Halmy, Kund. 2015a. *Beszéljenek az iratok.* Budapest: NEB.

———. 2015b. *Cenzúra? Az MSZMP KB Tudományos, Közoktatási és Kulturális Osztályának (TKKO) működése, 1982.* Lakitelek: Antológia Kiadó.

Horváth, Sándor. 2015. "Goodbye Historikerstreit, Hello Budapest City of Angels: The Debate about the Monument to the German Occupation." In *Forum Cultures of History,* Friedrich Schiller University Jena. http://www.cultures-of-history.uni-jena.de/debating-20th-century-history/hungary/goodbye-historikerstreit-hello-bud apest-city-of-angels-the-debate-about-the-monument-to-the-german-occupation/, accessed June 25, 2019.

Kaminsky, Anna, Dietmar Müller, and Stefan Troebst, eds. 2011. *Der Hitler-Stalin-Pakt 1939 in den Erinnerungskulturen der Europäer.* Göttingen: Wallstein.

Katona, András et al. 2014. *Tüntetések könyve. Negyedszázad 56 tüntetése Magyarországon (1988–2013).* Lakitelek: Antológia Kiadó.

Kávássy, János Előd. 2015. *Nyugati szélben. Adalékok a magyar-amerikai kapcsolatok 1989-es történetéhez; gondolatok a kelet-európai és a magyar rendszerváltáshoz.* Lakitelek: Antológia Kiadó.

Klimó, Árpád von. 2006. *Ungarn seit 1945.* Göttingen: Vandenhoeck & Ruprecht.

Kovács, András. 2011. *The Stranger at Hand: Antisemitic Prejudices in Post-Communist Hungary.* Leiden: Brill.

———. 2016. "Hungarian Intentionalism: New Directions in the Historiography of the Hungarian Holocaust." In *The Holocaust in Hungary: Seventy Years Later,* edited by Randolph L. Braham and András Kovács, 3–24. Budapest: CEU Press.

Kubik, Jan and Michael Bernhard, eds. 2014. *Twenty Years after Communism: The Politics of Memory and Commemoration.* Oxford: Oxford University Press.

Laczó, Ferenc. 2014. *Felvilágosult vallás és modern katasztrófa közt. Magyar zsidó gondolkodás a Horthy-korban.* Budapest: Osiris.

———. 2016. "Integrating Victims, Externalizing Guilt? Commemorating the Holocaust in Hungary in 2014." *Südosteuropa. Zeitschrift für Politik und Gesellschaft* 64 (2): 167–87.

———. 2018. "New Sensibilities, New Volatilities: Antisemitism in Contemporary Hungary." *Antisemitism Studies* 2018 (1): 75–108.

Mark, James. 2010. *The Unfinished Revolution: Making Sense of the Communist Past in Central-Eastern Europe.* New Haven, CT: Yale University Press.

Müller, Jan-Werner. 2012. *Wo Europa endet. Ungarn, Brüssel und das Schicksal der liberalen*. Frankfurt am Main: Suhrkamp.

Püski, István and István Gulay. 2015a. *"Ismertem az írók körüli mágneses teret."* *Püski Sándor élete hagyatékának tükrében I., 1929–1945*. Budapest: Püski Kiadó.

———. 2015b. *"A világszabadságot nem tudjuk elképzelni a magyar nemzet szabadsága nélkül." Püski Sándor élete hagyatékának tükrében II. 1946–1969*. Budapest: Püski Kiadó.

Riba, András László and Balázs Házi, eds. 2015. *Taxisblokád II. Egy belpolitikai válsághelyzet története. Dokumentumok*. Lakitelek: Antológia Kiadó.

Sáringer, János. 2015. *Iratok az Antall-kormány külpolitikájához és diplomáciájához I*. Budapest: Veritas.

Sáringer, János et al. 2015. *Súlypontáthelyezés a diplomáciában. A NEB Külügyi Munkacsoportjának tanulmányai 1*. Budapest: NEB.

Shapiro, Paul A. 2013. "The Trajectory of Democracy: Why Hungary Matters." March 19, 2013. https://www.csce.gov/sites/helsinkicommission.house.gov/files/The%20Trajectory%20of%20Democracy%20-%20Why%20Hungary%20Matters.pdf, accessed June 25, 2019.

Simon, Attila. 2014. *Magyar idők a Felvidéken, 1938–1945*. Budapest: Jaffa.

Snyder, Timothy. 2010. *Bloodlands: Europe between Hitler and Stalin*. New York: Basic Books.

Stone, Dan. 2010. *Histories of the Holocaust*. Oxford: Oxford University Press.

Szacki, Jerzy. 1995. *Liberalism after Communism*. Budapest: CEU Press.

Szántó, Gábor T. 2015. "Még nem késő." *HVG Online*, July 6, 2015.

Szekér, Nóra, and András László Riba. 2014a. *A Nagy Imre-kód. Nagy Imre újratemetésének politikai dimenziói*. Lakitelek: Antológia Kiadó.

Szekér, Nóra, and Zoltán Nagymihály, eds. 2015b. *Jeles napok, jeltelen ünnepek a diktatúrában. Pillanatképek a kommunista emlékezetpolitika valóságából*. Lakitelek: Antológia Kiadó.

———. 2015. *Taxisblokád I. Egy belpolitikai válsághelyzet története. Tanulmányok, interjúk*. Lakitelek: Antológia Kiadó.

Szeredi, Pál. 2014. *A Parasztpárt két évtizede. A Nemzeti Parasztpárt története, 1939–1960*. Pilisszentkereszt: Barangoló Kiadó.

———. 2015. *Nemzetépítő demokratikus ellenállás a Kádár-korban (1956–1987)*. Pilisszentkereszt: Barangoló Kiadó.

Szilágyi, Ákos. 2010. *A kékek és a zöldek. Hideg polgárháború Magyarországon*. Budapest: Új Palatinus.

Szilágyi, Gábor, and Stefano Bottoni. 2015. *Keletről Nyugatra. A kommunista mozgalom titkos pénzei*. Budapest: NEB.

Szűcs, Zoltán Gábor. 2010. *Az antalli pillanat. A nemzeti történelem szerepe a magyar politikai diskurzusban 1989–1993*. Budapest: L'Harmattan.

Tóth, Eszter Zsófia. 2015. *Antall József útja a miniszterelnökségig (1932–1989)*. Budapest: Veritas.

Tóth, Gábor Attila, ed. 2012. *Constitution for a Disunited Nation. On Hungary's 2011 Fundamental Law*. Budapest: CEU Press.

Ungváry, Krisztián. 2017. *A szembenézés hiánya. Felelősségre vonás, iratnyilvánosság és átvilágítás Magyarországon 1990–2017*. Budapest: Self-published.
Vági, Zoltán, László Csősz, and Gábor Kádár. 2013. *The Holocaust in Hungary: Evolution of a Genocide*. Lanham, MD: AltaMira Press.
Valuch, Tibor. 2015. *A jelenkori magyar társadalom*. Budapest: Osiris.

Chapter 3

Civil Society in an Illiberal Democracy

Government-Friendly NGOs, "Foreign Agents," and Uncivil Publics

Virág Molnár

Civil society has been assigned a central but often disputed role in the workings of modern political institutions. It has been defined in multiple, partially overlapping ways as the *realm of voluntary associational life* that is crucial for building cohesive societies by balancing the power of the state and the market; the *embodiment of "good society"* fostering estimable norms and values such as freedom, democracy, tolerance, and cooperation; and as the *public sphere*, the arena in which political ideas are formulated, deliberated, and evaluated (Bob 2011). The multitude of coexisting definitions attests to civil society's complexity and plurality but also its empirical elusiveness. In fact, the prominent U.S. sociologist Charles Tilly once remarked that the concept of civil society is "normatively admirable, [but] analytically useless" (Arato 2011, 195).

Nevertheless, in the socialist and post-socialist context, civil society always has been attributed causal force in accounting for political outcomes before, during, and after the democratic transition. A weak civil society was seen both as a cause and consequence of authoritarian state rule under socialism. Emerging civil society organizations during the last years of state socialism have been identified as essential in mounting an initial challenge to authoritarian rule as well as ensuring that formal democracy gets translated fully into substantive democracy (Arato 1991; Heller 2007). The current populist political backlash and illiberal turn is no exception. Political scientists have been quick to trace the malaise of democracy in Hungary to an ailing civil society. Jacques Rupnik, for instance, argued that the democratic setbacks in Central and Eastern Europe arose from the fact that constitutionalism and economic liberalization took precedence over citizenship and participation and that the democratic consolidation failed to transform civic culture (Rupnik 2007). While the exact causal impact of civil society on the quality of democratic governance continues to be contested, it is clear that it would be a mistake to try to understand the rise of illiberalism in Hungary without examining the interconnections between political and civil society, or politics and the public sphere (see also Kovács 1994; Kopecky and Mudde 2003a; Kotkin and Gross 2009).

The following chapter, therefore, aims to chart the main trends that have shaped the interstitial domain of civil society in recent years, especially since the introduction of the so-called "System of National Cooperation," which was imposed as a new social contract after the landslide election victory and return to power of Fidesz in 2010. This analysis operates with a broad defini-tion of civil society that encompasses all forms of societal self-organization regardless of value orientation. Unlike many contemporary political theorists who restrict the category of civil society to groups that pursue progressive and democratic causes, this chapter follows a Gramscian insight that sees civil society as a site of multiple struggles among various democratic and anti-democratic projects, a theater of history where the politics of affirmation and contestation play out (Gramsci 1971). Similarly, in contrast to dominant approaches that assess the vitality and contribution of civil society primarily through quantitative measures (number of organizations, number of employ-ees and members, the amount of financial resources available to civic organi-zations, and so on), the analysis focuses on capturing qualitative changes that underlie the sector. It identifies three general trends around which the chapter is organized: (1) increasing government control over and cooptation of civil society; (2) progressively intensifying attacks and repression of organizations critical of the government; and (3) the rise of "uncivil" society that embraces and promotes illiberal politics. The following sections delineate these trends with the help of detailed case studies that afford an in-depth look into the reconfiguration of the field, highlighting the ground-level dynamics through which the boundaries of political and civil society are being redrawn.

DISCIPLINING CIVIL SOCIETY

As a key figure of the pre-1989 democratic opposition, Fidesz leader and current prime minister Viktor Orbán always has been keenly aware of the significance of civil society for the practice of politics. In his MA thesis, which he completed at the Law School of Eötvös Loránd University (ELTE) in 1987, he dealt with theories of grassroots social movements based on a case study of Solidarity and other opposition groups in Poland in the 1980s (Orbán 1987; Dobszay 2014). It is no accident that throughout his political career he consistently has paid strategic attention to the relationship between civil society and the political system. After he lost the parliamentary elections to the socialists in 2002, he turned to civil society to contest the outcome by spurring a nationwide movement of the so-called "Civic Circles" to bring together various groups unhappy with the socialist victory in the hope of overturning the unfavorable results (Molnár 2016; Greskovits 2017). His new program of "National Cooperation," introduced after he regained power in 2010, therefore was bound to incorporate a set of formal and informal instruments for containing unfettered civil society activism to ensure that the "third sector" presents no challenge to his new political rule. Moreover, this program envisioned a new role for civil society in strengthening national sovereignty and fostering national interests (see also Hemment 2012 regarding Russia).

Consequently, the government has followed a three-pronged strategy in reshaping the institutional framework of the civil sphere: (1) the creation of an increasingly restrictive legal environment for civic actors, (2) the reorganization of the main government agency responsible for distributing public funds to civil society organizations, and (3) the establishment and support of civic associations that are seemingly independent but in reality are organized by the state and government-friendly groups while acting as a mouthpiece for government propaganda.[1]

First, a significant overhaul of the legal framework began with the passing of a new Nonprofit Law in 2012 and a new Civil Code in 2013. These new laws were meant to update and consolidate the existing fragmented legislation on the nonprofit and civil sector but actually have created the opposite effect. They have increased the uncertainty of the legal environment and the bureaucratic hurdles civil society organizations face in their daily operations. For instance, registration procedures have become more complicated and are plagued with constant delays. Especially, the bar to claim "public benefit status" (*közhasznúság*) has been raised, although this is a crucial requirement for organizations that hope to apply for government grants and other state subsidies (USAID 2017). Civic organizations in Europe are generally more dependent on public funds than those in the United States, and state support plays an essential role in the life of Hungarian nonprofit organizations. It makes up about 27 percent of the overall revenues of these organizations, while private donations count for about 18 percent; the rest are generated from membership fees (Sebestény 2001, 339).[2] Simultaneously, regulations pertaining to the economic activities and state monitoring of civil society organizations remain inconsistent. Official inspections occur more frequently and new financial audits have been introduced, also retrospectively, with regard to long-completed state-sponsored projects. In general, it is increasingly difficult to run these organizations without significant legal expertise, even though legal services in this field are scarce and costly while *pro bono* legal help is in short supply.[3] In its latest report on the sustainability of the civil sector, USAID downgraded the stability of the legal environment in which Hungarian civil society organizations operate to 3.3 from 3.1 in the previous year, which was already significantly lower than the average score of 1.4 for the period between 1998 and 2010 (USAID 2017).

Second, legislative changes have gone hand in hand with an extensive reorganization of governmental agencies that are in charge of allocating public funds to civil society groups. In 2011 the new Fidesz government established the National Cooperation Fund (*Nemzeti Együttműködési Alap*) to take the place of the National Civil Fund (*Nemzeti Civil Alap*) that used to be the flagship agency awarding state funds to civil society organizations. The change was not a simple act of renaming but involved more fundamental restructuring. For instance, while two-thirds of the board members of the former National Civil Fund were delegated directly by civil society organizations, their share shrank to a mere one-third in the new National Cooperation Fund (NCF). The head of the agency is no longer elected by its members but appointed by the minister for human resources. László Csizmadia, the current president of the NCF and a former businessman, never concealed his political sympathies for the Fidesz government, and he is also the founder of the pro-government civic association, the Civil Union Forum (*Civil Összefogás Fórum*). The NCF's annual budget was cut severely from its customary HUF 7–8 billion to HUF 3.5 billion, putting further strain on civic organizations that are generally dependent on state support, as noted earlier. At the same time, the number of applications to the fund by civil society organizations fell sharply from 17–20,000 to roughly 8,000, in part because organizations increasingly believe that only government-friendly groups will receive support. NCF's president has a right to veto every funding decision, and there is a special 10 percent ministerial quota that goes to organizations favored by the government minister overseeing the agency. Using a large grant from the European Union, the NCF also set up a nationwide network of the so-called Civic Information Centers (*Civil Információs Centrum*). Local civic organizations can apply for a certificate that designates them as an information hub for local civic groups in the area. These certificates for the most part have been awarded to openly pro-government organizations (like the government-sponsored think tank, *Századvég*) or to organizations that support the local implementation of public policies like the government's controversial workfare program.

Finally, since 2010 one could witness the rise of influential, formally independent but openly pro-government civic associations and activism that resemble "Astroturf" groups or GONGOs[4] in the service of disseminating and defending the government's official position. The Civil Union Forum undoubtedly has been the most active and conspicuous of these organizations. As mentioned above, the CUF is headed by the president of the National Cooperation Fund that oversees the allocation of public subsidies to civil society groups and is funded partly by a Fidesz-friendly foundation, the Civil Union Public Benefit Foundation (*Civil Összefogás Közhasznú Alapítvány*). The organization first had gained public visibility by organizing a series of adroitly orchestrated pro-government demonstrations that at their peak brought over 100,000 Fidesz government supporters to the streets of Budapest. Six of these so-called "Peace Marches" (*Békemenet*) had been organized between January 2012 and March 2014. The first "Peace March" on January 21, 2012 must have baffled the broader public, as there had been no real precedent for a pro-government rally in Hungary in the post-1989 period, in large part because such mass mobilization would have recalled the aims and choreography of government-organized mass demonstrations characteristic of the socialist era. Nevertheless, survey research carried out by Hungarian political scientists also has shown that many of the participants were not simply hired protesters but seemed to genuinely believe in the cause of the demonstrations (Susánszky, Kopper, and Tóth 2016). The signature banner of the inaugural Peace March that reverberated through traditional and online media might have confused non-Hungarian spectators, as it displayed the slogan: "We are not going to be a colony!" This motto became the emblem of the Peace March. It was meant to summarize the profound indignation Fidesz supporters felt over the flurry of harsh criticism directed against the Hungarian government by the European Union with respect to growing signs of anti-democratic tendencies in a string of new legislation, including the new Constitution, new Media Law, and the new Church Act regulating religious practice and freedoms, that were all passed relying on the Fidesz supermajority in the parliament. Peace Marchers portrayed the European Union as an authoritarian and oppressive institution, an instrument of foreign domination (even likened to the USSR) that meddles in Hungary's internal affairs and tries to erode its national sovereignty.

The Civil Union Forum also played a central and controversial role in the 2014 election campaign in which Fidesz and Viktor Orbán were reelected by openly endorsing a political party, which is in sharp conflict with its independent status as a civic group. Fidesz massively rewrote the rules for political advertising in election campaigns during its first term in office. Commercial television stations were barred from charging for political advertising. As a result, political ads virtually disappeared from commercial channels, while state-owned stations were limited to eight hours of political advertising over the 50 days of the official campaign. Outdoor advertising on billboards, lampposts, and other public places also was sharply restricted. However, the outdoor advertising restriction did not apply to "independent groups" like the

Civil Union Forum. CUF, taking advantage of this exception, launched an aggressive campaign that came to be known simply as the "clown ad," conveying the increasingly circus-like qualities of Hungarian politics.

The "clown ad" portrayed prominent socialist politicians – two former prime ministers, the president of the Socialist Party (MSZP), and the former socialist deputy mayor of Budapest who was the subject of a large-scale corruption trial at the time – standing in a police lineup, alongside a clown. The slogan printed below the lineup announced, "They Don't Deserve Another Chance." The "clown ads" were ubiquitous across Budapest, covering billboards, building facades, buses, and lampposts. Moreover, there were no counter images produced by other groups, which made the advertising initiative particularly overwhelming. Two years later, in 2016, a follow-up "clown ad" campaign simultaneously targeted the far-right *Jobbik* (Movement for a Better Hungary) and the leftist Democratic Coalition, the political party of the former socialist prime minister Ferenc Gyurcsány, for not supporting the government's anti-immigrant constitutional amendment. It has since been revealed that this smear campaign almost certainly was financed through covert government funds in the form of a "charitable donation" made by the state-owned monopoly power supplier, the Hungarian National Electricity Company (MVM), to the CUF-affiliated Civil Union Public Benefit Foundation.

The operation of CUF and similar groups has been likened to the "super PACs" of the American political process, a form of soft money covertly benefiting political parties (Hakim 2014). The main difference here is that in Hungary only the ruling party benefits from such "donations" and public funds most likely are channeled into supporting these pseudo-civic activities. The example of groups like the Civil Union Forum shows how the government is effectively instrumentalizing civil society to crowd out alternative political views and monopolize public debate.

CIVIC ORGANIZATIONS AS "FOREIGN AGENTS"

In tandem with multiplying legal hurdles and increasing the bureaucratic burden of civic organizations, the government also has launched direct attacks on civic groups. The gradually intensifying attacks have been directed primarily at organizations that receive funds from foreign donors based mostly in North America and Western Europe and whose chief mission is to strengthen democratic institutions, civil society, and human rights protection in Hungary. Government politicians and the conservative press repeatedly have described these civic organizations as "foreign agents," accusing them of pursuing foreign interests and agendas, thereby undermining Hungarian sovereignty.

This is an argument that is by no means unique to Hungary (Hemment 2012). It frequently also can be heard in Russia where the government turned its distrust of foreign donors into law in 2012, requiring all nonprofit organizations that receive foreign donations and engage in "political activity" to register and declare themselves as "foreign agents."[5] Since the "foreign agent" law went into effect, Russia also effectively has banned some organizations like the U.S. hedge fund billionaire and philanthropist George Soros' Open Society Foundations[6] from operating in the country by declaring their activities a security threat (Ablan 2015).

For years – roughly from 2010 to 2016 – in the new Fidesz era, the Hungarian government constantly skirted around the idea of introducing a similar registry, but it opted instead for a more *ad hoc* and diffuse strategy. In lieu of direct punitive measures, it relied on more pragmatic tactics including intimidation and public smear campaigns that were meant to signal a warning to civic groups while encouraging self-censorship. The government also labored to draw sharp symbolic and moral distinctions between "good" and "bad" organizations, with government-friendly organizations belonging to the former, while organizations critical and independent of the government exemplifying the latter category.

The first high-profile, direct attack on civil society after Fidesz's return to power was launched in 2014. It involved two unlikely protagonists: an ecological nonprofit organization called Ökotárs and the government of Norway. Ökotárs is the Hungarian member of the Environmental Partnership Association (EPA) that was set up by a consortium of U.S. private foundations in 1991 to bring together local organizations that promote and support civic green initiatives in Central Europe (Bulgaria, Czech Republic, Hungary, Poland, Romania, and Slovakia). Since its formal registration in 1994, Ökotárs has been active in supporting the nonprofit environmental movement and the cooperation of local and international NGOs and government organizations through grant-making, training, technical assistance, and consultancy. In the past two decades, the organization also has assumed an important intermediary role in administering grant schemes sponsored by various private, governmental, and intergovernmental donors, including, most recently, the NGO program of the European Economic Area/Norway Grants. It was this clearinghouse position for foreign donations that turned the organization into a target of government attack.

The EEA and Norway Grants were established in 1994 with the intention of reducing the development disparities between old and new member states of the European Union. Funding priorities are reexamined every five years, and the last two cycles (2004–2009; 2009–2014) have focused on former socialist states that joined the EU in and since 2004. In the latest full five-year scheme EUR 1.8 billion was distributed among 16 countries, with about 10 percent of the overall funds dedicated to NGOs. The NGO program is governed by bilateral agreements between Norway and individual countries. Until 2011, the funds were distributed through a highly centralized mechanism, through the Financial Mechanism Office (FMO) in Brussels and government agencies in the receiving countries. But in 2011 Norway Grants instituted a new distribution mechanism, transferring the distribution of funds from state bureaucratic organizations to local NGOs that were selected in a rigorous competition based on criteria that included experience in grant-making and management, independence, and general good rapport with the civil sector. The funders argued that this shift from governmental to civic intermediaries would improve the effectiveness of grant distribution because local NGOs are less bureaucratic and less prone to corruption while more skilled than government agencies at directing the funds where they really are needed.

It was through this competitive process that Ökotárs became one of the local Hungarian clearinghouses for the EEA/Norway Grants in 2011.[7] In the latest full funding cycle (2009–2014), they granted support to more than 400 organizations, with the grant amount ranging from typically HUF 1–2 million to HUF 40 million. The large awards are meant for a longer period (two to three years) and are smaller in number (23 such large grants were awarded in 2013).[8]

The areas that received the largest share of the budget in 2013 were human rights and democracy (21.6 percent), gender and equal opportunity (16.7 percent), and Roma integration projects (15.7 percent). Some of the specific organizations that have received funds included the Hungarian chapter of Transparency International (EUR 110,000) or the Asimov Foundation (EUR 105,000) that runs workshops on investigative journalism for independent websites, blogs, and social media activist groups and is also affiliated with the online portal Atlatszo.hu that promotes freedom of information initiatives to improve public accountability. Funds also were granted to Krétakör (EUR 117,000), one of Hungary's best-known, independent avant-garde theater companies that produces interactive plays on contemporary social issues, runs drama workshops and educational programs, and operates without any financial support from the government.[9] The Women's Organization, NANE ("Women for Women against Violence"), which fights against domestic violence and provides aid to victims of violence, and the Roma Press Center were also among the recipients to convey a sense of the range of initiatives that have been underwritten by the NGO Program of Norway Grants via Ökotárs in the most recent funding cycle.

Even though Ökotárs took over the management and distribution of Norway Grants from the government already in 2011, the government crackdown on the organization began in earnest only in 2014. The attack proceeded in three distinct phases. First, Ökotárs was accused of supporting direct political activity by funding political parties, more specifically, Hungary's remote equivalent of a green party, called LMP (*Lehet Más a Politika*, i.e., Politics Can Be Different), thereby violating the Hungarian Nonprofit Law that prohibits registered civic organizations from engaging in direct political activity. Second, the accusations shifted to Ökotárs directing funding to civic organizations that were linked to political parties. Third, Ökotárs was accused of financial irregularities and mismanagement of funds. The charges pragmatically mutated over time after earlier accusations of political influence peddling were refuted, underscoring that the real objective of the witch-hunt was to create a precedent and intimidate similar organizations.

With this political objective in mind, it is unsurprising that the nearly two-year public saga of this hitherto little-known civic organization was not short of dramatic scenes and was turned into a media spectacle. The government ordered a tax audit of Ökotárs to uncover financial irregularities and a simultaneous audit by the Government Control Office (KEHI), even though Norway Grants do not fall under the jurisdiction of the Government Control Office because they do not involve the distribution of government funds; their monitoring agency is the FMO in Brussels. At the height of the conflict, the Hungarian government even entered into a diplomatic row with Norway, which led to Norway temporarily suspending the funding of Norway Grants in Hungary.

The quarrel around Norway Grants also was cited explicitly in Viktor Orbán's notorious "illiberal democracy" speech (Orbán 2014) delivered in July 2014 in Tusnádfürdő (Băile Tuşnad). Orbán repeatedly called civil society actors "political activists paid by foreigners" who "are seeking to meddle with Hungary's state affairs by trying to exert influence over specific issues in strategic moments" (Orbán 2014). But the low point of the controversy was reached in September 2014 when, under heavy and armed police presence, the Anti-Corruption and Economic Crime Unit of the Hungarian National Bureau of Investigation raided and searched the premises of Ökotárs and five other NGOs, while the president of Ökotárs, Veronika Móra, was escorted by a group of police officers to her home where her personal computer and documents were seized.[10]

In a somewhat surprising turn of events, over a year later, in October 2015, the National Tax and Tariffs Agency (NAV) dropped all charges of financial mismanagement against Ökotárs and 17 other NGOs that received its support which also were investigated. Similarly, the Chief Prosecutor's Office found no evidence of unlawful practices in the operation of the accused NGOs. At the same time, the central district court ruled that the police search and seizure of documents at the headquarters of Ökotárs and other NGOs were unlawful and that there were no sufficient grounds for a search in the first place. The EEA/Norway Grants also conducted an independent audit of the

NGO program in Hungary with the help of the London-based multinational audit company PKF Littlejohn LLP which concluded that the fund operator's management and control systems were in line with legal regulations and requirements governed by bilateral agreements; only minor reporting errors were identified.[11] In other words, Ökotárs and the associated organizations were cleared of any wrongdoing by the end of 2015.[12]

On the one hand, this can be interpreted as a happy ending and a sign that the rule of law in Hungary has not been abandoned completely. On the other hand, the case exhibited typical characteristics of a public smear campaign in which news of acquittal and the clearing of the name of the organization never received the same media attention as the initial unsubstantiated charges. Moreover, the case helped to sow seeds of doubt among the public about the "true" intentions of civil society actors, while the eagerness of the government to criminalize civic organizations whose agendas and funding it cannot completely control remained a serious cause for concern and a clear threat to the independent civil sector.

Subsequently, Europe's refugee and migration crisis that erupted in the summer of 2015 introduced another significant turning point in government and civil society relations in Hungary. It renewed government accusations that Hungarian civil society groups are acting in pursuit of foreign interests. While North American and Western European media coverage of the dramatic developments in Hungary focused on condemning the actions of the Hungarian government, they generally failed to report about vigorous grassroots activism also triggered by the events. Several groups (e.g., Migration Aid, Migszol Csoport) sprang up literally overnight to help refugees stranded in Hungary. They relied entirely on volunteer work and private donations (primarily from individuals) to provide refugees with basic amenities, essentially stepping in to fill the role that the government was expected to perform. The government was taken by surprise by this grassroots mobilization and the unexpected vitality of these initiatives. Thus, soon various Fidesz officials began to spread the rumor that all these groups were financed and instructed by George Soros (Botos 2015).

The active role independent civil society organizations played in supporting migrants and refugees in the face of the Hungarian government's virulent anti-immigrant position finally pushed the government to take a more repressive stance against civil society actors. In June 2017 the Hungarian parliament passed a new NGO law "on the transparency of foreign-funded organizations" that was modeled closely on similar Russian and Israeli legislation. According to the official reasoning, this law was introduced to increase transparency and prevent civil society organizations from becoming instruments of foreign interference in Hungarian national affairs (including involvement in terrorism-related money laundering). But the NGO law was widely interpreted as an attack against civil society organizations critical of the government whose access to foreign financial assistance largely enabled them to maintain their independence.

The new law requires civil society organizations that receive more than HUF 7.2 million (USD 28,800) from any foreign sources in a tax year to register with the court as an "organization supported from abroad." Moreover, this information has to be made public by displaying the "foreign-funded" label on their websites, publications, and press materials, while it will also appear in the official CSO registry and the electronic portal of the Ministry of Human Resources. Failure to comply with the law will result in high fines and possible termination. Many prominent, "foreign-funded" civil society organizations loudly protested this legislation, and several (e.g., Hungarian Helsinki Committee, Ökotárs, TASZ) announced that they will refuse to register with the court as an act of civil disobedience. Fourteen civil society organizations also filed a complaint with the European Court of Human Rights in Strasbourg, while the European Commission initiated an infringement procedure against Hungary with regard to the law on foreign-funded NGOs for discriminating and disproportionately restricting foreign donations to civil society organizations, for restricting the right to freedom of association, and for raising personal data protection concerns.

The law on foreign-funded NGOs, however, also needs to be seen as part of a more elaborate policy package that the government designed to combine anti-civil with anti-immigration measures.[13] This is why George Soros became the central target of the attacks. Soros has been a key supporter of liberal civil society organizations in Hungary through his Open Society Foundations network, the founder of Hungary's most prestigious international private university, the Central European University, and an advocate of pro-immigration policies in the European Union. The attacks unfolded through a massive propaganda campaign in the summer of 2017 that used Soros to conjure up toxic stereotypes about Jews and bankers that have a long and disgraceful history in Central Europe. They now are culminating in the so-called "Stop Soros" package in 2018, further stigmatizing civil society by creating a new category of organizations that "support illegal migration"; by levying a 25 percent tax on foreign donations received by such organizations; and by upholding the government's right to shut down any civil society organization that is deemed a "security risk."

THE GROWTH OF "UNCIVIL SOCIETY"

In addition to the government's efforts to either discipline civil society organizations or crack down on critical groups as "foreign agents," the third robust trend that has reshaped the landscape of civil society activism in Hungary involves the emergence and rapid growth of "uncivil" publics (Molnár 2016). These "uncivil" publics include grassroots and civic associations that promote agendas that question, implicitly or explicitly, liberal democratic values. Especially since the 1990s, following the collapse of socialism and the end of the Cold War, civil society has been operationalized primarily as NGOs. As a result, the concepts of civil society, NGOs, and the nonprofit sector have been treated as largely synonymous (Aksartova 2006). Simultaneously, professional NGOs were assigned a key role in spreading and bolstering democracy in emerging post-socialist societies. The equation of NGOs with civil society, however, has significantly narrowed the definition of what groups, organizations, and activities constitute civil society. Moreover, this understanding has also been rooted in a powerful normative assumption that civil society organizations are imbued with both liberal and democratic values, and a stronger civil society inevitably means a stronger democracy.

In contrast, an empirical definition of civil society that encompasses the nonstate, nonmarket realm of associational life and the public sphere casts a much wider net. It includes, for instance, uncivil society as a tendency within civil society, which may be characterized by exclusivist and antimodernist predispositions – especially of ethnic or religious nature, and fundamentalism – or even the potential use of violence. There is an ongoing debate among scholars of civil society whether there is such a thing as uncivil society, how it can be delineated, and whether it should be included in the category of civil society (see, for instance, Kaldor and Muro 2003; Kopecky and Mudde 2003a, 2003b; Glasius 2010; Bob 2011). Yet, in the Hungarian case, the significant restructuring and illiberal shift of the public sphere only can be grasped fully by carefully scrutinizing the role of uncivil publics.

In the Hungarian context, the uncivil component of civil society comprises a broad range of organizations that advocate various forms of radical nationalism. It is this radical nationalist program that represents an exclusivist element because it generally translates into support for exclusionary politics (e.g., scapegoating of ethnic/racial minorities, anti-immigrant sentiments, chauvinism toward neighboring countries), hostility to the European integration project and globalization, and the re-ethnicization of the meaning of citizenship and cultural membership. In other words, the rise of uncivil publics has been closely coupled with a broader process of renationalization that has been identified as an important factor behind the spread of right-wing populism across Europe (Wodak 2015). Since at least the turn of the millennium in many post-socialist countries in general and in Hungary in particular, civil society has emerged as a key arena in which the symbolic repertoire of a new nationalism is being articulated (Feischmidt 2014; Trencsényi 2014).

Namely, it is not merely the state that plays a decisive role in recasting Hungarian nationalism but also civic actors, far-right political groups, and their media outlets backed by a vigorous industry that has turned nationalist identity politics into a profitable business (Feischmidt 2014). This is not an entirely new phenomenon in Hungary, for in the Reform era (from 1825 to 1848) and in the second half of the nineteenth century civic associations (reading clubs, ballroom societies, private literary salons, and so on) also played a crucial part in Hungarian independence efforts and the nation-state building project (Nemes 2001 and 2005).[14]

Contemporary uncivil publics remained outside the purview of academic research for a long time, in large part because they had low visibility in mainstream media channels. They generally lacked access to mainstream print and broadcast media and turned instead to online and social media to create an alternative public sphere to share and disseminate their ideas and activities. In an article in which I set out to reconstruct the landscape of radical civic activism I built on this important insight in conducting my empirical research (Molnár 2016). I began compiling a list of key organizations by first locating the websites of some of the best-known groups (the Goyim[15] riders, kuruc. info online news portal, nationalist rock bands) to quickly discover that their websites nearly always included a collection of links to other like-minded organizations. These were often designated as "links to our friends' websites" (*barátaink oldalai*) and "links to our supporters" (*támogatóink oldalai*), and it was chiefly by tracing these links that I mapped the network of uncivil publics in contemporary Hungary (see Figure 1 and Table A1 in Molnár 2016).

The inventory of these organizations is certainly not exhaustive, but it provides a comprehensive sampling of existing organizations to illustrate the wide range of social and cultural activities they pursue. They include cultural heritage associations that promote the preservation and cultivation of Hungarian "traditions" such as the learning of the Hungarian Runic alphabet; *baranta*, a Hungarian martial art; pre-Christian pagan religious practices (Hubbes 2011); or the preservation of traditional Transylvanian village and religious architecture. There are also several sports organizations, among them a women's handball team, motorcycle associations, and the fan club of one of the oldest and most iconic Hungarian football teams (*Ferencváros*). The rock bands represent a peculiar genre of political rock labeled "national rock."

Bookstores that specialize in the sale of nationalist and chauvinist literature, CDs of "national rock" bands, and other radical nationalist paraphernalia, concerts, or festivals like the so-called *Magyar Sziget* (Hungarian Island)[16] function as focal points for the socialization of right-wing radical groups. Radical nationalist media sources, especially online news portals, are particularly important because they play a similar role in unifying, modernizing, and diffusing radical cultural and political discourse.

These diverse groups draw on the symbolic imagery of Hungarians' historic independence struggles against the Ottomans in the sixteenth and seventeenth centuries and later against the Habsburg rule, the loss of Transylvania (and parts of northern and southern Hungary) after World War I, as well as popular legends about Hungarian ethnogenesis and history predating the conquest of the Carpathian Basin at the turn of the ninth and tenth centuries. They blend this medley of historical motifs into a contemporary antiglobalist rhetoric in which Hungarian independence is lost, for instance, to foreign multinational corporations and the European Union.

Dominant themes shared by these organizations echo the subjects of mythical nationalism that was invented and loosely codified in the process of nineteenth century nation-state formation and then complemented with motifs derived from the national trauma of the Treaty of Trianon and the interwar irredentism of Hungarian politics (for a critical summary, see Lőrincz 2010).[17] These shared themes are essential because they connect these organizations into a larger and fairly cohesive network while offering anchors of commonality that strengthen the cultural bond among members. The relevance of mythical nationalism also is emphasized in the case of other Central and Eastern European countries, especially in Poland (Zubrzycki 2011 and 2013).

Until the refugee and migration crisis in 2015, these civic organizations were more closely allied politically with *Jobbik* than with Fidesz. For instance, the *Magyar Gárda* (Hungarian Guard), a uniformed paramilitary formation, was founded by *Jobbik's* president. Some associations (e.g., an "independent" police trade union) formed official alliances with *Jobbik* before 2010, while most remained completely independent, beyond sharing intellectual kinship and frequenting each other's events. National rock bands, for instance, often performed at *Jobbik* party gatherings (Feischmidt and Pulay 2014). Since the migration crisis, however, *Jobbik* has been trying feverishly to reinvent and reposition itself as a more moderate populist party, and its (overt) ties to radical nationalist publics have loosened as a result, while many of these organizations shifted their allegiance and now openly support the Orbán government.

In the following I will use the example of the paramilitary organization *Magyar Gárda* (Hungarian Guard) to offer a more in-depth look at the types of organizations that make up the uncivil public sphere. The Hungarian Guard was one of the iconic organizations that played a key part in the right-wing radicalization of the public sphere and the rise of popular illiberalism, especially in the years leading up to Fidesz's landslide electoral victory in 2010. The organization was launched in August 2007 as an offshoot of *Jobbik*. The inauguration ceremony took place in front of the residence of the Hungarian president in Budapest's historic Castle District and was officiated by Lajos Für, Hungary's first post-communist minister of defense. The first fifty-six members of the Guard – a symbolic number chosen to recall the 1956 revolution – paraded in an outfit that was clearly intended to be a uniform: black boots, black trousers, white shirts with black waistcoats, and black caps emblazoned with the red and white stripes of the so-called "Árpád" flag. The Árpád stripes are a dubious symbol because even though they are part of Hungary's official coat of arms, they also are associated closely with the Nazi Arrow Cross regime, which ruled Hungary from October 1944 to March 1945 and incorporated the stripes into its own flag.

The second major public event, during which 600 new members were admitted into the Guard, was held in October 2007, coinciding with the anniversary of the 1956 revolution, in Heroes' Square, one of Budapest's major public squares that can accommodate large crowds and demonstrations. The recruits marched into the square in military formation while hundreds of onlookers clapped and cheered. In the following years several thousand members were initiated into the organization in similar inauguration ceremonies in Budapest and the countryside. These events also are filmed and made available on YouTube, attracting tens of thousands of viewers.

Unsurprisingly, the black uniform and military drills conjured up uneasy associations with the militia groups of the Nazis and Mussolini, which Gábor Vona, the president of *Jobbik* and founding member of the Guard, repeatedly denied. He explained that the Guard's uniform was nothing to be worried about as it only recalled the traditional outfit of Hungarian peasants: a testament to this is the fact that the black-pant–white-shirt–waistcoat combination topped with a black hat is a ubiquitous sight in Hungarian folk dance performances. By rejecting the Fascist symbolism, Vona was deliberately aiming to situate the Guard in Hungarian (folk) traditions and mainstream culture (LeBor 2008).

In fact, the Guard officially was registered as a cultural heritage association and was part of a broader call on the right to "reinvent civil society" (Németh 2007). The association's mandate included activities such as tending to soldiers' graves and memorial sites of historic battles as well as participating in disaster relief efforts, civil defense, and various forms of community service. At the same time, however, the Guard also was called upon to contribute to strengthening Hungary's "national self-defense" and to the "maintenance of public order." Jobbik always saw the Guard as the precursory base for the future establishment of a "National Guard" (*Nemzetőrség*) that would help protect Hungary in case of foreign aggression. Yet it is against the Hungarian constitution to form an armed civic association, so despite the strong military symbolism, the Hungarian Guard was never an arms-carrying organization. Additionally, setting up the Guard was a reaction to the experience of the 2006 street riots, police brutality, and the breakdown of public order as well as to perceptions of deteriorating public safety, particularly in the Hungarian countryside, that the far-right has attributed to the Roma minority and labeled as "Gypsy crime."

It is true that the Guard was active in local community service, disaster relief, and beautification of neglected graveyards, especially in more rural areas, but it was also engaged in openly discriminatory activities that eventually caused its demise, pushing it into illegality. Namely, besides their charity work, Guard members organized numerous demonstrative marches dubbed "health, mood, and public-safety-enhancing walks"[18] in villages and small cities of eastern and central Hungary. One of the marches, organized in December 2007 in Tatárszentgyörgy,[19] a small village in Pest County, south of Budapest, proved decisive in the subsequent legal suit against the Guard. Uniformed members of the Hungarian Guard partook in a procession against "Gypsy crime" and for the "public safety of the countryside," demanding the racial segregation of the Roma. Tensions in the village were riding high as the march, the chief purpose of which was to intimidate the Roma population, was met by the counter demonstration of human rights groups and Roma residents of the village. This event was treated as key evidence in the court proceedings that began in 2008 and ended with a ruling that ordered the disbanding of the Guard in July 2009. It demonstrated, namely, that the activities of the Guard were in sharp conflict with its stated goals; they aimed at invoking fear and inciting hatred against ethnic and racial minorities.

Although the Hungarian Guard was in many ways a singular and uniquely visible organization, it is embedded in a larger institutional field and a longer history of paramilitary organizations. Similar organizations were thriving in interwar Europe, including Hungary, and one in particular, the so-called "Ragged Army" (*Rongyosgárda*), which came to life in the wake of Hungary's failed Communist revolution of 1919, has been seen by the Guard as an important historical forerunner (Barotányi 2009). Likewise, there are several other smaller but analogous paramilitary organizations including the Highwaymen's Army (*Betyársereg*) or the Association for a Better Future (*Szebb Jövőért Mozgalom*) that have strong ties with the Guard and its successor groups constituting a closely knit network (Fomina 2013). Similar and more *ad hoc* vigilante groups also cropped up along Hungary's southern border at the height of the migration crisis in 2015 to scout out "illegal migrants" crossing into the country.

Paramilitary organizations certainly embody the most radical and alarming example of uncivil publics because they openly question the authority of the state and its monopoly over the use of legitimate force. They are a symptom of high levels of anomie and loss of faith in the existing public order. Nevertheless, they also highlight the centrality of violence in the symbolic repertoire of radical nationalism even if this violence is not necessarily acted out. They represent the most extreme form of uncivility, and most other organizations that make up a growing uncivil society embrace a more moderate agenda and do not openly violate the basic norms and rules of a democratic polity.

Uncivil groups have been in many ways the indirect beneficiaries of the Hungarian government's increasingly relentless crusade against liberal civil society. They are not entirely dependent on the government like "Potemkin NGOs" (Hemment 2012), such as the Civil Union Forum, but they profit from the discrimination of liberal civil society organizations. They are now more likely to have access to government support from various grants than before 2010, and their activities are seen as more legitimate despite their antidemocratic, nationalist, and exclusionary aspirations. Even though they are not necessarily actively endorsed by the government, they have gained in strength and visibility parallel with the stigmatization of liberal civility.

CONCLUSION

In Hungary the relationship between political and civil society has always been ambivalent and fraught with tension. There is widespread expectation to draw sharp boundaries between political engagement and civil society activism to underscore the independence and autonomy of civil society (Gerő and Kopper 2013). At the same time, there is a strong historical legacy bequeathed by socialism that suggests that only civil society organizations that are critical of the government can be truly genuine and authentic in their activities. As a result, more open and direct political activity by civil society groups always will be deemed suspect by one or the other political circle. The accusation of being a "bogus civil society actor" (*álcivil*) – referring to a civil society organization that is really just a political agent in disguise – can be frequently heard on either side of the political aisle. The government accuses NGOs of being political activists financed by foreign governments, while independent civic groups point their finger at associations that support government policies, describing them as frauds. Civil society's links to politics thus remain highly contested and controversial. The current government has been deeply troubled by this inherent indeterminacy, which has offered a strong incentive to contain and control the critical capacities of civil society actors. Since the refugee and migration crisis in 2015 the government has also seized the opportunity to intensify the crackdown on civil groups critical of the government by making them an integral part of its anti-immigration struggle.

The first two trends I highlighted in the paper show the tactical repertoire that the government has employed to extend its influence over the civil sphere. These tactics have at times been aggressive, at times indirect, and often inconsistent. The third trend I discern, in the form of an expanding "uncivil" society, tends to be overlooked by many researchers, partly because it requires a broadening of the definition of civil society to include groups that are self-organizing but are not necessarily "civil." I show that without taking this tendency seriously we cannot fully understand the restructuring of civil society in contemporary Hungary.

There is certainly cause for concern for the civil sector in Hungary in light of aggressive smear campaigns, shrinking funds, an increasingly hostile legal environment, and the growth of exclusionary publics. In the aftermath of the Ökotárs/Norway Grants affair there was some optimism that the rule of law can protect the civil sphere (Német 2016). At the height of the migration crisis in the fall of 2015 it came as a surprise that grassroots organizations can spring up quickly despite government hostility and lack of state financial support. In the run-up to the 2018 Hungarian parliamentary elections, however, the blatantly repressive and discriminatory treatment of civil society organizations that are not fully in line with the government's agenda has reached alarmingly new heights. Yet history shows that civil society can be remarkably resilient in the long run: despite sustained political harassment and repression, it ultimately remains an incubator of vitality, dynamism, and critical potential.

NOTES

1. The selective and discriminatory targeting of liberal civil society organizations that grew into a distinct trend after 2014 is discussed separately in the next section on civic organizations as foreign agents.

2. By comparison, in some Western European countries state support amounts to nearly, and in some cases, over more than 60 percent of civic organizations' revenues including France (57.8 percent), the Netherlands (59 percent), Germany (64.3 percent), Ireland (77.2 percent), and Belgium (76.8 percent). At the same time, this figure is only 30.5 percent for the United States (Sebestény 2001).

3. It is important to note, however, that the deterioration of the legal environment had already begun earlier around 2008 before Fidesz returned to power.

4. Acronym for government-organized non-government organizations.

5. This term conjures up images of Cold War–era espionage and sabotage, signaling to the public that these organizations are undesired, untrustworthy, and potentially threatening.

6. Soros funds a network of foundations that support human rights, freedom of expression, and access to public health and education in more than 70 countries. His foundations had been active in Russia from the late 1980s.

7. Ökotárs has performed this role as the lead member of a consortium of four local NGOs.

8. Ökotárs 2014.

9. In 2016 the theater company was awarded the prestigious Princess Margriet Award for Culture by the European Cultural Foundation for its work that turns theater into a social forum bringing different communities into dialogue.

10. Subsequently, the National Tax Agency suspended the tax ID of Ökotárs, which was a huge blow to the organization because without a tax ID it is unable to apply for grants or pay its employees. The lack of a tax ID also makes an organization ineligible for the 1 percent income donation program in the framework of which taxpayers can donate 1 percent of their income tax to a registered Hungarian civic organization of their choice.

11. See eeagrants 2015.

12. The incident was followed by a dubious bilateral agreement between the governments of Hungary and Norway about the future distribution of Norway Grants funds. And in an ironic twist of events, in November 2017 Ökotárs received a special prize from the Hungarian Prime Minister's Office for the successful management of EEA/Norway Grants in the 2009–2014 cycle.

13. It includes, for instance, the so-called "Lex CEU," an amendment to the Law on Higher Education regarding international universities, the specifics of which were carefully formulated to threaten the continuing operation of the Central European University (Trencsényi et al. 2017).

14. Although, at the time these associations were more committed to republican and liberal ideals of nationalism.

15. The word *Goyim* denotes a non-Jew in Hebrew.

16. The name of the festival recalls the name of Hungary's largest and most successful international summer festival, the *Sziget Fesztivál* that has taken place every August in Budapest since 2002. The original Sziget draws a large international crowd and a mix of internationally acclaimed and local performers, while the Hungarian Sziget emphasizes that both audience and performers are strictly Hungarian.

17. The online news portal kuruc.info also blends these themes with blatant racism and anti-Semitism more characteristic of neo-Nazi groups.

18. In Hungarian, "egészségügyi, közérzet- és közbiztonságjavító séta."

19. Two years later in 2009, this village became the site of one of the killings in the gruesome "Gypsy murders" case. A middle-aged Roma man and his five-year-old son were shot after their home was set on fire by far-right serial killers.

BIBLIOGRAPHY

Ablan, Jennifer. 2015. "Russia Bans George Soros Foundation as State Security Threat." *Fortune*, November 30, 2015. http://fortune.com/2015/11/30/russia-ban s-george-soros-foundation-as-state-security-threat/, accessed June 25, 2019.

Aksartova, Sada. 2006. "Why NGOs: How American Donors Embraced Civil Society after the Cold War." *International Journal of Not-for-Profit Law* 8 (3): 16–21.

Arato, Andrew. 1991. "Social Theory, Civil Society, and the Transformation of Authoritarian Socialism." In *Crisis and Reform in Eastern Europe*, edited by Ferenc Fehér and Andrew Arato, 1–26. New Brunswick, NJ: Transaction.

Arato, Andrew. 2011. "Afterword: Revis(it)ing Civil Society." In *The New Politics of European Civil Society*, edited by Ulrike Liebert and Hans-Jörg Trenz, 195–208. London: Routledge.

Barotányi, Zoltán. 2009. "A Rongyos Gárda története." *Magyar Narancs* 13, March 26.

Bob, Clifford. 2011. "Civil and Uncivil Society." In *The Oxford Handbook of Civil Society*, edited by Michael Edwards, 209–20. Oxford: Oxford University Press.

Botos, Tamás. 2015. "A Fidesz szerint a Migration Aid mögött is Soros György áll." *444* News Portal, September 21. http://444.hu/2015/09/21/fidesz-a-migration-a id-tuntetesekkel-kapcsolatos-kiadasait-soros-gyorgy-nagylelku-tamogatasa-fedezi/ , accessed June 25, 2019.

Dobszay, János. 2014. "A kurzus és a kurázsi: megroppantható-e a civil társadalom?" *Heti Világgazdaság*, October 4.

eeagrants. 2015. "Audit of NGO Programme in Hungary." https://eeagrants.org/New s/2015/Audit-of-NGO-programme-in-Hungary, accessed June 25, 2019.

Feischmidt, Margit. 2014. "Nemzetdiskurzusok a mindennapokban és a nacionalizmus populáris kultúrája." In *Nemzet a mindennapokban. Az újnacionalizmus populáris kultúrája*, edited by Margit Feischmidt, 7–51. Budapest: L'Harmattan.

Feischmidt, Margit, and Gergő Pulay. 2014. "Élmény és ideológia a nacionalista popkultúrában." In *Nemzet a mindennapokban. Az újnacionalizmus populáris kultúrája*, edited by Margit Feischmidt, 249–90. Budapest: L'Harmattan.

Fomina, Victoria. 2013. *Mapping the Network of Hungarian Extremist Group*. Research Report. Budapest: Athena Institute.

Gerő, Márton, and Ákos Kopper. 2013. "Mi a civil? Mit akar? Honnan jön? Mi köze a politikához? Vitaindító – Második rész." *Civil Szemle* 4: 47–51.

Glasius, Marlies. 2010. "Uncivil Society." In *International Encyclopedia of Civil Society*, edited by Helmut K. Anheier, Stefan Toepler, and Regina A. List, 1583–88. New York: Springer.

Gramsci, Antonio. 1971. *Selections from the Prison Notebooks*. New York: International Publishers.

Greskovits, Béla. 2017. "Rebuilding the Hungarian Right through Civil Organization and Contention." *EUI Working Papers* 2017/37, Robert Schumann Center for Advanced Studies. http://cadmus.eui.eu/bitstream/handle/1814/47245/RSCAS_ 2017_37.pdf?sequence=1, accessed June 25, 2019.

Hakim, Danny. 2014. "How Did Hungary's Election Become a Circus?" *The New York Times*, March 1.

Heller, Patrick. 2007. "Civil Society and Democracy in Post-transition South Africa." Unpublished manuscript.

Hemment, Julie. 2012. "Nashi, Youth Voluntarism, and Potemkin NGOs: Making Sense of Civil Society in Post-Soviet Russia." *Slavic Review* 71 (2): 234–60.

Hubbes, László-Attila. 2011. "A Comparative Investigation of Romanian and Hungarian Ethno-Pagan Blogs." *Reconnect Working Papers* 2. http://papers.ssrn.com/ sol3/papers.cfm?abstract_id=1984597, accessed June 25, 2019.

Kaldor, Mary, and Diego Muro. 2003. "Nationalist and Religious Militant Networks." In *Global Civil Society*, edited by Mary Kaldor, Helmut K. Anheier, and Marlies Glasius, 151–84. Oxford: Oxford University Press.

Kopecky, Petr, and Cas Mudde, eds. 2003a. *Uncivil Society? Contentious Politics in Post-communist Europe.* London: Routledge.

————. 2003b. "Rethinking Civil Society." *Democratization* 10: 1–14.

Kotkin, Stephen, and Jan T. Gross. 2009. *Uncivil Society: 1989 and the Implosion of the Communist Establishment.* New York: Random House.

Kovács, János Mátyás, ed. 1994. *Transition to Capitalism? The Communist Legacy in Eastern Europe.* New Brunswick, NJ: Transaction.

LeBor, Adam. 2008. "Marching Back to the Future: Magyar Garda and the Resurgence of the Right in Hungary." *Dissent*, Spring: 34–38.

Lőrincz, László, ed., 2010. *Egyezzünk ki a múlttal! Műhelybeszélgetések történelmi mítoszainkról, tévhiteinkről.* Budapest: Történelemtanárok Egylete.

Molnár, Virág. 2016. "Civil Society, Radicalism and the Rediscovery of Mythic Nationalism." *Nations and Nationalism* 22: 165–85.

Nemes, Robert. 2001. "The Politics of the Dance Floor: Culture and Civil Society in Nineteenth-century Hungary." *Slavic Review* 60: 802–23.

————. 2005. *The Once and Future Budapest*: DeKalb: Northern Illinois University Press.

Német, Tamás. 2016. "Kösz mindent Lázár János!" *Index* News Portal, April 20. http://index.hu/belfold/2016/04/20/norveg_civil_alap_tamadasok_okotars_civi lek/.

Németh, Miklós Attila. 2007. *Kettős kereszt avagy a Gárda jelenség.* Budapest: Masszi.

Ökotárs. 2014. "Annual Report." http://www.okotars.hu/en/annual-report-2014, accessed June 25, 2019.

Orbán, Viktor. 1987. *Társadalmi önszerveződés és mozgalom a politikai rendszerben (A lengyel példa).* Unpublished MA thesis. Budapest: ELTE Állam és Jogtudományi Kar.

————. 2014. Orbán Viktor teljes beszéde a 25. Bálványosi Szabadegyetem és Diáktábor rendezvényén. *Magyar Nemzet Online,* July 29, 2014. http://mno.hu/tusvan yos/orban-viktor-teljes-beszede-1239645, accessed June 25, 2019.

Rupnik, Jacques. 2007. "From Democracy Fatigue to Populist Backlash." *Journal of Democracy* 18: 17–25.

Sebestény, István. 2001. "A magyar nonprofit szektor nemzetközi és funkcionális megközelítésben." *Statisztikai Szemle* 79 (4–5): 335–55.

Susánszky, Pál, Ákos Kopper, and Gergely Tóth. 2016. "Pro-government Demonstrations in Hungary – Citizens' Autonomy and the Role of the Media." *East European Politics* 32 (1): 63–80.

Trencsényi, Balázs. 2014. "Beyond Liminality? The Kulturkampf of the Early 2000s in East Central Europe." *boundary* 2 (41): 135–52.

Trencsényi, Balázs, Alfred J. Rieber, Constantin Iordachi, and Adela Hîncu. 2017. "Academic Freedom in Danger. Fact Files on the 'CEU Affair'." *Südosteuropa* 65 (2): 412–36.

USAID. 2017. *2016 CSO Sustainability Index for Central and Eastern Europe and Eurasia.* USAID Bureau for Europe and Eurasia, Office of Democracy, Governance, and Transition.

Wodak, Ruth. 2015. *The Politics of Fear: What Right-wing Populist Discourses Mean*. London: Sage.

Zubrzycki, Geneviève. 2011. "History and the National Sensorium: Making Sense of Polish Mythology." *Qualitative Sociology* 34: 21–57.

———. 2013. "Aesthetic Revolt and the Remaking of National Identity in Québec, 1960–1969." *Theory and Society* 42: 423–75.

Chapter 4

Beyond Electioneering

Minority Hungarians and the Vision of National Unification

Gábor Egry

The extension of the right of ethnic Hungarians to acquire Hungarian citizenship was among the foremost measures of the freshly installed Orbán government in the summer of 2010. The law, accompanied by a bill that declared June 4, the day of the signing of the Peace Treaty of Trianon, as the "Day of National Cohesion" (*Nemzeti összetartozás napja*), was aimed to "heal the wounds" of the detachment of Hungarian minorities from Hungary. The new citizenship law entitled anyone who reasonably could claim that their ancestors lived in Hungary during any time in history and who could pass the test of being able to present their case to the authorities in Hungarian to apply for and receive Hungarian citizenship through a fast-track procedure of three to six months, irrespective of their place of permanent residence. Although Fidesz politicians initially evaded questions of voting rights, the new electoral law from 2013 enfranchised every Hungarian citizen to cast at least a single vote at the elections and established a process of dubious fairness and transparency to register, post, and count the postal votes of citizens living abroad. The 129,000 votes cast in 2014, of which Fidesz received 95 percent, were exactly how much the party needed to get the last seat to reach its second two-thirds majority.

Despite the growing popularity of hitherto "unorthodox" citizenship legislation in Europe, the new provisions generated an international echo, not the least because of the high number of those affected and the not so distant memory of Hungary's revisionist past and fractious relationship with some of its neighbors today (Faist 2007, especially 171–99).[1] Most of these often academic reactions focused on the dangers of granting citizenship on a purely ethnic basis (even if it was disguised as a seemingly neutral process) and the problems of enfranchising voters who do not bear the consequences of their political choices (Bauböck 2010). Especially in the light of the changes implemented in the electoral process, eliminating fair competition and favoring the governing party,[2] the whole story was mainly understood as being part of Fidesz's broader efforts to ensure its lasting grip on power.

In this essay I propose a different interpretation to this story. Notwithstanding the practical reasons and benefits for Fidesz, I will argue that this very symbolic first act of the parliament expressed the ideological foundations of the System of National Cooperation – an organic, integral, corporatist nationalism modeled on the 1930s. Thus, understanding how and why Fidesz attempted to integrate Hungarians living abroad sheds light on the nature of the System of National Cooperation and reveals its unexpectedly ideological character, often neglected by the dominant interpretation of Fidesz and Viktor Orbán as populist.[3] I will assert that citizenship, and more broadly the issue of Hungarians living in neighboring countries – covered by the Hungarian concept of *nemzetpolitika* (an untranslatable term for the politics of nation-building) – epitomizes the vision that Fidesz leaders hold of the national community and also exemplifies their nation and state-building efforts.

A PAINFUL REDISCOVERY? FIDESZ AND HUNGARIAN MINORITIES AFTER 1989

The fate of Hungarian minorities living in the neighboring countries was one of the most important symbolic issues of the regime change in 1989. The first legal mass demonstration on the streets of Budapest in 1988 protested against the deliberate destruction of Hungarian cultural heritage in the form of a program of "rationalizing" settlements by Nicolae Ceaușescu, Romania's ill-fated dictator. The discursive contrast between Ceaușescu's cold rationalist language and policy goals used to hide nationalist politics within the "progress towards of socialism" and the emotionally charged practice of destruction of villages not only made mobilization easier, but it also manifested the nature of the communist system and the desire for change. After his electoral victory, József Antall, the first prime minister after the regime change, declared in an often-cited speech that he wanted to be spiritually the prime minister of 15 million Hungarians. While his liberal opponents saw covert irredentism in this remark, the radical right wing of Antall's party, the Hungarian Democratic Forum (MDF), split from the party caucus over the issue of a Hungarian–Ukrainian basic treaty (1993) in which Hungary explicitly renounced all its territorial claims. These radicals, led by the writer and former vice-president of MDF, István Csurka, saw the collapse of the

Soviet Union a moment when Hungary could legally reclaim lost territories in Carpatho-Ukraine (Bárdi 2015).

Initially Fidesz belonged to the liberal section of the political spectrum, and while they showed concern for Hungarian minorities, they shared criticism of the right-wing government and its nationalistic tones in politics. Their attitude changed after 1994, after their shocking defeat to the Socialist Party and subsequent attempts to occupy the political center-right left empty by a collapsing Hungarian Democratic Forum. In an ironic twist it was the parliamentary debate over another basic treaty – this time concluded with Romania not long before the crucial presidential elections in 1996, when Ion Iliescu faced the common opposition candidate Emil Constantinescu – that enabled Fidesz to symbolically eject its liberal, antinationalist ballast and wholeheartedly embrace the nationalist line. Viktor Orbán rejected the treaty because it failed to include provisions granting administrative and territorial autonomy to the Hungarian minority. However, it was more telling that Orbán accused the socialist-liberal coalition of illegitimately consenting to the treaty, because it was rejected by the representatives of the Hungarian minority in Romania. According to Orbán, Hungary was bound to act as the country of the Hungarian minority, too, and its government could not pursue its own separate goals in foreign policy (Orbán 1996).

The rightist and nationalist turn of Fidesz was made easier by the party's embeddedness in Hungarian-speaking society in Romania. Since the very first moment of the change of regime in Romania, Fidesz politicians went about building a strong network there, which was later also transformed into a domestic resource. The dominant tone, initially, was more liberal, although Zsolt Németh, one of the party's founders and whose father was a preacher at a Budapest Calvinist congregation recruited from Transylvanian migrants, represented a more traditionalist, liberal nationalist variety, closer to Antall's views. A less visible aspect was the development of an economic network that slowly enabled businessmen and, in the 2000s, the Fidesz-led local governments to generate financial resources for the party. It also offered a recruitment field for party cadres, which initially also was limited in its extent but has become widescale since the turn of the millennium. The most visible aspect was how the party was able to use its connections with Hungarian minorities to further a nationalist discourse that also implied that Fidesz was to be the sole party that could represent the nation (Waterbury 2006).

Success was not immediate, especially when Fidesz could not control state resources in Hungary, and they had to overcome resistance from minority Hungarian elites, too. While the initial base of Fidesz was relatively strong in Romania, it lacked contacts in Slovakia and Serbia. But the absorption of parts of the failing Hungarian Democratic Forum and the Smallholders Party meant the use of their existing networks, too. Fidesz also attempted to overturn the existing minority elites by promoting alternatives (in Romania László Tőkés and the tiny Hungarian Civic and Transylvanian Hungarian People's Parties), actively contributing to the split of existing minority parties (such as the case of the Party of Hungarian Coalition in Slovakia that split in 2009 into *Most-Híd* and the Party of Hungarian Coalition, or favoring one among the several rival Hungarian organizations. The overall pattern was almost without exception that Fidesz backed dissidents or party wings that accused their opponents of betraying the true national cause: especially those parties that abandoned or toned down the demand for national autonomy in exchange for participation in the governments of the respective countries (Orbán 2009a).

The debate over the Hungarian-Romanian treaty signaled that an eventual Fidesz government would seek different means to integrate the nation. During its first tenure, between 1998 and 2002, Fidesz presented a bill, the so-called Status Law (2001), creating a special status for Hungarians living in neighboring countries. It was more symbolic than practical. The practical advantages included a moderate – EUR 30 – monthly allowance for every child attending a school with Hungarian as the language of instruction, reduced public transport fares in Hungary, and promised health care in Hungary up to the limited resources of a foundation set up for that purpose. Those who were eligible received a so-called Hungarian certificate (*Magyar igazolvány*), a passport-like document, with the Hungarian coat of arms on its cover, that certified eligibility to these benefits. For many it held great symbolic value: they saw it as an official recognition of their Hungarianness, and this understanding of the gesture was echoed by Fidesz politicians, too. More than 800,000 documents were requested.[4]

Nevertheless, the Status Law was an attempt to avoid opening the question of dual citizenship – a logical conclusion if one accepts the premise of nation-statehood based on ethnicity. In 2001 Fidesz refrained from granting citizenship, not the least because of the inner divisions over the demographic consequences of such a move. It was feared – and also hoped – that Hungarian citizenship will spur migration to Hungary as Hungarian communities were already declining due to emigration (in Romania and in the Yugoslav successor states) and assimilation (in Slovakia).[5] But by 2004, after an unexpected defeat by the socialist-liberal coalition in 2002, Fidesz decided to support an initiative for a referendum on dual citizenship. The plebiscite was held on December 5, and the very divided vote (51.57 percent in favor, 48.43 percent against) did not bind parliament due to a low turnout (37.49 percent).

Still, it was a moment of high symbolic importance. While the preliminary debate revealed how much Fidesz embraced integral, organic nationalism, the aftermath consolidated the party's hold on the imagination of minority

Hungarians. The rejection of dual citizenship by the socialists and liberals, and their alleged connection to the "welfare chauvinist" and xenophobic campaign material aimed at minority Hungarians, reinforced their image, actively promoted by Fidesz, as non-Hungarians who are not interested in the fate of Hungarians abroad. The "second Trianon" became an actively mediatized cultural trauma (Alexander 2004) that helped to stigmatize the political center and left in Hungary. Henceforward, reparation for the vote, the symbolic act of "healing the wounds," became a crucial part of Fidesz's promises, and it was gradually merged with the promise of redemption from the "trauma of Trianon" (Egry 2010; Egry 2015; Pytlas 2016).

But the debate preceding the referendum also revealed the deep divide in Hungarian politics concerning the understanding of the nation. Keen observers might have seen it already in the different programs of the late 1980s opposition organizations: the bottom-up vision of the liberals' new society and the overarching vision of national regeneration promoted by the right (Ripp 2006; Blokker 2011). The 1990s deepened the differences and transmitted it to an ever-broadening field, and it gradually eroded the consensus around the Hungarian minorities, too. After the 2002 electoral campaign in which criticism of the Status Law had a prominent role and the 2004 referendum, two hardly compatible visions confronted each other (Egry 2015).

The original consensus relied more on practical concerns than on principles. The foreign policy goals of post-1989 Hungary were embodied by three equally important priorities: (1) the Euro-Atlantic integration process, (2) good neighborly relations, and (3) a solution for the situation of Hungarian minorities with minority rights and autonomy in the long run. Certain parties put somewhat more emphasis on one or the other, but the general perception was that neither of these could be achieved without furthering the others. Thus, the issue of Hungarian minorities was carefully balanced with and positioned within Hungary's broad foreign policy goals (Bárdi 2015).

While the three priorities remained nominally intact until 2010, the initial differences regarding the proper means to further minority rights in neighboring countries gradually developed into an antagonistic understanding of what is Hungary's role in this matter and how it is related to the broader aims of the country. The socialists and liberals advocated a tactful approach to Hungary's neighbors in order to defuse support for nationalist parties who could invoke the Hungarian threat, and they also promoted the idea of European integration as the safest way to eliminate discrimination against Hungarian minorities and achieve minority rights on the basis of the Copenhagen criteria. As long as the prospect of European accession gave incentives, it was realistic and brought about real improvements. But it did not stop the demographic decline of these groups, and Fidesz argued that only national autonomy would provide the necessary means to abate the process.

Autonomy was a twofold concept ensuring the self-government of national minorities regarding their education, culture, and the use of their language in administration, the judiciary, and in public. For geographic areas inhabited by a majority Hungarian population (the narrow zone along the Slovak-Hungarian border, pockets along the Tisza River in Serbia and the Szekler counties in the middle of Romania), autonomy also meant administrative separation, that is, establishing special administrative units with regional assemblies holding the right of issuing laws on their internal affairs. For those who were living as local minorities, autonomy meant the right to join a national body that would govern minority education and culture and the right to use their mother tongue extensively. As large parts of minority communities were living in the latter situation, there was a division within minority parties accordingly, too. Proponents of autonomy were more inclined to abandon Hungarians within these internal diasporas, while the leaders of the minority parties tried to find a solution that would suit both groups, often accepting political compromises (in language use, education, the power of local governments, and so on) that fell short of autonomy but improved the situation of the internal diasporas.

Nevertheless, Fidesz postulated that only support for national autonomy – and, as a consequence, confrontation with mainstream majority parties – was true national politics, and good bilateral relations and European integration were only of secondary importance in this regard. To counteract the criticism that territorial autonomy and dual citizenship were at odds – as it was hard to expect from the neighboring countries to establish autonomous units inhabited by the citizens of other countries – Fidesz turned the argument upside down. They asserted that only dual citizenship and autonomy together can stop the decline, because minority Hungarians faced not one but two problems of recognition. They were denied autonomy by the respective majorities in their country, whereas the Hungarian state failed to acknowledge their membership in the nation by denying their citizenship.

Behind the issue of citizenship one can discern the relationship between the nation and the individual: how Hungarians are connected to the nation and how much this connection is formalized and institutionalized. Fidesz promoted the idea that every individual should have a legal bond with Hungary as their nation-state (special status or citizenship) and this relationship should mean an affirmation of their ethnicity. But while in 2001 the party juxtaposed and rejected citizenship as the appropriate realization of this idea with the special status enshrined in the Status Law, in 2004 it argued in favor. Some adherents of Fidesz, such as György Schöpflin, even argued that this specific ethnicity-based dual citizenship is not a return to a nationalist past but the post-modern citizenship of the future (Schöpflin 2005).

Liberals (most notably Tamás Bauer and János Kis) argued against this. They relied on the difference between cultural community and polity, the latter being a community of active citizens who bear the consequences of political decisions. In this worldview, minority Hungarians deserved support for their efforts to preserve their culture (for Kis it was even a moral obligation of Hungarians living in Hungary), but it should not entail political enfranchisement and rather be an act of pure solidarity. However, if they wished to migrate to Hungary, bureaucratic hurdles should be eliminated (Bauer 2004; Kis 2004a and 2004b). Finally, those in the Socialist Party and in the government (Csaba Tabajdi for the socialists and Erika Törzsök for the liberals) who were responsible for policy argued in favor of a conscious effort to support institution-building (cultural, social) in the minority communities and to help the economic efforts of Hungarian entrepreneurs, and from this perspective they looked upon them as distinct entities. From this perspective citizenship was either a purely symbolic (and thus secondary) issue that they either could reject or accept (Tabajdi was in favor) or an unnecessary complication of bilateral relations that threatened minority nation-building because of political repercussions (Törzsök 2003; Bárdi 2015; Tabajdi n.a.).

A key feature of the post-2010 transformation of Hungary was a specific understanding of the national community implied by Fidesz's vision. The nation became the only authentic political community, and existence outside it was presumed to be anomalous or even a death sentence (Varga 2009; Varga 2013).[6] As a consequence, the parties who rejected dual citizenship ceased to be legitimate representatives of the community because they denied its very foundations. Although after the failure of the plebiscite Fidesz sidelined this issue in its communication (given that it seemed to be less effective in attracting voters), they never made a secret of their intention to "remedy" the wounds inflicted by the negative result in 2004. As one of the first legislative measures in 2010, it turned out to be the symbolic start of national renewal.

Even before the moment of symbolic justice came, Fidesz used the stigmatization of its socialist and liberal opponents to undermine the position of the established Hungarian minority parties. Since 2004, publicized contacts with the Hungarian government could have been detrimental due to their negative image among minority Hungarians. Fidesz started to encourage its allies within minority parties to push for a more radical program of ethnic autonomy and try to take over leadership based on this program. In Romania, a series of new parties and organizations were established that challenged the Democratic Alliance of Hungarians in Romania (RMDSZ) and tried to mobilize Szekler counties within a popular movement for autonomy. But the new parties failed to make an electoral breakthrough and Fidesz eventually accepted a compromise with RMDSZ. In Slovakia, Fidesz's efforts to influence the Hungarian party led to divisions, and a group of influential politicians, who did not want to subordinate their politics to Hungary entirely, established a new Hungarian-Slovak party (*Most-Híd* – literally the Bridge) in 2009 that successfully competed with the traditional Party of Hungarian Coalition, now closely aligned with Fidesz. In Serbia, the largest party fended off the challenges, but its leadership accepted the influence of Fidesz in exchange for preserving their position within the party and the minority organizations.

THE IDEOLOGY OF NATIONAL UNIFICATION

Any government measure or activity concerning minority Hungarians almost automatically evokes the ghost of Hungary's revisionist past from the interwar era. Ironically, territorial revision is probably the only legacy of this era that Fidesz does not want to follow or at least instrumentalize. The reason is not necessarily modesty but rather geopolitical realism, not often associated with Fidesz and Viktor Orbán: the ethno-demographic reality of Romania, Serbia, Slovakia, or Ukraine makes it impossible to incorporate their territories into Hungary. The erstwhile territories of pre-1918 Hungary now are inhabited predominantly by Romanians, Slovaks, Serbs, or Ukrainians, and the largest compact region with a Hungarian minority, Szeklerland, is situated in the middle of Romania, 500 kilometers from the border. Even along the state borders, where long narrow zones, small patches, and enclaves, predominantly rural ones, still have a Hungarian majority population, the presence of the majority ethnicity is too significant to make reannexation possible. Moreover, Hungarian minority communities are aging and declining, even faster than in Hungary, not least because of emigration – not to Hungary but to the West.

This, however, has not meant abandoning a program of uniting all Hungarians in their own nation-state. Present-day Hungary, with its extended citizenship, is *the* state of Hungarians, the polity to which they pledge allegiance. The strong emphasis on the state as the only proper form of national existence, and thus the only way to redeem Hungarians from the oblivion awaiting them in neighboring countries, shows that dual citizenship was and is about much more than canvassing votes for the next election. It is not just rhetoric: the idea of the nation-state, in the sense of being the only legitimate and ultimate form of existence for an otherwise ethnically understood nation, pervades the political discourse of Fidesz, irrespective of whether they address the issue of Europe, the official historical narrative, the problems of (im)migration, or "unorthodox" economics. The idea of a strong Hungarian nation-state binds together disparate policy fields and policies, and not just superficially as a vague nationalism would do but in the form of concrete and specific policies and institution-building. Seen from this perspective, Fidesz's politics is the expression of a variety of national ideology that strives to establish a specific order and realize a strictly hierarchical vision of the unitary national community, built on the idea of duty and responsibility (Orbán 2009b; Ministry of Public Administration and Justice 2012).

This strong vision includes and equally applies to all Hungarians inside and outside Hungary. Duty and responsibility to the nation is the basis of their common polity, the often-invoked universal Hungarian nation in which individuals are subordinated to the community and its perceived destiny. Probably that is why unequal suffrage for minority Hungarians is not seen as a problem. Even though Hungarians residing outside Hungary have only one vote to cast for party lists and not two, one for party lists and one for a candidate in a single member constituency, the aim of the election in this system is not to select the most popular or most competent leaders or programs but rather *post festa* legitimization of the destined national leader, who has already proven his destiny by recognizing the nation's destiny.

The main elements of the understanding of the Hungarian nation were incorporated into the Preamble of the new constitution (Fundamental Law), the so-called National Avowal. Although it is part of a constitution (and it has legal force, too), the Preamble identifies the people with the nation in the very first sentence: "We, the members of the Hungarian nation." In the subsequent parts nation and state are consciously confounded, through historical references (to the foundation and continuity of the state by Saint Stephen and to the Holy Crown as the symbol of statehood and national unity), and through the disavowal of history in its entirety between the German occupation in 1944 and the regime change in 1990 as a period when the constitution was "suspended." Sometimes it happens indirectly, like with the declaration that national minorities in Hungary are also part of the political community and constituents of the state. The most explicit expression of this deliberate identification of the nation with the state is found in the following statement: "We deny any statute of limitations for the inhuman crimes committed against the Hungarian nation and its citizens under the national socialist and the communist dictatorship."[7] Although the text often refers to "citizens," it was passed after dual citizenship came into force; thus, the use of the concept of citizenship had not much limiting effect, as it entailed the whole nation as an ethnic unity.

The other strong theme present in the National Avowal is that of the decay and decline in the twentieth century and the idea of renewal. The nation – together with the family – figures as the only authentic framework for existence, and its strength is based on the labor and intellectual achievements of man. The Fundamental Law itself is just the expression of the Nation's will – a "living framework" that flows from this will and what is not based upon other considerations – and it is also "the form in which we want to live."

Renewal obviously was meant as reorganization of the state and nation at will. The theme of the alien character of the communist period is a common feature of the radical anticommunist interpretation of history, prevalent all over post-Soviet Europe (Mark 2010). However, in its Hungarian variety there is another discontinuity, the dissolution of historical Hungary in 1918–1920. The shrinking of the (ideal) nation-state and the appearance of Hungarian minorities in the successor states questioned the traditional, historicist reading of national history that wrought a narrative around the thousand years of continuous existence of a unitary Hungarian state. Henceforth the history of Hungarians outside Hungary was necessarily not part of the history of the nation that was identical with the history of the nation-state – unless it was reconceptualized and dissociated from statehood. A suitable substitute was found in the story of common suffering of all Hungarians because of the unbearable loss after the First World War, and this theme dominates the rightist historical narrative today. The Fundamental Law merges it with the idea of inauthentic history, a history entirely driven by external forces and people alien to the Hungarian soul, a notion applied to the Communist period, too, an era of common suffering again. But the ambivalence of confounding nation and state has not left history untouched in another respect. Instead of the uninterrupted existence of the state, the qualities of the nation became the focus and permanent core of national history. This approach served in the 1930s as the basis of the Hungarian *Volksgeschichte* (Romsics 2010), which tacitly was adapting national history to the dissolution of the unitary nation-state. The suffering of all Hungarians still remains central today to the historical narrative: postulating the existence of a permanent, unalterable national essence that posits national history outside historical time and makes the discovery of this essence the most important task of historians.

In the case of the Fundamental Law it has reversed the relationship between state and nation by declaring an otherwise continuous historical constitution as the expression of the nation's will and the form of its existence. In this logic national characteristics precede the state, and the state, including its constitution, acquires its form according to national specificities. It is, however, not limited to the state and its Fundamental Law. The idea of Hungarian specificities and peculiarities is so deeply rooted in Viktor Orbán's personal thinking that he always refers to them as the reason for his policies. He did it, for example, when explaining why Hungarians cannot tolerate any migrants.

STRUCTURES OF "NATIONAL COOPERATION"

In light of the ideology outlined above, the System of National Cooperation (SNC) is meant to be a restructured, reconfigured, and reinstitutionalized nation that encompasses every Hungarian. This ideology also stipulates that

every new institution is an expression of national specificities or the institutional embodiment of an authentic form of existence. The preference for
citizenship, an individual link between the nation-state and ethnic Hungarians
over autonomies, suggests that individuals are to be bound directly to their
nation and not through intermediary structures and institutions of their minority communities in the form of a "contractual nation."[8] It implies a certain
place in the fabric of the national community destined for these individuals
who are expected to fulfill their duty to the community. State-sponsored corporatism, favored also in the private sphere, is its institutionalization. Since
2010 teachers, public servants, doctors and nurses, and emergency services
personnel were all forced to join national professional bodies, hierarchical institutions whose leaders often are appointed by the government and
whom the government often used to consult as the only representation of
these professions or sectors. The tripartite bodies of government, employer,
and employee representatives were extended with rightist organizations and
churches and relegated to an advisory role. Public bodies in agriculture or
commerce and industry are led either by close associates of the prime minister (the Hungarian Chamber of Commerce and Industry) or by former Fidesz
politicians (the Hungarian Chamber of Agriculture).

Beyond the unmistakable and widespread economic nationalism, like
promoting Hungarian ownership of companies and arable land, Hungary's
social policy clearly reflects the intellectual sources of the System of National
Cooperation's ideology. The curtailment of social provisions (unemployment benefit, children's allowance) and the extension of tax credits in their
place, benefiting the highest 10 percent in terms of income, the linking of
the remaining benefits to certain social behavioral patterns, the introduction
of private bankruptcy that submits families to an external supervisor for as
long as five years (!), and the use of public works as the only means of reducing unemployment resembles the so-called "productive social policy" of the
1930s and the rightist social reform program of the same period (Hámori
2007; Szikra 2008; Szikra 2011). Before World War II, it was aimed at –
similarly to Fidesz's program – erecting a new social structure, a corporatist
one, establishing social harmony without eliminating or reducing social differences, and balancing out interests while linking them to the fulfillment
of national duties. In this vision of Christian corporatist social thinkers and
politicians like Pál Teleki and Gyula Gömbös, or even the radical rightist
Béla Imrédy, a nationally minded middle class served as the backbone of the
nation. It was led by the nation's destined leaders, conscious of their duty of
nationally educating workers and peasants, making them aware of their own
national responsibility, with their own sacrifice (Hámori 2007; Vonyó 2011;
Petrás 2013; Egry 2014).[9] This common work for a single and unquestionable
national destiny, defined by enlightened leaders, was meant to be a source of

social harmony. Party politics, understood as selfish politicking of every party apart from the one that represented the national interest, was condemned just as it is swept away today. Fidesz can only be the unquestionable party of a central position that is able to express national interests and issues in a natural and self-evident way, without "quarrelling" with its political competitors (Orbán 2010).

The position of Roma is undefined in the envisioned homogeneous Hungarian nation-state. The political discourse and public are ambiguous whether Roma are part of the Hungarian nation, but they are hardly seen as a nation, despite being listed among the officially recognized nationalities and ethnic groups. However, one thing is clear: they should fit into the new, organic, and hierarchical community and accept their role and duty as menial workers in public employment in order to deserve and merit state aid. Their social mobility is not conditioned upon simple talent and merit, and it ought to be accompanied with a selection process that ensures the adherence of this emerging Roma intellectual group to the values of the government.

It is thus hardly a coincidence that Fidesz tries to lay the foundations of a similar social elite with its policies and emphasizes similar national virtues also with regard to Hungarians living in the neighboring countries. Nonetheless, this kind of reinstitutionalization and reconfiguration of society has to stop at the borders. While granting dual citizenship managed to foster the necessary individual link between nation-state and members of the community (although the number of new citizens was left wanting, with around one million new citizens and a rapidly declining number of new applications out of the projected five million in four years), they hardly could have been integrated into the corporatist structures of the System of National Cooperation in Hungary. Nevertheless, Fidesz could not leave untouched their institutions and the relationship between their organizations and Hungary.

The changes were compatible with the shift toward integral nationalism and the corporatist turn outlined above. The government used three types of measures for this effect: a symbolic elevation of the issue in Hungary combined with a centralization of the institutions and elimination of the Hungarian minority organizations as autonomous mediators between Hungarian state organs and minority Hungarians. The last one also entailed the partial replacement or at least co-opting of the existing minority elites. As for symbolic elevation, the speaker of parliament, László Kövér, unfurled the Szekler flag and replaced the EU flag with it on the façade of parliament. It is significant, too, that this flag is a bone of contention in Romania, for administrative organs ban its use, while it is the symbol of the autonomy movement that challenged the more moderate policies of the largest Hungarian minority party for a long time.

The second Orbán government elevated the issue of Hungarians abroad to the level of creating not only a specific government office for it but also linking it to the figure of the deputy prime minister, Zsolt Semjén, whose main function is to oversee the policies toward Hungarian minorities. However, he has no ministry, and the administrative issues are dealt with by the state secretariat responsible for Hungarian minorities (*Nemzetpolitikai államtitkárság*) – between 2010 and 2014 as part of the Ministry of Administration and Justice and since 2014 as part of the Prime Minister's Office. The state secretariat was the foremost government unit in this respect since 2006, when the Office of Hungarians Abroad was eliminated, but its role was different. Earlier, it was rather a contact point for minority Hungarian organizations. It is also telling that neither Semjén nor the state secretaries (Árpád Potápi from 2014) or the deputy state secretaries who were the heads of the administration (Zsuzsanna Répás 2010–2014, Tamás Wetzel 2014–2015, Péter Szilágyi 2015–present) were of Hungarian minority origin. In the first 15 years after 1989 it was customary to nominate someone with such a background or with proven knowledge of and broad networks within these communities (like the socialist Csaba Tabajdi or the Fidesz politician Zsolt Németh). From 2014 state secretaries and deputy secretaries do not even have a significant past in this policy field, although it was at least a customary requirement earlier. So, the policy toward minority Hungarians was symbolically not just elevated but also mingled with other policies, losing its last distinctive trait.

The practical aspects of these symbolic steps were highlighted by the referendum on the refugee quota (or the "obligatory settlement of foreigners," as the government propaganda put it) in 2016. During the run-up to the vote, the government-initiated campaign abroad and the leaders of minority Hungarian organizations came out in support of the government's position – despite the fact that their communities either would not have been affected by the asylum-seeker quota system (Serbia) or their vote would not have affected the situation in their country of residence (Romania). The government also established a new public policy institution that replaced the previous European Comparative Minority Studies Foundation. The new Research Institute for National Politics (*Nemzetpolitikai Kutatóintézet*) was located in a decorative building in Budapest's castle district, opposite the coronation church, that was renamed the House of Hungarians (*Magyarság Háza*) and hosted representative events and a permanent exhibition.

The institutions dealing with budgetary expenses and financial subsidies were reconfigured, too. Earlier, a very fragmented system of public foundations assigned to different policy fields (economic cooperation, investment, vocational training, teacher training, and so on) and a central fund that announced calls for applications and made decisions with the participation of delegates from the Hungarian minority organizations managed the yearly amount allotted for Hungarian minority communities, apart from funds earmarked in the Status Law (Törzsök 2005). The Orbán government disbanded the public foundations and the central fund was transformed into a state-owned company, *Bethlen Gábor Alapkezelő Zrt.*, and Hungarian minority organizations lost their formal influence on the decisions.

As for the programs and activities, not all of the previous ones were eliminated; those that directly reached a large number of minority Hungarians were retained. The government looked upon itself as the government of all Hungarians and emphasized that every ministry should consider the Hungarian minority in their work and policies, as if they would live in Hungary (Ministry of Public Administration and Justice 2012). Citizenship applications were encouraged by political and social organizations, who helped to fill out, collect, and post the documents (and as a corollary collected data of future voters), and the government subsidized the network of offices for the same task. Specific emphasis was laid on programs that facilitated real-life contact between Hungarians from Hungary and from minority communities, and these were often aimed at "reviving" diaspora communities. A thematic year was announced annually to focus the activity of civic organizations, from the Year of Kindergartens in 2012 to the Year of Secondary Schools in 2015 and the Year of Young Hungarian Entrepreneurs in 2016. The *"Határtalanul"* (Without Borders) program finances the excursions of schools to and from Hungary, and the Kőrösi Csoma, Sándor Petőfi, and Mikes Kelemen Fellowships support individuals who spend longer periods either in the Western diaspora or in the neighboring countries and contribute to the civic activities of Hungarians, or help collecting and preserving Hungarian cultural heritage.

The boldest of all are the government's economic plans and programs. The then-minister of national economy, György Matolcsy, announced the so-called Wekerle Plan, a plan of Hungarian economic development in the Carpathian Basin that assumed the entire geographic zone to be a Hungarian economic sphere. As part of this effort every Hungarian community had to prepare a separate regional plan for its own region. The official aim of these programs is to facilitate economic cooperation among Hungarians (but not with non-Hungarians) and to reinstate a common Hungarian national economy. As a first step a HUF 50 billion development program for Vojvodina (northern Serbia) was announced, managed by the local Hungarian party, VMSZ, and accessible only to Hungarian citizens (Ministry of Economy of Hungary 2010; Pannonrtv.com 2016). In the next phase, similar programs were established with Romania, Slovakia, and Ukraine. These are always managed by a Fidesz client organization, with participation conditioned upon Hungarian citizenship, thus enabling the government to collect data on voters and reward or punish people. However, due to the lack of detailed analysis, it is hard to tell how much the distribution of these funds is based on political criteria.

These economic plans might reveal just how much these changes are aimed consciously at a change in Hungarian minority elites. The minority parties could not always rely on resources from their own countries (especially when they were outside government) and needed support from Hungary. While before 2010 the general rule was that the Hungarian government accorded subsidies to every significant minority organization, Fidesz started to discriminate against those who were not aligned strongly with it, withholding financial and other support. For example, Fidesz sponsored new alternative parties in Romania and Slovakia and used the infrastructure of the citizenship business in order to convey favors. The parties that were allowed to collect citizenship applications (thus aspiring for material help, offices, computers, and to legitimately collect data on potential voters) held an important advantage in symbolic and material terms over their rivals who were not afforded this privilege.

The outcome was mixed, suggesting that the total subordination of these communities is hardly possible. The Hungarian party in Slovakia split already in 2009 and the pro-Fidesz organization failed to gain enough votes for parliamentary representation in three successive elections (2010, 2012, and 2016), while its Hungarian-Slovak rival even became part of the government between 2010 and 2012 and after 2016. However, the Hungarian government did not accept this party as Hungarian, because it has Slovak membership as well; therefore, there is no official contact between them. In Ukraine, Fidesz achieved the resignation of the head of the Ukrainian Hungarians' Democratic Alliance, the less pro-Fidesz party of the two Hungarian organizations, but it was unable to undermine its support among voters significantly. However, both parties aligned their positions with Fidesz. In Romania minor parties challenged the dominant Democratic Alliance of Hungarians from Romania (RMDSZ/UDMR) for years without much success. Nevertheless, the previous leadership of RMDSZ, which tried to keep its distance from Budapest, was replaced with a new leadership that was much less successful in this regard, although still RMDSZ is the organization that has the most resources to fend off pressure from Budapest. However, they do not dare to contest the slogan of national autonomy that is used by Fidesz and its allies to discredit RMDSZ, which allegedly did not deliver anything in this respect. Finally, in Serbia the largest Hungarian party decided to accept Fidesz's influence in exchange for support to establish a political monopoly among Hungarians, but the unity has recently started to unravel.

Just like any other policy field of the System of National Cooperation, the politics of nation-building (*nemzetpolitika*) is prone to paradoxes and contradictions, not the least because of the inherent structural characteristics of the system. The foremost importance of the leader, Viktor Orbán, in every decision personalizes relations and enables certain figures to uphold or establish their own "fiefdoms" in the system, often competing with each other. The result is fragmentation despite centralization efforts. The fact that the citizenship process is managed outside the state secretariat for national politics was the first telling sign that this fragmentation could be deliberate. Soon after the Research Institute for National Politics was established, Jenő Szász, a friend of the parliament speaker, László Kövér, and the head of the failed Hungarian Civic Party from Romania, resigned and became head of the newly established Research Institute for National Strategy, an organization that recently started to focus on economic relations. In the economic realm, the case of Igazi Csiki Sör (Real Csiki Beer) manifested the importance of competing centers within the government. A businessman with a dubious past but with close ties to the powerful minister of the Prime Minister's Office, János Lázár, established a brewery in Csíkszentsimon (Sânsimion). When the company faced financial and legal problems and was brought to court by Heineken due to violation of company brand ownership, the Hungarian government stepped in to salvage the company and initiated legislation that would have banned the use of totalitarian symbols (including the red star featured in Heineken's brand) as commercial trademarks. The legislation would have hurt Heineken on the Hungarian market, and eventually the parties decided to abandon litigation and conclude an agreement (Bán 2018).

Fragmentation is, however, not the only paradox and contradiction surrounding the issue of Hungarian minorities. While the official discourse always refers to the Carpathian Basin as the natural sphere of existence of the nation and justifies policy with the goal of preserving Hungarians as Hungarians where they live, it is hard not to see signs of a conscious demographic management which uses Hungarian migrants to Hungary as a labor and demographic reserve. It was already part of the debate around dual citizenship in 2004, and László Kövér admitted it openly. It was also Kövér who recently announced that Hungarian national politics must develop a unitary, Hungarian, Carpathian Basin-wide workforce management system that would enable the mobilization of the Hungarian workforce in a way that also promotes the goal of preserving Hungarian settlements and communities where they are (Felvidek.ma 2016).

Another strange aspect of this politics is the latent tension between the centralized, corporatist reconfiguration of Hungary and its radical autonomist programs still upheld. Fidesz and its allies in the neighboring countries officially demand autonomy for minority Hungarians, but they also try to limit the choice of individuals. For example, Hungary sponsors the education of Hungarian minority teachers on the latest developments of pedagogy and new methods of teaching, yet schools in Hungary are deprived of financial, administrative, and pedagogical autonomy and teaching is increasingly uniform and conservative. After 2010, local autonomy was reduced to the level of city embellishment committees, and every administrative responsibility transferred from local governments to district and county level government offices. Thus, minority Hungarian parties are supporting publicly a Hungarian government whose politics are entirely the opposite of what they demand from the governments of their own countries for their own communities – communities that are supposed to form part of the Hungarian nation which has found its only authentic form of existence in the centralized Hungarian nation-state.

Finally, especially after 2014, Fidesz did just what it accused its predecessors of doing: it subordinated the issue of Hungarian minorities to bilateral relations and a geopolitical vision of a new Eastern European nationalist bloc, the new economic engine of the transformed EU (Orbán 2009b, *HVG* 2011, Fidesz 2015). The issue of Hungarian minorities was often swept entirely under the rug in bilateral relations and in the statements of Hungarian politicians about the necessity to focus on the mutually advantageous issues before turning to the contested ones in order to establish trust, which curiously resembles the argumentation of former prime minister Ferenc Gyurcsány. While previous socialist-liberal governments were accused of abandoning national autonomy to ease EU accession, now the Fidesz government remains silent in order to establish economic relations and find allies for an assault on the new enemy, the cosmopolitan, "heathen" Brussels. Hence, the new-found but strong alliance of Orbán and Robert Fico or Hungarian-Serbian rapprochement. One factor facilitating this cooperation was a common anti-migrant stance by these governments, but it is still striking in the light of Fico's earlier response to the Hungarian Law on Citizenship. The Slovak parliament passed a controversial law that stipulated the loss of Slovak citizenship for anyone who took a second citizenship. Nevertheless, the common struggle against Western European political norms erased this conflict, whereas with regard to other neighbors' minority grievances seem to have ceased to exist since Hungarian minorities could have the most important means to preserve their Hungarianness: Hungarian citizenship.

CONCLUSION

The System of National Cooperation is based on the vision of a unitary national society, detached from the outside world and relying mainly on its own resources. It is probably driven by a larger vision of changing geopolitics, the demise of the West due to its loss of global significance, which is considered a self-inflicted defeat because of unlimited liberalism and multiculturalism, and the eradication of traditions. To defy these trends, it makes the nation-state the ultimate bastion of existence for every Hungarian.

Its promise – a life without encountering others – makes it understandably popular among minority Hungarians, too, hence the appeal of Fidesz. Thus, the system is built at a larger, national scale, incorporating every Hungarian.

But developments within Hungary are crucial to understand the nature of the regime and the motives for its establishment. The reconfiguration of the state, its corporatism, and the hierarchical structures encompassing ever larger segments of society reflect the principles of organic nationalism. The role of the individual is subordinate to national destiny, and the moral foundations of participation are a sense of duty and responsibility proven by ceaseless work according to the guidance of the leadership and where individual liberty is exchanged for and dissolved in the collective freedom of a unitary and homogeneous nation. The nation-state is the authentic way of national existence, therefore the Hungarian state should become the state of all Hungarians, while Hungarians could have a proper national existence only as citizens of Hungary and members of its national community in every sense, including politics and institutions.

Paradoxically, this implies the dissolution of minority communities or at least their reorganization into mere dependents of Fidesz. Separate minority communities are replaced by a renewed vision of the authentic space of national existence, the Carpathian Basin, where the government proposes to establish unified structures for everyone. Out of these would emerge a unitary Hungarian national economy, an educational system, a health care system, a system of cultural institutions, and so on. It is not territorial revision, only the extension of Hungary to Hungarian citizens (and also to Hungarians who have opted to remain non-citizens). How realistic it is remains to be seen, all skepticism is well founded. But the offer is unmistakable, just as the tradeoff it implies, well known from the history of integral, organic nationalist regimes of the 1930s. Those who value ethnocultural "rights" more than individual freedom can exchange the latter for national existence devoid of individual liberty. They can exist within strict national hierarchies, spared of hard choices that are made for them by their leaders, but at least they can enjoy a refuge from the world within the familiarity of language and the illusion of a common, binding national destiny.

NOTES

1. Hungarian politicians stereotypically used to speak of 15 million Hungarians living in the world, of whom 5 million live abroad, while official statistics show that at least 3 million people are eligible and potentially conscious enough to make use of the new legal provisions. The number of new citizens reached 1 million by the end of 2017.

2. See the report of the OSCE observer mission on the elections in *2014 Hungary Parliamentary Elections*, April 6, 2014. OSCE/ODIHR 2014. See also *Budapest Beacon*, 2014.

3. Although Jan-Werner Müller recently defined populism in a way that encompasses Fidesz's nationalism, his approach seems to confound populism as a variety of political praxis and ideology as a vision of the community (see Müller 2015).

4. On the Status Law (legal texts and the debates around it), see Kántor et al. 2004.

5. For data on Hungarians, see Kapitány 2015. László Kövér, a member of Fidesz's inner circle since its establishment and the speaker of the parliament since 2010 publicly argued in a parliamentary debate that dual citizenship would be beneficial because of the positive migration effects. November 17, 2004. http://www.parlament.hu/orszaggyulesi-naplo-elozo-ciklusbeli-adatai?p_auth=4mdirEZY&p_p_id=pairproxy_WAR_pairproxyportlet_INSTANCE_9xd2Wc9jP4z8&p_p_li fecycle=1&p_p_state=normal&p_p_mode=view&p_p_col_id=column-1&p_p_col_c ount=1&_pairproxy_WAR_pairproxyportlet_INSTANCE_9xd2Wc9jP4z8_pair Action=%2Finternet%2Fcplsql%2Fogy_naplo.naplo_fadat%3Fp_ckl%3D37%26p_u ln%3D187%26p_felsz%3D145%26p_szoveg%3D%26p_felszig%3D145, accessed June 25, 2019.

6. Varga 2009 and 2013.

7. The original Hungarian also uses the word "*nemzet*" (nation) instead of the state (*állam*); otherwise, it is never used in this relationship, especially as "*állampolgárság*" explicitly refers to the state (*állam*).

8. For this concept, see Szarka 1999.

9. For the fate of the Christian middle class, see Rainer 2014.

BIBLIOGRAPHY

Alexander, Jeffrey C. 2004. "Towards a Theory of Cultural Trauma." In *Cultural Trauma and Collective Identity*, edited by Jeffrey C. Alexander, et al., 1–30. Berkeley: University of California Press.

Bán, Marina. 2018. "Memory Wars of Commercial Worth – The Legal Status of the Red Star in Hungary." VerfBlog. http://verfassungsblog.de/memory-wars-of-comm ercial-worth-the-legal-status-of-the-red-star-in-hungary/, accessed June 25, 2019.

Bárdi, Nándor. 2015. *Otthon és haza. Tanulmányok a romániai magyarság történetéből*. Miercurea Ciuc: Pro Print.

Bauböck, Rainer, ed. 2010. "Dual Citizenship foo Transborder Minorities? How to Respond to the Hungarian-Slovak Tit-for-Tat?" *EUI Working Papers* 75. Florence: EUDO Citizenship Observatory, Robert Schuman Center for Advanced Citizenship Studies.

Bauer, Tamás. 2004. "Válasz az MTA Etnikai-Nemzeti Kisebbségkutató Intézete és a Teleki László Intézet által a magyar állampolgárságnak a határon túl élő magyarokra való kedvezményes kiterjesztéséről megfogalmazott kérdésekre." A *Kettős állampolgárságról. Adatok, állásfoglalások, elemzések.* https://kisebbsegkutato.t k.mta.hu/kettosallampolgarsag/anket/ank_01.html, accessed June 25, 2019.

Blokker, Paul. 2011. "Dissidence, Republicanism and Democratic Change." *Eastern European Politics & Societies* 25 (2): 219–43.

Budapest Beacon. 2014. "OSCE Pronounces Hungarian Election Free But Unfair." *Budapest Beacon*, April 8. http://budapestbeacon.com/public-policy/osce-prono unces-hungarian-election-free-but-unfair/6552, accessed June 25, 2019.

Egry, Gábor. 2010. *Otthonosság és idegenség. Identitáspolitika és nemzetfelfog Magyarországon a rendszerváltozás óta.* Budapest: Napvilág.

————. 2012. "Strangers of Our Own. 'Nation,' 'Republic,' and 'Ordinary People' in Hungary after 1989." In *Nations and Their Others. Finland and Hungary in Comparison,* edited by Heino Nyyssönen and Mari Vares, 172–210. Helsinki: East-West.

————. 2014. "National Interactions: Hungarians as Minorities and Changes in Definition of Who Is Hungarian in the 1930s." In *Influences, Pressures Pro and Con, and Opportunities. Studies on Political Interactions in and Involving Hungary in the Twentieth Century,* edited by Zoltán Ripp, 75–98. Budapest: Napvilág Kiadó.

————. 2015. "A Fate for a Nation: Concepts of History and the Nation in Hungarian Politics, 1989–2010." In *Thinking through Transition. Liberal Democracy, Authoritarian Pasts, and Intellectual History in East Central Europe After 1989,* edited by Michal Kopeček and Piotr Wciślik, 505–24. Budapest: CEU Press.

Faist, Thomas. 2007. "Dual Citizenship: Change, Prospects and Limits." In *Dual Citizenship in Europe. From Nationhood to Societal Integration,* edited by Thomas Faist, 171–99. Aldershot: Ashgate.

Fundamental Law of Hungary. 2012. http://www.kormany.hu/download/e/02/0000 0/The%20New%20Fundamental%20Law%20of%20Hungary.pdf, accessed June 25, 2019.

Hámori, Péter. 2007. "A magyar kormány szociálpolitikája a visszacsatolt Felvidéken." In *Integrációs stratégiák a magyar kisebbségek történetében,* edited by Nándor Bárdi and Attila Simon, 167–86. Somorja: Fórum Kisebbségkutató Intézet – Lilum Aurum.

HVG. 2011. "Orbán: ismét Közép-Európa lesz az európai gazdaság motorja." *HVG*, June 17. http://hvg.hu/vilag/20110617_orban_kozep_europa_gazdasagi_motor, accessed June 25, 2019.

Kántor, Zoltán et al., eds. 2004. *The Hungarian Status Law: Nation-building and/or Minority Protection.* Sapporo: Slavic Research Center Hokkaido University.

Kapitány, Balázs. 2015. "Ethnic Hungarians in the Neighboring Countries." In *Demographic Portrait of Hungary 2015,* edited by Judit Monostori et al., 225–39. Budapest: KSH Népességtudományi Kutatóintézet.

Fidesz. 2015. "Képesek vagyunk arra, hogy Közép-Európa növekedési motorja legyünk." http://www.FIDESZ.hu/hirek/2015-10-02/kepesek-vagyunk-arra-hogy-k ozep-europa-novekedesi-motorja-legyunk/, accessed June 25, 2019.

Kis, János. 2004a. "Miért megyek el szavazni?" *Népszabadság,* November 22. http:// nol.hu/archivum/archiv-340838-157972, accessed June 25, 2019.

————. 2004b. "Nemzetegyesítés vagy kisebbségvédelem." A *Kettős állampolgárságról. Adatok, állásfoglalások, elemzések.* http://kisebbsegkutato.tk.mta.hu/ke ttosallampolgarsag/publicisztika/pub_159.html, accessed June 25, 2019.

Felvidék.ma. 2016. "KMKF: Létfontosságú a magyar munkaerő megőrzése a Kárpát-medencében." *Felvidék.ma*. http://felvidek.ma/2016/04/ma-plenaris-ulessel-fol ytatodik-a-karpat-medencei-magyar-kepviselok-foruma/, accessed June 25, 2019.

Mark, James. 2010. *The Unfinished Revolution. Making Sense of the Communist Past in Central-Eastern Europe*. New Haven, CT: Yale University Press.

Ministry of Economy of Hungary. 2010. *Wekerle terv. A magyar gazdaság Kárpát-medencei szintű növekedési startégiája*. http://2010-2014.kormany.hu/downloa d/1/45/a0000/Wekerle%20Terv.pdf, accessed June 25, 2019.

Ministry of Public Administration and Justice. 2012. *Magyar Nemzetpolitika. A nemzetpolitika stratégiai kerete*. Közigazgatási és Igazságügyi Minisztérium, Nemzetpolitikai Államtitkárság. http://www.nemzetiregiszter.hu/download/9/a2/ 00000/Magyar%20nemzetpolitika%20A4.pdf, accessed June 25, 2019.

Müller, Jan-Werner. 2015. "Parsing Populism. Who Is and Who Is Not a Populist These Days?" *Juncture* 22 (2): 80–89.

Orbán, Viktor. 1996. Debate of the Hungarian-Romanian Basic Treaty. September 3, 1996. http://www.parlament.hu/naplo35/197/1970016.htm, accessed June 25, 2019.

———. 2009a. "Fokozott szükség van a magyarok összefogására." http://2010-201 5.miniszterelnok.hu/beszed/fokozott_szukseg_van_a_magyarok_osszefogasara, accessed June 25, 2019.

———. 2009b. "Önfeladás a külpolitikában is." http://2010-2015.miniszterelnok.hu/ beszed/onfeladas_a_kulpolitikaban_is, accessed June 25, 2019.

———. 2010. "Megőrizni a létezés magyar minőségét." http://tdyweb.wbteam.com/ Orban_Megorizni.htm, accessed June 25, 2019.

OSCE/ODIHR. 2014. *OSCE/ODIHR Limited Election Observation Mission. Final Report*. Warsaw: OSCE/ODIHR. http://www.osce.org/odihr/elections/hungary/1 21098?download=true, accessed June 25, 2019.

Petrás, Éva. 2013. "A Vatikán és a magyar katolikus értelmiség. A magyar katolikus értelmiség útja a kereszténydemokrácia felé." In *Nyitott/zárt. Politikai és kulturális oreintáció 1914–1949*, edited by István Feitl, 77–92. Budapest: Napvilág.

Pytlas, Bartek. 2016. *Radical Rightist Parties in Central and Eastern Europe. Mainstream Party Competition and Electoral Fortune*. London: Routledge.

Rainer M., János, ed. 2014. *Búvópatakok – mélyfúrások: Magyar jobboldal – 1945 után*. Budapest: Széchenyi National Library, 1956 Institute, and Gondolat Kiadó.

Ripp, Zoltán. 2006. *Rendszerváltás Magyarországon 1987–1990*. Budapest: Napvilág Kiadó.

Romsics, Gergely. 2010. *Nép, nemzet, birodalom. A Habsburg Birodalom emlékezete a német, osztrák és magyar történetpolitikai gondolkodásban*. Budapest: Új Mandátum.

Schöpflin, György. 2005. "Új magyar nemzetfogalom felé." *A kettős állampolgárságról. Adatok, állásfoglalások, elemzések*. http://www.kettosallampolgarsa g.mtaki.hu/publicisztika/pub_209.html, accessed June 25, 2019.

Szarka, László. 1999. "Mozaiknemzetből szerződéses nemzet." *Európai Utas* 36 (3): 76–78.

Szikra, Dorottya. 2008. "A szociálpolitika másik arca. Fajvédelem és produktív szociálpolitika az 1940-es évek Magyarországán." *Századvég* 12 (2): 35–77.

————. 2011. "Produktív szociálpolitika." http://szuveren.hu/tarsadalom/produktiv-szocialpolitika.

Tabajdi, Csaba. n.a. *A magyar demokratikus baloldal és a nemzeti kérdés.* http://www.jadat.hu/ta02.pdf, accessed June 25, 2019.

Pannonrtv.com. 2016. "Temerinben megnőtt az állampolgársági kérelmek száma." https://pannonrtv.com/rovatok/tarsadalom/temerinben-megnott-az-allampolgars agi-kerelmek-szama-video, accessed June 25, 2019.

The Guardian. 2018. "Viktor Orbán's Reckless Football Obsession." *The Guardian.* https://www.theguardian.com/news/2018/jan/11/viktor-orban-hungary-prime-min ister-reckless-football-obsession, accessed June 25, 2019.

Törzsök, Erika. 2003. *Kisebbségek a változó világban.* Cluj-Napoca: The Miklós Misztótfalusi Kis Press of the Calvinist Church.

————, ed. 2005. *Szülőföld program. A határokon túli (Kárpát-medencében élő) magyarság gazdasági alapjainak és társadalmi kohéziójának támogatását célzó lépések előkészítése, valamint ezek lehetséges kapcsolódási pontjainak bemutatása. Stratégiai tanulmány.* Budapest: Cabinet Office of the Prime Minister.

Varga, Zs., András. 2009. "Nemzet és jogalanyiság." *Limes* 22 (4): 15–24.

————. 2013. "Megfontolások négy tételben a nemzet és alkotmány(a) összefüggéséről." *Magyar Kisebbség* 18 (3–4): 252–67.

Vonyó, József. 2011. "Gömbös kormánypártjának ideológiája." *Századok* 145 (1): 3–38.

Waterbury, Myra. 2006. "Internal Exclusion, External Inclusion: Diaspora Politics and Party Building Strategies in Post-Communist Hungary." *East European Politics & Societies* 20 (3): 483–515.

Chapter 5

The Role of Religion in the Illiberal Hungarian Constitutional System

Gábor Halmai

This chapter, dedicated to the role of religion in contemporary Hungary, deals with the practice of religious freedom in the new Hungarian constitutional order. After evaluating changes to legislation governing freedom of religion since 2010 in comparison to the situation following the democratic transition of 1989–1990, I discuss the possibilities of religious freedom in different models of state-church relationships. The main research question is whether the separation of church and state, formally maintained since Hungary's backslide to an illiberal constitutional system, still can guarantee secularism and autonomy for churches.

FREEDOM OF RELIGION BEFORE AND AFTER 1989

In 1568, the Transylvanian Diet at Torda (Turda in present-day Romania) was the first to announce religious tolerance in Europe. By 1848 Hungarian revolutionary legislation declared the equality of all accepted religions, although the emancipation of Jews did not occur until 1867. This period was characterized by cautious efforts to secularize and legislation proclaiming religious freedom for all but restricting the right of public worship to officially acknowledged communities, either incorporated or recognized. According to Act XLIII/1895, representatives from "incorporated" denominations were allowed to hold seats in the upper house of the parliament, while unrecognized religious communities only were able to practice their religion under police surveillance.

This development toward religious freedom and equality in the late nineteenth century was disrupted by the first major cataclysm of the twentieth century. The post–First World War regime of governor Horthy, which called

95

itself a "Christian course," led campaigns against unregistered small churches (sects in their terminology) and introduced anti-Jewish laws well before Nazi Germany. Right after the Second World War and before the communist takeover, "incorporated" churches lost their privileges when all religions were granted equal status, which basically amounted to the status previously enjoyed by "recognized" churches. But religious freedom became a moot issue in the 1949 communist Constitution: most religious orders were banned, the property of religious communities was confiscated to an overwhelming degree, numerous religious leaders were arrested and sentenced, and the separation of church and state was compromised altogether. Although state pressure began to relax to some extent from the 1960s, the general rules and practices of the regime did not change until the late 1980s. In 1964, the Holy See and Hungary signed a document that acknowledged the competence of the Holy See to appoint bishops under the condition of the oath of clergy to the Constitution.

The 1989 democratic transition ended the communist regimes' antireligious, atheist state model and introduced a liberal democratic constitutional system, which provided religious freedom and separation of church and state. This legal regime on freedom of religion and church-state relations was governed by Article 60 of the 1989 Constitution and Act No. IV of 1990 on Freedom of Conscience and Religion, and Churches. Article 60 of the Constitution of the Republic of Hungary read:

(1) In the Republic of Hungary everyone has the right to the freedom of thought, conscience and religion.

(2) This right includes free choice or acceptance of religion or other conviction and the liberty to publicly or privately express or decline to express, exercise and teach such religions and convictions by the way of religious actions, rites or in any other way, either individually or in a group.

(3) In the Republic of Hungary the Church functions in separation from the State.

(4) The ratification of the law on the freedom of conscience and of religion requires the votes of two thirds of the MPs present.

Furthermore, Article 8 of the same legislation, which required a two-thirds majority vote, declared that: "(1) Those following the same religious beliefs may, for the purpose of exercising their religion, set up a religious community, religious denomination or church."

Neutrality could be seen as the most important principle governing the state in regard to religious communities as well as to other ideologies. The state shall have no ideology. However, as the Constitutional Court stated: "from the right to freedom of religion follows the State's duty to ensure the possibility of free formation of personal convictions."[1] Neutrality meant, on the one hand, that the state shall not identify itself with any ideology (or religion) and, on the other hand, that it must not be institutionally attached to churches or to one single church. This indicated that the underlying doctrine behind the principle of separation (which was explicitly stated in the Constitution) was the neutrality of the state. Neutrality is not "laicism" (in the French sense of *laïcité*); the state may have an active role in providing an institutional legal framework as well as funds for the churches to ensure the free exercise of religion in practice. Separation (especially institutional separation), however, is stricter than in the German "coordination model" (Schanda 2001). Separation was defined by the Constitutional Court as respect of the autonomy of churches: "the State must not interfere with the internal workings of any church."[2] It also was understood as a principle stated in the act on religious freedom: "No state pressure may be applied in the interest of enforcing the internal laws and rules of a church."[3]

Under the 1990 law, a minimum of 100 persons were required to request the registration of a church from a court of law so long as they presented a charter of operations with a self-governing organizational structure and a declaration that the founders intended to pursue a religious activity (Article 8(1) and Article 9). The registry of churches was kept at the Metropolitan Court in Budapest. Registration was granted as a matter of formal compliance with the language of the 1990 statute, with no further in-depth inquiry. The 1990 law did not distinguish among various types of religious organizations; registration under the law meant that all religious communities received the same status. It was estimated and commonly accepted in parliamentary debate on the new legal regime that approximately 350 churches were registered under the 1990 law.

In this liberal democratic system with constitutional guarantees of religious autonomy, Hungarian society, even in comparison with other East Central European countries,[4] remained mainly secular: the proportion of churchgoers is under 15 percent, and the vast majority of citizens favor the strict separation of church and state, while opinion polls concerning restitution, funding, and similar issues show ignorance of these complex matters (Tomka and Zulehner 1999). When compared to the rest of Europe, Hungary belongs among the least religious countries (Tomka 2001). Both regarding religious beliefs and religious self-characterization Hungary is at 23rd place out of 31 European countries, regarding church membership at 24–25th place, regarding the percentage of monthly church attendance at the 21st–22nd (tied with Ukraine in these previous categories), and regarding daily prayer or several times a week at 18th place (EVS 1999). The 2011 census was a great disappointment for the Catholic Church, which lost 1.2 million people in a decade.[5] In 2013 Hungary was at the 11th place on the international atheism list, meaning that 23 percent of the population considered him/herself as atheist ("I don't believe in God and I never have") (Smith 2013).

Between 1990 and 2010, there were two, mostly failed attempts to deviate from the liberal democratic course. The first was a consequence of the main churches' attack on some small registered churches that were gaining more and more influence. In the so-called "sect debate," a draft parliamentary resolution deprived four small churches of their budgetary support. Notably, the attempt to ban these churches and to amend the law in order to force all registered churches to restart a new registration process finally failed.[6] The second attempt in 2000–2001 during the term of the first Orbán government tried to supplement the legal requirements of registration with the submission of the religious doctrines that then would be deliberated by the authorities. Another draft modification of the act would have allowed them to alter the general rule of church equality by law.[7] These amendments failed due to the lack of a two-thirds majority of the governing parties.

CONSTITUTIONAL CHANGES

The new constitution, entitled the Fundamental Law of Hungary, which was passed by parliament on April 18, 2011, shows the role of religion in national legitimation by characterizing the nation not only as the community of ethnic Hungarians but also as a Christian community, narrowing even the range of people who can recognize themselves as belonging to it. The preamble to the Fundamental Law, which is compulsory to take into consideration when interpreting the main text (see paragraph 3 article R), commits itself to a branch of Christianity, the Hungarian Roman Catholic tradition. According to the text of the preamble ("We are proud that our king Saint Stephen built the Hungarian state on solid ground and made our country a part of Christian Europe"), the members of the Hungarian nation recognize Christianity's "role in preserving nationhood," and honor the fact that the Holy Crown "embodies" the constitutional continuity of Hungary's statehood. Besides the sacral symbols, this choice of ideology is reflected – inter alia – in the Fundamental Law's concept of community and its preferred family model (paragraphs 1–9 of section L) and its provision regarding the protection of embryonic and fetal life from the moment of conception (section II).

The preamble, while giving preference to the thousand-year-old Christian tradition in Hungary, states that "we value the various religious traditions of our country." The choice of words indicates a model of tolerance in which various worldviews do not have equal status, although following them is not impeded by prohibition or persecution. It is, however, significant that the declared tolerance only extends to particular "religious traditions," especially

Christian ones but does not apply to more recently established branches of religion or to those that are new to Hungary or to nonreligious convictions of conscience. Clearly, the religious turn in Hungary started well before the refugee crisis of 2015, with the introduction of a System of National Cooperation (SNC), the multiconfessional setup of which gave space to Protestantism as well as Catholicism.[8]

The refugee crisis of 2015 demonstrated the intolerance of the Hungarian governmental majority, which styled itself as the defender of Europe's "Christian civilization" against an "Islamic invasion." At the beginning of the crisis, Prime Minister Viktor Orbán claimed that "Christian culture is the unifying force of the nation [. . . and] Hungary will either be Christian or not at all."[9] In another speech held in early September, Orbán went further by stating that "the Christian-national idea and mentality will regain its dominance not just in Hungary but in the whole of Europe." This new era should follow "the age of liberal blah-blah," because the origin of mass migration and the consequent refugee crisis is "the crisis of liberal identity."[10]

On December 23, 2017, Orbán went so far as to falsify the words of Jesus in order to protect his anti-migrant policy by saying that "we must love both our neighbors and ourselves" (Orbán 2017). As philosopher of religion György Gábor points out, Jesus does not command anyone to love himself; he simply states the degree of love that one ought to extend to one's neighbor.[11] The extremely conservative Hungarian Catholic as well as the Reformed Church echoed the government's antagonism toward refugees. Péter Erdő, the archbishop of Esztergom-Budapest and primate of the Catholic Church in Hungary, in opposing the guidance of the Pope, described helping refugees as "people-trafficking."[12] László Károly Bikádi, a Reformed minister of the small town of Hajmáskér, said the following about refugees in a sermon: "They come like ants. They move into our houses. What happens with mice, moles, and other creatures of the field? They come and beset us [. . .] we shouldn't make the mistake of throwing out our values just because people arrived among us who don't consider us their brethren."[13]

But should the alleged defense of Christianity from "Muslim hordes" be taken seriously? In a speech on July 26, 2012, Orbán explains why authoritarianism is needed to treat Hungarians: "Joining forces is not a matter of intentions, but of sheer force. With a half-Asian lot such as ours, there is no other way [GH: other than compulsion or force]."[14] In Hungary the unusual extent of religious plurality in early modern history is due to the territorial division of the country as well as to the bloody conflicts of the Reformation. Until after the First World War and the beginning of the Horthy era, no church could identify itself fully with the Hungarian nation. Although the Catholic Church dominated the Protestants, both numerically and politically, the Catholic Church played a minor historical role in preserving national consciousness, so that Catholicism never became equated with Hungarian patriotism. The Hungarian independentist, national tradition as well as the nineteenth-century national revival have strong Protestant, anti-Habsburg components. Even though the Roman Catholic Church in Hungary was very anti-communist immediately after 1945,[15] under communism they served neither as a symbol of national independence nor as a source of protection for the opposition as in Poland (Grzymala-Busse 2013).

In other words, Christianity and religion in general serve as reference points that Orbán's right-wing populism uses instrumentally. Fidesz originally was a liberal party with a militantly anticlerical view, but by the mid-1990s, when it shifted to conservative values, it embraced an openly positive stance toward religion. However, religion never was understood as a significant part of its identity and rather played a purely instrumental role in Fidesz's political strategy, even after they joined Europe's largest center-right party, the European People's Party (EPP), in the European Parliament. Thanks to Orbán's personal conversion to Protestantism and his opening to majority Catholic symbolism after 1998, Fidesz uses religious symbols in an eclectic way in which references to Christianity are often mentioned together with pagan traditions. This refers to the idea of "two Hungarys": a Western Christian and an Eastern pagan or tribal one (Ádám and Bozóki 2015). Orbán once voiced his conviction that the mythical Turul bird, a symbol of ancient Hungarians, is the "archetype into which Hungarians are born" (Orbán 2012). This means that Fidesz interprets pre-Christianity within the framework of nationalism; this ethno-nationalism provides a sufficient basis for political identification as a type of surrogate religion and is also suitable for winning extreme right-wing voters. In this respect Fidesz follows the authoritarian traditions of the Horthy regime, in which the "national religion" (*nemzetvallás*) played a crucial role, also serving as an attempt to overwrite the Catholic-Protestant divide. Another proof of Christianity being instrumental for Orbán is the fact that when he listed the illiberal regimes he admires – like China, Russia, Singapore, and Turkey – all of them were non-Christian or Orthodox.

The latest change of the Fundamental Law regarding Christianity was the Seventh Amendment adopted on June 20, 2018, which reads, "The protection of Hungary's self-identity and its Christian culture is the duty of all state organizations." The purpose of the proposed provision was questioned at the preparatory meeting of the judicial committee by members of opposition parties. The only explanation MPs of the governing Fidesz party, who initiated the new text, were able to provide was a paraphrase of an alleged sentence by Robert Schuman, the founding father of the European Union: "Without Christian culture there is neither Europe nor Hungary." Most probably, the same intention to legitimize his anti-European idea had led Orbán to recently reframe his concept of "illiberal democracy" as a fulfilment of "Christian democracy."

STATUTORY LIMITATIONS AND CASE LAW

Before January 1, 2012, when the new constitution became law, the Hungarian Parliament prepared a blizzard of so-called cardinal – or supermajority – laws, changing the shape of virtually every political institution in Hungary and making the guarantee of constitutional rights less secure. One of these cardinal laws was the law on the status of churches, passed on December 30, 2011, according to which the power to designate legally recognized churches is vested in the parliament itself.[16] The law listed fourteen legally recognized churches: eleven of them are Christian and three are Jewish. In February 2012, most probably in response to international pressure, particularly intervention by the United States, the parliament recognized an additional 13 groups, including Muslims, Buddhists, and smaller Christian groups, thereby raising the number of recognized churches to 27.[17] The law required all other previously registered churches (more than 200 religious organizations in total) to either reregister under considerably more demanding new criteria or continue to operate as religious associations without the legal benefits offered to recognized churches (like tax exemptions and the ability to operate state-subsidized religious schools). After this new law went into effect, only the mentioned 27 of the deregistered churches have been able to reregister, so the vast majority of previously registered churches have been deprived of their status as legal entities. Because registration requires an internal democratic decision-making structure and transparent finances, the majority of previously registered churches were unable to continue to operate with any legal recognition under the new regime, either because they did not elect their religious leaders or because anonymous donations constituted part of their financing. Nontraditional and nonmainstream religious communities – which had not faced legal obstacles between 1989 and 2011 – were facing increasing hardships and discrimination as a result.

Seventeen religious communities that previously had operated as churches but had lost their status due to the new act submitted constitutional complaints to the Constitutional Court. The applicants requested a review of the act on both procedural and substantive grounds. The procedural complaints mainly concerned the violation of the rule of law, the procedural rules of legislation, and the obligation to effectively consult other religious organizations. As regards the substantive complaints, the applicants' main concern was the prerogative of the parliament to decide over the legal status of churches by a two-thirds majority. The applicants contended that the legal provisions regulating the recognition of churches were contrary to the principle of separation of power, to the right to fair procedure, and to the right to legal remedy. The provision, without consideration for the constitutional principle of separation of powers, allowed the parliament to decide by itself on church status recognition without the right to appeal.

In February 2013, just before it was finally packed by the governing parties,[18] the Constitutional Court declared in Decision 6/2013 AB that, as a constitutional requirement, the State must ensure that religious communities get special status as "religions" based upon objective and reasonable criteria, and in harmony with the right to freedom of religion and the requirement of fair procedure. Furthermore, legal remedy against decisions on their special status must be ensured. However, it pointed out that it is not a constitutional requirement that every church has the same rights or that the state cooperates with all the churches to the same extent. Existing differences between religious communities could be considered by the legislator in accordance with the Fundamental Law, provided they are neither based on discrimination nor the result of discriminatory practice. The Court ruled that all religious associations have an equal right to apply for recognition by means of procedure that follows due process and ensures the right of effective remedy. Since the provisions for recognition set forth in the religious law had failed to do this, the Court restored the legal status of the deregistered churches.

In response to this decision, the Fourth Amendment to the Fundamental Law in April 2013 elevated the annulled provisions into the main text of the Fundamental Law, with the intention of excluding further constitutional review. Even though the Constitutional Court argued that the registration of churches by the parliament does not provide a fair procedure for the applicants, this procedure became part of the constitution.

Due to huge international criticism against the Fourth Amendment, the government again made cosmetic concessions. The Fifth Amendment to the Fundamental Law passed in September 2013 explicitly granted the authority to the parliament to select religious communities for "cooperation" with the state in the service of "public interest activities." An amendment to the Church law also adopted in September created a two-tiered classification consisting of "religious communities" and "incorporated churches."

The proof that these amendments did not really change the status of Hungarian churches is that the European Court of Human Rights (ECtHR) continued its procedure based on earlier complaints of nine religious communities and individuals. The Strasbourg Court, in its judgment of April 8, 2014, in the case of *Magyar Keresztény Mennonita Egyház* [Hungarian Christian Mennonite Church] *and Others v. Hungary*,[19] also found that Hungary's unconstitutional church law violated Article 9 on the right of religious freedom of the European Convention of Human Rights. Hungary appealed the decision. The Grand Chamber rejected that appeal, so on September 9, 2014, the decision became final and binding. Concerning Hungary's repeated assertions of the "state's broad discretionary power" to choose among religious communities with which to cooperate, the ECtHR argued: "In its choice of partners for outsourcing public-interest tasks the State cannot discriminate among religious communities. The neutrality of the State requires that, in case the State chooses to co-operate with religious communities, the choice of partners be based on ascertainable criteria, for example, as to their material capacities."[20] And despite the newly introduced second tier, the Court argued that such a demarcation does not satisfy the requirements of State neutrality and is devoid of objective grounds for differential treatment.[21]

In an early reaction to the decision, the state secretary of the Ministry of Justice pointed out that Hungary has no obligation to adhere to ECtHR rulings.[22] After the ECtHR judgment, the already packed Hungarian Constitutional Court decided several cases against the government. These cases were initiated by either deregistered churches or by judges who had to take into account whether the law was unconstitutional or was in contradiction with international treaties signed by Hungary and who turned to the Court. These petitions were submitted because the Church Law of 2011 ruled that more than 200 deregistered churches would lose their church status, and unless they were to apply for registration as private law associations within 30 days, they would cease to exist altogether. Religious groups previously registered as churches either not acknowledging the right of the parliament to terminate their status or being aware of the decision of the Constitutional Court that annulled these provisions of the law did not ask for registration or missed the deadline. After the Fourth Amendment to the Fundamental Law in 2013, ordinary courts were compelled to decide on the forced liquidation and termination of churches, even as associations. In a series of decisions the Constitutional Court ruled that, due to its Decision 6/2013 as well as the ECtHR judgment in the case of *Magyar Keresztény Mennonita Egyház and Others v. Hungary*, these judgments of the courts were not applicable, and the Constitutional Court also extended the deadline for application for the status of association.[23] In one particular case, besides the unconstitutionality of such court decisions, it also declared that they contradicted Hungary's international treaty obligations, and therefore it called upon the parliament to resolve this contradiction by October 15, 2015.[24]

As a reaction to the ECtHR judgment, in December 2015 the government submitted a fifth amendment to the Church Law. The amended law planned to replace the two-tiered system of classification for religious communities with a three-tiered system, consisting of "religious associations," "registered churches," and "certified churches." Future classification within the categories would be determined by a court. Additionally, the draft law allowed the state to enter into "cooperative agreements" with individual religious communities on a discretionary basis, in order to subsidize public interest activities performed by those religious communities.

The amendment would have marked a significant improvement over earlier versions of the Church Law in that it provided explicit rights and protections for religious communities classified in the lower tiers. It also would have curtailed the role of the parliament in allocating legal recognition to religious groups. According to the draft law, all groups previously recognized as "incorporated churches" (previously the highest tier) were to be automatically recognized as "certified churches" after the amendments went into effect. This meant that "incorporated churches" would have been exempted from applying at the court while religious associations would be required to do so. Groups belonging to the lowest tier, that is, "religious associations," would not be allowed to collect from the basket of the voluntary 1 percent church tax declaration that can be made when filing personal income tax in Hungary and which directly supports the activities of religious communities. Such discriminatory rules would be in explicit contradiction with the ECtHR judgment, as the entire "amendment fails to address the most serious violations of the right of religious freedom identified by the Court," because "transitional provisions with the proposed amendments would perpetuate, rather than correct the earlier violations of the ECtHR and discretionary powers afforded the state would continue the arbitrary recognition procedure criticized by both the ECtHR and the Venice Commission" (OSCE 2015).

Even this moderate amendment – according to which religious communities, with the exception of the "incorporated churches," still would not enjoy full religious freedom – was not enacted by the governing majority. Denied equality under the law and subject to opaque regulations, deregistered religious communities, similar to NGOs unpopular in the eyes of the government, would be subject to arbitrary and expensive audits, hindered or prevented from raising money, attacked in the government-controlled media, and harassed by local officials.

During the debate of the bill in September 2015 the government ignored all suggestions from opposition parties and NGOs that intended to improve it, and in December the bill was introduced unaltered to the parliament but failed to secure the necessary two-thirds majority vote needed to pass.[25] Since failing to pass the bill, the government has not taken any further steps to amend its church law nor has it taken steps to address the ongoing violations of the right of religious freedom identified by the ECtHR. Many deregistered religious communities in Hungary currently exist in a legal no man's land, recognized neither as churches nor as religious associations. As entities without a clear legal status they are unable to collect the one-percent voluntary church tax, their clergy are denied tax exemptions given to legally recognized churches, and their ability to maintain schools and enter into contracts is severely impaired.[26]

MODELS OF STATE-RELIGION RELATIONS AND LIBERAL DEMOCRACY

This change in the status of religious freedom in the Hungarian system of "illiberal democracy" after 2010 raises a question: what kind of state-religion relationship and religious systems are compatible with liberal democracy and which are not?

In his famous book, *The Clash of Civilizations and the Remaking of World Order*, Samuel Huntington says that the key characteristic of Western culture has been the separation of church and state, something that he sees as foreign to the world's other major religious systems (Huntington 1996, 217). His concluding question and answer is: "Where does Europe end? Where Western Christianity ends and Islam and Orthodoxy begin" (Huntington 1996, 158).

Alfred Stepan argued against Huntington that the greatest obstacle to liberal democracy, for instance, in Turkey or Egypt, is posed not by Islam but by military and intelligence organizations unaccountable to democratic authority. Both countries are more restrictive of freedom of religious expression within civil society and of freedom of organization within political society than that of any longstanding Western liberal democracy. On the other hand, the governing positions of the Muslim Brotherhood in Egypt and Erdoğan's anti-Atatürk governance had, and still represent, a different structure in these countries. Stepan also claims that "separation of church and state" and "secularism" are not intrinsic parts of the core definition of Western liberal democracy but the minimal boundaries of freedom of action that must be crafted for political institutions vis-à-vis religious authorities, and for religious individuals and groups vis-à-vis political institutions, what he calls "twin tolerations" (Stepan 2000). By "twin tolerations" Stepan means that (a) religious institutions should not have constitutionally privileged prerogatives that allow them to mandate public policy to democratically elected governments, and (b) at the same time, individuals and religious communities, consistent with our institutional definition of democracy, must have complete freedom to worship privately. In other words, the one toleration obliges the state to protect and "tolerate" the freedom of religious institutions to operate in civil society, while the other requires that the religious communities "tolerate" each other by not deploying constitutional privileges or state power to squelch their competitors. Stepan adds to this concept that this institutional approach to liberal democracy necessarily implies that no group in civil society – including religious groups – *a priori* can be prohibited from forming a political party.

Let us first see how West European democracies have met the requirements of "twin toleration." Some EU member states – Denmark, Finland, Greece, and the United Kingdom (in England and Scotland) – have established churches. Norway and Iceland, although not in the EU, are two other European democracies with an established church (only Sweden disestablished the Lutheran Church in 2000). Although Germany does not have an established church, Protestantism and Catholicism are recognized as official religions, and the majority of citizens pay state-collected church tax. The two European countries with "hostile" separations of church and state used to be France and Turkey, but the current Turkish situation fits here less and less. This means that three distinct models of state-religion relations can be discerned in contemporary Europe: those with an established church, the militantly secular, and a mixed model with a dominant but civil church. These are described by Silvio Ferrari through one country in each model: English multiculturalism, French secularism, and Catholic civil religion in Italy (Ferrari 2014). (Maybe the Dutch model can be considered as a fourth, where not even actual Calvinist believers are officially members of the Calvinist Church, and then there exists a symbolically subordinate but more organized and more numerous Catholic Church.) Ferrari concludes that there are sharp distinctions between the religious freedom of individuals, which all European states protect, and the status of religious communities and institutions, which are subject to restrictions. In another work speaking of Europe, Ferrari claims that it is necessary to go beyond the traditional classification of church-state relations and look at the common principles that are the basis of the European model of state-religion relations (Ferrari 2003). But the lesson from the European picture is that liberal democracies are compatible both with established churches and with unfriendly separation of church and state approaches as well. Therefore, the concepts of secularism and the separation of state and religion have a place in the Western European liberal democracy only in the context of Stepan's "twin tolerations." In other words, we have to leave room for democratic bargaining and the nonliberal public argument within religious communities that it sometimes requires.

CONCLUSION

It is not easy to characterize the relations between the state and religion in Hungary using Hirschl's (2010) models. It is certainly not theocratic constitutionalism and also not a religious establishment approach, which exists in some of Europe's most liberal and progressive polities, such as Denmark, Finland, Iceland, and Norway, having a formal, mainly ceremonial designation of a certain religion as the "state religion," or even in Germany, where the institutional apparatus of the Catholic, Evangelical, and Jewish religious communities are designated as public corporations and therefore qualify for state support from church tax.[27] Hungary's unique system is perhaps the closest to a more *de facto* scenario than a *de jure* model, where formal separation of church and state, as well as religious freedom more generally, are constitutionally guaranteed but where emerging patterns of politically systemized hegemony of the Catholic Church and religion-centric morality is present in the constitutional arena. The preamble of the Fundamental Law entitled National Avowal challenges the autonomy of individuals who do not accept normative life models defined on the basis of the Fundamental Law's ideological values, that is, "the form in which we want to live."

Constitutions in the modern world often have a great deal to say about religious liberty. Liberal constitutions require freedom of religious belief and propitious conditions for collective worship. Illiberal constitutions often combine religion and state authority to the point where an official religion dries out its contenders or where religious doctrine obtains direct legal status. Some illiberal constitutional bodies ban any religious influence on political life. In this chapter I tried to catalogue the different sorts of constitutional orders and provide a theoretical account of their differences. From this perspective, the growing importance of religion in national legitimation in Hungary can be considered as one of the reasons for the illiberal turn of this country.

One of the lessons to be learned from the Hungarian case study is that different constitutional models of state-religion relationships alone do not indicate the very status of religious rights in a polity. Even a theocratic model – as the one in Egypt under Mubarak with a relatively liberal jurisprudence of the Supreme Constitutional Court – can provide more religious freedom than a formal separationist approach such as the current Hungarian one. As the European Court of Human Rights stated in the case of *Magyar Keresz-tény Mennonita Egyház and Others*, Hungary violated the principle of state neutrality in the official justification of its laws silencing people with deeply held religious beliefs.[28] The political aspirations for more illiberalism after a liberal democratic period seemed to be the decisive element to find similarly restrictive measures for freedom of religion. Through the use of "abusive constitutional" tools,[29] a new Fundamental Law and its constitutional amendments to the illiberal constitutional model also became undemocratic,[30] enforcing conservative social and cultural norms not necessarily shared by the majority.

NOTES

1. Decision 4/1993.
2. Decision 4, 1993.
3. Article 15 (2) of Act No. IV of 1990.

4. Among the Visegrád countries only the Czech Republic can be characterized as more secular than Hungary. See World Values Survey, Fifth (2005–2008) and Sixth Waves (2010–2014), International Social Science Programme Data, 2003 and 2008.

5. See hungarianspectrum.org 2017a.

6. About the "Sect Debate," see Kis 1994.

7. About the 2000–2001 draft amendments, see Kis 2001.

8. Protestantism was represented in the Orbán government by Zoltán Balog, a Calvinist pastor who was minister of human resources from 2012 to 2018.

9. See Orbán 2015a.

10. See Orbán 2015b.

11. See hungarianspectrum.org 2017b.

12. See hungarianfreepress.com 2016.

13. See nol.hu 2019.

14. See Szabó 2012. The metaphor of Hungary's ill-fate stemmed from her inability to choose between Asia and Western Europe goes back to Endre Ady, one of the greatest Hungarian poets of the early twentieth century, as well as to Imre Kertész, a Nobel laureate in literature. See Kertész 2012.

15. See the fate of József Mindszenty, archbishop and primate, who refused to permit the Roman Catholic schools of Hungary to be secularized, which prompted the communist government to arrest him in 1948 and convict him in 1949 on charges of treason.

16. The first version of this law was passed by the parliament on July 12, 2011, as Act C of 2011 on the Right to Freedom of Conscience and Religion, and on Churches, Religions, and Religious Communities. The Constitutional Court in its Decision 161/2011 AB annulled the law for procedural reasons. Ten days after the Court's decision on December 30, 2011, a proviso was inserted into the First Amendment to the Fundamental Law to the effect that parliament, in a cardinal Act, determines "recognized churches" and the normative conditions for recognizing further religious organizations. Then, on December 30, 2011, parliament passed the Act on Churches, with virtually the same content as before.

17. The appendix to Act CCVI of 2011 lists a total of 27 churches. The Buddhist and Muslim "churches" are umbrella organizations for distinct religious communities. If we count those individual communities separately, there are 32 recognized churches. See Baer 2014.

18. In April 2013 eight out of fifteen judges were elected by the governing parties without any consent by opposition parties. For more about the process of packing the Court, see Halmai 2014.

19. Application Nos. 70945/11, 23611/12, 26998/12, 41150/12, 41155/12, 41463/12, 41553/12, 54977/12 and 56581/12.

20. *Ibid.*, 109.

21. *Ibid.*, 112.

22. See vg.hu 2014.

23. See Decisions 27/2014, 35/2014, 15/2015, 3144/2015.

24. Decision 23/2015.

25. Due to by-elections in early 2015, Fidesz lost its two-thirds majority by two votes.

26. The Forum for Religious Freedom (FOREF Europe), in its recommendation dated September 27, 2016, urged the government of Hungary to address the current violations of religious freedom occurring in Hungary. See osce.org 2016.

27. See Hirschl, 29.

28. See a similar definition of state neutrality in Kis 2012.

29. The category of "abusive constitutionalism" was introduced by David Landau using the cases of Colombia, Hungary, and Venezuela. See Landau 2013.

30. As Jan-Werner Müller rightly argues, it is not just liberalism that is under attack in Hungary but democracy itself. Hence, instead of calling them "illiberal democracies," we should describe them as illiberal and "undemocratic" regimes (Müller 2016).

BIBLIOGRAPHY

Ádám, Zoltán, and András Bozóki. 2015. *The God of Hungarians. Religion and Right Wing Populism in Hungary*. Unpublished manuscript.

Baer, David H. 2014. "Testimony Concerning the Condition of Religious Freedom in Hungary," submitted to the U.S. Commission on Security and Cooperation in Europe (the Helsinki Commission). In *A vallásszabadság védelmében/Essays in Defense of Religious Freedom*. Budapest: Wesley János Kiadó.

EVS. 1999. *EVS – European Values Study 1999 – Integrated Dataset*. GESIS Data Archive, Cologne. ZA3811.

Ferrari, Silvio. 2003. "The Legal Dimension." In *Muslims in an Enlarged Europe*, edited by Brigitte Marechal, Stefano Allievi, Felice Dasseto, Jorgen Nielsen. Leiden: Brill.

———. 2014. "Models of State-Religion Relations in Western Europe." In *The Future of Religious Freedom. Global Challenges*, edited by Allen D. Hertzke. Oxford: Oxford University Press.

Grzymala-Busse, Anna. 2013. "Whither Eastern Europe? Changing Political Science Perspectives on the Region. Studying Religion and Politics in East Central Europe." University of Michigan.

Halmai, Gábor. 2014. "In memoriam magyar alkotmánybíráskodás." *Fundamentum* 2014 (1–2): 36–64.

Hirschl, Ran, 2010. *Constitutional Theocracy*. Cambridge, MA: Harvard University Press.

hungarianfreepress.com. 2016. "Migrant Crisis and the Shameful Silence of Cardinal Péter Erdő." http://hungarianfreepress.com/2016/08/17/migrant-crisis-and-the-s hameful-silence-of-cardinal-peter-erdo/.

hungarianspectrum.org. 2017a. "They Don't See Eye to Eye: Pope Francis and the Hungarian Bishops." http://hungarianspectrum.org/2017/12/27/they-dont-see-e ye-to-eye-pope-francis-and-the-hungarian-bishops/, accessed June 25, 2019.

hungarianspectrum.org. 2017b. "Viktor Orban Rewrites the Bible and Falsifies the Words of Jesus." http://hungarianspectrum.org/2017/12/26/viktor-orban-rewrites-the-bible-and-falsifies-the-words-of-jesus/, accessed June 25, 2019.

Huntington, Samuel P. 1996. *The Clash of Civilizations and the Remaking of World Order.* New York: Simon & Schuster, 1996.

Kertész, Imre. 2012. "La Hongrie est une fatalité." *Le Monde,* February 10.

Kis, János. 1994. "Erkölcs, hit, tolerancia." *Kritika* 1994 (2): 2–9.

———. 2001. "Egyház, állam, társadalom." *Világosság* 2001 (6): 58–66.

———. 2012. "State Neutrality." In *Oxford Handbook of Comparative Constitutional Law,* edited by M. Rosenfeld and A. Sajó, 318–34. Oxford: Oxford University Press.

Landau, David. 2013. "Abusive Constitutionalism." *UC Davis Law Review* 47: 189–260.

Müller, Jan Werner. 2016. "The Problem With 'Illiberal Democracy.'" *Project Syndicate,* January 26.

nol. 2019. "Jönnek mint a sáskák." http://nol.hu/belfold/hajmasker-lelkesz-reformatus-menekultek-video-1631467, accessed June 25, 2019.

Orbán, Viktor. 2012. "Minden magyar a turulba születik." *Népszabadság,* September 29.

———. 2015a. "Magyarország keresztény lesz vagy nem lesz". Speech in Debrecen on May 18, 2015. http://index.hu/belfold/2015/05/18/orban_magyarorszag_kereszteny_lesz_vagy_nem_lesz/#.

———. 2015b. Speech in Kötcse on September 5, 2015. https://vastagbor.atlatszo.hu/2015/09/17/a-vagatlan-kotcsei-beszed/.

———. 2017. "Meg kell védenünk a keresztény kulturát." *Magyar Idők,* December 23.

OSCE. 2015. *Hungary: Amended Church Law Remains at Variance with OSCE Standards and the European Convention on Human Rights.* OSCE Human Dimension Implementation Meeting, Warsaw, September 30.

osce.org. 2016. "Hungary: Two Years After Ruling by ECtHR Church Law Remains Unaltered." http://www.osce.org/odihr/268711?download=true, accessed June 25, 2019.

Schanda, Balázs. 2001. "Church Autonomy and Religious Liberty – National Report on Hungary." In *Church Autonomy: A Comparative Survey,* edited by Gerhard Robbers. Frankfurt am Main: Peter Lang.

Smith, Tom, W. 2013. *Beliefs about God across Time and Countries.* NORC/University of Chicago. April 18, 2012. Updated February 12, 2013. *Report for ISSP and GESIS GSS Cross-National Report* No. 32.

Stepan, Alfred. 2000. "The 'Twin Tolerations.'" *Journal of Democracy* 11 (4): 37–57.

Szabó, Brigitta. 2012. "Félázsiai származékoknál, mint mi, csak így megy." *Népszabadság,* July 27.

Tomka, Miklós. "Hagyományos (vallási) értékek a modern társadalomban." *Education* 2001 (3): 419–33.

Tomka, Miklós, and Paul M. Zulehner. 1999. *Religion in den Reformländern Ost(Mittel) Europas.* Ostfildern: Schwaben.

vg. 2014. "Itt a kormány válasza a strasbourgi ítéletre." http://www.vg.hu/kozelet/jog/itt-a-kormany-valasza-a-strasbourgi-iteletre-425267, accessed June 25, 2019.

Chapter 6

The Right Hand Thinks

On the Sources of György Matolcsy's Economic Vision

János Mátyás Kovács

WHY MATOLCSY?

The hero of my chapter, György Matolcsy, is the governor of the Hungarian National Bank and the former minister of the national economy, a scholar and a columnist, the economic visionary of Viktor Orbán, and the architect of what he calls "unorthodox" economic policy.

From a bird's eye view, everything seems fine. During the past decade, Matolcsy's career as a top policymaker has been unbroken: as a minister, he managed to survive a deep economic crisis that threatened sovereign default in the early 2010s; as a central banker, he has contributed to restarting and sustaining economic growth in the country. He has strong views of all fields of economic policy with thousands of pages written, half a dozen books published, and a magnum opus, entitled *Equilibrium and Growth*,[1] completed. The latter celebrates his unorthodox program and serves as a principal textbook at "his" publicly funded János Neumann University in Kecskemét.[2] Yet, the more I read Matolcsy's writings, the deeper my hesitation became: would applying standard procedures of intellectual history-writing to understand his work as a visionary not blow up its academic significance?

Nonetheless, I decided to prepare this chapter but in the back of my mind Helmut Schmidt's witty remark was preserved: *wer Visionen hat, sollte zum Arzt gehen.* If Matolcsy did not maintain a symbiotic relationship with Orbán (who called him his "right hand"),[3] I certainly would confine my analysis to a series of sarcastic remarks ridiculing a self-conceited voodoo economist[4] who happened to be in the right place at the right time. However, what if Orbán was correct by saying, with a large dose of self-praise, that "the [present Hungarian] prime minister is a quasi-Adenauer, and the minister for economic affairs is a quasi-Erhard"?[5] What if Matolcsy really found a recipe for a lasting economic miracle in Hungary—a "veritable fairy tale,"[6] as he likes to brag?

This chapter will not check whether that recipe has been successful. Instead, I will be interested in its composition and genesis, and examine the main ingredients of György Matolcsy's economic thinking in both communist and precommunist times. First, the major components of his current unorthodoxy will be presented. Then, in identifying the historical sources of unorthodox economic policy (UEP), I will highlight some crucial similarities between moderate reformism under communism and prewar étatism, and reveal a surprising continuity of state interventionism in Hungary over almost an entire century; an economic paradigm that survived the allegedly neoliberal era after 1989.[7]

However, before becoming immersed in intellectual history, let me indicate the kind of juicy stories of "everyday Matolcsyism" that the reader will not hear from me. I will leave it in the good hands of critical-minded journalists in Hungary to portray him as a kitchen-table historian indulging in the heroic past of ancient Hungarians who, in Matolcsy's view, excelled in gastronomy and brain surgery. Similarly, no mention will be made of his thesis of genetic bonds connecting ethnic Hungarians and Japanese, and I will also disregard his attraction to numerology (he fears the number 8).[8] Furthermore, although it would take us closer to the sociology of the Orbán regime, I will not devote even a single paragraph to Matolcsy's nepotist and protectionist allures that manifest themselves by employing his own girlfriend and future second wife (and her sister and mother) in the National Bank and in its foundations, allocating large credits to his cousin (and, through him, to Matolcsy's two sons) as well as to spending public funds for the establishment of his "personal" university of economics, or subsidizing his PhD supervisor's department at another university.[9] More importantly, all informed guesswork describing Matolcsy's role as Orbán's kingmaker will be ignored. Ostensibly, after 1994, during the periods in which Fidesz was in opposition, he mobilized his business network, which emerged in the turbulent times of privatization before and after 1989, in order to assist his future boss in financing the "national side" of Hungarian politics.[10]

Political analysts still owe the public an explanation for the lasting relationship between this "odd couple." Why did Orbán decide to elevate Matolcsy's unorthodox economic policy to the level of *Staatsideologie*, knowing the political risk of supporting an economic advisor of dubious fame who is, in addition, a rather arrogant, snobbish and narcissistic communicator?[11] Nevertheless, aside from unconditional loyalty, Matolcsy also had a spectacular intellectual commodity to sell to his idol. He offered the Fidesz government in both 1998 and 2010 an easily digestible and applicable economic philosophy. It embraced all necessary properties of a populist program, ranging from harsh attacks on the harmful economic policy of socialist-liberal governments, through naming the wrongdoers—including the Western "principals" of the domestic "agents"—to a simplistic economic plan of overcoming hardships and substantially increasing the autonomy of the Orbán administration against global and regional economic organizations.[12] This program also promised to contribute to a rapid consolidation of the national-conservative elites and an efficient mobilization of their electorate. Apparently, the old wisdom of "the Moor has done his duty, the Moor can go" does not apply here because, after a while, the prime minister fell in love with the economic policy package advocated by his aide and kept glorifying it as a cornerstone of his System of National Cooperation.

CELEBRATING UNORTHODOXY

Calling his own economic program "unorthodox," Matolcsy provokes two kinds of reactions from critical observers. On the one hand, one can interpret the UEP as a manifestation of sheer ignorance about the economic orthodoxy of our time and decide not to go beyond a hasty analysis of the program's *political* rationality. In this case, the UEP will be regarded as a postmodern product of politics, a *bricolage* of poorly defined economic principles that often exclude each other.[13] What is actually unorthodox in Matolcsy's policy mix is that, as ironic as it may be, in formulating his interventionist agenda he borrows heavily from a body of thought he vehemently attacks most of the time. Introducing the flat tax and trusting in its trickle-down effects,[14] preferring workfare to welfare, supporting transnational companies and weakening the trade unions, etc.—that is, policies he should have rejected as "neoliberal delusions," to cite his favorite stigma—became principal constituents of the UEP.[15] By means of this mix one cannot offer an exhaustive description of "Matolcsyism" for good. Any other idea he deems useful (or just fashionable) may be taken on by him at any time. In 1990, Matolcsy said this in an interview:

> I do not regard myself either as a liberal or a neo-conservative economist. I see my place in an intellectual coalition, in which Keynesian and neoconservative ideas coexist perfectly, but also the practice of social market economy or even liberal techniques of finance.[16]

On the other hand, his program also can be considered a thought experiment that has something to do with interventionist theories of *economic* policy along a Third Way between capitalism and communism; theories that look back on a considerable past in the Hungarian history of ideas. Here, an obvious object of scrutiny is Matolcsy's role as a moderate socialist reform economist in the 1980s.[17] In a search for further historical analogies, prompted by the stubborn attempts of the Orbán regime to return to the 1930s, it is also child's play to discover some of the main ingredients of Matolcsy's economic doctrines in the works of agrarian populists on both the left and the right. An eminent member of that group was Mátyás Matolcsy, a leading economist of the national-socialist camp in Hungary,[18] and a distant relative of our hero. Child's play can be dangerous though. It is really not too difficult to demonstrate the similarity between core elements of Hungarian economic thought at these stages and Matolcsy's agenda today, and even telling personal links between the three can be revealed. However, let me stress upfront that even a strong evidence of similarity does *not* lead to the conclusion that (1) the moderate socialist reformers were semi-fascist thinkers,[19] or that (2) Matolcsy has borrowed ideas from his ancestor on purpose. He may not be familiar with and is not responsible for the thoughts and deeds of his relative in retrospect. What is the gist of Matolcsy's proud unorthodoxy? Let him speak first:

> In 2010, Hungarian economic policy returned to pragmatic economic thinking. Its core is that it is labor, capital, and knowledge (technology) that produce new value. As a contrast, redistribution . . . does not create new value. (Matolcsy, 2015, p. 211)

By and large, these three sentences summarize his "theory of value" as presented in his voluminous book *Equilibrium and Growth*,[20] in which he tries to canonize the UEP-generated "breakthrough in economic history" (*ibid.*, 9–35). In Matolcsy's opinion, this breakthrough was due to a clear formulation of a series of other scholarly theses of his own. Reading his works,[21] one has the impression that he regards the following insights as his most significant scientific discoveries:

• Economic equilibrium is contingent on growth, and both depend on increasing employment while restrictions reduce effective demand and the pace of growth and, as a consequence, reproduce crisis.
• Crisis has many faces: underconsumption, underinvestment, growing external debt, and budget and current account deficits. In Hungary, the global crisis was preceded and/or complemented by an employment and demographic crisis, a growth crisis, and a structural crisis—all leading to a "neither equilibrium, nor growth" combo representing a "transition crisis."
• The "equilibrium or growth" dilemma can be solved with the formula of "growth + employment = sustainable equilibrium," in which raising the level of employment (cf. "work-based society") is the salient point. With

its help, the familiar symptoms of economic malaise such as high budget deficit and public debt can be "grown out." In the short run, however, the "balanced budget + employment = growth" rule has to be followed.

- Imbued with neoliberal illusions, the international economic organizations force a therapy of severe and counter-productive restrictions (shocks) upon the countries in crisis, and guide them along the "Mediterranean Road" toward new crises.
- Following the advice of these organizations, Hungary has replaced state ownership with foreign ownership, public monopolies with private monopolies of large transnational firms (particularly in the banking and energy sectors), and a wasteful planned economy with a wasteful market economy. Incomes were channeled from the "real" economy to the financial sector.
- Meanwhile, "the West" began to be outcompeted by "the East," the economic success of which is based on enhanced state intervention, a large share of public ownership, cheap labor, hard work, strong family ties, and a high level of exports supported by a weak currency. Hungary also needs such a "developmental state." Matolcsy describes his ideal hybrid regime in the following way:

> From the Anglo-Saxon model, we have to borrow the flexibility of the labor market and the tax system of low rates. However, the unlimited market, the dismantling of state control in all fields, and the principle of ownership without responsibility, must not be taken on. [. . .] As for the economy, the patterns to follow can be the North-Italian, Bavarian, Austrian, Slovene . . . medium-sized family enterprises from which a majority of jobs, tax revenues, and even innovation emerge. [. . .] My sympathy lies with the Asian family-centered model—I think it fits Hungarian habits perfectly. . . . [This model] is based on self-reliance . . . it does not need large public pension and healthcare systems. [. . .] The transfer of value patterns, diligence, morals and reliability, knowledge, and expertise do not emerge from market entrepreneurship, but primarily from family frameworks. The family does not work along the lines of profit-making, but is based on feelings of love and belonging.[22]

- In the lack of a strong developmental state, the country was forced to sacrifice many of its comparative advantages (especially in agriculture, transportation and tourism), let its economy deindustrialize and turn into an "assembly line" for transnational companies. Thereby, it became fatally exposed to global forces that siphon off capital from Hungary.

In what follows, it will not be my intention to contest the above platitudes, prejudices or blatant fallacies often hailed as original scientific inventions. This had been done by some of my distinguished colleagues during the past three decades.[23] Yet, why conceal the fact that as a member of the Hungarian research community of economists I also feel challenged by every second sentence of Matolcsy, especially when he speaks, in a patronizing tone, of mental traps that allegedly constrain the fantasy of "neoclassical-liberal" economic theorists and political elites.[24] Fortunately, putting on the cap of a historian of ideas, I am privileged to focus on locating his work in the history of economic thought in Hungary rather than submitting it to a quality test.

Matolcsy's economic discourse has not changed much during the past thirty years: its main pillars had been cemented under late communism. True, it became a bit more sophisticated by borrowing the "music" of the Stiglitz-style critique of the Washington Consensus and that of the Eastern European version of the "Varieties of Capitalism" school,[25] not to speak of other new-collectivist interpretations of current capitalism.[26] At the same time, these intellectual impacts produced an "anything goes" blend of economic principles reinforcing the Eastern European type of state-oriented conservatism and contradicting the "neoliberal" elements of the UEP mentioned above. Matolcsy's rhetoric grew more self-confident with the global financial crisis of 2008 and the subsequent calamities within the Eurozone. Today, when he is fully convinced that his unorthodox approach managed to reverse the decay of the Hungarian economy, his "narrative of the savior" reached hitherto unknown heights of self-praise.

In the time of the first Orbán government between 1998 and 2002, Matolcsy as the minister of the national economy was not yet authorized to convert each and every one of his pet ideas into an all-embracing package of economic policy. The subsequent eight years of the socialist-liberal coalition reinforced his conviction that combining the socialist "fire" of forcing economic growth, impeding liberalization and pursuing egalitarian social policies with the liberal "water" of equilibrium-oriented restrictions and further steps toward the privatization of welfare services leads nowhere. He decided to release the economic program of the socialists from the captivity of the liberals, and to accomplish what the socialists never dared/could/wanted to accomplish: a sovereign state-capitalist regime with a fast-growing economy and moderate welfare performance. Matolcsy realized that any cautious development policy requires close cooperation with international economic organizations and was persuaded that external assistance would constrain the government's room to maneuver. Austerity measures would imply huge political costs while providing no guarantee to avoid the trap of dependency.[27]

He was confident that the theoretical insights listed above were confirmed by the "lost decade" of socialist-liberal rule and laid the foundations for the following aims and means of UEP:

- In order to stabilize the economy, the government has to radically loosen its relationship with international economic organizations (in Matolcsy's words, launch a "freedom fight" to end "colonization") in order to avoid a strong conditionality that would block the use of unorthodox means of crisis management such as the nationalization of private pension funds or levying special taxes on banks (a "tactical nuclear weapon" as he says). The country must turn its back on the IMF, that is, no bail-out programs, not even stand-by arrangements are to be accepted.

- Similarly, the supervision of domestic economic policies by the EU (and the IMF-EU cooperation in reviewing the country's economic performance) need to be weakened by meeting the Maastricht criterion for the budget deficit. The IMF can be asked to leave the country ("We threw them out," in Matolcsy's parlance),[28] but jeopardizing EU transfer payments would be too high a price to pay for national sovereignty. This is the final limit of provoking Brussels with a peacock dance, to use Orbán's favorite metaphor. A substantial weakening of national currency[29] (and pursuing a loose monetary policy in general) is an adequate technique of attaining the goals of the UEP; a technique the government would not be allowed to apply if Hungary had introduced the Euro. Thus, joining the Eurozone must be delayed as long as possible.
- While temporarily risking sovereign default and capital flight, the government can rely on societal support resulting from economic growth, an increase in employment and consumption, redistribution of incomes to the upper and middle classes via flat tax, state subsidies for domestic capitalism, or privileges offered to public servants and part of the cultural elite, etc., and a containment of poorer social groups up until incomes of the better-offs begin to trickle down. The means of containment include public works, tax cuts (e.g., family tax relief), price controls (e.g., of utility services), and so on, which will sugarcoat the pill of provisional welfare losses in the first phase of the UEP.
- The main sources of stabilization through accelerating growth are the EU's development funds, remittances of Hungarian migrant workers, confiscation of private pension funds, restructuring the budget by curtailing "unproductive" expenditure (cf. welfare retrenchment), levying special taxes on banks, telecommunication, commercial, utility companies, etc.—that is, preferably on foreign capital from the West—while promoting capital inflow from the East (e.g., through a "residency by investment" program), channeling savings into government bonds, reducing income taxes and raising VAT,[30] etc. These sources are exploited to make a first push. The momentum of stabilization is further maintained by massive government intervention ranging from the renationalization of "strategic firms," the launching of large-scale public credit programs and development plans of "reindustrialization," to use the official label,[31] to employment subsidies. To secure firm political background for these policy measures within the

EU, the subsidies should benefit a selected group of companies, primarily German car manufacturers, which will also be exempted from special taxes. Evidently, the strength of the first push depends on the consolidation of the institutional setup of the Orbán regime, above all on the rapid elimination of constitutional checks and balances on central economic decision-making (paradoxically, including that of the independence of the National Bank)— a precondition Matolcsy expected his "Adenauer" to satisfy.

• Regarding the cultural/psychological sources of the "growth turn," they are granted by "national cooperation," i.e., to quote Albert Hirschman, by the "loyalty" of the winners of the UEP and the "exit" of the losers. In the near future, the regime will reproduce itself almost automatically. Given the risks of a devastating reaction to the UEP by the global markets, this Grand Design must be well-protected inside the country. It not only has to be backed by a supermajority in parliament, a party-state under control and a wide network of vested interests, but, being an ingeniously uncomplicated construct ("simplicity" is Matolcsy's favorite term), it also needs to become comprehensible and acceptable by ordinary citizens, or at least they must not see any alternatives to replace it with. The UEP's path is as narrow as the razor's edge. Therefore, one needs to "dream big," to use Orbán's phrase, about the future, and take huge risks. To mobilize for the "revolutionary" process, the economic architects of "national cooperation" also have to promise big (e.g., create one million new jobs in ten years, introduce one-digit income and profit taxes, reduce public debt to 50 percent of GDP, become the center of industrialization in Europe, catch up with Austria in 20 years, etc.), "talk big" using newspeak (e.g., work-based society, "Eastern wind," "Hungarian Miracle," etc.), and radiate optimism as well as invincibility.

ON THE LEGACY OF MODERATE REFORMISM

Below, I will skip the question of whether these aims have been attained and the means have proven appropriate during the past decade. Also, it will not be asked what the price of this vast experiment in social engineering has been. Similarly, the proportions between deliberate action, spontaneous developments, luck and improvisation will not be examined, just as I will also disregard the cases in which Matolcsy made a virtue of necessity.[32] What really interests me here is his toolbox of ideas, or more exactly, the question of when and how the main instruments may have been placed in it in the past.

I had a tormenting feeling of *déjà vu*. Orbán's arrogant reference to similarities between Ludwig Erhard and György Matolcsy was correct in one respect: both economists had spent their formative years under authoritarian regimes. However, while the father of the "German miracle" emerged from the Nazi era as a veritable (social) liberal, our hero carried over from communism and beyond a much heavier legacy of state interventionism, irrespective of the fact that from time to time he also takes pride in presenting himself as a devotee of *Soziale Marktwirtschaft*.[33]

In trying to comprehend Matolcsy's recent texts, I was traveling in time, first back to the 1980s into the thick of reform economics (market socialism). The methodology, many of the key concepts, the style and the sociological position of the author all reminded me of the moderate reformers (and the fallacy cherished by a number of foreign analysts of economic thought in Hungary prior to 1989). Frequently, these analysts mistook exception for rule. In focusing on the radical wing of reform economists, a small minority of the research community at the time, they often forgot about the overwhelming majority, the moderates. Today, one can hear their voice from Matolcsy's writings.

In the second part of the 1980s, Matolcsy drifted to the camp of radical reformers, and took part as a co-author in formulating their emblematic manifesto "Turnaround and Reform."[34] At the same time, he remained cautious, did not flirt with the Democratic Opposition (a loose network of anti-communist activists), and did not publish in *samizdat*. Accepting a high-level position in the national-conservative government in 1990 proved to be a point of no return. He found a political home there (he joined Fidesz later) but has not ceased to measure himself against his former colleagues among the radicals.

Here I cannot dwell upon the "speculative" (verbal) institutionalism of reformist thought, the affinity of reformers for artificial designs of reconciling the "plan" with the "market," or their embeddedness in high politics in the communist era.[35] Rather, a cursory distinction will be made between the radicals and the moderates. While the moderates believed in a gradual evolution from *socialist* to *social* market economy (*nota bene*, to a rather statist version of the latter), and accepted a slow change in major institutional regimes of the planned economy, the radicals demanded a rapid dismantling of the communist party-state and central planning as a prerequisite to shifting to a less statist (but not neoliberal) version of capitalism.[36] If a bigger picture were needed, one could add that, in contrast to the radicals, the moderate reformers, many of them unreconstructed socialists, had strong reservations against reestablishing the hegemony of large-scale private property, opening up to the West, and introducing resolute austerity measures to stabilize the economy. They showed a clear preference for what we call today a "developmental state," that is, a large public sector surrounded by small- and medium-sized semi-private enterprises regulated by a strong government that does not always bother itself with protecting property rights and other market freedoms under the rule of law. Some of them did not even mind a national-protectionist conversion of the party-state. When, in 1990, Matolcsy joined the government of József Antall, he subscribed to the elements of the moderate program almost word-by-word.

Observers tend to trace the origins of Matolcsy's current unorthodoxy by referring to his rediscovery of Keynes during the 1990s,[37] to the attraction of the Chinese success story of managed capitalism, and the heartfelt approval by him of the critique of the Washington Consensus all over the world. In my view, however, these sources are to be regarded as nothing but the whipped cream on the cake, as we say in Hungarian. His views had already been affected by old-school Keynesian concepts earlier, in the community of moderate reform economists. Similarly, the success stories of the Little Tigers had seemed to the less liberal-minded economists in Hungary already more than attractive by the 1980s, and much of the post-1989 condemnation of the Washington Consensus had been anticipated by them when they pondered how Hungary could escape from the trap of indebtedness before the collapse of communism.

Moderate reform economics served as a net collecting such concepts floating in the air during the agony of planned economy. At the time, Matolcsy, as a ministerial official and later as a researcher, was primarily interested in reforming state ownership. He conceived of marketization *without* genuine (competitive) privatization either by assisting small entrepreneurship at the border of formal and informal economies, or by integrating large state-owned firms in huge government holdings reminiscent of the Japanese or Italian regimes of industrial organization.[38] When, in 1986, János Kornai termed the latter strategy of state-led modernization "Galbraithian socialism,"[39] he used an over- and an understatement at the same time. I am afraid that he overestimated the impact of Keynes upon moderate reformers, and, simultaneously, underestimated their propensity for state-collectivism, and even *dirigisme*.

Many of them (especially those representing branch ministries and big state companies)[40] were enchanted by large public development programs to be executed by robust government agencies. Instead of privatizing the big firms, they demanded empowerment of the managerial elite (the "technostructure"), the acceleration of export-led growth, as well as the expansion of consumption and public investment even at the risk of upsetting the macroeconomic equilibrium. The moderate reformers were right to fear that a transition to liberal democracy would hamper the implementation of their far-reaching modernization strategies. Imbued with technological optimism and with a strong belief of promulgating cutting-edge institutional schemes of modern capitalism, they talked about the radical reformers as "ultra-liberals" with the same contempt as Matolcsy when he places curses on those whom he calls neoliberals today. To tell the truth, at the time he did not share each and every interventionist views of the "Galbraithians," but rather swung back and forth between them and the radicals. Ironically, he may be farther from the latter in our days than he was at the end of the 1980s.[41]

MEDIATING BETWEEN TWO MATOLCSYS

There is no reason to further invoke the memory of long-forgotten Hungarian economists here, though I cannot help settling on the name of Sándor Kopátsy who has been the chief mentor of Matolcsy ("my second *alma mater*," as he says) for about four decades now.[42] Over 90, he still served Matolcsy as an advisor. Born into a Protestant lower-middle-class family in a provincial town, Kopátsy became a regional leader of the National Peasant Party after the war, turned to communism rapidly, but kept his agrarian leanings, and worked as a self-made economist in the Planning Office. He was a 1956-er who was approached by the secret police to serve as an agent after the revolution,[43] a middle-level official in the Finance Ministry, as well as an active supporter of the New Economic Mechanism in 1968—a not-so-untypical career path in communist Hungary. It was the end of the 1960s when he became a family friend of the Matolcsys (György was 13 in that year).[44] Since the late 1970s, they worked in the Finance Ministry, made research, published, did business, and played politics in close cooperation. Both were party members before 1989. No doubt about it, until recently, the theory provider (the *Ezzesgeber*) in their tandem was Kopátsy, who in his most creative phase of life used to write a book almost every year.[45] An interesting difference between them today is that—while Matolcsy enthusiastically identifies himself with the parvenu political culture of the Orbán regime as a whole—Kopátsy often attacks its neo-feudalistic patterns and romantic politics of history from a puritanical-plebeian perspective.[46]

Kopátsy belonged to the moderates among the reform economists (he still considers himself a left-liberal thinker),[47] and his early ideas on how to smuggle limited and informal private property rights into the institutions of state ownership—that is, by turning large public firms into holding enterprises and opening vistas for SMEs and cooperatives—provided Matolcsy with fresh food for thought. The latter wrote his first study on these topics in 1981. While Kopátsy planned to keep the holdings in state property, transferring their shares to public pension funds, and sell only a small minority of the shares to private persons, Matolcsy designed a more tricky, rapid, and down-to-earth procedure of privatization by suggesting a gradual evacuation of company centers through selling the individual factories, workshops, commercial agencies, etc., of the companies to insiders or other firms (cf. cross-ownership) at very friendly prices. This scheme was called "spontaneous privatization" (a term coined by him).[48]

Matolcsy borrowed from Kopátsy, besides the holding model, the idea of a dual economic structure dominated by large firms in industry and small- and medium-sized companies in agriculture, the critique of restrictive economic policies, fast liberalization, and of ignoring the "Eastern" markets, the admiration of state-led development based on reflationary policy and the like,[49] as well as a peculiar style of economic thought. This style abounds in pompous propositions without proper verification by formal models and with a parochial contempt for modern economics.[50] As the titles of Kopátsy's works demonstrate, his economic views are underpinned by a shallow culturalist discourse in history concerning "missing the road," the "society of quality," the "way out," the "history of human race," and the "forgotten village." I am sure these phrases ring a bell even with readers who have just read Kopátsy's name the first time. If I add what the word *TETT* means in the title of the book on the "society of quality," they will not have to think twice to identify an important birthplace of Matolcsy's moralizing-psychologizing economic vision. This acronym, denoting "act" or "action" in Hungarian, refers to nature, morals, knowledge, and talent (*természet, erkölcs, tudás, tehetség*) and invokes the activist spirit of the radical social movements in the Hungary of the 1930s.[51]

As a young man, Kopátsy found himself on the left wing of the national-populist (*völkisch*) movement, idolizing Imre Kovács, the chief ideologue of the National Peasant Party—a devotion Kopátsy has cherished up till now.[52] Why do I mention Kovács's name? Because he was a friend of another leading agrarian expert, one of the most talented young economists of the populist camp in the interwar period who turned to national socialism and became an MP and a prominent intellectual of Ferenc Szálasi's Arrow Cross Party. While Kovács campaigned against citizens of German origin in Hungary (*Donauschwaben*), his friend wanted to get rid of the Jews. At the same time, both hated Hungarian aristocrats almost as much as the two ethnic groups in question. The reader will already know that the name of the economist was Mátyás Matolcsy.

An engineer by training, he also studied economics (for example, at the London School of Economics), and—following the defense of his doctoral dissertation in economics in 1932—joined the Hungarian Institute for Economic Research (MGKI) as an expert of national income statistics. With time, he became a passionate advocate of land reform who regarded the coalition of landed aristocracy and Jewish plutocracy as the main obstacle to a fair redistribution of land among ethnic Hungarian smallholders. At this juncture, he was a typical adherent of Third Way ideology located between feudal capitalism and communist planning. In 1935, he entered politics as an MP of the national-conservative government party of Gyula Gömbös, then joined forces with left-wing populist writers and agrarian sociologists and the Smallholders Party, finally arriving in the national socialist camp and becoming a top politician of the Arrow-Cross Party in 1942/1943. Matolcsy was known as an Italian-style fascist rather than a Nazi fanatic, someone who called for the total expropriation of Jewish fortunes and the deportation of all Jews, but did not dream of an *Endlösung*. In his parliamentary speeches and newspaper articles, however, he demanded the sharpening of anti-Jewish legislation by resorting to a harsh racist discourse that contained phrases such as "total dejewification," "concentrating the Jews in labor camps," and compared the Jews to ulcers that should be "removed from the nation's body" (cf. Ungváry, 2001; Matolcsy, 1941b, 1942a,b).[53]

Although to my knowledge György has not quoted Mátyás (yet),[54] he must have read some of his works, or at least heard family stories about his famous relative, an economist like him, at the dinner table.[55] Be as it may, many of György Matolcsy's current economic views sharply remind the observer of those advocated by his ancestor. It is of secondary importance, I believe, whether György actually read Mátyás's texts. Maybe, he simply "reinvented the wheel." Thus far, it has been either dangerous or uncomfortable in Hungary to talk publicly about a high-ranking fascist relative. Therefore, even if György had been familiar with each and every work written by Mátyás, he would not have been keen to admit it. It is also possible that even Sándor Kopátsy avoided speaking with György about Mátyás. Nevertheless, the Kopátsy-Kovács connection may be the missing link in understanding the transfer of ideas from Mátyás to György.[56]

I have four salient points of resemblance between Mátyás Matolcsy's thoughts and the UEP in mind:[57]

1. the combination of large public property with small- and medium-sized private properties;
2. the violability of private property rights;
3. the superiority of state interventionism in a "managed economy" (*irányított gazdaság*)[58] over the free market; and
4. the concept of a work-based social state (*szociális munkaállam*).

The following brief quotations from Mátyás Matolcsy's 1938 book *New Life on Hungarian Land* (*Új élet a magyar földön*) reveal many similarities:

Economic liberalism is replaced by the managed economy. . . . This subjects the goal of maximum utility to the universal interests of the nation. The fundamental characteristic trait of the managed economy is the loosening of the rigid principle of the inviolability of private property. . . . The assets remain in private hands, but the owner will be responsible not only for himself, but also for the state. Instead of the pagan concept of private property in Roman law, we will define a concept matching Christian civilization. . . . The mandatory maximum of the utilization of production factors, the maximum of capital gains of production goods, and the maximum of personal incomes is to be stipulated [by the state].[59]

The concept of a "work-based state" is central to his political speeches, in which he pays tribute to Mussolini's corporatist regime, and demands a large increase in employment and welfare for laborers, particularly the rural poor.

One might easily add another four (or even fourteen) points to the four points above. They would range from the adoration of the Japanese model of state capitalism, welcoming industrial policies and price controls and blaming the banks, through taking pride in a Hungarian *Sonderweg*, and a predilection for grandiose master plans of social transformation (in his case with a special emphasis on land reform and family farms), to the reinforcement of the Christian middle class and the stimulation of population growth. In principle, Third Way thinkers in Central Europe could evolve in a liberal direction as demonstrated by the example of the Freiburg School in Germany. It should also be noted that not all agrarian populists in Hungary became national socialists during the late 1930s.[60] Thus, György Matolcsy could have inherited a less inglorious relative who harbored similar ideas (say, Imre Kovács) than Mátyás Matolcsy. In any event, the similarity between the interventionist agendas of the two Matolcsys is not tantamount to sameness: Mátyás was a staunch critic of feudal legacies, a supporter of agricultural cooperatives, and—most importantly—a politician with a high level of social responsibility, demanding steeply progressive taxation and the leveling of incomes. Last but not least, Mátyás did bother with statistics.

I began my chapter by referring to a book of our hero published some years ago, and a few pages later ended up first in the 1980s and then back in the 1930s. In fact, this has been a rather slow move. Normally, we Hungarians do this trip in only a second by switching on the public radio or television today.

NOTES

1. Matolcsy (2015). Books with over six-hundred pages and a title like this are usually published by Nobel laureates.
2. This is the hometown of Matolcsy's family (the mayor is his relative). Our hero managed to allocate public funds, much of them originating from the EU, to build a new campus.
3. In Orbán's words "Nobody can promise me so much money, for which I would be willing to sacrifice my right hand." See index.hu (2010).

4. Matolcsy's close colleagues from among the reform economists in the Finance Ministry and/or the Institute of Financial Research before 1989, with whom I have had ample opportunity to speak during the past thirty years about his academic and political career. use sharp words to criticize his ignorance of economic theory. The ironic question asked by the former minister of finance István Hetényi, following one of Matolcsy's self-admiring conference presentations—"Gyuri, you do not bother with statistics, do you?"—is still widely remembered among Hungarian economists (Dudás 2010). Regarding his activities as a minister or central banker, they consider him a maverick, a self-conceited gambler who, if *Fortuna* happens to like him, may reap the harvest of unsown seeds (cf. free-riding on "quantitative easing" in the United States, or the fall of energy prices after the global economic crisis). In the eyes of these experts, many of whom became leading policymakers of the socialist-liberal coalition, Matolcsy has always been a skillful specialist in politicking and economic counselling—a job that made him rich during privatization in the late communist period—rather than a luminary in economics (cf. Várhegyi 2013).

Younger experts who were brought up in the world of neoclassical economics over the past quarter of a century show even less compassion. See origo.hu (2014). They look down on Matolcsy as a parochial government *apparatchik* who, in his lack of mathematical knowledge, is unable to understand a text written in the language of modern economics. He is regarded by them as an aborted old-Keynesian who thinks that the substance of *General Theory* can be confined to a simplistic growth formula based on boosting consumption and employment through government spending. In their view, Matolcsy is best described as an adventurer who likes to cherish antineoliberal conspiracy theories and spread geostrategic blah-blah about the inevitable decay of the West (see also Máriás 2013a,b).

5. See index.hu (2010).

6. See cnn.com (2012).

7. For another element of the interventionist tradition in Hungarian economic thought, see László (2014). He wonders whether the "Hungarian twins" in the United Kingdom, Thomas Balogh and Nicholas Kaldor, would endorse something like the UEP if they were still alive.

8. See index.hu (2011a, 2012), magyarnarancs.hu (2018).

9. See Dudás (2010), Keller-Alánt (2019a,b), Máriás (2013a,b), Mészáros (2012). Matolcsy decided to write his dissertation some years ago.

10. As his mentor Sándor Kopátsy—more about him later—said, "Matolcsy conjured up so much money with his progrowth economic policy and trickery, that the elections [in 2002] must not have been lost" (Kopátsy 2002a).

11. To be on the safe side, Orbán has always counterbalanced Matolcsy in the government with experts in fiscal policy during the past nine years – for example, with the dry, accountant-like economist Mihály Varga.

12. Among economists, Matolcsy was called "seven-percent Gyuri" after he promised Orbán to attain such a high rate of growth in the Hungarian economy already at the end of the 1990s. He discovered Keynes and introduced Orbán to his views long before the global economic crisis. Apparently, there was no cultural gap between the prime minister and his *intimus*. The former required exactly what was distilled by the latter from a large variety of Keynesian thoughts, namely, the slogans of full

employment and rapid growth (as guarantees of political stability) as well as the opportunity for the regime to increase the ratio of state redistribution (as a guarantee of feeding its cronies and winning the elections). See Mészáros (2012).

13. For more on this, see the notion of "simulacrum," to be introduced in the Conclusion of this volume.

14. Matolcsy provided Hungarian comedians with an easy joke when he said in the Hungarian parliament in 2012 that the introduction of the flat tax had increased the number of births in Hungary in some months.

15. See Matolcsy (2007).

16. See Matolcsy/Lindner and Horváth (1990a).

17. For a summary of the stages of his academic and political career before 2010, see Mihályi (2010, 452–55), Dudás (2010).

18. For his biographical details, see the last section of this chapter.

19. To take the example of racism, it would be unfair to draw a parallel between a top politician of the Hungarian fascists who wanted to deport all Jews from the country and Orbán's right hand, who "only" contends, in line with the new Fundamental Law, that the persecution of Hungarian Jewry began only at the onset of the German occupation in 1944 (Matolcsy 2013). The only fascist economist who became a leading figure in various communist governments after 1945, and finished his career as a moderate reformer was Béla Csikós-Nagy.

20. Symptomatically, no renowned academic economist wrote a review of this book. Apart from Matolcsy's aides, the only person who took his "theory" seriously was the journalist Zoltán Farkas (2016), who published a devastating criticism of it in an economic weekly. For critical assessments of the UEP by other journalists, see, e.g., Keller-Alánt (2019a,b).

21. What comes below is a concise summary of Matolcsy's unorthodox views without detailed references to these books, journal articles and interviews: (books) Matolcsy, (1981, 1991, 1998, ed, 1999, 2003, 2004, 2008, 2009, 2015); (articles) Matolcsy (1981, 1988a,b, 1989a,b,c, 1990b, 1995, 1996a,b,c, 1997a,b, 1998a,b,c, 1999a, 2002, 2007, 2011, 2013); (interviews) Matolcsy/Lindner and Horváth (1990a), Matolcsy/Farkas (2000), Matolcsy/Tardos (2010).

22. See Matolcsy/Tardos (2009, 204–6), Matolcsy (2007).

23. These are perhaps the most thorough critical assessments of Matolcsy's UEP: Antal (1998), Farkas (2011), Mihályi (1992), Pete (1999), Surányi (2016), Várhegyi (2013, 2016, 2019a,b). See also the chapters by János Köllő, Péter Mihályi, and Dorottya Szikra in this volume. A former deputy governor of the National Bank, Júlia Király, condensed the criticisms in one sentence: "Unorthodoxy is when one does not read the textbooks" (Király 2013). Today, a majority of experts are ready to disapprove of Matolcsy's thoughts only anonymously.

24. Even if members of the economic research community in Hungary had not been frustrated by the roughness of Matolcsy's attacks on neoclassical theory and economic liberalism, the fact that he demolished the excellent research base of the National Bank and spends a colossal amount of taxpayers' money on his antiliberal obsession in higher education would have irritated them. As stated by leading economists of the Hungarian Academy of Sciences, the National Bank intervenes in higher

education without any quality control and violates the autonomy of universities by forcing them to adjust to the expectations of the donor. See mta.hu (2015), Laki (2015).

25. cf. Kovács (2013).

26. Matolcsy published many dozen brief pseudo-reviews of English-language books in the conservative weekly *Heti Válasz* between 2002 and 2013 (see valasz. hu 2019). In these, he does not analyze the selected works in detail, but picks those ideas of the authors, leading social scientists in the West, that underpin his own policy proposals. The lessons he draws at the end of each review revolve around some kind of new (non-leftist) collectivism based on conservative values along a "Fourth Road." Matolcsy prefers to choose authors with an antiliberal thrust, condemns 68-ers, applauds the success stories of state capitalism in the East, attacks "casino capitalism," speaks of the "pirates of the money world," calls for a Green New Deal, and unveils anti-Hungarian conspiracies.

27. For more on Fidesz's learning curve, see the Conclusion.

28. See index.hu (2011b).

29. A controversial result of weakening the Hungarian forint was a steep rise in the revenue of the National Bank, which—instead of being transferred to the country's budget—has been used by the newly established foundations of the Bank to finance Matolcsy's ambitious educational programs and his personal network. By the way, loosening monetary policy to stimulate growth belongs in the most orthodox toolboxes of economic policy.

30. In 2012, the general rate of VAT in Hungary was increased to a record-high 27 percent.

31. The development plans of the government were named after Ignác Darányi, István Széchenyi, Kálmán Széll, and others, i.e., leading politicians of the Monarchy and the Horthy regime, respectively.

32. Critical analysts agree that the "Matolcsy moment" of growth *and* equilibrium could not have been reached during the past couple of years if Hungary had not received generous subsidies from the EU (and sizable remittances from her citizens working abroad), and had not been able to free-ride on the post-crisis recovery of the world economy. They also contend that the country's success is temporary, since it has not been underpinned by a remarkable rise in productivity as well as in private savings and investments, and is threatened by a tremendous decline of the quality of its economic and legal institutions due to the political consolidation of Orbán's cronies. According to a well-documented and most disturbing criticism (Király 2019), Matolcsy first had to dig a deep hole to climb out of it later. As a minister, he inherited in 2010 an economy that survived the global crisis and began to stabilize itself when the Orbán government pushed it back into recession by applying UEP.

33. See Matolcsy/Tardos (2010). In this interview, Matolcsy stresses the importance of the reformist legacy of late communism in developing a "renewed liberal and social market economy." (See also Matolcsy 2009.) Here, instead of "liberal," he uses the word's old Hungarian translation, "*szabadelvű*." During the 2010s, even this term vanished from his rhetoric.

34. cf. Antal et al. (1987).

35. For an analysis of "reform economics" as a research program and a political project, see Kovács (1990, 1991, 1992).

36. Let me mention here some of the then well-known moderates: Iván T. Berend, Péter Ákos Bod, Béla Csikós-Nagy, István Hagelmayer, István Hetényi, Róbert Hoch, Mihály Kupa, Péter Medgyessy, Rezső Nyers, Gábor Révész, Tamás Sárközy, and János Tímár. The group of radicals included László Antal, Tamás Bauer, Lajos Bokros, István Csillag, Mihály Laki, László Lengyel, András Nagy, Attila Károly Soós, György Surányi, and Márton Tardos. As usual, the works of András Bródy, Ferenc Jánossy, János Kornai, and Tibor Liska resist even such a rough classification.

37. See Matolcsy (1996a). This study anticipated nearly all key ideas and policy goals that would feature in the UEP. In an effort to rehabilitate Keynes, Matolcsy celebrates the theory of his supposed predecessor as a bible of crisis management, catching up with the advanced world, correcting the mistakes of the monetarist turn, and strengthening the state. To illustrate the sloppiness of his reasoning, here are two sentences from the core argument he presents without any proof: "There emerges a simple difference between advanced societies and Hungary. While in the former 70 percent of society are able to stabilize the economy through their demand and 30 percent destabilizes it through decreasing demand, in the latter the proportions are almost exactly reversed" (*ibid.*, 192).

38. cf. Mihályi (1992, 82–83), Kovács (2018, 143–72).

39. Kornai (1986, 1730–32).

40. Here I think of authors such as the industrial managers and policymakers László Kapolyi, László Horváth, and Ádám Juhász, or the economists Ferenc Kozma and Andrea Szegő.

41. See, e.g., Matolcsy's numerous articles in *Heti Világgazdaság* on ownership reform between 1985 and 1989, as well as Matolcsy (1988a,b, 1989a,b,c, 1990b).

42. Matolcsy's former colleagues also mention other persons that he chose to respect and/or to follow. They include his former superiors in the Finance Ministry István Csillag, István Hetényi, Péter Medgyessy, and—currently—Viktor Orbán.

43. According to my research in the archives of state security in Hungary, Kopátsy was "asked" to work as an informant in 1957, but it is not clear whether he filed reports after 1960 (Kopátsy 1957–60, 2011a; see also Lengyel 2014). In 2002, it was leaked out by members of the so-called Mécs Commission (a parliamentary body investigating the past of government officials) that Matolcsy had reported to the secret police before 1989, but to date there is no public evidence for his collaboration. See also Kovács (2008).

44. Kopátsy wrote the script of a television series, in which a certain "Dr. Brain" explained the New Economic Mechanism to ordinary citizens (*Magyarázom a mechanizmust*). It was produced by a film studio (with an affiliation in Kecskemét) managed by Matolcsy's father, a Protestant intellectual who became friends with Kopátsy.

45. This is a selection of Kopátsy's books: Kopátsy (1983, 1989a,b, 1992, 1993a,b, 1995, 1996a,b, 1998, 2000, 2001a,b,c, 2002a,b,c, 2005, 2006, 2011b,c, 2013).

46. cf. Kopátsy (1996a,b, 1998a, 2001a,b). See also Lengyel (2014).

47. For his reformist creed, see Kopátsy (1989a,b).

48. See Kopátsy (1969, 1988, 1989), and Matolcsy (1981a, 1988a,b, 1989a,b,c, 1990b). For a comparison of the two schemes, see Mihályi (2010, 82–83). During the 1980s, these reform projects were part of a whole series of proposals for restructuring state ownership. At the time, some of them (e.g., those designed by István Csillag and László Lengyel or by László Antal and Márton Tardos) counted as more radical than these two. For a thorough analysis of "cross-ownership," see Stark (1996).

49. In 2002, this is how Kopátsy recalled his views before and after 1989: "I did not approve a rapid exit from the Eastern markets. They have remained valuable even for rich Western countries [. . .] I did not approve that loss-making companies were driven into bankruptcy with no reason. Even a loss-making firm is better than mass unemployment. It is better not only from the perspective of budgetary equilibrium but also from that of the moral state of society. [. . .] I did not approve a much faster liberalization than the Hungarian society and economy could digest. [. . .] A fundamental insight of mine in economics is that . . . without deliberate depreciation of money one cannot carry out economic development catching up with rapid technological progress. [. . .] As an economist, my most important message is that inflation is one of the greatest inventions of the twentieth century." (Kopátsy 2002c)

50. Matolcsy praises his mentor thus: "It will be the time of veritable intellectual globalization when Kopátsy's thoughts will circulate at big universities in China and India, and be cited in both Bakonybél [a small Hungarian village] and Paris." (Matolcsy 2011) Matolcsy follows Kopátsy's style of writing in republishing large segments of his earlier articles and books in later ones, and "sparing" the reader from a precise definition of his main scientific terms as well as from a minimum number of notes and references to present the state of the art he wants to surpass. Probably the best example for this approach is Kopátsy's 360-page book *New Economics* (*Új közgazdaságtan*, 2011c). While Kopátsy is the sole author of his works, in Matolcsy's case it is difficult to judge the share of his collaborators in the research and writing of his books.

51. One of Kopátsy's idols was the novelist and playwright László Németh, who envisioned the "revolution of quality" in the 1930s. Kopátsy borrowed from him the emphasis on morals, knowledge and talent, and transmitted these concepts permeated by ethnic essentialism to Matolcsy, who quotes his mentor's views extensively. For instance, in his *Equilibrium and Growth*, Matolcsy writes about "talent capital" and the "two invisible sources of economic growth: morals and talent." Moreover, he suggests the following magic formula: "knowledge x talent x morals = value," adding that the breakthrough made by the Orbán government in the first half of the 2010s was contingent on a "hidden moral turn" and the exploiting of the advantages of the "Hungarian way of thinking" (Matolcsy 2015, 217–22).

52. cf. Kopátsy (1996b).

53. See also Matolcsy (1934, 1938a,b, 1941a,b), csaladitemeto.hu (2019).

54. In his article on Keynes (Matolcsy 1996, 197), he cites Kovács's famous work *Silent Revolution (Néma forradalom)*, for which Kovács collected research materials in a long study tour across Hungary together with Mátyás Matolcsy.

55. Recently, Mátyás's son, Mátyás Matolcsy Jr., published a very detailed family history (cf. csaladitemeto 2019), and the family has organized so-called "Matolcsy

meetings" since 2002. When, some years ago, György was blamed for not dissociating himself from his "uncle's" anti-Semitic ideas, he responded through an official letter by the National Bank, stating that Mátyás was not the uncle of György. (See hvg.hu 2013.)

56. Another source of information could be an opinion leader among young officials and researchers of the Finance Ministry and a close colleague of Matolcsy, László Lengyel. In the 1980s, he studied the history of economic thought in Hungary during the 1920s and 1930s, and published about István Varga who – as director of the Hungarian Institute for Economic Research – worked and published together with Mátyás Matolcsy (Lengyel 1986, 2014).

57. These are some of Mátyás Matolcsy's most important books: Matolcsy (1934, 1938a,b, 1941).

58. Sometimes he even used the term "managed *planned* economy" to express the level of state interventionism he considered appropriate and his respect for central planning in the Soviet Union (Ungváry 2001).

59. Matolcsy (1938b, 15, 59, 61).

60. cf. Trencsényi et al. (2018, 142–61, 225–41), Kovács (1993). At any rate, one did not have to be a populist thinker to be part of the interventionist consensus of the interwar period. The German concept of *gelenkte Wirtschaft* (managed economy) was taken over by the former Czechoslovak minister of finance, Karel Engliš whose 1936 book entitled *Regulierte Wirtschaft* (Regulated Economy) was translated into Hungarian immediately. Its etatist message was accepted in a way or other even by more liberal-minded scholars in Hungary such as Farkas Heller, Ákos Navratil, Tivadar Surányi-Unger, and István Varga.

BIBLIOGRAPHY

Antal, László. 1998. "Kiigazítás – ahogy én látom." *Közgazdasági Szemle* 45 (2): 97–122.

Antal, László, Lajos Bokros, István Csillag, László Lengyel, György Matolcsy. 1987. "Fordulat és reform." *Közgazdasági Szemle* 34 (6): 642–63.

cnn.com. 2012. "Hungary: Economy in Transition." https://edition.cnn.com/videos/business/2012/06/07/marketplace-europe-matolcsy-hungary-economy.cnn.

csaladitemeto.hu. 2019. "Matolcsy Mátyás pályafutása." http://www.csaladitemeto.hu/dok/sir17-13.pdf, and "A Matolcsy család gyökerei." http://www.csaladitemeto.hu/mcsgy.pdf, accessed June 25, 2019.

Dudás, Gergely. 2010. "A számok nem zavarnak, Gyuri?" *HVG.hu*, May 25.

Farkas, Zoltán. 2011. "Önkénygazdaságtan – A Fidesz erőltetett menete." *Mozgó Világ* 37 (6): 3–15.

———. 2016. "Vigyázat, csalás! Újraolvastuk Matolcsy 644 oldalas öndícséretét." *HVG*, May 1.

hvg.hu. 2013. "Matolcsy családja érintett volt." https://hvg.hu/itthon/20130204_Ungvary_Matolcsy_csaladja_erintett_volt_a, accessed June 25, 2019.

index.hu. 2010. "Orbán megtartja Matolcsyt." https://index.hu/gazdasag/magyar/20 10/10/05/orban_megtartja_matolcsyt/, accessed 25 June, 2019.

———. 2011a. "Matolcsy. A siker láthatatlan." https://index.hu/belfold/2011/11/19/ matolcsy_a_siker_lathatatlan/.

———. 2011b. "Kipateroltuk az IMF-et." https://index.hu/gazdasag/magyar/2011/05 /03/matolcsy_kipateroltuk_az_imf-et/.

———. 2012. "Megtaláltuk Matolcsy piros pöttyeit." https://index.hu/tudomany/ egeszseg/2012/11/19/megtalaltuk_matolcsy_piros_pottyeit.

Keller-Alánt, Ákos. 2019a. "Matolcsynak malaca van vagy tényleg korszakos zseni?" *Magyar Narancs*, March 7.

———. 2019b. "Tisztogatások, műkincsláz, ügyeskedések: a Matolcsy-éra kemény ügyei." *Magyar Narancs*, March 14.

Király, Júlia. 2013. "A jegybankárok mindennapi ethoszán is múlik." *Magyar Narancs*, March 28.

———. 2019. *A tornádó oldalszele. Szubjektív válságtörténet 2007–2013*. Budapest: Park Könyvkiadó.

Kopátsy, Sándor. 1957–1960. Állambiztonsági Szolgálatok Történeti Levéltára, II/6c H 15914, Somogyi B dosszié.

———. 1969a. "Önálló tulajdonosi szervezetekről." *Pénzügyi Szemle* 13 (3).

———. 1969b. "A vállalati tevékenység komplex és többéves értékelésének problémája." *Pénzügyi Szemle* 13 (11): 929–36.

———. 1983. *Hiánycikk: a vállalkozás*. Budapest: KJK.

———. 1988. "Gondolatok a tulajdonreformról." In *Tulajdonreform*, edited by László Lengyel, 51–58. Budapest: Pénzügykutató Rt.

———. 1989a. *Húsz év után*. Budapest: Pénzügykutató Rt.

———. 1989b. *Levél a magyar reformerekhez*. Budapest: KJK.

———. 1991a. "Még soha, sehol elő nem fordult feladat." *Valóság* 34 (2): 1–11.

———. 1991b. "Nagyüzem? Kisbirtok? Farmergazdaság!" *Társadalmi Szemle* 46 (11): 24–34.

———. 1991c. "A privatizáció társadalmi és gazdasági háttere." *Vezetéstudomány* (9): 12–18.

———. 1992. *Beszélgetések Adyval*. Budapest: Száminform Kiadó.

———. 1993a. *A fogyasztói társadalom közgazdaságtana*. Budapest: Privatizációs Kutatóintézet.

———. 1993b. *Gazdaságpolitikai úttévesztés*. Budapest: Privatizációs Kutatóintézet.

———. 1995. *Van kiút*. Budapest: Belvárosi Könyvkiadó.

———. 1996a. *A mi XX. Századunk*. Budapest: Belvárosi Könyvkiadó.

———. 1996b. *Az elfelejtett falu*. Budapest: CET Belvárosi Könyvkiadó. http://mek .oszk.hu/01400/01412/01412.htm.

———. 1998a. *Nyugat felé*. Budapest: Kairosz Könyvkiadó–Növekedéskutató.

———. 1998b. "A magyar privatizáció stratégiája." *C.E.T* 6 (7): 45–53.

———. 1999. "Mire építhetünk?" In *Növekedés és globalizáció*, edited by György Matolcsy, 143–73. Budapest: Kairosz Könyvkiadó–Növekedéskutató.

———. 2000. *TETT. A minőség társadalma*. Budapest: Kairosz Könyvkiadó. http:// mek.oszk.hu/02900/02930/html/01.htm.

———. 2001a. *Az igazi történelem.* Budapest: CET Belvárosi Könyvkiadó. http://mek.niif.hu/03000/03060/03060.htm.

———. 2001b. *Harmadszor Nyugat felé.* Budapest: CET Belvárosi Könyvkiadó. http://mek.oszk.hu/03000/03062/03062.pdf.

———. 2001c. *Kádár és kora.* Budapest: CET Belvárosi Könyvkiadó.

———. 2002a. *Az Orbán-jelenség.* Budapest: CET Belvárosi Könyviadó. http://mek.oszk.hu/02900/02955/02955.htm.

———. 2002b. *A magyar marslakók titka.* Budapest: CET Belvárosi Könyvkiadó. http://mek.oszk.hu/02900/02956/02956.pdf.

———. 2002c. Mária Börcsök. *Szerencsés ember.* Budapest: CET Belvárosi Könyvkiadó. http://mek.oszk.hu/03000/03061/html/.

———. 2005. *Kállai kettős. Magyarország: 1945–1990.* Budapest: CET Belvárosi Könyvkiadó.

———. 2006. *1956 – Az igazat mondd, ne csak a valódit.* Budapest: CET Belvárosi Könyvkiadó.

———. 2011a. "Miért kellene visszakozni?" *Válasz.hu,* December 21. http://valasz.hu/uzlet/miert-kellene-visszakozni-44230.

———. 2011b. *Az emberi faj története.* Budapest: Mundus Novus.

———. 2011c. *Új közgazdaságtan. A minőség társadalma.* Budapest: Akadémiai Kiadó.

———. 2013. *Történelemszemléletem.* Budapest: Vinczemill Műhely. http://kopatsytort.blogspot.com/p/blog-page.html.

Kornai, János. 1986. "The Hungarian Reform Process. Visions, Hopes, and Reality." *Journal of Economic Literature* 24 (4): 1687–737.

Kovács, János Mátyás. 1990. "Reform Economics: The Classification Gap." *Daedalus* 119 (1): 215–48.

———. 1991. "From Reformation to Transformation: Limits to Liberalism in Hungarian Economic Thought." *East European Politics and Societies* 5 (1): 41–72.

———. 1992. "Compassionate Doubts about Reform Economics (Science, Ideology, Politics)." In *Reform and Transformation: Eastern European Economics on the Threshold of Change,* edited by J. M. Kovács and Márton Tardos, 299–333. London: Routledge.

———. 1993. "Which Institutionalism? Searching for Paradigms of Transformation in Eastern European Economic Thought." In *The Political Economy of Transformation,* edited by Hans-Jürgen Wagener, 85–96. Heidelberg: Physica-Verlag.

———. 2008. "Accomplices without Perpetrators. What Do Economists Have to Do with Transitional Justice in Hungary?" *Totalitarian Movements & Political Religions* 9 (2–3): 311–34.

———. 2013. "Tradition, Nachamung, Erfindung. Neue Kapitalismen in Osteuropa." *Transit* 43: 32–52.

———. 2018. "From Two to One (And Only)? Theorizing Ownership in Communist Hungary." In *Populating No Man's Land. Economic concepts of Ownership under Communism,* edited by J. M. Kovács, 143–72. Lanham, MD: Lexington Books.

Laki, Mihály. 2015. "A Magyar Nemzeti Bank közgazdasági kutatást és oktatást támogató tevékenysége 2013 után." https://www.mtakti.hu/blog/a-magyar-nemz

eti-bank-kozgazdasagi-kutatast-es-oktatast-tamogato-tevekenysege-2013-utan/ 3750/.
László, Géza. 2014. "Unortodox kalandozásaink." *Magyar Narancs*, May 7.
Lengyel, László. 1986. "Két személyiség a válsággal szemben (Varga István és Cs.
Szabó László eltérő pályaíve a harmincas években)." *Valóság* 29 (10): 51–64.
———. 2014. *A szabadság melankóliája*. Budapest: Kossuth Kiadó.
magyarnarancs.hu. 2018. "Matolcsy és a számmisztika." https://magyarnarancs.hu/ belpol/matolcsy-es-a-szammisztika-112966, accessed June 25, 2019.
Matolcsy, György, and László Lengyel, eds. 1981. *Viták a gazdasági mechanizmus reformjáról*. Budapest: Pénzügykutató Rt.
Matolcsy, György. 1981a [1999]. "A beruházási tőke, értékesítési piac és a hatékony mechanizmus együttes szükségességéről." In *Viták a gazdasági mechanizmus reformjáról*, edited by László Lengyel and György Matolcsy. Budapest: Pénzügykutató Rt., 97–122.
———. 1988a. "Az állami vállalattól a társulásig." *Valóság* 31 (6): 66–79.
———. 1988b. "Változatok a tulajdonreformra." *Gazdaság* 22 (4): 21–41.
———. 1989a. "Egy naplóolvasó egy olvasónaplóról. Lengyel László: Végkifejlet." *Valóság* 32 (12): 108–13.
———. 1989b. "Helybenjárás." *Mozgó Világ* 15 (11): 3–15.
———. 1989c. "Spontán bűvészet." *HVG*, October 28.
———. 1990a. Lindner András and Horváth Zoltán. "Portré: Matolcsy György." *HVG*, June 23.
———. 1990b. "A spontán tulajdonreform védelmében." *Külgazdaság* 34 (3): 38–59.
———. 1991. *Lábadozásunk évei (A magyar privatizáció - trendek, tények, privatizációs példák)*. Budapest: Tulajdon Alapítvány – Privatizációs Kutatóintézet.
———. 1995. "Privatizáció: Gyors befejezést!" *Figyelő*, April 20.
———. 1996a. "John Maynard Keynes—olvassuk, ne temessük!" In *Akik nyomot hagytak a 20. századon*, edited by Tibor Erényi, 178–99. Budapest: Napvilág Kiadó. http://tek.bke.hu/keynes120/docs/matolcsy.pdf.
———. 1996b. "Gazdasági és társadalmi sokkterápiák 1990 és 1995 között Magyarországon." *Társadalmi Szemle* 51 (5): 3–14.
———. 1996c. "A társadalmi sokkterápia kísérlete 1995-ben." In *Magyarország politikai évkönyve*, edited by Sándor Kurtán et al., 240–47. Budapest: Demokráciakutatások Központja.
———. 1997a. "Eredeti tőkeátcsoportosítás Magyarországon. A tőkeszivattyú működése." *Századvég* 2 (5): 37–60.
———. 1997b. "Kiigazítás recesszióval." *Közgazdasági Szemle* 64 (9): 782–98.
———. 1998. *Sokk vagy kevés?* Budapest: Kairosz Kiadó.
———. 1998a. "Emlékeim a privatizációról." *C.E.T* 6 (6–7): 3–17.
———. 1998b. Zsófia Mihancsik. "Engem a nagy történelmi kihívások mindig elcsábítanak." In *Lámpások az Alagútban. Emlékek a Pénzügykutatóról*, edited by Hédi Volosin, 342–62. Budapest: Pénzügykutató Rt.–Perfekt Rt.
———. 1998c. "Vagyonvesztés a kilencvenes években Magyarországon." *C.E.T* 6 (6–7): 55–60.
———, ed. 1999. *Növekedés és globalizáció*. Budapest: Kairosz Növekedéskutató.

————. 1999a. "Globális csapdák és magyar megoldások." In *Növekedés és globalizáció*, edited by György Matolcsy, 68–104. Budapest: Kairosz Növekedéskutató.

————. 2000. Zoltán Farkas. "Belföldi motorok a növekedéshez." *Népszabadság*, August 4.

————. 2002. "Gyógyuló és gyógyító Magyarország." In *Jobbközéparányok*, edited by Gyula Tellér, 13–26. Budapest: Kairosz Kiadó.

————. 2003. *Élő emlékeink. A Széchenyi Terv világa*. Budapest: Válasz Könyvkiadó.

————. 2004. *Amerikai birodalom. A jövő forgatókönyvei*. Budapest: Válasz Könyvkiadó.

————. 2007. "A neoliberális gazdaságpolitika téveszméi." *Polgári Szemle* 3 (7–8). http://epa.oszk.hu/00800/00890/00028/EPA00890_Polgari_Szemle_205.html.

————. 2008. *Éllovasból sereghajtó. Elveszett évek krónikája*. Budapest: Éghajlat Könyvkiadó.

————, and Zoltán Cséfalvay, eds. 2009. *Jövőkép. Megújított szabadelvű és szociális piacgazdaság Magyarországon*. Budapest: Magyar Gazdaságfejlesztési Intézet.

————. 2010. Károly Tardos. "A polgári Magyarország gazdasági műhelyében." In *Felárkózás vagy lemaradás?*, edited by Károly Tardos, 184–208. Budapest: Gondolat.

————. 2011. "Előszó: A történész Kopátsy." In Sándor Kopátsy, *Az emberi faj története*, 5–6. Budapest: Mundus Novus.

————. 2013. "Egymillió városlakó hiányzik." *Heti Válasz*, January 30. http://valasz.hu/uzlet/egymillio-varoslako-hianyzik-60066.

————. 2015. *Egyensúly és növekedés*. Budapest: Kairosz Könyvkiadó.

Matolcsy, Mátyás. 1934. *Az új földreform munkaterve*. Budapest: Révai Nyomda. http://www.mtdaportal.extra.hu/books/matolcsy_matyas_az_uj_foldreform_munkaterve.pdf.

————, and István Varga. 1938a. *The National Income of Hungary, 1924/25–1936/37*. London: P. S. King and Son Ltd.

————. 1938b. *Új élet a magyar földön*. Budapest: Cserépfalvi Kiadó. http://mtd aportal.extra.hu/books/matolcsy_matyas_uj_elet_a_magyar_foldon.pdf.

————. 1941a. *A zsidók útja*. Budapest: Nyilaskeresztes Párt. https://web.archive.org/web/20130513195602/http://betiltva.com/files/matolcsy.php.

————. 1941b. "Felszólalás." *Képviselőházi Napló*, 1939, vol. XI (November 21, 1941): 525–27. Budapest: Atheneum.

————. 1942a. "Felszólalás." *Képviselőházi Napló*, 1939, vol. XII (November 28, 1941): 176–78. Budapest: Atheneum

————. 1942b. "Felszólalás." *Képviselőházi Napló*, 1939, vol. XIII (June 3, 1942): 338–44. Budapest: Atheneum.

Máriás, Leonárd. 2013a. "Orbánnak nem kellett az új közgazdász-nemzedék." *HVG.hu*, February 14. https://hvg.hu/gazdasag/20130214_kozgazdasz_alternativa.

————. 2013b. "Közgazdászok az Orbán-korban." *HVG.hu*, February 19. https://hvg.hu/gazdasag/20130219_Kozgazdasz_alternativa_2.

Mészáros, Bálint. 2012. "Egy összeillő ember." *Magyar Narancs*, June 14.

Mihályi, Péter. 1992. "Privatizálás magyar módra." *BUKSZ* 4 (1): 48–53.

————. 2010. *A magyar privatizáció enciklopédiája*, vol. I, II. Veszprém–Budapest: Pannon Egyetem–MTA Közgazdaságtudományi Intézet.

mta.hu. 2015. "A IX. Osztály állásfoglalása." https://mta.hu/data/dokumentumok/ix_osztaly/KTB%20ALLASFOGLALAS%202015%20DECEMBER%2010.pdf, accessed June 25, 2019.

origo.hu. 2014. "Én nem tudom, micsodák Matolcsy tanai." https://www.origo.hu/gazdasag/20140911-en-nem-tudom-micsodak-matolcsy-tanai.html, accessed June 25, 2019.

Pete, Péter. 1999. "Matolcsy György: Sokk vagy kevés?" *BUKSZ* 11 (2): 188–96.

Stark, David. 1996. "Recombinant Property in East European Capitalism." *American Journal of Sociology* 101 (4): 993–1027.

Surányi, György. 2016. "Cél és valóság." *Népszabadság*, May 14.

Trencsényi, Balázs, et al. 2018. *A History of Modern Political Thought in East Central Europe, Volume II: Negotiating Modernity in the "Short Twentieth Century" and Beyond, Part I: 1918–1968*. Oxford: Oxford University Press.

Ungváry, Krisztián. 2001. "Értelmiség és antiszemita közbeszéd." *Beszélő* 6 (6): 74–92.

valasz.hu. 2019. "Szerzői oldal." http://valasz.hu/szerzo/ujsagiro/matolcsy-gyorgy-2 9, accessed June 25, 2019.

Várhegyi, Éva. 2013. "Matolcsy veszélye az, hogy felkészületlen." *Népszabadság*, March 24.

————. 2016. "Az alapítványokon túl." *Magyar Narancs*, March 17.

————. 2019a. "Szerencsés csillagzat alatt. Matolcsy György jegybankelnöki ciklusa." *Élet és Irodalom* 63 (8) (February 22).

————. 2019b. "A bankszektor elrablása." *Mozgó Világ* 45 (2): 3–14.

Part II

FACES OF SOCIAL ENGINEERING

EXCLUSION, CO-OPTATION, AND REDISTRIBUTION

Chapter 7

Toward a "Work-Based Society"?

János Köllő

Viktor Orbán's second government inherited one of Europe's worst performing labor markets. Prior to the global financial and economic crisis, in 2008, the employment rate of the Hungarian working-age population stood at 57 percent, far below the European Union-27 (EU-27) average (66 percent) and the unweighted mean of other postsocialist member states (65 percent).[1] The economic crisis brought about a further decline to 55 percent in April–June 2010 when Fidesz – Hungarian Civic Alliance won the election and the new government took office.

Employment was critically low in three social groups. Unskilled people with only a primary education background, who accounted for one-fifth of the working-age population, had a meager 26 percent probability of being employed.[2] The employment rates of elderly men and mothers raising young children were also far below the European and (Organisation for Economic Co-operation and Development (OECD) averages. Among 50–64-year-old men, 53 percent was employed: this was the second lowest rate in Europe (after Poland), ten percentage points below the mean of Eurostat member countries (author's calculation using the European Labor Force Survey of 2005). The employment probability of mothers raising 0–5-year-old children was the single lowest in the OECD, while the employment level of women with older or no children was close to the cross-country average (OECD 2007).

In this chapter we discuss how Hungarian Prime Minister Viktor Orbán and his policymakers diagnosed Hungary's "employment disease" and what kind of therapy they proposed. We then look at the short-run outcomes and the likely long-run consequences of the radical reforms, which took place in and after 2010.

HOW TO CREATE ONE MILLION JOBS?

Already during the election campaign of 2010, *Fidesz* announced an ambitious plan of adding one million new jobs to the existing 3.7 million in ten years (400,000 in the first five years) and, in general, turning Hungary from a welfare state to a "work-based society" where no able-bodied person would be entitled to income without working. A master plan of how to achieve an extraordinary 2.6 percent annual employment growth rate, required to reach these targets, was elaborated in 2011.[3]

The document set four objectives: (1) creating one of the most flexible labor markets in Europe, (2) providing competitive knowledge in a renewed system of vocational training, (3) enhancing job creation by direct (mostly EU-funded) support to small- and medium-sized firms and maintaining a stable regulatory environment for all businesses, and (4) putting an end to "unemployment holidays" by creating proper incentives for reemployment and by providing jobs in public works schemes for the long-term unemployed instead of paying them cash benefits. The reforms that followed affected a wide area of labor market regulations, educational policies, unemployment assistance, and welfare provision as well as labor legislation and taxation.

A New Labor Code

The new Labor Code enacted in December 2011 reduced the costs of dismissals by setting limits to severance pay and allowing employers to state vague reasons (such as the loss of trust) for firing an employee. It also endowed employers with increased authority in determining the place of work and the distribution of working time over the day, week, and year. The protection of union representatives and the right to strike were also curtailed. Neumann, Laki, and Nacsa (2013) provide a detailed account of how the regulations shifted the balance of power from employees to employers.

Making Work Pay

In several steps, between 2010 and 2013, the government introduced a flat-rate personal income tax, which reduced the marginal tax rate on high earnings from 40 to 15 percent. Raising labor supply on the intensive margin was an explicit goal of this reform.[4] Further measures were aimed at widening the gap between wages and benefits at lower tiers of the labor market. The minimum wage–average wage ratio was increased from 36 percent in 2010 to 42 percent in 2015 (HLM 2015, 275). At the same time, the duration of insurance-based unemployment benefit (UI) was drastically cut from nine to only three months, an unprecedented level in OECD countries. The flat-rate unemployment assistance allowance (UA) was maintained as an open-ended, means-tested benefit, but its amount was decreased from 21 percent of the national net average wage in 2010 to only 15 percent in 2013 (HLM 2015, 267).

Public Works Instead of Benefits

Public works, a large-scale program for the long-term unemployed, was initially introduced by Viktor Orbán's first government in May 2000 and was maintained by the socialist administrations in office between 2002 and 2010. The program employed about 30,000 participants on average prior to the crisis and 53,000 between the autumn of 2008 and the 2010 elections according to the Labor Force Survey (author's calculation).[5] The public works programs were financed by the central budget, predominantly organized and managed by municipality-level local governments, and typically provided simple jobs in street cleaning, road and park maintenance, forestry, water management, and (less frequently) social services. The second *Fidesz* government decided to expand the scheme and put it in the center of its unemployment support policies. The rules of participation, the sanctions against noncompliers, and the level of remuneration changed drastically. Since 2011 a person registered as unemployed can be called to do public works on short notice, at any time and for any duration. Declining a call may imply exclusion from UA benefits for three years, irrespective of the type of job that was offered and the educational level of the person. The remuneration, formerly equal to the minimum wage, was set at 75 percent of the minimum wage. The degree of expansion is shown by the skyrocketing levels of participants (an average annual stock of 208,000 in 2015) and expenditures (220 percent of the combined amount spent on other active labor market policy programs.)

Closing the Pension Gate

The *Fidesz* government continued to raise the mandatory retirement age, in accordance with a scenario laid down in 1997, and further tightened the terms of early retirement and access to disability payments. The plan of reactivating 100,000 out of 350,000 disability pension recipients younger than the retirement age was also announced with audits starting in 2011.[6]

Assisting Mothers in Returning to Employment

Hungary traditionally spent large amounts of cash benefits on parents at home with their babies. According to the OECD Family Database (OECD 2007),

Hungary expended three times as much on such benefits (per child, as a percentage of per capita GDP) as the OECD average. The amount of full-time equivalent parental leave (calculated as the number of subsidized weeks times the ratio of childcare allowance to the national average wage) was also the highest within the OECD. Accordingly, Hungarian mothers stayed at home with their children for protracted periods, 4.7 years on average according to estimates by Bálint and Köllő (2008). While entry to full-time employment without losing GYES (a flat-rate, low-amount childcare benefit) was allowed by a socialist government in 2006, working parallel with taking up GYED (an earning-related, high-amount allowance) was prohibited. The *Fidesz* government removed this barrier in 2014.[7]

Transforming the Educational System

The educational reforms taking place since 2010 have been based on the conviction that the Hungarian economy primarily needs well-trained blue-collar workers and engineers rather than bunches of educated unemployed produced *en masse*, allegedly, in general secondary schools and faculties of humanities and social sciences. Accordingly, the government started a major reshaping of the educational system. The reform put forth that the share of uncertified vocational schools should increase to 35 percent at the secondary level. The duration of training should be shortened to three years from its previous length of four years. Significantly less time (a maximum of 30 percent) should be devoted to general education and the development of basic competences. To make this reform compatible with regulations on school leaving-age, the age floor for compulsory school attendance should be decreased from 18 to 16 years. The curriculum should be geared toward the development of practical skills, already from age 15, and the school need not prepare students for *Matura* examinations required for further studies. The reform proposed that Hungary needs a dual system of training with the active participation of businesses, similar to those of Germany and North European countries. The supervision of vocational training should be shifted from the Ministry of Education to the Ministry of Economy. The decreasing share of secondary grammar schools (*gimnázium*) and vocational secondary schools (*szakközépiskola*) which also grant a Matura in addition to providing vocational qualification, automatically limits the number of potential applicants to colleges and universities – a desirable outcome given the "overeducation" of the young generation and the existence of several "useless" fields of study. The structure and content of education should be driven by the demand for labor, best known by the Chamber of Commerce and Industry and other employer organizations, which should become key players in the planning of vocational education.

Steps outside the Mainstream

In 2011, a new regulation allowed women, who had accumulated at least 40 accrual years to retire and receive full pensions irrespective of their age. The decision was most probably motivated by pronatalist considerations (retired women taking care of their grandchildren can substitute missing nurseries) and were fully incompatible with the announced war on early retirement. Similarly, the introduction of job retention subsidies in 2012 for workers younger than 25 or older than 55, GYES and GYED recipients returning to work, workers in unskilled jobs, and newly hired long-term unemployed seem to be at odds with attaining "flexicurity" in the labor market, i.e., making job separations easier but less painful by means of sufficiently high compensation for the unemployed. The job retention subsidies amounted to Hungarian Forint (HUF) 14,500 a month for periods of three or more years for most of the target groups, and HUF 27,000 a month for shorter periods in the case of school leavers in their first jobs, working childcare recipients, and newly hired long-term unemployed.[8] To put these figures in perspective, we estimate that they amounted to 30 and 57 percent of the total tax burden on two-thirds of the net average wage in 2012.[9]

Table 7.1 collects a number of indicators showing how the above-mentioned reforms were put in practice and how far they reached in the first five years *Fidesz* spent in office. We compare 2010 and 2015 for which published sources are available. At some points, we use microdata from the first quarter of 2015 compared to the same quarter of 2010. Evolutions after 2015 will be discussed briefly later. The six blocks of the table contain indicators on taxes, unemployment insurance and assistance, retirement, childcare assistance, and enrollment in secondary and tertiary education.

Starting with taxes, we find that a major cut of the marginal personal income tax rate, and a resulting minor one of the average rate, did not imply a decrease in the total tax burden on net wages. On the contrary, the tax wedge on the median wage grew by 5.2 percentage points and that on the minimum wage jumped from 36 to 49 percent. Actually, in sharp contrast to what Viktor Orbán regularly claims, the tax wedge on Hungarian wages is not "one of the lowest in the world" but the second highest (after Belgium) within the OECD.[10] Curtailing UI benefits had strong impact, with the number of recipients falling from 160,000 in 2010 to less than 55,000 in 2015. Given only three months until expiry of the benefit, the fraction of UI recipients leaving the register for a job fell substantially, from almost 40 percent in 2010 to only 27 percent in 2014.

The data on other forms of unemployment support suggest that despite the expansion of public works the share of nonemployed people receiving some kind of unemployment assistance (UI, UA, or public works) fell from 17.5 to 13.3 percent. A part of those dropping out of unemployment assistance were

Table 7.1   Key Indicators of Reforms – Evolutions between 2010 and 2015

	2010	2015	Source
Tax wedge on 67% of the average wage[a] (%)	43.8	49.0	1
Tax wedge on the minimum wage[a] (%)	36.2	49.0	1
UI recipients (thousands)	159.6	55.0	2
Fraction leaving UI because of entry to employment[b] (%)	38.9	27.2	2
Nonemployed, received UI or UA and/or did public works[c] (%)	17.5	13.3	3
Nonemployed, received other transfer[c] (%)	53.9	55.5	3
Nonemployed, unassisted[c] (%)	28.6	31.2	3
Retirement under the mandatory age (thousands)			
Male	29.9	2.4	4
Female	5.8	26.6	4
Male, 2010 and annual average in 2011–2015	29.9	9.0	4
Female, 2010 and annual average in 2011–2015	5.8	40.2	4
Median age of retirement (pensioners, both genders)	60.3	60.0	5
Childcare allowance recipients: fraction at work (%)[d]			
GYED (earning-related, high-amount, maximum 2 years)	2.2	4.5	6
GYES (flat rate, low-amount, maximum 3 years)	11.5	8.2	6
GYET (flat rate, low amount, conditional, maximum 10 years)	11.5	13.5	6
Any kind of childcare allowance	8.5	7.6	6
Enrollment in three types of secondary schools (%)			
Vocational training	35.4	30.3	7
Vocational secondary school	46.2	38.2	7
General secondary school	42.5	44.8	7
Application and admission to colleges/universities (thousands)[e]			
Applications	140.3	105.6	8
Admissions	98.2	72.3	8
Of which state-financed (no tuition fee)	68.7	55.9	8

Sources: (1) HLM (2015, 276). (2) HLM (2015, 235). (3) Author's calculation using LFS microdata. First quarters. (4) HLM (2015, 271). (5) HLM (2015, 270). (6) Author's calculation using LFS microdata. First quarters. (7) HLM (2015, 249). (8) Available online: http://www.felvi.hu/felveteli /ponthatarok_rangsorok/ elmult_evek/!ElmultEvek/elmult_evek.php?stat=1.

Notes: (a) 100 (Total wage cost-Net wage)/(Total wage cost). (b) All exits from the UI register = 100. (c) Aged 15–61, not in employment, not in school = 100. Other transfers include pensions child allowance and social benefits. (d) GYES and GYET are flat-rate, low-amount benefits up to age 3 and 10 of the child, respectively. GYED is an earning-related, high-amount benefit up to age 2 of the child. "At work" stands for employment defined by ILO-OECD standards. (e) Courses starting in September.

absorbed by other welfare system programs (pensions and childcare allowances), while others have been left without any kind of financial support. The share of the latter group increased slightly, from 28.6 percent in 2010 to 31.2 percent in 2015. The tightening of retirement rules in 2010, and a complete ban on paying old-age pension to people below the mandatory age in 2011, resulted in the near disappearance of early retirement by men but not by women. The annual flow to female early retirement jumped from 6,000 in 2010 to 40,000 in 2011 and remained at relatively high levels afterward, resulting in a 42,800 average annual flow in 2011–2015. As a result, the median age at retirement of men and women together did not change.

The possibility to combine GYED and paid work after a baby reached age one resulted in a minor rise of employment among mothers on this type of allowance: their share rose from a negligible 2.2 percent to an almost negligible 4.5 percent. The effect of this small positive change was more than offset by fall in the employment rates of parents on GYES and GYET. The overall employment rate of childcare support recipients actually fell from 8.5 to 7.6 percent.

Changes in the structure of secondary-level education only partly matched the reformer's intentions and were modest until recently. General secondary schools managed to absorb a larger fraction of the 2015 cohort (that was smaller by 5.5 percent than the one of 2010) compared to 2010. The share of vocational training schools stayed constant, while vocational secondary schools lost three percentage points of their initial share.

The plan of curbing tertiary education by means of restricting tuition-free places and setting upper limits to the number of admissible students in general (by fields of study and teaching institutions) seems to have reached its goals. While the combined size of the typical entry cohorts (age 18–20) decreased by 15 percent in 2010–2015, the number of applications fell by 25 percent and the number of admissions dropped by 27 percent, promising a halt to harmful "overeducation."

REFORMS AT WORK – FIRST FIVE YEARS

The time elapsed since 2010 is too short to allow a proper, evidence-based evaluation of Orbán's employment and educational policies. Therefore, in this short section we only present the basic facts on aggregate employment growth, the main purpose and promise of the reforms, without assuming causal links between particular policy measures and the observed outcome. After reviewing the evidence on employment growth we will discuss the *likely* consequences of the reforms in the longer run, relying on research results and the experience of other countries.

Table 7.2   Employment in January–March 2008, 2010, and 2015 (Head count, thousands)

	In Hungary excluding public works	Abroad	In public works	Total
2008	3,789	28	27	3,844
2010	3,581	45	53	3,679
2015	3,836	105	176	4,117
Changes				
2010–2015	255	60	123	438
2008–2015	47	77	149	273

Source: Labor Force Surveys, author's calculation. The observations are weighted with the census-based revised weights provided by the CSO.

The data on aggregate employment suggest that Orbán's second and third governments reached their principal aim: between the first quarters of 2010 and 2015 employment grew by 398,000, which almost exactly matches the target of 400,000 new jobs created (net) in five years. (For the levels in 2010 and 2015, see Table 7.2 below.) At first sight, the figures seem to justify the reforms briefly introduced in the previous sections. While the educational reforms could hardly have an impact within such a short period, other measures may have contributed to what indeed looks like a march toward a work-based society. This is what every Hungarian can learn, day by day, from the government-controlled media and the speeches of *Fidesz* representatives.

At a closer look, the data call for a less triumphant interpretation. A large part of the net growth in employment came from two sources, which had apparently little to do with "job creation" in the standard meaning of the expression: a threefold increase in the number of public works participants and a twofold rise in the number of Hungarians working abroad between 2010 and 2015. (The latter category includes those who work abroad at the time of the interview without having left their Hungary-based households. Those leaving the country and their families on a permanent basis are unobserved in the LFS and accounted as part of the decline in the resident population.) While the members of both groups are engaged in gainful work and are justifiably included in the aggregate employment figure – as it happens in other countries – the growth in their number hardly can be interpreted as a success in job creation. The jobs for migrant workers have mostly been created in Austria, Germany, and the United Kingdom, while public works can be regarded as a program for the unemployed rather than an economic sector providing full membership in the workforce.

Table 7.2 presents more precise statistics on the sources of employment growth between the first quarters of 2010 and 2015. Data on January–March 2008, yet unaffected by the crisis, are added. As shown in the fourth row,

183,000 "new jobs" out of a total of 438,000 were created abroad or in the public works scheme.

In evaluating the rest of the total growth (255,000, still an impressive figure) one has to consider the fact that the *Fidesz* government came back to power at the depth of a cyclical downturn. A crisis has long-term and even permanent effects, but it also implies a temporary loss of jobs for several reasons. Firms facing uncertainties tend to postpone their hiring decisions and suspend their investment projects. The crisis also confuses their trade connections. When the crisis seems to be over, a part of the postponed hirings are realized, some suspended projects are restarted, and trade links are partly restored or replaced by new ones. While employment recovers slowly after a deep crisis, a partial recovery can take place without any intervention or positive external shock. Therefore, we have reasons to believe that a part of the job growth after 2010 represents a recovery of this kind.

Employment was higher by only 273,000 in 2015 relative to 2008. As much as 55 percent of this surplus came from the expansion of public works programs and 28 percent was explained by a growth in the number of Hungarians working abroad. Net growth in the number of domestic employment in standard jobs amounted to only 47,000, or 17 percent of the entire surplus. It seems that Orbán's unconventional employment policies could not galvanize the Hungarian labor market as yet. It may be the case, however, that the reforms will bear fruit in the longer run.

CHANGES AFTER 2015

The Hungarian economy grew relatively fast after the European markets had recovered from the crisis.[11] The acceleration of GDP growth brought about a further increase of employment as shown in Table 7.3. This time the bulk of the growth came from the primary labor market resulting in a surplus of 420,000 above the precrisis level of market-based employment. Concomitantly, the number of Hungarian residents working abroad slightly fell, and participation in the public works programs was cut after peaking in 2016.

Table 7.3   Employment after 2015 (Head counts, thousands)

	In Hungary excluding public works	Abroad	In public works	Total
2015	3,923	111	176	4,210
2016	4,027	117	208	4,352
2017	4,118	110	194	4,409
2018*	4,209	103	155	4,467

Source: Labor Force Surveys, author's calculation. The observations are weighted with the census-based revised weights provided by the CSO.
(*) January–September.

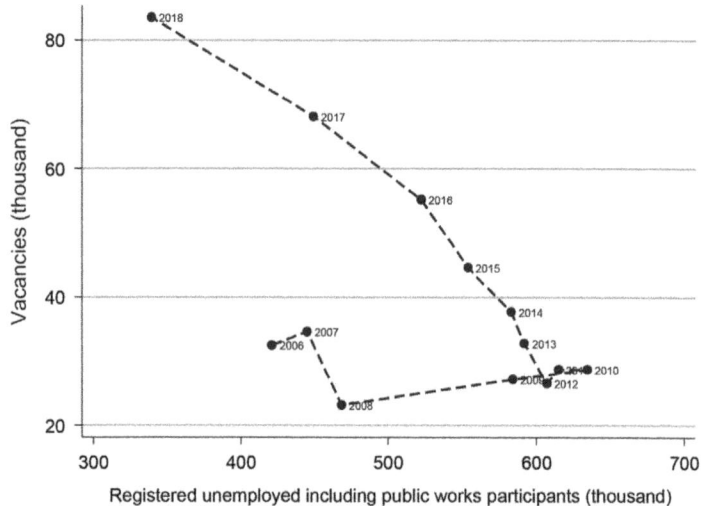

Figure 7.1   Unemployment and Vacancies in 2006–2018. *Sources*: Unemployment: Labor Force Survey micro data, own calculation. Vacancies: Central Statistical Office Stadat Database, http://www.ksh.hu/docs/hun/xstadat/xstadat_evkozi/e_qli027c.html? down=262 downloaded on April 10, 2019.

Employment growth was accompanied by a fast rise in unfilled vacancies. By the end of 2018, the share of unfilled jobs relative to all (filled or unfilled) jobs reached 2.7 percent, a high level in European comparison (Eurostat 2019). Figure 7.1 shows how the Hungarian labor market moved in the space of unemployment and vacancies (the UV or Beveridge space) after 2006, when the collection of vacancy data based on the Eurostat methodology started. Unemployment is measured with the combined number of registered unemployed and public works participants, that is, people out of market-based employment and registered in labor offices prior to and after participation in a PW program.[12] Vacancies based on Eurostat figures are measured on the vertical axis.

The figure shows that market shifts outward in the Beveridge space, which hints at worsening structural frictions and mismatches. The growing demand for labor apparently hits supply-side constraints and seems unable to sufficiently reduce the number of people without standard jobs.

HALF A MILLION JOBS SO FAR AND MORE TO COME?

The plan of creating one million jobs in ten years clearly failed, but the market performed better than expected on the basis of forecasting models.[13]

However, as the end of the period of postcrisis recovery and low interest rates is approaching, further improvements can only be achieved through properly designed reforms in the labor market. We now discuss the scope for such policies in the major fields of intervention.

Flexibility

Tax cuts and measures decreasing adjustment costs (due to the lower costs of dismissals, less job protection, and weaker unions) are potentially important drivers of flexibility. The returns to these measures could be substantial in a rigid labor market but predictably low in Hungary where employment protection has never been strong, unions have always been relatively weak, and fiscal vulnerability sets limits to further reducing taxation. International comparative research in the frame of the Wage Dynamics Network (Kátay 2011) suggested that already before 2010 Hungary ranked among the countries with the lowest degree of downward real wage rigidity. Nominal rigidity was higher, but still below the overall cross-country average, and only the minimum wage remained an important source of downward wage rigidity. Cazes and Nesporova (2003) showed that Hungary's employment protection legislation index (EPL) was equal to 1.65 at the millennium, halfway between that of the United Kingdom (0.75) and continental EU countries such as Austria, the Czech Republic, Germany, and Poland with values above 1.9. In the Central and Eastern European (CEE) region, only Slovakia had a lower EPL index (1.44) than Hungary's.

There are at least two further specifics, suggesting that the kind of flexibility conducted by the *Fidesz* governments should have a limited impact. First, the budgetary effect of major cuts in some taxes like PIT and profit tax had to be compensated by the introduction of more than 30 new types of taxes, many of them announced unexpectedly and enacted overnight, and some of them being openly discriminative. (The examples range from special taxes levied on banks and telecommunication companies to a tax specifically targeted at large multinational retail trade companies. The EU ruled out most of these special taxes later.) A high degree of uncertainty generated by these unsustainable and *ad hoc* measures diminish the returns to tax cuts by raising country risk. In their microsimulation model Benedek, Kátay, and Kiss (2012) predicted that the 2013 tax reform package could have increased employment by about 100,000 (between two equilibrium states), but a 50-base-point increase in the yield of government bonds was expected to decrease the return to 58,000 and a 100-point increase was predicted to reduce it to about 30,000.[14] Second, making dismissals easier for firms without providing proper support to the job losers is likely to generate strong resistance against downsizing and reduces rather than boosts flexibility.

Supply-Side Incentives

The available estimates (Kiss and Mosberger 2011, Benczúr et al. 2014) suggest that labor supply elasticities are relatively low in Hungary (a range of 0.1–0.2). Economically significant effects were found with high-income people having second jobs. For the unskilled, Benczúr et al. (2014) estimated the elasticity of labor force participation with respect to the gap between income while employed and income while nonemployed to be about 0.18. Taking this estimate at face value, we get that doubling the gap (a purely theoretical possibility) could induce a seven percent growth of activity, which translates to about 35,000 additional jobseekers and somewhat less jobholders.

Methodologically sound studies of past cuts in UI benefits (Micklewright and Nagy 1994, Galasi and Nagy 2002, 2003) also detected weak effects and found that waiting behavior is characteristic of a small minority of the benefit recipients (Micklewright and Nagy 1999). In an experiment on how stricter monitoring affects outflows to jobs from the unemployment register, Micklewright and Nagy (2010) found no significant effect except for women in their thirties.

Minimum Wage Policy

A first wave of increasing the minimum wage by Orbán's first government in 2001–2002 was analyzed in several studies. Kertesi and Köllő (2003) found that doubling the minimum wage, a rise from Ft 25,500 to 50,000 in the course of 13 months, had a negative effect on the employment and no measurable impact on search intensity among the nonemployed. The implied demand elasticities were high in the small-firm sector (-0.57) but much weaker (-0.06) in large firms with more than 300 employees. Both Köllő (2011a) and Harasztosi and Lindner (2019) estimated demand elasticities to fall between -0.13 and -0.25 for 2001–2003 in firms employing more than 20 workers. The latter paper demonstrated that the negative effect of the minimum wage was offset partly by increases in sales prices, mainly in services. In brief, past experience did not support that the minimum wage was an effective instrument to stimulate labor supply, while it had a weak negative effect on labor demand in general and a stronger one in the small-firm sector. The available evidence on benefit and minimum wage effects hint at the presence of demand-side constraints at lower tiers of the labor market.

Public Works

Public works, as it is used in Hungary, is a unique attraction in the employment policy landscape. Such programs – organized by local governments and set as a condition for benefit receipt – do exist in several European countries but at a much lower scale, and usually integrated into packages of various programs. Public works was also part of the federal *Welfare to Work* program in the United States, until 2004, and is still operated in about half of the states. Currently, only Slovakia runs a big public works program with a "workfare" character, but participation rates and especially expenditures fall short of the Hungarian levels. The programs closest to Hungary's in terms of magnitude and design were Argentina's already abandoned *Trabajar* and *Jefes y Jefas* projects in 1997–2001 and 2000–2009, respectively. Impact studies on them by Fachelli et al. (2004), Ronconi et al. (2006), and Ravallion et al. (2001) suggested that they were precisely targeted, alleviated poverty in the short run, but did not help the participants in returning to the primary labor market and strengthened their dependence on the welfare system.[15]

Research into public works in Hungary also suggests that the participants' chances of reintegration are poor. Cseres-Gergely and Molnár (2016) found that 13 percent of the workers who left the program did market jobs six months after exit. This is a strongly upward biased estimate of the exit to job rate since a public works spell is more likely to terminate if the worker expects, or already found, a market job. LFS data suggest quarterly exit to market job rates of 5.8 percent for 2012–2013, the period studied by Cseres-Gergely and Molnár.

The setup of public works teams does not help reintegration effectively since the overwhelming majority of participants work in isolated groups rather than real work organizations. Köllő (2015a) found that the median participant worked at an employer, where the share of public workers among all workers amounted to 88 percent (all educational levels) and 98 percent (unskilled). Furthermore, the rules of call hinder job search and informal work. Neither international experience nor Hungarian research results support that public works is an effective way of reintegration. Given its specifics like mandatory participation, biased occupational composition, and substandard wages, the slots created in the program can hardly be accounted as "employment" in the sense this term is customarily used.

Education

Orbán's education reforms have been criticized in many ways, including mass demonstrations in 2016, and for many reasons. Criticisms have been directed toward full centralization of the school system, restrictions imposed on schools' choice of their curriculum, and the allocation of resources without clear rules. Further components, such as choosing between compulsory Bible classes and "ethics" classes, which incidentally forces parents and children to reveal their cultural and political preferences, are also under attack. Here, we restrict the attention to problems relevant for the employment prospects of the next generation.

There is considerable criticism of reshaping the secondary level of education in favor of vocational training schools. Hajdu et al. (2015) show that vocational training schools develop the basic competencies of students less than other types of secondary schools, even after controlling for primary school test scores and parental background. The gap between types of schools predictably will widen further after the radical curtailing of general education for apprentices. Insufficient basic competencies have grave consequences in a country where the demand for literacy, numeracy, and communication skills is on the rise. Narrow skills lose their value within a short time, while general skills have high returns even within blue-collar occupations. The returns to secondary school (*Matura*) attainment over basic vocational qualification steeply rise over the life cycle (op. cit.).

The government argues that Hungary needs a "German-type dual training system," but any formal similarity between the present and planned Hungarian education and training regime and those of Germany and several Northern European countries is misleading. German trainees, for instance, get 7,950 or 7,155 hours of general training prior to entering vocational training, while Hungarians get 5,742 during their eight-year studies in primary school (Eurydice 2013).[16] Denmark operates a three-year dual system of apprentice-based vocational training (Cort 2002), but it starts after nine years of general training and develops the basic competences of the students much more efficiently than Hungarian training schools. A comparison of data from the International Adult Literacy Survey (IALS) suggests that Danish vocational school graduates have more years in school, perform much better in skills tests, and significantly fewer have severe problems in reading, writing, and solving simple quantitative tasks. As many as 65 percent of them speak English in contrast to only 0.8 per cent of Hungarians. Danish former apprentices have much higher employment rates and relative wages, they are twice as likely to be upwardly mobile than Hungarians and perform a much wider variety of tasks involving literacy at work. They are also three times as likely to participate in retraining and to change jobs as Hungarians (Köllő 2011b). It is fairly unlikely that the shortening of training and the radical cut in hours devoted to the development of basic competencies will move Hungary in the direction of Denmark or Germany.

Observers familiar with international comparative data note that the share of 26–35-year-olds with a college or university diploma is still only 25.5 percent in Hungary (LFS data, 2011 Q1), well below the Lisbon target of 40 percent and the European average.[17] There is no evidence of "overeducation" at the tertiary level. The returns to diploma are high by international comparison. Furthermore, the data do not support that humanities and social science graduates perform poorly in the labor market (Hajdu et al. 2015).

Last but not least, the reform is criticized for a lack of effort at integration. As shown in Jenkins et al. (2008), analyzing PISA 2006, the impact of family background on test scores is nowhere as strong within the OECD as it is in Hungary. The results are similar in PISA 2009. Further survey data show that Hungary has the highest ratio of between schools to total variance in student performance (OECD 2007). Furthermore, using TIMSS and PIRLS data, Csapó et al. (2009) demonstrate that a large part of what seems to be within-school variance at first sight actually comes from between-class and between-premises variance. Most of the children directed to low-quality schools and classes in the primary school continue their studies in the dead-end of the uncertified vocational training system.

The practice of routing disadvantaged children to segregated schools and classes affects the Roma minority disproportionately. Havas and Liskó (2005) estimate that while there was a twofold increase in the share of Roma children in primary schools between 1980 and 2003, the number of 100 percent Roma classes grew by a factor of 8. Furthermore, they found the share of Roma children to be 30 percent in normal classes, 15 percent in special classes for high-achievers, and 70 percent in special classes for low-achievers.

Orbán's "system of national cooperation" deliberately strengthens these attributes at several points. Grade repetition in primary education, which presupposed the parents' consent from the early 2000s onwards, was reintroduced. The school leaving age was cut from 18 to 16 years (with the original plan being a limit of 15 years).[18] Several programs supporting integrated education have been abolished and new channels have been opened for segregation, through the takeover of many schools by churches and private schools. In sum, restricting tertiary education, directing 14-year-old children to dead-end vocational training, and restricting their curriculum to practical skills required at the *current* state of technology will predictably deteriorate rather than improve the employment prospects of young people.

LIFE OUTSIDE THE WORK-BASED SOCIETY

Responding to failures with the exclusion and separation of those who fail or are assumed to fail is a common characteristic of recent Hungarian policies addressing such diverse social problems as school failures, homelessness, and long-term unemployment. Approving segregated education and early tracking, cutting the school leaving age, efforts to keep homeless people out of sight, drastic cuts to unemployment assistance, and active labor market programs other than workfare are just a few examples of the practices that, taken together, seem to constitute a consistent policy of secluding the laggards and directing people to pathways according to their assumed abilities and "merits."

The reproduction of a sizeable, poorly educated minority of the labor force and leaving this minority without assistance are all the more risky as Hungary (similar to other CEE countries) is apparently unable to provide its low-educated populace with jobs. Massive unskilled unemployment is a region-wide problem. Only in Romania and Slovenia – the top performers in the region in this respect – do the absolute and relative employment rates of the unskilled exceed Belgium's, the laggard within the EU-15. All other CEE countries score worse than any of the old Member States, with the ratio of unskilled to skilled employment rates falling short of 0.45 in Bulgaria, Estonia, Hungary, and Latvia; 0.4 in the Czech Republic and Poland; and 0.35 in Lithuania and Slovakia (Köllő 2015b).

Data on how low-educated workers and jobs are matched in these countries point to deficiencies that stem directly from the common past of the former state-socialist countries. These economies offer more simple jobs than Western and Northern economies do but far fewer than the South European ones. The unskilled cannot rely on a network of family-owned and family-managed small firms – a shelter for many unqualified Greeks, Italians, Spaniards, and Portuguese. At the same time, the low-educated lack the competencies, which enable low-educated West-Europeans and, particularly, North-Europeans to do complex jobs. In CEE, the data hint at an extreme degree of social isolation, which constrains the low-educated in informal learning and participation in civil activities, enhancing both cognitive and noncognitive skills.

While Orbán's governments should clearly not be blamed for the region-wide problem of high unskilled unemployment, their response to the problem seems to rest on mistaken assumptions. Both his first and second governments regarded high unskilled unemployment as a supply-side problem that needs to be addressed by "making work pay," on the one hand, and workfare, on the other. The available evidence on these policies suggests that they tend to isolate the unskilled from the rest of the society rather than integrate them. The fragmentation of society is risky: it is likely to damage the quality of institutions and constrain potential growth through linkages described in Easterly et al. (2006).

NOTES

1. HLM (2009, 305). Hungary had the second lowest employment level in Europe after Malta (55.2 percent), where female labor force participation has always been notoriously low. The data relate to the population aged 15–64.

2. Author's calculation using the January–March 2008 wave of the quarterly Labor Force Survey.

3. The full document, entitled the National Work Plan (*Nemzeti Munkaterv*), is no longer available on official government websites. For the full text of Version 6 of the plan, see tbinfo.hu 2019.

4. The system was further simplified by the abolishment of tax credits for low earnings. At the same time, new tax credits were introduced for families raising children. This reform was also motivated by a wish to keep up with Slovakia and the Baltic states in a "tax competition" for foreign direct investment.

5. The data stand for average quarterly stocks in the indicated periods.

6. See mfor.hu (2010).

7. Note that while childcare allowances are available for both parents, the overwhelming majority of the recipients (98.5 percent in January–March 2015 according to LFS data) are women.

8. One dollar was about HUF 280 and one euro was about HUF 320 in 2019. See munkaugyiaudit 2012.

9. Two-thirds of the net average wage was equal to HUF 96,500 and the tax wedge was 47.9 percent in 2012. (See Table 7.1.) The tax burden is calculated as the net wage times the tax wedge.

10. See data oecd.org (2019).

11. Real GDP per capita grew by 3.3 percent in 2013–2018. In this respect, Hungary compared favorably to the Czech Republic (2.9 percent), was in line with Slovakia (3.1 percent), but lagged behind Poland (3.4 percent) and Romania (4.4 percent) according to World Bank data.

12. Note that public works participants are temporarily excluded from the register when they join a public works project.

13. A full macroeconomic model built by Vincze (2011) estimated employment growth to fall between -40,000 and +187,000 in 2011–2020, depending on assumptions made on the paths of exports and the fiscal balance. Major (2012) predicted that labor force participation would grow by a maximum of 250,000 in the same period.

14. Hungary's CDS spread was below 2 percent in early 2010 and about 3 percent in 2012–2013 mostly because of measures increasing country risk (Kondor 2014).

15. India's *National Rural Employment Guarantee* (NREG) program is often labeled the world's largest public works program but, in fact, its design is completely different as NREG *offers* employment opportunities to voluntary participants. See Azam (2012) and Zimmermann (2012) among others.

16. The duration of general education varies across regions in Germany.

17. Hungary was ranked 19th in the EU-27 in 2013, according to data of the EU LFS.

18. Mártonfi et al. (2015) suggest that increasing the age floor from 16 to 18 years brought about an increase in completed school years and graduation with Matura exam. Econometric estimates by Adamecz (2016) support these conclusions, albeit she also finds increased dropout rates from basic vocational schools among students whom the increased age limit "enforced" to stay in education.

BIBLIOGRAPHY

Adamecz, Anna. 2016. "When Higher Compulsory School Leaving Age Increases Dropping Out. The Heterogeneous Effects of a Compulsory School Leaving Age Raise with Respect to Parental Education." Manuscript. Budapest: Central European University.

Azam, Mehtabul. 2012. "The Impact of Indian Job Guarantee Scheme on Labor Market Outcomes: Evidence from a Natural Experiment." World Bank and IZA Discussion Paper No. 6548, May 2012.

Bálint, Mónika, and János Köllő. 2008. "A gyermeknevelési támogatások munkaerő-piaci hatásai." *Esély* 1: 3–27.

Benczúr, Péter, Áron Kiss, and Olivér Miklós Rácz. 2014. "Income Taxation, Transfers and Labour Supply at the Extensive Margin." Banque de France Working Paper No. 487.

Benedek, Dóra, Gábor Kátay, and Áron Kiss. 2012. "Microsimulation as a Tool for Assessing the Impact of Tax Changes." In *The Hungarian Labor Market – Review and Analysis*, edited by Károly Fazekas, Péter Benczúr, and Álmos Telegdy, 115–33. Budapest: Institute of Economics and OFA.

Cazes, Sandrine, and Alena Nesporova. 2003. *Labour Markets in Transition. Balancing Flexibility and Security in Central and Eastern Europe*. Geneva: International Labour Office.

Cort, Pia. 2002. "Vocational Education and Training in Denmark." CEDEFOP Panorama Series. Luxembourg: Office for Official Publications of the European Communities.

Csapó, Benő, Gyöngyvér Molnár, and László Kinyó. 2009. "A magyar oktatási rendszer szelektivitása a nemzetközi vizsgálatok tükrében." *Iskolakultúra* 4: 3–13.

Cseres-Gergely, Zsombor, and Gyöngyvér Molnár. 2016. "Labour Market Situation Following Exit from Public Works." In *The Hungarian Labor Market – Review and Analysis,* edited by Károly Fazekas and Júlia Varga, 148–59. Budapest: Institute of Economics and OFA.

data oecd.org. 2019. https://data.oecd.org/tax/tax-wedge.htm, accessed June 25, 2019.

Easterly, William, Jozef Ritzen, and Michael Woolcock. 2006. "Social Cohesion, Institutions and Growth." *Economics and Politics* 18 (2): 105–20.

Eurostat. 2017. Newsrelease – Euroindicators, 171/2017 – November 14, 2017. http://ec.europa.eu/eurostat/documents/2995521/8444168/2-14112017-BP-EN.pdf/2de0034c-e53f-4bf7-ac31-c553a2ce7de5, accessed June 25, 2019.

Eurydice. 2013. "Comparative Overview on Instruction Time in Full-time Compulsory Education in Europe." 2013/14 European Commission Eurydice Report. http://eacea.ec.europa.eu/education/eurydice/documents/facts_and_figures/Instruction_Time_2013_14.pdf, accessed June 25, 2019.

Galasi, Péter, and Gyula Nagy. 2002. "Járadékjogosultsági időtartam és elhelyezkedés." *Közgazdasági Szemle* 2: 480–497.

Galasi, Péter, and Gyula Nagy. 2003. "A munkanélküli-ellátás változásainak hatása a munkanélküliek segélyezésére és elhelyezkedésére." *Közgazdasági Szemle* 7–8: 608–34.

Hajdu, Tamás, Zoltán Hermann, Dániel Horn, Gábor Kertesi, Gábor Kézdi, János Köllő, and Júlia Varga. 2015. "Az érettségi védelmében." Budapest Working Papers on the Labor Market 2015 (1).

Harasztosi, Péter, and Attila Lindner. 2019. "Who Pays for the Minimum Wage?" *American Economic Review* 109 (8): 2693–2727.

Havas, Gábor, and Ilona Liskó. 2006. *Óvodától a szakmáig*. Budapest: Oktatáskutató Intézet – Új Mandátum.

HLM. 2009. *The Hungarian Labor Market – Review and Analysis.* Budapest: Hungarian Academy of Sciences and National Employment Fund.

————. 2015. *The Hungarian Labor Market – Review and Analysis.* Budapest: Hungarian Academy of Sciences.

Jenkins, Stephen P., John Micklewright. Sylke V. Schnepf. 2008. "Social Segregation in Secondary Schools: How Does England Compare with Other Countries?" *Oxford Review of Education* 34 (1): 21–38.

Kátay, Gábor. 2011. "Downward Wage Rigidity in Hungary." European Central Bank Working Paper No. 1372.

Kertesi. Gábor, and János Köllő. 2003. "Fighting 'Low Equilibria' by Doubling the Minimum Wage?: Hungary's Experiment." IZA Discussion Paper No. 970.

Kiss, Áron, and Pálma Mosberger. 2011. "The Elasticity of Taxable Income of High Earners: Evidence from Hungary." Hungarian National Bank Working Paper 2011 (11).

Köllő, János. 2011a. "The Consequences of Doubling the Minimum Wage." In *The Minimum Wage Revisited in the Enlarged EU*, edited by Daniel Vaughan-Whitehead. Cheltenham: Edward Elgar.

————. 2011b. "A német rendszerű duális képzésről." http://www.szuveren.hu/ve ndeglap/kollo-janos/a-nemet-rendszeru-dualis-kepzesrol, accessed June 25, 2019.

————. 2015a. "Where Do Public Workers Work?" In *The Hungarian Labor Market – Review and Analysis*, edited by Károly Fazekas and Júlia Varga, 160–65. Budapest: Institute of Economics and OFA.

————. 2015b. "Patterns of Integration – Unskilled Employment in Norway, Italy and Hungary." *Economics of Transition* 23 (1): 105–34.

Köllő, János, Zsanna Nyírő, and István János Tóth. 2017. "The Evolution of Basic Indicators of Labor Shortage." In *The Hungarian Labor Market*, edited by Károly Fazekas and János Köllő, 63–72. Budapest: MTA KRTK.

Kondor, Péter. 2014. "Megvan, mi rángatja a forintot." *Index*, June 10, 2014.

Major, Klára. 2012. Az inaktívak és az aktívak (foglalkoztatottak és munkanélküliek) létszámának előrejelzése ágazati, foglalkozási és iskolai végzettségi bontásban. Manuscript. MTA KTI.

Mártonfi, György, et al. 2015. *A 18 éves korra emelt tankötelezettség teljesülése és (mellék)hatásai.* Edited by György Mártonfi. Budapest: Oktatáskutató és Fejlesztő Intézet.

mfor.hu. 2010. "Reform a munkaerőpiacon." http://www.mfor.hu/cikkek/Reform_a_munkaeropiacon__sokaknak_fog_fajni.html, accessed June 25, 2019.

Micklewright, John, and Gyula Nagy. 1994. "How Does the Hungarian Unemployment Insurance System Really Work?" *Economics of Transition* 2: 209–32.

————. 2010. "The Effect of Monitoring Unemployment Insurance Recipients on Unemployment Duration: Evidence from a Field Experiment." *Labour Economics* 1: 180–87.

munkaugyiaudit. 2012. "Munkavédelmi akcióterv." http://munkaugyaudit.hu/a-munk ahelyvedelmi-akcioterv-adokedvezmenyei/, accessed June 25, 2019.

Nagy, Gyula, and John Micklewright. 1999. "Living Standards and Incentives in Transiton: The Implications of UI Exhaustion in Hungary." *Journal of Public Economics* 3: 297–319.

Neumann, László, Mihály Laki, and Beáta Nacsa. 2013. "Az új Munka Törvénykönyve hatása a munkahelyi érdekképviseletre." *Munkaügyi Szemle* 4: 96–112.

OECD. 2007. Family Database. https://www.oecd.org/social/family/database, accessed June 25, 2019.

Ravallion, Martin, Emanuela Galasso, Teodoro Lazo, and Ernesto Philipp. 2001. "Do Workfare Participants Recover Quickly from Retrenchment?" World Bank Policy Research Working Paper No. 2672, September.

Ronconi, Lucas, Juan Sanguinetti, Sandra Fachelli, Virginia Casazza, and Ignacio Franceschelli. 2006. "Poverty and Employability Effects of Workfare Programs in Argentina." PMMA Working Paper No. 2006 (14).

tbinfo.hu. 2019. "Nemzeti Munkaterv." www.tbinfo.hu/files/nemzeti_munkaterv.do c, accessed June 25, 2019.

Vincze, János. 2011. "Ágazati kibocsátás." Budapest: MTA KTI. http://elorejelzes. mtakti.hu/publikaciok/TaMOP-2-3-2-09-1-muhelytanulmanyok/16/, accessed June 25, 2019.

Zimmermann, Laura. 2012. "Labor Market Impacts of a Large-Scale Public Works Program: Evidence from the Indian Employment Guarantee Scheme." University of Michigan and IZA Discussion Paper No. 6858, September.

Chapter 8

The Fear of Population Replacement

Attila Melegh

In 2018 Hungary became a battlefield in a government propaganda campaign that has cast a mysterious enemy allegedly fighting for uncontrolled immigration ("population exchange") against a heroic government that intends to defend Hungary, and very importantly Europe, from the ongoing "invasion." The campaign prominently suggests that this effort to invade Hungary and Europe itself is supported by "agents" in Brussels and the United Nations (UN) who are financed by George Soros. As billboards across the country spelled out in February 2018, Soros plans to settle millions of people from Africa and the Middle East in Hungary.

Already in 2017 on the anniversary of the 1956 Hungarian Revolution Prime Minister Viktor Orbán presented the fight against "globalists" in the following way:

> The truth is that, thirty years after communism, there is once again a world power which seeks to turn the European nations into a monochrome, homogeneous mass. Like all cultured European nations, we Hungarians have always had our own notion of our country: a vision of freedom and civilization; a vision of how to be human and how to live as human beings. This is how, throughout history, we've always rebuilt Hungary, once we've rid ourselves of our oppressors. This is how it was after we tore down communism and sent the Soviets packing. The truth is that now, three decades down the line, everything that we think about Hungary and the order of life in Hungary is once again under threat. The truth is that after we regained our freedom in 1990, we have once again arrived at a crossroads in our history. We wanted to believe that the old troubles could no longer return. We wanted to believe that the deranged dream that the communists had of turning us Hungarians into *Homo Sovieticus* could never return, ever again. And now here we are, astonished to see that the forces of globalism are trying to force our doors open, and are working on turning us

Hungarians into *Homo Brusselius*. We wanted to believe that never again would we have to deal with political, economic and intellectual forces seeking to sever our national roots. We also wanted to believe that in Europe there was no room for terrorism and violence.[1]

This and other texts from the prime minister and his government use a language full of references to a political vocabulary prevalent before World War II, evoking the old discursive patterns of "race suicide" (Ashford 2014, 107–33). This becomes exceptionally clear in the following excerpt from László Kövér, a chief ideologue of Fidesz and speaker of the Hungarian parliament, in 2015:

> The world as it existed for thousands of years on the basis of traditional types of values is falling apart, and this is leading to dramatic consequences; namely, the vision of the death of the nation which inspired the literature of the reform period is actually very close. Not only in the case of Hungarians: the situation is more or less the same for all native populations of all European member states; namely, that we are so close that we cannot stop going down the demographic slope and, practically, we will die out. [. . .] Now we can see that when the global population increases, thus in a certain way there is overpopulation, population decline occurs only in Europe, and sooner or later this will lead to an invasion by those who see a living space for themselves here.[2]

The defense of Hungary is linked to another pattern, namely, the defense of Europe against an overly cosmopolitan West and global organizations representing the dangers of unregulated "immigration," termed as "invasion" or a "modern-day mass movement." The January 2018 speech that Viktor Orbán addressed to leaders of the Visegrád Group (Czech Republic, Hungary, Poland, and Slovakia) highlights the common rejection of becoming an "immigrant society" as he terms it, even against the "manipulative" efforts of the United Nations:

> I would like to draw everyone's attention to the fact that the support, the positive presentation and the development of a model European programme for migration did not start in 2015, and did not start with *Willkommenskultur*. It began in 2004, when a UN Secretary-General called Kofi Annan went to the European Parliament and gave a speech. He said that this would be the great question for the future, and outlined what Europe should do. He said that immigrants would need Europe, and Europe would need immigrants. He said that we must put aside our prejudices, open channels for immigration, and that societies in Europe must adapt. Migration, he said, is not a problem, but a solution. Between 2004 and 2015 we failed to realize that this process was actually underway in Western Europe. All this was revealed to us by the 2015 crisis, which brought all of us – Hungarians included – face to face with a dilemma: whether we

wanted to accept the advice of Kofi Annan and history, by following the path being taken today by the Western European countries – the majority of which have turned themselves into immigrant countries; or if we did not want to become an immigrant country. We help those who need help – there can be no debate about that. We shall give protection to those who need it. But we shall not accept migrants, either now or later, because we do not want to become an immigrant country. We don't want to solve our internal problems – such as population problems – with immigration, but with a family policy. So this is the new situation that we are all faced with. I frankly tell you that in the immigrant societies of Western Europe what I see are parallel societies, terrorism, the deterioration of public security and native populations losing the feeling that they are at home in their own countries. I find no attraction in any of these things, nor anything that would reassure Hungary. Instead we must distance ourselves from that and preserve our traditional ways of life.[3]

Taken together, we can see that the most important theme for Orbán is to avoid immigration in general and to defend the so-called traditional way of life against "global powers," for the sake of which radical steps are justified. He speaks against migrants in general when actually he refers to people from outside Europe "illegally" crossing European borders. He avoids mentioning those who legally cross the border, or Hungarians from Romania, Serbia, Ukraine, or other former Hungarian territories who settle in Hungary. They are not included in this category of migrants. At the same time, by deliberately misinterpreting the arguments of the "globalists" "promoting" migration, the key Hungarian politicians effectively destroy the discourse of migrants' human rights used by international actors. Such rhetoric relies on racial and national distinctions and creates the impression of a large-scale war between globalists and defenders of Hungary and Europe.

While this may appear to be a strange and ludicrous discursive construction, the central elements resonate with the Hungarian public. In the spring of 2016, almost 70 percent of Hungarian respondents thought that the most important problem for Europe was immigration, well above the EU average and similar to citizens of many other small East European states (*Eurobarometer* 85, 2016). By the autumn of 2017, together with respondents in the Czech Republic and Estonia, Hungarian interviewees ranked immigration as a top priority for Europe (*Eurobarometer* 88, 2017). Notably, in both years immigration was not a top priority when citizens were surveyed about national concerns, which certainly shows a twist in Hungarian and East European public opinion: namely, that Europe and Europeanness is to be defended from migrants outside their own region.

When we look at the reasons to refuse "immigrants," a 2016 survey reveals that around 90 percent agree on the protection of Hungary from the point of view of culture and security. According to the respondents, Hungary is not wealthy enough to support immigrants. They also agree that if there is even the remotest probability that terrorists are among them, then no one should be allowed in. The culturally homogenous country should remain so, and accordingly 74 percent of respondents believe the mixing of cultures threatens basic cultural values (Ságvári 2017).

The themes used by Orbán have a clear and hegemonic position, and we need to look at the discursive and structural logic behind them as similar public opinion patterns can be seen in other East European countries. As opposed to many critiques, the shift cannot be attributed to one person, and one should go beyond asserting that public opinion is simply being misused and distorted.

How should we understand such discursive patterns? From where do the involved mental maps come from, which we understand as key ideational mechanisms about how knowledge on demographic and migratory processes are structured? How are various demographic developments and actors of the world represented? How should we interpret anti-immigration demographic nationalism, which can be understood as a combination of selective anti-immigration discourses and regulations with straightforward, state-sponsored pronatalism and the use of "own resources" for the sake of improving our standing within Europe? How can we link these discursive and political events and the underlying mental maps to demographic structures and changes? What challenges do the structural processes of fertility, migration, and mortality show, and how can we interpret the political reaction given to them during the Orbán regime? First, I shall provide a historical-structural analysis of demographic processes and then review policies and institutionalized norms that shape mental maps and that are shaped by mental maps.[4] Finally, I will look at the interrelationship between material structures, processes, and political discourses in order to complete a complex and dynamic analysis of Hungarian demographic nationalism in the 2010s.

HISTORICAL-STRUCTURAL ANALYSIS: REGIONAL CHALLENGES AND DEPENDENCIES RELATED TO MIGRATION AND DEMOGRAPHIC CHANGE

Since the late 1980s, due to the increasing competition in the world economy, evolving EU integration, changes in the international environment, and the shifts in demographic and labor market processes, the role of migration as a source of labor force and human capital began to grow as opposed to local fertility. During the last thirty years global migration has become more intensive and relative ratios of migrant versus nonmigrant population have increased, especially in the case of the European Union

(Melegh 2017). On a macrolevel these processes are linked to capital flows and other historical-macrostructural changes due to persistent and increasing economic inequalities within the EU countries (Sassen 1988; Sanderson-Kentor 2008; Melegh 2011 and 2013; Böröcz 2014; Fassmann et al. 2014; Melegh 2016).

Eastern Europe has shown an increasing diversification of net migration rates over the course of the past sixty years. In the 1950s it was more or less homogenously a net emigrant region (with the exception of some of the western republics of the Soviet Union). After changes that took place between the 1960s and 1990s, it lost this homogeneity and some parts became immigrant areas, while others became or remained emigrant areas. At one time Hungary followed a path toward becoming an immigrant country, but since the mid-2000s it has moved toward an emigrant pattern, which we also can observe in the case of Romania and Bulgaria. However, in contrast to these countries, here especially the younger, better educated, and/or skilled labor has moved in massive numbers to Austria, Germany, and the United Kingdom (Blaskó and Gödri 2014).

As Böröcz has shown, in terms of GDP per capita, Hungary was a relatively rich country in Eastern Europe from a global perspective in the 1950s, and it increased its well-being with regard to the world average till the 1980s (reaching levels over 140 percent of the global average), when it started a period of stagnation and then a fall after the regime change of 1989, a drop that has been partially compensated (Böröcz 2009, 131–39). This loss of developmental dynamics is especially visible when compared to the trajectory of other, previously migrant-sending countries such as Austria and Italy, which improved their relative positions dramatically after the 1970s and became predominantly migrant-receiving countries. Around 1980, a new cycle of globalization of the world economy began, which resulted in the worsening of Hungary's foreign indebtedness and stagnation, which also characterized most socialist planned economies in the region in the 1980s (Chase-Dunn et al. 2000; Böröcz 2009, 134–35). The economic restructuring in the late 1980s and 1990s was following neoliberal economic policies (almost total privatization, cutting of subsidies, large-scale bankruptcy, opening the national consumer market to the global economy), and these changes, combined with the collapse of Comecon, led to the decline of productive capacities (e.g., around 30 percent of industrial capacities), jobs (more than 1.3 million), and most importantly job security, the memory of which has had major longer-term consequences concerning migration.

This period of shock economics, together with labor market changes and refugees coming from neighboring countries, especially from ex-Yugoslavia, contributed to an increase in negative attitudes toward immigrants among groups who lost stable jobs, especially the long-term unemployed hoping to qualify for disability pensions (Fábián and Sík 1996, 399–400; Bernát et al. 2015). These negative attitudes amplified later during the so-called Status Law debate and again during the last refugee crisis. But the structural factors go well beyond these points, most importantly containing those that shaped or did not change popular mental maps of outright Eurocentrism and that saw the country as an unequal partner of the West while being "superior" to the "East" (Melegh 2006).

During the last sixty years the target countries of Hungary's emigration have not changed significantly, which shows how important historical links are to mass migration and how related mental maps have changed. Hungarian emigrants have chosen consistently Austria, Germany, North America (United States and Canada), the United Kingdom, and to some extent Australia. There was one exception in the 1970s, namely, Israel (Melegh 2013, Melegh and Sárosi 2015). Regardless of the striking resilience, we can also argue that Hungary, like the whole region, has become more Eurocentric in its external relationships and has become more loosely connected to non-European emigration destinations. It should also be mentioned that during state socialism Hungary maintained an intensive economic relationship with North Africa (Libya, Egypt) and the Middle East (Syria) where Hungarian professionals and workers served for longer periods on various industrial projects. These contacts subsided after the regime change and the collapse of the target regions.

This lack of substantial contact with non-Europeans did not change, even if we look at the refugee flows since 1989 when Hungary signed the Geneva Convention, and especially from 1997 (when geographical limitations were lifted for the convention) till early 2015 when the cyclical inflows were based on incoming Hungarians (in the early years), Bosnians (1994–1995), and Kosovars, while Afghanis, Pakistanis, and Iraqis played a smaller role. Moreover, until early 2018 only a small percentage of asylum applicants received protected status. According to the Central Statistical Office, 320,298 people entered Hungary from 2000 to 2017, from whom 177,135 arrived in 2015 alone, and from whom only 9,427 qualified for some form of (mainly temporary) protection (KSH Stadat 2018). A very high proportion of asylum seekers actually left the country without completing the asylum process. Thus, Hungary has not established new migratory links this way. Even the massive outflow of refugees due to the dramatic crisis in the Middle East produced by Western and regional powers (Iran, Saudi Arabia, and Turkey) and the crossing of the Hungarian border by hundreds of thousands of people did not change the migratory picture substantially. Almost no one wanted to stop in Hungary, even well before the Hungarian refugee system was hardened with the closure of the country's existing refugee camps and the building of two fences along the Hungarian and Serbian border. Asylum seekers now must wait in containers set up by the Hungarian state until they can submit applications.

Concerning immigration, the key feature is that the whole region, including Hungary, sends large numbers of people to the West following historical links but only receives migrants from the immediate region, and further links are rare and relatively weak (like China, Vietnam, or other areas of the world). Thus, we see an unequal exchange with the West and the loss of massive populations. According to the United Nations (UN) in 2015, more than 25 million people who were born in Eastern Europe did not live in their country of birth, while the total number of immigrants, mainly from the region, just exceeded 10 million, indicating huge demographic challenges.

Hungary has not been the worst off among these countries. From the late 1980s till the early 2000s Hungary's relative richness in contrast to other Eastern neighbors increased the country's attractiveness for prospective migrants living in even deeper crises, like in Romania or the former Soviet Union. In this context, due to strong ethnic-historical links, Romania became a major source of migrants to Hungary during and after the collapse of state socialism, followed by other neighboring areas inhabited by people of Hungarian origin (Serbia and Ukraine). According to the Hungarian microcensus in 2016, among the foreign-born population aged 25–64 almost two-thirds speak Hungarian only, which shows that Hungary has attracted mainly immigrants who already had a linguistic link (Melegh and Papp 2018). Immigration from China and Vietnam has been continuous since the late 1980s, and in the early 1990s there was a larger inflow from China. The number of immigrants exceeded 14,000 in the case of China and came close to 5,000 in the case of Vietnam. These immigrants had various motives, including higher education, but the majority sought self-employment and formed an isolated ethnic niche within Hungary (Nyíri 2010; Várhalmi 2017).

Based on United Nations statistics, since the early 2000s, a growing emigration stock is visible as related to Hungary and the emigrant stock by country of birth increased by 52 percent until 2017, when in the whole period after 1990 it was altogether 65 percent (UN 2017). According to the estimates of the SEEMIG project, utilizing UN migration matrices based on censuses and the stock data on country of birth, Hungary had an increasingly negative balance of migration since 2010, losing some 10,000 individuals per year, as opposed to periods of positive migration balances in the mid-2000s (Földházi et al. 2014, 36). This rise of emigration and parallel economic restructuring also led to a greater dependency on remittances that can be observed in other former socialist countries (Böröcz 2014). The diversification in the destinations of the migration of Hungarian speakers from neighboring countries (going to other European countries) has led to the situation in which the main immigrant groups do not counterbalance emigration in numbers and also do not match the "lost population" in composition. Since 2011 the number of Hungarian emigrants within the EU went up, and they now approach levels estimated to be between 300,000 and 400,000 (Eurostat 2017). According to the United Nations, the figure is even higher, with the total number of Hungarian citizens living abroad estimated to be 595,000 in 2015. If we compare the educational and employment levels of the emigrants and immigrants, then we can see that the qualifications of immigrants born in China, Romania, and Vietnam match the levels of the emigrants, whereas other migratory links do not provide such "remedies" (Melegh and Sárosi 2015; Melegh and Papp 2018). Thus, there is an "emptying" process whereby unequal exchanges in population both in numerical terms and with regard to the educational level have an unfavorable impact on Hungary and the surrounding region.

Since the 1960s, fertility in Hungary has followed a decreasing or stagnating trend like in other developed countries, but it started from a much lower level as compared to European and East European averages. In certain periods it showed unexpected trends (a very quick decline in the 1960s, some growth in the 1970s, and then a quick decline around the regime change) (UN 2015a). Nevertheless, Hungary has lingered around or below a low level of 1.5 children per female of child-bearing age for a long period of time, which has had a huge impact on aging and age composition. Fertility has staggered back from very low levels since 2010, but this has no significant impact on the total number of births as the more numerous cohorts of women in their fertile period (often termed descendants of the so-called Ratkó era in the early 1950s when abortion was banned) have already gotten much older. This is a crucial factor for the demographic composition of the country and may prove to be very important in terms of maintaining various systems of social protection.

Mortality has been seriously gendered, showing different tendencies over the long run in terms of average life expectancy at birth. The country started to increase its global advantage in terms of male and also female mortality in the 1950s and early 1960s (mainly due to the decrease of infant mortality and the control of infectious diseases) – but kept the negative lag with regard to European levels – while later adult male mortality started stagnating and diverted from global trends (UN 2015a). It caught up with improving global trends only in the early 1990s. Female mortality has followed European patterns till the mid-1970s, then stagnated and it was in the mid-1990s when it started to follow global and European trends again, up until the present day mainly due to a delayed "cardiovascular revolution" without improving relative positions in the region (Kovács 2018; Meslé and Vallin 2017). It seems that in the last four years there has been a pause in this improvement, entering a new phase of stagnation (showing thus somewhat similar tendencies like neighboring Romania) and increasing the relative distance from European

Union averages (Kovács 2018). Overall, we can say that the decrease of mortality does not compensate for the loss of the population since the early 1980s, and even more importantly the data highlights the impact of increasing social inequalities on individuals' health status (Meslé 2004; Kovács and Bálint 2014; Kovács and Tóth 2015).

Hungary faces serious demographic challenges, and structural changes have not been favorable for a positive narrative. Instead, they have pointed toward developmental frustrations within a system of Eurocentric migratory linkages. The consequence of this move toward unequal exchange with Western countries (capital enters and labor moves in the other direction; loss of labor and skills; an increasing mismatch between labor demand and labor supply; loss of social and tax payments; and especially the overall process of aging) seems especially serious when we analyze Hungary's case from the point of view of the nation-state and its social welfare system. According to SEEMIG population projections and forecasts, the shift to an emigration pattern based on the current demographic trend may lead to an extra loss of population of over one million people by 2060, and it would produce extremely unfavorable age pyramids (Földházi et al. 2014). Actually, we can argue that there is a threat that most countries in East Central Europe would not be able to avoid huge tensions in their social welfare systems, caused by demographic and migratory processes. This can be a key factor in explaining why some of them, and most importantly Hungary, are so prone, at least on the level of public opinion, to fears of a population exchange, which can be manipulated by political elites. In the following, we will look at what population and migration policies have been institutionalized in Hungary and what discourses have been in operation after 2010 in the light of the above-described demographic challenges, historical migratory links, and related unequal exchanges.

POPULATION POLICIES AND INSTITUTIONALIZED DEMOGRAPHIC NATIONALISM

In order to understand the development of population policy measures and institutions, we need to go back to at least the 1960s when the Hungarian state socialist system introduced a rather developed set of social and population policy measures to counterbalance the rising costs of bringing up children (for the literature on this development, see Tárkányi 1998; Melegh 2006; Szikra 2010 and 2014; Kristó 2015). Thus, among other policies during the 1960s, family allowances were increased and made universal, and a paid one-year – and later (from 1973) a three-year – maternity leave was introduced, providing a fixed monthly allowance for mothers. In addition, families having or planning to have children also were given extra public housing privileges in a rather imbalanced housing market. Since the early 1960s, these policies and the lack of "success" of pronatalist measures were accompanied by the anxieties of populist writers, who repeatedly raised the threat of the "death of the nation," providing a major discursive heritage for later contemporaries (Heller et al. 1990; Melegh 2006, 82–88).

In the 1980s, with the introduction of a special policy to help working mothers, the country began to institutionalize inequalities and develop a new type of pronatalism supporting "higher-quality" parents (i.e., better-educated and better-paid) as opposed to "less educated" parents (Melegh 2006, 86–88). Once Hungary opened its borders and economy, it was caught between rising consumerism and increasing economic difficulties, yet it continued on a path toward selective pronatalism, which became more systematic under the second and third Orbán governments. This path followed many twists and turns. First, there was a major shift in order to reduce budget spending and take away support from higher-income families. Thus, the universal system of family allowance collapsed, along with a special policy supporting higher-income earning mothers under the socialist government and its finance minister, Lajos Bokros. Bokros's reform package introduced an income threshold, limiting the total amount of support under the maternity leave package for working mothers, which led to a substantial fertility decrease. The first Orbán government reintroduced the universality in key aspects of the family support policy, thus reintegrating middle- and upper-class groups into the system of family-related welfare benefits. At the same time his administration started to "penalize" "undeserving" lower social groups if they, for instance, took their children out of the school system. After 2010, the new Orbán governments did not increase the value of the family allowance above the 2008 level. Meanwhile the governments started providing tax allowances for families with children, meaning that families who had taxable revenue as specified by the legal system received support. This preferential support also appeared in state-sponsored housing loans, which could be utilized by families with enough economic and social capital to participate in the real estate market. This combination of universality, middle-class preferences, and utilitarian elements not only remained in place after the first Orbán government, but some elements were further strengthened by subsequent governments. Very clearly, the second and third Orbán governments simply radicalized and extended the same logic with an ideological underpinning of national revitalization as exemplified by László Kövér's 2015 speech quoted in the introduction to this chapter.

In 2010, the new Orbán government faced dramatic economic difficulties, in particular hundreds of thousands of families who had mortgages or loans in foreign currencies and who were facing indebtedness spurred by high interest rates and the collapsing value of the Hungarian forint. This form of foreign currency housing loans for Hungarian citizens had emerged during a period of lax financial regulation and initially was believed to provide financial relief for families and generate extra demand within the economy. The first Orbán government had signaled its support for such loans, but it was the later socialist governments that fully supported this "opening" of credit to potential home owners. Controlling the impact of these loans was of paramount importance for the Orbán government because of its financial and economic consequences, as well as the impact on their population policies. After the 2008 economic crisis, the "middle class" was collapsing and the government wanted to be its "savior." However, after "saving" some of the groups from improperly regulated loans of commercial banks, the Orbán government reverted to its original ideas of promoting the "working" and "middle" classes and the housing market with substantial support coming from the budget. These measures included new types of housing support, for instance, the so-called "family housing support" (in Hungarian, CSOK) and then rapidly afterward the so-called National Housing Communities (in Hungarian, NOK). The family housing system, with all its (not minor) risks, aims to provide varying free or low-interest (subsidized) money for building new houses differentiated according to the number of children promised or living within the family. NOK is just a high-risk pool that provides financial resources beyond the banking system, but whether or not this can be efficient in any way is debatable (Kapitány 2016; Szikra 2018).

Major maneuvering has been also aimed to exclude the "undeserving" poorer groups from these measures in order to avoid higher fertility among them, steps that have implicit ethnopolitical and anti-Roma underpinnings (Szikra 2014, 492–95; 2018). At the same time, at least in the first phase of implementing these ideas, the government also tried to build in other conservative, "traditionalist" family policy goals, like more marriages, longer-lasting marriages, and stronger control over abortion, but social reactions and the wish to avoid a backlash in public opinion resulted in a retreat in some (but definitely not all) areas during the policymaking procedures and legislative steps (Szikra 2018, 236). These conservative intentions remained present in antiabortion campaigns and a massive funding allotted to conservative movements promoting a family model of three children, but only among "deserving" families (for example, the Association of Large Families and "Three Princes and Three Princesses" movement, in addition to various congresses on family life). It is also important to point out that some of the effects of these policies did not secure their original goals and that family support reached those social groups that were originally not targeted. A case in point is the family tax allowance, which not only changed during the Orbán governments but also became more inclusive toward groups without substantial income.

The class bias of the Orbán government is much clearer from the perspective of "penalizing" groups with lower socioeconomic status via changing social policy measures, pushing them into an almost compulsory public work system, and never adjusting the family allowance, while linking such benefits to a normative code of behavior (Szikra 2014 and 2018). Here, the central issue is not the complete exclusion of the lower-class groups from middle-class-oriented policy measures but the taking away or freezing of any non-work-related income, thus making the family life of the very poor unmanageable in most respects. This shows without a doubt the selective pronatalism of the Hungarian government and its aim to "discipline," "penalize," and selectively "reward" the national population body. Such biopolitical moves have been promoted instead of changing social relations around social policy target groups that would allow families to change their demographic behavior without the "disciplining" and "rewarding" measures of the government. Groups with higher educational levels (and with much better labor market opportunities) actually have higher fertility than those with secondary education (Kapitány and Spéder 2015). In this respect, the institutional system of population policies mirror the conservative, nationalistic, and repressive regimes between the two world wars, which also aimed at disciplining the nation in order to better perform in the global competition for various resources and territories. Although far more lenient than those systems were in practice (not in discourse), the logic is strikingly similar.

Interestingly, neither longevity nor reducing mortality have become targets of the Orbán government, despite banning smoking in public spaces or requiring everyday physical exercise in schools. The government refrained from major structural reforms of health care, especially after the failures of the previous socialist governments. Additional efforts were made, including the monopolization of tobacco sales into so-called "National Tobacco Shops" and promoting sport. However, these measures were not just health-oriented policies: they also served the business clientele of the Orbán government. Simultaneously, the health care system and the working conditions of health care workers deteriorated to crisis levels.

Overall, the established institutional framework has been rather stable and the process of demographic "decline" has not led to a change in some of the key institutional frameworks. The focus on fertility has remained. Family formation ideologies have become far more conservative with a special stress on anti-genderism (Kovács 2017) and "traditional" procreation. Kövér linked all these elements, castigating "the trumpeters of the culture of death, who say that there is no future, that [. . .] there is only today and that is where we should live."[5] This radicalization process has clear parallels with conservative-fascist discourses between the two world wars (Quine 1996; Bashford 2014). Look no further than Mussolini who said, "[n]ational demographic strength provides a subsidiary but fundamental evidence of nations' political as well as economic and civic strength" (Mussolini 1957, 364). This can be clearly related to the speech of Orbán in January 2017 at the so-called Lámfalussy conference:

> Europe is getting weaker [. . .] Hundreds of thousands live with us about whom we do not know what they are looking for. That nation or community, which is not able to reproduce itself, surrenders its right to exist. This problem cannot be solved [. . .] with tricks, migrants and settlement [. . .] from outside [. . .] as then that nation partially or totally gives up its national identity.[6]

Thus, the mental map underlying the institutional framework is that the decline in the global proportion of Europe's and Hungary's population means the loss of privileged positions and control capability. This is to be counterbalanced by strengthening demographic nationalisms in Europe, promoting local and desirable fertility, and opposing migration at least from the unprivileged areas.[7]

MIGRATION POLICIES AND INSTITUTIONALIZED DEMOGRAPHIC NATIONALISM

Hungary was a country where emigration was the key concern of politics between the late nineteenth century and the mid-twentieth century (Brunnbauer 2016, 145–207). During the socialist period, there was near total political silence over emigration and even immigration, and the subject was basically taboo (Tóth 1997). This can be also shown by the fact that the main journal in population studies, *Demográfia*, did not publish any study on international migration among its 339 articles between 1958 and 1968. This might well be an important factor in explaining the undeveloped discourse on migration over the long run and the exclusive focus on fertility.

For a long time after the regime change and the collapse of the Iron Curtain, Hungary did not have an overall document on migration policy and the integration of migrants. In 2007 a government draft was leaked, and rightwing opposition politicians panicked about a rumored one million Chinese immigrants arriving in Hungary (Melegh 2007). In 2013 the Orbán government produced an official "Migration Strategy" white paper in order to justify its programs financed by various migration-related funds of the European Union.[8] This paper focused only on immigration and mainly on those non-Hungarians coming from the so-called Third Countries (non-EU, neither Norway nor Switzerland), and very importantly, it concentrated on security issues and adaptation requirements regarding migrants. Thus, growing emigration was ignored, and policy elements such as the integration of immigrants were either very brief or contained promises of further governmental actions including an "Integration Strategy" that never has been completed.

As a set of institutional practices and norms, Hungarian migration policy can be understood as resting on four pillars (Melegh et al. 2017). The Hungarian state clearly endorses migratory and other links with Hungarian minorities living in neighboring countries. It is not alone in this approach, as many European states maintain preferential treatment to people "linked" to them (Joppke 2005). This preferential link can be ethnic and/or colonial and/or historical (for instance, previously emigrating groups and their offspring), and in migration policy we see an increase of such measures as many countries try to establish preferred "reservoirs" for their labor markets, which might face overall or relative shortages in the future (for examples of flexibility in national citizenship, see Sassen 2006). Most Eastern, Southern, and South Eastern European states follow somewhat similar lines, but it seems that the motivation behind such an approach in Hungary is a complex "nation-building" agenda transcending state borders. Hungary declares itself to be fully responsible for the legacy of "historic" Hungary in terms of ethnic composition and culture, and it has built up direct legal links with the "affiliated" groups living outside Hungary in a gradual process (see Gábor Egry's study in the present volume).

Before 2010, there were already various attempts concerning legally prescribed privileges like the so-called Status Law in 2001[9] and a failed referendum in December 2004 for establishing "double citizenship" for Hungarians living outside the country, which were severely attacked by the Socialist Party on grounds of defending the national labor market. These campaigns were important events that inadvertently strengthened anti-immigration attitudes well before Orbán came back to power in 2010. These political moves were based not only on "xenophobic" sentiments but also on using imagined East/West hierarchies, for example, saying that "Eastern" hordes were at the gates of Hungary, when actually preferential treatment was offered for those with ethnic-historic links to Hungary (Melegh and Hegyesi 2003).

In 2011, special legislation was passed with the aim of offering citizenship without residence in the country itself. Now the country offers full citizenship to all Hungarians who can claim an ancestor who lived on former Hungarian territories. The procedure has been made very expedient, and since its implementation the government has issued more than one million passports that have allowed these groups to access the labor market in Hungary as well as the Schengen Zone – which was not open for many of them under their original citizenship. Beyond the ethnic-historical nation-building process using transborder legal and citizenship linkages, Hungary offers its institutional support for the free movement of people within the EU and fully respects the

Schengen Agreement. The maintenance of a privileged zone of "Europeans" has been a clear governmental priority as it allows free movement and open labor market maneuvering of Hungarian citizens.

In contrast, for the last two decades Hungary has followed a rather harsh and unsupportive policy toward third-country nationals (non-EU members) of non-Hungarian origin. In this respect it basically followed the logic of EU legislation, which was implemented quickly during the EU accession negotiations. But by not establishing institutionalized integration policies and maintaining further discriminatory practices, this separation of certain pillars increased and has led to a segregated system of immigration. In this system strong conditions must be satisfied for settling down in the country and gaining citizenship. Importantly, the institutional support is incomparable with the one available for the above-mentioned privileged groups. Discrimination appears also in the integration of these groups in education (Feischmidt 2005) or in providing citizenship and/or longer-term residence for non-Hungarian third-country nationals (Kováts et al. 2011). Repeated empirical analyses on integration have shown that, in education and various institutionalized cultural encounters, the local population and teachers are basically trying to downplay the importance of cultural diversity, and especially the need for handling such complex social relationships. Foreignness is a handicap, and integration is the responsibility of the immigrant only.

Intriguingly and seemingly contradicting the ethnocentric and Eurocentric logic of the current government, a special process for immigration, the so-called "Residency Bond Program" was created in 2012. It provided easy residence and settlement in case of "national economic interest" for those persons who invest EUR 250,000 into a special personal treasury bond issued by the Government Debt Management Agency.[10] However, this is actually an exception to the rule as only very large sums of money can increase the "status" of third-country nationals. Importantly, this special privilege was attacked severely by opposition parties that raised the problems of security risks of this program (receiving mainly Chinese, post-Soviet, and Middle Eastern citizens) and the clear appearance of private interests (as the companies managing these bonds are registered offshore and linked to prominent figures of Fidesz). Such discourse in some ways reinforced the hegemonic anti-immigration block in public opinion.

In terms of discrimination the clearest institutional closure is in the case of refugees. With the EU accession in 2004, Hungary fully implemented the relevant EU regulations as an exercise in constrained compliance. Following the arrival of a large number of asylum seekers from Kosovo – because of the panic about "Roma" asylum seekers misusing the system – from 2013 onward (2,155 in 2012, 18,895 in 2013, and 42,775 in 2014),[11] Hungary experimented with various symbolic and legal changes in order to slow down or even stop entirely the incoming flow. A more dramatic change started in the winter of 2014 and 2015 when the number of asylum seekers, mainly from Middle Eastern countries, climbed exponentially, reaching 177,135 in 2015, out of whom, however, only a few remained In Hungary. In 2016 it went back to 29,435,[12] while in 2017 it was only 3,397.[13] The approval rate of the authorities was never high due to the disappearance of asylum seekers and restrictive policies, but in 2017 around 1,300 people were approved for provisional protection. This later move showed that the restrictions and the amazingly harsh language against the EU and the refugees were mostly for political purposes as the government was eventually satisfying the "quota" needs of the European Commission.

In a series of legislative acts parallel to the actual flows, the government changed the legal status of Serbia and various other countries to safe countries. Following the examples of Bulgaria, Spain, and the French port city of Calais, it built a border fence along the Hungarian–Serbian and later along the Hungarian–Croatian border, criminalized illegal border crossing attempts, introduced a "crisis situation" due to extreme migratory pressure, and restricted many of the basic rights of people who were seeking international protection. In addition, it commenced a (to a large extent symbolic) battle against the dominance of the EU that was pressing for "forced settlement" of immigrants, which culminated in an inconclusive national referendum in October 2016 and a failed attempt to change the constitution that same year. Later, the legislative acts were extended to block civic groups allegedly supporting immigration, including a requirement that any foreign funding over a relatively low threshold had to be declared as "support from abroad," in concert with numerous other administrative barriers for NGOs. In the run-up to the 2018 elections, the so-called "Stop Soros" law also was accepted by the parliament. This series of radical constraints increasingly was "explained" by the need to preserve Hungary's cultural homogeneity and its refusal to "mix."

Overall, even on an institutional level, Orbán and his government have been hugely dependent on a path of institutional heritage relying on the radicalization of demographic nationalism. The above-analyzed migration policy is extreme: open only toward the "kin" and "true Europeans," building walls to protect privileged European spaces, and seeking to guarantee the Hungarian nation a better standing in imagined geopolitical hierarchies. Showing the linkage between institutional and cognitive structures, the selection of the two privileged groups as opposed to everybody else is very much in line with the mental map of the wider population with its focus on a "stronger" and "more secure" Europe and Hungary.

Taken together with other population policies, we can see that the institutional inertia and policy developments show discrepancies with the demographic processes described above. Hungary is confronting massive demographic losses, especially with regard to migration and an ongoing brain drain – processes that are occurring despite the government's major demographic "revitalization" plans.[14] Beyond the mechanical fight against "population replacement," it has no rational contingency policies for higher levels of outmigration or for migration coming from non-European countries. The institutional framework for handling refugee flows replicated from the "Western" models was not integrated into the whole system of immigration and remained an "isolated" element, to be dismantled easily. Thus, the inherited as well as recreated institutional framework and the current discursive patterns disregard a multitude of policy options that might be able to handle the negative consequences of emigration. These could create more integrative immigration policies beyond the focus on ethnically and historically linked Hungarians and thus counterbalance unequal exchanges with richer Western European countries in social transfers. Finally, they could provide an institutional framework for poorer or marginalized groups to strengthen their labor market positions (beyond public work) and social integration in order to achieve not only better social frameworks but also higher demographic potentials.

POLITICAL CONTROL AND DISCURSIVE FIGHTS OVER HIERARCHIES

When reviewing the discursive and political structures in relationship to the above developments, we can see that Orbán's only "consistent" motive is to show domestically and internationally that the most important goal is to regain national pride and to discipline the post-socialist, post-liberal "political chaos." We can understand this perspective as a form of resistance-based identity in the system of perceived hierarchies globally and most importantly within Europe (as described by Manuel Castells). By constructing such an identity (changing the terms of hierarchies), the marginalized actors (or those who perceive themselves as such) can resist the system that is absorbing them (Castells 2006, 30; Melegh 2006).

The Orbán regime portrays itself as the defender of Hungary's collective national interests as framed by nationalist ideologies in various fields: reducing foreign currency debt, selective and highly materialized pronatalism for "stable" parts of the society, recalling emigrants, penalizing emigrating students, building fences against refugees who "threaten" local culture, and so on. The promise is that Hungarian society can remove itself from global and European dependencies if its citizens follow the government's attack on "liberal taboos" that hinder its desired policies. The main targets of these attacks are "liberal" civic groups that allegedly maintain and serve "foreign interests" and promote values such as human rights. These invectives are embedded in a national emancipation discourse against global and European hierarchies, which has been able to achieve discursive hegemony through siphoning the idea of liberation from individual onto collective levels. This maneuvering can be seen clearly in the following excerpt of Orbán's talk given at the Hungarian Diaspora Council:

> The principal danger we can see lies in the debate between globalists and nations. Europe has decided to set out on a post-Christian and post-national era. In other words, it has envisaged a new era in which it will replace policy built on Christian traditions and national consciousness with something different. For want of a better term, we call it policy for a "United States of Europe." Europe is working to replace an alliance of nations with a federation of states: a United States of Europe, similar to the USA – with all its accompanying spiritual and cultural consequences. This is the only logical explanation for millions of people being transported to Europe from other cultures – as there must be some sort of explanation for why this is happening now. [. . .] I think the political forces intent on creating a United States of Europe have been deliberately transporting to Europe – and will continue to transport – multitudes of people from other cultures, who in many cases truly deserve our pity and compassion.[15]

Protecting the nation against "migrants" is presented here not as a direct attack on the human rights of people escaping from war zones but as a "just" fight against "transporters" who want to build a United States of Europe with these tools. This is a very peculiar story, but it is very important because it shows that, on a discursive level, Orbán's focus is multiple, shifting the view from individuals and victims to the nation – which is to be defended against the victims as they are tools in the hands of a globalist conspiracy.

It is vital to see that the overall discursive logic is not just local but also pan-European and aims at building a "new" future of the radical right in Europe while rearranging intra-European hierarchies. According to him, Europe should be strengthened and should restore its historical privileges (lost in terms of economic and population weight) with the help of Central Europe as a faithful guardian of fundamental values against a weakened West. In this argument, he recycles parts of the intellectual heritage of the so-called Central Europe debate taking place in the 1980s, discussing the special role of this region within European history (Kundera 1984).

On a discursive level Orbán clearly fights for protecting the privileges of East Central European emigrant workers as opposed to "illegals" and "outsiders." This can be clearly exemplified by the exchange of Britain and the Orbán-led Visegrád countries in the midst of a global refugee crisis in early January 2016. It is notable how such East-West exchanges happen among conservative and/or radical nationalists and in what ways the Hungarian government wants to export its ideas for the sake of a new Europe. According to the *Guardian*, the then British prime minister David Cameron was told by his Hungarian counterpart, Viktor Orbán, not to treat Hungarians in the United Kingdom as migrants.

> We would like to make it quite clear that we are not migrants into the UK. But we are the citizens of a state that belongs to the European Union who can take jobs anywhere freely within the European Union. [. . .] We do not want to go to the UK and take something from them. We do not want to be parasites. We want to work there, and I think that Hungarians are working well. They should get respect and they should not suffer discrimination.[16]

So we can learn from this exchange that migrants are parasites. Hungarians (and other EU members) are not migrants and they work, while others want to take something away from the "locals." Hungary is thus against discrimination in case other "Europeans" are hurt. Only East Europeans should be entitled to take the labor side of the capital-labor relationship in Europe. In a paradoxical way the "migrants" become common enemies within the "European family," just the discursive angles and thus even the groups themselves can be different in the above hierarchical exchanges. The fight for the protection of the labor rights of Hungarian "migrants" across Europe has further increased after Brexit as more and more states (among them, Germany and Austria) have started "reforming" their welfare system in order to avoid the provision of welfare support for immigrant workers.

Orbán also attacks intra-European and interregional prestige hierarchies in other ways. He argues that Hungarian demographic and migration policies should not be formulated by the interest of the great powers like Germany and its large-scale capital. Orbán thus sought to consolidate Hungary's otherwise very weak EU positions by challenging EU discourses and the prevalent Western European narrative about the position of "internal Orientals" (i.e., "East Europeans") as passive and dependent objects of Western policymaking.[17] This is foregrounded by calls to rescue "Christian Europe" against "terrorists," "economic migrants," "Muslims," and even "barbaric hordes."

CONCLUSION

The history of the population and migration policy and the radicalization of demographic nationalism can be understood as a dynamic that has evolved during the era of globalization out of an interplay between demographic challenges (most importantly population loss, larger-scale emigration, the consequent change of population composition, and the need to have extra labor force), institutional heritages of pronatalist measures, and political discourses aiming at "national revitalization." This complex relationship brims with tensions and contradictions. The way Hungary has been integrated into migratory linkages not only shows how the global economy has developed unequally but also sets up what experiences and mental maps are created over the long term, meaning that a dramatically Eurocentric mental map and the internal fight for status within the EU is built into its structures. This is why Hungary is not alone in showing signs of radicalization since the other Visegrád countries share similar structural positions. The structural background, institutional path dependencies, and mental maps show congruencies, and here we can observe a "moment of hegemony" and a "new historical-political block" as described by Gramsci among others (Gramsci in Forgacs 2000, 194). Thus this new authoritarian historical-political block is not an accident, but its structures and political processes remain fragile, subject to contradictions, and are exceedingly difficult to manage.

Overall, based on a selective nationalist institutional heritage, Orbán developed a set of ideas to make Hungary far more competitive and to free it from certain "dependencies." This he termed as a "Hungarian race car" (full national sovereignty and centralized control) or a "speed boat" maneuvering among huge ships. In theory, this could be an ideological formulation of some kind of a nationalist developmental state as seen in postwar Japan, South Korea, or even Brazil during the 1970s and 1980s. Such a model was popular due to ideological inclinations and a preference for political control and a "hidden" reallocation of resources over development of more complex policy measures for understanding and managing complex global dependencies and inequalities (Evans 1969). As we noted above, in Hungary demographic and migratory structural problems were not confronted head on, and they were mainly put to use to buffer an institutional heritage of selective pronatalism. Discursive campaigns were favored over balanced policies formulated by cooperation among the state, NGOs, and academia, whereby a clear policy could be developed for solving some of the key social concerns of the decline of stable and meaningful employment instead of its artificial improvement in numbers.

Taken together, this becomes a trap of semi-peripheral demographic nationalism that fights mainly on symbolic levels, the inefficiency of which is covered by a conscious demographic and/or biopolitical hysteria and panic. This hysteria can be understood as claiming to "defend" the population against various "enemies" as set by relevant historically developed mental maps. These maps buttress symbolic references to the fight over dependencies and challenges without actually formulating substantial policies to handle them or at least attenuate some of the occurring negative consequences. Moreover, the discourse functions merely to symbolically point at some of the problems but actually legitimizes inaction and passivity. This implies a clear right-wing radicalization of the inherited patterns of demographic nationalism, with certain elements of social processes (like ethnic composition) being turned into direct targets of violent state intervention. This radicalized framework reminds us of the population discourse of "racial suicide" from the interwar period. It is a sad irony of history that all this happens in a region that suffered the most because of those policies and being seen as inferior to the Great Powers. Now they themselves have become pioneers of a dubious experiment in ethnocentric authoritarianism, covered with the slogan of "defending Europe."

NOTES

1. Orbán (2017a).
2. Info Rádió (2015).
3. Orbán (2018).
4. In order to see how mental maps can influence demographic behavior, see the project of Developmental Idealism Studies initiated by Arland Thornton (https://developmentalidealism.org/, accessed June 25, 2019). See also Thornton (2005).
5. Info Rádió (2015).
6. Orbán (2017b).
7. For the loss of global weight and EU building up strategies to counterbalance, see Böröcz (2009).
8. Governmental Decree 1698/2013 (X.4).
9. Act of XII/2001.
10. Introduced by Act CCXX of 2012 and terminated in 2018.
11. *Eurostat.* "Population on January 1 by Age Group, Sex, and Citizenship [migr_pop1ctz]." Last update September 17, 2015.
12. *Eurostat.* "Asylum and First Time Asylum Applicants by Citizenship, Age and Sex, Monthly Data (rounded) [migr_asyappctzm]." Last update: March 13, 2017.
13. The figure of the Immigration and Naturalization Office (2018). *Menedékjogi kérelmek* (2017).
14. University students who receive state support and leave for work on abroad after completing their studies have been targeted by a measure that makes three years of participation in the Hungarian labor market compulsory. If they emigrate immediately after completing their studies, they will face a stiff bill to reimburse the state for their studies.
15. Orbán (2017c).
16. *The Guardian* (2016).
17. See the concept of the internal Orient in the classic book of Todorova (1997).

BIBLIOGRAPHY

Bashford, Alison. 2014. *Global Population: History, Geopolitics, and Life on Earth.* Columbia Studies in International and Global History. New York: Columbia University Press.

Bernát, Anikó, Endre Sik, Bori Simonovits, and Blanka Szeitl. 2015. *Attitudes toward Refugees, Asylum Seekers and Migrants*. Budapest: TÁRKI. http://www.tarki.hu/ hu/news/2015/kitekint/20151203_refugee.pdf, accessed June 25, 2019.

Blaskó, Zsuzsa, and Irén Gödri. 2014. "Kivándorlás Magyarországról: szelekció és célország-választás az „új migránsok" körében." *Demográfia* 57/4, 271–307.

Böröcz, József. 2009. *The European Union and Global Social Change: A Critical Geopolitical Economic Analysis*. London: Routledge.

———. 2014. "Regimes of Remittance Dependency: Global Structures and Trajectories of the Former Soviet 'Bloc.'" *Demográfia* [English Edition] 57 (5): 5–37.

Brunnbauer, Ulf. 2016. *Globalizing Southeastern Europe. Emigrants, America, and the State since the Late Nineteenth Century*. London: Lexington Books.

Caporali, Arianna, and Antonio Golini. 2018. "Births and Fertility in Interwar Italy: Trends, Images, Policies and Perceptions." https://cdn.uclouvain.be/public/Exp orts%20reddot/demo/documents/Caporali.pdf, accessed June 25, 2019.

Castells, Manueal 2006. *Az identitás hatalma – Az információ kora – Gazdaság, társadalom és kultúra – II. kötet*. Gondolat Kiadó, Budapest

Chase-Dunn, Christopher, Yukio Kawano, and Benjamin D. Brewer. 2000. "Trade Globalization Since 1795: Waves of Integration in the World-system." *American Sociological Review* 65 (1): 77–95.

Eurostat. 2017. "Population on January 1 by Age Group, Sex, and Citizenship [migr_ pop1ctz]." Last update: September 17, 2015.

Evans, Peter B. 1989. "Predatory, Developmental, and Other Apparatuses: A Comparative Political Economy Perspective on the Third World State." *Sociological Forum*. Special Issue: Comparative National Development: Theory and Facts for the 1990s. 4 (4): 561–87.

Fábián, Zoltán, and Endre Sik. 1996. "Előítéletesség és tekintélyelvűség." In *Társadalmi riport*, edited by Rudolf Andorka, Tamás Kolosi, and György Vukovich, 381–413. Budapest: TÁRKI, Századvég.

Fassmann, Heinz, Elisabeth Musil, Ramon Bauer, Attila Melegh, and Kathrin Gruber. 2014. "Longer-Term Demographic Dynamics in South-East Europe: Convergent, Divergent and Delayed Development Paths." *Central and Eastern European Migration Review* 3 (2): 150–72.

Feischmidt, Margit, and Pál Nyíri. 2005. *Nem kívánt gyerekek? Külföldi gyerekek magyar iskolákban (Immigrant Children in Hungarian Schools)*. Budapest: Hungarian Academy of Sciences. Institute of Minority Studies.

Földházi, Erzsébet, Branislav Bleha, Branislav Šprocha, and Boris Vaňo. 2014. "Population Projections for Hungary and Slovakia at National, Regional, and Local Levels." http://www.seemig.eu/downloads/outputs/SEEMIGPopulationProjection sHUSK.pdf, accessed June 25, 2019.

Forgacs, David, ed. 2000. *The Gramsci Reader. Selected Writings 1916–1935*. New York: New York University Press.

Heller, Mária, Dénes Némedi, and Ágnes Rényi. 1990. *Népesedési viták Magyarországon 1960–1986*." Budapest: KSH Népességtudományi Kutató Intézetének kutatási jelentései 37: 13–125.

Info Rádió. 2015. "Interview with László Kövér." http://indavideo.hu/video/Info Radio_-_Arena_-_Kover_Laszlo_-_1resz_1, accessed June 25, 2019.

Joppke, Christian. 2005. *Selecting by Origin: Ethnic Migration in the Liberal State.* Cambridge, MA: Harvard University Press.

Kapitány, Balázs. 2016. "Lakáshelyzet és gyermekvállalás: fontos, de nem a legfontosabb: A csok termékenységi hatásairól." *Korfa – Népesedési Hírlevél* 16 (1): 1–4.

Kapitány, Balázs, and Zsolt Spéder. 2015. "Gyermekvállalás." In *Demográfiai Portré*, edited by Judit Monostori, Péter Őri, and Zsolt Spéder, 41–56. Budapest: KSH NKI.

Kovács, Eszter. 2017. "The Emergence of Powerful Anti-Gender Movements in Europe and the Crisis of Liberal Democracy." In *Gender and Far Right Politics in Europe*, edited by Köttig, Bitzan, and Pető, 175–89. New York: Palgrave Macmillan.

Kovács, Katalin. 2018. "Halandóság." In *Demográfiai Portré 2018.* By Judit Monostori, Péter Őri and Zsolt Spéder. Budapest: KSH Népességtudományi Kutató Intézet.

Kovács, Katalin, and Bálint Lajos. 2014. "Education, Income, Material Deprivation and Mortality in Hungary between 2001–2008." *Demográfia* [English Edition] 57 (5): 73–89.

Kovács, Katalin, and Gergely Tóth. 2015. "Egészségi állapot." In *Demográfiai Portré*, edited by Judit Monostori, Péter Őri, and Zsolt Spéder, 95–114. Budapest: KSH NKI.

Kováts, András, ed. 2011. *"Magyarrá válni": bevándorlók honosítási és integrációs stratégiái.* Budapest: MTA Etnikai-nemzeti Kisebbségkutató Intézet.

Kristó, Katalin. 2015. "Tervek és a valóság – A pénzbeli családtámogatási ellátások vizsgálata a kormányprogramok tükrében." PhD Dissertation, Nemzeti Közszolgálati Egyetem. http://akk.uni-nke.hu/uploads/media_items/kristo-katalin-disszert acio-tervezet.original.pdf, accessed June 25, 2019.

KSH Stadat. 2018. Népesség és népmozgalom. http://www.ksh.hu/docs/hun/xstadat/ xstadat_eves/i_wnvn003.html, accessed June 25, 2019.

Kundera, Milan. 1984. "The Tragedy of Central Europe." *The New York Review of Books*, April 26.

Melegh Attila. 2011. "Globalizáció és migráció Magyarországon." *Educatio* 2: 206–19.

———. 2013. "Net Migration and Historical Development in Southeastern Europe since 1950." *Hungarian Historical Review* 1 (3–4): 144–82.

———. 2017. "Európa a globális migrációban 1990–2015 között az ENSZ és a Világbank statisztikái tükrében." *Demográfia* 17 (1). http://demografia.hu/kiad vanyokonline/index.php/korfa/issue/view/549, accessed June 25, 2019.

Melegh, Attila, and Adrienn Hegyesi. 2003. "'Immár nem mi vagyunk a szegény rokon a nemzetközi világban.' A státustörvény és az Orbán-Nastase-egyezmény vitájának sajtóbeli reprezentációja és diskurzív rendje." In *Kampánykommunikáció*, edited by Erika Sárközy and Nóra Schleicher, 135–71. Budapest: Akadémiai.

Melegh, Attila, Anna Vancsó, Dorottya Mendly, Márton Hunyadi, and Vivien Vadasi. 2017. "Hungary and Migration." In *The European Migration System and Global Justice: A First Appraisal*, edited by Enrico Fassi and Sonia Lucarelli, 125–34. Bologna: AMSActa, University of Bologna Institutional Repository. http://doi. org/10.6092/unibo/amsacta/56, accessed June 25, 2019.

Melegh, Attila, and Annamária Sárosi. 2015. "Magyarország bekapcsolódása a migrációs folyamatokba: történeti-strukturális megközelítés." *Demográfia* 58 (4): 223–67.

Melegh, Attila, and Attila Z. Papp. 2018. *Historical Links and Integration of Migrants from Neighbouring Countries. Manuscript for Population Europe.*

Meslé, France. 2004. "Mortality in Central and Eastern Europe: Long-term Trends and Recent Upturns." *Demographic Research*, Special Issue 2: 45–70.

Meslé, France, and Jacques Vallin. 2017. "The End of East-West Divergence in European Life Expectancies? An Introduction to the Special Issue." *European Journal of Population* 33 (5): 615–27.

MTA TK Kisebbségkutató Intézet. 2017. *A nemzeti integráció magyarországi elfogadottságának és támogatottságának vizsgálata.* Kutatási beszámoló.

Mussolini, Benito. 1957. "Discorso dell'Ascensione." In *Opera Omnia di Benito Mussolini*, vol. XXII, edited by Edoardo Susmel and Duilio Susmel, 360–90. Firenze-Roma: La Fenice.

Nyíri, Pál. 2010: "Kínai migránsok Magyarországon: mai tudásunk és aktuális kérdések." In Változó migráció – Változó környezet, edited by Ágnes Hárs and Judit Tóth, 147–72. Budapest: MTA Kisebbségkutató Intézet.

Orbán, Viktor. 2017a. "Prime Minister Viktor Orbán's speech on the 61st anniversary of the 1956 Revolution and Freedom Fight." http://www.kormany.hu/en/the-prime-minister/the-prime-minister-s-speeches/prime-minister-viktor-orban-s-speech-on-t he-61st-anniversary-of-the-1956-revolution-and-freedom-fight, accessed June 25, 2019.

———. 2017b. "Többpólusúvá kell tenni Európát." http://www.kormany.hu/hu/ a-miniszterelnok/hirek/miota-nincs-ellenzekben-az-mnb-latvanyos-a-gazdasagi -fejlodes, accessed June 25, 2019.

———. 2017c. "Prime Minister Viktor Orbán's Speech at the 7th Plenary Session of the Hungarian Diaspora Council." http://www.kormany.hu/en/the-prime-minister/t he-prime-minister-s-speeches/prime-minister-viktor-orban-s-speech-at-the-7th-ple nary-session-of-the-hungarian-diaspora-council, accessed June 25, 2019.

———. 2018. "Viktor Orbán's speech at the Visegrád Group conference 'The Future of Europe'." http://www.kormany.hu/en/the-prime-minister/the-prime-minister-s-speeches/viktor-orban-s-speech-at-the-visegrad-group-conference-the-future-of-eu rope, accessed June 25, 2019.

Quine, Maria Sophie. 1996. *Population Politics in Twentieth-Century Europe.* New York: Routledge.

Sanderson, Matthew R., and Jeffrey Kentor. 2008. "Foreign Direct Investment and International Migration: A Cross-National Analysis of Less-Developed Countries, 1985–2000." *International Sociology* 23 (4): 514–39.

Ságvári, Bence. 2017. "Looking behind the Culture of Fear: Lessons From an Attempt to Segment Hungarian's Attitudes on Migration." Lecture at the workshop: *Inequality, Demographic change and Political Reactions in South Eastern Europe from a Global and Historical Perspective.* Karl Polanyi Research Center of Global Social Studies at CUB, Hungary, June 16, 2017.

Sassen, Saskia. 2006 [1988]. "Foreign Investment: A Neglected Variable." In *The Migration Reader: Exploring Politics and Policies*, edited by Anthony M. Messina and Gallya Lahav, 596–608. London: Lynne Rienner Publishers.

———. 2006. *Territory-Authority-Rights. From Medieval to Global Assemblages.* Princeton, NJ: Princeton University Press.

Szikra, Dorottya. 2010. "Családtámogatási rendszerek Európában történeti perspektívában." In *Családpolitikák változóban*, edited by Ágnes Simonyi, 9–19. Budapest: Szociálpolitikai és Munkaügyi Intézet.

———. 2014. "Democracy and Welfare in Hard Times. The Social Policy of the Orbán Government in Hungary since 2010." *Journal of European Social Policy* 24 (5): 486–500.

———. 2018. "Ideológia vagy pragmatizmus? Családpolitika az orbáni illiberális demokráciában." In *Lépték és irónia: Szociológiai kalandozások*, edited by András Bozóki and Katalin Füzér, 219–41. Budapest: L'Harmattan; MTA Társadalomtudományi Kutatóközpont.

Tárkányi, Ákos. 1998. "Európai családpolitikák: a magyar családpolitika története." *Demográfia* 2–3.

The Guardian. 2016. "Don't Treat us as Migrants, Hungarian PM Tells Cameron." http://www.theguardian.com/politics/blog/live/2016/jan/07/osborne-interest-rates-speech-cameron-eu-for-an-interest-rate-rise-politics-live, accessed June 25, 2019.

Thornton, Arland. 2005. *Reading History Sideways: The Fallacy and Enduring Impact of the Developmental Paradigm on Family Life.* Chicago: University of Chicago Press.

Todorova, Maria. 1997. *Imagining the Balkans.* Oxford: Oxford University Press.

Tóth, Pál Péter. 1997. *Haza csak egy van? Menekülők, bevándorlók, új állampolgárok Magyarországon (1988–1994).* Budapest: Püski Könyvkiadó.

United Nations, Department of Economic and Social Affairs. 2017. *Trends in International Migrant Stock: Migrants by Destination and Origin* (United Nations database, POP/DB/MIG/Stock/Rev.2017).

United Nations, Department of Economic and Social Affairs, Population Division. 2015. *World Population Prospects: The 2015 Revision*, DVD Edition.

Várhalmi, Zoltán. 2017. "Migráns gazdasági klaszterek működésének jellemzői" című doktori disszertációjának védése. Doctoral dissertation. Budapest: ELTE.

Chapter 9

Votes, Ideology, and Self-Enrichment

The Campaign of Renationalization after 2010

Péter Mihályi

In 1990 Hungary became a parliamentary democracy in which private property was enshrined in the constitution and strong new institutions were designed to meet the requirements of a planned European Union accession. Subsequently, the country became a pioneer in the post-communist transformation process for roughly a decade. The second decade was much less spectacular and, by and large, all structural reforms (in public administration, defense, health care, pensions, agriculture, and so on) ended in 1998 when Viktor Orbán became prime minister for the first time. The privatization process continued but slowed down, and the many state-owned enterprises (SOEs) that remained were used by incumbent governments for short-term political gains. Two of these bad habits became visible even to the general public. First, the board seats of these companies were "donated" to loyal party figures, and when parliamentary elections brought a new party into a government position, the entire management was replaced. Second, larger state-owned or partially state-owned firms were used as a *caisse noire* of the government. The fantasy of subsequent governments proved to be unlimited: the largest SOEs were instructed to buy government bonds or pay for certain public outlays instead of the government; state-owned firms were directly instructed to buy inputs from government-loyal private firms and/or support government-loyal media outlets with paid advertising and so on.

Despite these troubling patterns, the first two decades still were reasonably successful in many dimensions. Hungary joined the community of Western-type political democracies (NATO, EU) and managed to diminish the per capita GDP gap vis-à-vis the most advanced OECD countries. Unemployment, inflation, and social inequalities remained subdued. The Hungarian model of privatization brought a large amount of privatization revenues in convertible currencies – in relative terms much more than anywhere else.[1]

Around the mid-1990s Hungarian policymakers presumed that selling virtually each and every "crown jewel" of the Hungarian economy to the "multis" was not merely a short-term financial necessity (to keep servicing the National Bank's convertible currency debt) but helped an imperative long-term policy goal: to integrate the Hungarian economy into the value chains of the largest European and U.S. multinational firms. In fact, this was thought to be the only conceivable way to put Hungary firmly on an export-led growth path – something that Hungarian policymakers had urged in vain for two decades prior to 1989. The expectation was that the majority of foreign strategic investors would come to Hungary with the aspiration to use it as a cheap production site for exports back home. And this is exactly what happened. In other post-communist countries, legislators understood this connection only five to ten years later. Compared to other OECD countries, Hungary became one of the most *liberalized* and *globalized* economies by 2010.

To the great surprise of the outside world, the spring election in 2010 brought a complete reversal in the liberalization process as well as Hungary's commitment to Western values, European integration, free markets, and privatization. Kornai (2015) called this rightly a sharp and unique U-turn. Nobody in Hungary then thought that soon another autocratic leader, the Pole Jarosław Kaczyński, would follow Orbán's steps in many dimensions, including a U-turn on privatization (Błaszczyk 2016).

In 2010–2011 a new constitution, the so-called Fundamental Law,[2] together with an unprecedented raft of new laws, was approved by the Hungarian parliament, all of which pointed toward more administrative centralization and the creation of an unlimited maneuvering space for the government. In retrospect, the surprise inside and outside of Hungary was not entirely justified. Those who had a good memory and could recall the various policy actions and public communications of the first Orbán government might have expected something like this. There was only one crucial difference between the policies of the two periods (1998–2002 and 2010–2018). In the first period Orbán and his Fidesz party did not have a supermajority of votes in parliament, and *therefore* Orbán was fully determined to use his newly acquired two-thirds majority in 2010 to the maximum possible extent. He was aware that a supermajority can be lost quickly after a few by-elections.

This chapter will present an overview of the most spectacular renationalization transactions after 2010[3] and will offer the author's opinion on the most likely drivers of the process. As the title already indicates, my assertion is that there is more than one explanation of why things happen in the way they happen. This is not a trivial statement. Inside Hungary, and among the country's foreign observers, there has been an ongoing debate since 2010 about the order of importance of these three factors. The order in the title reflects the author's persuasion, but I am aware and the readers of this book should also know that others prefer different orders.[4] There is an additional remark, which needs to be made at the outset. Since 2010 Viktor Orbán has been ruling his party and the country as a third-world autocratic ruler who is not subject to any institutional limitations. Therefore, throughout this chapter, his name, his party, and his government are used interchangeably. Every decision made by the country's parliament, its president, or its government are Orbán's personal decisions, even if they do not look that way at first sight.

THE BROADER PICTURE

The renationalization campaign was only one element of Orbán's one-person rule – and not the most important one.[5] As I already noted above, right after the 2010 election, he initiated a new constitution, which was adopted in a few months. This new Fundamental Law took away a lot of discretionary power and property from the municipalities (e.g., schools, in-patient health-care facilities, fire brigades, museums, and archives) and shifted them to the central government.[6] What matters most from the vantage point of the present chapter is the fact that even the concept of "private ownership" was removed from the constitution. Moreover, virtually all acts affecting the scope of state ownership were converted to cardinal laws requiring a two-thirds majority to be amended.

The constitutional two-thirds majority between 2010 and 2015[7] and after 2018 allowed Orbán to initiate a large-scale transformation of the entire domestic political institutional system that involved – *inter alia* – the restructuring of the territorial administration, the abolition of the remainders of self-government and the three major pillars of social security (pension, health, and unemployment benefits), the control and supervision of public education (primary and secondary schools), the curtailment of autonomies in higher education through the nomination of chancellors above rectors, and so on.[8]

The new strategy had an important foreign policy dimension, too. Much of the statements and acts of the prime minister carried anti-EU and anti-American sentiments, as well as revanchist allusions to the detriment of Hungary's neighbors (chiefly Romania but also Serbia and Ukraine). "Opening toward the East" was a newly invented slogan for this purpose. This meant a EUR 10–12 billion loan deal with Russia on the delivery of two 1,000 megawatt nuclear power electricity generating blocks, a EUR 2–3 billion loan deal with China for the modernization of the Budapest to Belgrade railway track, and unsuccessful government efforts to make trade deals with Central Asian republics, as well as in the Far and the Middle East. Among the 1,366 laws passed by parliament in 2011–2018, many were designed purposely to limit the free conduct of businesses. The political calculation was that it would take years until the EU could enforce the *acquis communautaire* on Hungarian legislators, and by the time this would happen, Hungarian public opinion would lose interest in the matter. And indeed, this tactic worked well for a while (Bugarič 2010). The tacit support of Washington was "bought," primarily with an unconditional support of the NATO alliance in foreign military campaigns (Afghanistan, Iraq, and Syria). But then, to the great surprise of Orbán's foreign policy team, Hungarian-American bilateral relations started to worsen, and the election of Donald Trump did not bring any change until May 2019.

OWNERSHIP CHANGES

Even before Orbán became prime minister in 2010, he did not hide his renationalization plans. As the leader of the opposition between 2002 and 2010, he systematically opposed any newly emerging privatization proposal of the government and regularly criticized the big privatization transactions from the previous two decades. With the benefit of hindsight, it is clear that this criticism was politically effective only because the ruling Socialist Party had displayed a half-hearted attitude toward privatization, too. In many cases, when the future of entire industries was discussed in parliament, the anti-market creed of Fidesz and the Socialist Party were surprisingly close to each other. The mutual understanding and cooperation were most noticeable in the energy and the banking sectors.

For many reasons, it is difficult to get a grip on the true size of the ongoing Hungarian renationalization campaign. There is a deliberate policy of keeping as much information hidden as possible. The transactions on the government's side have been carried out by different institutions, such as the Hungarian National Asset Management, Inc. (MNV Zrt.), the legal successor of the former privatization agency,[9] the Prime Minister's Office, the national bank, branch ministries, existing state-owned corporations, and so on. This is, of course, on purpose. The government has been trying to withhold information from the public. Another major problem is the way the deals are structured. Often the initial purchase price for which the state buys the companies' equity is relatively small compared to the size of future payment obligations in the form of debt and restructuring costs. A good example is the renationalization of the Hungarian Foreign Trade Bank in 2014. The government paid only EUR 55 million for the shares, but the total costs that were absorbed later ran up to EUR 215 million.

In spite of these technical hitches, Table 9.1 below gives a clear enough indication of both the total volumes and the sectoral proportions. The method

Table 9.1   The Size and Scope of the Most Important Renationalization Transactions of the Second and Third Orbán Government, 2010–2019

	Number of companies affected	Total value of (re) nationalization transactions of shares, immoveable property and tangible assets (HUF Bn)*	Percentage
Equity purchase from which			
- energy companies	16	1319	43
- financial institutions**	140	371	12
- other utilities	4	34	1
- telecommunication, IT, transportation	8	387	13
- manufacturing	4	26	1
- miscellaneous***	27	146	5
Total equity	199	2,282	75
Real estate (agricultural land, housing, office buildings)****	n.a.	353	12
Agricultural land	n.a.	91	3
Tangible assets (e.g. works of arts)	n.a.	18	1
Total value of equity obtained free of charge after the confiscation of pension fund assets	n.a.	297	10
Total	n.a.	3,042	100

Notes: * All known transactions executed by public authorities. ** Of which 128 are co-operative banks. *** Of which 19 were created in the framework of Public-Private-Partnership projects. **** Including 28,000–30,000 houses and/or apartments purchased from defaulted foreign exchange borrowers. This table does not cover the purchases of local governments due to the lack of comprehensive data collection. Exchange rate (as of end of 2018): HUF 322 = EUR 1.
Source: Author's compilation with the collaboration of Professor Éva Voszka from different official sources and daily newspapers.

used here to compile the total figures from individually reported transactions was tailored to be as close as possible to the statistical rules according to which the privatization figures have been compiled since 1989 – both in Hungary and internationally.

For the Hungarian general public, the total amount of money spent on renationalization, HUF 3,042 billion (≈ EUR 9.5 billion) as reported above is a colossal number. The combined privatization revenue for the 1990–2010 period – after the conversion of all types of revenues into euros – amounted to EUR 13.1 billion. In other words, 72 percent of the money "earned" in privatization was already "paid back." On the other hand, it is important to see that in a macroeconomic national accounting framework, both the sales and the repurchase numbers were minor. If the HUF 3,042 billion figure from Table 9.1 is compared to the combined annual GDP of Hungary between

2010 and 2019, this amounts to less than 1 percent of the cumulative GDP. If the HUF 3,042 billion is compared to the annual budgetary outlays of a recent year, the proportion is still small (about two percent), since the expenditure side of the Hungarian public sector amounts to roughly 50 percent of GDP.

Another dimension in which it is inspiring to compare the costs of rationalization is the total value of assets acquired by the Orbán government through the renationalization of the country's private pension funds that came as a total surprise even for well-informed economic analysts. This plan was made public a few months *after* the 2010 general election. At year-end, the government scrapped the mandatory private pension fund pillar and seized the savings amassed by nearly three million pension fund members during the previous 13 years.[10] The savings channeled back to the government coffers from the private pension funds equaled roughly HUF 3,000 billion, or 10 percent of GDP in 2010. In other words, this single move was a grab of similar size as the entire renationalization process described above.

THREE EXAMPLES FROM THE ENERGY SECTOR

As Table 9.1 revealed, the most affected segment of the economy was the energy sector (49 percent). Right after the 2010 election, Orbán used the country's half-privatized, half-state-owned electricity industry to pay for certain renationalization deals and absorb the losses arising from mandatory price cuts.[11] Instead of the state asset management company, which is MVM's owner, MVM was instructed to purchase natural gas trading and storage companies from their previous German strategic owner (E.ON). MVM also was "asked" to be involved in telecommunication and construction businesses. One of the reasons why this solution was chosen was to have the possibility to retain information from the public. The fact that these new burdens quickly undermined MVM's own financial viability and the capability to focus on its core activity did not bother the prime minister or the state apparatus. In the public discourse, they justified every measure at the macroeconomic level very much in the same way as the communist planners did for decades: the state must occupy the "commanding heights" of the economy.[12]

Another important reversal went through in the natural gas distribution sector. Already in early 2010 – i.e., before the national elections – the then-ruling Socialist cabinet signed a deal with E.ON and acquired an option to buy back the gas storage companies and the gas trading company that held the Russian-Hungarian long-term gas delivery contract in its portfolio. As it soon turned out, this step was done in agreement with Orbán, who already wanted to buy back these companies during his first premiership in 1998.[13]

In the same fashion, but in different roles, the two Hungarian sides of the political spectrum (the Socialists and Fidesz) agreed behind the scenes to buy back 22 percent of the shares of the Hungarian oil company, MOL, from its Russian proprietor, *Surgutneftegaz*, for EUR 2.2 billion. Although MOL has been listed on the Budapest Stock Exchange since 1995, with this purchase, the Hungarian state suddenly became the largest shareholder of the company. To help understand the personal motives behind this deal, it is important to note that MOL has been run since 2000 by Zsolt Hernádi, president and CEO and a close personal friend of Orbán, who got this position during the first Orbán premiership. Hernádi is entirely in Orbán's hands. As the top manager of MOL, he has been charged with corruption in Croatia, where MOL acquired a subsidiary earlier, and the prime minister could extradite him to the Croatian authorities at any moment, if he wishes to do so.

SOFT DEALS AND SWEETHEART DEALS

At first glance, the large number of company renationalizations (approximately 200) looks suicidal, especially if and when foreign owners were affected. After all, Hungary is not only a United Nations (UN) and EU member but also bound by bilateral investment treaties (BITs), some of which preceded the 1989 regime change.[14] However, after close inspection of all the nationalization deals, we can see that what happened was not a ferocious expropriation but rather a "regulatory taking" in the language of Anglo-Saxon jurisprudence. In economic terms, this is a policy with which the government regulates the use of a property to such a degree that the regulation effectively amounts to an exercise of the government's eminent domain power,[15] without actually divesting the property's owner of title to the property. Thus, what has been happening in Hungary under the Orbán regime is *indirect coercion* in everyday parlance, and as a result of which targeted foreign owners find it more advantageous for themselves to sell their assets to the Hungarian state rather than to absorb the losses arising from the newly enacted rules. This was not even covert. As early as 2005, when Orbán was still in opposition, he declared bluntly at a public rally: "We don't need to be pusillanimous. If a government tells someone, please return this property, the government's word will have enough weight."[16]

There were only a handful of attempts of "taking" – i.e., forced confiscation without compensation – a procedure analogous with the Russian "corporate raiding" phenomenon (Rachlitz 2014). But even in these cases, after the initial fierce verbal threats, the government finally chose a soft form. The first well-publicized case was the continued harassment of the French

Suez Environment Co., the majority owner of the city of Pécs's water com-pany.[17] Shortly after Zsolt Páva, the new Fidesz mayor took office in 2009, security officers in the dead of night locked out the employees of Suez and the city forcibly took over the company. The head of the company could not even enter the building. *Suez* naturally sued. After four years (!) of negotia-tions – including one prime-ministerial meeting between the two countries concerned – the parties settled with a payment of HUF 7.5 billion for *Suez*, which – ironically – was paid by the central government (instead of the city of Pécs) in the end. Another similar story developed when a grave industrial accident occurred in 2010 at a privatized aluminum company (MAL Zrt.) in the Western part of Hungary.[18] In anger, parliament adopted a new law and nationalized the firm under the pretext of its interest in national defense. Some months later, however, this initiative was entirely forgotten and the relevant clauses of the nationalization act were repealed. Instead, various state authorities – including those responsible for the environment – forced the company into bankruptcy, from which, in turn, the state asset manage-ment company purchased the physical assets and incorporated them into new companies under new names. The establishment of criminal responsibility for the industrial accident (if there was any at all) was still in the hands of the courts in mid-2019.

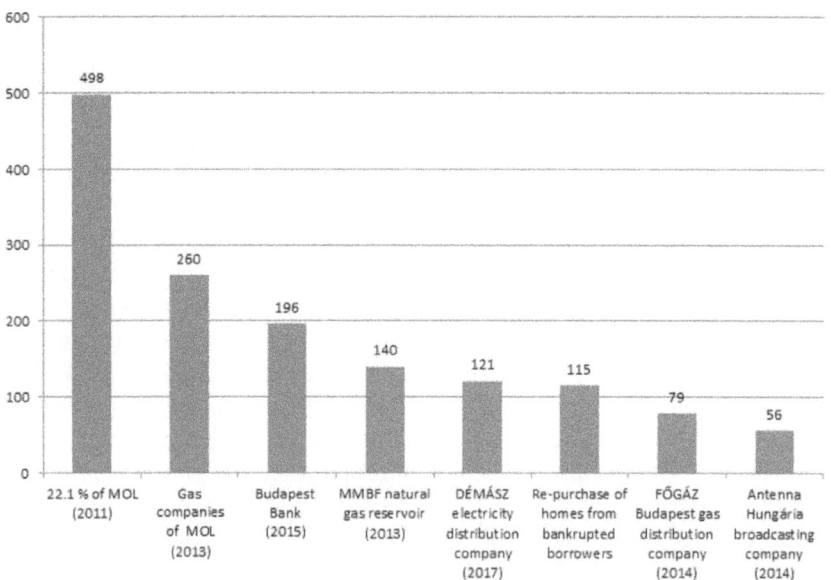

Figure 9.1 The Largest Renationalization Deals, 2010–2017 (HUF Billion). *Source*: Author's compilation with the collaboration of Professor Éva Voszka from different official sources and daily newspapers.

As I showed earlier, some important renationalizations, including the French *Suez* case just mentioned above, have turned out to be *sweetheart deals* – i.e., unbelievably favorable contractual arrangements for foreign sellers. The buying prices in the four most notable cases – the purchase of one-fifth of MOL shares from a Russian company (*Surgutneftegaz*) closely linked to President Putin, the 100 percent repurchase of the natural gas division of E.ON from Germany, and the acquisition of Budapest Bank and the Hungarian Foreign Trade bank previously owned by *General Electric* and the German *Bayerische Landesbank*, respectively – were all two to three times higher than the intrinsic market value of these firms. How can we explain this? My answer is that through such deals Orbán wanted to win good marks in Paris, Moscow, Berlin, and Washington at the cost of Hungarian taxpayers. In other, less important cases, the beneficiaries of such sweetheart deals were Hungarian political friends and supporters of the Fidesz regime.

The data so far suggest that this policy of sweetheart deals was successful. The inflow of capital from the outside world did not stop, as many had feared at the beginning. But it has slowed down. There are signs of capital flight, but the problem is manageable. All in all, Hungary improved its relative position among the leading ex-communist countries in terms of FDI/capita – at least until 2016.[19] The same can be said about the outward movement of capital: in terms or ranking, Hungary's position improved somewhat (see Table 9.2).

Another complicated matter is the *fiscal implication* of renationalizations. Intuitively, one would think that state money used for buying equity would – *ceteris paribus* – directly increase the government's fiscal deficit that was above three percent most of the time since 1990. But this is not the case. According to Maastricht Treaty rules, the costs of nationalization do not appear as a negative item among the current expenditures, just as it happened during the heyday of privatization, when privatization revenues did not increase budgetary revenues. While the net debt is increasing with every renationalization deal, if the public sector's cash position is deteriorating, this figure is not taken into consideration in the so-called Excessive Deficit

Table 9.2   Ranking of the Leading Post-Communist States in Foreign Direct Investment, 2007 and 2016

		Inward FDI					Outward FDI			
		2007			2016			2007			2016
1	Estonia	8 507	1	Estonia	13 966	1	Estonia	3 133	1	Estonia	4 742
2	Czech R.	7 380	2	Czech R.	10 333	2	Slovenia	2 714	2	Slovenia	2 766
3	Croatia	7 098	3	*Hungary*	7 705	3	Russia	1 772	3	*Hungary*	2 378
4	*Hungary*	6 745	4	Slovakia	7 635	4	*Hungary*	1 175	4	Russia	2 165
5	Slovakia	5 405	5	Kazakhstan	7 564	5	Croatia	598	5	Lithuania	895

Notes: Equity + reinvestment of earnings + debt instruments from 1992. Excluding special purpose entities (SPE).
Source: WIIW FDI Database.

Procedure, where the target indicator is gross debt rather than net debt. The explanation is that in accounting terms, for the state budget privatizations and (re) nationalizations are merely asset swaps:

Privatization = equity (-) vs. cash (+)
Nationalization = cash (-) vs. equity (+).

LIMITATIONS OF FREE COMPETITION

The reprivatization process cannot be understood in itself because it was closely interlinked in different ways with at least 60 precisely targeted anti-market measures. However, for the sake of brevity, I will highlight only a few of these measures in order to provide the reader with a sense of the large variety of the hastily implemented measures. A more detailed but compressed overview can be found in Table 9.3.

Literally from its very first days, the government has assumed special power to control the *prices* of basic services, such as electricity, gas, water, district heating, waste management, and so on. Using the opportunity offered by falling energy prices on international markets, the government introduced five rounds of nominal price cuts in 2013–2014, cumulatively amounting to almost 25 percent. This policy had far-reaching consequences. First, it turned out to be extremely effective to boost the ruling party's popularity. Second, it has eroded quickly the profitability of the utility companies, many of which were already earmarked for renationalization. In addition to this, the system of *taxation* was revamped: direct taxes on households were reduced, while many new taxes were devised to dent the profits of multinational companies, energy firms, banks, and retail food chains.

In February 2012, the Hungarian parliament voted to make the sale of tobacco a state monopoly. At that point in time, 40,000 stores sold cigarettes (including cafés, restaurants, petrol stations, and so on). These firms all lost their licenses from one day to the next. Instead, 7,000 new sales points were opened in which the clientele of Fidesz was given an opportunity to start new businesses on a concessionary basis. The alleged reason for establishing these tobacco shops was the government's desire to decrease the number of smokers and protect the health of underaged youth. The real reason, as investigative journalists quickly found out, was to help one domestic tobacco company and discriminate against foreign firms like *Philip Morris*, and *Imperial Tobacco*. After making the wholesale trade of handling tobacco products also a state monopoly, the Hungarian state could decide which products the shops would stock and indirectly impact on the prices of these products in the tobacco shops. There were only a few determined shop owners who were ready to go to Strasbourg to complain at the European Court of Human Rights. Those who did finally were awarded compensation, but their businesses were lost forever. The fate of Hungarian entrepreneurs who made their living from the operation of slot machines in special stores and cafés was very similar – altogether in 18,000 locations. In three steps, these operators were deprived of their lucrative businesses, as the government limited the licensing to two large casino operators (both who happened to be close friends and political allies of Orbán). This issue also landed on the desk of a pan-European court. And the Hungarian government lost again. In its verdict the court explained, "When the national legislature revokes a license that allows its holder to exercise an economic activity, it must provide a reasonable compensation system or a transitional period of sufficient length to enable that holder to adapt."[20]

A colorful example of the interventionist, discriminative measures was the "Sabbath Law," as it was labeled by the local correspondent of the *Financial Times*.[21] From March 15, 2015, on a historical national holiday, large supermarkets were forced to shut their doors on Sundays. Orbán defended his measure saying he was protecting Sunday as a Christian day of rest. In other communication channels, the government simultaneously told the public that the aim was to weaken the position of supermarket chains such as *Tesco* (UK), *Aldi* (Germany), and *Auchan* (France) and help Hungarian family owned shops and other smaller retailers. In the end, the move did not work; smaller family shops could not improve their relative positions, and the public at large was frustrated, so this measure was abolished after a little more than a year. This was one of the handful examples of unorthodox economic policy measures where the government backstepped. But it was probably too late. The owner of the largest Hungarian chain recently announced that he was willing to sell his chain of shops to *Aldi* or *Lidl* – before the market value of his shops drops even more.

There is simply not enough space in the present chapter to go systematically through all the new legislative measures which aimed at limiting competition and trying to cherry-pick the winners according to the whims of the prime minister. Table 9.3 below offers a manageably short summary of these measures – laws and lower level regulations. In the third column of the table, I marked separately those policy measures that were similar to the plans or the actual acts of the two socialist-liberal coalition governments that ruled Hungary between 2002 and 2008. Just like in the case of the renationalization of energy companies and banks, there are important parallels in many other sectors. Therefore, the politicians and the communication messengers of Fidesz were often right when they defended their new measures by saying that similar methods or policy tools were already introduced during the rule of the previous governments. And indeed, in many cases, the difference was only in size and/or the scope of the measure.

Table 9.3 Discretionary Laws and Economic Policies, 2010–2017

Sectors affected by the changes	Impact was significant	Similar measures were implemented between 2002–2010	European Commission (EC)	International fora adjudicated on it		
				(Court of Justice of the European Union) CJEU	ECHR (European Court of Human Rights)	International Centre for Settlement of Investment Disputes (ICSID)
Foreign trade, payments and investments (8)						
Limiting FX lending to households	x	x	x	x		
Mandatory conversion of FX loans to HUF	x		x			
Limiting households to buy cars abroad	x	x		x		
Limiting the purchase of agricultural land by foreigners	x	x	x	x		
Limiting the rental agreements on agricultural land to foreigners	x		x	x		
Limitation of foreigners' right to buy real estate other than land	x					
Prohibiting the operation of foreign-owned public notary firms		x	x			
Prohibiting the imports of sperm for artificial human insemination						

Price control (17)

—for households (consumers)

gas for heating and cooking	x	x	x	x	
bottled LPG gas for cooking	x				
electricity	x		x	x	
distance heating	x			x	
wood and coal for heating					
tap water					
liquid waste disposal					
solid waste disposal	x		x		
selective waste disposal			x		
chimney supervision and cleaning					
maintenance of elevators					
railway passenger tickets		x			
— for firms (providers)					
minimum hourly charge for selected services	x				
taxi prices, including prohibition of discounts	x	x			
mark-up on tobacco	x				
mark-up on imported food products					
loan intermediation fees	x				
Wage control (5)					
civil servants entitled to severance payments exceeding HUF 2 million	x				x

(Continued)

Table 9.3 Discretionary Laws and Economic Policies, 2010–2017 (*Continued*)

Sectors affected by the changes	Impact was significant	Similar measures were implemented between 2002–2010	European Commission (EC)	International fora adjudicated on it		
				(Court of Justice of the European Union) CJEU	ECHR (European Court of Human Rights)	International Centre for Settlement of Investment Disputes (ICSID)
mandatory wage rise for low-wage workers of the private sector	gradually abandoned					
wage commandos	abandoned					
maximum wage of EU project managers at universities						
maximum monetary compensation of blood donors						
Mandatory zero price (free service) (5)						
cash withdrawal from ATMs, twice in a month	x					
news service by state-owned news agency (MTI)	x					
funerals	postponed					
approximately 20 permits and licenses from the authorities	x					
water use in agriculture for irrigation						
Special (new) taxes and/or tax rates (16)		x				
mobile service providers	x					
networked public utilities	x					

banks and other financial institutions	x			
insurance companies	x			
producers of "sin" foods				
pharmaceutical companies	x		x	
hypermarkets	x		x	
public relations and media companies	x		x	x
solar panel manufacturers				
manufacturers of central heating devices				
internet providers	revoked			
tobacco manufacturers	x		x	
extra tax on the import license for e-cigarette				
--preferential VAT rates	x			
pork, poultry, fresh milk, eggs, restaurant catering services, housing construction, and music festivals	x	x		
-- preferential excise duty on certain alcoholic drinks		x	x	
-- preferential social security contributions	x	x		
Limitations on the operation of... (10)				
retail shops with low profits	introduced and revoked			
mandatory closing on Saturday and holidays				

(Continued)

Table 9.3 Discretionary Laws and Economic Policies, 2010–2017 *(Continued)*

Sectors affected by the changes	Impact was significant	Similar measures were implemented between 2002–2010	European Commission (EC)	International fora adjudicated on it		
				(Court of Justice of the European Union) CJEU	ECHR (European Court of Human Rights)	International Centre for Settlement of Investment Disputes (ICSID)
opening of new hypermarkets and malls	x		x			
minimum staff size for hypermarkets	not introduced					
teaching of foreign languages						
adult education						
obligation to audit invoices in certain sectors						
mandatory employment of consumer protection experts						
limitation of fishing at Lake Balaton	x					
limitation of eviction of home owners in case of personal bankruptcy		x				
Limitation of the Competition Act (4)						
loosening the anti-cartel provisions						
abolishing the right of merger control			x			
loosening the rules of public procurement	x					
loosening the rules of construction permits	x	x				

Purposeful creation of monopolies and oligopolies (212)

	C1	C2	C3	C4	C5	C6
market of lunch tickets and similar fringe benefits	x					x
retail trade of tobacco products for retail pharmacies		x				x
tax holidays for sponsors of five popular sports			x	x		x
race horse betting			x			x
slot machines		x	x			x
mobile telephone payment systems	x				x	x
allocation of state-financed advertising in the media						x
waste metal trade						
first-aid at open public events						
services of forensic experts						
sales of baby bonds						
management of EU-funded tenders						
participation of engineering design bureaus on EU tenders						
representation of the Hungarian State in front of foreign courts						
broadcasting the football matches of the Champions'' League						x
prohibition of Uber taxi services						x

(Continued)

Table 9.3 Discretionary Laws and Economic Policies, 2010–2017 (*Continued*)

Sectors affected by the changes	Impact was significant	Similar measures were implemented between 2002–2010	European Commission (EC)	International fora adjudicated on it		
				(Court of Justice of the European Union) CJEU	ECHR (European Court of Human Rights)	International Centre for Settlement of Investment Disputes (ICSID)
limitation of the market of professional company liquidator firms	x					
privileged position of state-run prison firms in the delivery of hospital textiles and nurses' uniforms	x					
broadening the scope of mandatory membership in industrial chambers	x					
housing lottery						
Total number of sectors: 69						

Source: Author's compilation.
Abbreviations:
EC = The Commission of the European Union
CJEU = Court of Justice of the European Union
ECHR = European Court of Human Rights
ICSID = International Centre for Settlement of Investment Disputes (Washington)

CONCLUSION

At the beginning of this chapter, I called the Orbán regime an autocratic one – in line with countless domestic and many Western analysts (Fukuyama 2012; Scheppele 2012 and 2013). Since the middle of 2015, the pan-European refugee problem has become the strongest factor in strengthening Orbán's personal popularity among voters. But in present-day Hungary, as a member state of the European Union and NATO, even autocratic rulers need continuous political legitimization through elections as well as through the results of public opinion surveys. The Orbán government has been fully cognizant of this, and in many dimensions of policymaking – including ownership changes and the anti-market measures – it has been acting accordingly. Such a measure was the punitive and retroactive taxation of the banking sector. This policy brought cash to the treasury, and it was popular at the same time. But such actions alone cannot be converted into votes easily. Therefore, during the last years (after 2015), generous income policy measures were used as an important vote and support generating mechanism.[22]

The renationalization policy worked in the same direction. From the very beginning of the post-2010 period, the prices of public utility services, such as gas, electricity, water, district heating, communal waste disposal, and so on were not only frozen but reduced in nominal terms by a cumulative 20–25 percent. In fact, this type of regulatory policy was the prime reason why the foreign owners of the affected companies were ready to sell their firms to the Hungarian government or to anybody else for that matter.

As already noted, the punishment of the financial sector – including insurance companies, brokerage firms, and so on – was initially driven by fiscal motives. Between 2010 and 2014, the government desperately needed revenue to keep public debt under control and to spend fresh money on pet projects (e.g., building new football stadiums and other sports facilities).[23] The attempt to discredit banks and bankers in the eyes of the public served ideological purposes, too.[24] In a similar way, as it happens in many other countries, it was very easy to generate hate and anger against bankers and banking as such, especially if in the country concerned the banks are predominantly foreign owned – as it is the case in Hungary. To this end, the government mobilized the state-controlled media, repeatedly sent letters to each and every household,[25] and these two subjects – utility prices and the sinfulness of the banks – have been kept carefully in the center of the public discourse still in 2019.

Centralization measures implemented within the public sector, such the reorganization of schools, hospitals, museums, courts, and so on serves simultaneously an ideological purpose (e.g., the change of the school curricula) and an administrative objective. The reorganization is used as a legal pretext to replace the top management of these institutions. In this way, a broad stratum of new clients has been created, the members of which are strongly incentivized to remain loyal to the Orbán regime in the years to come. The ideology, which has often and rightly been labeled by foreign observers as a populist interpretation of the world (Brodsky 2015), resonates with many former Socialist voters, too.

As noted in the introduction, it is a widely shared view both inside and outside of Hungary that the Orbán regime's most important objective is self-enrichment and the entire renationalization campaign serves this objective. According to this view, renationalization is merely transit-renationalization, because the most valuable renationalized assets are going to be privatized to Orbán's own family and his clientele. On the basis of the evidence available at the time of finishing this overview in July 2019, there were only a few deals where the last part of the "privatization ➜ renationalization ➜ privatization" chain was realized. The nine largest renationalization transactions listed in Figure 9.1 have not been reversed yet. All these companies are still state-owned. There are only two smaller transactions – or more precisely two series of very complex ownership changes and redrafting of the companies charters – that did seem to go in such a direction. In both cases, banks were affected.

From the summer of 2013, 128 provincial cooperative banks were stripped from their independence step-by-step. At the end, they were all integrated into a complex web of financial institutions that is under the control of *FHB Mortgage Bank Company Plc.*, a company listed on the Budapest Stock Exchange. Sources close to the information suggested that, sooner or later, the most influential beneficiary owner of FHB Bank, Zoltán Spéder – a close ally of Orbán – would take possession of all the co-operative banks. But this did not happen in the end, because Spéder fell out of the favor of the prime minister. Thus, this huge, newly created financial network of 12 regionally centralized banks ended up in the hands of Orbán's childhood friend, Lőrinc Mészáros (the second richest business person in Hungary). Another, equally complicated, multistep transaction was the reprivatization of *MKB Foreign Trade Bank* – after a renationalization in 2014. This bank, owned by the German *Bayerische Landesbank* since 1994, was renationalized under the pretext of the newly instituted solvency procedure (required by the European Central Bank). True enough, something must have happened, because both the German mother bank and its Hungarian subsidiary made huge losses during the international financial crisis. At the end, MKB went into receivership controlled by the National Bank, which also has undertaken the task of finding a new private owner. It took quite a while and there were several temporary new owners, but finally, this bank landed in the hands of Mészáros, as well.

Nevertheless, in my opinion, the renationalization campaign only indirectly served private enrichment of the prime minister (and/or) his friends. From the perspective of Orbán, the outright divestment of the newly acquired assets to friends and relatives would have been a politically very risky technique generating potentially dangerous oligarchs. Orbán was not a disciple of Boris Yeltsin; his role model is Vladimir Putin. Just as the present Russian leader, Orbán understood from the very early period of his political career that excessive individual wealth of oligarchs is a potential threat to his regime,[26] a state of affairs where you cannot trust anyone, not even your best friend. He put this astutely on one occasion in September 2014, when he had to break with his oldest personal ally, Lajos Simicska, then treasurer of Fidesz: "The trees cannot grow into the sky."

Rather than trying to build a clientele through reprivatization of renationalized firms, he has chosen another channel – the allocation of public procurement assignments. Through hundreds of manipulated tenders, hundreds of billions of forints were also channeled to a very broad clientele of the Fidesz party. Small fish were supported, and among them very many very small fish. Everybody knows that the flow of these friendly orders can be stopped at any moment, while confiscating companies, lands, forests, hotels, or any other type of real assets takes time and creates a lot of noise in the media for a prolonged period of time. For autocratic leaders, power, fame, popularity, and instant gratification matter most while private enrichment is of little real importance.

NOTES

1. For a detailed overview, see Mihályi (2010).
2. See kormany.hu (2011).
3. Beyond the publications of the present author – Mihályi (2014, 2015, 2016), Mihályi and Sztankó (2015) – there are only a few scholarly papers on the ongoing renationalization process. See Bod (2012), Szanyi (2014, 2016), and Voszka (2013).
4. On the one extreme, Bálint Magyar is the main proponent of the "*mafia state*" theory, according to which the prime motivation of the subsequent Orbán governments is their wish to enrich themselves (i.e., the ministers) and their "extended family" that includes not only family members but also their political and business clientele (see Magyar's paper in the present volume). The other extreme position has been taken – *inter alia* – by the writer and essayist Rudolf Ungváry. He has been arguing for many years that the Orbán regime is a "fascistoid mutation" primarily driven by a backward-looking ideology inspired by the regimes of Mussolini, Hitler, and Horthy. For an English-language summary of the latter, see hungarianspectrum. hu (2014).
5. For describing the rationale of the mechanism of political campaigns, see Soós (1987), a path-breaking paper, which was a summary of his book, published in Hungarian only.
6. For a detailed analysis of the centralization process, see Kornai (2011, 2012, and 2015) and Mihályi (2016).

7. Until 2015, the Fidesz government enjoyed the privilege of having a two-thirds majority in parliament, but then this was lost in subsequent by-elections. Between 2015 and 2018 not a single cardinal law has been passed.

8. These were all very important changes, in fact, more important than the rena-tionalization campaign, but for obvious reasons the present chapter cannot cover them.

9. For minimum information, see mnvzrt.hu (2019).

10. Hungary had a three-pillar pension system, with the state-funded pay-as-you-go scheme being the first pillar. It was complemented with a mandatory private pension-fund regime introduced in 1997 as the second pillar, where payments toward future pensions were deducted from gross wages and invested on the market to gen-erate additional returns. There was (and there is still) an optional third pillar, which enables future pensioners to save more money for their pension by contributing some of their net income to private pension funds.

11. The Hungarian Power Companies Trust (MVMT) was set up in 1963. With more than 20 subsidiaries, the Trust enjoyed a monopolistic position, based on its exclusive import rights and the ownership and operating rights of the entire system. In 1995, at the inspiration of the junior coalition partner, the liberal SZDSZ, the government accepted the concept of a liberalized model, according to which there should be no ownership relations between power stations and distributor compa-nies, and transactions should be regulated by commercial contracts. This would stop cross-financing, and the cost of electricity production and distribution could be clearly separated. In order to enhance competition, the members of the MVM-group should have been sold separately to prevent one investor from gaining excessive power. The remaining task of MVM would have been system operation and whole-sale of electricity. In fact, the blueprint suggested by the British advisory company (*Schroders*) was similar to what the EU Directive 96/92 introduced (the so-called single buyer model). The management of MVM objected to the concept from the very beginning. They considered the decentralization and privatization of the holding unnecessary. As MVM was the largest company in the country in 1991, the reduction of the power and size of the holding firm was not an attractive alternative. Whenever possible, managers emphasized that the control, monitoring, and development of the electricity system is of strategic importance. In the end, they managed to water down the liberal, pro-market concept. First, the bids for the nuclear power station as well as for some smaller power generating companies were rejected. Second, the grid was not even offered for sale. Third, MVM also could keep blocks of shares in the distributing companies. As a result, the "privatized" MVM did not become a small holding company; it became merely a smaller-than-before vertical holding. In the period between 1996 and 2010, there was a well-orchestrated cooperation among the MVM management and the key energy specialists of the ruling party to rebuild the vertically integrated monopoly.

12. This phrase comes from V. I. Lenin who used this in one of his last speeches. Shortly before his death in 1922, he spoke in front of the congress of the Communist International. He had to defend his economic reforms – the so-called New Economic Policy – from leftist critics. Lenin's main line of argumentation was that, in spite of the state support given to private ownership and the revival of markets, the most

important firms are and will remain in state ownership. Subsequently, in the 1930s, this metaphor surfaced in the vocabulary of the British Labour movement and later was widely used in India where planning was introduced into the existing market relations.

13. Already at that time, he made steps toward nationalizing the natural gas arm of MOL, but he literally ran out of time, as he unexpectedly lost the 2002 elections.

14. For the full list of Hungary's 58 BITs, see investmentpolicyhub.unctad.org (2019).

15. In many countries, the reference to the state's eminent domain power is simply called "public interest."

16. Orbán was quoted as saying this in the run-up to the 2006 general elections on August 27, 2005 at a widely publicized Fidesz convention. See index.hu (2015).

17. Pécs is the fifth largest town in Hungary with a population of 150,000.

18. The accident occurred in the wake of a flood of sludge from a ruptured reservoir. The waste, produced during bauxite refining, poured through three neighboring villages, killing eight people and wounding 200 others.

19. It is true, however, that after the 2008 financial crisis, a large part of Hungarian FDI was an involuntary transfer of money in the order of EUR three billion. Foreign banks had no choice; they had to recapitalize their subsidiary companies in Hungary (but also in other Central and Eastern European countries). In other words, the flow of fresh FDI into the Hungarian banking sector was not the vehicle of future growth but rather the vehicle of damage control.

20. See curia.europa.eu (2015).

21. See ft.com (2014).

22. Per capita, after-tax real incomes were 20 percent higher in 2017 than in 2010, although the rise of GDP within this period was not more than 16 percent. Source: Central Statistical Office.

23. See hungarianspectrum. hu (2013).

24. This policy included a smear campaign against George Soros with unmistakable anti-Semitic undertones. See, e.g., Guerrero and Schonberger (2017).

25. In the political discourse, the government preferred to call this kind of unidirectional correspondence as "national consultations," because the addressees were invited to answer the "yes or no" questions contained in the letter. From 2010, eight round of consultations have been organized covering a broad range of topics (e.g., pensions, taxes, social security contributions, migration, demography, and so on).

26. As we explained elsewhere at greater length, the same logic drives the Chinese post-communist autocratic leader, President Xi Jinping. Both Putin and Xi captured their own homegrown oligarchs after a period in which their predecessors had been captured by the oligarchs of that time. Mihályi and Szelényi (2017).

BIBLIOGRAPHY

Åslund, Anders. 2006. "The Folly of Russian Re-nationalization." *Moscow Times*, May 23 http://www.themoscowtimes.com/opinion/article/the-folly-of-re-national ization/204898.html.

Błaszczyk, Barbara. 2016. "Some Aspects of Privatization Reversal in Transition Countries: The Case of Poland and Hungary." *Studia Ekonomiczne – Economic Studies* 40 (4): 527–554.

Bod, Péter Ákos. 2012. "Non-conventional Economic Policy Measures – Hungarian Style." *Hungarian Review* 3, January: 16–23.

Brodsky, Clava. 2015. "Hungary's Dangerous Constitution." *Columbia Journal of Transnational Law.* http://jtl.columbia.edu/hungarys-dangerous-constitution/, accessed June 25, 2019.

Bugarič, Bojan. 2014. "Protecting Democracy and the Rule of Law in the European Union: The Hungarian Challenge." *LSE 'Europe in Question' Discussion Paper Series* 79, July.

curia.europa.eu. 2015. "Hungarian Legislation which Prohibits the Operation of Slot Machines Outside Casinos may be Contrary to the Principle of Freedom to Provide Services." http://curia.europa.eu/jcms/upload/docs/application/pdf/2015-06/c p150069en.pdf, accessed June 25, 2019.

ft.com. 2014. "Hungary to Force Supermarkets to Close on Sundays." https://www.ft. com/content/9066c9f0-83b7-11e4-9a9a-00144feabdc0, accessed June 25, 2019.

Fukuyama, Francis. 2012. "What's Wrong with Hungary." *The American Interest* 6, February. http://www.the-american-interest.com/2012/02/06/whats-wrong-with-hungary/, accessed June 25, 2019.

Guerrero, Eszter Susan, and Schonberger, Adam. 2017. "The Nationalist Hungarian Government Is Endangering Jewish People with its Smear Campaign against Philanthropist George Soros." http://www.independent.co.uk/voices/hungary-govern ment-george-soros-viktor-orban-antisemitism-a8089621.html, accessed June 25, 2019.

hungarianspectrum.hu. 2013."Viktor Orban on Football." https://hungarianspectrum .wordpress.com/2013/08/04/viktor-orban-on-football/, accessed June 25, 2019

———. 2014. "Rudolf Ungváry on the Fascistoid Mutation." http://hungarianspec trum.org/2014/11/29/rudolf-ungvary-on-the-fascistoid-mutation-in-todays-hun gary-part-i/, accessed June 25, 2019 and http://hungarianspectrum.org/2014/11/30/ rudolf-ungvary-on-the-fascistoid-mutation-in-todays-hungary-part-ii/, accessed June 25, 2019.

index.hu. 2015. "Hazaárulók és privatizáció." http://index.hu/belfold/kamp1525/, accessed June 25, 2019.

investmentpolicyhub.unctad.org. 2019. "Investment Policy Hub." http://investme ntpolicyhub.unctad.org/IIA/CountryBits/94#iiaInnerMenu, accessed June 25, 2019.

kormany.hu. 2011."The Fundamental Law of Hungary." http://www.kormany.hu/ download/e/02/00000/The%20New%20Fundamental%20Law%20of%20Hungar y.pdf, accessed June 25, 2019.

Kornai, János. 2011. "Taking Stock." *Népszabadság*, January 6. http://nol.hu/gazdas ag/janos_kornai__taking_stock-938851, accessed June 25, 2019.

———. 2012. "Centralization and the Capitalist Market Economy." *Népszabad-ság*, 28 January 2011. http://nol.hu/belfold/centralization_and_the_capitalist_mark et_economy-1297262, accessed June 25, 2019.

————. 2015. "Hungary's U-Turn." *Capitalism and Society* 10 (2): 1–24.

Mihályi, Peter. 2010. *A magyar privatizáció enciklopédiája, 1–2. Kötet.* Veszprém: Pannon Egyetemi Kiadó and MTA Közgazdaságtudományi Intézet.

————. 2014. "Re-nationalization in Post-communist Hungary, 2010–2013." *The Privatization Barometer Report 2013/2014.* Milan: Fondazione Eni Enrico Mattei and KPMG, 46–50. http://www.privatizationbarometer.net/PUB/NL/5/3/PB_AR2 013-2014.pdf, accessed June 25, 2019.

————. 2015. "A privatizált vagyon visszaállamosítása Magyarországon 2010–2014." Centre for Economic and Regional Studies, Hungarian Academy of Sciences, *Discussion Papers*, MT-DP 2015 (7), February.

————. 2016. "Re-nationalization and Recentralization in Hungary, 2010–2016." *Studia Ekonomiczne – Economic Studies* 90 (4): 579–597.

Mihályi, Peter, and Éva Sztankó. 2015. "A tőzsdei bevezetés jelentősége két magyar óriásvállalat példáján – MOL és MVM." Centre for Economic and Regional Studies, Hungarian Academy of Sciences, *Discussion Papers*, MT-DP 2015 (8), February.

Mihályi, Péter, and Iván Szelényi. 2017. "The Role of Rents in the Transition from Socialist Redistributive Economies to Market Capitalism." *Comparative Sociology* 16: 13–38.

mnvzrt.hu. 2019. "Magyar Nemzeti Vagyonkezelő." http://www.mnvzrt.hu/en, accessed June 25, 2019.

Müller, Jan-Werner. 2014. "Moscow's Trojan Horse. In Europe's Ideological War, Hungary Picks Putinism." *Foreign Affairs* 6, August. http://www.foreignaffairs .com/articles/141825/jan-werner-mueller/moscows-trojan-horse, accessed June 25, 2019.

Rachlitz, Michael. 2014. "Corporate Raiding and the Role of the State in Russia." *Post-Soviet Affairs* 30 (2–3): 89–114.

Scheppele, Kim Lane. 2012. The Unconstitutional Constitution." Posted to Paul Krugman's blog "The Conscience of a Liberal" for *The New York Times.* http://kru gman.blogs.nytimes.com/2012/01/02/the-unconstitutionalconstitution/#more-27 941, accessed June 25, 2019.

Scheppele, Kim Lane. 2013. "Hungary, the Public Relations Offensive." Posted to Paul Krugman's blog "The Conscience of a Liberal" for *The New York Times.* http://krugman.blogs.nytimes.com/2013/04/08/guest-posthungary-the-public-re lations-offensive/?_r=0#more-34278, accessed June 25, 2019.

Soós, Károly Attila. 1987. "Informal Pressures, Mobilization, and Campaigns in the Management of Centrally Planned Economies." *Economics of Planning* 21 (1): 39–48.

Szanyi, Miklós. 2014. "Privatization and State Property Management in Post-Transition Economies." *Centre for Economic and Regional Studies of the Hungarian Academy of Sciences – Institute of World Economics Working Paper* 2011. December 2014.

Szanyi, Miklós. 2016. "The FDI-led Development Model Revisited? The Case of Hungary." Centre for Economic and Regional Studies of the Hungarian Academy of Sciences – Institute of World Economics Working Paper 220, February 2016.

The Washington Post. 2014. "The Post's View: Hungary's 'Illiberalism' Should Not Go Unchallenged." August 17. http://www.washingtonpost.com/opinions/hungar ys-illiberalism-should-not-go-unchallenged/2014/08/16/b2dc72d4-1e5c-11e4-82 f9-2cd6fa8da5c4_story.html, accessed June 25, 2019.

Ungváry, Rudolf. 2014. *A láthatatlan valóság: A fasisztoid mutáció a mai Magyarországon.* Bratislava: Kalligram.

Voszka, Éva. 2013. "Államosítás, privatizáció, államosítás." December: 1289–1317.

Chapter 10

Viktor Orbán's Propaganda State

Miklós Haraszti

Media freedom went from endangered to extinct in Hungary after Viktor Orbán's third election victory in a row in April 2018, in what amounts to his fourth term in office. All legal, institutional, and economic guarantees of a free press were eliminated during the previous eight years of Orbán's rule. While there are a few free-thinking journalists holding on in a few struggling media outlets, they argue with and within a well-established regime that purposefully eradicates pluralism and independence of the media, freedom of information, and meaningful public debates.

Orbán's transformation of the nation's media into a centralized propaganda machine is part of why Freedom House's 2019 survey categorized Hungary's political system as "partly free," the first such mark registered inside the European Union.[1]

Before 2010, Hungary shared the woes typical of new democracies but also had protective laws and institutions and a politically and culturally multi-centered media. Orbán's rule has not only ruined them; it has also funneled an unchecked amount of taxpayer money into a dominant media empire steered by the government regardless if owned by the state or by its cronies. The purpose of this media system was unconcealed and already has been achieved: monopolization of the information flow and the inundation of society with uncontested electoral propaganda.

Viktor Orbán's media governance highlights the fundamental role of censorship and propaganda in illiberal metamorphoses of democracy. Restricting and streamlining the information flow is crucial for the basic endeavor of illiberal governance, which consists of engineering multiparty elections while depriving the electorate of an informed choice. These transformations invariably combine an initial demagogic popularity grab with an abusive power grab. In turn, the captured public institutions will be used to streamline public opinion, all in the service of repeating previous electoral successes. Even when illiberal state capture evolves into a mafia-like control scheme, with enrichment of the leader's family and clan at its core, just as Bálint Magyar demonstrated in Hungary's case,[2] it can be sustained only through a perpetuation of electoral victories. Viktor Orbán's meticulous censorship and propaganda machine is as efficient in suppressing choice as dictatorships used to be, while the system is clearly neither a remnant nor a remake of the old, communist one.

In Orbán's propaganda state, populist persuasion of the electorate is joined by quasi-rule of law and quasi-market-compatible operations. Restrictive institutional, legal, administrative, financial, ownership, licensing, advertising, and punitive regulations of the media are paired with government-aided private media acquisitions. All these measures are employed in combination, devised to starve political diversity in the media, and sustain the government's practical monopoly on messaging.

Being part of the European Union still does make a difference in comparison to post-Soviet variations in illiberalism. In Orbán's system, existential intimidation is more or less limited to the menace of joblessness, de-licensing, revenue loss, and bureaucratic harassment. The more direct forms of bullying, such as journalistic offences punished by prison, bogus criminalization, or outright violence, are avoided. However, constant discrimination against independent journalists, and their depiction as foreign agents bent to destroy the nation's good fortune, push public discourse ever further from fact-based dialogue.

ORBÁN'S ROAD

Throughout his decades spent in politics, Orbán has operated with a wealth of textbook methods that have aimed at achieving his current quasi-total domination of Hungary's public sphere. After a few years wasted in the liberal, freedom-conscious political camp, Orbán turned to managing his own media business by the early 1990s. Ever since, he has followed that path – both in opposition and in government – by way of piecemeal and grand-scheme alterations alike. Furthermore, he has been persistent in ridding himself of any economic or personal dependencies that would constrain his influence over the acquired media, even if it meant routing loyal allies. What follows is a brief list of the main stages of his media policies.

During the first cycle of Hungary's freely elected legislature – from 1990 to 1994 – Orbán subscribed to the purist creed: "Politicians, hands off the media." A fierce debater, he joined critics[3] of the government of József

Antall for trying to politically dominate the state media and for sabotaging legislation to make the media independent. However, his rigor lasted only until 1993, when the first opportunity arose for his opposition Fidesz party to hold some media power of its own. Thanks to behind-the-scenes governmental ties, Fidesz treasurer Lajos Simicska could privatize *MAHIR*, the state advertising company. Simicska's city posters had served Orbán's electoral campaigns up until 2014, when the two comrades fell out.

Already in 1994, with the help of the outgoing government of the Hungarian Democratic Forum (MDF), *MAHIR* took hold of *Magyar Nemzet*, a venerable liberal-conservative daily founded in 1930; then it founded another daily, *Napi Magyarország*, and finally the Simicska holding amalgamated the two papers, this time on a nationalist-conservative editorial line. In the 1994–1998 parliamentary cycle, Orbán – still in opposition – integrated the splintered right-wing spectrum. Part of his popularity with the nationalist-conservative political camp rested in switching from a defender of the liberal press to its vehement critic.

In 1998, when Fidesz came to power through a coalition with the Smallholders' Party of József Torgyán, Orbán's tactics mainly consisted of circumventing media laws and the Constitution. The coalition possessed less than two-thirds of the parliamentary mandates required for passing laws related to press freedom. Thanks to a consensus media law, adopted in 1996 also by Fidesz, the regulations already guaranteed freedom of expression and pluralism. Or at least so it seemed until Orbán set his mind on circumventing the outspoken constitutional ban on government domination. Exploiting ambiguities of the media law, he staged the coup of the "truncated boards."[4]

The maneuver was based on the legal requirement of an equal representation of governing and opposition parties in the praesidia of state-owned *Hungarian TV* and *Hungarian Radio*. However, the far-right MIÉP party of István Csurka blocked the joint nomination on the opposition side by insisting on an extra candidate for the party. (While legally in opposition, Csurka enthusiastically agreed with Orbán's vow to fight the "liberal-communist" media.) Finally, in December 1998, citing the lack of the opposition's agreement about their candidates, house speaker and Fidesz politician János Áder, today president of Hungary, put only the government's candidates to a vote and excluded the opposition's. As a reward for Csurka's "selfless" cooperation in the ruse, MIÉP cadres were given top editorial positions. Chief prosecutor Kálmán Györgyi declared the election of a government-only board a breach of the Constitution, advising parliament to correct the procedure. Instead, he was called by speaker Áder to a meeting behind closed doors, and the next day Györgyi resigned without explanation.

At that time, as a diverse media was on guard, such moves still alarmed the public. Despite Orbán's media warfare, or perhaps partly because of it, he lost the 2002 elections. He took away two conclusions from his defeat, and neither of them suggested that he should play by liberal standards. The first was that he should not be fighting against the letter of the law; rather, all the laws should change. The other was that controlling the state-owned media is insufficient if the rest remains pluralistic and populated with journalists eager to scrutinize the government; all media of any clout must be controlled.

The defeat of the first Fidesz government in 2002 forced Orbán to spend eight years in opposition, during which time he acquired further media power. Under the socialist-liberal government, Fidesz was left with plenty of partisan support, even in the public media. *Hungarian Radio*, for example, was allowed to keep its Fidesz-leaning presidents (Katalin Kondor, 2001–2005, and György Such, 2006–2010).

Fidesz's main financier, Lajos Simicska, retained the daily *Magyar Nemzet* and founded Hungary's first cable news channel, *Hír TV*, in 2003. In 2005, *Echo TV* and the liberal daily *Magyar Hírlap* turned pro-Fidesz once industry tycoon Gábor Széles purchased them. In 2009, in a scandalous licensing deal between Fidesz and the Socialist party, Simicska acquired the national radio *Class FM* while entrepreneurs close to the Socialists launched another national channel, *Neo FM*. In protest against the backroom bargain, László Majtényi, president of the National Radio and Television Authority (ORTT) resigned from his position and membership.

The sizable Fidesz media machine played a crucial role in Orbán's return to government in 2010. In September 2006, *Hungarian Radio* orchestrated the dramatic leak of then-prime minister Ferenc Gyurcsány's notorious "lie speech," his admission at a closed Socialist party gathering that he had won the 2006 elections by "lying day and night." The scandal led to violent demonstrations, during which far-right activists stormed the headquarters of the *Hungarian TV* and set it on fire. Simicska's *Hír TV* gave a live transmission of what it called a "revolution," with no compassion for the colleagues and the police trapped in the burning building. A month later, during the October 2006 commemorations of the 1956 uprising, the police took violent revenge against the protesters. These media events pushed the government into a (deserved) freefall, concluding with Fidesz's landslide election victory in 2010.

In the 2010 election campaign, Simicska's private media empire provided Orbán with a platform where his talent at delivering antagonizing messages could flourish. While avoiding a prime ministerial debate, a practice he has followed ever since, he could portray his opponents as willful enemies of Hungary. In fact, he did not really have opponents, because the socialist-liberal coalition had collapsed under a series of corruption and credibility debacles.

In 2010, Orbán's second government switched from circumvention of the law to the creation of his own legal universe, accomplishing the long-prepared illiberal makeover. In the 2010 elections, Fidesz captured 51 percent of the votes, which, in turn, yielded two-thirds of the parliamentary mandates, sufficient to change any law, even the Constitution. Revealingly, the very first of the cardinal alterations was a "media law package," tabled in June 2010, less than a month after the new parliament convened. The package struck down the Constitution's Article 61/4, the media pluralism tenet, which had obliged parliament to adopt a law aimed to "preclude information monopolies."[5] ORTT was replaced by a National Media and Infocommunications Authority, with jurisdiction over all broadcasting, print, and Internet media, governed by the Media Council (MC). Unprecedented in a democracy, the almighty MC had solely ruling-party appointees.

The media package set off the first international scandal of Orbán's illiberal rule. In Europe at the time, only Russia's *Roskomnadzor* and Belarus's *Ministerstvo Informatsii* had this pyramid-like, unmitigated governmental control over the media. However, Orbán used the consternation of fellow democracies to his political benefit by depicting the uproar as an attack on the nation itself and posing as the defender of Hungarians' pride.

Neelie Kroes, information commissioner of the EU, and Thorbjørn Jagland, secretary general of the Council of Europe, convinced Hungary in 2011 and 2013 to relent on a few of the more outrageous items of the media law.[6] However, these partial concessions only helped Orbán to claim that the international community had endorsed the rest, including the most contentious part: the one-party composition of the Media Council.[7]

In just two months after taking office, Orbán managed to write into law his domination over the public-service media, something he had struggled to achieve by circumventing the law between 1998 and 2002. The Media Council soon demonstrated its might by closing down *Neo FM*, leaving Simicska-owned *Class FM* as the only nationwide commercial radio.

However, the limits of a purely authority-conducted media capture were shown in the case of *Klubrádió*. The country's only independent radio station had employed several critical-minded journalists who had been fired from state radio during Orbán's first premiership. Citing arbitrary reasons, such as that the empty back pages were not signed by the applicant, the Media Council declared *Klubrádió*'s frequency tenders unsuccessful in 2010, and the radio sued. Amid demonstrations supporting the radio, the courts rebuffed the Council, and since 2012 *Klubrádió* operates a Budapest frequency. However, it lost all its frequencies in the countryside.

Klubrádió's legal fight – and the residual independence of some courts – indicated that the conquest of privately owned media was going to be a more protracted endeavor than the subordination of state-owned outlets. Still, the media owners – mostly Western companies at the time – understood the message: they should fear for their markets, revenues, or their continued functioning. They took on the task of disciplining their editors or simply sold their media properties to Fidesz allies.

In 2014, after his third electoral victory, Orbán changed tactics in his quest for an information monopoly: he no longer relied only on the Media Council's partisan decision-making; instead, he switched to state-assisted oligarchic buy-outs. Putin had already implemented such a tactic in Russia with success. Orbán also abruptly quit relying on Lajos Simicska as his sole oligarch, which in many cases had constrained his own decision-making sovereignty and had provided Simicska with an independent say about strategy and appointments. The two seemed to have a lifelong covenant since sharing a college dormitory room. Orbán, as prime minister, made Simicska the perpetual winner of EU-supported investment projects, and he went on to not only pay Fidesz back with rock-solid media and campaign support but also to assist the Orbán family with its own enrichment.

However, in 2014, Orbán dropped Simicska for a dozen freshly empowered cronies. By diversifying state corruption, he secured his new partners' absolute dependence on his will. A "Khodorkovsky moment" seems inevitable for any budding dictatorship. The need to replace self-made, self-confident oligarchs with hand-picked, submissive ones was another Putin teaching that Orbán has keenly followed.

Open war between the duumvirate chiefs who until then had run the country together broke out on "G-day," February 6, 2015, named after Simicska's four-letter insult that he publicly hurled on Orbán after learning that the latter enticed journalists to collectively quit Simicska's outlets for the newly founded Fidesz-friendly media.[8] The ensuing mafia-style showdown petrified Hungary's public for four years, until Simicska's capitulation.

Simicska turned his media from loyal to oppositional in a week's time. Paradoxically, this basically unprincipled revenge provided the country with an unexpected vestige of media pluralism, temporarily at least. The journalists who remained with Simicska's *Magyar Nemzet*, *Hír TV*, and *Lánchíd Rádió* were nevertheless delighted to be able to finally scrutinize corruption. Orbán's response was no less furious. Simicska was immediately enlisted among the enemies of the nation. Giant posters depicted him and George Soros as fellow puppet masters of the opposition.[9] Hungary's manually controlled procurement authorities now worked in reverse gear, squeezing the Simicska businesses out of all their revenues.

After Orbán swapped Simicska for several new cronies, he also changed the ideology he had provided with his media appropriations. The claim of an "anti-liberal political rebalancing" was exchanged for the stated goal of "a mostly Hungarian-owned media" in order to incubate "a class of national owners." "What critics call corruption is the government's main policy," an Orbánist ideologue admitted frankly.[10]

"Hungarization," that is, Orbanization, of the media was made easier by involving several loyal owners. Before the swap, much of the independent media had still been foreign-owned, including the nationwide televisions, most nationwide radios, and most of the printed press. It would have been hard to immediately concentrate them under a sole owner. On the other hand, a diversified oligarchy was also the solution to unobtrusively liberate the media of the professional and decency standards set by the foreign investors who had never engaged in partisan propaganda or extremist causes.

Orbán picked an elementary school classmate, Lőrinc Mészáros, to replace college dormitory roommate Simicska as the admiral of his media armada. In 2015, Mészáros became the absolute winner of EU and state procurements, and skyrocketed in status from the mayor of Orbán's home village Felcsút to Hungary's richest person and its first Forbes billionaire.[11] By 2018, Mészáros's endless empire extended to hundreds of media outlets.

Other new (albeit temporary) guardians of the pro-Orban media included Andy Vajna (deceased in 2019), the former Hollywood producer of the *Terminator* film series; Árpád Habony, the local business partner of the late U.S.-Israeli campaign guru Arthur Finkelstein and coauthor of the campaigns slandering George Soros[12]; Austrian Heinrich Pecina, Orbán's "good" foreigner, transitory front owner of *Népszabadság*, the country's strongest left-liberal quality newspaper, which he shut down overnight in 2016. Even the son of National Bank president György Matolcsy was assigned to provisionally take over Hungary's largest portal site, Deutsche Telekom's *Origo.hu*.

Orbán's third consecutive victory in the 2018 elections brought yet another surprising policy twist: he re-centralized his multi-owner media empire under a single hand. First, defeated Simicska agreed to sell the remnants of his media portfolio to a business partner who then immediately passed it on to the Mészáros empire. Then in November 2018, 476 government-friendly media outlets – which make up 80–90 percent of all the media in Hungary[13] – were "donated" by their owners to a recently established *Central European Press and Media Foundation (Közép-Európai Sajtó- és Média Alapítvány, KESMA, or CEMPF)*.[14] The Foundation's managers are long-time Fidesz operatives. Orbán's transitory agents of the last four years now surrendered their huge media holdings not just voluntarily but also for free, as if acting to illustrate Bálint Magyar's mafia state theory. Orbán wrapped up the rapid monopolization by immediately issuing a decree, designating the Foundation's acquisitions "a matter of national strategic importance," thus exempting *KESMA* from any market share scrutiny by the Competition Authority or the Media Council.[15] *KESMA*'s credo states: "The goals are clear: to counteract fake news and disinformation from progressive sources; to take action against political correctness, and to strengthen the national-civic side, so that truly conservative-Christian thinking can be present in public discourse with the same force as its left-liberal counterpart."[16]

BUILDING BLOCKS OF A PROPAGANDA STATE

An illiberal state's propaganda machinery is not a totalitarian uniformity. It just switches off any meaningful competition in coverage of political issues in the electorally important media markets, and is especially keen on isolating pivotal audiences from reports of governmental corruption and abuse. It is Huxleyan rather than Orwellian in that political diversity is not outlawed but constrained, and its remnants get buried under a fake diversity of entertainment.

The print press has been completely taken over. By 2018, there remained one independent national daily in all of Hungary, left-wing *Népszava*, founded in 1877 and currently owned by entrepreneurs close to the Socialist party. It is not a market hit, despite its rarity. *Magyar Nemzet*, Hungary's conservative newspaper of record, followed the path of left-liberal *Népszabadság*. Simicska shut it down on the day after the 2018 elections. Reopened by Mészáros, it has been operated by *KESMA* since 2019. All other national and local dailies had landed in the hands of government-sustained oligarchs, and were transferred in 2019 to *KESMA's* portfolio.[17] They are strictly coordinated editorially; their sections on politics are identical word for word.[18]

In television, the last outposts are under siege. The actual venue where elections get decided remains the couch where families watch the evening news. Orbán's television holding is not complete, but it is already sufficiently vast and dominating to carry the day. The multichannel public-service media, the most-watched news source in the countryside, was swept at once after the 2010 elections. Nationwide commercial *TV2* also became saturated with opposition-bashing and migration-cursing messages after the *ProSiebenSat.1*-owned station ended up in custody of Andy Vajna in 2014.

Orbán could not score a similar success with the other foreign-owned network, *RTL Klub*. It survived the onslaught in 2014, when Orbán's parliament hit *RTL Klub* with a pre-profit advertisement revenue tax. In response, the channel defiantly enriched its evening news with corruption stories, borrowed from web-based investigative outlets. To the surprise of skeptics who had assumed only tabloid news could be popular, its newscast won top ratings. It has become the proof that resistance is possible, provided the outlet is profitable; has an influential foreign owner, such as German-American-held Bertelsmann; and the owner encourages the editorial team to strike back with the most unexpected weapon: a proper journalistic job.[19] It is widely assumed that Orbán will not relent his efforts to either conquer *RTL Klub* or smash this last independent stronghold.

After Simicska's *Hír TV* was ceremoniously re-appropriated by Fidesz,[20] one cable channel, the Faith Church–owned *ATV* may remain tolerated in the role of the token independent, albeit not without paying a price, just like *Dozhd TV* in Russia. Affiliated with Pat Robertson's U.S.-based televangelist network, *ATV*, while being unbiased in domestic party politics, turned supportive of Orbán's war on refugees from time to time.

Radio is another wall-to-wall victory for Orbán's media strategy. Both the state radio channels and the private radios are now part of Orbán's propaganda machine. Simicska had to give up his nationwide *Class FM* already in 2016, and his temporarily anti-Orbán *Lánchíd Rádió* fell silent the day after the 2018 elections. *Klubrádió* remained the only independent voice on air, an exception that proves the rule, similarly to *Ekho Moskvy*, the showcase independent radio in Vladimir Putin's Russia. Music radios in Hungary are incentivized to carry government propaganda. Since 2014, authorities have provided them with an inexpensive daily package of readymade three-minute hourly news, produced by a former spokesperson of Viktor Orbán.[21] As a result, all people in Hungary listening to music radios while driving, cooking, or shopping in the malls are persistently bombarded with uniform political messages.

Since 2014, state-aided oligarchs have started biting into the online media market. *Origo.hu*'s takeover doubles as a story of political acquiescence by a huge international media owner. Deutsche Telekom not only agreed to maneuver the site into Orbán's fleet, but before doing so it helped remove its independent editors. The German communications giant has lucrative state contracts. The next huge bite could be *Index.hu*, the second-largest portal site. In September 2018, *Index.hu*'s parent company was purchased by investors with ties to Fidesz's satellite party, KDNP.[22] They claim to be driven by profit expectations alone – but this is how the debacle started with *Népszabadság*, *TV2*, and all bought-up and then re-tuned outlets.

MTI, the state news agency, has efficiently contributed to the emasculation of the Internet. The 2011 Media Law cleverly ordered *MTI* to make all its news available free of charge to any subscribing media. Alternative news production more or less died in Hungary the day *MTI* has started its "news for free" service. Today, the independent online media can publish critical-minded opinion pieces, but they elaborate on the same uniform, state-manufactured news.

Investigative journalism is bravely fighting the tide, but it is mostly Internet-based, with no proper home in the legacy media. A few specialized investigative sites, such as *Átlátszó* and *Direct36*, are supported by foundations, and labeled therefore as foreign-paid enemies. The fragmented and mostly urban Internet media may enable occasional mobilizations, such as the 2014 protest march against Orbán's proposed Internet usage tax.[23] However, electoral public opinion is clearly shaped by the victorious pro-governmental media empire.

Parliament has, step-by-step, constrained the right to access information in the last eight years. Back in 1992,[24] Hungary was a proud model of access to information rights. In 2011,[25] Orbán abolished the independent office of information ombudsman, and replaced it with an information authority.[26] The watchdog became a lapdog. The Constitutional Court, packed and streamlined in 2011, has raised no objection.

By 2018, pro-government owners have overwhelmed the billboards and public posters which are arguably the second most important media of election campaigns, following television. When in 2017 Simicska lent *MAHIR*'s poster stands to the Jobbik party's anti-corruption election campaign, with personal depictions of Orbán as a thief,[27] the prime minister retorted with a barrage of legal measures, and that settled the war. The municipalities (most of which have been Fidesz-controlled since 2010) were given the right to separately regulate the size and placement of the billboards on their territories. In parallel, a "Lex Simicska" was passed, banning the billboard companies from giving concessions off their list rent prices to any political party – as if Simicska had not allowed Fidesz to use the *MAHIR* billboards for virtually free in the last quarter century.

Strangely, the regular courts have remained the only institutions that still defend journalists' rights in Hungary. Their judges often oblige businesses and government agencies to disclose requested data to journalists. Just as in defamation cases, the key distinction of "information in the public interest" still survives in the courts for the time being. But time may soon run out. In 2019, parliament passed the creation of a separate administrative court system operated by government-picked judges; due to Western criticism, its actual setting up was postponed recently. Complaints against rulings by the Media Council or denials of data disclosure would be redirected from the regular judiciary to the new courts.

With completion of the KESMA super-monopoly, the model of the propaganda state was born, inside the EU:

- The Media Council provided the necessary licenses, merger permissions, or denials.
- The parliament passed special restrictions, such as special taxes levied on advertisement revenues or Internet usage, pushing the still independent media into selling on the cheap.

- State development banks were ordered to lend money to the chosen media-shopping oligarchs, thus creating a taxpayer-paid but privately owned media empire out of nowhere.
- All advertising in any media by any government agency or enterprise was concentrated in a *National Communication Agency* under the supervision of Orbán's cabinet minister Antal Rogán.[28] His budget for "government information" (advertisements and posters proclaiming achievements or identifying enemies) has exponentially grown to reach seventy billion forints for the year of 2018.[29]
- Independents were starved, while the state advertising bonanza helped the oligarchs pay back the banks and fund their new, loss-making acquisitions.[30]
- The post-communist re-monopolization of the media, underway since 2010, was completed in 2019, with the "voluntary" establishment of *KESMA* by the media oligarchs.[31]

CONCLUSION: TRIUMPHANT POPULISM – FROM FAKE NEWS TO FAKE MEDIA

Without controlling the media, Orbán could not have perfected his populism to become an irresistible, monothematic, post-factual propaganda mantra. Beyond fake news, a centrally guided fake media has been created in Hungary. It is not just spreading "alternative facts" – the aim is to squeeze out all alternatives to fake news.[32]

Just as Vladimir Putin before him, Orbán proved that the method Hannah Arendt described as totalitarian propaganda could be replicated in a multiparty democracy's multi-owner media scene. For the propaganda state to succeed, she said, it first has to annihilate access to real news; and meaningful pluralism had been censored away early on by Orbán's media governance. The essence of the method, Arendt told, was a concentrated state effort to actually build the claimed fake realities, and then give up on argumentation, and keep pointing at that convenient new reality. Think of the fake civil war in Ukraine to convince the public of a "fascist danger," or the building of the border fence in Hungary in order to convince the nation that it is being protected from the "demise of its civilization" and an omnipresent "Soros plan" to subjugate Europe's nations.

Before 2015, Orbán quarreled with abstract enemies: the International Monetary Fund, "Brussels," liberalism, the communists, and the multinationals. But stirring up fear of external enemies and local quislings has its own dynamics; Orbán now turned to enhancing and weaponizing the region's dormant ethnic prejudices. The government saturated Hungary's public space with a convenient new version of xenophobia, transforming the entrenched aversions toward Roma into anti-migrant feelings, and topping it with the coded anti-Semitism of the anti-Soros propaganda campaign. The giant posters depict "caravans" of invading dark-skinned aliens who are led and financed by a grinning "speculator."[33] Billions of taxpayer money have been spent on fake referenda asking the electorate to reject a nonexistent Soros Plan and nonexistent EU obligations.[34] Fake "National Consultation" surveys, sent to every Hungarian citizen, ask leading questions, such as: "Do you agree with the government that instead of allocating funds to immigration we should support Hungarian families and their children yet to be born?" With the 2018 amendments to the Fundamental Law, the propaganda state stepped over yet another European anathema: it ordered the criminalization of its critics. The "Stop Soros" bill explicitly empowers the secret services to control NGOs and to determine if their communications amount to punishable support for migration.

The author of this chapter was among the organizers of a press conference in December 1989, together with Orbán, to reveal that the communist secret services were still spying on the opposition groups, despite the fact that at the roundtable talks we already had agreed about the transition to democracy. That scandal was a final blow to the old order before the first free elections.

Of course, at that time, there was a free media to convey the news to the voters.

NOTES

1. See freedomhouse.org 2019.
2. See his study in the present volume.
3. Such as the writer of these lines, an SZDSZ MP from 1990 to 1994.
4. Or "csonka kuratórium" in Hungarian.
5. Amendment of the Constitution, passed July 6, 2010. Disclosure: The writer of this account is the unhappy but still proud author of the pluralism tenet of the 1989 Constitution.
6. See reuters.com 2011.
7. See mertek.eu 2013.
8. See theorangefiles.hu 2019.
9. See 24hu 2017.
10. See 444.hu 2015.
11. See forbes.com 2019.
12. Grassegger 2019.
13. See mertek.atlatszo.hu 2019.
14. See cepmf.hu 2019.
15. Ibid.
16. Ibid.

17. See ipi.media 2017a.
18. See azonnali.hu 2018.
19. See ipi.media 2018.
20. See reuters.com 2018a.
21. See origo.hu 2014.
22. See reuters.com 2018b.
23. See nytimes.com 2014.
24. Law 1992 LXIII.
25. Law 2011 CXII.
26. National Authority for Data Protection and Freedom of Information.
27. See 444.hu 2017.
28. See politico.eu 2018.
29. See g7.hu 2019.
30. Cf. Bohlen 2018.
31. See nytimes.com 2018.
32. See ipi.media 2017b.
33. See lokal.hu 2018.
34. Cf. Gall 2016.

BIBLIOGRAPHY

azonnali.hu. 2018. "Az összes megyei napilap szerkesztője ugyanarra gondolt ma reggel," http://azonnali.hu/cikk/20180407_az-osszes-megyei-napilap-szerkesztoje -ugyanarra-gondolt-ma-reggel, accessed June 25, 2019.
Bohlen, Celestine. 2018. "Can Hungary's Fourth Estate Survive?" *New York Times*, September 23, 2018, https://www.nytimes.com/2018/09/23/opinion/can-hungarys -fourth-estate-survive.html, accessed June 25, 2019.
cepmf.hu. 2019. "Preambulum", "Announcement", "Goals," https://cepmf.hu, accessed June 25, 2019.
forbes.com. 2019. "Lorinc Meszaros," https://www.forbes.com/profile/lorinc-me szaros/#11a89cd44868/, accessed June 25, 2019.
freedomhouse.org. 2019. *Freedom in the World*, https://freedomhouse.org/report/fre edom-world/2019/hungary.
Gall, Lydia. 2016. "What Does Hungary's Migrant Quotas Referendum Mean?" https://www.hrw.org/news/2016/10/06/what-does-hungarys-migrant-quotas-refer endum-mean-europe, accessed June 25, 2019.
Grassegger, Hannes. 2019. "The Unbelievable Story of the Plot Against George Soros," https://www.buzzfeednews.com/article/hnsgrassegger/george-soros-c onspiracy-finkelstein-birnbaum-orban-netanyahu, accessed June 25, 2019.
g7.hu. 2019. "Júliusra elfogyott…" https://g7.hu/kozelet/20190719/juliusra-elfogyott- a-kormanyplakatokra-szant-20-milliard-de-jut-meg-ra-penz/, accessed July 19, 2019.
ipi.media. 2017a. "Orban Completes Takeover," https://ipi.media/orban-completes-t akeover-of-hungarian-regional-media/, accessed June 25, 2019.

———. 2017b. "Hungarian Taxpayers Fund Unique Fake News Industry," https:// ipi.media/analysis-hungarian-taxpayers-fund-unique-fake-news-industry, accessed June 25, 2019.

———. 2018. "Amid Media Takeover," https://ipi.media/amid-media-takeover-hu ngarys-largest-tv-station-proves-tough-nut-to-crack/, accessed June 25, 2019.

lokal.hu. 2018. "Jelentősen szigoritják a 'Stop Soros" törvénycsomagot," https:// www.lokal.hu/2018-02-szigoritott-formaban-nyujtjak-be-a-stop-soros-torvenycso magot-kedden/, accessed June 25, 2019.

mertek.eu. 2013. "Letter of Hungarian NGOs on Media Legislation," http://mertek.e u/en/2013/02/04/letter-of-hungarian-ngos-on-media-legislation-to-mr-thorbjorn-ja gland-secretary-general-council-of-europe/.

mertek.atlatszo.hu. 2019. "Fidesz-Friendly Media Dominate Everywhere," https:// mertek.atlatszo.hu/fidesz-friendly-media-dominate-everywhere/, accessed July 27, 2019.

nytimes.com. 2014. "Proposed Internet Tax Draws Hungarians to Streets in Protest," https://www.nytimes.com/2014/10/30/world/europe/hungarians-march-against-pr oposed-tax-on-internet-use.html, accessed June 25, 2019.

———. 2018. "No News Is Bad News for Hungary. The Autocrat Viktor Orban has Taken Control of Much of the Country's Media," https://www.nytimes.com/2 018/12/03/opinion/hungary-orban-media-suppression.html.

origo.hu. 2014. "A kormányszóvivő volt cége közszolgálati híreket gyárt," http: //www.origo.hu/itthon/20140211-atlatszo-a-kormanyszovivo-volt-cege-kozszolg alati-hireket-gyart.html, accessed June 25, 2019.

politico.eu. 2018. "Orban's Media Puppetmaster," https://www.politico.eu/articl e/viktor-orban-media-empire-hungary-election-antal-rogan-fidesz-propaganda/, accessed June 25, 2019.

reuters.com. 2011. "Hungary Amends Media Law, Defusing EU Criticism," https ://www.reuters.com/article/us-hungary-media-vote/hungary-amends-media-law-d efusing-eu-criticism-idUSTRE7265RN20110307, accessed June 25, 2019.

———. 2018a. "Orban Loyalists Take Control," https://www.reuters.com/article/us- hungary-orban-media/orban-loyalists-take-control-of-prominent-hungarian-new s-channel-idUSKBN1KM4VT, accessed June 25, 2019.

———. 2018b. "Gloom in the Newsroom," https://www.reuters.com/article/us-hunga ry-orban-media-insight/gloom-in-the-newsroom-as-hungarys-independent-media- recedes-idUSKCN1M40SP, accessed June 25, 2019.

theorangefiles.hu. 2019. "Lajos Simicska," https://theorangefiles.hu/lajos-simicska kozgep/, accessed June 25, 2019.

24hu. 2017. "Ime a Fidesz válaszkampánya a Jobbik plakátjaira," https://24.hu/belfol d/2017/04/27/ime-a-fidesz-valaszkampanya-a-jobbik-plakatjaira/, accessed June 25, 2019.

444.hu. 2015. "Amit korrupciónak neveznek az gyakorlatilag a Fidesz legfőbb poli- tikája," https://444.hu/2015/12/21/lanczi-tamas-amit-korrupcionak-neveznek-az-g yakorlatilag-a-fidesz-legfobb-politikaja, accessed June 25, 2019.

———. 2017. "Ti dolgoztok, ők lopnak," https://444.hu/2017/04/01/ti-dolgoztok-o k-lopnak-oriasi-plakatkampanyba-kezdett-a-jobbik, accessed June 25, 2019.

Chapter 11

Ideology or Pragmatism?

Interpreting Social Policy Change under the "System of National Cooperation"[1]

Dorottya Szikra

The welfare state has a special place in Hungary's "System of National Cooperation" (SNC), and this status determined Hungarian social policy reforms since 2010. While preceding post-communist/liberal governments also deserve criticism for austerity measures or failed welfare state reforms (e.g., Ferge 2012; Lakner 2015), the post-2010 coalition was the first one in the history of the new democracy to explicitly declare that it did not aim at building a welfare state. Under the second and third Fidesz cabinets, the unwritten contract between the state and society to protect the social security of Hungarian citizens has more or less ceased. The state, in the understanding of the SNC, does not hold responsibility to "embed" society (Bohle and Greskovits 2012) and protect the most vulnerable from the consequences of the global (and local) economic crises.

The limited understanding of social rights is reflected in the Fundamental Law of 2011. According to Article XIX, the state "shall strive to provide social security to all of its citizens," a step back compared to the 1989 Constitution, which, at least in theory, provided social security for its citizens (Juhász 2015). At the same time, social rights became linked to responsibilities of citizens in a rather vague manner: "The nature and extent of social measures may be determined by law in accordance with the usefulness to the community of the beneficiary's activity" (Art XIX (3) of the 2011 Fundamental Law). What kind of "activity" was needed to receive social protection from the state? And who defined the "usefulness" of one's activity? Clearly, Hungarian citizens, and especially those who fall back upon the solidarity mechanisms of the state, became more exposed to arbitrary decisions.

Viktor Orbán, in his critical manifestations about Western welfare states, further nuanced the fundaments of the SNC's social policy. Already in 2012, he declared:

All the states have to accomplish the correction of the welfare state. This is more difficult in the West because they have full-fledged welfare states but not so difficult in Central Europe as welfare states are not yet created here. We tumble among the ruins and semi-finished buildings of post-communism, but here we have no welfare state. Our program is to establish, instead of the Western-type of welfare state that is not competitive, a *work-based society*. (Orbán 2012 – emphasis and translation by Szikra)

In the summer of 2014, Orbán explained that "the Hungarian solution is the approaching era of a *work-based society*" [*munka-alapú társadalom*], one that would overcome the liberal state and the welfare state (Orbán 2014 – emphasis by Szikra).

The prime minister did not talk to the wind: his turn away from the idea of the welfare state has been manifest in a general drop in social spending since 2010. Hungary was the only country within the OECD cutting social spending in the harshest years of the crisis (OECD 2014).[2] Austerity, however, did not affect all areas of welfare equally. In fact, spending in some fields, like family policies, was increased substantially. These extra resources were, as we will show in this chapter, directed toward the better-off, while cash-transfers for the poor were curtailed severely. In other words, austerity measures were applied selectively to punish the unemployed and the poor and, in the case of the pension reform, people with reduced work capacities.

Despite this general trend, when looking at the underlying ideological considerations of social policy reforms, we found a surprising diffusion of opposing ideologies, incorporating neoliberal, conservative, and *étatist* elements (Szikra 2014). In this chapter, we will ask if there is a guiding principle of social policy reforms of the SNC at all? Or are pragmatic considerations stronger than underlying ideological aims?

To this aim, we will first map different interpretations about the role of ideologies in general, and "post-communist traditionalism," as defined by Csillag and Szelényi (2015), in particular, in the policymaking processes of the SNC. Then we will turn to analyzing two distinct social policy areas, namely pensions and family policies. The 2011 pension reform shows how changes hurting the interests of millions of employees and influential private companies can be carried out without substantial public resistance. We will argue that, besides the weakness of organized civil society, the ideology of *nationalist étatism*, resonating with the attitudes of people, played an important role in the political success of this reform. The elimination of the disability pension scheme – that received much less scholarly and media attention – provides a luminous example of the creation of a division between "deserving" and "non-deserving" groups through the means of social policy. Family policy, on the other hand, is traditionally loaded with ideology, and thus has been an ideal field for the conservative coalition to communicate its preferences about moral values and gender roles. In the chapter, we disclose possibilities and limits of such ideologically driven social policy-making. To conclude, we will assess the role of ideologies, and especially how "post-communist traditionalism" can be considered to be the greatest common factor in social policy measures between 2010 and 2016.

THE ROLE OF IDEOLOGIES IN PUBLIC POLICY-MAKING UNDER THE SNC

Current scholarly standpoints about the role of ideology in public policy-making under the SNC can be grouped into three distinct categories. The first line of argument, what we call "pragmatic policy-making," argues that policy decisions since 2010 do not show any particular ideological orientation but are ultimately driven by the interests of the ruling parties and the government. Politically, reforms aim at maximizing electoral support and strengthening the power of the ruling elite. Economically, the aim is the (re)distribution of assets for those in power and/or loyal to the executive branch. While this interpretation is most pronounced in the "mafia state" argument of Magyar (2013; see also his chapter in this volume), interestingly, it can also be grasped in the thinking of some of the influential spin doctors of the Orbán government (Lánczi quoted by Mándi 2015, 26–27).

The second approach accepts that pragmatism has been present in decision-making since 2010 but argues that ideologies have also played an important role in public policy reforms. Rather than having one particular ideology, however, a "bricolage" of different paradigms is present that "results in a heterogeneous set of public policies" (Carstensen 2011 quoted by Körösényi 2015, 414; see also Szikra 2014).

The third approach, what we call "ideologically-driven policy-making," is in strong opposition with the first argument and claims that, because of the still existing rules of majoritarian democracy, the post-2010 government needs an ideology "which would appeal to 'ordinary people' . . . with strong national and religious collective identity" (Csillag and Szelényi 2015, 27). According to the authors, this ideology is "post-communist neoconservatism/traditionalism" that features the usual essential values of conservative ideology such as "patria, church and the (traditional) family" and resembles the once popular Tea Party movement of social conservatives in the United States. The major difference is that the post-communist variant is essentially *étatist* "not only in social issues but also in matters of economic policy" (*ibid.*, 26–27). Post-communist neoconservatism/traditionalism is rather appealing in the whole region but is especially tangible in the rhetoric and political decisions of Putin since the early 2000s (*ibid.*, 40), of Viktor Orbán since 2010, and recently also of Jarosław Kaczyński. Main characteristics of the post-communist traditionalist ideology, as described by Csillag and Szelényi (2015), are summarized in the box below:

Post-communist Traditionalism

- Initiates extra parliamentarian actions around socially conservative issues like abortion and LGBT rights
- Makes a critical distinction between workers and people who "do not work"
- Opposes any "hand outs" to the "undeserving poor"
- Is anti-immigrant and generally against affirmative action and positive discrimination
- Is manufacturing a common enemy
- Is *étatist* – favoring the big "caring" state
- Celebrates traditional family and related gender roles

Source: Author

If social policy bears the features of post-communist traditionalism, it will certainly create a sharp division between "deserving" and "undeserving" social groups, where the "undeserving" serve as one of the common "enemies" of the SNC. Policy decisions, furthermore, must show visible signs of nationalist *étatism*. The "traditional family" and hetero-normative values are also of central concern to this ideology, which is often played out in anti-gay movements as well as attacks against gender equality. Furthermore, post-communist traditionalists think that Christian religion and churches should play a key role in an envisioned "good society" in the making. We will argue in the chapter that the majority of social policy reforms pass the "test" of the post-communist traditionalist ideology. The project of fully creating a social policy driven by statist neo-conservatism, however, faces serious obstacles in the social reality of a twenty-first century post-industrial post-communist society.

2011 PENSION REFORM

Fidesz's 2011 pension reform was carried out with extreme speed and without any consultation with stakeholders (Simonovits 2011). Trade unions, civil society, and experts found it especially difficult to trace the steps of the pension reform for two reasons. First, because changes were made parallel to other crucial legislative processes, including the unilateral adoption of the Fundamental Law and the new Labor Code. Second, the pension reform consisted of several important elements approved simultaneously with each other and not revealed to the wider public prior to the adoption of the bills.

We can now see, retrospectively, that the "systemic change of the pension system"[3] [*nyugdíjrendszerváltás*] consisted of three major elements: first and foremost, the state confiscated the assets of private pension funds, finally eliminating the compulsory private pillar. Second, various parametric changes were carried out, including the ceasing of early retirement schemes and introducing the "Women 40" program. Third, the disability pension scheme was removed from the pension system altogether and transferred to a state fund financed from general taxes.

The first and most fundamental element of the reform affected the private pillar of the pension system. The so-called mixed pension system, in existence between 1998 and 2011, consisted of a public pillar (on a pay-as-you-go [PAYG] basis), a compulsory private pillar, and a voluntary private pillar. The private pillar, propagated by the World Bank in the 1990s, was introduced following the "Argentinean model" by the socialist-liberal coalition in 1997 (Müller 1999). Despite high administrative costs, a low level of transparency, and low returns (e.g., Augusztinovics et al. 2002), the private pillar became surprisingly popular. Three-quarters of all employees (approximately three million people, including about two million older employees for whom the private pillar was not mandatory) entered private funds that accumulated an amount equal to about 10 percent of Hungary's GDP by 2011. From the very beginning, Fidesz opposed the privatization process on anti-capitalist and nationalist grounds. Under its first term, it already shrank the private pillar, and by 2010, the Fidesz government turned to a more radical solution (see Szikra and Kiss 2017) blaming private pension funds for the "misuse" of members' money.

As a first step, the contributions due to the private pension funds were directed to the treasury for fourteen months (Act CI/2010) to ease the burden of the budget under the crisis. Still, in 2010, the parliament adopted a bill to completely eliminate the private pillar without public debate, consultation, or substantial resistance. Instead of directly confiscating private pension assets, the new legislation announced that those who stayed in private pension funds would not be eligible for the future accrual of a state pension (75 percent of one's total pensions), although their employers would be obliged to contribute to that scheme. Furthermore, contributions paid by employers were renamed (using an odd pleonasm) as a "social contribution tax" [*szociális hozzájárulási adó – szocho*] to which no future claims could be attached (Act CLVI/2011). Meanwhile fiscal laws were removed from the jurisdiction of the

Hungarian Constitutional Court to prevent the court from interfering in the nationalization process. Originally meant as a temporary measure, this later was made into a firm part of the new Fundamental Law, with the consequence that "the Parliament can now enact fiscal laws that violate the constitution and individual rights, and the Constitutional Court is not just temporarily but permanently barred from reviewing them" (Halmai and Scheppele 2012, 12). Facing administrative difficulties and assuming that they would not receive their public pensions, 97 percent of private pension fund members "opted" for the public scheme. In short, Hungarian private pension fund members were blackmailed successfully by their own state, while their assets were nationalized. We can regard the procedures of the 2010–2012 pension reform as an essentially *étatist* move and a dress-rehearsal for Hungarian illiberal democracy.

The other two main elements of the pension reform, the ceasing of any early retirement possibilities and severely limiting the social rights of disability pensioners seem to be typical neoliberal measures (Szikra 2014). Taking a closer look, however, it becomes clear that the intention of the government was something other than simple austerity. Besides cuts, substantial increases were issued in some areas and new possibilities opened up for certain social groups.

The reason given for ceasing of early retirement benefit schemes (Act CLXVII/2011) was to "eliminate fraud and privileges" within the old-age pension scheme and to meet spending commitments of the Structural Reform Programme required by the EU. But instead of issuing, as experts suggested, a gradual change that would encourage people to stay longer in the labor market and retire later, a very rigid system was established: the rule became that no one can receive old-age pensions under the age of sixty-two after 2012. Thus, the official pension age and the de facto pension age became almost the same.

Two further parametric decisions, however, sharply contradicted these activation aims. First, in the case of civil servants and judges, it was no longer an option but mandatory to retire at the age sixty-two according to the 2011 pension reforms. Here, the aim of activation was overruled by ideological considerations. Although no official explanation has been given, it is quite likely that the anti-communist ideology of Fidesz to dismantle "clotted structures," that is, to replace the "old" elites with ones who are loyal to Fidesz was the major driving force behind this reform step, later copied by the Polish PiS-government to force judges to retire.[4] In 2012, the European Court of Justice ruled that Hungary's decision to lower the compulsory retirement age of judges to sixty-two was illegal as it violated equal treatment rules of the EU.[5]

The "Women 40" program was another major exception to the rigid retirement rules. According to the program, women can retire earlier than the compulsory official retirement age in cases when they have made forty years of social insurance contribution. Years of higher education do not count as contributory years, whereas time spent on maternity and parental leave does for a maximum of eight years. The intention of the cabinet was to encourage grandmothers to look after their grandchildren. The "Women 40" scheme is thus an innovative attempt to link conservative, pronatalist aims with the old-age pension system. It also reflects the traditionalist view of the coalition about gender roles, in which (elderly) women are rewarded for their past and current caring activities. In this case again, not only the general aim of activation but also rational economic calculations were overruled by ideological considerations.

The third element of the pension reform, the exclusion of disability pensions from the pension system from January 2012 (Act CXCI/2011) meant that people below the retirement age would receive disability and rehabilitation assistance [*rokkantsági és rehabilitációs ellátás*] rather than a social insurance pension. The intention of the government was to "purify" the pension system from disability-related benefits. Pushing disability pensioners out of the pension scheme and into social assistance is a historically important but often overlooked aspect of the pension reforms: disability pensions, widows', and orphans' pensions as a joint pension system has been in place since 1928 providing much stronger social rights to beneficiaries than social assistance eligibility. During the post-communist years, disability pensions were used widely as a way out of the labor market, as a better option to unemployment benefit.[6] Fidesz's intention to decrease the number of beneficiaries of disability pensions was thus understandable both for budgetary reasons and as a means of activation.

The revision of the status of disability pensioners has been humiliating and punitive, and the activation policies (including training, mentoring, and social work) were not established to help former disabled pensioners to (re-) enter the labor market. Out of the total number of 470,000 people receiving disability pensions (including those above retirement age), approximately 100,000 people were "pushed out" of both systems and were directed to the unemployment benefit system and public works programs with much stricter conditions of eligibility (see also János Köllő's contribution in this volume). Others received the new assistance payment but no social services to help to engage in gainful employment.

Although it is difficult to disentangle pragmatic, interest-driven, and ideological elements in the 2010–2012 pension reforms, overall the reform process bears strong ideological marks and pronounced elements of post-communist traditionalism. No doubt, the confiscation of private pension assets was an *étatist* move celebrating the "caring state" and underpinned by nationalist arguments while scapegoating multinational banks and insurance companies. Certainly, the nationalization of pension assets provided extra resources to the cabinet (and thus could be viewed as an interest-driven policy decision), but studying the causes behind this radical decision, a central ideological aim of the Orbán government becomes apparent: the decreasing of personal income tax (PIT) of the "hard working" as opposed to the "work-less" or even those who earn the minimum wage or have low incomes (for whom PIT increased).

The elimination of the disability pension scheme explicitly aimed at the creation of a strong division between the "healthy," "able-bodied," "work-ing" population and the "disabled" and "non-working" population, pushing the latter out of the social insurance system. Given that the social insurance system is not only the most important means of state-run redistribution but also a symbol of nationwide solidarity, we have good reasons to argue that the government pushed the "disabled" out of the system of national solidarity while questioning their overall eligibility for state help.

FAMILY POLICIES

Family policies are traditionally heavily loaded with ideologies as they can easily show the moral values and beliefs of governing elites (Morgan 2006). In the case of post-2010 family policies under the SNC, we can distinguish symbolic elements from concrete policy measures. Assuming that the "lib-eralization" of relationships in the past decades is one of the main reasons for declining birth rates, the Orbán government initiated the restoration of "traditional family values" and has issued a symbolic fight against gender studies and homosexual relationships. The centrality of the "traditional fam-ily" in present-day conservative ideology is best illustrated by the fact that this notion has been incorporated into the new constitution. The National Avowal of the 2011 Fundamental Law states that "the family and the nation constitute the principal framework of our coexistence." Article L (1) stresses that "Hungary shall protect the institution of marriage as the union of a man and a woman established by voluntary decision, and the family as the basis of the survival of the nation." Article II goes on to declare that "the life of the foetus shall be protected from the moment of conception," opening the way to the restriction of abortions in Hungary. However, the cabinet did not always implement these norms into its actual family policy reforms.

Among policy proposals, a "celibacy tax" was raised by one of the key advisors of Orbán, former prime minister Péter Boross, in the summer of 2010 but was soon taken off of the agenda after widespread criticism pointing out the origins of this tax under the Rákosi era in the 1950s.[7] The same idea, together with the suggestion to only let women with at least three children serve in leading positions in public service, was put back on the table in January 2016 by the Christian Democratic Party (KDNP).[8] Another controversial concept, that of a "family vote" was picked up by Fidesz politicians in the course of the preparation of the Fundamental Law of 2011.[9] The government also launched campaigns promoting family and marriage, including the "Week of Marriage"[10] [*Házasság Hete*] organized every year or the short-lived "Find Your Partner" [*Párválasztó*] program in 2013.[11] As a harbinger of a new adversary communication campaign, László Kövér, president of the parliament said in December 2015 that the ruling party had "enough" from the "gender craziness" [*gender-őrület*] and that "we would like our daughters to think that the highest quality of their self-fulfillment is to give birth to grandchildren for us."[12] These statements provoked strong reactions by opposition parties as well as civil groups' actions, for example, the sending of negative pregnancy tests to Kövér.

Later on, especially during its third governmental term, high-ranking members of Fidesz confessed their commitment to a patriarchal gender order and, especially since 2017, issued "anti-gender" campaigns similar to right-wing extremists throughout Europe (Grzebalska, Kováts, and Pető 2017). For example, alongside the attack against George Soros and the Central European University (CEU), an adversary campaign against the Gender Studies Department at CEU as well as the new Gender Program at the Social Sciences Faculty of Eötvös University was launched by government-friendly media.[13] Meanwhile, communicated as a counter-action against gender studies programs, the government decided to set up a program of Family Studies within the Corvinus University Budapest.[14] These examples show clearly that the promotion of families is framed by Fidesz as being in sharp opposition to gender equality as well as the diversity of sexual identities and orientations.

In contrast to the lack of resistance to pension reforms, there was more visible opposition against the traditionalist communication of the government on gender issues. It seems that a wide segment of society is sensitive to the interference of the state into family life and the extension of traditional family values upon them. Statistics underpin that the behavior of society has changed rapidly towards more flexible and nontraditional family forms in the past decades. For example, according to the 2011 census, only 65 percent of Hungarians lived in "traditional families" as opposed to 80 percent in 1990. Furthermore, more than 50 percent of children were born out of wedlock by 2015, similarly to the UK (OECD Family Database 2017). The number of marriages has been among lowest within the OECD (the crude marriage rate[15] dropping from 5.2 to 3.9 between 1995 and 2014). Despite the notable decrease in the number of divorces recently (that can partially be attributed to policies that prefer married couples), more than every second marriage has ended up in divorce in 2014, which was among the highest rates within the post-communist region (Transmonee Database 2016). Furthermore, the over-whelming majority of Hungarians support the idea that carrying a pregnancy to term should be the decision of women, which is in line with the legislation and the actual practice.[16]

Moving from symbolic to *concrete* family policy reforms, we must mention the 2011 "cardinal law" on Family Protection (Act CCXI/2011), which has quasi-constitutional legal status.[17] It states that "the promotion of families is distinct from the system of social provision for the needy. The state provides support primarily to the responsible upbringing of children" (§2. Act CCXI/2011) and this refers to "working" families who have sufficient resources to raise their children. We must meanwhile remember that Roma families often are depicted by the media as "irresponsibly" having "too many" children.

The 2012 demography program of the Ministry of National Economy named "The New Baby Boom. Revolution of Middle-class Fertility" [*Az Új Baby Boom. A középosztály gyermekvállalási forradalma*] repeatedly disclosed the preference of the government to increase fertility among the middle class and not in all strata of society. According to the document, increased fertility rates were the "prime interest of the Hungarian economy" as "with every child a future taxpayer is born!" (NGM 2012, 97). Demography and economic development thus were interlinked once again like the interwar years and later under communism (Szikra 2011; see also Melegh's article in this volume). The government translated these ideas into action primarily through redistributive means, and much less so via the restriction of abortions. However, a government campaign against abortion, in 2011, was paradoxically financed from EU resources.[18] In 2017, some hospitals (primarily run by churches) were allocated extra government resources in return for refusing abortions.

Overall, an increase in the fertility rates of the middle (and upper) classes was to be reached through a vast increase in the financial well-being of better-off families. The primary means has been a new family tax allowance system. Families with one or two children have gained seven percent of the average salary per child per month in 2012 (HUF 10,000/month – approximately EUR 30), while families with three or more children could keep 23 percent of the average salary per child (HUF 33,000 – approximately EUR 100). For example, the net income of a family with four children may have increased by the amount of the average salary in case they have enough deductible income (see detailed tables in Inglot, Szikra, and Rat 2012). Families with lower income could, at the same time, only utilize a smaller portion of the aforementioned amounts due to a lack of refunds. Meanwhile, the minimum income, formerly exempt from PIT, became subject to the 16 percent tax, and the tax refund of low-income earners was ceased, decreasing the net income of the lower social strata substantially. Naturally, unemployed parents did not receive a penny through the new tax allowance system. Although "large families" were the prime targets of the extended tax allowance system, the bottom two income deciles, even those with three children, lost out in the new tax system compared to the top two deciles who were the absolute winners of the reform (Tóth and Virovácz 2013, 394). This shows that in fact the financial situation of families was a more important criterion of "deservingness" than the number of children.[19] Family tax allowance, being the second largest amount in family policy spending by 2012, was further extended to social insurance contributions [*családi járulékkedvezmény*] from January 2014, which allowed more families to utilize this benefit, thus meant a slight correction of the above-mentioned problems. Since 2016, the flat PIT was decreased further to 15 percent, while the allowance of families with two children was increased.[20]

In 2014, reforms to the two-year-long earnings-related parental leave system, GYED [*gyermekgondozási díj*] were issued. "GYED-extra" allowed women who work full-time after the first birthday of their children to receive the full amount of GYED (HUF 108,780 per month or EUR 350). This option was extended to parents of six-month-old babies in 2016. Meanwhile, the so-called sibling GYED [*testvér-GYED*] was adopted, providing the possibility to receive parental leave in "parallel" for two or more children who were born within three years of one another. While parents holding a stable labor market position gained a lot from the new programs, no changes were issued for parents with weak or no work records. The amount of flat-rate universal GYES remained at an extremely low level (at HUF 28,500 or EUR 90 monthly, with no adjustment since 2008).

During 2015 and 2016 Fidesz also subsequently reformed the long-existent housing social policy program [*szociálpolitikai támogatás – szocpol*]. As a symbolic gesture, the name was changed to "family home-building benefit" [*családi otthonteremtési kedvezmény – CSOK*]. Eligibility criteria were changed so that pronatalist aims and upward redistribution were strengthened in the program. Most importantly, unemployed and public workers were excluded from the program. New couples can now "promise" to have one, two, or three children and receive the benefit. They have to be married and have to have three children within ten years to get the maximum amount of HUF 10 million (approximately EUR 32,000) as well as an extra HUF 10 million as a credit. Housing benefits for newly wed couples were one of the few instances when the cabinet, according to its ideology, explicitly discriminated against unmarried (including same-sex) couples. In the case of parents who already have three or more children, there is no need to be married – so the criteria are not applied consistently.

As we have seen, programs for upper-middle-class families (tax allowance, GYED, and CSOK) were boosted. Meanwhile the most important elements of the Hungarian family policy system, universally available family allowance and GYES, were not upgraded and thus lost approximately 40 percent of their real value since 2008. From 2013, the "truancy of children" [*hiányzás*], defined as being away from school for fifty or more classes (approximately ten school days) in a year, became sanctioned by the temporary withdrawal of full family allowance and also with the exclusion of parents from the public works program and social assistance. Between 2011 and 2014, no less than 10 percent of children (altogether 189,650)[21] were excluded from the family allowance system, either through the above rules or the decrease of the compulsory education age from eighteen to sixteen years in 2011. These policies punish poor families overwhelmingly, and among them many Roma who live in segregated settlements to a disproportionate extent.

In terms of services for families, the state promoted the transfer of social and educational facilities to churches. This was done by providing higher state subsidies to church-run educational institutions as compared to state-run and privately run schools. Consequently, the share of children enrolled in religious kindergarten and schools tripled between 2001 and 2016, with the bulk of the increase taking place after 2010 (Varga 2017, 138).

In the case of family policies, the post-communist traditionalist/conservative ideology effected a *double division* among families, creating intersecting situations of privileges and exclusions. Despite the strong and often adverse communication of the cabinet, the gendered dimension of the traditionalist ideology has rarely been implemented in practice. On the other hand, the second and third Orbán cabinets made an especially sharp divide between so-called "responsible" and "irresponsible" families and this has been consequently implemented in its family policies.

CONCLUSION

As we have shown, strong ideological elements have underlined the social policy decisions of the second and third Orbán cabinets. Reforms, at the same time, have benefited almost exclusively the middle and upper classes. Ideological and pragmatic considerations thus were paired together winningly in the social policy of the SNC.

In the next table, we assess whether and how post-communist traditionalism was present in pension and family policy reforms under the SNC. The government insisted on some of its central ideological concerns, even if they went against strong international or internal interests or produced costly and inefficient policy solutions. Seemingly pragmatic, economically driven aims to nationalize private pension assets were accompanied by ideological considerations. Throughout the welfare reforms "deserving" and "undeserving"

Table 11.1 Ideological Features of Pension and Family Policy Reforms in Fidesz's Hungary

	Pension Reform	Family Policy
Initiates extra parliamentarian actions around socially conservative issues	YES. Adversary campaign against multinational banks and private insurance companies.	YES. Anti-gender equality and pro-family campaigns with popular civil actors. Homophobic statements. Increased role of churches in family-related services.
Makes a critical distinction between workers and people who "do not work"	YES. Ceasing of disability pensions. Increasing pensions for high-income earners.	YES. Institutional division of families to "working" and those who are a "burden" on society. Boosting work-related benefits.
Opposes any "hand-outs" to the "undeserving poor"	YES. Ceasing of disability pensions. Freezing minimum pensions.	YES. Freezing all universal family benefits. No means-tested social assistance for families.
Against affirmative action and positive discrimination	NO. "Women 40" program is positively discriminating for women. YES. Negative changes to the disabled and people with low income.	YES. Promoting the "hard working" and opposing any increase in family policies for the poor and the Roma. Segregation in schools.
Creating a common enemy	YES. The "fight" against multinational banks and insurance companies.	YES. "War" against "gender ideology." Communicating heteronormativity and homophobia.
Étatism – in favor of the big "caring" state	YES. Nationalizing private pension funds. Caring state for the "hard working." NO. Exclusion of the disability pensions from the social insurance system.	YES. Boosting public spending on family policies. Caring state for the "hard working" and their families.
Celebrates the traditional family and related gender roles	YES. "Women 40" program.	YES. Fundamental Law. Pro-family and pro-marriage campaigns. Preferential treatment of married couples in CSOK. Excluding women from decision-making positions.

Source: Author, based on Csillag and Szelényi 2015.

social groups were delineated sharply from each other, in which the first over-lap with the "hard working" and the second with the "workless" population. Such a division was pronounced in the case of tax and family policies as well as disability pension reforms.

In the case of family policy reforms, the division between "hard working" and "workless" families was more consequently implemented than tradi-tional family norms. While better-off, "hard working" families received vast resources through the tax allowance system, unemployed and poor families were excluded from being the target group of family policies per se on the basis of their "irresponsible" child bearing. In this employment- and/or class-based division, the wider public did not revolt against increasing exclusion of the nonworking and low-income earners from benefits, and there was no widespread outcry about discrimination against Roma families, including increased school segregation.

The division of society into "deserving" and "undeserving" categories is not unprecedented in Hungarian history: this idea was central to the social policy of the Horthy era as well as state socialism, as both negated handouts to the "workless" and linked benefits to employment. The more generous, post-1990 social policy efforts that aimed at the creation of a welfare state (not at all without contradictions) and promoted the development of certain social transfers as universally available to all citizens who need them have been fading away. In the understanding of the SNC, social rights are not based on "needs" any more but rather on "deservingness" measured accord-ing to one's performance – as stated in the Fundamental Law.

NOTES

1. This paper was supported by the János Bolyai Research Scholarship of the Hungarian Academy of Sciences.
2. In fact, decline already started under the Bajnai government in 2009 when pen-sions were severely cut and the most important universally available family-related cash transfers, as well as means-tested benefits, were frozen.
3. The expression of the ruling coalition defining the 2011 pension reform, which refers to the "systemic change" of the economic and social system in 1989.
4. The expression "clotted structures" comes from a major ideologist of Fidesz, Gyula Tellér, advisor to the prime minister. See mandiner.hu (2015).
5. On the decision of the forced retirement of Hungarian judges, see curia.europa. eu (2012).
6. See, for example, Scharle (2008).
7. See hrportal.hu (2010).
8. See hvg.hu (2016).
9. See index.hu (2011).

10. See hazassaghete.hu (2019).
11. See mno.hu (2013).
12. See mno.hu (2015).
13. See index.hu (2017a).
14. See elteonline.hu (2017).
15. The number of marriages per 1,000 inhabitants.
16. This ratio has, however, decreased from 88 percent in 2007 to 78 percent in 2017. Data is based on a research of a representative sample of 1,000 respondees. See index.hu 2017b.
17. Cardinal acts, similarly to the constitution, need a two-thirds parliamentary majority to be amended, and thus work as long-term guarantees for the fulfilment of new policies beyond one political term. To avoid rules of civil consultation and public debate about cardinal acts, individual MPs of Fidesz, rather than the government, proposed these legislations.
18. See europarl.europa.eu (2011).
19. This is partly due to the fact that the flat-rate 16 percent PIT was applied to previously nontaxed, low-income earners, thus while high-income earners were the absolute winners of the tax reforms (decreasing the highest PIT rate from 38 to 16 percent), low-income earners and especially those on the minimum wage lost out.
20. The family tax allowance in case of a two-child family was increased to 12.500 HUF which translates to app. 40 EUR per child.
21. Authors' own calculation using HCSO Stadat 2015.

BIBLIOGRAPHY

Augusztinovics, Mária, Róbert I. Gál, Ágnes Matits, Levente Máté, András Simonovits, and János Stahl. 2002. "The Hungarian Pension System before and after the 1998 Reform." In *Pension Reform in Central and Eastern Europe*, Vol. 1–2, edited by Elaine Fultz. Geneva: International Labour Office.
Bohle, Dorothee, and Béla Greskovits. 2012. *Capitalist Diversity on Europe's Periphery*. Ithaca, NY: Cornell University Press.
Csillag, Tamás, and Iván Szelényi. 2015. "Drifting from Liberal Democracy – Neo-Conservative Ideology of Managed Illiberal Democratic Capitalism in Post-Communist Europe." *Intersections. EEJSP* 1 (1): 18–48.
curia.europa.eu. 2012. "Judgement of the Court." http://curia.europa.eu/juris/docume nt/document.jsf?text=&docid=129324&pageIndex=0&doclang=EN&mode=re q&dir=&occ=first&part=1&cid=7080, accessed June 25, 2019.
Drahokoupil, Jan, and Stefan Domonkos. 2012. "Averting the Funding–gap Crisis: East European Pension Reforms after 2008." *Global Social Policy* 12 (3): 283–99.
elteonline.hu. 2017. "Családtudományi mesterképzést indít a Corvinus Egyetem, válaszul az ELTE gender képzésére." http://elteonline.hu/kozelet/2017/03/08/csala dtudomanyi-mesterkepzest-indit-a-corvinus-egyetem-valaszul-az-elte-gender-k epzesere/, accessed June 25, 2019.

europarl.europa.eu. 2011. "Anti-abortion Campaign in Hungary." http://www.euro parl.europa.eu/sides/getDoc.do?pubRef=-//EP//TEXT+OQ+O-2011-000139+0+D OC+XML+V0//EN, accessed June 25, 2019.

Ferge, Zsuzsa. 2012. *Vágányok és vakvágányok a társadalompolitikában.* Budapest: L'Harmattan.

Fundamental Law of Hungary. 2011.

Halmai, Gábor, and Kim Lane Scheppele. 2012. "Opinion on Hungary's New Constitutional Order." Amicus Brief for the Venice Commission.

hazassaghete.hu. 2019. http://hazassaghete.hu/, accessed June 25, 2019.

hrportal.hu. 2010. "Nem érzelmi kérdés a gyermektelenségi adó." http://www.hrpo rtal.hu/c/nem-erzelmi-kerdes-a-gyermektelensegi-ado-20100915.html, accessed June 25, 2019.

hvg.hu. 2016. "A szingliadóról indít vitát a KDNP." http://hvg.hu/itthon/20160107_ A_szingliadorol_indit_vitat_a_KDNP, accessed June 25, 2019.

index.hu. 2011. "Előkerült a gyerek utáni extra szavazati jog a Fideszben." http:// index.hu/belfold/2011/02/11/elokerult_a_gyerek_utani_extra_szavazati_jog_a_fid eszben/, accessed June 25, 2019.

———. 2017a."Nem rombolja le a társadalmat, ha gondolkodunk a nemi szerepekről." http://index.hu/belfold/2017/02/23/tarsadalmi_nemek_gender_mesterkepzes_az_ elten/, accessed June 25, 2019.

———. 2017b. "Többen akarnak halálbüntetést, mint tíz éve." https://index.hu/bel fold/2017/10/30/a_magyarok_negyede_szeretne_halalbuntetest/, accessed June 25, 2019.

Inglot, Tomasz, Cristina Raţ, and Dorottya Szikra. 2012. "Reforming Post-communist Welfare States: Family Policy in Poland, Hungary and Romania since 2000." *Problems of Post-Communism* 59 (6): 27–49.

Juhász, Gábor. 2015. "Államcélok, paradigmaváltás és aktuálpolitikai alkotmányozás. A szociális jogok védelme az Alaptörvényben." *Esély* 2015 (1): 3–32.

Körösényi, András. 2015. "A magyar demokrácia három szakasza és az Orbánrezsim." In *A magyar politikai rendszer – negyedszázad után*, edited by András Körösényi, 401–22. Budapest: Osiris – MTA TK.

Lakner, Zoltán. 2015. "Az átmenet alagútja. A szociálpolitika-alkotás magyarországi politikai környezete." PhD dissertation. Budapest: ELTE Social Sciences Faculty.

mandiner.hu. 2015. "Orbán Viktor valósitja meg a rendszerváltást." http://mandiner .hu/cikk/20150702_orban_viktor_valositja_meg_a_rendszervaltast_interju_lanc zi_andras_teller_gyula.

Mándi, Tibor. 2015. "Politikai gondolkodás." In *A magyar politikai rendszer – negyedszázad után*, edited by András Körösényi. Budapest: Osiris – MTA TK.

Mesa-Lago, Carmelo. 2014. *Reversing Pension Privatization: The Experience of Argentina, Bolivia, Chile and Hungary.* ILO, ESS Working Paper, No. 44.

mno.hu. 2013. "Tizmillióból segiti a párválasztást a kormány." http://mno.hu/belfol d/tizmilliobol-segiti-a-parvalasztast-a-kormany-1152081, accessed June 25, 2019.

———. 2015. "Politikai vihart kavartak Kövér László szavai." http://mno.hu/politi ka/vihart-kavartak-kover-laszlo-szavai-1319148, accessed June 25, 2019.

Morgan, Kimberly, J. 2006. *Working Mothers and the Welfare State. Religion and the Politics of Work-Family Policies in Western Europe and the United States.* Stanford, CA: Stanford University Press.

Nemzetgazdasági Minisztérium (NGM). 2012. *Az Új Baby Boom. A középosztály gyermekvállalási forradalma.* Budapest.

Orbán, Gábor, and Dániel Palotai. 2005. *The Sustainability of the Hungarian Pension System: A Reassessment.* MNB Occasional Papers 40. Budapest: Central Bank of Hungary.

Orbán, Viktor. 2012. "Speech at the EPP Congress." Speech in Bucharest, Romania, October 17–18, 2012. http://www.fidesz.hu/hirek/2012-10-19/orban-nem-joleti-allam-hanem-munka-alapu-tarsadalom-epul-kepek/, accessed June 25, 2019.

———. 2014. "The Era of the Work-based State Is Approaching." Speech in Tusnádfürdő (Baile Tusnad, Romania) at the 25th Bálványos Summer Free University, July 29. http://www.kormany.hu/en/the-prime-minister/news/the-era-of-the-work-based-state-is-approaching, accessed June 25, 2019.

Romano, Serena. 2014. *The Political and Social Construction of Poverty: Central and Eastern European Countries in Transition.* Chicago: Policy Press.

Scharle, Ágota. 2008. "A Labour Market Explanation for the Rise in Disability Claims." In *The Hungarian Labour Market: Review and Analysis*, edited by Károly Fazekas et al., 91–103. Budapest: Institute of Economics, HAS and Hungarian Employment Foundation. http://econ.core.hu/file/download/mt/2_eleje.pdf, accessed June 25, 2019.

Scharle, Ágota, and Dorottya Szikra. 2015. "Recent Changes Moving Hungary away from the European Social Model." In *The European Social Model in Crisis: Is Europe Losing Its Soul?*, edited by Daniel Vaughan-Whitehead, 229–61. Cheltenham: Edward Elgar.

Simonovits, András. 2011. "The Mandatory Private Pension Pillar in Hungary: An Obituary." *International Social Security Review* 64 (3): 81–98.

Szikra, Dorottya. 2011. "Tradition Matters: Child Care and Primary School Education in Modern Hungary." In *Children, Families, and States: Time Policies of Childcare, Preschool, and Primary Education in Europe*, edited by Karen Hagemann, Konrad H. Jarauscha, and Cristina Allemann-Ghiond, 364–84. New York: Berghahn Books.

———. 2014. "Democracy and Welfare in Hard Times: The Social Policy of the Orbán Government in Hungary between 2010 and 2014." *Journal of European Social Policy* 5: 486–500.

Szikra, Dorottya, and Diána Kiss. 2017. "Beyond Nationalization. Assessing the Impact of the 2010–2012 Pension Reform in Hungary." *Review of Sociology* 27 (4): 83–107.

Tóth, G. Csaba, and Péter Virovácz. 2013. "Nyertesek és vesztesek. A magyar egykulcsos adórendszer vizsgálata mikroszimulációs módszerrel." *Pénzügyi Szemle* 58 (4): 385–400.

Varga, J. 2018. *A közoktatás indikátorrendszere 2017.* HAS KRTK-KTI. Budapest, Hungary.

Chapter 12

The Central European University in the Trenches

Zsolt Enyedi

Hybrid regimes are typically analyzed from the point of view of competitiveness, checks and balances, pluralism, individual rights, and media freedom. Their various social sectors like economy, sport, education, or religious life tend to receive little attention. Without the capture of these nonpolitical spheres, however, regimes cannot consolidate.

Universities are relevant institutions in this regard because they have a central role in socializing citizens, selecting elites, and legitimizing government policies. A decisive influence over universities is particularly important for those regimes that have an ideological agenda. Without such an influence they face a constant intellectual challenge even if they have a monopoly over the central arenas of power.

In non-totalitarian regimes governmental control over the nonpolitical spheres will always be limited and contested. Citizens learn about the locations of the boundaries of freedom from the official rules and regulations and from prominent controversial cases. Governments may initiate conflicts against NGOs, churches, companies, or universities – not because these organizations are political challengers but in order to signal the costs of autonomy. In 2017 the Central European University (CEU) became one of those prominent controversial cases that indicate the degree of democratic regression and the remaining social pluralism in Hungary.

THE ORGANIZATIONAL AND LEGAL BACKGROUND

The CEU is a graduate higher education institution with MA and PhD programs in the social sciences and humanities. Currently, the university has about 1,500 students from about 120 countries. Several of its programs are ranked among the 100 best in the world (see *Times Higher Education* or *Quacquarelli Symonds* rankings).

The CEU was established in 1991 by dissident intellectuals and scholars from the Soviet bloc and by their Western supporters, primarily the investor and philanthropist George Soros, who provided the necessary financial means. During its first years of existence the CEU worked in Prague, Budapest, and Warsaw, but by the mid-1990s, it consolidated its operations in Budapest, Hungary. The university was chartered in the State of New York, its academic programs were registered with the New York State Education Department, and it received institutional accreditation from the Middle States Commission on Higher Education. The CEU is one of the many higher education institutions (e.g., American University in Cairo, American University of Paris, American University in Bulgaria, American University of Central Asia, and so on), which have their seat in the United States but have no campus on American territory. In Hungary, the CEU was recognized as a foundation-based university, a category that exempted foreign professors from having to obtain Hungarian work permits.

For about twelve years, the CEU functioned in Hungary exclusively as a foreign university. In 2004 the Hungarian parliament passed a law that created a Hungarian institution of higher education under the Hungarian translation of the name of the CEU (*Közép-európai Egyetem* or KEE). The purpose of the law, as stated in its preamble, was to enrich Hungarian academia by providing full-fledged membership to the CEU in the Hungarian higher education sector.[1] Subsequently, the KEE obtained Hungarian accreditation and the university's American and Hungarian units functioned as one integrated academic community. As all academic programs are registered in the United States, all students receive an American diploma. A smaller group of programs have Hungarian accreditation. Those students who enroll into these programs and who comply with the special Hungarian requirements have the possibility of receiving a Hungarian diploma as well.

The rector of the KEE and the rector and president of the CEU are one and the same. The leader of the university is, on the one hand, elected by the board of trustees, while as rector of the KEE he or she is appointed by the president of Hungary. The professors have an employment contract with KEE, but the contracts include the obligation to participate in the delivery of the CEU's programs. The CEU-KEE agreement established an integrated framework for the two units and specified that KEE facilitates the CEU's educational activities in Hungary using the "license-agreements" formula of the Hungarian higher education law, which allowed Hungarian universities to contribute to the functioning of foreign universities.

This brief legal review was important to underline the fact that the 2004 law created a complex legal structure, implying one academic community and one administrative structure but two legal seats and two institutional accreditations. While this complexity hardly was sensed by the university's students and by its professors and was perfectly in line with both Hungarian and American law, it amounted to a vulnerability that could be exploited by a hostile government in 2017.

Notwithstanding its legal structure, the CEU is a complex case also in terms of its actual location on the national – international continuum. On the one hand, the CEU is one of the most international universities in the world.[2] About 80 percent of its students and 60 percent of its professors are non-Hungarian, its language of operation is English, and its rectors have been, so far, all foreigners. On the other hand, the university is well embedded in Hungarian academia. The university employs about 400 Hungarian employees and teaches about 350 Hungarian students each year. Its facilities (e.g., its library) are used by thousands of local citizens. It cooperates intensively with Hungarian universities. The long list of common projects includes a jointly operated medievalist library, the participation of Hungarian "college of excellence" students in CEU courses, the teaching of CEU doctoral candidates at various Hungarian universities, and many more. Every year about 200 Hungarian students receive a full or partial fellowship, and the CEU makes great efforts to attract talented Hungarian scholars back to Budapest. In 2017 the CEU was able to attract close to HUF 10 billion to Hungary from foreign research funds and contribute the same magnitude to the Hungarian budget.

THE TENSIONS PRECEDING THE LEGAL INITIATIVE

While achievements such as the ones listed earlier fostered a sense of belonging and confidence at the university, a darkening political atmosphere after 2010 led to growing unease. Given its support for the principles of open society and given its specialization in humanities and social sciences, a considerable part of the research and teaching activities at the university focus on issues such as the quality of democracy, rule of law, corruption, nationalism, gender- and ethnicity-based discrimination, European integration, and social justice. This agenda fits uneasily with nationalist and centralizing ideology and the increasingly xenophobic and authoritarian rhetoric of the ruling party. But neither Fidesz's opposition to liberal constitutionalism nor the one-party control of the state apparatus necessitated a direct conflict between the university and the government. Due to its financial independence the university could feel relatively safe.

A more immediate threat presented itself by the intensification of government attacks against George Soros, the founder of the CEU. He became a target of criticism as a supporter of civic organizations (primarily human rights and anti-corruption organizations like Helsinki Committee, Transparency International, and Amnesty International). In 2015 a new issue emerged that polarized the relationship between Soros and the prime minister of Hungary, Viktor Orbán – the issue of asylum seekers. Orbán presciently identified immigration as the principal issue of the coming years, not a self-evident observation in a country in which the number of immigrants has never been above two percent. It soon became clear that he needed someone to personify the threat of immigration, and George Soros was considered to be ideal for the purpose.

In the meantime, the CEU received a new rector and president, Michael Ignatieff, a widely respected historian, public intellectual, and former Canadian liberal politician. On September 6, 2016, the state secretary responsible for education visited the CEU. At the meeting, he reassured the new rector that the ongoing attacks against the founder of the university would not affect the university. Ignatieff's inauguration ceremony in October included a welcoming speech in Hungarian, a Hungarian poem, and a folksong (performed by a choir from a local university), reflecting the new rector's ambition to emphasize the Hungarian dimension of the university. The future of the university seemed secure. In reality, the preparation for the attack against the university, supervised by a small circle within the government, was already in full swing.

Government officials devoted the fall and winter months to a thorough scrutiny of the vulnerable components of the university's legal structure. The re-examination of the CEU's license of operation started in October. Originally the focus of investigation was on confirming the validity of the U.S. accreditation of the CEU and its programs. The officials expressed doubts concerning the CEU's proper American registration and legal status. This suspicion was backed by the fact that the institutional accreditation document of the CEU issued by the Middle States Commission on Higher Education contained the Budapest and not the New York address. During the coming months the CEU supplied all the necessary documents[3] to prove that its legal seat is in the state of New York. The Educational Authority confirmed at a meeting with university officials that the matter is solved. But, in fact, no decision was issued, simply because the bureaucrats did not dare to make any positive statement concerning the university. While the statutory deadline for closing such files is sixty days, at the time of writing this chapter more than two years and three months passed, and the case is still without an official verdict.

In the meantime, a general audit of foreign universities was launched. Irregularities were detected in virtually all institutions. In the case of the CEU, it was found that not all of its American academic programs have been registered in Hungary (even programs not leading to Hungarian degrees need to be registered), and the university does not report information about its operation properly to the Higher Education Information System. The CEU acknowledged the administrative error concerning the first point, swiftly registered its programs, and committed itself to more accurate data reporting, although it pointed out that some of the categories of the statistical system simply do not fit its American mode of operation (semesters instead of trimesters, four years of doctoral studies instead of six years, and so on). None of these matters appeared particularly significant.

The more worrying sign surfaced on February 2, 2017, when the magazine *Figyelő* published an article with the title "Can the Soros School Stay?" speculating about the intensions of the government to close down the CEU. The well-connected journalist claimed that a government minister leaked already before Christmas that the CEU was on the government's black list, with the final goal of forcing the university to leave Hungary. The article considered the CEU as a natural target given its ability to out-compete Hungarian universities in obtaining research funds and because of its Gender Studies program. As it later turned out, this early publication correctly identified some of the arguments used against the university in the upcoming campaign, although many more were added in the coming months.

The *Figyelő* article attracted considerable attention. The English-language *Budapest Beacon*, for example, reported the next day that "Budapest's Central European University (CEU) may come into the cross hairs of the Hungarian government in 2017 as part of the broader war it is declaring on civil society." The rector of the CEU promptly issued a response to the *Figyelő* piece, concluding with the statement: "The article implies that the government is considering steps against the CEU. On the contrary, for more than 25 years, we have had professional working relationships with every Hungarian government, including the current administration; we expect to maintain these good relations in the future." In order to dispel any lingering doubts, the rector sent an invitation to the minister of human capacities. The minister was unwilling to meet, and suddenly the once amicable secretary of state became unavailable, too. Finally, after many unsuccessful attempts at learning what the government's plans were, the minister of justice agreed to meet the rector on March 20, 2017. Unfortunately, the meeting proved to be only moderately informative: the minister confirmed that some changes were being contemplated concerning foreign universities but could not provide details about them as the legislative initiative was drafted within the Ministry of Human Capacities.

The question whether the CEU would become a target of a governmental campaign was finally clarified by the article of the pro-government website *Origo* on March 28. The title of the piece left little doubt: "Severe wrongdoings at the Soros university." Based on a government audit of foreign universities (which was at that time not public), the article accused the CEU of "concrete fraud." The website reported that the government plans legislative actions for a more proper regulation of the field, concluding with the statement "Evidently, it is a question whether the university will close once the law is modified."

When the executive summary of the audit was finally released, it turned out that it contained a much more nuanced and balanced picture than the *Origo* summary. While it indeed referred to the lack of registration of some courses, it acknowledged that "the registration applications for these programs have since been submitted, and are currently being assessed." In fact, a few days later the registration was approved. The audit also mentioned that countries such as the United States have no European-style accreditation of individual programs but added that

> certain program elements are subject either to periodic internal audits – which typically apply to the whole institution – or to periodic audits by an external validating organization, which also apply to the institution as a whole. An example of an institution in this category is the Central European University (CEU): the Middle States Commission on Higher Education *sets out very detailed and strict conditions* (emphases added by author) which the CEU has had to fulfil and must continue to fulfil in order to remain an accredited institution in the United States.[4]

THE HIGHER EDUCATION BILL
AND FIRST REACTIONS

Within a few hours, however, the CEU came to realize that the problem was not a hostile article that misconstrued a government report but the actual legislative change. The amendment of the higher education bill was published on the website of the Hungarian parliament on March 28. The text of the amendment substantiated the worst fears of the university. The amendment demanded foreign universities must have educational activities in their home country (and be recognized by the authorities as universities operating in the territory of the country), and to have a name that does not resemble the name of another university recognized by Hungary. Furthermore, the universities originating outside of the European Economic Area (EEA) will be allowed to operate in Hungary only if there exists an international agreement between the Hungarian government and the respective country's government. Finally, it also deprived universities originating in non-EEA OECD countries of the right to enter into a license agreement with Hungarian universities and removed previous exemptions from work permits.

While the law was formulated to affect all foreign universities, most of its clauses were relevant only for the CEU. The CEU was the only foreign university without a campus in its home country, the only one that had a name issue (because the Hungarian name is a direct translation of the American name), and the only non-EEA OECD university that had a contract with a Hungarian university. The CEU was also one of the two universities that were affected by the change of the work permit policy, and the only one having a considerable number of non-EU nationals on its faculty (including its rector). Finally, while the demand for international agreement affected nominally seven universities, the CEU was the only one with a politically "problematic" background. Given that the signing of treaties is a discretionary right of governments, the CEU had the most reason to worry about the eventual signature of such an agreement.

On the next day, on March 29, CEU management held a community forum and a press conference, pointing out the discriminatory nature of the amendment, the threat to academic freedom, the lack of consultation, the short deadlines, and the political undertones behind the media attack, and asked the government to withdraw the proposal and to start negotiations with the affected universities about the new regulation of the sector.

The response to the press conference arrived fast, delivered by the prime minister through an interview on public radio on March 31. In the interview he consistently called the CEU "the university of George Soros" or "Soros university." He said, among other things, that "the Soros university, which issues foreign diplomas too, confessed itself that it does not conduct education abroad, which is against Hungarian rules," "cheating is cheating, whoever commits it," and "not even billionaires stand above the law." He said of potential talks with the CEU: "We don't need to discuss the issue with them, they are not the American government." Then he went on saying that Hungarian universities have justified grievances against the CEU because the university issues both American and Hungarian diplomas, putting other Hungarian universities in a disadvantageous position. He concluded that "there is a clear rule according to which a foreign diploma can be issued only if the university operates abroad" (Orbán 2017).

In fact, there was no such rule; the prime minister accused the university of not following rules that he planned to pass through parliament in the coming days. The rest of the interview was mainly about the alleged long-term plan of George Soros to abolish borders and to undermine national sovereignty.

In spite of the references by the prime minister to the interests of Hungarian universities, the representatives of Hungarian academia responded negatively to the legislative initiative. The most important forum – the Presidium of the Rectors' Conference – met on April 3 and asked the government at least to extend the deadlines.

Originally the debate in parliament concerning the higher education law was supposed to take place on April 5, but the government fast-tracked the legislation. The amendment was submitted to parliament on April 3, the text of it was further amended by Fidesz representatives on the same day, and the law was accepted on April 4.[5] As a result, the new regulation was accepted within a week of its publication, and the time allotted for debate in parliament was limited to a couple of hours. No more than twenty-four hours passed between the starting time of the parliamentary debate of the bill and its adoption.

The MPs of the government party made two changes to the original proposal. The first one was bringing the deadlines of compliance even closer – despite the request of the Presidium of the Rectors' Conference to the contrary. The final text stipulated that unless all conditions are met, no new student can be accepted after January 1, 2018 (as opposed to September). Regarding the international agreement requirement, the final amendment demanded that "such international agreement be based on the previous agreement with the central government of the state in case of a federal state, where the recognition of the binding effect of an international agreement does not fall into the scope of the central government." This convoluted sentence implied that the CEU will need not one international agreement but two to continue to operate in Budapest: one between Budapest and the State of New York and one (the "previous agreement") between Budapest and Washington, DC. The latter was supposed to be finalized within six months, by October 11, 2017.

The public reacted with a storm of indignation. A 10,000-strong demonstration on April 2 was followed by one of the largest demonstrations ever against the Orbán government, in which close to 80,000 people took to the streets. The aim of the second demonstration was to put pressure on the president of Hungary to veto the law. Hundreds of universities across the world sent petitions with the same request, joined by political authorities in Europe and the United States.

On April 10 the president signed the bill into law. His decision triggered further protest actions, not only in Budapest but also in many other university towns. Once it became clear that a protracted legal and international process would decide whether the university can stay, the demonstrations became smaller and less focused on the CEU.

While the decision of president Áder was disappointing, he tried to distinguish his own position from parliament's in an extraordinary statement in which he called for negotiations between the government and the affected universities. In line with the request of the president, the government set up a negotiating team that was supposed to prepare intergovernmental treaties. Another committee was established to discuss the issues of implementation with the universities. But in the first months the former team focused on other cases than the CEU, while the second, consisting of mid-level administrators from many ministries, showed to have neither competence for working out a mutually acceptable settlement nor knowledge concerning crucial questions like what the requirement of education in the country of origin actually means at the only meeting with CEU officials (on May 17, 2017).

The uproar against the new regulations and the attitude of the government led to an unprecedented move in parliament: representatives of the left and the radical right turned together on April 21 to the Constitutional Court to investigate the constitutionality of the law and the way it was accepted.

The international response (discussed in more detail below) was similarly unequivocal. When the state secretary of education visited Brussels after the adoption of the law, he confidently claimed to journalists: "I don't think that the opinion of the European Commission will have any negative opinion of the law" (HVG 2017). In fact, two weeks after the promulgation of the bill, on April 26, the European Commission started infringement proceedings against the Hungarian government, pointing out that the law is incompatible with freedom for higher education institutions to provide services anywhere in the EU, with the right of academic freedom, the right to education, the freedom to conduct business, and with the EU's legal obligations under international trade law. Similarly, on April 27, the Parliamentary Assembly of the Council of Europe (PACE) called on Hungary to suspend the implementation of the law. It also requested the opinion of the European Commission for Democracy through Law (i.e., the Venice Commission) on the compatibility of lex CEU (as the law became widely known) with Council of Europe standards.

The Hungarian government vigorously defended the new regulations in various international fora. The most public stage of this defense happened in front of the European Parliament (EP) on April 26. The prime minister claimed in front of MEPs that the law abolishes privileges and loopholes and distributes rights across universities in an equal fashion. Neither parliament nor the EPP, Fidesz's party family, accepted this interpretation. On May 17 the EP passed a resolution calling for repeal of lex CEU and to suspend immediately all deadlines. Following up on a statement by the Governor of the State of New York issued on May 24, urging a discussion about the matter, the EP also called for talks between New York and Hungary. In the coming days, bowing to the increasing pressure, the government began a series of talks with the Governor of New York Andrew Cuomo's team.

Global attention on the issue continued unabated for the next months: on June 14, the Cultural and Education Committee of the European Parliament urged the government to solve the issue and the rapporteurs of the Venice Commission visited the CEU on June 30. In the meantime, the government's suggestion for a federal level agreement was turned down – politely – by the education secretary of the Trump government in the U.S. In a letter dated June 15, Betsy DeVoss informed the minister of human capacities that education matters belong to the jurisdiction of the individual states in the United States. Apparently, Hungarian authorities decided to accept this letter as "the previous agreement with the central government" stipulated by the text of the new law. This seemed to be a less embarrassing move than to modify the law. On July 14 the minister of foreign affairs signed a treaty with Maryland regarding McDaniel College, the only other relevant American institution of higher education (Boston and Webster universities showed no interest in continuing their activities in Hungary). By August the treaty was voted on in parliament and turned into law.

The treaty on the McDaniel College was important for the government in order to show that it was not waging an all-out war against American universities, but the text of the treaty undermined one of the crucial arguments used in the debate with the CEU. The agreement explicitly stated that the Maryland authorities do not take any responsibility for the activities of the Budapest campus of McDaniel College. This ran counter to the argument that international agreements are necessary because foreign authorities must take responsibility for their universities operating in Hungary. The government nevertheless signed the agreement as it badly needed it for its propaganda efforts.

While the government could disregard the parliamentary assembly of the Council of Europe, it had to respond to the European Commission's "reasoned opinion" sent in April. The response sent by the Ministry of Justice on May 25 was found unsatisfactory by the European Commission. On July 13 the Commission reconfirmed its previous negative opinion and gave another month to the Hungarian government to reconsider the case. On August 14 the minister of justice replied, showing no willingness to modify the regulations. Finally, on December 7 the Commission referred Hungary to the European Court of Justice.

In the meantime, the Venice Commission issued its own preliminary opinion on August 11 (reconfirmed by a final decision on October 6). According to this opinion the law, even if it was justifiable in principle, should make an exception for the universities that have been already functioning in the country prior to the amendment. Extra guarantees such as international agreements were considered by the Venice Commission as superfluous for universities that have been established in the country for many decades.

In the communication with European bodies, the government admitted no fault whatsoever, but then, on October 13, 2017, the Hungarian Parliament suddenly modified the law. But the modification concerned only the deadlines: they were extended by one year. The government presented the move as a concession and as a belated response to the requests of the Hungarian Rectors' Conference and the Venice Commission. In reality it was simply a tactical move, postponing the final decision.

For the CEU the postponement of the deadlines was not a concession but a cold shower. In order to understand the disappointment of the university, one needs to go back to the negotiations that took place between the representatives of the Hungarian government and the Governor of the State of New York across the summer months. These negotiations resulted in an agreement that was acceptable to the CEU. The university learned from the talks that the Hungarian government no longer insisted on a federal-level agreement and that the requirement of education in the home country could be fulfilled by a single higher education program run jointly with an American higher education institution. In other words, there was no need for a full-scale campus or for accreditation of programs that lead to degrees.

In order to meet the criterion of education in the country of origin, the CEU swiftly signed a memorandum of understanding with Bard College in New York state in September and launched a new Advanced Certificate Program in Inequality Analysis. With exemplary speed, the American authorities registered the program and added Annandale-on-Hudson, New York, to the teaching sites of the CEU in their registries by early October. Only the signature of Hungarian officials was missing.

In the August version of the draft agreement, the Hungarian government committed itself to submit the signed treaty to the Hungarian parliament for a vote by November 15, 2017. But the only event on that day was a phone call by the Hungarian negotiator to his American counterpart, saying that while the prime minister approved the text of the negotiations, the final settlement should happen only after Hungarian officials inspected the program in Annandale. Since actual courses could begin only in February 2018, this decision meant the postponing of the signature of the agreement for at least three months, possibly a year. Unofficially, the government informed the press that the issue was taken off the table until the April 2018 elections. The leaked position of the Constitutional Court was the same: the CEU issue was too sensitive politically to address prior to the elections. The fact that this prolonged the legal limbo of the university, with many harmful consequences for the operation of the institution, did not resonate with the representatives of the legislative, executive, and judiciary branches of the government.

The negative turn in the attitude of the government was most likely a product of the intensification of the anti-Soros campaign. Around the end of August, the government decided to launch a so-called national consultation (a postal ballot) on the issue of the "Soros Plan." The questionnaire, sent to all citizens in the second part of September, contained several questions specifically focused on the alleged plan of George Soros. Here is one example:

> George Soros would also like to see migrants receive lighter sentences for the crimes they commit. George Soros, with significant amounts of funding, supports numerous organizations that assist immigration and defend immigrants who have committed unlawful acts. . . . Do you support this point of the Soros Plan? YES/NO.

During the coming months the country was flooded with anti-Soros posters. A Fidesz MP likened Soros to Satan, and the prime minister identified the stakes of the upcoming election as a battle against Soros to rescue European Christian civilization. While the university stopped being the primary focus of the anti-Soros campaign, hardly a day passed without a negative reference to the CEU in the pro-government press.

In the meantime, hopes for the intervention of the judiciary were dashed by a very unusual decision of the Constitutional Court. The Court was silent on Lex CEU for an entire year, in spite of the appeal of MPs. Then, in June 2018, it declared that it would not rule on the issue until the European Court of Justice (ECJ) also investigated the law. This was the first time that the Hungarian Constitutional Court suspended the review of a legal act citing the need for a "constitutional dialogue" with the ECJ.

The CEU found itself in a Kafkaesque situation. The Ombudsman refused to deal with the complaints of the university, claiming that the Constitutional Court was investigating the case. The Court pointed to the European Court of Justice, knowing that the ECJ has authority to examine only a narrow range of issues, and therefore a large majority of constitutional concerns will remain unaddressed. The president, who earlier publicly suggested the cooperation with an American university, refused to comment on the fact that the university's legal limbo continued even after his advice was formally accepted.

SUPPORT AND INTERNATIONAL CONTEXT

The mobilization against the law was spectacular. As far as Hungarian society was concerned, it produced a wave of petitions and mass demonstrations that had not been seen for many years. Citizens took to the streets right after the news about the law broke. Most activity took place in Budapest, but smaller-scale demonstrations happened in virtually all the larger cities in Hungary. Instead of perceiving the CEU's dual identity as an unfair advantage, the Hungarian Academy of Sciences and the representatives of most universities considered in their statements the CEU's bridge function as beneficial for Hungarian academia. Reputed Hungarian legal scholars, including a former president of Hungary and president of the Constitutional Court, expressed their dismay at encroachment on the rule of law. A number of *amicus curiae* criticizing the law were submitted to the Constitutional Court, signed by some of the most prestigious constitutional scholars in the country. Professors of the largest Hungarian university organized a day of lectures in the defense of academic autonomy and in solidarity with the CEU. The students of Budapest universities expressed their sympathy through various imaginative gestures, including erecting gates with the labels "CEU should stay" and "CEU should go," and filming how the crowds chose to pass through the former.

The support from international academia was equally overwhelming. More than twenty Nobel laureates expressed their opposition to the law. The protesters included the presidents of Oxford, Harvard, Duke, New York University, Princeton, Berkeley, Yale, and several other universities, and professors of hundreds of higher education institutions. Altogether more than 700 universities expressed their solidarity with the CEU. Academies (British, Swedish, Austrian, and so on), and professional organizations like the European University Association, the Canadian Association of University Teachers, the Europaeum, the World International Studies Committee, and the International Association of Universities, also joined in, representing tens of thousands of researchers and students worldwide, urging the government to withdraw the amendment of the law. Hungarian intellectuals and academic organizations from Romania also issued petitions.

Virtually all relevant political authorities in Europe expressed their concerns about the bill, ranging from the assembly of the Council of Europe to the European Parliament on to the president and chancellor of Germany. The vote in the European Parliament about launching the Article 7 procedure revealed that the government cannot count on the solidarity of sister parties. As a number of participants noted (see, for example, the comments of Judith Sargentini MEP[6]), the CEU affair created deeper divisions within EPP than previous conflicts. At the same time, the vote also showed that the majority of British, Croatian, German, Italian, and Spanish conservatives are against sanctions, while most Austrian, Bulgarian, and French center-right politicians are indifferent. The fact that many German Christian Democrats were ready to give the benefit of the doubt to Orbán saved the Hungarian government from a consequential defeat. The subsequent victories of populist parties across Europe created a situation in which the leaders of EPP no longer dared to challenge the Hungarian prime minister.

It is difficult to assess whether the widespread – cultural, political, academic, and popular – protest eventually made a difference or not. The fact that the U.S.-Hungarian negotiations ended with a draft that allowed the CEU to continue to exist in Budapest in roughly the same structure that it had in the past – with the important change that CEU launched a new program in the U.S. – was perceived as a concession in 2017, at least compared to the belligerent statements made by the representatives of the government and the government party in the first phase of the conflict. On the other hand, the postponement of the final settlement shows that the government was actually resistant to the pressure. Its propaganda war against the CEU served the wider anti-Soros campaign well, while causing considerable harm to a Soros-related

institution via keeping it in a legal limbo for at least a year. In order to understand what the actual alternatives were to solve the issue, one needs to return
to the discussion of the legal and institutional framework of the university and
to the government's vision of the optimal model.

INSTITUTIONAL ALTERNATIVES

According to the official justification of the law (i.e., the justification submitted as part of the amendment), foreign education institutions are welcome as a
"means" for achieving the goals of Hungary's cultural policy. The regulations
must make sure that the implemented arrangements are in line with Hungary's foreign policy objectives and national security concerns. Following
the same instrumentalist-paternalistic logic, the secretary of state responsible
for education justified the need for a campus in the home country, saying that
foreign universities have a legitimate reason to be allowed in a country only
if they bring in knowledge that was produced elsewhere and that is missing in
the host country. This is why the existence of a campus in the home country
is a necessary requirement. The CEU's counterargument, that its American
style of education, its American curriculum, and administration, all approved
and certified by American educational authorities, constitute enough added
value to fulfill this logic, was dismissed. The government insisted on physical
facilities in the home country.

Many Fidesz politicians expressed a preference for the departure of the
CEU from Hungary, while allowing the continuing functioning of the Hungarian unit, the KEE. The CEU resisted the government's pressure to transform into a Hungarian private university for several reasons. The ability to
issue American diplomas was only one of them. Virtually as important was
the attachment to the idea of being an American-Hungarian integrated university, and the fear of interference by the government if the American shell
would be removed. This fear received confirmation in 2018 when the government banned MA programs in Gender Studies at Hungarian universities.

The model preferred by the government was unattractive also because it
implied splitting the university in two and leaving only the Hungarian accredited programs in Budapest. The American and Hungarian research and educational programs form a symbiosis and their separation would present major
academic and logistical challenges. Additionally, for international students
and scholars, the fact that the CEU, while operating in Hungary, is part of the
American higher education system used to be an important point of attraction.

It was clear that the government would never acknowledge that it made
a mistake with the law, although concerning the demand for a federal level
agreement, for example, it must have realized that the requirement was a

legal impossibility. The question was whether a face-saving solution could be identified, and if so, whether the government would embrace it. One option could have been to exempt existing institutions from the new conditions, as suggested by the Venice Commission.

Another solution would have been to acknowledge that the KEE has grown out of, yet is inherently linked to, the CEU. The preamble of the original 2004 Law on the CEU could have been the right starting point. The lawmakers at that time expressed their will to incorporate the American university into the Hungarian system. The solution that they chose, to duplicate the legal personalities, was, arguably, suboptimal. They could have affirmed simply that the American university is considered a Hungarian university by virtue of the fact that it complies with Hungarian rules and regulations and because it is supervised by the Hungarian Accreditation Committee. This solution, which could have simplified issues for the Hungarian state bureaucracy as well, however, would have implied building upon a legal document issued at the time when Fidesz's opponents were in government. This proved to be too much to ask, even though the original 2004 Act on the CEU was supported by Fidesz MPs at that time.

The model that was preferred by the government was to build some of the specificities of the CEU's legal structure into the New York state and Hungary agreement. The fundamental drawback of such a solution was that it based the continuation of the university on the discretionary decision of politicians (as opposed to accreditation agencies), and it expressed the vision of the universities as a "means" in the hands of the governments to achieve their foreign policy goals (as described by the justification of the law cited earlier). While in principle opposed to such an approach, the CEU appreciated the idea of the international treaty because this framework was seen as providing a higher level of safeguards for its survival as an autonomous institution than any domestic rule. An ideal agreement would have contained an explicit ban on sudden and unilateral changes in the legal status and operation of the university and would have committed the partners to an international arbitration forum. Despite the fact that these extra guarantees were rejected by the Hungarian delegation, the university would have welcomed the treaty had it been signed, as planned, during the fall of 2017.

Throughout the crisis the university faced the classic dilemma of exit, voice, and loyalty. Loyalty, that is public silence and behind-the-door lobbying, appeared not only as morally problematic but also as ineffective given the ferocity of the attacks and the fact that they were preceded by a long and secret preparatory phase. Exit, that is moving the university to another country, was an option, given that many cities invited the CEU and even offered premises. But the university refused to surrender without a fight and opted for a critical voice against the law. Next to meeting government officials (i.e., the few who were ready to talk to CEU administrators), the university turned to the public and to international decision-makers. The most important activities aimed at swaying the opinion of politicians, judges, state bureaucrats, and ordinary citizens who were flooded by government propaganda by issuing press releases, organizing press conferences, sending letters to MPs, MEPs, the Presidium of the Rectors' Conference, meeting officials in Washington, DC, New York, Brussels, and Strasbourg, responding to defamations, and providing the Constitutional Court and the Venice Commission with facts and arguments.

Another layer of the campaign focused on public opinion and the supporters of the CEU. The production of "*I stand with CEU*" badges, the launching of hashtag campaigns on social media channels, and the encouragement of friends and alumni to turn to their legislators, the government, or to the president, led to a particularly successful mobilization. As an external appreciation of the work of the communication team, CEU was awarded the Council of Advancement and Support of Education (CASE) Circle of Excellence Gold Award in the Crisis Communications category.[7]

The CEU employed a wide spectrum of legal arguments against the law. The university pointed out that the parliament adopted the law without consultation, violating the rules of due process, even though Hungarian regulations (the 2010 Law on the Participation of the Community in the Preparation of Laws) demand social dialogue, consultation with relevant institutions, and an impact study. In fact, the relevant institutions, in this case the Hungarian Academy of Sciences and the Hungarian Rectors' Conference, were kept in the dark as much as the university itself. The CEU also argued that, in line with the current constitution of Hungary, no law can give a discretional right to the government to determine whether an institution of higher education can operate or not.

The CEU also added that there is no aspect of quality assurance that justifies the examination of whether a foreign higher education institution runs a program in its country of origin. Setting up programs in the United States was considered not only to entail a considerable new financial burden but also to lack academic and Hungarian "patriotic" justification, as the channeling of resources into American higher education will not improve the quality of education in Budapest.

Against the charge that the CEU lacks European-style program accreditation, the university pointed out that this has no relevance for the quality of education (CEU followed the same rules as e.g. Harvard). The U.S. system is simply different from the European systems – programs are "registered" and not "accredited" – but the substance is the same: the relevant agency checks whether the qualifications of the professors, the quality-insurance mechanisms, and the infrastructure is adequate for a graduate-level program (in the case of the CEU, Columbia University, New York University, and so on, it is the New York State Education Department). Additionally, the institutional accreditation is more demanding than a similar procedure in Europe. The issue of discrimination was also central to the arguments of the university. As most clauses of the law apply only to one university (the CEU is the only foreign university in Hungary without a campus in its country of origin, the only university from an OECD country that relied on license agreements, the only university that has a large number of third-country national faculty, and so on), the case for discrimination was seen as solid not only by the CEU but also by the Venice Commission and the European Commission. The CEU particularly complained that the discontinuation of the cooperation agreements between universities of non-EEA OECD countries and Hungarian universities has no other purpose than to undermine the way KEE participated in the delivery of the CEU's programs. Finally, in line with the opinion of virtually all observers, the CEU considered the deadlines punitive and unrealistic.

The university tried to explain that the ability to issue U.S. degrees is not a privilege but a right earned by complying with the relevant American legal and academic criteria, a possibility that is open to anyone. Those students who wish to receive Hungarian degrees are required to complete assignments that were not asked for by American authorities (particular forms of exams, different deadlines, and so on).

The CEU also pointed out that while in the past OECD and EEA universities were treated by Hungarian regulations similarly, the new regulations discriminate against the former group of countries. From an academic point of view there was no immediate rationale for considering American or Canadian universities worse than European ones.

Some of the arguments of CEU were not directed to the law itself, but to the discourse that surrounded its introduction. The university found particularly problematic that the prime minister called the CEU a "secondary battlefield" in the political war he was and still is waging against the founder of the university and that, parallel to the consistent refusal of the relevant minister to meet the representatives of the university, government propaganda described CEU as an institution that is unwilling to cooperate. While typically government officials denied that the law was motivated by the anti-Soros campaign, on a number of occasions they were rather blunt about their motivations. Most importantly, the minister of the Prime Minister's Office (the number two in the Hungarian government) at a press conference on July 6, 2017, admitted that the "CEU and the Fidesz government used to live in peace with each other. The change happened when George Soros announced his program to open the borders of Europe and to call into Europe millions of immigrants" (Német 2017).

Perhaps most importantly, the university was successful in showing the link between the law that can lead to the withdrawal of the license of operation of particular universities and – academic – freedom. The government's line, according to which the state does not wish to determine what is taught in the classrooms and therefore this is simply an issue of regulation and not of academic freedom, was received with skepticism even by those who otherwise agreed with the attack on the CEU. Reassuringly, those who rejected both the hypocritical explanations and the hostility against the university outnumbered the supporters of the government's propaganda in the streets of Hungary. The main slogan of the demonstrations was "Free Country, Free University!"

The university was less successful in convincing the public about its autonomy from its founder. While it was important to point out that, in the twenty-one-person board of trustees, Mr. Soros sits together with the vice chancellor of Oxford, the chancellor of the University of California, Berkeley, the former president of Stanford, the former provost of Columbia, the former Republican governor of the State of New York, and many other established intellectuals and public figures, the "Soros University" phrase remained ubiquitous. Given the fact that George Soros was targeted by an unprecedented and vicious state campaign (reminding many of Orwell's *1984*), the university also considered it vital to show solidarity with him, thereby inevitably reconfirming the association.

ANTI-CEU ARGUMENTS AND DISCOURSE

The arguments of the CEU and its supporters of course were met with the counter-arguments of the anti-CEU campaign. The original *Origo* article and the first interview of the prime minister on the topic have been already cited. They were followed by hundreds of articles and statements, repeating that the "Soros University cheats" by not having a campus in the United States or that CEU has an unfair advantage compared to the Hungarian universities. All these articles followed the pattern of the statement of the Ministry of Human Capacities issued on April 4:

> The Soros University enjoyed privileges that were not secured for any other higher education institution in Hungary. The university could issue two different degrees, a Hungarian and an American one, while students pursuing these degrees were required to complete only one single program. While this was a good business for George Soros, it is an unfair advantage [for CEU] in the competition among [Hungarian] universities. This discriminatory situation of the business regulations was abolished by the amendment of the law, which closed a loophole and created fair relations between universities.[8]

A longer version of the above frame was circulated to members of the European Parliament and to all Hungarian diplomats, who were asked to repeat the arguments in letters to the editor, like the Hungarian ambassador to Austria did,[9] and use it in their local communication.

The less sophisticated attacks simply focused on the fact that that Soros, the founder of the university, is a financial speculator. The journalist and sometimes writer Tibor Fischer, for example, alleged in *The Guardian* that in its current fight the university is after "bums on seats and dollars" (Fischer 2017), disregarding the simple fact that the CEU is a university where, thanks to a generous scholarship policy, the per-capita amount spent on students is much larger than the amount collected from fees. The relevant university budget reports, all publicly available, reflect the fact that the CEU – in order to ensure that talented students from modest backgrounds can receive high-level education – selects students based on merit. While these facts were all known to the representatives of the government, they made sure that in all attacks against the university there was some reference to "dollars" or "market advantage."

The labeling of the CEU as a virtual, phantom, offshore, or fake university had a long-lasting popularity in the smear campaign. Ironically and tellingly, these phrases were used even by the spokesperson of the government who received a PhD at the CEU and prior to the campaign was proud of his *alma mater*. Contrasting the CEU and the KEE, the Hungarian unit that was established after more than a decade-long operation of the CEU, by calling the first a fake university and the second a real one, was a favorite rhetorical trick during the first wave of the campaign. The goal was to legitimize the expulsion of the American unit from Hungary and to make the impression that the CEU had some "privilege." The latter term was the leading slogan of the anti-CEU campaign for many months to come. The executive summary prepared by the Cabinet Office of the Prime Minister and circulated at embassies featured the term "privilege" six times, without ever defining it.

The administrative irregularities detected at foreign universities only were mentioned in the first weeks, as they turned out early on to be too minor and not at all related to the content of the debated law. Similarly, the accusation that issuing an American degree in a European city is suspect also lost some of its traction when it turned out that the children of the prime minister and of the president of Hungary both attended universities (in Switzerland and in the United Kingdom, respectively) that had the same rights.

The rhetoric of more moderate officials was more nuanced but still full of distortions of the facts. The president of Hungary's April 25 lecture in front of secondary school pupils is a good example of the subtle biases pervading the official discourse. He acknowledged that at the CEU "very serious value-added activities happen," but he also repeated the claim that only KEE conducts education and the CEU does not, disregarding the fact that all of the students of the university are enrolled in the CEU, that most of the programs have exclusively CEU accreditation, and that all professors have in their contract the obligation to participate in the delivery of the CEU's educational programs. The president also claimed that some Western countries have more restrictive regulations, forgetting that the Hungarian legal amendment did not simply erect high barriers in front of potential newcomers to the educational market but it undermined existing institutions. In no other case did a European government introduce legislation leading to the discontinuation of established, law-abiding universities.

In the discourse surrounding the CEU, it became customary to contrast the university to the other foreign universities who remained silent on the matter, meaning that they showed respect to the authority of the Hungarian government. In fact, most of the other universities under review either stopped operating in Hungary prior to the audit or their presence had been marginal (e.g., running a study abroad program or a joint degree program with a Hungarian university). Even those institutions that were affected, like Boston University, simply faced the danger of losing one or two programs, co-offered with a Hungarian university. Less than 1 percent of their activity was in jeopardy. Additionally, most foreign universities were from EU countries, and therefore were not affected by the law.

More importantly, these criticisms expressed the view that active opposition by a university to a governmental decision was in some way "improper," even if the university's own existence is at stake. When the rector of CEU protested against the lack of consultation and against the discriminatory character of the law and lobbied for the withdrawal of the bill, the pro-government media and the government officials interpreted his actions as proof that he "politicized" the situation and behaved as a liberal ex-politician and not as an academic official.

In its most vicious attacks the government talked about CEU not as a university but as a fifth column of hostile external political forces. As the minister of human capacities, for example, put it in Echo TV on June 23 "we are dealing here with an international lobby organization, an international conspiracy."[10] The issue of the CEU was linked to the new rules on NGOs and the fight against the "compulsory settlement of migrants" (i.e., the quota on the evaluation of asylum-seekers' application that the EU contemplated in those months). As the justice secretary phrased it in the pro-government daily *Magyar Idők* on June 27: "These three subjects are linked. They all serve the purpose that Hungarian interests prevail in Hungary" (Jakubász 2017).

The negative international reaction was rebuffed with the claim that education is a national matter, the European Union has no jurisdiction over it, and that many democratic countries have similarly restrictive regulations against foreign universities. The danger faced by the CEU was belittled by claims that the solution was underway, the government was consulting the university (which was not the case), and by then emphasizing that even if the CEU must close down eventually, the Hungarian-accredited unit of the university would be able to continue its activities without any change.

During the spring and summer months virtually no day passed without an article in the right-wing press against the CEU. Some publications alleged that the 2004 declaration by the Governor of the State of New York and Prime Minister of Hungary about the CEU was invalid because the two politicians were not in the same town on the day of signing the document. Others implied that the CEU's American accreditation was a fraud. Again, others attacked the university because of its gender studies program. Right-wing journalists went through the 15,000 MA and PhD thesis titles, selected the dozen that were about queer subculture or transgender issues, and claimed that the university aimed to undermine Hungarian families with fake science and teaches homosexuality. The Department of Gender Studies featured in virtually all of the many hundreds of articles written against the CEU (and even in speeches and interviews of Fidesz MPs and officials), while none of the other fourteen departments were mentioned, showing the deep cultural irritation of conservative circles against a small academic program.

While the campaign against George Soros proved to be useful in 2017 for mobilizing government supporters, the CEU's utility in this regard was limited. NGOs could be more easily portrayed as dangerous political organizations, and Fidesz turned its legislative and propaganda machinery against them. The Stop Soros bills introduced to the legislature in February 2018 threatened targeted NGOs with fines and ultimate prohibition, but because no specific deadline was introduced these attacks did not have the same dramatic aspect as the assault against the CEU. Ironically, even if at this point the government preferred to leave the CEU out of the political battles, and even if the CEU itself preferred to stay out of the campaign, the logic of a witch hunt, according to which any association with George Soros was a crime, kept the CEU in the same basket as the NGOs.

CONCLUSION

As Hungary's justice minister mentioned in his parliamentary speech (Trócsányi 2017), no Hungarian law attracted as much international attention and criticism as the higher education law, not even the new constitution – introduced unilaterally by Fidesz – in 2011. In some sense this should come as no surprise given how unambiguously the law was designed to target an institution that operated for twenty-two years as a law-abiding university in

Hungary, and how partisan was the campaign that surrounded the introduction of the law. While countries differ from each other in the ways they regulate higher education, the outright harassment of a university is uncommon in democracies.

It was also not accidental that the Hungarian public came to see the CEU as a political symbol. When a previous rector of a major Hungarian university was asked whether any of the universities in Hungary can be considered autonomous in academic and financial sense, he answered that there is only one, the CEU (Népszava 2017). Clearly, many considered the CEU affair as an attack against western education, a service that is considered important by (middle-class) citizens irrespective of political affiliation.

On the other hand, there is something perplexing – or miraculous – behind the fact that many tens of thousands of people went to the streets for a small, postgraduate, highly specialized higher education institution, while, for example, the private pension funds were nationalized without any serious opposition and the abolishment of fair elections was met with international silence. The dramatic configuration of the story, a David *vs.* Goliath-type of duel between a party-state and a university, may have motivated many people inside and outside Hungary to mobilize.

In the spring of 2017, when the crisis broke out, the government party lost popularity and the support of some high-profile conservative intellectuals. But in a few months its popularity recovered, and the anti-Soros and anti-migrant campaign proved to be very successful. By prolonging the deadlines, the government undermined the dramatic appeal of the CEU story. The attention of the public shifted elsewhere.

The prospects are bleak. During the year of 2018, the comfortable electoral victory, the contraction of the domestic critical media, the success of populist parties around the world, and the slowness of the European judicial mechanisms have emboldened the government. The university is indebted to the Hungarian society that showed support in so many ways, but it can remain in Hungary only if neither the quality of its teaching and research, nor its freedom of speech is compromised. So far the government has been unwilling to guarantee either.

NOTES

1. The preamble of Act LXI/2004 (Law about the State Accreditation of Középeurópai Egyetem) stated: "in order to achieve the goals set out in the joint declaration issued by the Parliament, the Prime Minister of the Republic of Hungary and the Governor of New York State on April 5, 2004, for the purposes of recognizing

Közép-európai Egyetem (Central European University) recognized in the State of New York (United States of America) as a Hungarian, private university, and in order to strengthen the international character of national higher education, introduce foreign experiences, and extend higher education expertise obtainable in foreign languages."

2. One ranking put the CEU in second place: THE 2018.

3. Its charter, the certificate showing that the CEU is a tax subject of the USA, an American bank account statement, and so on.

4. "Jelentés a kormány részére," http://www.kormany.hu/download/b/32/0100 0/Jelent%C3%A9s%20a%20k%C3%BClf%C3%B6ldi%20fels%C5%91oktat%C 3%A1si%20int%C3%A9zm%C3%A9nyekr%C5%91l.pdf, accessed June 25, 2019.

5. Act 25/2017 was accepted by 123 votes against 38.

6. See the interview with her: Langowski (2018).

7. See https://www.case.org/awards/circle-excellence/2018/istandwithceu-centr al-european-universitys-campaign-academic-freedom, accessed June 25, 2019.

8. See Kovács-Angel (2017).

9. Perényi (2017).

10. "Mélymagyar," https://www.youtube.com/watch?v=ZIKGhzgHHYU, accessed June 25, 2019.

BIBLIOGRAPHY

Fischer, Tibor. 2017. "I Don't Recognize Viktor Orbán as a Tyrant." https://www.the guardian.com/commentisfree/2017/apr/20/viktor-orban-tyrant-western-media-hu ngarian-leader-democracy-antisemite, accessed June 25, 2019.

HVG. 2017. "Hátrál a kormány? Palkovics mintha a lex CEU módosítását vetette volna fel Brüsszelben." http://hvg.hu/gazdasag/20170411_Palkovics_tudni_ve li_hogy_Brusszelt_nem_zavarja_a_Lex_CEU, accessed June 25, 2019.

Jakubász, Tamás. 2017. "Hazánk nem nyitja ki a kapukat." https://magyaridok.hu/bel fold/hazank-nem-nyitja-ki-kapukat-1873858/, accessed June 25, 2019.

Kovács-Angel, Marianna. 2017. "Emmi: A Soros-egyetem megtéveszti a közvélemé-nyt, a tudósokat és a nemzetközi intézményeket." https://24.hu/belfold/2017/04/ 04/emmi-a-soros-egyetem-megteveszti-a-kozvelemenyt-a-tudosokat-es-a-nemzetk ozi-intezmenyeket/, accessed June 25, 2019.

Langowski, Judith. 2018. "Már a veszélyzónában vagyunk." https://merce.hu/201 8/07/21/mar-a-veszelyzonaban-vagyunk-interju-judith-sargentinivel/, accessed June 25, 2019.

Német, Tamás. 2017. "Lázár elárulta, miért nem működhet tovább békében a CEU." https://index.hu/belfold/2017/07/06/lazar_elarulta_miert_nem_mukodhet_tovab b_bekeben_a_ceu/, accessed June 25, 2019.

Népszava. 2017. "Egyetemi autonómia – 'Lassan elérjük a pinceszintet'." https://ne pszava.hu/egyetemi-autonomia-lassan-elerjuk-a-pinceszintet, accessed June 25, 2019.

Perényi, János. 2017. "Hektische Tiraden gegen Ungarn." https://derstandard.at/20
00055573911/Hektische-Tiraden-gegen-Ungarn, accessed June 25, 2019.
THE. 2018. "International Student Table." https://www.timeshighereducation.co
m/student/best-universities/international-student-table-2017-top-200-universities,
accessed June 25, 2019.
Trócsányi László. 2017. "Trócsányi László expozéja." http://www.kormany.hu/hu/
igazsagugyi-miniszterium/a-miniszter/beszedek-publikaciok-interjuk/trocsanyi-las
zlo-expozeja20171018.

Part III

HUNGARIAN *SONDERWEG* OR REGIONAL BACKSLIDING?

Chapter 13

The Post-Communist Mafia State as a Criminal State*

Bálint Magyar

WHY MAFIA STATE?

In the past few decades, new areas of research have not emerged from the many categories designed to characterize the institutional systems of liberal democracy. New categories like "illiberal democracy" (Zakaria 1997), "electoral democracy" (Howard and Roessler 2006), "defective democracy" (Merkel 2004), or "semi-authoritarianism" (Ottaway 2003) simply apply the appropriate adjective prefix, reflecting the logic of transitology. Transitology in this understanding appears both as a transformation of social systems and as a reference to its own literal meaning: these systems are underway and form different models according to their distance or deviation from liberal democracy. The fraudulent nature of this approach presupposes the universality of the logic of the dynamics of liberal democracy and fails to notice the qualitatively different logics and dynamics of regimes. It relegates constituent phenomena of the system to a secondary category of importance and marks defining traits as mere deviancies that are surmountable and are to be surmounted.

In post-communist regimes the four most important constituent phenomena that a proposed new analytical framework must be built on and correspond with are the following:

- a rudimentary or completely absent separation of the spheres of social action (Offe 2004);
- a privatization process that is managed to create new property owners (Magyar 2018);

* This chapter is republished with permission from The Post-Communist Mafia State as a Form of Criminal State, originally appearing in Twenty-Five Sides of a Post-Communist Mafia State (CEU Press, 2017).

- an operation of executive power in informal organizations according to a patron-client system (Hale 2015);
- a "privatization" of public authority – using Max Weber's categories (1978).

The political and sociological effects of these phenomena – autocratic tendencies and widespread corruption – have been noted by scholars (Karklins 2002; Grødeland and Aasland 2011; Cieślik and Goczek 2015), but they have either been regarded by transitologists as side effects or were arbitrarily put into the center of analytical frameworks without taking other elements and their relative positions into account. For example, some scholars have moved to sociological factors and directly linked issues of power concentration and wealth accumulation, creating categories like "clientelist regime" (Roniger 2004), "crony capitalism" (Kang 2002), and "kleptocracy" (Dawisha 2014). In post-communist systems, these categories are misleading. "Clientelist," as an adjective, does not express the illegitimacy of the relationship; the term "crony," in the context of corrupt transactions, assumes parties or partners of equal rank. And as for the arrangement connoted by the term "kleptocratic," the term neither implies an aggressive takeover of property nor a system based on permanent and monopolized patron-client relations of subservience.

To remedy these problems, I offer a framework of categories that breaks with the underlying presuppositions of the transition paradigm. It does not merely change the words used to label the regimes but also conceptually reestablishes its components accordingly. It considers the four constituent phenomena mentioned earlier and understands autocratic tendencies and deep corruption as fundamentals – and not side-effects – of post-communist regime development and operation. The new multilevel analytical framework puts the relational economy and post-communist autocracy in its center, and it features a coherent system of categories, defined in context and covering the relevant – economic and political – layers holistically.

However, if we want to understand the nature of corruption as a governance regime, then we have to clearly distinguish between three levels.

The first level is so-called day-to-day corruption, which is characterized by scattered, sporadic, face-to-face corruption transactions, involving players from the economy and the public authorities.

The second level is when corruption reaches the higher layers of governance and when these are not only occasional but regular transactions. The cooperation among players becomes more complex both on the side of the supply of corruption and on the side of the demand for corruption: namely, corruption partners within the economy are often oligarchs or criminals from the organized underworld. (Here, we need to distinguish between the two groups: criminal organizations carry out illegal "economic" activities supported by illegitimate access, while oligarchs usually conduct *lawful* economic activities, mostly with illegitimate access.)

This level is referred to as the realm of state capture, and we can speak about this phenomenon when only certain segments of the public authority are captured and not the governmental structure in its entirety. Within this level political competition appears to continue, governmental change is still possible under constitutional circumstances, and the oligarchs still maintain their relative autonomy, as they are not tied infinitely to certain political actors. Both sides can enter and leave corruption transactions relatively freely. Organizational criminology refers to this stage as state crime. In the case of *the third* level it is inappropriate to talk simply about state crime as a phenomenon that we have observed as a criminal state. No longer are oligarchs or an organized underworld capturing the state, but instead, a political enterprise, an *"organized upperworld,"* captures the economy, including the oligarchs themselves. Some post-communist countries may be classified as such already: for example, Azerbaijan, some Central Asian countries that were once Soviet republics, Hungary within the European Union (EU), Montenegro in the Balkans, and Russia. This level becomes possible when two conditions are met: (1) the monopolization of power by one political actor, accompanied by the systematic surrendering of the institutions of checks and balances, along with (2) a lack or practical non-existence of private property when regime changes occurred and extensive distrust as privatization took place in these countries afterwards (Denisova 2009).

The emerging post-communist criminal states, where the governance bears the features of a criminal organization, can be described as *post-communist mafia states* (Magyar 2016; Magyar and Vásárhelyi 2017; Magyar 2018). That is, a *privatized form of a parasite state*. In this case the central bodies of the state itself operate in concert as a criminal organization, that is, as an organized upperworld.

The basic features of the corrupt criminal state may follow ten points:

- *Both the concentration of political power and the accumulation of wealth of the adopted political family (the new clan-type form of the ruling elite) occur in unison.* Public benefit becomes subordinated permanently to private interests, and in a manner that influences political decision-making in a fundamentally determinant, systematic way.
- *As a consequence of a change of the political elite, an alternation and systematic replacement of the economic elite takes place as well;* these changes are not driven by the instruments of democracy and market economy.
- Together with the legalized instruments of state monopoly of coercion, *the mafia state coercively extracts private fortunes* – sometimes indirectly

through *different forms of nationalization* – to serve its own interests and redistributes them amongst clients of the adopted political family.

- The corruption of the organized criminal upperworld is neither a matter of incidental – even sporadic – backdoor dealing nor an occasional irregularity or deviance, but a centrally directed and rationally transacted plunder, a centrally orchestrated collection of protection money. *The concentration of power and the increase in wealth of the adopted political family cannot be operated in disjointed systems.* While the traditional mafia reaches its objectives through blackmail, intimidation, and open violence, the spheres of influence in the mafia state can be shaped by quasi-lawful instruments of coercion accomplished by public authorities.

- The *key actors* in this type of corrupt criminal state include the following:
  1. The *poligarch* is someone who uses his/her legitimate political power to secure illegitimate economic wealth – while his political power is visible, his economic power remains hidden. The poligarch manages his family business in the form of a political venture.
  2. The *oligarch* is someone who from more or less legitimate economic wealth builds political power for himself – in this case his economic power is visible, while the political power, if it exists at all, remains hidden.
  3. The *front man* is someone who has no real power, neither in politics nor in the economic sphere, but serves as a bridge over the gap between the real nature of power and its required legitimacy.
  4. The *corruption broker* brings the partners of the corrupt transaction together in the role of mediator or expert lawyer.

- *Decisions are taken outside the competence of formalized and legitimate bodies* of democratic institutions and brought about in the topmost, tightly-knit, informal circle of the adopted political family, the chief patron's court.

- Formalized and legal procedures of governance give way to *arbitrary actions of disposition*. The head of executive power does not govern but illegitimately disposes of the country as if s/he owned it. State institutions, including parliament, government, tax offices, and the prosecutor's office, do no more than rubberstamp and attend to the bookkeeping. They become the institutions of politically selective law enforcement. The "law of rule" substitutes for the "rule of law." Proper jurisdiction is replaced by an arbitrary practice of justice. Legislation is no longer the field of lawful, normative regulations that are valid for all and brought to bear upon all equally, but where laws are tailored to fit the needs of those in power. *Equality before the law is replaced by inequality after the law.*

- In place of legally protected autonomous positions, a *patron-client chain of vassal relationships* comes into being, which results in a liquidation of the grounds that uphold individual autonomy and forcing livelihoods into an order of dependences.

- This new form of vassal dependency should not be called feudal or patrimonial because *the material nature of power and its formal legitimacy do not converge.* The gap between them is bridged by state coercion and hypocrisy using quasi-democratic procedures by restricting civil rights, clamping down on the freedom of press, and manipulating the electoral system. It is neither a liberal democracy nor a dictatorship.
- *The mafia state is not ideology-driven.* It builds on various ideological templates that suit its political agenda. While inconsistent in terms of public policy expertise, emotionally it remains consistent. This is also its strength: it resists rational critique. The coherence of its "values" is ensured by the *cultural model of the dominance of the head of the patriarchal family.*

THE CRIMINAL CHARACTER OF THE REGIME

Organizational criminology has systematized criminal acts according to the type of organization that commits them. David O. Friedrichs (2010) makes a distinction between corporate crimes and state crimes. However, government and business may occasionally collaborate and even directly encourage and assist each other in committing certain crimes. Three separate categories follow from this: (1) state-facilitated corporate crime, (2) corporate-facilitated state crime, and (3) state-corporate crime, which occurs when the two act together on an equal basis.

In addition to the existence of *state crime*, a *criminal state* may also exist that systematically, deliberately, and perniciously violates and impairs the fundamental rights of its citizens. Within such a state, both economic entities that depend on public procurements and tenders and civil society organizations – that in reality function as political puppets and serve the interests of power – are interwoven very tightly within the state and government. In such cases, those involved in corrupt activities and those in a repressive regime are connected to each other in manifold ways (Friedrichs 2010).

According to the Hungarian Criminal Code, a "criminal organization [is] a group of three or more people, formed for an extended period of time and acting in concert, with the objective of . . . intentionally perpetrating criminal offenses."[1] In applying this law, "acting in concert" means that the members of a criminal organization "share tasks related to criminal activities," which "obviously presumes prior planning and a certain degree of direction and organization." A legal harmonizing resolution by the Supreme Court of Justice in 2005[2] also provides guidance on understanding the functioning of a criminal organization for different specific trial situations, as follows:

- A criminal organization is qualitatively different from individuals simply acting together; the *criminal organization has to be formed for an extended period of time, and must act in concert*;
- "Acting in concert" is a conceptual component of the *criminal organization*, which, in terms of content, is a set of *mutually-reinforcing effects on those acting in it*; however, the existence of acting in concert does not follow from being in direct contact with actors in a criminal organization, nor specific knowledge of other actions or the identity of other actors; behavior as *a member of a criminal organization* can only be attributed to a perpetrator who has engaged in activities in a criminal organization formed by a division of functions, and in a manner based on superiors and subordinates, with full knowledge of the organization, and collaborated while in constant contact with its members;
- The existing provisions of the Criminal Code do not distinguish among the *hierarchy* (or "posts") *of actions within the criminal organization* in terms of their activity or intensity, as these conditions only are considered during the sentencing phase;
- A person outside of a criminal organization does not become a member of it by receiving a contracted job from the organization, as integration into the organization requires knowledge of the organization's inner workings and active involvement within it; a clear distinction must be made between substantively judging a criminal act committed as a member of a criminal organization, and *a criminal act committed on a contracted job from a criminal organization (or any of its members)*;
- If there is evidence that a criminal offense was linked to the operation of an actual criminal organization, or committed within the context of such, then due to the conditions it was carried out – particularly due to the nature of a specific behavior presuming the prior or later *linked actions* of others, and due to events that are necessary and therefore likely to occur – it can be concluded that the action of the occasional perpetrator (participant) is recognized as being committed within a criminal organization.

The language of the code reflects a clear understanding. Although the legal harmonizing resolution grants a unified interpretation of human trafficking, prostitution, drug trafficking, and other classic activities of a similar nature in the organized underworld, neither the Criminal Code nor the definitions in the resolution exclude the possibility of applying these provisions in cases when a large part of the members of a criminal organization are leaders at the highest levels of public authority institutions. In fact, it does not even exclude this from being the element that moves and defines the criminal organization, the organized upperworld.

The Palermo Protocols against transnational organized crime, adopted in 2000 by the United Nations and ratified by Hungary in 2006,[3] do not rule out the narrative that the struggle might take place not only between organized groups in the underworld and representatives of state authority but that the representatives of the state can themselves form the core of a criminal organization.

Following the Palermo Protocols, the Council of Europe's Committee of Specialists on Criminal Law and Criminological Aspects of Organised Crime (PC-S-CO) also defined the criteria that, when present, provide evidence of a *criminal organization*. Their definition includes both mandatory and optional criteria. As will be seen, the criteria used by the expert group to define the mafia, or the organized underworld, which also regulates Hungarian criminal law, may also be used to describe the organized upperworld or the functioning of the mafia state. The Palermo Protocols distinguish between mandatory and optional criteria as follows:

Mandatory criteria:
- collaboration of three or more people;
- for a prolonged or indefinite period of time;
- suspected or convicted of committing serious criminal offenses;
- with the objective of pursuing profit and/or power.

Optional criteria:
- having a specific task or role for each participant;
- using some form of internal discipline and control;
- using violence or other coercive means suitable for intimidation;
- exerting influence on politics, the media, public administration, law enforcement, the administration of justice, or the economy by corruption or any other means;
- using commercial or business-like structures;
- engaged in money laundering;
- operating on an international level.

It should not be particularly difficult even for the lay reader to see that the mafia state conveniently fits into these criteria.[4] "What is picking a lock compared to buying shares? What is breaking into a bank compared to founding one?" asks Mack the Knife in Brecht's *Threepenny Opera*. In terms of the mafia state, one might ask what lawbreaking is compared to passing legislation. What is robbery compared to the expropriation of property through laws and decrees? What is abuse committed by one's boss compared to centrally planned purges? What is hacking a website to illegally depriving a station of its radio frequency? And one can keep scrolling down the list covering all areas of life where it is evident that institutions of public authority are not guardians of legality and equality before the law but just the opposite: institutionalized bodies serving arbitrary personal interests.

The question is no longer how it should be interpreted in a legal sense when "three or more people collaborating" – contrary to the expectations of Hungarian legislators or the Council of Europe's group of specialists – does not mean the underworld mafia but the organized upperworld, sometimes even those with official duties. The question remains how the machinery of justice can be put in motion at all in a mafia state, and how society and the immune system of public authority being paralyzed can be activated. The answer would naturally go beyond the "descriptive" and "understanding" genre of sociology.

The central figure in the mafia state is not an arbitrarily structured power elite with an incidental culture but an adopted political family with powers granted by the chief patron, powers that are then extended across the entire nation through illegitimate means by a supreme, narrow group of decision-makers working as a non-formalized, non-legitimate body. In this case, the agent of action, the criminal organization perpetrating criminal offenses, is the *chief patron's court* itself, in which some members have senior-level public authority duties at the very top of the branches of power, including all key institutions. But there are also "advisory" members who have not been incorporated into the institutions of public authority, as well as trusted oligarchs and possibly their front men as well. Perhaps one or two dozen individuals make up the "polypburo" of the mafia state.[5] The criteria for a criminal organization applies to them: "three or more people," "a group formed for an extended period of time and acting in concert" that has a "hierarchy" and "mutually-reinforcing effects on those acting in it," and includes "the objective of perpetrating criminal offenses," "dividing up tasks" required for this, and if necessary, "contracting" persons outside of the criminal organization.

CRIMINAL ORGANIZATIONS
EXPROPRIATING PROPERTY

From isolated violations of the law, the contours of relationships within the mafia state are outlined by the *linked actions* of organized crime. These include acts that are unlawful in and of themselves (such as extortion, fraud and financial fraud, embezzlement, misappropriation, money laundering, insider trading, agreements that limit competition in a public procurement or concession procedure, both active and passive bribery, abuse of authority, abuse of a public service position, buying influence, and racketeering) combined with acts that are not unlawful in and of themselves (such as motions submitted by independent parliamentary representatives instigating tax audits and so on).

A linked action may be made up of a wide range of variations of the aforementioned situations. Let me demonstrate the action of a state-sponsored criminal organization and take the case of an outdoor advertising company, ESMA. With ministerial collaboration, an offer is made to ESMA's owner by a potential new owner who belongs to the leading oligarchs of the adopted political family. ESMA's owner does not accept the offer, upon which the tax authorities appear at his door as a means of persuasion through non-physical violence. This still does not convince the owner of the desired company to rid himself of his property, upon which, again as a means of bloodless violence, an *ad hoc* legal amendment proposed by a parliamentary representative and adopted by parliament deprives the company of its concession-based activities. The company's value begins to drop precipitously, and as a final step, a second amendment exempts his rival from any possible negative consequences stemming from the amendment that destroys the business in question. The entire operation takes place within a very short period of time. After the company is starved for several years, the owner sells his hopeless business when one of the godfather's new, favorite oligarchs makes an offer for it at a moderate price. Once the business is sold, the discriminatory legal provision that made the business impossible to run also is repealed by parliament, so that the new oligarch loyal to the godfather can operate his firm at full capacity. Unlike the traditional mafia, public authority in Hungary uses bloodless means to enforce its will.

This case bears the characteristics of the activities of a mafia state criminal organization in the following ways:

- intentional perpetratration of criminal offenses (extortion, abuse of authority, and so on);
- acting in concert – as a wide range of the branches of power (ministerial, governmental control and law enforcement institutions, the legislature) and individuals (oligarchs and chosen beneficiaries who change from time to time) are required to coordinate the actions according to a specific schedule;
- constitution of a hierarchical group, in which those who comprehend the entire operation are isolated from those carrying out the actions (e.g., public servants conducting tax inspections or parliamentary representatives submitting legal amendment proposals);
- mutual reinforcement of the effects of the actions of the members of criminal organization — since they would not be able to reach their desired goal (expropriation of property) by acting independently.

Since the political regime under study has been defined as a mafia state, it is only appropriate to illustrate the mechanism of change of ownership carried out by state coercion using the example of slot machines and casinos. The operation of *slot machines*, generating a tax revenue worth approximately HUF 70 billion (EUR 220 million), was overseen on behalf of the authorities by the state-owned Szerencsejáték Zrt. It is worth examining the rearrangement of this branch of business step-by-step as it was integrated into the political family's circle of interests:

Step one: The re-regulation of the operation of slot machines primarily placed in catering industry premises took place in 2011, when the monthly tax per machine was raised from HUF 100,000 (EUR 330) to five times that amount by an unexpected amendment motion in parliament, whereby operators were obliged to change their existing machines to server-based machines by October 2012. As a result of the measure, operators handed in 60 percent of the slot machines within a month of the amendment being passed.[6] Their numbers decreased further over the next year from 22,000 to 2,000.[7]

Step two: In October 2012 the operation of slot machines, as well as game rooms and electronic casinos, was banned by means of an amendment pushed through parliament in a couple of days. Only casinos were exempt and allowed to continue operating the machines. The ban also affected approximately 1,000 businesses that had invested in the server-based slot machines in line with the amendment that had been introduced a year earlier. According to the government:

> The earlier measures had only achieved their objective in part, trying to ensure that those who lived in the most disadvantaged situations did not dump their money into slot machines, while on the other hand, serious national security risks had also been raised in regard to the activities of those with interests in the gaming industry.[8]

The government intended to make up for some of the losses in tax revenue that followed from these actions by taxing online gambling.

Step three: Casinos were exempted from the ban on the operation of slot machines, and the maximum number of machines that could be installed in one premise was set at 300. Then in 2013 the maximum number of casinos that could be operated in the country was set at 11.

Step four: According to reporting from the independent Hungarian weekly *HVG*:

> Amending the law on gambling in the middle of November 2013, parliament decided that the minister for national economy could sign concession contracts for the operation of at most five casinos without making a

public tender, but taking an exceptionally high concession fee, with those contractors whom he considers reliable. . . . The other important change in the November amendment was that the gaming managers could deduct the amount of the concession fee from the tax on the games. The Las Vegas Casino, one of Andy Vajna's [a Hungarian-born film producer in Hollywood] firms, is best served by this change: thanks to the amendment he could pay HUF 1.6 billion less to the state budget. In 2012 the Las Vegas Casino had paid HUF 1.1 billion in gambling taxes at a rate of 30 percent on the net income of HUF 3.8 billion, as well as HUF 791 million as fee for the concession. Thus, altogether HUF 1.9 billion was paid to the state. According to the new regulations, they should only have to pay about HUF 300 million in taxes.[9]

Step five: In May 2014, of the eleven casino concessions that can be issued, five in Budapest were granted by the ministry for national economy to Andy Vajna's Las Vegas Casino Kft., while two were issued to Gábor Szima's Aranybónusz 2000 Kft., for the eastern Hungarian cities of Debrecen and Nyíregyháza. All of these were issued in spite of the fact that the state-owned Szerencsejáték Zrt., had also applied for the casino operator concessions. It seems they had proved less "reliable." As previously recounted, until his death in January 2019, Andy Vajna, the former film producer, was the government commissioner who disposes with state support for the production of Hungarian films and was a close confidant of Viktor Orbán. Gábor Szima, on the other hand, had been involved in the gambling business earlier, and he once owned the Debrecen football team, his role with the team now being filled by his son. "According to the ministry of national economy they will pay HUF 4 billion in concession fees and HUF 1 billion in VAT to the state budget."[10]

Step six: Yet, the parliament, in parallel to distributing the casino concessions, made it possible for casino owners to deduct the concession fee from the gaming tax, and even made it VAT exempt.[11]

Step seven: According to the Hungarian portal *Népszabadság Online*, which has since ceased publication in retribution for its critical reporting:

> With the involvement of Andy Vajna and Gábor Szima, the large international companies operating online casinos and card game websites – such as PokerStars or Bet365 – could legalize their presence in Hungary. This opportunity is made available to the businessmen close to the government by an amendment that was handed in by the cabinet to parliament as part of the omnibus bill on changes to tax regulations for the following year. One item of the proposal made it possible also for someone other than the owner of the concession to pay the concession fee. Thus, even offshore companies can pay the fee, out of funds whose origin is not transparent, and on top of this, the owner of the permit is still allowed to deduct the fee from the gambling tax. Furthermore, according to the proposal, online card

game websites and casinos can only be operated by people who have Hungarian concessions for the operation of casinos – i.e., Vajna and Szima.[12]

Step eight: According to the daily *Világgazdaság*, the taxes paid by the casinos owned by Andy Vajna and Gábor Szima – unlike tax regulations on retail units – allegedly

> are based on self-declaration, because the National Tax and Customs Administration of Hungary does not really have an overview of slot machines. On the one hand, the integrated online inspection device of the tax authorities was not fitted into these slot machines, which would have collected and recorded the data created in the course of their operation, and, on the other, there is no mention of a server-based network. So in the age of online cash registers the state is completely in the dark as far as the income of casinos is concerned.[13]

Notably, "various parties involved in this industry estimate that the income generated at Andy Vajna's five casinos in the capital should be around HUF 15 billion."[14]

Step nine: All that is left is to launch a money-laundering machine called the Stability Savings Accounts, which enables poligarchs, oligarchs, and front men to deposit their funds under state protection.

Step ten: Vajna is given a monopolistic grant for organizing online gambling as well.

This is how the adopted political family of the mafia state manages gambling and acquires casinos: expulsion, establishing a monopoly, favoring friends in concessions, special tax benefits, state-supported money laundering. And not a drop of blood has been spilled. This case bears the characteristics of the activities of a mafia state criminal organization as well. The actions are as follows:

- intentional perpetration of criminal offenses (extortion, abuse of authority, purchasing influence, and so on) by causing serious damage to law-abiding companies that changed their machinery to server-based machines and by causing massive losses in tax revenues directly by the uncommon and large-scale tax amnesty, and indirectly by not enforcing the use of electronic cashiers connected to the network of the National Revenue and Tariff Office. There is no positive societal goal behind this law, and it is clearly discriminative for every other company in the country that had to introduce the costly electronic cashiers.
- acting in concert, as a wide range of the branches of power (ministerial, governmental) and individuals (the chosen beneficiaries) are required to coordinate their actions according to a specific time and sequence;

- constituting a hierarchical group, in which those who comprehend the entire operation are isolated from those carrying out the actions (e.g., parliamentary representatives submitting legal amendment proposals);
- mutual reinforcement of the effects of the actions of the members of criminal organizations — since they would not be able to reach their desired goal (expropriation of concessions) by acting independently;[15]
- involvement in money laundering because both PokerStars and Bet365 are offshore companies that could benefit from the introduction of Stability Savings Accounts.

In other cases, the redistribution is not about possession of property itself but positions from which tributes can be extracted when the state taps the private sector. But since, according to the rationale of the system, *the political family must be built, extended, and fed on middle and lower levels of society as well*, new segments in areas that were formerly operated neutrally by the market constantly must be harassed, occupied, and repositioned as direct state tribute extractors of sorts.

This is what happened in the case of tobacco shop concessions, when first, on false health protection grounds, a state monopoly was imposed on the retail of tobacco products, and once the previous small shop owners had been driven out, the new clientele of the regime were provided higher profitability through legislative means (see also Péter Mihályi's chapter in this volume). At the same time – having been stripped of their right to sell tobacco products – tens of thousands of rural grocery and newspaper shop owners and other small property holders were ruined. In this case the mafia state appeared as an organized structure with candid self-assurance. When it came to the distribution of large fortunes the deals between a limited number of actors took place behind closed – at times, government – doors. In contrast, the tobacco shop concessions were run past the whole network of the adopted political family and reviewed by Fidesz-led municipalities and the rest of the government clientele. "Basically, what is important is that the people chosen must be committed to the political right, . . . so the socialists don't win," said the Fidesz mayor of Szekszárd at the meeting where he and the Fidesz councilors reviewed the list of those applying for the tobacco shop concessions.[16]

The case of tobacco shop concessions is a great demonstration of what typifies the mafia state, in part because this is not classic corruption, where many independent, small cases of corruption are carried out within a large application procedure in a decentralized and unsynchronized way. On the contrary, centrally planned by the adopted political family, a group of people are divested of their property – that is, a concessionary right – legalized by a parliamentary amendment of law. Then comes the centrally directed robbery by selection of the new owners who belong to the family. The first phase of the process is also an example of market-grabbing nationalization, where it is not the property itself, that is, the shop that is taken away, but the right to sell a range of products there. Obviously, the case of the tobacco shop concessions is not a bunch of individual "scams" but the coordinated functioning of the mafia state, which only aimed in small part to satiate the oligarchs, and to a large extent aimed to sustain the "small shareholders" of the regime. Before the rearrangement of the retail market of tobacco products, the guaranteed trading margin was three percent. The new law already had stipulated the margin at four percent, and following the manipulated selection process the parliament raised this to ten percent with another amendment. In other words, the revenue generated from raising the levies on tobacco products – contradicting the declared ideological aims – is not directed into the health care system or prevention programs but ensures the profitability of shops granted by the state to lower ranks of the adopted political family. This guaranteed deal did not even serve the kind of social goals that go back to the praxis of the interwar period, when the state supported disabled war veterans, war widows, or war orphans with the income from these concession rights. Of the 5,415 winning bids, only 280 went to people with disabilities. But the action did not leave the small food and convenience stores, especially in villages, undisturbed: five percent of them had to shut down already in 2014 due to a major decrease in income, being deprived from the right to sell tobacco.[17]

The redistribution of tobacco retail rights was followed by the nationalization of wholesale rights as well. As *Népszabadság Online* reported:

> Without a public tender, as the only applicant, *British American Tobacco* and *Continental Group* owned *Tabán Trafik Zrt.*, was given the exclusive right to wholesale of tobacco by the government. The company, with strong ties to the network around the governing party, was not only one of the big winners of the tobacco shop tenders, but as a result of a small technical glitch it had also been revealed that earlier it had even participated in drafting the tobacco concessions law.[18]

This case bears the characteristics of the activities of a mafia state criminal organization as well by

- intentional perpetration of criminal offenses (extortion, abuse of authority, and so on);
- acting in concert, as a wide range of branches of power (legislation, governmental control, and Fidesz factions in the local governments) and individuals (to a smaller degree the oligarchs of the adopted political family, mostly

the least significant beneficiaries of the current regime); they are required to coordinate their actions according to a specific sequence;

• constituting a hierarchical group, in which those who comprehend the entire operation are isolated from those carrying out the actions (the local organizers of the nationwide plan are presumably not overseeing the whole process, but the process itself definitely materializes on a local level);

• mutual reinforcement of the effects of the actions of the members of criminal organizations, since they would not be able to reach their desired goal (the distribution of concessions in the adopted political family) by acting independently;

• stalling to provide data of public interest and the destruction of losing applications; the whole procedure was aimed at covering up corruption and obstructing investigative inquiries.

A multitude of cases mentioned earlier (e.g., that of the biased lease of state-owned land) could also be discussed in a similar framework.

CLASSIFYING CRIMINAL ORGANIZATION ACTIONS

The *nature of damage* caused by criminal organization actions of the state can be classified in the following way:

Damage to public property and revenue:

• diverting potential state revenue to private parties (e.g., a gas deal between MVM [Hungarian Electricity Company] and MET Holding AG, related to István Garancsi, one of Orbán's closest oligarchs);

• forgoing potential tax revenue (e.g., forgiving billions of forints in tax debts without audits by the tax authority);

• diverting potential state dues to private parties (e.g., the residency bond, providing foreigners with a free entry to the EU at EUR 250,000 per bond, in addition to a EUR 29,000 fee, which is collected by some half-dozen firms close to Fidesz that are entitled to deal with the bond);

• diverting state concessions to private parties (e.g., online gambling);

• expropriating leasing rights (e.g., on the basis of civil law, dispossession of rights to pre-lease state land that is rightfully due to private lessees);

• diverting municipal or government real estate properties to individuals within the political family's sphere of interest at below-market prices (e.g., the downtown Budapest real estate racket, which has given rise to alleged misappropriation);

- illegitimately diverting tender funds to overpriced bidders within the political family's sphere of interest (e.g., a series of tenders won by Orbán's favorite oligarchs like Simicska, Mészáros, or Tiborcz who is Orbán's son-in-law).

Damage to private property and income:
- expropriating property (such as the dispossession of savings accumulated in private pension funds and also including the forced nationalization of the savings cooperatives and their subsequent transfer to third parties);
- expropriating private enterprises (e.g., 300–400 private companies by media estimates, such as the case of ESMA discussed above);
- introducing mandatory state concessions for private enterprise activities (e.g., retail and wholesale tobacco sales discussed above);
- expropriating state concessions and leasing rights (e.g., slot machines, allocating state-owned land leasing rights to targeted members of the political family regardless of prior relationships with lessees or producers).

Causing both public and private damage
- manipulating the concessions for slot machines and casinos

The *connectedness of the actions* by a criminal organization can be single-stage and multi-stage. The *institutional scope of managing corrupt transactions* by a criminal organization may have the forms intra-institutional or inter-institutional. Finally, the *extent of the authority* of the institutions involved can be local or nationwide.

The *types of collaborating institutions and their major actions* according to their branch of power are as follows:

- *Legislative*: since 2010, parliament has passed a mass of custom-tailored laws that mostly served as a framework for any subsequent manipulation, as well as laws that generally support the functioning of the mechanisms of state corruption, such as:
  ○ Raising price limits on public procurements (thereby contributing to a higher degree of corruption in procurements);
  ○ Facilitating an undue classification of public interest data (under the pretext of national strategy and national security considerations);
  ○ Facilitating money laundering;
  ○ Eliminating conflicts of interest as an obstacle to applying for tenders and subsidies;

○ Upholding the confidentiality of official asset declarations by the relatives of politicians;
○ Abusive disqualification of applicants from public procurement tenders, on occasion or for longer period.
- *Executive*: the list of collaborating institutions ranges from central bodies (e.g., the tax authority) to municipalities and chamber associations.
- *Justice*: elective law enforcement, in which the number of cases prosecuted on corruption-related charges has fallen to an unprecedented extent.
- Or any combinations thereof.

The statutory definition of crimes committed by a criminal organization can be

> extortion, fraud and financial fraud, embezzlement, misappropriation, money laundering, insider trading, bribery, bribery of officials (both the active and passive forms of the last two), abuse of authority, abuse of a public service position, buying influence, racketeering, and so on.

In most cases, there is no need even to run through the entire criminal process, since the victims understand that the "offer" from the adopted political family, backed by the full arsenal of state power, "cannot be refused." And so businesses created through threats and extortion take the appearance of being voluntary, which will usually reduce the victim's losses if he can take the hint and is willing to reach an agreement. As with the mafia, the proportion of those who suffer physical violence following a "voluntary understanding" is minimal compared to those who pay protection money or offer their services; it is usually sufficient for the mafia state just to display the range of illegitimate state coercion, accompanied by an offer for a "voluntary" deal. (Needless to say, achieving similar goals in a real dictatorship does not have to be so complicated or done in a way that imitates the functioning of a democratic institutional system.)

As the institutionalized immune system of liberal democracy is neutralized, the process of the socialization of obedience and submission advances forward. If the monitoring power of the public is restricted, if the chances to change the government are reduced by manipulating the electoral system, and if faith is effectively lost in the fair operation of fora for legal redress due to selective enforcement of the law, then the effect will be in the direction of acquiescence and accommodation. One cannot help but notice that chief prosecutor Péter Polt (a long-time Fidesz appointee) is also part of the polypburo, a colluding member of the team, and so *there is no means* by which the machinery of legal redress or justice can be set in motion against the criminal organization. In fact, in the course of selective law-enforcement, it is not the only question who is not charged with a crime, so that she can be left to run or just continue to "work" obediently according to instructions of the vassal order, but who is charged merely with criminal intent. For instance, one can face a preliminary trial initiated by Hungarian prosecutors for protective purposes, so that she can be "immunized" by the courts and relieved from having to stand trial in front of international law enforcement agencies.[19]

As a result of this socialization process, the number of crimes reported between 2010–2013 for three types of criminal activities related to corruption, both active and passive forms of official bribery as well as racketeering, decreased to one-half to one-third of the amount in the preceding four years (Oroszi and Tóth 2015). One reason for this may be that "citizens were previously more likely to see the value of reporting crimes, or even that they had less fear of reprisals" (*ibid.*), meaning that reporting on others for a crime turns into reporting on oneself. But even more telling is that – as an illustration of selective law-enforcement – the number of crimes that were reported but later rejected by the authorities has tripled, and the rate of investigations that were started but then terminated has doubled.

CONCLUSION

In this chapter, I analyzed a set of phenomena related to a peculiar merger of spheres of social action in post-communist regimes. I understand this merger as well as the consequential economic and political system, identified as a "mafia state," not as a deviant form of the Western types of market economy and democracy. Instead, it is treated as an independent social setting with its own internal logic, dynamics, and actors. The mafia state is established via the parallel replacement of the political and economic elite for the benefit of the adopted political family, a single-pyramid patronal counterpart to the ruling elite of liberal democracies. In the established system, trade is generally not based on the voluntary cooperation of economic actors, but it is initiated by the adopted political family, resulting in transfers of political services and economic goods. The oversight the adopted political family exercises is ensured through bloodless, illegitimate coercion of the state, which is transformed into a criminal state where, under the autocratic control of the chief patron, the concentration of power and ownership go hand in hand.

I used the notion of criminal state as a more general category for mafia-type regimes. The notion of a criminal state is embedded in the literature on criminal law as well as international treaties against mafias, such as the Palermo Treaty. Reconceptualizing the "mafia state" theory into the analytical framework of the "criminal state," a vast array of phenomena in post-communist regimes can be understood in a systemic way.

NOTES

1. See net.jogtar.hu (2019).
2. See lb.hu (2005).
3. Act CI of 2006 on the promulgation of the United Nations Convention against Transnational Organized Crime, as established in Palermo on December 14, 2000.
4. For more on classifying the public legal system as one that stretches the conceptual limits of a criminal organization, see Vörös (2014).
5. While the "politburo" was the top-level body of the Bolshevik-type communist parties, Fidesz, the ruling party of the mafia state in Hungary, has no politburo and its highest formal organ is the Presidium. The actual top power center is, however, an informal close network, the virtual feelers of which are like arms of the octopus. The film series about the Sicilian mafia, titled in Italian *La piovra*, was highly popular in Hungary during the 1980s.
6. See feol.hu (2011).
7. See hvg.hu (2012).
8. *Ibid.*
9. See hvg.hu (2013a).
10. See origo.hu (2014).
11. See napi.hu (2014).
12. See nol.hu (2014a).
13. See vg.hu (2015).
14. *Ibid.*
15. See hir24.hu (2015).
16. See hvg.hu (2013b).
17. See hvg.hu (2015).
18. See nol.hu (2015); propeller.hu (2015).
19. See nol.hu (2014b). "The following is from an audio recording published in the Polish weekly *Wprost* on Monday. In it, Jacek Krawiec, president of the Polish petroleum company PKN Orlen, is in discussion with Treasury Minister Włodzimierz Karpiński and the latter's deputy, Zdzisław Gawlik. The meeting took place in January 2015 in Sowa and Friends, a restaurant in Warsaw. Among other things, the petroleum company chief talked about his visit to Budapest and the discussions he conducted with Zsolt Hernádi, president and CEO of MOL, in this passage (quoted):

Jacek Krawiec: Listen, I'll tell you something that proves how different our situation is from that of the Hungarians. I went to see Hernádi because he can not leave Budapest. I ask him, 'How many years are you going to get?' Relaxed and smiling, he says, 'Y'see, my lawyers realized that if this case goes to trial in any EU country and I am acquitted of the charges, then the verdict has to be recognized by every EU member state, letting me travel around Europe.' I ask him if the case will be tried in Hungary. He tells me it will. So I say, 'But then it may take two or three years.' And he says, 'We'll have a ruling in April.' Sitting next to him is this guy, the legal director, a real self-important type named Ábel (referring to Ábel Galácz, who is not the legal director but the group-wide sales director). He (Hernádi) turns to him and says, 'Ábel, tell Jacek who the prosecutor is going to be for this trial in Hungary.' He says, 'My wife.' You see? Just imagine such a situation! The wife is the prosecutor, he gets an acquittal, and everything is taken care of. Can you imagine this happening over here?

Zdzisław Gawlik: Maybe it does happen and we just don't know about it.

Włodzimierz Karpiński: This is what Kaczyński dreams about, these are the kind of internal political conditions he would like."

BIBLIOGRAPHY

Cieślik, Andrzej, and Łukasz Goczek. 2015. "On the Evolution of Corruption Patterns in the Post-Communist Countries." *Equilibrium* (1689–765X) 10 (1): 33–53.

Dawisha, Karen. 2014. *Putin's Kleptocracy: Who Owns Russia?* New York: Simon & Schuster.

Denisova, Irina, et al. 2009. "Who Wants to Revise Privatization? The Complementarity of Market Skills and Institutions." *The American Political Science Review* 103 (2): 284–304.

feol.hu. 2011. "A félkarú rablók kivégzése." http://feol.hu/gazdasag/a-felkaru-rablok-kivegzese-1123941, accessed June 25, 2019.

Friedrichs, David O. 2007. "Transnational Crime and Global Criminology: Definitional, Typological, and Contextual Conundrums." *Social Justice* 34 (2): 4–18.

———. 2010. *Trusted Criminals*. Belmont, CA: Wadsworth Publishing.

Grødeland, Åse Berit, and Aadne Aasland. 2011. "Fighting Corruption in Public Procurement in Post-Communist States: Obstacles and Solutions." *Communist and Post-Communist Studies* 44: 17–32.

Hale, Henry E. 2015. *Patronal Politics – Eurasian Regime Dynamics in Comparative Perspective*. Cambridge: Cambridge University Press.

hir24.hu. 2015. "Törvényben szabályozta az online kaszinójátékot a parliament." http://www.hir24.hu/belfold/2015/07/06/torvenyben-szabalyozta-az-online-kaszinojatekot-a-parlament/, accessed June 25, 2019.

Howard, Marc Morjé, and Philip G. Roessler. 2006. "Liberalizing Electoral Outcomes in Competitive Authoritarian Regimes." *American Journal of Political Science* 50 (2): 365–81.

hvg.hu. 2012. "Megszavazták a nyerőgépek betiltását." http://hvg.hu/itthon/2012 1002_Megszavaztak_a_nyerogepek_betiltasat, accessed June 25, 2019.

———. 2013a. "Többezer félkarú rabló lepi el Magyarországot." http://hvg.hu/gazdas ag/20131209_Tobbezer_felkaru_rablo_lepi_el_Magyarorsz, accessed June 25, 2019.

———. 2013b. "Megszereztük: hangfelvétel bizonyítja a trafikmutyit." http://hvg .hu/itthon/20130509_trafik_Szekszard_Fidesz_hangfelvetel?utm_source=mandine r&utm_medium=link&utm_campaign=mandiner_201502, accessed June 25, 2019.

———. 2015. "Tömegesen zárnak be a boltok a trafikrendszer miatt." http://hvg.hu/ enesacegem/20150603_Tomegesen_zarnak_be_a_boltok_a_trafikok_m, accessed June 25, 2019.

Kang, David C. 2002. *Crony Capitalism: Corruption and Development in South Korea and the Philippines*. Cambridge: Cambridge University Press.

Karklins, Rasma. 2002. "Typology of Post-Communist Corruption." *Problems of Post-Communism* 49 (4): 22–32.

lb.hu. 2005. "Resolution 4/2005 by the Criminal Legal Section of the Supreme Court of Justice." http://www.lb.hu/hu/print/joghat/42005-szamu-bje-hatarozat, accessed June 25, 2019.

Magyar, Bálint. 2016. *Post-Communist Mafia State: The Case of Hungary*. Budapest: CEU Press.

———. 2018. "Towards a Terminology for Post-Communist Regimes." In *Stubborn Structures: Reconceptualizing Post-Communist Regimes*, edited by Bálint Magyar, 97–176. Budapest: CEU Press.

Magyar Bálint, and Júlia Vásárhelyi, eds. 2017. *Twenty-Five Sides of a Post-Communist Mafia State*. Budapest: CEU Press.

Merkel, Wolfgang. 2004. "Embedded and Defective Democracies." *Democratization* 11 (5): 33–58.

napi.hu. 2014. "Ezért kap milliárdos adókedvezményt Vajna." http://www.napi.hu/ado/varga_ezert_kap_milliardos_adokedvezmenyt_vajna.585449.html, accessed June 25, 2019.

net.jogtar.hu. 2019. TV, 459. §(1). http://net.jogtar.hu/jr/gen/hjegy_doc.cgi?doc id=A1200100, accessed June 25, 2019.

nol.hu. 2014a. "Vajna zsebére nyilnak aszázmilliós kiskapuk." http://nol.hu/belfold/vajna-a-neten-is-mindent-visz-1497253, accessed June 25, 2019.

———. 2014b. "Lengyel lehallgatási botrány." http://nol.hu/gazdasag/ujabb-botran yos-hangfelvetel-1469927, accessed June 25, 2019.

———. 2015. "Valami nagyon furcsa az Orbán-kormány álomüzletében." http://nol .hu/gazdasag/valami-nagyon-gyanus-az-orbank-kormany-alomuzleteben-1539525, accessed June 25, 2019.

Offe, Claus. 2004. "Political Corruption: Conceptual and Practical Issues." In *Building a Trustworthy State in Post-Socialist Transition*, edited by János Kornai and Susan Rose-Ackerman, 77–99. New York: Palgrave Macmillan.

origo.hu. 2014. "Andy Vajna kapta a Budapest környéki kaszinókat." http://www .origo.hu/gazdasag/20140506-a-kormany-het-kaszinora-adott-ki-engedelyt.html, accessed June 25, 2019.

Oroszi, Babett, and Balázs M. Tóth. 2015. "Polt Péter kinevezése óta meredeken zuhan a politikai korrupciós ügyekben indított büntetőeljárások száma." *Átlátszó*, February 6, 2015. http://atlatszo.hu/2015/02/06/polt-peter-kinevezese-ota-mere deken-zuhan-a-politikai-korrupcios-ugyekben-inditott-buntetoeljarasok-szama/.

Ottaway, Marina. 2003. *Democracy Challenged: The Rise of Semi-Authoritarianism*. Washington, DC: Carnegie Endowment for International Peace.

propeller.hu. 2015. "Kihúzta a gyufát a kormány a nemzetközi dohánycégeknél." http://propeller.hu/itthon/3118393-kihuzta-gyufat-kormany-nemzetkozi-dohany cegeknel, accessed June 25, 2019.

Roniger, Luis. 2004. "Political Clientelism, Democracy and Market Economy." *Comparative Politics* 36 (3): 353–75.

vg.hu. 2015. "Felépült a Vajna-birodalom." http://www.vg.hu/gazdasag/felepult-a-vajna-birodalom-448456, accessed June 25, 2019.

Vörös, Imre. 2014. "'Alkotmányos puccs' Magyarországon, 2010–2014." In *Magyar polip – posztkommunista maffiaállam*, edited by Bálint Magyar and Júlia Vásárhelyi. Budapest: Noran Libro Kiadó.

Weber, Max. 1978. *Economy and Society: An Outline of Interpretative Sociology.* Edited by Guenther Roth and Claus Wittich. Berkeley: University of California Press.

Zakaria, Fareed. 1997. "The Rise of Illiberal Democracy." *Foreign Affairs*, November 1, 1997.

Chapter 14

Democracy for Losers

Comment on Bálint Magyar

Stephen Holmes

Using the mafia analogy to illuminate the predatory injustices perpetrated by territorially anchored political states echoes an ancient and venerable tradition. Still popular today, as the influential writings of Charles Tilly demonstrate (Tilly 1985), the analogy goes back at least to Saint Augustine:

> Remove justice, and what are kingdoms but gangs of criminals on a large scale? What are criminal gangs but petty kingdoms? A gang is a group of men under the command of a leader, bound by a compact of association, in which the plunder is divided according to an agreed convention. (Augustine 1972, IV, 4)

Bálint Magyar uses the mafia state analogy masterfully to classify and dissect the government of Viktor Orbán, with special emphasis on the way "the plunder is divided." Rather than trying to criticize or correct his penetrating look into contemporary Hungarian politics, which I am in no position to do, I will concentrate on his remark that the post-communist mafia state in Hungary is "not ideology driven."[1] There is a good deal of truth in this claim, and especially in the notion that the regime's worldview is eclectic, erratic, internally inconsistent, and instrumental to wealth accumulation by regime insiders. Without aspiring in any way to refute this highly original use of the mafia state analogy, I nevertheless think something important can be learned by focusing more explicitly on the instrumental role of ideology in bringing about and sustaining the Orbán system, a role that the "mafia state" metaphor does not encourage us to explore.

Nothing I say is meant to diminish the role of clientelism, cronyism, nepotism, and self-dealing in building and sustaining the current system. Orbán and his circle can no doubt be understood as kleptocrats whose methods of rule are quixotic. They have managed to seize the heights of power only because they were able to rally and sustain significant public support. This support cannot be explained, as Bálint Magyar is the first to admit, by focusing solely on their criminally corrupt behavior. This is what he means when he describes the post-communist mafia state as marked by a "gap between the real nature of power and its required legitimacy." In explaining the public legitimacy it has managed to garner, we should also look closely at the way Orbán describes the world to his supporters, a task made all the more urgent by the fact that his perspective on past developments and current trends is plausible and is spreading rapidly beyond Hungary. Given that classical mafia networks and groupings are sustained partly by patriarchal, traditionalist, and tribal allegiances and often resort to quasi-religious symbols and rituals, the blanket assertion that the post-communist mafia state in Hungary is "not ideology driven" may distract needlessly from some less scandalously acquisitive dimensions of the system Orbán has built.

I will explore the ideological underpinnings of Hungary's mafia state by reexamining Orbán's notorious and eye-opening July 26, 2014, speech in Băile Tuşnad, Transylvania in which he reaffirmed his commitment to building an illiberal state in Hungary. It was an audacious and politically resonant speech. The era of liberal democracy is over, Orbán announced, suggesting that the train of illiberal democracy already had left the station and that those who refused to clamber aboard will be left miserably behind.

Those of us who are haunted by thoughts of a relapse into the cultural climate of 1930s Europe are acutely aware of the dark side of anti-liberalism. But we should not allow historical memories and current anxieties to dominate the way we understand the disturbingly broad appeal of Orbán's anti-liberalism. He is consciously inverting our anxieties, stressing the dark sides of liberalism, and doing so with considerable political success. Rather than dismissing such talk as mere propaganda designed by a criminal elite conspiring to delude the unthinking masses, we need to understand what he and his supporters have in mind.

As my reference to the 1930s was meant to suggest, there is nothing new about anti-liberalism. On the contrary, anti-liberal ideology developed in tandem with liberalism itself. It found its first great historical expression in the theorists of the French and German counter-Enlightenment. But the flame of an incendiary ideology is only politically dangerous when public emotions become exceptionally flammable. Today, around the world, authoritarian, xenophobic, and even racist public sentiment seems all-too-easy to ignite by anti-liberal grown-ups playing with fire. What I want to try to explain, using the Hungarian example, is why.

Orbán presents himself as a reformer able to speak unpleasant truths that liberal politicians have been unwilling to confront or admit. Hungary's *liberal* democracy, over the previous two decades, has failed to defend the country's national interest, he says. As a result of the disappointments doled out by liberalism, "we have to abandon liberal methods and principles of organizing a society, as well as the liberal way to look at the world."[2]

What is remarkable about the entire speech is the way Orbán casts himself as a non-ideological reader of global events, an observer of liberalism's historical decline. He implies that he has come to his illiberalism reluctantly, as if an anti-liberal were a liberal who has been mugged by reality. He has embraced illiberalism, he tells an electorate aware of his earlier political views, only after being profoundly disappointed in the performance of liberalism as an ideological framework for guiding political and economic development in post-communist Hungary. The Hungarian regime today may not be ideology-driven, but its legitimacy derives in large part from the claim that liberal ideology, for its part, has simply not worked. In drawing this conclusion, Orbán is being (or pretends to be) very empirical and practical. He was compelled to jettison the liberalism of his youth because of its miserable failure to fulfill its most solemn promises. So what chronic shortcomings of liberalism does he claim to see and what remedies does he propose?

First, the liberal definition of freedom has proven to be a terrible disappointment. Open borders, which represented the hope of travel abroad in 1989, now represent an easy-to-exploit public fear of immigrants flooding the country. Liberal toleration increasingly is derided as a euphemism for the interests of wealthy families and businessmen who need cheap domestic help and poorly remunerated workers, but who do not have to live in the run-down neighborhoods where immigrants and lower-class Europeans uncomfortably rub shoulders. Another negative side-effect of open borders is parochial and provincial resentment against "devernacularized," mostly Anglophone or Germanophone, elites. They regularly are smeared as potential defectors and traitors. And the fact is that open borders mean that they can easily leave the country and flourish.

Next, liberalism's emphasis on individual rights obscures the nature of political abuse after 1989, which took the form of the privatization of the public patrimony, a kind of industrial-scale corruption that violated no individual rights and was indeed consolidated by the creation of individual rights to own private property. This is what Orbán means when he says that "in Hungary liberal democracy was incapable of protecting public property that is essential in sustaining a nation." Similarly, focus on individual rights fails to capture the experience of humiliation and fears of national decline that have played such a large role in post-communist political life. Moreover, liberalism's justification of economic inequality by the myth of meritocracy masks the central role of luck in the arbitrary distribution of wealth in society, a masking which is humiliating for the losers of the economic lottery because it encourages the winners to attribute their success to their superior talent and greater personal effort. The myth of meritocracy is additionally offensive in the region's historical context because of the privileged access to economic success provided, after 1989, to those who occupied important political positions in the previous oppressive system.

As a skilled populist demagogue, Orbán has exploited such themes to discredit liberal politics in favor of authoritarianism and xenophobia. What gives his stance resonance around the world is his rejection of the liberal idea, shared by all leaders of rich Western countries, that we still live in a post–Cold War world. The rest of the world has a quite different vision of where we stand today. Indeed, most agree with Orbán that we live in a post-colonial world. In this vision of recent history, the West does not represent freedom and progress but rather bullying interference in the sovereign affairs of other countries. One example is the strong conditionality enforced by the EU on newly admitted states (with no mention made of ongoing EU subsidies in Hungary). Another is the American invasion and occupation of Iraq. The easiest of Orbán's claims to defend, in fact, is that the age of *exporting* liberal democracy is over.

The American approach, exporting liberal democracy by conquest and occupation, has proved a spectacular failure. And the European approach, exporting liberal democracy by expansion of and integration into the European Union, is facing, especially now after the Brexit referendum, what could well prove to be a terminal crisis. In any case, the experience of outsiders trying to control your country while looking down at you as hapless contestants in the great "liberal imitation game" naturally creates a politics of resentment. As Nietzsche and Max Scheler have explained, resentment works by ideologically devaluing, and indeed rejecting as valueless, the ideals that one cannot oneself attain, in this case the ideal of a liberal political order on the Western model. Orbán's silly fantasy of creating an "iron dome" around Hungary appeals to a populist desire to be insulated from Western interference as well as from the quick-paced and all-corrosive forces of globalization. The proposal is unrealistic, but the anti-liberal worldview behind it has become easy to sell politically to the extent that publics everywhere now smell fatal weakness in the West. Ironically, Brussels' apparent incapacity to discipline Hungary for its defiance of liberal orthodoxy confirms Orbán's claim that the West has grown hopelessly weak.

To be sure, anti-liberalism would not have proved to be such a politically effective and (to Orbán's supporters) attractive ideology if Hungary were not an ideologically fragmented society where highly articulate pro-European forces have by no means been vanquished wholly. But the wholesale pro-European self-identification of Hungary's post-transition elites has made the anti-elitist backlash even more virulent as American-led liberalism and the European Union have fallen into parallel crises of legitimacy.

No doubt about it, the America-led postwar international order is being shaken, most notably by the declining global influence of America, the world's leading liberal democracy. Notice in this regard the way Orbán derides America by weaving together traditionalist and anti-capitalist themes, stating on the one hand that "the strength of American 'soft power' is deteriorating, because liberal values today incorporate corruption, sex and violence, and with this liberal values discredit America and American modernization," and then adding that "the internet, understood by the liberal world as the greatest symbol of freedom for many long years, is being colonized by big corporations." He also mentions "the global economic" and "global military power shift that emerged in 2008," treating the world financial crisis as a watershed because it revealed capitalism run amok, that is, the extent to which the ostensibly free international financial system was colonized by gamblers who almost single-handedly destroyed the world economy with their greedy schemes for personal enrichment devoid of any restraining concern for the public interest. More recently, Orbán has ratcheted up his attack on the liberal capitalist order by a flurry of anti-Soros propaganda with strong anti-Semitic overtones.

Other signs of the regime change on an international level which is happening before our eyes are the weakening of the "Atlantic Alliance" between the United States and the major European powers and China's success at bringing more people out of poverty than any country in world history. The latter has undermined the belief that economic prosperity necessarily is linked to liberal democracy.

China's success, in particular, plays a central role in the new global appeal of anti-liberalism. Confidence in the political superiority of liberal democracy in the post-Second World War period, and especially after 1989, hinged on two factors: first (in Western perceptions), on the military victory of America over the Nazis and, second, on the political victory of America over the Soviet Union. These twin victories were thought to prove the ideological superiority of liberal democracy over all forms of autocracy, communist and capitalist alike. The rise of China seriously has undermined this flattering narrative, suggesting that liberal democracy beat the Nazi version of capitalist autocracy only because America was much bigger than Germany and therefore that capitalist autocracy in China is by no means destined to lose its competitive struggle with America (Gat 2009). While refusing to imitate Western-style political and economic arrangements, China's political and economic success cannot be denied. This helps explain Orbán's assertion that Hungary should concentrate on improving trade relations with China rather that absurdly lecturing the Chinese on human rights.[3] The non-liberal Chinese miracle is an important part of the global context that make's Orbán's virulent anti-liberalism look like a sign of the times. His love affair with Trump is also interesting from this perspective, not to mention the preferential treatment of Putin that he and Trump conspicuously share.

By stressing the anti-liberal *Zeitgeist* visible around the world today, I do not mean to diminish the importance of specific Hungarian factors that obviously play a large role in Orbán's political appeal. The great territorial amputation of Hungary performed at Trianon in 1920 left cultural scars easy for nationalistic political entrepreneurs to exploit and provides the basis for a rather unique form of xenophobic authoritarianism, which, especially when combined with the specifically Hungarian form of the post-communist mafia state analyzed by Bálint Magyar, we might hazard to call "goulash anti-liberalism." The Trianon trauma might seem to be buried in the distant past. But Hungary is a small and linguistically isolated nation. The fact that the population speaks a rare language can create a sense of existential vulnerability and can even engender unspoken fears of extinction. Liberalism provides no remedy for the existential fears of being obliterated as a people that arguably are expressed in a continuing obsession with Trianon. Orbán can exploit politically such artificially pumped-up anxieties by suggesting that Hungarian liberals have betrayed extraterritorial Hungarians and by urging the country's new anti-liberal political class "to recognize that Hungarian diaspora around the world belongs to our nation and to try and make this sense of belonging stronger with their work."

On the other hand, the irredentism driving Putin's seizure of Crimea, accompanied as it was by claims to have rescued ethnic Russians stranded abroad after the collapse of the USSR in 1991, makes Orbán's ploy seem representative of larger trends rather than being exclusive to Hungary. Above all, Orbán's focus on the grievances of extraterritorial Hungarians represents a bitter *j'accuse!* against the Wilsonian international order that could commit such a wicked crime against the people, unilaterally shrinking the borders of the state so they no longer align with the territory inhabited by the nation in the sense of a moral community within which "we" want to live.

One reason why West Europeans find the politics of contemporary Hungary so difficult to understand is Western skepticism about "minority rights" when applied to "co-nationals" allegedly imprisoned inside the territory of other, usually contiguous, nation-states. Because Nazi propaganda invoked such *Minderheitsrechten* to justify a policy of aggressive annexationism, the liberal democracies of the West proved unwilling to include minority rights in the postwar Universal Declaration (Mazower 2004). The nonchalance with which Orbán and Putin appeal to their stranded diaspora to justify violations of the liberal international order may even reflect the failure of anti-Nazi revulsion at minority rights to penetrate Russian and Hungarian political cultures. The lack of any association between the rights of extraterritorial nationals and National Socialism, due in Hungary to a failure to come to terms with Hungarian complicity in the Holocaust, is one factor that makes these cultures especially susceptible to anti-liberal appeals. (This is not to deny that Hungarian irredentism – which in many ways resembled the French pattern after 1871 – predated Nazism or that some of the countries that protested most vocally against this irredentism became willing Nazi collaborators after 1939.)

Whether anger at Trianon remains a real motivation for the Orbánistas or is merely a pretext that matters very little. One way or the other, Hungarian public opinion today is pervaded by a feeling that being integrated into the liberal-capitalist economic order is a trauma. The remedy that Orbán offers is to insulate Hungary to some extent from this malign influence. When he says that "a democracy is not necessarily liberal," and adds, "Just because something is not liberal, it still can be a democracy," he is addressing himself directly to those who view the transition after 1989 as a losing proposition. His admiration for developmental dictatorships in China and Singapore, as well as his manipulation of elections and crackdown on dissent, makes his claim to be building an illiberal *democracy* easy to mock. His interest in genuine democracy is obviously negligible, as demonstrated by his persistent efforts to destroy local self-government and access to information, as well as his resort to strategic gerrymandering and quasi-democratic referenda.[4] But before feeling triumphant, we must remember two things: first, that the traumatic transition of 1989 was not democratic either (since wild privatization was not popularly selected in a competitive election), and second, that however Hungarian voters voted in the twenty years before Orbán's rise to power, the policies of the governments did not change, Hungary's political elites remaining fully in accord with the demands of Brussels.

So, here again, Orbán's political success stems in part from his ability to speak to the losers of 1989, to empathize with their suffering and give it a voice. (This is not to deny the social heterogeneity of Fidesz voters who ranged from lower middle-class losers to yuppies and middle-class winners, not to mention national oligarchs.) The similarity of Orbán's mixture of nationalism and class resentment that in 2016 fueled both the Brexit referendum and the rise of Donald Trump becomes clear in a famous passage from his 2014 speech in Transylvania. After declaring that Hungarian politics from 1989 to 2010 was based on the liberal principle "that we are free to do anything that does not violate another person's freedom," he goes on to unmask this principle as class ideology, since self-satisfied westernized Hungarians were the ones who decided what constituted a harm:

We constantly felt that the weaker were stepped upon. It was not some kind of an abstract principle of fairness that decided upon conflicts originating from a recognition of mutual freedoms, but what happened is that the stronger party was always right: the stronger neighbor told you where your car entrance is. It was always the stronger party, the bank, that dictated how much interest you pay on your mortgage, changing it as they liked over time. I could enumerate the examples that was the continuous life experience of vulnerable, weak families that had smaller economic protection than others during the last twenty years.

Such politicized nostalgia for a precapitalist, feudal-style protection racket lends some support to the mafia parallel. Orbán is addressing himself here directly to those who think the dark science of traumatology offers a better picture of their country's post-1989 development than the sunny science of transitology. He is offering himself as the leader of a democracy for losers. The losers of the transition speak directly through him. He draws support, for instance, from those who feel offended by the orthodox Brussels view that Hungary under Orbán is "backsliding." The real backsliding, they believe, occurred after 1989. The losers of 1989 include those who borrowed money in Swiss francs and then, after a radical devaluation of Hungary's currency, had to make skyrocketing monthly payments in depreciated forints. This is what Orbán has in mind when he remarks that "the liberal Hungarian state did not protect the country from indebtedness. And – and here I mostly mean the system of foreign exchange loans – it failed to protect families from bonded labor." Such crushing burdens reinforced the sense that integration into the global economic system was humiliation and impoverishment not freedom, as it had been originally presented by its liberal cheerleaders.

True, the amount of boilerplate anti-liberal rhetoric that Orbán recycles in his public statements is impressive. Using "rootless cosmopolitan" as a code word for Jew is not unprecedented, to say the least. The same can be said of claims that liberalism is hyper-individualistic and erodes the common life of "we Hungarians." This is what he has in mind when he says that "liberal democracy was not capable of openly declaring, or even obliging, governments with constitutional power to declare that they should serve national interests. Moreover, it even questioned the existence of national interests." Along these same lines, he claims that the liberal picture of society as a spiritually empty network of producers and consumers cannot capture the moral depth of the Hungarian nation.

We could take such off-the-shelf anti-liberal sloganeering as a sign that Orbán's talk is just that, talk, and need not be taken seriously. But this would be a mistake. Resentment against liberal politics, and especially against liberal internationalism, is real and consequential. Liberal ideology itself emphasizes impersonal markets and the unbiased rule of law. But liberal arrangements always favor certain social groups over others and distribute society's benefits and burdens not fairly but according to the power of one's social networks. The Polish example proves that populist breakthroughs do not always depend on an economic downturn. What gives populism its grip on the public mind is the way its proponents "unmask" liberalism's hypocrisy, exposing the systematic favoritism underlying its superficial fairness. This is why populists always blame the ex-communist new rich first.

Those who see themselves as the losers of liberal politics naturally gravitate toward a self-appointed "leader" who speaks the unvarnished truth about liberal hypocrisy and promises to defend their interests just as well as the liberal elites hiding behind markers and the rule of law once defended the interests of the well-connected winners of the transition. We may deride cult-of-personality style governance as institutionally weak. But we should not underestimate the appeal of political systems dominated by a strong leader. First of all, strong-leader populism is a system easy for most people to understand. Unlike the EU, a virtually leaderless system in which thousands of tiny decisions are made anonymously and therefore unaccountably, leader-dominated politics is oriented toward bold decisions as well as inviting hope that the leader will rescue the losers from their plight. The accession of Emmanuel Macron to the French presidency shows that this shift has now penetrated the core of Western democracy, too.

In other words, far from being unique to Hungary, Orbán's way of describing the contemporary crisis is spreading to ostensibly better-established liberal democracies as well. To associate Orbán with Putin, Miklós Haraszti has described the former's foreign policy as "drifting in a Western boat propelled by an Eastern wind." But Orbán's boat also is propelled by a "Western wind." The ineffectiveness of the EU in addressing Hungary's authoritarian turn is due in part to the power of Eurosceptic and "the boat is full" anti-immigrant parties in the West. Punishing Hungary for xenophobia when paranoid fears of being swamped demographically are on the rise throughout Europe is an obvious non-starter. This is the context in which Orbán has been able to emerge, grow, and thrive. He was an early and remarkably prescient detector of the evolving illiberal *Zeitgeist*.

The eclectic anti-liberal ideology that Orbán has stitched together for purely instrumental purposes is an amalgam of many "antis": anti-globalization, anti-capitalism, anti-EU, anti-gay, anti-immigrant, anti-pluralism, anti-multiculturalism, and anti-American. This negative list is much richer and more suggestive than his perfunctory nods to a positive vision of a Christian workfare state. Consider first the odd suggestion that there is some kind of dark alliance between Brussels and Africa, EU policy, and the immigrant crisis. The two are connected, in the anti-liberal mind, because both are viewed as threatening to dilute the national identity of Hungarians. Anti-Americanism comes into the picture here as well, since the world's greatest liberal democracy, the United States, played a leading role in fomenting the current immigration crisis by its warmongering in Afghanistan, Iraq, Libya, and Syria.

A major contribution of Bálint Magyar's diagnosis of Orbán's authoritarian clientelism is to undercut exaggerated and unhelpful comparisons of the
current Hungarian regime with European fascism. The regime's nationalism
is in many ways a mirage: "The Hungarian octopus creates a collectivist,
nationalistic ideology under the pretext of the so-called national and social
justice, which is just a tool to justify their egotistic aspirations for concentrating power and wealth."[5] Thus, the regime uses the illegitimacy of privatization wealth not to renationalize the public patrimony but rather to redistribute
it to political supporters. In Bálint Magyar's words: "With the legalized
instruments of state monopoly of coercion, the mafia state coercively extracts
private fortunes – sometimes indirectly through different forms of nationalization – to serve its own interests and redistributes this amongst clients of
the adopted political family." This is the sense in which "national capitalism" displays a more than passing resemblance to the fascist original, at least
to the extent that companies like *Krupp, I. G. Farben*, and so forth played
an essential role in the workings of the Nazi economy. Orbán promises to
insulate Hungary from interference by Brussels even while living hypocriti-
cally off EU subsidies. More generally, Orbán promises order, but his rule is
more haphazard, arbitrary, and unpredictable than oppressive. This is what
distances the mafia state from genuinely fascist precursors. His government is
oppressive but (so far) not bloody. The paramilitary groupings involved in the
rise of fascist and Nazi regimes in the 1920s and 1930s were partly a legacy
of World War I. This source of mass political violence in the psychology of
war-traumatized veterans is not available to populist politicians today. (Until
now, the border guard-vigilante dynamic that Orbán cynically unleashed
remains a pale replica of early twentieth-century paramilitarism, but the possibility remains that he will resort to more violent means to stay in power if
the less violent ones lose their efficacy.)

Yet the family resemblance between soccer-stadium democracies in the
1930s and today is not entirely unrevealing. For one thing, Orbán consistently
invokes Hungarian solidarity to discourage expressions of solidarity with less
fortunate members of Hungarian society, appealing to the "true" nation to
attack the poor, elderly, gays, Jews, NGOs (considered foreign-paid agents),
Roma, and especially liberals as "foreign" to the genuine community. This is
a natural turn, since any regime which elevates loyalty to the highest virtue
is bound to obsess about conspiring traitors lurking in its midst. To distract
attention from the government's poor economic performance it helps to identify scapegoats and fuel the idea that Hungary is surrounded and infiltrated
by "enemies."

The costs of this way of ruling the country are obviously high. First, by
encouraging resentment against privileged Anglophone elites, the government also increases the brain drain of talented individuals who arguably

have something valuable to contribute to society. This is what Bálint Magyar means when he writes that "the nationalism of the mafia state is not targeted at other nations, but rather the expulsion from their own nation of all those, who are not part of the adopted political family, or are not built into the order of vassals. Since they are not part of the 'patriarch's household,' they must face all the consequences of being outsiders" (Magyar 2014).

Emigration may reduce domestic opposition to Orbán, but it obviously bodes ill for the country's future development, which is not to say that it is irrational from the regime's point of view. Second, the tendency of this sort of government to prize loyalty over competence means that everyday governance is suffering. Third, direct and indirect censorship of the press not only covers up corruption but also fosters a culture of rapidly circulating unsubstantiated rumors, which degrades the public mind and political life in general. Most of all, the tendency of Hungary's current Godfather and his vassal dependents to seek political legitimacy for their self-enrichment schemes by creating imaginary enemies from whom the government can protect the people not only fosters public paranoia but also is extremely unlikely to end without unleashing the kind of uncontrollable violence that it has avoided mercifully thus far.

NOTES

1. Unless otherwise indicated, all citations of Bálint Magyar are to his chapter in this volume.
2. All passages from Orbán's speech are cited from budapestbeacon.com 2014.
3. See kormany.hu (2017a, b).
4. For a persuasive argument that populist democracy is a contradiction in terms, see Müller (2016).
5. See aspeninstitute.cz (2014).

BIBLIOGRAPHY

aspeninstitute.cz. 2014. "Bálint Magyar. 2014. "Post-Communist Mafia State – The Hungarian Case." http://www.aspeninstitute.cz/en/article/4-2014-post-communist-mafia-state-the-hungarian-case, accessed June 25, 2019.
Augustine. 1972. *City of God*. Harmondsworth: Penguin.
budapestbeacon.com. 2014. "Full Text of Viktor Orbán's Speech." http://budapestbeacon.com/public-policy/full-text-of-viktor-orbans-speech-at-baile-tusnad-tusnadfurdo-of-26-july-2014/10592, accessed June 25, 2019.
Gat, Azar. 2009. *Victorious and Vulnerable: Why Democracy Won in the 20th Century and How it is Still Imperiled*. Lanham, MD: Rowman & Littlefield.

kormany.hu. 2017a. "Prime minister Viktor Orbán's speech at the Lámfalussy Conference, January 23, 2017." https://www.kormany.hu/en/the-prime-minister/the-prime-minister-s-speeches/prime-minister-viktor-orban-s-speech-at-the-lamfalussy-conference

———. 2017b. "The Old Globalisation Model Is Obsolete." http://www.kormany.hu/en/the-prime-minister/news/the-old-globalisation-model-is-obsolete, accessed June 25, 2019.

Magyar, Bálint. 2014. *Post-Communist Mafia State – The Hungarian Case*. Budapest: CEU Press and Noran Press.

Mazower, Mark. 2004. "The Strange Triumph of Human Rights, 1933–1950." *The Historical Journal*, 47 (2): 379–98.

Müller, Jan-Werner. 2016. *What Is Populism?* Philadelphia: University of Pennsylvania Press.

Tilly, Charles. 1985. "War Making and State Making as Organized Crime." In *Bringing the State Back In*, edited by Peter Evans, Dietrich Rueschemeyer, and Theda Skocpol, 173–87. Cambridge: Cambridge University Press.

Chapter 15

Nothing But a Mafia State?

Balázs Váradi

Is it ethical to tear down government-sponsored public service billboard posters? Should an opposition politician who accepts to serve as an ambassador be ostracized by her colleagues? How acceptable is it for a Hungarian citizen to petition the European Parliament to punish his or her own government? Making moral judgments and forging political strategies to topple a government are difficult without a clear definition of the political system one lives under.

In this short chapter, I argue that Bálint Magyar's vivid and insightful diagnosis of the present political regime in Hungary as a "mafia state," as developed in his chapter may be an incomplete or even misleading description of the Orbán regime since 2010. To start with, I have two methodological quibbles. One concerns the genre: is Magyar's "mafia book" an extended essay, a political pamphlet, or the diagnostic part of a political strategy to fight Orbán? Another asks about the method: does the proof of the existence of a mafia state in Magyar's bold claims lie in sociology or journalism?[1]

This is the way I interpret his contribution – which is a summary of his book, a set of his articles, and an ongoing stream of volumes edited by him[2] : if we strip down Magyar's analysis from the inventive neologisms he creates combining terms such as the state, the family, and the mafia, he tells us the following:

(1) The Orbán regime in power since spring 2010 in Hungary
    (a) has a well-defined essential sociological-political nature.
    (b) is no more a liberal democracy.
    Rather, it is a regime that is
    (c) within the European Union, *sui generis*.
    (d) essentially *post-communist*.

(e) moreover, it is a regime in which the political and economic power is wielded by a concentric hierarchy organized around loyalty and gains from redistribution, whose internal and external relationships are reminiscent of certain kinds of organized crime.

(2) The regime has *no ideological or policy-related goals concerning the whole of Hungarian society* beyond their one objective to retain power and to milk it for economic gain.

First things first: I agree with claim (1) (b). Political and legal analysis by the Tavares report,[3] Kim Lane Scheppele and her coauthors in 2014, Bánkuti 2015, Pech 2017, the OSCE-ODIHR observers of the 2014 election, scores by international watchdogs like Freedom House,[4] as well as an admission by Viktor Orbán himself in Băile Tuşnad can be taken as sufficient evidence that Hungary is no more a liberal democracy.

Although I wonder about the right method to establish such a strong claim in political sociology, and whether it was followed by Magyar and his coauthors, I do not want to argue with the many instances illustrating the claim under (1) (e). I think while it plays down the fact that there are still thousands upon thousands of civil servants designing and implementing policies in the best Weberian tradition, it is an inventive, thought-provoking, and plausible description of many elements of the way Hungary is governed under Orbán.

My squabble is with the remaining four claims. Let me address them one-by-one.

THE ORBÁN REGIME IN POWER SINCE SPRING 2010 HAS A WELL-DEFINED ESSENTIAL SOCIOLOGICAL-POLITICAL NATURE (1)(A)

Are power relations in Hungary now stable and well-delineated enough to try to look for the system's essence? An argument can be made that they are not or at least not yet. Even if we do not put too much trust in their methods and allow for some cautious delay, Hungary's descent does not seem to be over according to its Freedom House (2018) democracy scores: the deterioration of Hungary's headline democracy score from 2013 to 2016 (0.4) is similar in size to the change in 2010–2012 (0.47) when the constitutional foundation of the new Orbán regime was laid, or to the 0.42 deterioration in the most recent 2016–2018 period.

We can find both mainstream political scientists like Lise Herman (2015) and discerning domestic observers like Ákos Szilágyi (2015) who consider the regime to be on a trajectory away from an imperfect liberal democracy and toward something that we have yet to define: maybe tracing out a lamentable excursion that ultimately takes the country back to liberal democracy or maybe making a descent to a hegemonic authoritarian regime. In either case, trying to identify a fleeting stop along the trajectory of change as a final destination can be misleading.

But even if we allow for the premise that there *is* such a thing to describe as the Orbán regime, searching for its essence could prove a wild goose chase. Essentialism is dangerous. What is the essence of an elephant? Its size? Its thick skin? Its trunk? An unexpected metaphor ("an elephant is nothing but a slow giant rat") could give us an "aha" experience. Still: a naturalist would never look for an answer for this question. Her description, useful for both the conservationist and the hunter, would be concerned with the anatomy, the ethology, the evolutionary taxonomy, and so on of the animal.

THE ORBÁN REGIME IS, WITHIN THE EUROPEAN UNION, SUI GENERIS (1) (C)

If looking for a definition, the most useful is one fitting in a taxonomy, identifying the *genus proximum* and the *differentia specifica.* One such categorization of political regimes, using differences in how democratic they are was proposed by Howard and Roessler (2006) who distinguished between regimes based on yes/no answers to consecutive questions: (1) Is there pluralism/freedom/rule of law? (2) Are elections free and fair? (3) Are elections contested? (4) Do elections take place?

While this might not yield a concrete "aha" concerning the nature of the regime, since contested elections took place in Hungary in 2014 and 2018, depending on our answers to the questions whether "freedom, pluralism, and the rule of law" still sufficiently prevail and whether we judge the most recent general elections "free and fair," the country can be put conveniently in one of three boxes: Liberal Democracy / Electoral Democracy / Competitive Authoritarian regime. If the reader accepts my "no" answer to the first question mentioned earlier, the two alternatives that remain are Electoral Democracy or a Competitive Authoritarian regime.

A *sui generis* term like Magyar's mafia state, under which Hungary stands alone in the EU, might reveal something about the workings of the regime, but it would tell us little about where it fits.

THE ORBÁN REGIME IS ESSENTIALLY POST-COMMUNIST (1) (D)

This term is an integral part of Magyar's definition. He says that "the System of National Cooperation came about on the foundations of a communist dictatorship, as a product of the debris left by its decay" (Magyar 2016, 68). He takes this notion so much for granted that his comparisons are exclusively with other ex-Soviet or ex-Soviet-ruled countries. While culturalist frameworks stressing the importance of path-dependence have been repeatedly applied to Hungary by political analysts (János Kis, János Széky, or Péter Tölgyessy), it is not clear why it is the historical period of communism in Hungary (1949–1989) that should be the main defining element of its emergence. Most of the analysts mentioned above as well as the apologists of the regime concentrate on the turbulent years between 1989 and 2010, while some (like János Kis) put quite a bit of the blame on social and cultural divisions predating the communist regime.

Indeed, while there is undoubtedly cronyism in some post-communist countries like Azerbaijan, the systems of cronyism Magyar describes as mafia state are easier to compare with descriptions of Brazil or Tunisia under Ben Ali than many ex-communist states like the Baltic countries or Georgia.

THE REGIME HAS NO IDEOLOGICAL OR POLICY-RELATED GOALS CONCERNING THE WHOLE OF HUNGARIAN SOCIETY BEYOND THEIR ONE OBJECTIVE TO RETAIN POWER AND TO MILK IT FOR ECONOMIC GAIN (2)

"Par excellence public policies are eliminated: decisions have no professional motives only consequences," writes Magyar (2016, 73). This is a central point for him, which, if true, is the best argument for amplifying the "mafia state" metaphor to a monocausal explanation of the Orbán regime: he thinks that not ideology, not the public good however construed, not any policy goal, but private monetary gain is the only explanation for what it does.

This extreme claim is by no means beyond mainstream political science. Indeed, it can be interpreted as an answer to the old question whether politicians' behavior can be explained based on their motive to grasp and keep power alone (office-seeking behavior), or it helps to assume that they have extrinsic goals (policy-seeking behavior). If it is exclusively the office-seeking motive that drives politicians (as is assumed in many public choice models), then that is not very far from the answer Magyar gives us.

The Orbán regime itself does provide a plethora of ideological and policy-seeking explanations for what it does: it claims that it aims to tweak the system of redistribution so as to favor the better off, especially households with children ("strengthen the middle class/families"), to annihilate putative social networks still surviving from communist times (cf. the "clotted structures" argument of Fidesz ideologue Gyula Tellér), to achieve higher participation in the labor force (a "work-based society"), to inch away from the West that is perceived as decadent ("opening toward the East"), and to change the proportion of foreign versus domestic ownership in the economy ("a strong country, independent of multinationals"). But Magyar interprets all of the regime's policy measures carried out under these slogans as serving nothing but office-seeking and pecuniary motives.

He has two strong general arguments on his side. First, he argues – starting with their U-turn from a classical liberal to a center-right party around 1994, to the radical-populist party of the right it is at present – that the declared policy goals of Fidesz have frequently changed: from anti-clerical it turned staunchly Christian; from pro-Tibet to pro-China; from pro-market to *dirigiste*. I agree that if they had been more constant, the charge that they were a mere front for completely unprincipled mafia rule would have been harder to make stick. But frequent changes in policy stances also can be pragmatic responses to changing economic and political conditions, while the political party in question carries on pursuing unchanged selfless goals. Indeed, it is not hard to identify swift and complete policy turnarounds in the track record of many political parties, abroad or in Hungary (e.g., the turnaround about decreasing/increasing taxes by the Hungarian Socialist Party and the Alliance of Free Democrats in 2005–2006 comes to mind – to mention two other parties close to power for more than one four-year term since 1990).

His second argument is inductive. He and his coauthors advanced policy area by policy area, case-by-case, from government communication to banning the development of new shopping malls, stressing that those in power and their minions stand to materially gain from the measures in question. This, however, even if convincing, cannot exclude the alternative explanation that lucre is a mere side-effect but not the actual goal. An instructive case is the change in how the retail trade of tobacco is regulated (Laki 2014). The introduction of a new system of licensing tobacconists and distributing those licenses to Fidesz supporters based on a speedy and secretive sham tender fits very well in Magyar's frame. Did changes in the rules of wholesale tobacco trade create a chance to reward (or to extort money from) companies involved in that business? Well, these measures were accompanied by others (a tax hike, ban on smoking in certain spaces, and so on) ostensibly meant to restrict smoking in Hungary for reasons of public health. May the goal have been as much fighting the prevalence of smoking-related disease and death as helping supporters to gain? Magyar's answer is no. The World Health Organization gave a high award to Viktor Orbán in 2013, so their answer can be read as yes.

The best way to counter the blame that everything stems from the greed of the mafia state is to try to enumerate government measures that do not serve the enrichment of the "concentric elites," the maintenance of their loyalty, or dependence or the re-election of Fidesz. I think there are quite a few such policy measures. Let me just list three, all from the earlier years of the regime, so that we have a chance to see them run their full course.

(1) The 2011–2012 personal income tax reform.[5] Replacing the progressive schedule with a flat rate, plus adding a very generous tax break for having children to the child benefit system, left a gaping hole in the budget. It also left tens of billions of forints in the pockets of the top income decile of households. Many of these households are hostile to the Orbán government. It is questionable if this costly fiscal measure, instituted years before the next election, was a cost-effective way to garner votes. Moreover, the same amount could have been spent on all kinds of subsidies made conditional on loyalty or economic and political support. It is much easier for me to believe that the declared policy goal, widespread across center-right parties worldwide – leaving more money with high earners, augmenting the incentives for them to work harder, and make the tax system simpler and less distortionary – was the primary one.
(2) The regime has instituted a number of changes that they claim are meant to reintroduce and foster a more traditional, more conservative, more religious lifestyle. These range from integrating religious education in the curriculum of state schools to deregistering smaller churches to a ban (by now lifted) on keeping shops open on Sunday. These measures have been unpopular with the bulk of the population, which is less religious than the EU average[6] (in fact, the government revoked the Sunday ban when the threat of a referendum against it manifested itself), and are at most a very wasteful way to help churches or friendly retailers. Is it not more likely that they simply mean it? That they desire to use these few levers an EU member state has to make families more Christian?
(3) Orbán's foreign policy turn toward Russia (the so-called opening toward the East) is certainly not a vote-getter on the hardly-Russophile Hungarian right. It palpably hurt the country's relations with a number of other countries from the United States to Poland. Under the right conditions, it would have been certainly possible to find another unprincipled partner to provide financial support for upgrading the Paks nuclear power plant. If we want to explain this shift in the international relations of Hungary, we have to look for reasons of policy, perhaps even of geopolitics (e.g., increasing leverage within the EU), not of office-seeking or gain.

While I readily accept that the mafia-like mechanisms Magyar and his coauthors describe can be an important element of the political sociology of Fidesz's rule, I am unsure if there is a well-enough-defined political system yet in Hungary for us to make this label stick. Even if we accept the premise that there is something solid enough to characterize, I doubt his description can stand as a full explanation of its own. In fact, reducing one's diagnosis to the claim that a mafia-like conspiracy to bleed the country dry, devoid of any ideology or policy goal whatsoever has taken over, leaves a lot of the regime's behavior unexplained.

I think the analytical route to follow is to combine traditional political science categories as suggested earlier with a better understanding of the trajectory along which less-than-completely consolidated liberal democratic political systems can transform relatively peacefully into electoral democracies and, from there, into competitive authoritarian regimes, and the structural drivers that goad Hungary along that road.

While the exploitative and hierarchical nature of Orbán's rule, as described in Magyar's witty contribution in this volume as well as his books, can perhaps contribute to the understanding of that path, it cannot, and does not, tell us why and where Hungary is going, at what speed, and whether it will stop short of turning into full-fledged authoritarian regime.

NOTES

1. These concerns are expressed in more detail in a critical essay in Hungarian upon which this piece is based (Váradi 2015).
2. In English: Magyar 2016 and Magyar and Vásárhelyi 2017. Since the contribution in this volume is an abridged version of Magyar's argument in all of these, I think it is fair that I concentrate on his books. My quotes come from the English-language volumes.
3. EP Resolution 2012/2130(INI) – 03/07/2013. Situation of Fundamental Rights: Standards and Practices in Hungary
4. See Freedom House (2018).
5. Cf. Eurostat (2013).
6. See European Commission (2010, 204).

BIBLIOGRAPHY

Bánkuti, Miklós, Gábor Halmai, and Kim Lane Scheppele. 2015. "Hungary's Illiberal Turn: Disabling the Constitution." In *The Hungarian Patient: Social Opposition to an Illiberal Democracy*, edited by Péter Krasztev and Van Til Jon, 37–46. Budapest: Central European University Press.

European Commission. 2010. *Special Eurobarometer/Biotechnology*. Brussels: European Commission.

Eurostat. 2013. "Taxation Trends in the EU." https://ec.europa.eu/taxation_customs/sites/taxation/files/docs/body/report.pdf, accessed June 25, 2019.

Freedom House. 2018. "Nations in Transit 2018." https://freedomhouse.org/report/nations-transit/2018/hungary, accessed June 25, 2019.

Herman, Lise Esther. 2015. "Re-evaluating the Post-communist Success Story: Party Elite Loyalty, Citizen Mobilization and the Erosion of Hungarian Democracy." *European Political Science Review* 8 (2): 251–84.

Howard, Marc and Philip Roessler. 2006. "Liberalizing Electoral Outcomes in Competitive Authoritarian Regimes." *American Journal of Political Science* 50: 365–81.

Laki, Mihály. 2014. "A trafikpiac átalakulása és átalakítása" (The Re-shaping of the Tobacconist Market). MTA KTI *Discussion Paper* MT-DP 10

Magyar, Bálint. 2016. *Post-Communist Mafia-State: The Case of Hungary*. Budapest: CEU Press and Noran Press.

Magyar, Bálint, and Vásárhelyi Júlia, eds. 2017. *Twenty-Five Sides of a Post-Communist Mafia State*. Budapest: CEU Press.

OSCE-ODIHR. 2014. Hungary, Parliamentary Elections April 6, 2014. Warsaw: OSCE. Available online: http://www.osce.org/odihr/elections/hungary/121098?download=tue.

Pech, Laurent, and Kim Lane Scheppele. 2017. "Illiberalism Within: Rule of Law Backsliding in the EU." *Cambridge Yearbook of European Legal Studies* 19: 3–47.

Scheppele, Kim Lane. 2014. "Hungary and the End of Politics." *The Nation*, May. Available online: https://www.thenation.com/article/hungary-and-end-politics/.

Szilágyi, Ákos. 2015. "Vezérdemokrácia vagy Cezarizmus?" *2000* (5): 1–65.

Váradi, Balázs. 2015. "Polip-e?" (Is It an Octopus?). *BUKSz* (Budapest Review of Books), 3–4.

Chapter 16

What, If Anything, Can the EU Do?[1]

Jan-Werner Müller

Liberal democracy is under threat in Hungary and Poland. What, if anything, can the EU do in this situation? In this chapter, I shall first address the question whether the EU has the authority to act as a guardian of liberal democracy in Member States, or, to put it differently, whether it can establish a form of supranational militant democracy – with authority understood both in a broader normative and a narrower legal sense. Second, I shall examine whether the Union has the capacity to fulfill such a role, looking closely at a number of existing legal instruments but also evaluating a range of more direct political strategies which have been proposed in recent years. I shall argue that all existing approaches are problematic, and I shall suggest – but, given the constraints of this volume, only in passing – that a new institution, a "democracy watchdog" tentatively labeled the "Copenhagen Commission," could serve to remedy the Union's deficits in democracy protection. Third, and in a more speculative vein, I shall ask whether the EU has what it takes by way of legitimacy – not in a theoretical normative sense but as an empirical matter: Would there not be a tremendous nationalist backlash against Brussels if the Union started prescribing "correct" understandings of democracy to its Member States?

IS THE UNION AUTHORIZED TO PROTECT DEMOCRACY IN MEMBER STATES?

The answer to this question is often short-circuited by the argument that an undemocratic institution like the EU cannot act as a credible defender of democracy: the EU, it is said, is part of the problem and not part of the solution for democracy in Europe today. A number of responses are plausible in the face of such a blunt charge. The minimal one would be to say that Member States, as *liberal democracies*, have freely delegated specific tasks and powers to the EU – and that those tasks include the defense of democracy. In other words, the Union derives its legitimacy not from being a full continental democracy (at least at this point in time) but rather from national parliaments that have voted freely to bind themselves and follow European rules – and they have freely established certain sanctions for those not following said rules, in particular Article 7 of the Treaty on European Union (TEU).

Article 7 provides for the option to suspend the voting rights of a Member State in the European Council, if that Member State is in persistent breach of fundamental European values, as specified in Article 2 TEU. Yet this argument might be a little too quick, if one assumes the question to be specifically about democracy protection: after all, Article 7 does not really mandate anything like intervention *within* a Member State or, put more dramatically, the salvation of a national liberal democracy by the EU. Rather, the core of Article 7 consists of a mechanism to insulate the rest of the Union from the government of a particular Member State deemed no longer fully in compliance with the values of democracy, rule of law, human rights, and so on. Put simply: the Article enables a *moral quarantine* not an actual intervention. So, while clearly political in its intent, Article 7 can only bring about direct political change in the form of a kind of "isolationism" of the EU and its Member States vis-à-vis one "rogue state"; it cannot immediately change the internal politics of the Member State (although one might say that a Member State's inability to articulate and defend its core interests in EU fora is bound to have knock-on effects inside the country: if the Union decides to cut infrastructure subsidies for a Member State, and that Member States' government cannot make its case in response in the European Council, one would think that this situation has consequences for domestic politics, whether in the form of a government losing support or perhaps in the form of a nationalist backlash against the EU – I shall write more about this toward the end of the chapter).

On the more positive side, it is worth emphasizing that Article 7's moral quarantine has a robust normative justification in democratic theory: the principle of all-affected interests. It has often been argued that this principle cannot be operationalized if one focuses on all the effects that political decisions and laws could have beyond the borders of the country where specific laws apply:[2] any kind of causation – who is affected by what? – is simply too hard to specify when we try to ascertain who plausibly can be affected by a political decision (and who, according to democratic theory, ought ideally to have a say in the decision). In the context of the EU, however, a more modest claim can be made for a specific *legal* interpretation of the all-affected principle (along the lines of Beckman 2008): EU law applies across national borders, after being created by individual Member States acting together. More important still is that Hungarian and Polish courts are also EU courts – they apply EU law, and their decisions have to be recognized across the Union. In sum, then, literally *every* European citizen has an interest in not being faced with an authoritarian Member State in the EU (or one where the rule of law has been seriously undermined): that state will make decisions in the European Council and therefore, at least in an indirect way, govern the lives of *all* citizens; the institutions of that state – above all courts – will also issue judgments that all others will then have to recognize. Just think of the European Arrest Warrant, which relies on the idea of mutual recognition of judicial decisions (and ultimately on trusting that all Member States guarantee the rule of law and the independence of the judiciary).[3]

Even beyond this concern about what one might call the "cross-border output" of governments and legal systems in breach of fundamental values, there is a concern about how actions within a state can affect those who make use of their right of free movement (and could thus be subject to arbitrary, unfair procedures in another EU state). Combine all this with the fact that Member States cannot retaliate against other Member States directly ("you nationalize our companies, we nationalize yours"), and one can see that a government going "rogue" actually puts into jeopardy the entire European edifice. That edifice is built on notions of mutual recognition of law and a certain degree of mutual trust of governments – and if those go, everything goes.[4]

More bluntly: it may well be true that there are far-away countries containing people about whom many other Europeans know nothing, but as long as they are in the EU, they do concern them.[5] This sheer fact of interdependence has been brought home to virtually all Europeans by the Eurocrisis, but there interdependence mostly has been understood in financial and economic terms. However, there is a broader, freely chosen *political* interdependence, too. Countries have given up direct control of many areas of political, social, and economic life – which is another way of saying: their capacity to defend their citizens' interests – because they trust Brussels to live up properly to the commitment to exercise its delegated powers and agreed tasks.[6] And precisely because Brussels has to mistrust Member States, Member States can then trust each other.

Now where does this leave any mandate for interventions in a Member State? Let me explore two further arguments: first of all, one might claim that de facto an overarching supranational EU constitutional order has emerged and that, in the absence of any legal possibility actually to eject a Member State – this option is simply not provided for in the treaties at all – this order implies a right to safeguard this constitutional settlement through interventions within Member States. In other words, it does not matter whether the EU is on the way to becoming something resembling a federal state or not. What matters is that every political community (and the EU surely is a political community, one that defines itself partly on the basis of shared fundamental values) either has instruments for internal intervention or something like a right to expel one of its parts. At the moment, the EU certainly lacks the latter as states can only leave voluntarily.[7]

Concretely, such a view of the EU would imply that the European Commission – as the designated guardian of the treaties – could start infringement proceedings on the basis of Article 2.[8] Of course, this scenario looks like an unelected institution which is *not* a court empowering itself comprehensively to review the political and legal systems of Member States. De facto, the Commission already has been moving in such a direction, in particular through "Justice Scoreboards" that evaluate national judiciaries (but usually without assessing the quality of the rule of law as such). In any case, the Commission makes precisely such evaluations every time it has to decide whether to admit an applicant state into the Union. An acceptance of the idea of the EU as a distinct political order, which is predicated on the Member States being liberal democracies does imply that the EU has the required *authority* to ensure that the Member States remain liberal democracies – or to exit from this particular order if they so desire.

There is a further justification for democracy protection that can bolster the EU's authority (and also its empirical legitimacy) but that is not based so much in legal or political theory. This is the idea of the EU as a political insurance scheme or even, put more bluntly, of the EU as a kind of policeman who will "save us from ourselves." One of the explicit goals of European enlargement to the East was to consolidate liberal democracies (or complete the transition to liberal democracy in the first place in the case of Romania and Bulgaria). The region's governments sought to lock themselves into Europe precisely so as to prevent what is now often referred to as "backsliding"; it was like Ulysses ordering his sailors to bind him to the mast in order to resist the siren songs of illiberal and antidemocratic voices in the future.

Considered against this background, Hungarian and Polish leaders are wrong to accuse Brussels of some form of "Eurocolonialism." Viktor Orbán, comparing the EU to former colonial powers who oppressed the Magyars, has complained that "they are trying to tell us how to live." In fact, "they" are only reminding Hungarians (and Poles) how they wanted to live when they joined the Union in 2004 (which is not to say that it is never legitimate to criticize the EU because of an initial commitment to membership – it is just not reasonable to do so when Brussels lives up to the very commitments a Member State population once sought).

DOES THE EU HAVE THE CAPACITY TO PROTECT
LIBERAL DEMOCRACY IN MEMBER STATES?

I have argued so far that the EU does have authority to protect liberal democracy in Member States – as paternalistic as this might sound in the ears of some. The question now is whether it has the capacity to do so. It is here that the EU certainly has come up short. Let me substantiate this claim by briefly examining existing legal approaches and more political strategies, which have been proposed to rein in "rogue governments."

First, Article 7 itself. The idea for such an article was pushed by two paragons of West European liberal democracy, Italy and Austria, in the run-up to enlargement, out of fear of what uncouth Eastern Europeans might do (the irony being that sanctions – though not under Article 7 – were first applied against Austria in 2000).[9] Nowadays, Article 7 is considered widely as a "nuclear option," even by the former president of the European Commission, José Manuel Barroso. In other words: it is deemed unusable. Countries seem too scared that sanctions might also be applied against them one day; sometimes regional solidarity (especially in Central and Eastern Europe) also plays a role.

To be sure, these are all contestable empirical hypotheses. If, let's say, the Greek colonels of the junta from 1967 to 1974 came back tomorrow, would we repeat the mantra that Article 7 is a "nuclear option" that can never be used? Still, from what we know now, there are reasons to be skeptical about the efficacy of Article 7. In the cases of Hungary in 2011 and Romania in 2012, the relevant actors could not even agree that there was a "risk of a breach of fundamental values" (just a risk!); in the case of Poland, the European Commission finally has moved toward the invocation of Article 7 – but at the time of writing, it still seems to put its faith in further "dialogue" instead of actually triggering the article. Moreover, it seems highly unlikely that the Commission will be able to succeed in convincing a sufficient number of Member States in the Council to go along.

What about the Commission acting on its own, in its capacity as the (supposedly) impartial guardian of the treaties? The problem is that the instruments the Commission has at its disposal are often not a good match for the specific political challenges to liberal democracy. Infringement proceedings can, of course, only be based on EU law – which often does not cover the relevant areas of democracy and the rule of law, other than in the very generally worded Article 2 TEU. This makes it harder to address systemic problems and comprehensive efforts to undermine checks and balances in particular.

The most striking example here remains the Hungarian government's 2011 de facto decapitation of the judicial system by lowering the retirement age of judges from 70 to 62. Under Article 285 TFEU the Commission eventually took Hungary to the European Court of Justice for age discrimination – and won its case (meanwhile the Hungarian Constitutional Court also had ruled against the Hungarian government). But the judges were never reinstated (the new Fidesz government loyalists who were appointed have stayed in place), and despite its nominal legal success Europe appeared impotent in getting at the real issue, which was political and had nothing to do with discrimination against individuals.

While the Commission – after the initial experience with Hungary's government in 2010–2014 – added a "rule of law mechanism" to its repertoire of instruments, that particular instrument can only lead to the triggering of Article 7 in the end – with all its apparent problems. Moreover, the mechanism is heavily reliant on the idea that "dialogue" can solve any conflicts between the Commission and a Member State government. True, the EU is based on practices of constructive dialogue and compromise (if not outright consensus). But such practices often are only plausible from a certain – to put it crudely but not inaccurately – technocratic perspective. "We" are trying to solve problems together – so the assumption runs. In the cases of Hungary and Poland, this is of course an illusion. Fidesz and PiS have a political agenda, and their conflict with Brussels is political in nature (and they have used that conflict – portrayed as one between the nation and an unelected supranational bureaucracy – to gain support in domestic politics).

It occasionally might be helpful for EU-level actors to pretend that the conflict is not political – after all, that makes it easier for everyone to save face at the end of a conflict. But there can also be times when the Commission has to find a way to make good on its claim to be impartial – and yet *de facto* fight a political fight. One instance of such a recognition is Frans Timmerman's decision to address the Polish public directly in a newspaper article – in order to explain that he, as the Commission's vice president tasked with rule-of-law issues, was trying to defend common values (as opposed to attacking Polish national sovereignty).

Clearly, whether one can win such fights will depend also on the quality of a national public sphere and whatever there is by way of a European public sphere. Given that rogue governments tend systematically to reduce media pluralism and the fact that there still is not much transnational public discourse, the deck is likely to be stacked against the Commission. This makes it all the more probable that the latter will declare victory on the basis of compromises reached behind closed doors or revert to a strategy of treating conflicts as always being amenable to technical solutions.

One might be tempted to think, then, that plainly political challenges should be met with plainly political responses. In a sense, Article 7 does fit this requirement – it is a distinctly political and comprehensive judgment by EU institutions and by a country's peers in the EU. But given its seeming ineffectiveness, an alternative would appear to be party politics outside EU institutions. What does this mean? It has often been said that the crisis of the Euro currency brought about the *politicization of Europe* – and that it is now time for the *Europeanization of politics*: as mentioned earlier, citizens of many Member States – possibly all Member States – have woken up to the fact that what happens elsewhere in Europe has a direct impact on their lives; what we need are ways to internalize these externalities and reach common European policies that can be justified on the basis of election outcomes across Europe.

Alas, a less desirable effect of such Europeanization of politics has also become apparent: the nominally "mainstream" conservative/Christian Democrat European People's Party (EPP) has often decided to shield Orbán from criticism and potential sanctions. Leading EPP politicians time and again issued stern warnings to the Hungarian prime minister – for instance, when he publicly mused about reintroducing the death penalty in Hungary, an absolute no-no for Christian Democrats in particular. But they have come close to excluding Fidesz from their ranks only recently. The reasons seem simple: Fidesz has a relatively large number of deputies in the European Parliament, and the EPP is firmly committed to keeping its plurality in the parliament (Helmut Kohl once insisted that Christian Democrats had not built Europe to then leave it to socialists). Orbán also has been useful for individual Christian Democrats to achieve their short-term political purposes: leading Bavarian politicians, for instance, have made a spectacle of celebrating Orbán at their meetings in order to mark their opposition to Angela Merkel's temporary opening of German borders to refugees (not to speak of Bavarian business interests which are being very well served in Hungary).

It is true that in September 2018 a significant number of EPP deputies at last changed their minds and supported triggering Article 7 against the Hungarian government. On the one hand, this proved that the European Parliament could be a significant actor in European democracy defense, after all. But the EPP still has not excluded Fidesz, and one could be forgiven for thinking that the EPP leadership played a careful double game: being seen as uncompromising on European values but keeping Fidesz (and its large number of deputies in the fold) – while knowing full well all along that, given the likely response of the European Council, no real sanctions against Budapest will follow.

All these dynamics might be contingent – after all there was one case in the past when a supranational party family suspended a member (the Party of European Socialists *de facto* excluded Slovakia's SMER after the latter entered a coalition with the extreme-right SNS), and a change of tune of the EPP leadership in September 2018 was not trivial. And yet there are also reasons to believe that, ultimately, the problem here is structural: as the

American political scientist Dan Kelemen has argued, Europe's party system is developed enough for party loyalty across borders to matter – hence the EPP's de facto continuing support for Orbán. Yet the party system (not to speak of the European public sphere) is not developed enough truly to Europeanize political issues – which matters because pockets of authoritarianism within larger democratic structures usually only are dissolved by "federalizing" the problem.[10] Kelemen calls the EU's current state an "authoritarian equilibrium" – a somewhat shocking but ultimately plausible label for a situation in which democratic actors de facto supporting undemocratic actors tend not to pay a price for their conduct. As long as election campaigns for the European Parliament remain national affairs, it is unlikely that this fateful equilibrium will become destabilized.

WHAT CAN BE DONE?

Let us take a few steps back. What precisely was the problem again? The theoretical challenge, I submit, is to locate an *agent of credible legal-political judgment* as to whether a country is systematically departing from what one might call the EU's *normative acquis* – a task which is different both from assessing compliance with EU law and from ascertaining belief in values (whatever the latter might mean concretely: a Committee on "Un-European" Beliefs and Activities in the European Parliament?). Technical-legal judgment of rule compliance in and of itself is insufficient; philosophical consensus about values is simply not the issue (all governments in the Union continue to profess faith in democracy and the rule of law); nor, as I argued in the previous section of this essay, is it all a matter of fundamental rights violations. We are dealing with systemic, mostly constitutional challenges, which will require some understanding of context, some sense of proportion, and, not least, some meaningful capacity for comparison of *what is actually happening* within different political systems (as opposed to the claims about what is happening within these systems by local elites). A simple checklist, as so often used in the EU accession process ("Do the judiciary's offices have computers? Check!"), will not do[11]; somebody needs to see and understand the whole picture and also the particular *sequencing* of the creation – and possibly the dismantling – of a liberal-democratic system.[12] As Dimitry Kochenov has shown, we simply cannot take the Copenhagen criteria off the legal (or perhaps, more accurately, normative) shelf and pretend, on the basis of the experience with accession processes, that "protection of liberal-democratic values" equals compliance with these very general criteria (let alone compliance with the *acquis*): they never were defined sufficiently and they were often inconsistently applied (Kochenov 2015). To go back to checklists or to set up "scoreboards" would mean that it is actually the Commission who is backsliding (that is: going back to old sins of thinking that capacity to implement the *acquis communautaire* and paying lip service to liberal democracy equals fulfilling the Copenhagen criteria).

What follows from framing the problem this way? First of all, Article 7 ought to be left in place – but it also ought to be extended. There might arise situations where democracy is not just slowly undermined or partially dismantled but where the entire edifice of democratic institutions is blown up or comes crashing down, so to speak (think of a military coup). However, in such an extreme case, the Union ought actually to have the option of expelling a Member State completely. As said earlier, under the TEU, states may decide to leave voluntarily, but there is no legal mechanism for actually removing a country from the Union. True, these all might seem remote scenarios, but then again, what has happened in Hungary and Poland in recent years also once was considered a remote scenario.

This still does not answer the question of *who* a consistent and credible agent of political judgment could be. "The Commission" seems to remain the most plausible answer – especially in light of the fact that it has acquired new powers in supervising and changing the budgets of Eurozone Member States. But many – possibly all – proposals to increase the legitimacy of the Commission (seen as a necessary complement to such newly acquired authority) contain the suggestion essentially to *politicize* the Commission: ideas to elect the president directly or to make the commissioners into a politically uniform cabinet government would render the body more partisan – *on purpose*.[13] And such partisanship makes the Commission much less credible as an agent of impartial legal-political judgment.

My suggestion is to create an entirely new institution, which could act as a main guardian of Europe's *acquis normatif*.[14] One could think of a "Copenhagen Commission" (as a reminder of the "Copenhagen criteria," flawed as they might have been), analogous to the Venice Commission – a body, in other words, with a mandate to offer comprehensive and consistent political judgments.[15] The hope is also that such a body – ideally composed of legal experts and statesmen and stateswomen with a proven track record of political judgment – could become sufficiently visible so as to effectively raise an alarm across a common European political space (though here, once again, the weakness of the European public sphere is an issue).

However, the real question is of course: *and then what?* What if a country undermines systematically the rule of law and restricts democracy? My suggestion is that the Copenhagen Commission ought to be empowered to investigate and then trigger a mechanism that sends a clear signal (not just words) that remains short of the measures envisaged in Article 7. Following the advice of the Copenhagen Commission, the European Commission should be required to cut funds, for instance, or impose significant fines.[16] Cuts of EU-specific funds would reinforce the message that a country undermining the rule of law is doing something that concerns the Union as a whole – and that the response is a genuinely European one.

A major concern here is that financial sanctions tend to punish populations and not governments. The Hungarian government attempted at one point to constitutionalize the principle of visibly passing EU-related fines on to all citizens, clearly hoping that such "democracy taxes" will increase resentment vis-à-vis Brussels. However, there is credible evidence that it is not always exactly the poorest of the poor who benefit from Brussels subsidies – but oligarchs close to what has been described as the "Hungarian post-communist mafia state" (see Bálint Magyar's chapter in this volume). EU funds function here like oil revenues for despots in parts of the Middle East: an effectively free resource that can be distributed by governments to buy political support or reinforce authoritarian structures (one might be tempted to speak of a European resource curse).

Having said that: all the existing tools should remain at the disposal of the relevant actors. Article 7 could still be invoked; the Commission could take a Member State to the European Court of Justice; the Court could try to protect the substance of EU citizenship; and politicians could have a serious word with one of their peers in another Member State, if they feel that the State in question is leaving the broad European road of liberal democracy.

THE (ALL-IMPORTANT) QUESTION OF CRITERIA

It is one thing to identify a plausible agent of judgment; it is another to specify criteria on the basis of which judgments can be made. Especially against the background of the experience with the Copenhagen criteria and with the conflicts between the Hungarian government and the European Commission in 2010–2014, one may well wonder whether Europeans really agree on how they want to live politically speaking? The concern here is that there actually are no shared European values – let alone norms and standards that could be operationalized to judge the shape of a particular democracy and a particular legal system. Yes, there is a single *market* but no single model of liberal democracy – and therefore such a line of criticism would continue, even if all efforts to protect democracy in Europe are arbitrary.

Let me offer three responses to this worry, which could be rephrased as: who ought to face a burden of justification vis-à-vis the rest of the EU, when they embark on significant political changes (and not just individual fundamental rights violations, which could be very serious, of course, but which can be dealt with by the Luxembourg and the Strasbourg courts)? First, from a *historical* perspective, I believe it can be shown that the whole direction of political development in postwar Europe has been toward delegating power to unelected institutions, such as constitutional courts.[17] And that development was based on specific lessons that Europeans – rightly or wrongly – drew from the political catastrophes of the mid-twentieth century: the architects of the postwar West European order viewed the ideal of popular sovereignty with a great deal of distrust; after all, how could one trust those who had brought fascists to power or extensively collaborated with fascist occupiers? Less obviously, elites also had deep reservations about the idea of *parliamentary sovereignty*. Had not legitimate representative assemblies handed all power over to Hitler and to Marshal Pétain, the leader of Vichy France in 1933 and 1940, respectively? Hence parliaments in postwar Europe were systematically weakened, checks and balances were strengthened, and non-elected institutions (constitutional courts are the prime example) were tasked not just with defending individual rights but with defending democracy as a whole.[18] In short, distrust of unrestrained popular sovereignty, and even of unconstrained parliamentary sovereignty are, so to speak, in the very DNA of postwar European politics. (I emphasize again that these are empirical observations, not normative arguments; the point here is not to justify this particular political model.) In fact, it is fair to say that these underlying principles of what I have elsewhere called "constrained democracy" were almost always adopted when countries were able to shake off dictatorships and turned to liberal democracy in the last third of the twentieth century: first on the Iberian peninsula in the 1970s, and then in Central and Eastern Europe after 1989. Going out on a conceptual limb, one might even consider this model of democracy as a European "basic structure" analogous to the basic structure doctrine of the Indian Constitutional Court.

European integration, it needs to be emphasized, was part and parcel of this comprehensive attempt to constrain majority decisions: it added supra-national constraints to national ones.[19] This logic was more evident initially with institutions like the Council of Europe and its European Convention on Human Rights, but the desire to "lock in" liberal-democratic commitments became more pronounced in a specific EU (or then: EEC) context with the transitions to democracy in Greece, Portugal, and Spain in the 1970s.

History is not destiny, and its lessons do not automatically generate legitimacy. But it seems a reasonable presumption that radical departures from this postwar model of politics place a special burden of justification on Member State governments embarking on such a departure. This thought applies to Hungary and Poland, where constitutional courts to which these countries committed after 1989 *in the name of solidifying democracy* are being systematically weakened. But it does not apply to a country like Britain, where de facto constraints on – in theory unlimited – parliamentary sovereignty have had a more informal character, at least up until recently, and where the observance of such constraints can by and large be expected (perhaps too optimistic an assumption). Not all countries in the EU will necessarily converge on constrained democracy. But in judging individual cases, overall context and, in particular, an account of *historical trajectories* and *sequencing* are crucial.[20] The whole may well be something quite different than the sum of the parts, which is – to stress the point again – the main reason why simplistic "check-lists" in judging constitutions or political systems in their totality will not do. The Venice Commission made this argument very plain in its opinion on the proposed fourth amendment to the new Hungarian Fundamental Law in 2013:

> In constitutional law, perhaps even more than in other legal fields, it is necessary to take into account not only the face value of a provision, but also to examine its constitutional context. The mere fact that a provision also exists in the constitution of another country does not mean that it also "fits" into any other constitution. Each constitution is the result of balancing various powers. If a power is given to one state body, other powers need to be able to effectively control the exercise of this power. The more power an institution has, the tighter control mechanisms need to be constructed. Comparative constitutional law cannot be reduced to identifying the existence of a provision the constitution of another country to justify its democratic credentials in the constitution of one's own country. Each constitution is a complex array of checks and balances and each provision needs to be examined in view of its merits for the balance of powers as a whole.[21]

This attempt at "weaponizing" comparative constitutional law by governments in Warsaw and Budapest has to be comprehensively rejected. The fact that certain provisions also exist in other countries regarded widely as democratic does not in and of itself prove that there is no problem with such provisions. Someone judging the situation needs to see the whole, instead of simply checking up on the plausibility of highly selective comparisons. At the same time, appeals to the particularity of the whole cannot be used as a kind of shield against outside criticisms: it is not just comparative constitutional law that has been weaponized but also the notion of "constitutional identity."[22] The idea of preserving such identities finds significant support in the European treaties. Yet it cannot function as a deflector for all concerns about a dismantling of democracy and the rule of law.

In this context, it is also worth emphasizing the traps set by another strategy prominently adopted by Budapest and Warsaw. Orbán has been very effective to reframe the conflict with the EU as one of "mere politics" or to put it even more bluntly, subjective value choices. Liberals, as he and other defenders of his vision of an "illiberal state" or a "twenty-first-century

Christian Democracy" will charge, simply do not like his conservative family policies, his defense of strong nation-states inside the EU, and, most of all, his rejection of immigration and the settlement of refugees in Hungary.[23] One can legitimately disagree about these issues in a democracy. But by focusing all attention on them, Orbán has remade what should be a debate about basic democratic institutions into yet another culture war (with an appeal to conservatives everywhere in Europe to join his side since, in the eyes of one of his intellectual supporters, his concept of illiberal democracy "is most congruent with the Burkean version of conservative thought").[24]

Once the conflict has been declared a matter of seemingly subjective value commitments, it becomes easy to accuse the liberals of being the real illiberals: even though they are supposed to be the defenders of diversity, they cannot tolerate an ethnic nationalist like Orbán who seeks to deviate from a supposed Western mainstream of multiculturalism and "the anti-nationalist political culture of the EU."[25] Hungary is even said to have "become the object of cosmopolitan resentment,"[26] while Poland can appear as the victim of liberal technocrats in Brussels who pursue their ideology with religious zeal.[27]

A number of observers have been willing to concede that "illiberal democracy" might be a legitimate reaction to undemocratic liberalism. The EU appears as an obvious instance of a liberal technocracy against which "the will of the people" needs to be asserted. Yet the EU prescribes neither a uniform legislative stance on controversial questions such as same-sex marriage nor a single model of democracy. Its members just have to be democratic enough according to the (admittedly flawed) Copenhagen criteria. When EU leaders have criticized the Hungarian and Polish governments, Budapest and Warsaw have countered that they are defending national sovereignty against liberal diktats from Brussels. Alas, the Union has played into their hands by making it seem that democracy always belongs to the nation-state, and that the liberal repair crew from Brussels only turns up if there is some drastic malfunction with the rule of law. Instead, EU representatives should have been much clearer that, by defending an independent judiciary as well as civil society and critical media, they are defending nothing less than democracy itself. Put differently: one can have many legitimate *policy* disagreements in the EU. What one cannot get is this: having one's preference for an undemocratic *polity* realized inside the Union.

This still leaves the question of more precise criteria that might be used to trigger sanctions or some other kind of intervention. Observers have worried that calls for EU intervention might become the stuff of symbolic politics; in particular, there has been a concern that only *small* (and *newer*) Member States will ever be picked on. This is a common interpretation of what happened when Jörg Haider's far-right party came to power in Austria in 2000.

Leaders like Jacques Chirac and Gerhard Schröder – unable to do anything about Jean-Marie Le Pen's National Front or the neo-Nazi NPD, respectively, at home – could moralize about small countries at no cost internationally or so it seemed, while also scoring some points against their domestic opponents.[28] Meanwhile, nobody ever dared to touch Berlusconi's Italy, no matter how much political *bunga-bunga* was going on.

However, it would be a mistake to conclude from a comparison between the cases of Austria, Hungary, Italy, and Poland (and also Romania in 2012) that only weaker and newer Member States get picked on. There are important differences here. First, the problem with the "Haider Affair" was partly that sanctions were imposed *before* the new government had taken any significant actions. This is a marked contrast with the cases of Hungary and Poland: in both countries, governments have a very clear track record; what they were doing also had a systematic character and could not be excused as a matter of one-off mistakes.

Second, there is a significant difference between Berlusconi's Italy, Orbán's Hungary and Kaczyński's Poland. True, the *Cavaliere* also tried to weaken checks and balances. But the opposition, despite its generally sorry state, remained strong enough to resist major constitutional re-crafting; throughout his time in office, Berlusconi was constrained by the fact that he headed coalition (i.e., not single-party) governments; the media was not dominated completely by Berlusconi's own empire; crucially, the judiciary kept putting up a fight; and various Italian presidents – Giorgio Napolitano, in particular – would block Berlusconi's plans.[29] He also lost popular referenda, especially the 2006 constitutional referendum, which would have introduced far-reaching changes. In short: there were reasonable grounds for thinking that the situation would self-correct over time through internal political struggle.

I want to suggest three criteria that need to be met for an actual negative opinion by an entity like the Copenhagen Commission (or other EU actors, for that matter): first, a Member State government has to have a *track record* of violating core liberal-democratic political principles. There is no case for purely preemptive action, only evidence-based sanctioning. Second, that track record also should show a government's general conduct to have a *systematic* nature: one-off violations might be deeply problematic, but they can be dealt with by courts, and they should be seen in context. To be sure, mistakes simply cannot be excused by context, but they can be explained, and such explanations might also make it plausible that a particular government, despite mistakes, is fundamentally well-intentioned. Third, intervention is about enforcing commitments which were entered into voluntarily in the past. If there is reasonable hope that such commitments can, in the end, mostly be enforced internally, intervention should wait. *Self-correction* remains the best outcome, but whether it will actually happen is a matter of political judgment – as is the question how long one should wait for such an outcome, and what price is reasonable for individual Member State citizens to pay before such an outcome materializes.

SOME FURTHER CONCERNS

What is distinctive about the EU as a polity? For a long time, a plausible answer seemed to be: unity in diversity or *pluralism*. The Union promises tolerance instead of homogenization and mutual opening and respectful peer review instead of a centralized institution coercing Member States (aka a supranational state). Some of the suggestions made in this chapter would seem to be contrary to this picture – a centralized review of democratic and rule of law standards appears incompatible with this received wisdom about the Union. In contrast with this Panglossian view of European pluralism, one has to remember that the EU has always been about *pluralism within common political parameters*. The accession process itself has not had as its goal something like maximizing difference but in fact has been meant to ensure sameness in certain regards (democracy, rule of law, state capacity, and so on). And as long as it has been taking in new members, the EU has been in the business of making definitive judgments on whether a country really is a liberal democracy or not (even if the Copenhagen criteria might have given a false sense of certainty about these judgments) and, more broadly, judgments on where the limits of pluralism are to be located. In that sense, mandating a distinct and highly visible body while keeping an eye on whether everyone is remaining a liberal democracy does not constitute a fundamental break with EU principles and practices.

Let me here also address a related concern: If supposedly technocratic "new constitutionalism" is partly to blame for authoritarian tendencies (for instance, as Paul Blokker forcefully has argued in 2013), then is some form of "democracy oversight" from on high not just adding to the problem? If constitutionalism never becomes part of lived political experience in newer Member States in particular but is instead created and enforced by distant bodies of experts, then will more paternalistic "guardianship" by Brussels not reinforce the lesson that constitutionalism is something that a particular "we" does not do autonomously, is incapable of internalizing, and so on? My – perhaps too flippant – answer is this: nothing prevents one from starting a European Citizens' Initiative to express concern about the rule of law in a Member State; nothing prevents a transnational European civil society from what governments will always condemn as "meddling in internal affairs." The alleged "technocracy" of the EU and "grassroots initiatives" are not mutually exclusive: here it makes little sense to play off popular democracy against "liberal technocracy."

Democracy protection in the EU is not analogous with the "authoritarian liberalism" which some critics have seen emerge as a result of the Eurocrisis (Wilkinson 2013). To be sure, it can look like both are punitive approaches, which result in disciplining national democracies and which effectively limit the diversity of expressions of the will of democratic majorities across Europe; both can look like a project to make the economy and the rule of law respectively safe from popular democracy.

Yet such an equation is ultimately implausible for two reasons: first, uniform austerity policies and surveillance of national budgets by the European Commission – as well as economic prescriptions that are not even logical (not all countries can become "more competitive" at the same time) – these are all about making Member States converge on an ability to fulfill very specific economic and financial criteria (even if they do not require a complete convergence of economic models). This kind of specificity is absent from proposals for democracy protection. Having such specificity would amount to an insistence, for instance, that every country must have a particular constitutional court. But nobody is proposing such constitutional micro-management or an undue narrowing of "pluralist constitutionalism" (Dani 2013); democracy protection is about guarding boundaries to pluralism, not about reducing, let alone abolishing, pluralism.

Second, "austerianism" and prescriptions for a Europe under the surveillance of a European Commission enforcing budget discipline clearly have been accepted under duress. But it is a stretch to say that Member States adopted the values mentioned in Article 2 TEU under pressure from the most powerful actors inside the EU (the initial political decision to join the Union is a different matter than pre-accession strategies and the conditionality imposed by the Commission as a result of that initial decision). Along the same lines, I would also reject the argument that challenges to liberal democracy have been caused directly by the EU itself – which is not to say that the EU is blameless or that the single market has not de facto led to clear injustices in the newer Member States in particular. At least from a purely economic point of view, the impact of the EU has been positive – even if the abrupt end of the post-accession boom in 2007 exacerbated underlying political weaknesses in the newest Member States.[30]

Which brings us to a final worry – the answer to which is necessarily more speculative. By now, we have some record of the conflicts between the European Commission and Hungary and Poland (as well as Romania in 2012). But when it comes to a more general empirical assessment, we simply do not know whether financial sanctions, for instance, would create a great nationalist backlash, as is often asserted, turning entire countries from Euroenthusiasm to Euroskepticism. I would offer two thoughts:

First, for Europe to try to "hold back" or try somehow to remain "neutral" in highly charged domestic conflicts about matters of *polity* (and not just *policy*) is not costless and, in the end, actually also not really "neutral" at all. A reluctance to try to protect liberal democracy in a Member State will betray the hopes of all those citizens of the country in question who did put their trust in the Union as some sort of guarantor against new forms of illiberalism or outright authoritarianism. In any case, a government eager to dismantle checks and balances, for instance, will on some level know that it is heading for a conflict with European institutions – hence it has every incentive to whip up Euroskeptic sentiments, whether the EU actually does very much or not. In other words, preemptive nationalism is likely to be promoted – quite irrespective of any particular approach the Union adopts.

Second, there is little evidence that any of these nationalist campaigns have worked or, for that matter, that strong exercises of EU leverage have produced any severe backlashes. Orbán's self-declared "war of independence," or so polls suggest, has not proven popular,[31] nor was the infamous "Stop Brussels" campaign a clear-cut success (there is no clear evidence that it helped win the April 2018 elections). Even very heavy-handed forms of conditionality by the EU in the past (think of Slovakia in the late 1990s) have not obviously rendered the EU illegitimate in the eyes of the populations of a Member State subject to conditionality. Neither law nor political theory can proceed on the basis of measures of popularity – but it is worth remembering that approval ratings for (and trust in) the EU remain among the highest in Hungary and Poland.[32] Huxit or Poxit do not appear to be credible threats at this point.

What has to be admitted is that serious sanctions would always go against the very EU ethos of consensus finding, mutual accommodation, and even mutual normative self-relativization which has worked so well, so often, and which is ultimately predicated on a shared willingness not to push things to the limit. They would also, prima facie, go against notions of constitutional tolerance, which valorizes particular national understandings of political values. Yet the actual choice might not be between upholding these ideals or serious sanctions. The choice is more likely to be between, on the one hand, accepting the (inevitable) risks of sanctions and, on the other, condoning a process where the core of the EU slowly rots. Ultimately, it is not in the Union's interest to have a periphery where everyone knows that things are not quite okay and yet no one dares to do anything.

NOTES

1. This chapter draws extensively on three previous pieces: Müller (2015, 2017, 2018).

2. For the general problems and dilemmas associated with the all-affected principle, see Goodin (2007).

3. See also the recent ruling by the European Court of Justice that a court in Ireland could refuse to extradite a defendant to Poland if there are legitimate concerns that the defendant would not face an independent court in Poland, given the recent "reforms" to the Polish judicial system. See "Judgement of the court," http://curia.europa.eu/juris/document/document.jsf;jsessionid=9ea7d2dc30ddba6fe80880c04b469954cee8b8500263.e34KaxiLc3qMb40Rch0SaxyOax10?text=&docid=204384&pageIndex=0&doclang=EN&mode=req&dir=&occ=first&part=1&cid=156791, accessed June 25, 2019.

4. I am grateful to Jan Komárek on this point.

5. There may well be decisions that for the moment only affect locals – but institutional re-engineering does pose a permanent possibility of someone exercising their free movement becoming subject to unjust institutions created by a "rogue" government.

6. I am grateful to Jan Komárek on this point.

7. I thank Dan Kelemen for discussions on this point.

8. Some lawyers hold that Article 2 is simply a declaration that imposes no obligations on Member States. I thank Bruno De Witte on this point.

9. See Sadurski (2009).

10. See R. Daniel Kelemen (2017a, b).

11. Scheppele (2013). See also Nicolaïdis and Kleinfeld (2012).

12. Thanks to Renáta Uitz on this point. See also her excellent study: Uitz (2015).

13. Not that the Commission today is truly "apolitical" – but the fiction that Commissioners, upon taking office, lose their party-political identities does have some disciplining effect. In the scenario envisaged by proponents of the Commission as de facto (and possibly even in name) a European government, the whole point is that the body would be – and ought to be – visibly partisan.

14. One might be tempted to think of decentralizing such an agency, for example, having ombudsmen or something analogous to discrimination agencies in each country – the obvious counterargument being that such actors and agencies would likely be subject to national capture.

15. I am indebted to Rui Tavares for discussions on this point.

16. I am indebted to Kim Lane Scheppele for discussions on this point.

17. I have made this argument at greater length in Müller (2011).

18. One might add that dignity – and not freedom – is the master value of postwar constitutions.

19. One might ask in what way does "constrained democracy" differ from "guided" or simply "defective" democracy? The answer is that in the former, genuine changes in who holds power are possible and that all constraints are ultimately justified with regard to strengthening democracy. In the latter, no real change is allowed.

20. I am indebted to Renáta Uitz for making me understand the importance of sequencing.

21. "Hungary: fourth amendment to the Constitution," http://www.venice.coe.int/Newsletter/NEWSLETTER_2013_03/1_HUN_EN.html, accessed June 25, 2019.

22. As an example of this strategy, see Szájer and Ablonczy (2012).
23. See, for instance, Furedi (2018).
24. *Ibid.*, 117.
25. *Ibid.*
26. *Ibid.*, 74.
27. Vermeule (2017).
28. See also Merlingen, Mudde, and Sedelmeier (2001).
29. I am grateful to Giovanni Capoccia and Gianfranco Pasquino on this matter.
30. Jacoby (2014), and Bruszt (2015).
31. Hungarian Spectrum (2013).
32. See, for instance, Polen Analysen (2018).

BIBLIOGRAPHY

Beckman, Ludvig. 2008. "Democratic Inclusion, Law and Causes." *Ratio Juris*: 348–64.

Blokker, Paul. 2013. *New Democracies in Crisis? A Comparative Constitutional Study of the Czech Republic, Hungary, Poland, Romania, and Slovakia*. New York: Routledge.

Bruszt, László. 2015. "Regional Normalization and National Deviations." *Global Policy* 6 (1): 38–45.

Dani, Marco. 2013. "The 'Partisan Constitution' and the Corrosion of European Constitutional Culture." *LEQS Paper* 68.

Furedi, Frank. 2018. *Populism and the European Culture Wars: The Conflict of Values between Hungary and the EU*. New York: Routledge.

Goodin, Robert E. 2007. "Enfranchising All Affected Interests and Its Alternatives." *Philosophy and Public Affairs* 35: 40–68.

Hungarian Spectrum. 2013. "Hungarian Public Opinion on Viktor Orbán's 'War of Independence'." http://hungarianspectrum.wordpress.com/2013/07/11/hungarian-public-opinion-on-viktor-orbans-war-of-independence, accessed June 25, 2019.

Jacoby, Wade. 2014. "The EU Factor in Fat Times and in Lean: Did the EU Amplify the Boom and Soften the Bust?" *Journal of Common Market Studies* 52: 52–70.

Kelemen, R. Daniel. 2017a. "Europe's Other Democratic Deficit." *Government and Opposition*. Vol. 52: 238–52.

———. 2017b. "Europe's Authoritarian Equilibrium." *Foreign Affairs*, December 22, 2017. Available online: https://www.foreignaffairs.com/articles/hungary/20 17-12-22/europes-authoritarian-equilibrium.

Kochenov, Dimitry. 2008. *EU Enlargement and the Failure of Conditionality*. The Hague: Kluwer.

Merlingen, Michael, Cas Mudde, and Ulrich Sedelmeier. 2001. "The Right and the Righteous? European Norms, Domestic Politics and the Sanctions Against Austria." *Journal of Common Market Studies* 39: 59–77.

Müller, Jan-Werner. 2011. *Contesting Democracy: Political Ideas in Twentieth-Century Europe*. London: Yale University Press.

————. 2015. "Should the EU Protect Democracy and the Rule of Law inside Member States?" *European Law Journal* 21: 141–60.

————. 2017. "If You're Not a Democracy, You're Not European Anymore." *Foreign Policy*, December 22, 2017. http://foreignpolicy.com/2017/12/22/if-youre-not-a-democracy-youre-not-european-anymore/.

————. 2018. "'Democracy' Still Matters." *New York Times*, April 5, 2018. https://www.nytimes.com/2018/04/05/opinion/hungary-viktor-orban-populism.html.

Mungiu-Pippidi, Alina. 2007. "EU Accession Is No 'End of History.'" *Journal of Democracy* 18: 8–16.

Nicolaïdis, Kalypso and Rachel Kleinfeld. 2012. "Rethinking Europe's 'Rule of Law' and Enlargement Agenda: The Fundamental Dilemma." Sigma Paper 49.

Polen Analysen. 2018. "Zivilgesellschaft und Demokratie in Polen und den anderen Visegrád-Ländern." http://laender-analysen.de/polen/pdf/PolenAnalysen217.pdf, accessed June 25, 2019.

Sadurski, Wojciech 2009. "Adding Bite to the Bark: The Story of Article 7, E.U. Enlargement, and Jörg Haider." *Columbia Journal of European Law* 16: 385–426.

Scheppele, Kim Lane. 2013. "The Rule of Law and the Frankenstate: Why Governance Checklists Do Not Work." *Governance* 26: 559–62.

Szájer, József and Bálint Ablonczy. 2012. *Gespräche über das Grundgesetz Ungarns: Bálint Ablonczy im Gespräch mit József Szájer und Gergely Gulyás.* Budapest: Elektromédia.

Uitz, Renáta. 2015. "Can You Tell When an Illiberal Democracy Is in the Making? An Appeal to Comparative Constitutional Scholarship from Hungary." *International Journal of Constitutional Law* 13: 279–300.

Vermeule, Adrian. 2017. "Liturgy of Liberalism." *First Things* (Spring 2017). https://www.firstthings.com/article/2017/01/liturgy-of-liberalism.

Wilkinson, Michael. 2013. "The Specter of Authoritarian Liberalism: Reflections on the Constitutional Crisis of the European Union." *German Law Journal* 14: 527–60.

Chapter 17

Supply Side Revolution

The Consequences of the
2015 Polish Elections

Radosław Markowski

When first invited to contribute a chapter from the Polish perspective to this volume analyzing the case of Hungary, I was certain I would concentrate on why democratic consolidation proved successful in Poland and why it did not work as expected in Hungary. I still am inclined – at least partly – to consider the Polish case as considerably different from the Hungarian one. However, the main message I wish to convey is the following: at the end of 2015 there were no real reasons for Poles to embark on a wholesale and revolutionary change of their country as most Poles were satisfied with their salaries, jobs, households, and life in general. Yet what happened after the election – which was partly due to the unexpected results of electoral technicalities and procedural accident (almost never under proportional electoral rules does 18.6 percent of eligible votes for a party translate into a majoritarian composition in parliament which is precisely what happened in Poland) – was an attempt to engineer a comprehensive across-the-board change of society and the state.

Before we move to the details of the main theme, several caveats are due at this point. First, both the academic literature and journalistic accounts too readily claim the existence of parallels between Poland and Hungary. I myself have contributed to this comparison (see Markowski and Tóka 1995; Kitschelt, Mansfeldova, Markowski, and Tóka 1999), yet in most cases the alleged similarities were tested critically against reliable data and drew the conclusion that any existing correspondences were shallow and essentially divergent.[1] The story in this chapter will follow such an approach. Second, social science scholars typically are impatient and very eager to offer universalistic interpretations; political phenomena in particular often are interpreted in general terms and grand theories are utilized to depict the purported macro-developments. Ideally, scholars need a sense of the ontology of time and an awareness of the nature of causality that is behind the changes under scrutiny before reliably claiming the working of any grand theories. Briefly, even if the eight-year period under Hungary's Fidesz government and a previous crisis-ridden period allow for – in my view – only tentative theoretical explanations, the Polish case is still a matter of speculation about the trajectory of the last years. Third, in order to understand the recent Polish developments, one has to contextualize it in a broader Central European context, and the parallel with Hungary in this instance is of utmost relevance. Fourth, making sense of the populist, xenophobic, and anti-EU drive in Europe in recent years is complicated by two simultaneous yet often contradictory stories offered, on the one hand, by "public intellectuals" and, on the other hand, by empirically oriented social sciences. The former pictures a dramatic state of democracy in its fatal, final years, whereas the latter soberly indicates important, still minor changes in normative expectations and performance evaluations of European democracies (Levitsky and Way 2015; cf. Ferrin and Kriesi 2016; Markowski 2016; Alexander and Welzel 2017; Voeten 2017). This controversy has to be addressed, in particular, if one is inclined to offer advice on what to do. Fifth, Polish politics, both historically and today, is decided by the Polish Catholic Church to an extent unknown elsewhere in Europe. This influence is both indirect via early childhood to adult general axiological (normative) socialization and direct via pressure on politicians and delivering open instructions to parliament or government indicating preferred policy solutions. These normative and policy "preferences" are backed by open blackmail and threats (ranging from soft advice not to show up to receive communion to sheer blackmail of excommunication). It is still an open question who is the "mover" in this relationship, but for this chapter it is important to note that majority of the current Polish Episcopate as well as the lion's share of the grassroots clergy are a political asset in the hands of the governing party (for details, see Markowski 2018).

BACKGROUND TO THE 2015
PARLIAMENTARY ELECTION

In this section I present my main argument for a "supply side revolution" and that hardly any evidence existed in the form of social "demand" for radical change in the fall of 2015. This section will present numerous data, ending with public opinion polls made as late as October, November, and December 2015, that is, up to two months after the election.

The 2015 parliamentary election in Poland had a number of specific features. Above all, it was not primarily about the economy: evaluations of Poland's economic performance seem not to have been relevant for the decisions made by voters. It should be recalled at this point that under the two-term coalition of Civic Platform (PO) and Poland People's Party (PSL) between 2007 and 2015 – a period approximately spanning the global crisis – Poland achieved remarkable cumulative GDP growth of approximately 25 percent accompanied by a decline in income inequalities (a Gini coefficient of 0.29, down from 0.36 in the early 2000s), inflation bordering on zero, and single-digit unemployment in 2015 for the first time in two decades (Czapinski and Panek 2015; EUROSTAT 2016). During this period, Poland became a more active and recognized international player and partner; this was particularly the case in the EU, where Jerzy Buzek and Donald Tusk – both major figures of the ruling senior coalition party, PO – were appointed to key EU positions. Yet the response of Poles was ambiguous: by the end of 2015, 70 percent and 80 percent of Poles, respectively, were satisfied with their jobs and lives in general as well as with their household situation (CBOS 2015 and 2016), but they remained dissatisfied from a political perspective, distrusting elites, parties, and parliamentarians, and expressing a preoccupation with alleged threats to Poland and the Polish way of life emanating from wider global forces (Markowski and Tworzecki 2016).

This mood of political distrust and suspicion played a significant role in the campaign. Law and Justice (PiS), the major opposition party during the 2007–2015 electoral term, sought to persuade voters that Poland was in the hands of a corrupt elite; that Polish economic development, while good, nevertheless was proceeding more slowly than it might have; that Poland was a "Germano-Russo condominium" that has been left "in ruins" by the maladministration of the previous government; and that former prime minister Donald Tusk and ex-president Bronisław Komorowski were "traitors" who deliberately conspired to bring about the death of former president Lech Kaczyński in the Smolensk plane crash of April 2010. The relentless repetition of these narratives worked to demobilize a part of the governing coalition's electorate, which came to believe in the existence of widespread corruption in spite of the fact that – according to internationally recognized institutions – the previous decade has seen significant improvement in Poland's standing. This demobilization was most clearly in evidence among the rural population yet was also present among the urban population of previous PO supporters.

PiS also benefited from offering a number of irresponsibly costly but popular pledges: a universal child benefit, reversing the PO-PSL government's unpopular but necessary plan to increase the retirement age to 67 for people of both sexes, and increasing tax-free income thresholds. These and other less profound promises were aimed at attracting those who had lost out as a result of the otherwise successful modernization of Poland.

Nevertheless, PiS's most important campaign decision was to withdraw its truly radical and divisive politicians from the frontline, including the leader Jarosław Kaczyński. This trick was successful, with more moderate PiS politicians appearing attractive and unthreatening to the smooth functioning of democratic polity.

The success of *Nowoczesna* (Modern) heralded the emergence of an important new structural phenomenon. The appeal of this party resonated with younger, well-educated, mainly urban and entrepreneurial voters who were attracted by the economically liberal stances associated with PO in the early 2000s. During its term in office, the PO alienated many of its followers by departing from its market-oriented roots. Nowoczesna initially benefited from these policy shifts by PO, only to disintegrate and almost disappear by the end of the parliamentary term. However, it was not policy mismanagement that triggered the most significant blow to the government and the PO leadership but the "tape affair."

A year prior to the election the news weekly *Wprost* (closely associated with PiS and, as some claim, at their disposal) published selected tape recordings of private meetings in a restaurant between government ministers and prominent public figures. The tapes did not reveal any instances of corruption or other illegal actions.[2] However, the emergence of this affair and its subsequent development prompted the prosecutor general to open a formal investigation to identify its prime mover, while the vulgar language used by the politicians recorded on the tapes stoked popular anger.

The outcome of the May 2015 presidential election was also a contributory factor. This election saw the incumbent, Bronisław Komorowski, defeated in a run-off with the obscure PiS politician Andrzej Duda. This outcome was completely unexpected: only six months before the beginning of the campaign Komorowski enjoyed a confidence rating in excess of 70 percent. Yet the complacency this popularity bred was part of his downfall; secure in his own mind of victory, he avoided running a genuine campaign and providing a clear vision for his second term of office, indicating instead that his second term would be very much a continuation of the previous one in policy terms. Komorowski's PO party also took the decision not to provide substantial funding for the presidential campaign, motivated by the pragmatic assessment that an expensive campaign would be superfluous given his popularity, and also for political reasons PO preferred the president to have a weaker popular mandate, than the one that stems from an outright first round landslide victory. By comparison, Duda was highly motivated and his campaign was ambitious, targeting a range of dissatisfied and excluded social groups with a slate of eye-catching but largely unrealistic policy promises. Economists have estimated that the cost of the campaign promises of the incumbent president and the contender were in the ratio of 1:10.

Table 17.1   Results of the Parliamentary Elections in Poland on October 25, 2015

Party/Coalition	Parliamentary Elections of: 2015			2011		
	Number of seats	Votes (thousands)	Votes (%)	Number of seats	Votes (thousands)	Votes (%)
Law and Justice – PiS	235	5,712	37.58	157	4,295	29.89
Civic Platform – PO	138	3,662	24.09	207	5,630	39.18
Kukiz' 15	42	1,339	8.81	-	-	-
Nowoczesna (Modern)	28	1,155	7.60	-	-	-
United Left – ZL/ Democratic Left Alliance – SLD 2011	-	1,147	7.55	27	1,184	-
Peoples Party – PSL	16	780	5.13	28	1,202	8.36
KORWIN/ Nowa Prawica 2011	-	723	4.78	-	152	1.06
Razem	-	550	3.62	-	-	-
Other	-	133	0.87	-	152	1.05

Source: Official data of PKW (the State Electoral Commission).

Finally, the Catholic Church also played an important role, conveying clear partisan preferences. According to a poll conducted after the 2011 election, of those respondents who reported that parish priests had indicated openly the party for which a Catholic should vote, nine out of ten said that the party in question was PiS. In the 2015 election, the political interference of the Church was more overt, including open mobilization of the electorate of their favored party as well as assisting voters in getting to the polls.

FREE AND FAIR ELECTIONS WITH UNFAIR CONSEQUENCES

In this section the details of the Polish parliamentary election of October 2015 will be presented in order to illustrate that the pervasive media opinion of a landslide victory by PiS and the allegedly overwhelming support for radical change in Poland was unsubstantiated once one pays rudimentary attention to the details of the electoral results. This section will show that, until the very end of 2015, nothing significant – be it in terms of political radicalism or right-wing populism or xenophobia – haunted Poles' minds. The majority of the adult population of Poland were, until the end of 2015, very Euro-enthu-siastic, happy with their lives, jobs, incomes, household situation, and so on.

The October 2015 parliamentary election in Poland resulted in the vic-tory of a single party, Law and Justice, which returned to power after eight years in opposition. For the first time in the history of democratic Poland, the winning party was able to create a government without long negotiation, horse-trading, and compromises with coalition partners. The major point to be made, however, is that this was due not so much to significant switches in the preferences of voters but rather the result of a very high number of wasted votes (almost 17 percent of active voters) due to thresholds for parties (5 percent) and party coalitions (eight percent). The lack of coordination among leftist parties was of utmost importance in this instance, as these parties wasted approximately 12 percent of the vote. As a consequence, Gallagher's disproportionality index surged to 11 percent (see Table 17.2). Let us recall that in three of the seven previous parliamentary elections, the victorious party attracted a higher percentage of active voters than that achieved by PiS in 2015 (37.6 percent) but was unable to form a single-party government (Markowski, Czesnik, and Kotnarowski 2015: 19–23). The senior coalition partner in the 2011–2015 government, Civic Platform (PO), lost a significant share of the vote, but if the newly established party Nowoczesna (Modern) was considered to be a direct heir of the liberal policy platform and almost identical to the early (i.e., 2001) PO, then the center-liberal camp together obtained 32 percent of the vote. It should also be kept in mind that the 2015

Table 17.2 Indicators of the Party System Format, Poland 1991–2015

Indicators	1991	1993	1997	2001	2005	2007	2011	2015
Turnout (percentage of active voters)	43	52	48	46	41	54	49	51
Fractionalization	0.93	0.90	0.78	0.78	0.83	0.70	0.73	0.78
Number of effective parties (Laakso & Taagepera), votes	13.86	9.80	4.59	4.50	5.86	3.32	3.74	4.45
Number of effective parties (Laakso & Taagepera), seats	10.45	3.88	2.95	3.60	4.63	2.82	3.00	2.75
Disproportionality (Gallagher)	4.14	15.74	9.75	4.42	5.61	4.39	5.67	10.55
Wasted votes, percent	8.37	34.44	12.1	9.37	10.93	4.12	4.12	16.61
Sum of two biggest parties (votes), percent	24.31	35.81	60.96	53.72	51.13	73.62	69.07	61.67
Sum of two biggest parties (seats), percent	26.52	65.87	79.35	61.09	61.96	81.52	79.13	81.09
Biggest to second party ratio (votes)	1.03	1.32	1.25	3.24	1.12	1.29	1.31	1.56
Biggest to second party ratio (seats)	1.03	1.29	1.22	3.32	1.14	1.26	1.32	1.70

Source: Own calculations based on PKW official data.

PiS party list contained candidates from two other parties, Polska Razem (PR)[3] and Solidarna Polska (SP), and actually was a three-party coalition. Two additional phenomena are worth mentioning: the absence of parties of the left in the new parliament and the poor result of the Polish Peasant Party (PSL), the only Polish political party that has survived under the same name and leadership since 1989. The poor result of the agrarian PSL in the countryside among peasants and farmers undoubtedly has made a significant contribution to PiS's strong showing. One must emphasize that only 12 months earlier PSL performed far better in the local elections, enjoying the support of almost 24 percent of the Polish electorate, meaning that it lost approximately 19 percentage points in a year and barely passed the threshold in October 2015 with an unimpressive 5.3 percent. Two factors seem to have contributed to their worst ever result. First, the alleged rigging of the 2014 election, which de facto turned out to be a shameful technical error in the creation of the ballots, and second, a very manipulative yet skillful PiS campaign aimed at farmers' dissatisfaction with agriculture by outmaneuvering former governments with promises of generous rural policies.

PiS emerged as the sole winner of the elections, gaining 235 seats (in a 460-seat lower house) and thus the ability to form a one-party government (see Table 17.1). This outcome was surprising, since it is rare in the Polish party system for a party to be able to govern alone with only slightly more than 37 percent of the vote.

Three parties have achieved higher electoral support during the short history of Polish democracy. In 2001, 2007, and 2011 the winning parties received a larger percentage of the vote, yet because of the overall results of these elections – in particular the number of wasted votes – those winning parties were unable to form single-party governments. In 2015 almost 17 percent of votes were wasted, a figure much higher than in any previous election, with the exception of 1993, which was subject to a then new electoral law introducing thresholds (see Table 17.2). Journalistic accounts of the 2015 election have tended toward the interpretation that this was a landslide victory for PiS and indicative of a fundamental change in the political preferences of Poles. However, this was not borne out by the overall figures.

Let us inspect the results more closely. If one assumes – and it is a correct assumption – that the average support for PiS in the last two years prior to the election was around 30 percent (plus/minus three percent), and if one adds an approximately five percent joint contribution of the two small rightist "sofa" parties of Zbigniew Ziobro and Jarosław Gowin, then the overall result is around 37 percent, which nearly matches the official result of the election. Briefly, if PiS alone managed to enlarge its support in the year or two prior to the election, it should be estimated at two to four percent maximum. This hardly can be called a landslide victory or a call for revolutionary change. The calculations below add to the story: The centrist camp – composed of previous incumbent coalition partners, PO and PSL, both belonging to the European Peoples Party bloc in the EU – was able to attract almost 30 percent, which combined with an additional above seven percent of the new centrist liberal party, Nowoczesna, amounts to an identical 37 percent.

The Polish electoral outcome, seen from the perspective of voters' preferences, is substantially different from the outcome of the 2010 election in Hungary where 14 percent more citizens voted than in Poland and resulted in a landslide victory for Fidesz, which enjoyed 53 percent support, not to mention the impressive result of the even more nationalistic and radical Jobbik, which came third with 17 percent of the vote. In other words, 70 percent of politically active Hungarians voted for radical change to not only policies but to the regime in general, and the governing party enjoyed a constitutional majority. In Poland, the vote for national-populist parties, as they pretended[4] to be in the campaign, amounted to about 45 percent.

The – broader than simply partisan – ideological preferences of Poles are fairly stable since 2001 (see Figure 17.1).

As one can see from the ideological self-identification of Poles on the classical left-right scale, the changes during the previous decade are totally insignificant – clearly above 40 percent identifies itself with the "right," 45 to 50 percent with the "center" and between 10–15 percent with the "left" (data of the Polish National Election Study Series). What is probably even more

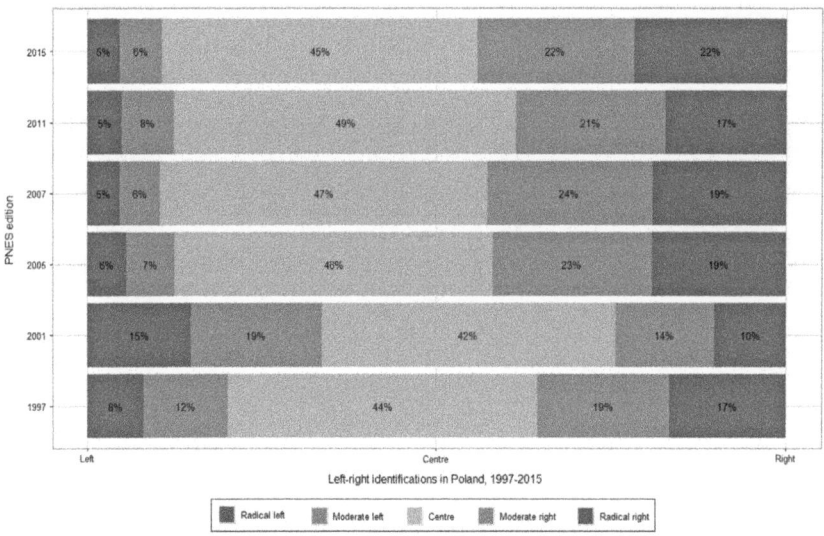

Figure 17.1 Political Preferences of Poles in National Elections since 1997. *Source:* Polish National Election Study Series.

important is the issue-content of the "left" and "right" in Poland. Unlike many other societies, Polish ideological "left-right" orientations are almost exclusively attributable to sociocultural issues (public role of the Catholic Church, pro-life versus pro-choice on abortion, foreigners, symbolic-historical issues, previously – in the 1990s – strongly related also to the issue of former communist *nomenklatura*). The socioeconomic issues (taxes, social security, privatization) either do not matter at all for Poles' ideological leaning or matter only marginally. The significant change in the past twenty or so years is that currently the EU issue became an important constitutive component of the "left-right" ideological orientations of Poles, to be sure; the left and the center are significantly more pro-European than the "right." Figure 17.2 shows the changes in time in the content contribution to "left-right" identities of Poles.

The turnout in this election was low and in line with Polish tradition whereby about half of the eligible voters participate in a parliamentary election. In 2015 just short of 51 percent of the electorate voted, which means that 5.7 million citizens who voted for PiS constitute 18.6 percent of eligible voters. Let us recall again that the PiS electoral committee actually constituted a three-party coalition; while PiS was clearly the dominant entity, the minor parties PR and SP commanded approximately two to three percent support, which means that in terms of absolute numbers they added about 700,000–750,000 votes to the success of the PiS electoral list. As evidence

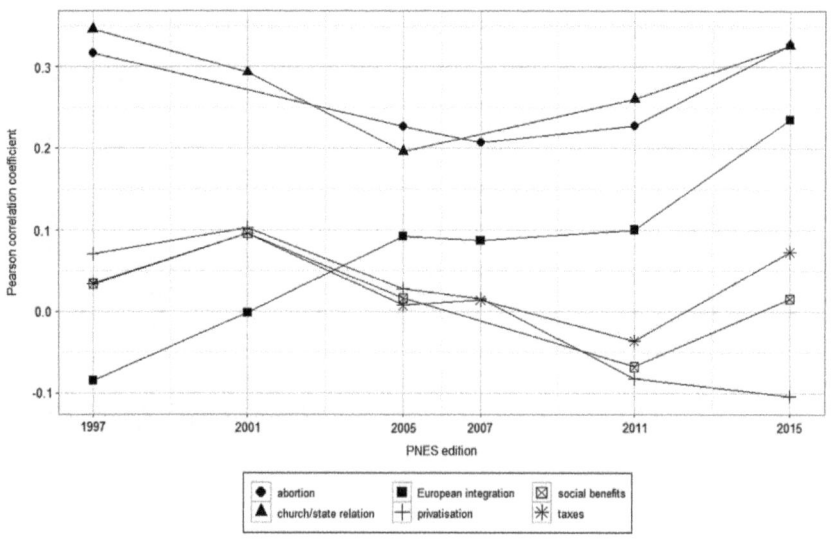

Figure 17.2   Left-Right Identifications and Attitudes toward Political Issues in Poland since 1997. Author's calculations based on the Polish National Election Survey 2015.

that these two parties are not negligible, we can observe that both their leaders became important figures in the PiS-led government, with PR leader Gowin appointed as one of the deputy prime ministers and Ziobro appointed as a powerful minister of justice and chief prosecutor.

The 2015 election – in terms of voters' support – can hardly be called *critical* and was far from reshaping the face of Polish party politics. Its results generally confirmed the presence of a divide that has been in place over the course of the previous decade between two roughly equal nationalist-populist and centrist-liberal camps. The most striking difference between the outcome of the 2015 election and the previous twenty-five years was the complete absence of parliamentary representation for the left. The traditional post-communist left, embodied by the Democratic Left Alliance (SLD), participated in the 2015 election as the main party of the United Left (Zjednoczona Lewica or ZL) electoral coalition. While some of the new left parties also joined this coalition, the brand new Razem (Together) party belied its name by refusing to cooperate with it and running as a separate entity. This split had significant consequences: while ZL fell just short of the eight percent threshold for coalitions, Razem failed to clear the five percent threshold for parties. As a result, a significant proportion of the wasted votes (around 12 percent out of almost seventeen of the total) was attributable to the failure of the left to coordinate its actions.

The unexpected fate of the left, notwithstanding their inability to coordinate their activities, obviously is determined by the fact that PiS itself has a very "leftist" socio-economic appeal and their redistributive promises in the 2015 campaign could hardly be met by any classical leftist party. To be sure, PiS, in terms of socioeconomic and redistributive policies, is indeed a "leftist" party, comparable to Fidesz's redistributive etatism, yet in the case of Fidesz there are more policies (and ideologies) *à la carte*: the new rich receive a rather liberal taxation rate, elderly pensioners receive "socialist generosity," and the lower-middle class receives nearly no financial benefit other than national pride coupled with religious exultation. Poland's PiS seems to be less flexible and inventive.

The election also showed that the Polish party system remains open to the emergence of entirely new parties and movements, with the success of the populist Kukiz' 15. This movement is named after its leader, the rock star Paweł Kukiz, whose second career as a campaigner began some three years ago when he emerged as a fierce critic of the PO-PSL government and as an advocate of a first-past-the-post electoral system. Aside from electoral reform, Kukiz's campaign was populist in character, combining radical anti-elitism and rejection of established political institutions with economic nationalism.

Public opinion polls and the results of an exit poll conducted on the day of the election point to the following sociopolitical alignments in Poland.

For reasons of space, I will limit my comments to the overrepresentation of major socioeconomic groups among the electorates of major parties. Among the electorate of the winning party – PiS, which constituted 37.6 percent of those who participated in the 2015 election – there is a significant overrepresentation of:

(a) people with primary (53 percent) and vocational (56 percent) education;
(b) peasants and farmers (53 percent);
(c) people above 50 years of age (48 percent);
(d) pensioners (49 percent);
(e) workers and rural residents (47 percent).

Among the electorate of the second strongest party, PO, which constituted 24 percent of those who participated in the 2015 election, there is an overrepresentation of residents of big cities (30 percent), those with high professional status (29 percent), and those with university degrees (27 percent). However, the PO electorate is rather old: those above sixty years of age constitute 29 percent of its following. Followers of the newly-established Nowoczesna, whose official electoral result amounted to a mere 7.6 percent of those participating, are overrepresented among the younger middle-aged cohort of those between thirty and thirty-nine years of age (11 percent), those with a university degree (12 percent), those with higher professional status (14 percent), and those living in metropolitan areas (13 percent). Finally, support for Kukiz' 15, which attracted 8.8 percent of active voters, is disproportionately high among those aged between eighteen and twenty-nine (21 percent), and as a consequence, among students (21 percent) and among workers (13 percent). The PSL electorate does not differ from previous years: they are more likely to be found in the countryside, are rather old, and have lower levels of educational attainment.

Table 17.2 illustrates that even if the 2015 parliamentary election falls short of being a "critical" one in terms of the voting results and their consequences for the composition of parliament, there are nevertheless significant changes compared with the relative stability of the previous decade.

Overall, we note greater party system instability between 2011 and 2015, as an increase in the number of effective parties in terms of votes, levels of disproportionality not seen since the early 1990s, and considerable growth in both aggregate and individual-level volatility (the latter derived from self-declarations of respondents to the Polish National Election Survey) are visible,[5] see Table 17.3.

It should be kept in mind that these figures refer to a party system that consistently reflects the choices of barely half of the citizens eligible to vote. This is an important caveat, since it should be expected that volatility statistics in

Table 17.3 Voter Volatility in Poland 1991–2015 (Percent)

Aggregated	1991–1993	1993–1997	1997–2001	2001–2005	2005–2007	2007–2011	2011–2015
Global (Pedersen Index)	34.78	19.19	49.30	38.39	24.96	13.74	30.10*
Between Block Volatility (BTW)@	18.90	7.58	18.72	26.16	11.06	2.36	26.30#
Individual	1991–1993	1993–1997	1997–2001	2001–2005	2005–2007	2007–2011	2011–2015
Between Party Volatility	-	62.26	55.94	62.64	34.48	23.12	26.72*
Between Block Volatility (BTW)	-	15.47	20.24	27.69	15.36	17.24	18.15#

@ Between Block volatility for years 1993 through 2011 has been calculated for the "left-right" divide. From 2007 onward, however, this divide does not define Polish politics, and as a consequence we do not calculate it anymore.
*In the 2011–15 period, this figure is calculated under the assumption that the new party – Nowoczesna (Modern) – is an absolutely new entity, unrelated to PO.
In the 2011–15 period this figure is calculated under the assumption that the new party – Nowoczesna (Modern) – is an ideological splinter from PO and as such a continuity of PO program and policies.
Source: author's calculations based on the Polish National Election Survey 2015.

political systems with much higher rates of participation might have a propensity to be less stable than in those political systems where only those truly interested in politics participate in elections.

An attempt has been undertaken (Markowski and Stanley 2016) to depict and explain Polish party politics with the theory of cleavage politics, and in particular to answer the main question in this tradition, that is: whether voter-party relationships have been "frozen" in time. The analyses – several distinct hypotheses tested – show that the whole post-1989 period in Poland can be divided into at least three phases, the last one starting after the 2005 election and unveiling features of (weak yet visible) "freezing," that is, party system stability measured by voter loyalty across time – from election to election. The tendency is there if one looks at the numbers of loyal voters and their linkage to cleavage voting pattern (Knutsen and Scarbrough 1995; Tóka 1998), the pattern indicating that loyal voters are better represented and that the loyalty of vote is associated with the perception of institutionalized (and not "wild" or chaotic) social conflicts. Briefly, the analyses of the alleged political cleavage and freezing of the sociopolitical relationships shows it is far from a strong, durable phenomenon, even if we detect certain features of structuring these relationships. The 2015 election has shown that the Polish party system is still fairly open, allowing new entrants to succeed in parliamentary presence. The overall party system instability has grown, yet the major two rival blocks remain in both their ideological and programmatic position as well as the size of their followers' support.

THE NEW GOVERNMENT: UNEXPECTED POST-ELECTORAL DEVELOPMENTS

It should be emphasized at this point that the 2015 parliamentary election in Poland was free and fair, with no indication of any fraud or procedural misconduct. PiS won the election, attracting over a third of the active electorate and gaining 52 percent of seats in parliament. The government PiS formed after the election had a mandate to run the country and to implement the policies they promised in the campaign, regardless of how realistic those pledges were. However, once it became clear that PiS could form a government without the need to coordinate its plans with a coalition partner, the party embarked on a course of action unrestrained by democratic procedures, constitutional provisions, and the "good manners" of pluralism.

Almost immediately, it became apparent that the "hiding" of divisive and unpopular figures was a campaign tactic: Antoni Macierewicz became minister of defense; Zbigniew Ziobro became minister of justice, and Mariusz Kamiński was given special responsibilities for coordinating the work of the security forces. With the government comprised of such figures, the tone of Polish politics rapidly became nationalist, anti-European in general, and anti-German in particular, and served to alienate Poland's most important global partners. Domestically, the radical turn consisted of a campaign to persuade Poles that their country was "in ruins" after the PO-PSL government, and the use of insulting and divisive rhetoric by major PiS figures – including the president – about political opponents, dubbing them, "traitors," "gangsters," and "cronies." Those protesting against the government's violations of the Constitution were referred to as "the worst sort of Poles" and "genetically prone to treason."

Unfortunately, the actions of the new government were not restricted only to symbolic divisions and vulgarity. In the first few months after the election, PiS already made significant "advancement" in turning back democratic progress in Poland: (1) it effectively paralyzed the Constitutional Tribunal, and in doing so clearly breached the Polish Constitution of 1997 on several counts (for details, see: Opinion of the Venice Commission, published on March 11, 2016); (2) it assumed direct control of the public media, turning it into a state media with a distinctly nationalist narrative and one-sided, partisan news coverage, resulting in a dramatic decline in viewing figures, estimated to be in the hundreds of thousands[6]; (3) it assumed direct control over the appointment and dismissal of civil servants, who can now be fired on the grounds of mere suspicion of misconduct, suggesting that the new government finds such fundamental legal values as the presumption of innocence suspicious in its own right.

Certainly, Orbán's Hungary serves here as a role model. Kaczyński's promise that "one day Budapest will arrive in Warsaw" came – even if accidentally and with all differences to be noted – true. The rule of PiS changed the political reality faster and was more illegal than in the Hungarian case. Kaczyński was crystal clear that PiS's 5.7 million supporters, that is, less than 19 percent of almost thirty-one million eligible voters, will never in the foreseeable future translate again into a single-party parliamentary majority. He had to be fast. The essence and the sequence of "reforms" in Poland resembled the ones implemented in Hungary: first, dismantling the separation of powers, by paralyzing the Constitutional Tribunal (accompanied by other changes to the autonomy of the judiciary, in particular the Supreme Court's Chief Justice); next, new media legislation allowing the reasonably well functioning public media to be turned into a party-driven propaganda machine; then attacking the autonomy of NGOs, altering the rules and institutional design of the Electoral Commission, and so on (for an in-depth and detailed description of these developments, see Sadurski 2018). But the important difference between the two systems is that the Polish developments have been based on clear violations of the Polish Constitution of 1997.

That Poles expressed no fundamental dissatisfaction with the changes during the twenty-five years prior to the 2015 elections already has been emphasized in this chapter. Moreover, studies conducted by the Polish Central Statistical Office and other prominent research projects like *Social Diagnosis* (Czapiński and Panek 2015) provide consistent evidence that Poles are among the most EU-enthusiastic in Europe, their attitudes toward Germans have improved enormously over the previous twenty-five years (a mere four percent claim the relationship between the two nations is poor), and Polish national identity has changed from ascriptive and ethnic to formal and civic (CBOS 2015 and 2016). On the other hand, the PiS government, since its grip and control of many state and cultural institutions, has launched a megalomaniac "historical politics," with newly created heroes, in particular, of the period during and after the Second World War as well as of the first "Solidarity" phase, the latter resulting in Lech Wałęsa and other important leaders of the "S" movement being erased from historical handbooks and museums. The Second World War Museum in Gdańsk is being "invented anew," replacing a cosmopolitan and sensitive vision about all victims of wars, in particular those of the Second World War, with one giving priority to the "Polish point of view." The idea of the new narrative dominating the museum's message is to promote heroism and positive values related to resistance, sacrifice, and the values wars create, instead of giving priority to the suffering and fate of victims, whichever nationality they happened to be. Such an example is only one in a series of changes attempted (fortunately, not all successful) in museums across Poland. Moreover, during a diplomatic crisis with Israel and the World Jewish Congress (as well as with the majority of NATO and EU members) in 2018 over a new law that aimed to silence critical voices concerning the role of Poles in the Holocaust, a revanchist proposal was put forward by an important Polish education authority that guided tours in Auschwitz-Birkenau can only be performed by Poles.

There is, however, one aspect of the public domain where the picture is more complex: the political domain. While we find a clear majority of Poles (75 percent) declaring satisfaction with the quality of local government in Poland, a significant minority (40 percent, up from 33 percent in 2007) experience a "sense of neglect" by the authorities. Yet a clear majority of Poles are in favor of the liberal version of democracy, preferring freedom to equality, modernity to tradition, and entrepreneurship to solidarity as the main goal of the state (Polish NES 2015 data file; Markowski and Kotnarowski 2016; Markowski and Tworzecki 2016). By early 2018, irrespective of the popular – and generous by Central European standards – family allowance of "500+,"[7] the main PiS campaign promise implemented since 2016, along with other generous social policies (retirement age reduced to sixty and sixty-five years for women and men, respectively; free prescriptions for seniors, and so on), no increase in support for this party has been recorded – in absolute numbers it oscillates around 5.5 million, slightly less than during the 2015 election. What we witness in public opinion institutes' (poorly conducted and analyzed) data is definitely lower support and distaste for most opposition parties, which are unable to prevent PiS from executing their policies in violation of constitutional procedures and clearly stated rules.

THE NEW ORDER: WHAT FOR?

Dozens of well-informed commentators on Poland are asking the questions: why and what for? As indicated in the introduction, I am hesitant to generalize, but an outline can be sketched out. In my view the PiS government's actions indicate that they do not have an overarching blueprint or a positive plan, and instead they opt for a "radical change," even if its justification is obscure and ambiguous.

First, Kaczyński's objective is discontinuity. Discontinuity in all domains. Historically, his mindset is a *fin de siècle* one – borders, industry, nation, enemies, nationalization, and the like dominate his imagination and linguistic repertoire. His distaste for the liberal world is well documented; it springs from his alienation from the world, derived from linguistic and digital illiteracy, and generally his infantile presence in the social environment.[8] Such a description is nothing personal for a public personality and former prime minister of a country of nearly forty million people in the EU.

Second, Kaczyński's aim is to rewrite the contemporary history of Poland, starting from the First Solidarity (1980–1981) movement and his negligible status at the time to the reconstruction of the reality surrounding the period of late 1980s and the Round Table accords of 1989; the latter being labeled by PiS and its leaders as "treason" of elites leading to the formation of an anti-national alliance of communists and liberals. Generally, the new historical narrative claims that the twenty-seven years of democratic Poland is a period of civilizational disaster, lack of sovereignty, semi-independent status and loss of "Polishness" at the expense of decadent Western liberal values. The above is just a short sample of the language being used to socialize PiS followers to the new social order and the new state.

Third, historical confabulations are necessary to achieve this and to justify the radical change. On the one hand, we witness – in cultural and educational policy, in particular – a paramount revival of national megalomania and religious fundamentalism (the latter in Poland is tightly linked to xenophobic narratives). For example, in everyday life, open support is expressed by PiS and the Catholic Church for the most obsolete, radical traditions of interwar

Poland like ONR[9] or a new invention and sheer confabulation about the role of so-called cursed soldiers (*żołnierze wyklęci*).[10]

Fourth, a full-blown exchange of elites, and consequently the distribution of social prestige, is another priority of the PiS government. The removal or sheer firing starts with the judiciary, public administration, and the media, but quickly jumps after business (the management of state treasury-owned enterprises being the focal point), education (including attempts at limiting university and academia autonomy),[11] and – obviously – the apparatus of intelligence agencies and special military forces. The analyses of this particular aspect of radical change envisaged by PiS points to the theory of an open versus closed access social order (North et al. 2013). In a nutshell, an exchange of the elites is the first step to withdraw from open, meritocratic recruitment based on competence and skills and embark on closed access order criteria – loyalty, ascribed status traits (e.g., religiosity), "patriotism," national sensitivity, and the like.

Fifth, we definitely live in an era of increased influence of semi-democratic to openly despotic regimes, the latter gaining economic importance in a globalized world. The systems are being named with a fair amount of invention: soft authoritarianism, electoral autocracy, unfree democracies, illiberal democracies, and so on. Some of these regimes are openly "modern," claim "democratic" principles, persuade their people that they are more "effective" than liberal democracies – allowing for faster growth and development – and skillfully criticize existing and confabulated shortcomings of democracies, in particular their elitism and alleged sluggishness in decision-making. Total control over media and deliberate misinformation of "the people" as to the exact state of affairs is one of the fundamental objectives to be accomplished first. The role model is Viktor Orbán and his accomplishments, and rarely are other personalities mentioned as alternative models; certainly, and for obvious historical reasons, Putin cannot be the idol. A *patron-client* relationship in the public domain is another feature. Permanent media campaigns actively distort reality, spreading a mixture of fears and threats concerning freedoms and property rights as part of a concerted effort to control the citizens. These new autocrats effectively make use of democratic vocabulary but refurbish it with its illiberal and populist versions. They pay lip service to the key principles of liberal democracy, yet they are very much interested in running elections as mechanisms legitimizing the de facto nondemocratic rule; elections are treated as an effective mechanism to control their own dissidents, manipulate any opposition, and ultimately to have an in-depth view of people's preferences, allowing them to react accordingly by establishing vital patronage linkages and clientelistic exchanges.

PiS's Poland, appears to be on a path to illiberal democracy, and even to electoral authoritarianism. Already all – without exception – reliable rankings of democracy, rule of law, media freedom, and so on (Freedom House, Polity, Bertelsmann Index, Rule of Law Index of the World Justice Forum, etc.) have unveiled a dramatic deterioration of Poland's position. Some of the aforementioned phenomena are already in place, that is, in the many bills adopted by the PiS-dominated parliament (violation of property rights concerning land ownership, public media autonomy, nontransparent invigilation provisions in the anti-terrorist act, the role and unconstrained prerogatives of the prosecutor general, and many more).[12]

Today, answers to the questions of "why" and "what for" are difficult; more time should be allowed to detect the ultimate new social and political order conceived by PiS. If I were, however, to search for well-established historical examples of the PiS regime blueprint I would opt for two. First, even if unconscious, the end-product of PiS activities might be – a bit more populist-democratic than the original – a version of *Estado Novo* (Schmitter 1975) in Portugal. Most of Salazar's inventions are close to Kaczyński's heart: restrained modernization, nationalism, conservatism in sociocultural domain, fundamentalist Catholicism, and above all a clear drive toward corporatist solutions at the expense of civil society and civil freedoms. And even if the literal Portuguese pluricontinentalism is – for obvious reasons – missing, a similar idea of a Polish-led Intermarine (Commonwealth) region is a strong foreign policy alternative to the current reliance on NATO and EU. If one adds the strong hierarchical, organic, and integralist orientation of the *Estado Novo*, and moreover together with the key idea that desirable, yet national, modernization has to be controlled by "decent" Catholic-rural-popular forces, then the above-mentioned case shows a mosaic similar to the future end-product of PiS's Poland.

Second, and again, a significant part of PiS policy ideas are simply emulated from Fidesz policies; the question remains open whether PiS's Poland will also end up with the level of illiberalism and sheer corruption Orbán's regime managed to achieve after eight years in power (Magyar 2016). Nevertheless, there are several differences between the Polish and the Hungarian cases. The most important one being that Kaczyński's regime lacks a constitutional majority and all its illiberal moves as well as clear violations of the effective 1997 Constitution provisions have allowed the international democratic community to act more decisively against these violations in accordance with the Copenhagen criteria and Article 7 of the Lisbon Treaty. The recent developments, even if considered by many to be sluggish, as most EU decisions, mean clear criticism of Polish government decisions. For the first time in its history, the European Commission, on December 20, 2017, took the unprecedented step of triggering "Article 7" of the EU treaties against Poland. This "nuclear" option and extraordinary decision comes as the EU accused Poland of violating democratic values, principles of the rule of law, and basic norms of a democratic polity as well as standards of the European Union.

A fundamental distinction, however, lies in the economic and moderniza-tion development of the two countries in the three decades after 1989. The dynamics of change – a very important experience of *Homo Politicus* – taught Poles that economic and civilizational miracles happen. Even if they were deservedly critical of the PO/PSL government of 2007–2015, the psycho-logical imprint of a country that has changed dramatically and caught up with Hungarian GDP per capita nevertheless is part of the Polish political experience. True, the explosive economic growth in this period (Poland's cumulative GDP has grown by above 25 percent) was not quite repeated in the subsequent four years, especially if considered comparatively. Another difference is the relationship with the immediate neighborhood. No Polish prime minister had ever dreamed of claiming he or she represents citizens of neighboring countries, and – so far – Polish foreign policy was marked by exceptional self-restraint as far as historical legacies are concerned. Last but not least, Polish parliamentary as well as extra-parliamentary opposi-tion seems to be in better shape than its Hungarian counterpart. Hundreds of thousands of Poles took part in manifestations against violations of the Constitution (or the paralysis of the Constitutional Court), in favor of the European Union and Polish membership, and supporting the so-called Black Protest of women against further restrictions of the abortion law, reminding us of the vibrancy of Polish civil society thus far. The health of the Polish party system also differs considerably from that of Hungary in that the ruling party in Poland is – using a spatial metaphor – much more radically located at the outskirts of both the classical "left-right" dimension as well as the more sophisticated multidimensional, issue-defined spaces of competition.

It is difficult to predict whether this relative weakness of PiS vis-à-vis other political and social actors in Poland (unlike Fidesz's hegemonic position) will force them to embark on even more radical policies and activities or – the reverse – will compel them to more moderate policies. The first four years of their rule point to the first scenario, as the option chosen by Kaczyński testifies.

Finally, the little that might serve as an explanation of the marginal victory of the nationalist camp in Poland in 2015 is twofold[13]:

(a) a century-long narrative of the "cultural lag theory" by William Ogburn (1922) might serve as the starting point. His enduring intellectual legacy is the theory of social change and disorganization. Ogburn – oversimplifying the matter – suggested that technology is the primary engine of progress but tempered by social responses to it. Space does not allow to elaborate on the details of the four stages of technical development he proposed (invention, accumulation, diffusion, and adjustment), but what is crucial for us here is that technological inventions are always paving the way to modernization and change. The social reaction and cultural adjustment of the technological invention always lags behind. As long as the lag is moderate, no social disorganization follows; however, once the lag becomes too broad, maladjustment creates problems and dysfunctions of the social machinery, leading to disorganization, anomie and, ultimately, the destruction of social order might follow.

If one is ready to translate this social modernization language into a political one, and define democratic institutional infrastructure (the general political system design, electoral rules, the logic of bicameralism, the prerogatives of the Constitutional Court, and the like) as politico-technological inventions that occurred in CEE countries via the process of diffusion (another important phase in the chain of Ogburn's theory) from the West, then one can formulate the following interpretation. Apparently, the effort at familiarizing the public of the new democracies to these – de facto – technocratic innovations has been relatively unsuccessful in socialization terms. Briefly, the essence and the logic of institutional opportunity structure of a democracy evidently has not been "nested" in the public mindset and political culture at large. In other words, the mechanical and the psychological effects (Duverger 1954) of institutional infrastructure have been temporarily detached. In David Easton's (1965) parlance, the *diffuse political support* for liberal democracies has apparently not been embedded deeply and still remains contextually determined.

(b) The other theoretical opportunity at explaining what has happened in Poland derives from simple "relative deprivation" accounts, like Gurr's or Davies' proposals, which concentrate on the juxtaposition of objective developments vis-à-vis the public's growth in expectations. It applies to the Hungarian case much better than to the Polish one, but only if we focus on socioeconomic issues alone. If one, however, broadens the universe of human goals to noneconomic phenomena, such as prestige, pride, symbolic issues, political efficacy, feeling of participation, and avoiding political alienation (a number of indicators shows that in the last years Poles did consider strictly political phenomena to be worsening, irrespectively of how justified these evaluations were), then the Polish developments might be explained by it as well. Had space allowed I would have discussed here another accompanying phenomenon which is the so-called accountability neurosis among post-communist CEE democracies; briefly, the new democratic citizens of CEE countries are – *en masse* – unprepared for a realistic assessment of the accomplishments of governments.[14] Democratic theory is convincingly serious about the necessity of the *responsiveness* of the government to citizens' preferences as the absolute requisite of qualitative democracy, yet empirical democratic theory insists that this requisite has to be "matched" by *responsible* citizens (Soroka and Wlezien 2012). The logic and mechanism of this relationship is fairly obvious: if citizens use ameritocratic, non-rational, or otherwise non-empirical criteria for evaluating the deeds of the incumbents, then there is little incentive on the side of politicians to behave both responsibly and responsively. Why would they, since their policy efforts, calculation of alternatives, and reasoned decision-making do not count. This phenomenon, considering the peculiarities of PiS supporters' socio-demographics, can also serve to explain the minor shift that has occurred prior to the 2015 election.

CONCLUSION

Neither during the eight years of PO-PSL government nor at the time of the 2015 election was there any evidence to suggest a significant public appetite for the radical post-electoral change implemented by the PiS government. Yet a party boasting the support of less than 19 percent of eligible voters opted for making fundamental changes to the constitutional reality, social order, and the practice of an EU state. In a nutshell, the Polish state has been captured by a revolutionary sect of sorts, which is pursuing the objective of dismantling the foundations of Poland's liberal democratic order. Instead of a legal culture based on checks and balances and the separation of powers, sheer political will is to drive political developments. According to this vision, the state replaces the market, civil society, and the rule of law; it is to follow anti-capitalist, anti-globalist policies, and to be driven by non-meritocratic recruitment principles. The sociocultural aspects of this new system focus on the redistribution of prestige and go along with historical confabulations, the politicization of history. These objectives are accompanied by the dismissal of pluralism, an anti-elitist and anti-intellectual mood, and the "management of fear" (Jews, Germans, migrants), which resembles the political and cultural code of the interwar narrative offered by the far-right-wing nationalist camp (*Endecja*).

The conquest of the state and its institutions by PiS is portrayed as national liberation, and the contempt for the existing legal order as a desire for natural justice. The 2015 Polish parliamentary election and its unexpected consequences certainly raise new questions for the literature on the path and sequence of democratic transition and consolidation[15] and force us to rethink the historical accounts in which authoritarian regimes (may) originate by democratic means. The recent developments in Poland also call for an in-depth theoretical explanation of how nationalist-populist political options might gain in strength in spite of the apparently unfavorable context of social progress and economic success.

This chapter was completed just before the 2019 parliamentary elections in Poland. (the editors)

NOTES

1. For a recent in-depth comparison of the historical and contemporary Hungarian-Polish differences, see Magyar and Mitrovits (2016).

2. Among others, the participants of these – scattered in time – dinners comprised the then minister of finance, minister of internal affairs, minister of foreign affairs, the president of the central bank, and the like. The views exchanged by these politicians can be summarized as a critical overview of the quality of governance and the state itself. Still, apart from selected strange opinions, inappropriate language, and a bit too informal inquiry into what can be done in policy terms, none of the tapes have indicated any corruption deals, violation of law, or the Constitution. In fact, the narrative can be characterized predominantly as deep concern about Poland, its economy, and the state capabilities to implement necessary policies.

3. Not to be confused with the leftist Razem (Together) party.

4. PiS pretended during both the presidential and the parliamentary campaigns that its political goals were limited to serious changes in implemented policies, with no intention of any radical change in the nature of democracy, the role of Constitutional Tribunal, nor ideas about total control over public media, and so on. Moreover, during the campaign, the most controversial figures of PiS – and negatively perceived by the public, with 50 percent (or more) of a "distrustful" rating – Antoni Macierewicz, Zbigniew Ziobro, and the leader himself, Jarosław Kaczyński were "hidden" from the public. The candidate for the premiership Beata Szydło, when asked by journalists, openly promised, for instance, that Macierewicz will not become the future minister of defense.

5. The volatility figures for the 2011–2015 period are shown in two versions, the first assuming that the new party Nowoczesna (Modern) is a brand new entity and entrant to the parliament; the second accounting for the extent to which the voters of Nowoczesna are former PO followers who see the party as a continuation of PO's previous programmatic and policy orientation.

6. Data available online: http://www.wirtualnemedia.pl/wiadomosci/telewizja/wyniki-ogladalnosci\.

7. Program 500+ is aimed at providing 500 Polish zloty (equivalent of about EUR 120) per month per child, except to well-to-do families with only one child. It reaches most Polish families, either with two or more children in the family or poorer families with one child. The overall yearly cost of the program for the budget is approximately PLN 25 billion (slightly below EUR 6 billion), it reaches about 3.6 million children (55 percent of all children below age eighteen) and 2.8 million parents.

8. An increasing number of analysts in Poland claim sociology and political science are incapable of explaining the Kaczyński phenomenon and one has to resort to social psychology or even more sophisticated disciplines dealing with human psychology. Space allotted to this chapter does not allow me (nor does my professional background) to follow a psychological investigation; nevertheless, what I call the "civilizational illiteracy" of a person who heads an EU member state of nearly forty million people poses a very serious problem. Moreover, apart from his inability to use a computer, drive a car, effectively use his own bank account, his personal conduct

also matters. Kaczyński's inability to accomplish simple daily routine tasks (shopping) as well as his personal life (void of any close relationship to another human being, save closest family) is not only strange but scary. His unaccountable political status after the 2015 election is one thing, but his unaccountable personal status (not being responsible for any important relationship) allows him to behave in a completely unpredictable manner. He simply "doesn't care," no matter what happens.

9. ONR, Obóz Narodowo-Radykalny [National Radical Camp], is a far-right movement, by some described also as neo-Nazi. Their program claims affinity to Polish nationalism, national radicalism, antisemitism, anti-communism, Euroscepticism, and ideas of anti-globalization. Save the last two, preceding ideological traits easily can be linked to the Polish movement that existed in the interwar period and shares the same name.

10. A complex group of post–World War II soldiers who continued their fight with the communist regime. Many were true patriots and heroes, numbering only several thousand individuals. Yet certain groups across Poland also had been involved in murdering Jews and committed several documented mass murders of Belarussians as well as Poles and Ukrainians. To be sure, these atrocities of the postwar era should not obscure their core activities – fighting for an independent Poland. But one needs in-depth knowledge about the precise groups and their actions in order to arrive at historical justice. The current PiS government does not distinguish between those who were heroic and those who committed crimes.

11. First hints at PiS's willingness to "review" the scholarly degrees and titles was mentioned in April 2016. The practical side of the proposal is unclear yet the justification is fairly serious.

12. For many other changes and "policies," see Sadurski (2018).

13. For broader and more in-depth theoretical explanations, see Markowski (2018).

14. Apart from limited skills for the adequate (or just, if you will) evaluation of the government's accomplishments by citizens, an additional problem stems from the practice of unconstrained overbidding during electoral campaigns that result in paramount "promise inflation," usually objectively unattainable.

15. For an in-depth discussion of this issue, see Markowski (2018).

BIBLIOGRAPHY

Alexander, Amy, and Christian Welzel. 2017. "The Myth of Deconsolidation: Rising Liberalism and the Populist Reaction." *ILE Working Paper Series*, No. 10, University of Hamburg, Institute of Law and Economics. https://www.econstor.eu/bitstr eam/10419/170694/1/ile-wp-2017-10.pdf, accessed June 25, 2019.

CBOS 2015/106. Komunikat z badań: Tożsamość narodowa i postrzeganie praw mniejszości narodowych i etnicznych.

CBOS 2016/004. Komunikat z badań: Zadowolenie z życia.

Czapiński, Janusz, and Tomasz Panek, eds. 2015. *Diagnoza Społeczna 2015*. Warsaw: Rada Monitoringu Społecznego.

Cześnik, Mikołaj, Michał Kotnarowski, and Igor Lyubashenko. 2016. "Kto kształtuje polską politykę – o aktywności i nieaktywności wyborczej." *Studia Socjologiczne* 4 (223): 39–66.

Davies, James C. 1962. "Toward a Theory of Revolution." *American Sociological Review* 27 (1): 5–19.

Duverger, Maurice. 1954. *Political Parties*. London: Methuen.

Easton, David. 1965. *A System Analysis of Political Life*. New York: Wiley.

Eurostat 2016. http://ec.europa.eu/eurostat/tgm/table.do?tab=table&language=en& pcode=tessi190, accessed June 25, 2019.

Ferrin, Monica, and Hanspeter Kriesi, eds. 2016. *How Europeans View and Evaluate Democracy*. Oxford: Oxford University Press.

Gurr, Ted. 1970. *Why Men Rebel*. Princeton, NJ: Princeton University Press.

Kitschelt, Herbert, Zdenka Mansfeldova, Radosław Markowski, and Gabor Toka. 1999. *Post-communist Party Systems: Competition, Representation, and Inter-Party Cooperation*. Cambridge: Cambridge University Press.

Knutsen, Oddbjorn, and Elinor Scarbrough. 1995. "Cleavage Politics." In *The Impact of Values*, edited by Jan van Deth and Elinor Scrabrough, 492–523. Oxford: Oxford University Press.

Levitsky, Steven, and Lucan Way. 2015. "The Myth of Democratic Recession." *Journal of Democracy* 25 (1): 45–58.

Magyar, Bálint. 2016. *Post-Communist Mafia State: The Case of Hungary*. Budapest: CEU Press.

Magyar, Bálint, and Miklós Mitrovits. 2016. "Lengyel–magyar párhuzamos rendszer-rajzok." *Élet és Irodalom* 32, 33. August 12, 19.

Markowski, Radosław. 2018. "Backsliding into Authoritarian Clientelism: The Case of Poland." In *Democracy under Stress: Changing Perspectives on Democracy, Governance and their Measurement*, edited by Petra Guasti and Zdenka Mansfeldova. Prague: Institute of Sociology, CAS.

———. 2016. "Determinants of Democratic Legitimacy: Liberal Democracy and Social Justice." In *How Europeans View and Evaluate Democracy*, edited by Monica Ferrin and Hanspeter Kriesi. Oxford: Oxford University Press.

Markowski, Radosław, Mikołaj Cześnik, and Michał Kotnarowski. 2015. *Demokracja – Gospodarka – Polityka*. Warsaw: Wydawnictwo Naukowe SCHOLAR.

Markowski, Radosław, and Michal Kotnarowski. 2016. "Dlaczego zadowoleni Polacy wybrali partię niezadowolenia." *POLITYKA* 6: 26–30.

Markowski, Radosław, and Ben Stanley. 2016. "Rozłamy socjopolityczne w Polsce: iluzja czy rzeczywistość?" *Studia Socjologiczne* 4: 15–38.

Markowski, Radosław, and Hubert Tworzecki. 2016. "Czy Polacy mają skłonność do autorytaryzmu?" *POLITYKA* 10: 32–35.

Markowski, Radosław, and Gábor Tóka. 1995. "Left-turn in Hungary and Poland Five Years after the Collapse of Communism." *Sisyphus* 75–100.

North, Douglass C., John Joseph Wallis, Steven B. Webb, and Barry R. Weingast. 2013. "Limited Access Orders: An Introduction to the Conceptual Framework." In *In the Shadow of Violence: Politics, Economics, and The Problems of Development*, edited by Douglass C. North, John Joseph Wallis, Steven B. Webb, and Barry R. Weingast. Cambridge: Cambridge University Press.

Ogburn, William Fielding. 1922. *Social Change with Respect to Culture and Original Nature.* New York: B. W. Huebsch.

Sadurski, Wojciech. 2018. "How Democracy Dies (in Poland): A Case Study of Anti-Constitutional Populist Backsliding." Sydney Law School. Legal Studies Research Paper, No. 18/01.

Schmitter, Philippe. 1975. *Corporatism and Public Policy in Authoritarian Portugal.* London: Sage.

Soroka, Stuart, and Christopher Wlezien. 2010. *Degrees of Democracy: Politics, Public Opinion and Policy.* Cambridge: Cambridge University Press.

Tóka, Gábor. 1998. "Party Appeals and Voter Loyalty in New Democracies." *Political Studies* 46 (3): 589–610.

Venice Commission. 2016. "Opinion on Amendments to the Act of 25 June 2015 on the Constitutional Tribunal of Poland." Adopted by the Venice Commission at its 106th Plenary Session, Opinion No. 833/2015. Venice, Italy. March 11–12, 2016.

Voeten, Erik. 2017. "Are People Really Turning away from Democracy?" *Journal of Democracy*, web exchange. https://www.journalofdemocracy.org/online-exchange-"democratic-deconsolidation", accessed June 25, 2019.

Chapter 18

Regime, Parties, and Patronage in Contemporary Romania

Silvia Marton

The primary interest of this chapter consists in focusing on party patronage as both a selective distribution of resources and means of production of consensus among rival political parties and their electorates (Shefter 1977, 403–51; Shefter 1993; O'Dwyer 2006), in order to understand the way that the contemporary Romanian political regime and party system function, and how political parties relate to the state. In this sense, patronage in post-communist Romania represents a remarkable vantage point for grasping the pitfalls of the party system, state building, and democratization.

Patronage is especially relevant for the nature of the Romanian political system as it throws light on the moving sands of the private-public distinction and on the procedures guiding the transgression of this boundary (Thompson 2013). Political parties are essential for understanding this process, as they are the primary vectors for organizing elections and for recruiting the political personnel for coveted positions in the state. With parties, the clientelistic exchange is an excellent way of politicization, since patronage is not only the political expression of social domination but also determines how political domination takes shape when it relies on the resources distributed by public office holders (Briquet 1997, 101 and 108–9).

This chapter does not assume a normative position[1] on party patronage. Rather, its aim is to capture degrees of tolerance about power relations, favors, and patronage practices that adapt to new forms of managing interests and competition for power (Monier 2014, 15, 17). Cultural and political categories such as public interest, loyalty, impartiality, civic duty, private interest, and abuse are historically and politically constructed as the consequence of debates and conflicts on practices considered at a given moment to be corrupted. From this perspective, patronage is politically neutral as a category of political analysis, and it is a technique for governing that changes over time (Engels 2014, 33–50; Engels 2008, 68–86).

The first part of this chapter will show that the Romanian post-communist state has not generated sufficiently autonomous state institutions meant to embody and enact a publicly shared sense of general interest. Parties substitute themselves for the state by generalized patronage, and state institutions thus are unable to develop their autonomy. The second part will analyze the president's role in reconfiguring the nature of patronage practices, while the third part examines the shifting political cleavages against the background of the persistence of party patronage practices. Such an analysis might shed light on the important differences between the evolution of the Romanian and Hungarian political systems but also points at common challenges and some points of structural similarity, which usually are disregarded when the more stable and openly ideological Orbánist regime is compared to the much more volatile Romanian configuration.

COMPETITIVE BARGAINING PROCESSES AND PATRONAGE PRACTICES

Romania's accession process to the European Union (effective in 2007) was guided and conditioned by the institutional and political criteria of democratic consolidation (Grabbe 2006). However, still caught in the party-state web, the Romanian bureaucracy is not wholly autonomous but mostly controlled by political parties and subordinated to them. Patronage practices, whether national or local, greatly influence the functioning of bureaucracy and the general perception of its efficiency and impartiality – and by extension, perceptions of the state itself.

The functional and structural model of the communist party-state continued after 1989 and was included in the first electoral laws of 1990. The new regime was conceived initially around a large and disciplined party dominating the political scene – the National Salvation Front (FSN) and its successors: the National Salvation Democratic Front, the Party of Social Democracy in Romania, and finally the current Social Democratic Party (PSD) (Ionescu 2007, 257–66). The result was major and difficult negotiations between rival political actors and fragile coalitions that continuously contradict this original intent.[2] FSN's vision was the organizational vigor of a majoritarian governmental party, achieved in 1990–1992, in 2000–2004, and again since 2016 by PSD, while all major post-1989 parties aim to copy this model. FSN/PSD coopted the bulk of the communist political, administrative, and local elites, and then became the transition's paradigmatic post-socialist, post-political, neoliberal, technocratic party. Its vision was (and mostly still is) of a society devoid of legitimate political cleavages and able to be represented integrally by a dominant political party that successfully administers and integrates its various actors and constituencies – regional strongmen, business tycoons, unions, technocrats, nationalists, Europeanized cosmopolitan elites, and so on. Throughout the 1990s and ever since, all parties were willing (though not always successful) to use the resources of the state to acquire a mass base and electoral support and had every incentive to restrict bureaucratic autonomy (Preda and Soare 2008, 118–22, 159–67; Ionescu 2009, 263–71, 283–302). In a sense, the situation of the early 1990s is similar to the emergence of modern Romanian parties during the 1880s (Marton 2014, 141–66). The absence of significant groups demanding bureaucratic autonomy is explained by the typology of governmental patronage (Ionaşcu 2006, 62–77). From 1990 to 1996, party-affiliated ministers appointed and dismissed high civil servants in the context of a rather high continuity of political and bureaucratic personnel with the pre-1989 period (Grosescu 2007, 199–231; Ştefan and Grecu 2014, 202–3). From 1996, when the domination of the FSN and its successors ended with the electoral victory of the opposition coalition, up to 2000, all governmental levels were politicized by the coalition parties (according to a much-publicized "algorithm"), and the notion of "political clean-up" (with "neo-communists" as main targets) accompanied the discourse on reform. From 2000 to present, after each parliamentary election the majority coalition again "cleaned up" the administration down to its deepest layers, based on the algorithm imposed by the parties (since most governments are coalition governments). While under pressure from European institutions, a law on the status of civil servants was adopted in 1999, patronage practices do not disappear. Since 2000, in actual fact, patronage has been orchestrated more systematically and in a more disciplined manner, with parties manipulating the flaws and omissions in the legislation. In other words, there is a continuous reconfiguration of strategies in order to control the administration (Ionaşcu 2006, 62–77). The "purge" in the wake of elections or coalition changes includes effectively all the directors and boards of public companies, schools, and hospitals, as well as all the territorial bureaucratic and economic entities under the administration of the central government representative (prefect). Thousands of such positions are negotiated and filled by every new government – a process that usually takes a good part of its first year of mandate.

Despite the EU accession criteria and professionalization of especially the younger generation of public officials, bureaucracy remains captive to the party-state relationship. Recent research further confirms that parties in government seek to impose their own personnel and associates rather than trying to coopt the existing ones. The instability of administrative personnel is heightened by the frequent rotation of ministerial mandates (Ionaşcu 2007, 71–89).

Political appointments are not limited to Romania; they are common practice in all democracies: a change of government requires major changes in the main institutions. But the problem for Romania is the far-reaching level of political appointments and the frequently low concern for the professional expertise of the actors. Romania's specific patronage makes positions that normally should be accessed as a result of competitive selection procedures (in line with what is usually called "classic bureaucracy") to be influenced politically. For example, members of the selection boards for competitions in administrative institutions are appointed by political parties. Another well-known example is the appointment, politically negotiated by parties, of members of various administrative boards of public institutions or state-owned large enterprises. Legal and constitutional inconsistencies (e.g., an unclear boundary between civil servants and public dignitaries,[3] or the possibility for middle- and low-level civil servants to be party members) diversify the dependency of administration on political parties both nationally and locally (Bojin 2010, 146–55). The Romanian contemporary regime, as defined by the parties, is not only a regime that politically controls bureaucracy: it is also a regime that seems not to accept or trust the very existence of a bureaucracy in Weberian terms (impartiality, expertise, etc.). Those few institutions that seem to escape this strict logic of party subordination (e.g., the National Anti-corruption Directorate, DNA) are few and far between and under immense pressure.

Patronage also creates a certain kind of successful political party. Its success is measured by its ability to mobilize and "control" (i.e., anticipate) voting and the ability to survive while in opposition (in the context of a very tense political climate). Since bureaucracy is unprofessional and without credibility, the Romanian state is compelled to let political parties control it. It is a vicious circle that persists since the second half of the nineteenth century when modern Romanian parties formed (Marton 2014). Paradoxically, parties make bureaucracy tangible for the large circle of people who are part of the patronage networks, people who are really active in politics, are politically mobilized, and who are politically relevant. Romania has a rather low political participation rate, and citizens are not particularly active by conventional measuring standards. Participation in the November 2014 presidential elections, for instance, was exceptionally high at 64.1 percent (since 2000 it varies between 56 and 57 percent), while for the 2016 parliamentary elections it was 39.5 percent (41.7 percent in 2012).[4] Moreover, several recent referenda were invalidated by the Constitutional Court on grounds of insufficient participation. With the exception of PSD (which concentrates more than half of all party members in Romania), party membership is rather low, and participation in street demonstrations was generally low during the 2000s.

Since 2012, however, street protests and mobilization grew rapidly and have been surprisingly effective.[5] Yet this mobilization had little effect on electoral participation itself. Political parties have a "captive" electorate, consolidated over the last thirty years, which does not vary much. PSD, for instance, rarely has varied outside its traditional 30 to 40 percent electoral percentage. Networks of patronage are the active part of the electorate on which parties rely in order to have good electoral results, and committed party voters ready to be mobilized. Therefore, parties are interested only in mobilizing their "captive" electorate and patronage networks and do not necessarily wish a larger citizen participation. Each party counts in reality on the opponent's voter demobilization, which explains the importance of negative electoral campaigns. A "captive" electorate is maintained by the direct or indirect access to resources (subsidies, public works, contracts, office positions) and only marginally by ideology or by resorting to political passions. It is the main explanation for the importance of patronage networks. Corrupt funding of political parties (Ionaşcu and Soare 2012a, 17–43; Ionaşcu and Soare 2012b, 56–64) is part of the public debate after each election but with few institutional answers aside the occasional prosecution by the DNA.

For a while, most major Romanian parties aimed to create a cartel (Mair and Katz 1995, 5–28; Crowther and Suciu 2013, 369–406). Patronage networks allow, in a cartel party system, strategies for survival in opposition after losing the election: since cartel party systems minimize the risks associated with electoral loss and maximize policy convergence and state colonization, losing parties do not really fear being isolated from society as the winning parties do not enact massive changes. On the contrary, they usually are perfectly capable to rapidly pick up and integrate the patronage system once their electoral support improves. From this perspective, there is no major difference in the political philosophy and the organizational culture of the main political parties (PSD, the National Liberal Party – PNL, or the Liberal-Democrat Party – PDL[6]), which are in many ways interchangeable. Yet the sheer electoral dominance of PSD after 2012 made this party less interested in cartel politics and explains its current drive towards majoritarian winner-takes-all approaches. The other main political party (the center-right PNL) oscillates uneasily between the elusive chances of resuming the cartel with the PSD (with whom it formed a political alliance between 2011–2014) and the more radical anti-PSD rhetoric of new political parties, especially the centrist-technocratic Save Romania Union (USR) that formed in 2015.

Such newer political parties, even while employing a more radical discourse of political reform, confirm in their *modus operandi* the difficulty of elaborating alternative models for a political party. Their recruitment strategies are based on a pool of technocratic elites and NGO personnel, and sport expertise and integrity as their main values but at the same time fail to capitalize on the political cleavage based on these contrasts. In effect, their *raison d'être* is to contest patronage politics and the deprofessionalized governance of PSD. But while USR sprang to eight percent in the December 2016 parliamentary elections after only several months of existence, it stagnated thereafter in the polls. Their territorial presence is weak and tends to lack instruments for organizational coherence. Therefore, such parties are heavily concentrated in several major cities.

In contrast, the traditional big parties are fairly decentralized locally. Starting with the PSD after the electoral loss of 2004, the importance of the local networks of patronage for ensuring the party's resilience in opposition reinforced the relative power of the local party leaders in its governing bodies. This model has since been replicated by the other parties as well. Recent research has shown that national and local elites are rather separated, local-national career mobility is reduced, and prominent local party leaders prefer a career at the local level (Ştefan and Grecu 2014, 204–6, 209–11). Local political or economic leaders (the so-called barons) have had ample organizational and political freedom (at least from the early 2000s until today). Funding of these local leaders follows the partisan logic: governments favor their local party leaders and their constituencies (Preda and Soare 2008, 50–57).[7] The promise of "barons" to influence voters and win elections in the districts they control in exchange for preferential economic and financial support from the government (especially for infrastructure works). Local "barons" are protégés of the government; they distribute the money – through preferential contracts – to local businesses. In some cities and counties, it is hard to conduct a successful economic activity without party affiliation or without the support of a party. In this way, parties control their local members. However, sometimes it happens that local leaders rebel against party leaders in the capital as a means to get more benefits.

Inter-party mobility of elected officials is a practice that strengthens partisan patronage even while delegitimizing the overall party system. A large number of national and local cadres (MPs, mayors, civil servants, and so on) tend to "migrate" and register with the winning party after an election or just before an election with a foreseeable result. There is thus often a way for such local notables to benefit from the limited competition among the main parties. Their tendencies for shifting affiliations increase the incentives of the parties to reward and protect them through ever more extended patronage networks.

Under the 2004 law, mayors and members of local county councils lose their mandate if they migrate and leave the party they were affiliated to when elected. Yet while prohibited for locally elected officials, inter-party mobility in the national parliament is not legally limited: rather, it is the easiest way for governments to build a majority (including the situation when a governing coalition partner leaves the coalition). It is why all parties accept coalition governments so that they can negotiate in parliament. As a corollary, there are no clear losers within an electoral cycle: an opposition party always can become, even midway through the election cycle, a governing coalition partner, and coalitions can change any time. Given that alliances are done and undone in parliament, it is a rivalry between adversaries who practice the same strategy and finally get along. Moreover, it is the constitutional prerogative of the president to appoint a new prime minister who does not already have a parliamentary majority, since he or she can build that majority *via* subsequent negotiations with the different parliamentary groups.[8] In a sense, this is the reason for the utmost importance of presidential elections – in a regime that otherwise leaves the president's office with little constitutional resources to affect actual politics. This recalls a typical feature of pre–Second World War Romanian politics, where the king would nominate a prime minister who would proceed then to organize elections and systematically win a parliamentary majority.

The MPs' political migration cannot be prohibited constitutionally, as this would entail an imperative mandate. In recent years, there are indeed many debates on constitutional reform to include such a provision. The scale of migration justifies the relevance of such a debate: from 2008 to 2012, at least 20 percent of MPs have changed their party affiliation at least once.[9] There are frequent cases of multiple migrations (changing several parties) during a single term. MPs may be elected on behalf of a party and then be active in parliament as members of another party. They sometimes negotiate with the governing party for financial advantages for the benefit of mayors within their constituency.[10] Local notables usually press the MPs from their region to change party affiliation, so de facto Romanian MPs, despite the principle of national representation, have little autonomy with respect to local notables that facilitate their local electoral support. For example, in 2013 and 2014, most MPs from People's Party-Dan Diaconescu (PP-DD) migrated to the National Union for Romania's Progress (UNPR) (most often following pressures from local party leaders), while others migrated directly to the powerful PSD that, *via* local notables, built a parliamentary wing composed of former PP-DD MPs.[11] In such situations, the vocabulary commonly used is "transfers" (like in football).

Several smaller parties, in fact, act as dedicated transit points for MPs migration. Such parties have no specific ideological affiliation and rarely advance any significant ideological credentials. UNPR, in recent years, was born *in parliament*, by defectors from PSD, the Conservative Party (PC),[12] then PNL and PDL, and was a quasi-constant coalition partner from 2009 to 2015 of PDL, PSD, and PNL, which successively led the governing coalition (Ştefan and Grecu 2014, 198). The Liberals and Democrats' Alliance Party

(ALDE) is another party that formed in 2015 as a splinter parliamentary group separating from the PNL once the latter quit the governing coalition, and it professed immediate support for the then-existing coalition led by the PSD. In a sense, such parties provide the guarantee that existing patronage relations are not significantly disturbed by electoral cycles, thus ensuring continuity and a win-win logic.

The importance of migration for political parties and their clientele is further illustrated by the government's emergency decree in the fall 2014 to allow local elected officials, for forty-five days, including the period of the November 2014 presidential campaign, to migrate from one party to another without losing their mandates. Even if the government's decree was rejected later by the Constitutional Court on grounds of unconstitutionality and (in February 2015) by the Chamber of Deputies, it had already produced practical effects. It should be noted that the deputies did not sanction those who migrated under the decree, so no locally elected official that changed party lost his/her mandate. The party that benefited most from the decree was – predictably – the PSD, in government at that time (in forty-five days, the PSD gained 404 mayors and lost 3).[13]

The patronage system produced by the Romanian parties explains, in many ways, the political stability after 1989, the absence of physical violence between political actors, the relative latency of aggressive nationalist rhetoric shared by all parties, and the ability of rival actors to negotiate and mitigate incessant political conflicts. The purpose of patronage is manifold: to win elections by using the administrative apparatus to win the majority, to maintain monopoly in the distribution of public goods and state employment/functions, and to give access to preferential contracts and local investment (colloquially, the so-called pork barrel). In a context in which national homogenization policies are (quasi) unanimous, patronage plays its integrating role to satisfy the ambitions of all strata of the national and local elite. Partisan rivalries rather than ideological rivalries are the major sources of political conflict: the opponents are opponents precisely because they engage in the same – but rival – patronage practices.

Hence there is no occurrence of one-party super-majorities in Romania like the case in Hungary in 2010 when Fidesz got two-thirds of the parliamentary mandates that allowed it to make profound and unilateral (non-negotiated) transformations of the constitutional structure. Fidesz shuns cartel situations by claiming that only it embodies the whole nation and by having the actual supermajority that makes any political compromise void of meaning. Romania came close to a coalition supermajority in 2012–2013 (the Social-Liberal Union, USL,[14] after the December 2012 parliamentary elections, had a little less than two-thirds majority in parliament). USL had the rhetoric of exclusive (with its satellites) control over all institutions. But its governing was conflict-ridden and broke up in February 2014 when the PNL went into opposition, while in the November 2014 presidential elections, PNL-supported Klaus Iohannis defeated PSD's Victor Ponta and a new cohabitation began. Thus, there was no individual party with a supermajority after 1992, when FSN failed to repeat its previous record, namely 66 percent of parliamentary seats after the May 1990 elections. In a sense, the 1990s still made possible massive ideological mobilization, while after 2000, such party mobilization relied exclusively on parliamentary elections for patronage networks support.

Lack of ideological mobilization is a crucial distinction between PSD and Fidesz, which may sport similar political convictions but had till recently very different strategies. It was only after 2014 that PSD progressively started to incorporate nationalist rhetoric as a complementary mobilization repertoire, and it is a repertoire that is regularly toned town in part because of PSD's ongoing tacit alliance with the Hungarian minority's political party (UDMR/RMDSZ) as well as, regionally, with Viktor Orbán. Moreover, conservative-nationalist mobilization cannot distinguish PSD from its rival parties (especially PNL) that have systematically included religious conservative constituencies. The October 2018 citizens' initiative for constitutional change – promoted by religious and conservative organizations that aim to constitutionally make impossible any future legalization of homosexual marriage – received support from both the PSD and the PNL and hence cannot meaningfully differentiate their similar conservative ideological positioning.

THE PRESIDENT AND THE PARTIES: SHIFTING NATURE OF THE POLITICAL REGIME

At best, the president in Romania holds the symbolic means of public pressure to oppose patronage, since his constitutional prerogatives are limited or shared with the prime minister. Furthermore, his electoral prospects depend on the party structure and capacity for mobilization of an existing party; therefore, presidents tend to seek and protect such a relationship. The president cannot oppose the parliamentary majority and only has instruments to insulate certain institutions from complete governmental domination. He has control over the National Security and Defense Council (CSAT) – hence over key institutions such as the secret services and the regulatory framework of national defense and security (the president and the security services press for an increasingly large concept of security); he nominates several top positions in the judicial system; and crucially, he can constitutionally nominate another prime minister than from the party that has a relative majority after elections.

But overall, the president is dependent de jure on the parliament and de facto on the political parties (Constantin 2010, 217).

Romania has had several types of presidents so far, if one considers the relationship between presidents and prime ministers. In the aftermath of the 1991 constitution, the dominant political vision did not include the notion of cohabitation. The new leadership during president Ion Iliescu's first two terms (1990–1996) did not accept cohabitation since the 1989 regime change was considered as an opportunity for bureaucratic reforms and for the adoption of a one-party pluralism of reform communism (rather than Western-type pluralism). Hence their "ideology of consensus," with its technocratic base (competence and expertise) of political neutrality, was understood as diminution of politics and exclusion of competitive bargaining processes (Siani-Davies 2005, 206–19, 244–61), delegitimization of any opposition (at least until 1992), and domination of FSN. The new leadership had a profile of apparatchiks of the second or third echelons of the Communist Party, representing the generation of technocrats of the 1970s who replaced the older communist leaders associated with the personal concentration of power in the hands of Ceauşescu and his nationalist-autarkic rule. Several wings of the FSN split during the 1990s to create new parties that purported to recruit more Europeanized technocrats and oppose the older elites.

President Emil Constantinescu's term (1996–2000) brought atomized coalition governments to the forefront. He was supported by the Democratic Convention of Romania (CDR), itself a coalition of the "historical" parties (notably the Christian-Democratic National Peasant Party, PNŢ-CD, and the National Liberal Party, PNL), in alliance with UDMR and the Democratic Party (PD, a splinter group from FSN). He proved that a president without his party's support cannot influence governmental coalition (Ionescu 2007, 265). CDR disintegrated in 2000, while its main party (PNŢ-CD) never won parliamentary seats again. This was an extreme example of fragmentation and conflict within the governing coalitions, and therefore by the mid-2000s the idea of changing the proportional system of representation into a majoritarian one made important headway. Ultimately, however, as we will see further on, the parties opted for variants of proportional systems, thereby conserving the overall patronage logic as well as the necessity for governmental coalitions. Majoritarian electoral systems probably would have propelled PSD to supermajorities due to its vast and resilient local patronage networks, but the hybrid proportional system already has ensured its parliamentary dominance since 2012.

The third mandate of president Iliescu was inaugurated in 2000 after an election that saw the emergence of a far-right nationalist party (Greater Romania Party, PRM) whose leader, Corneliu Vadim Tudor, reached the second round of the presidential elections. As before 1996, Iliescu and his party

PSD perfected the consensus discourse and exponentially developed local patronage relations with strict scrutiny from the party's national headquarters and the personal control of Prime Minister Adrian Năstase.

Traian Băsescu's two terms (2004–2012) inaugurated a new round of conflict-ridden cohabitation that capitalized on the emerging political cleavage centered on the issue of corruption. He was supported in 2004 by the PDL-PNL coalition (Truth and Justice, DA). His terms were marked by numerous political scandals, crises, and governmental instability, and he pressed for a majoritarian two-party system. He oversaw a modification of the electoral law that amended the proportional system yet did not – because of resistance in parliament – result in a "first past the post" system. He pressed for a focused state, as he often referred to the metaphor of the ship commander and the "active president" (*președinte jucător*). Băsescu envisioned his presidential role as a supra-head of government, notably when announcing major governmental policies, commenting on legislation, or expressing views on government activity. He went through two unsuccessful impeachment procedures: April 2007 (impeachment rejected by Romania's Constitutional Court, then voted for by parliament; the president was suspended but a referendum reconfirmed him) and July 2012 (the Constitutional Court expressed an unclear opinion about the impeachment; the parliament voted for it; the referendum was overwhelmingly in favor of the impeachment, but the Constitutional Court invalidated the popular vote because the electoral participation narrowly missed the legal quorum). Unable to govern *via* parties as he wished and faced with two difficult cohabitations, Băsescu inaugurated alternative mechanisms that avoided the parliament altogether such as presidential commissions on various subjects[15] and encouraged the increasing influence of secret and security services in politics.

Klaus Iohannis, elected in a landslide popular vote in 2014, tried to reorient the idea of the presidency. He rejected the idea of "active" presidency as embodied by Băsescu and was faced from the onset with a cohabitation context. With no influence on parliamentary majorities throughout his mandate, his approach to the equilibrium within the political regime was markedly different from his predecessors. His one-year (2016) experiment with minority technocratic government ended in one of the largest electoral victories of PSD. In November 2015, a tragic fire at a concert venue (*Colectiv Club*) left sixty-five dead and generated massive street protests in Bucharest under the slogan "Corruption kills" – a reference to the shady authorizations that the venue obtained from corrupt local officials. The PSD government resigned, and a new government was formed – led by the former European commissioner Dacian Cioloș. The particularity of this government was that it enjoyed broad support across the political spectrum in parliament. As a self-identified "technocratic" government with a limited mandate, its aim was to transcend political conflict and implement several consensual policies. Its dependence on mainstream political parties in parliament, however, made it impossible for the technocratic government to challenge the patronage networks of the parties, especially the ones engrained in the local administrative structures. At the end of the year, PSD came back to power with a landslide victory.

Each time, presidential elections tend to reconfigure the political sphere, and with each new president Romania adapts its political regime. The president's apparent lack of constitutional instruments conflicts with being the elected position with the largest political participation and electoral legitimacy. Therefore, presidents attempt to reshape the political regime in order to find ways of dealing with the ubiquitous patronage party network and their parliamentary domination. But while the president is dependent for electoral mobilization and parliamentary cooperation on the parties, the parties also need the support of winning candidates who may generate significant premiums for their party structure and improve their credentials within the networks of local notables and citizens.

SHIFTING POLITICAL CLEAVAGES AND PATRONAGE

After the major political cleavage of the 1990s centered on communism's legacy faded, during the past fifteen years, the dominant political cleavages focused on corruption (Iancu 2019, 161–86) and national identity. The origin and the carriers of the anti-corruption discourse are the presidents, the NGOs, and actors within the justice system (notably the DNA). Conversely, the major political parties prefer nationalist and conservative repertoires partly to deflect the anti-corruption discourse that targets their core patronage mechanisms. The recently formed Save Romania Union is the only exception of a parliamentary party fully engaged in the anti-corruption discourse.

Political parties in Romania are understood as instruments for governing, while their representative role is rather marginal.[16] Patronage also explains the absence of left-right ideological cleavages between political parties and the stabilization of the party system: the major parties govern with the help of several small partners (UNPR, ALDE, and UDMR). UDMR – the Hungarian minority's party – was built in the 1990s using the same logic as the PSD – as a party with powerful and resilient local patronage networks that aim to have uninterrupted access to the central government's resources. It participated in governing coalitions and supported minority governments almost continuously after 1996. Since 2012, however, governing coalitions can be formed without its support and therefore its access to the Romanian government's resources is somewhat more limited. A new political patron (Fidesz and

Viktor Orbán) has now emerged and UDMR gradually has aligned itself with Orbán's identity politics.

Since there has been a significant convergence of public policies of all political parties and very limited left-right ideological differentiation in Romania, political distinction is projected on the adversary's intrinsic corruption. Much of the political debate revolves around the idea that the other party is more corrupt. It is the reason each party records all episodes of fraud in order to make the difference politically in the absence of other criteria. There is an ongoing rhetorical struggle over the meaning of "corruption": while the street protests define corruption as the ultimate reason for the country's problems ("corruption kills"), over time political parties have developed a defense against this by pointing to the legitimizing effect of electoral support.[17] Due to the electoral system for local elections, local party officials can be reelected with very few votes – and the parties have capitalized on the notion that mayors accused of corruption may get reelected to claim popular democratic support that invalidates the DNA's prosecution. Moreover, parties convince their most active constituencies that anti-corruption prosecutors lack impartiality and thus try to delegitimize the DNA.

This corruption-centered political cleavage has displaced the dominant antagonism during the 1990s, namely (neo-)communists versus anticommunists (Gussi 2007, 117–32; Gussi 2011), which emphasized the ideological opposition over the meaning of the 1989 events and the continuity of the pre-1989 institutions and political personnel. By comparison, in Hungary, the former communist-anticommunist cleavage has been overwritten by the national-antinational cleavage by Fidesz, as illustrated notably by Prime Minister Viktor Orbán's rhetoric when defining Fidesz's political legitimacy as a governing party and Hungary's role in Europe.[18] In general, such a rhetoric is a revival of the idea that the majority's will should have no boundaries, not only in terms of numbers (parliamentary supermajority) but also in terms of the added legitimacy by ethnic and cultural dimensions.

In Romania, however, the radicalization of nationalism has had only a limited effect to date. Several reasons stand out: first, as mentioned above, the nationalist rhetoric can only partly displace the political cleavage based on anti-corruption (former prime minister Victor Ponta's nationalist discourse was defeated by Klaus Iohannis' anti-corruption platform during the 2014 presidential elections); second, the two narratives – nationalist and anti-corruption – have not yet been mobilized together like in Hungary. Fidesz successfully depicted its main adversary, the Socialist Party (MSZP), as both corrupt and anti-national; rather, in Romania both anti-corruption and nationalist rhetoric tend to be used in contradiction and rarely in conjunction. However, the current leadership of PSD has started to include significant elements of Fidesz' political discourse, including the antagonistic references to George Soros who has sponsored a large amount of liberal civil society projects in Romania since the 1990s.

Anti-corruption discourses delegitimize almost integrally the political class and political parties and feed citizens' distrust in politics in general. The circularity of the anti-political discourse highlights, moreover, the difficulty of the simultaneous process of regaining trust in the political class *and* enlarging the autonomous sphere of administration that would mean reducing the influence of the political class. Trust (Tilly 2005) – a key variable of any process of democratic consolidation – becomes an elusive element, and this further nourishes the anti-political and populist dimensions of Romanian political culture (Soare 2010, 87–118; Pârvu 2015, 259–74).

The contextual differences notwithstanding, there are striking similarities between contemporary Hungary and Romania in terms of anti-pluralist and anti-political attitudes and discourses. Fidesz and PSD view political opposition as radically illegitimate. According to their current practices, solely Fidesz or PSD can represent the nation, and conflict with the party is described as conflict with the nation. But a technocratic mirage is a frequent narrative of the newer parties such as the USR. In this sense, all these parties converge on the idea that "real" problems need rapid and clear solutions, preferably dealt with by loyal party members in the case of PSD or Fidesz (for party loyalty equates with national loyalty as the party is the nation itself) or dealt with by experts and "technocrats" in the case of their opposition. Public debate on major policies thus is seen as futile by most actors involved.

The delegitimization of political parties and of their role for governing and recruitment of the political personnel, and of politics as such, is illustrated by the 2016 local elections in Romania. Wishing to gain electoral support, USR's candidates explicitly wanted to "save Bucharest from politicians,"[19] as if common interests and priorities could be dealt with solely by expertise, that is, without politics. This follows the recent liberalization of the legislation governing the formation of political parties and the emergence of new parties that claim – in contrast to the mainstream parties – to be repositories of expertise and managerial competence, and not of political skills and partisan interests. However, their weak organizational skills prevent them from seriously challenging the existing hegemony of the (new) PNL and PSD in regional and local elections.

Romanian political parties' policy convergence is exemplified by the fact that there are no left-wing parties. PSD never had a genuine left orientation but rather a developmentalist one (and a constant focus on economic growth). Having embraced legitimation through expertise, and with the capacity to populate governmental and administrative positions – hence, to recruit experts and top bureaucrats for policymaking – its ideological credentials on the left were deemed superfluous. At the same time, the PNL is very socially conservative and is also allied (as PSD) with the major religious organizations. Both embrace neoliberal economic policies, the only difference being in rhetoric: while PNL adopts positions that condemn the "socially assisted" population (a discourse that, when it is not overtly racialized and directed against the Roma population, moralizes poverty as personal debauchery), PSD alternates policies for diminishing poverty with highly regressive forms of fiscal reform.

This is a manifest paradox in Romanian politics: while the ubiquitous public discourse denounces PSD from a neoliberal standpoint as "communist" (during the anti-corruption street protests PSD is called "the Red Plague"), its actual policies are neoliberal. Moreover, most other parties repositioned themselves several times and generated scissions and alliances around an elitist view on society coupled with a neoliberal view on economy with a minimal state. The perception that the only politics is a politics on the right produced ideological U-turns such as the striking example of the Democratic Party, a splinter-party from FSN, initially defined as social-democratic and affiliated to the Socialist International until 2005; in 2006, it joined the European People's Party and in 2007 it became the PDL (after a merger with the smaller Liberal Democratic Party and a split from the National Liberal Party). This was to be the main party on the right, especially after the 2014 merger with PNL. The vast majority of the new parties formed after the liberalization of party formation legislation (in 2015) are now to the right of PNL.

As elsewhere in East Central Europe, an older political cleavage (autochthonism *vs.* liberalism/cosmopolitanism) is seeing new life. In Romania, where the two main parties – PNL and PSD – have a significant convergence in policy and personnel, this cleavage is not pitting one against the other nor against challenger parties from the margins of the political regime. Instead, all these parties (old and new) pick up autochthonism as the primary political discourse, with the corresponding risks of legitimizing the most untenable positions. The cleavage is enacted mostly in opposition to a "Soros-sponsored globalist civil society" in stark similarity with Hungary. In effect, memorial culture in the region always was ambivalent about incorporating fascism into national anticommunist memory (Mark 2011, 93–125). The nationalist rhetoric and stereotypes become especially salient during elections. For instance, during the 2014 presidential campaign, the PSD candidate (incumbent prime minister Victor Ponta) ran on a failed attempt to create a new national "social contract" focusing on ethnic elements (*Mândri că suntem români*/Proud to be Romanians). After 2004, PDL and president Traian Băsescu also used a heavy nationalist rhetoric, especially on the issue of unification with the Republic of Moldova. This means that, in contradiction with the Fidesz example, a generalized but somewhat desubstantialized ethnic (and often racist) nationalism, irredentism, and xenophobia are consensual and widespread among all Romanian political actors, and they are mobilized whenever considered to be useful for ritualized popular campaigns or political strategy (during elections, national holidays, defense of "national" values against "foreigners," multinational companies, etc.) accompanied by sporadic flare ups of anti-foreign capital rhetoric (e.g., supermarkets and prices) and anti-Hungarian messages that rarely have translated into actual policy. The universal, but conformist, adoption of nationalism by all parties may explain the current inadequacy of the previously salient and powerful right-wing extremist nationalist parties in Romania like the Greater Romania Party (Gallagher 2005),[20] despite fertile ground for the reception of such positions.

While Hungary had a radical and strident position rejecting European initiatives on refugees and built walls to protect the "Hungarian nation" against them, the Romanian government adopted a low-key position that shared the underlying fears yet resulted in few policy choices. This is partly due to the absence of actual refugees at the borders but also because there is little political advantage in enacting radical nationalism when most parties are positioned similarly. Moreover, the Romanian elites still share a substantial positive consensus on European affairs and avoid (contrary to Hungary) transforming European policy antagonisms into an internal political cleavage. Importantly, while Viktor Orbán openly challenges EU policy toward Vladimir Putin, in Romania signs of rapprochement with Russia would mean instant political suicide. This can be explained on a historical scale in part because of Romania's unique discomfort with its Eastern position and consensual rejection of any discourse that would reclaim its regional cultural position in the Balkans or Eastern Europe (Todorova 1997).

In Hungary, Fidesz and Viktor Orbán devised an antagonistic collective grand narrative about Hungary and the ethnically defined nation, about comprehensive social and political change, about Europe and the world characterized by insecurity and disorder, suggesting self-inclusion and reinforcing "national" values. Orbán's ambitious rhetoric is about Hungary's "mission," "rebirth," "survival," and "truth," a rhetoric of crisis and survival, a moral revolution. A corresponding systematic autochthonist grand narrative is less relevant in Romania for the reason that it is suffused in all political parties' discourses, alternating with technocratic pro-European legitimation and anti-corruption discourses.

In this sense, Romanian political elites and citizens alike are overwhelmingly pro-EU; there is little significant anti-EU rhetoric or movement. The "West" still remains, at least rhetorically, a normative standard Romania should admire. The "West" concentrates both institutions (EU, NATO, IMF, WB, etc.) and values. These legitimize the dominant and widespread neoliberal view on society and economy. The slogan of the USL coalition when trying to impeach (in 2012) the president (in a conflict that was also about which one of them is the real westernizing force) was *"Vreau o țară ca afară"* or "I want a country like in the West,"[21] meaning that he was not westernized enough.

CONCLUSION

Romanian political parties do not seem to have the power to oppose the National Anticorruption Directorate's (DNA) increased prosecutions, also strongly pushed by the EU, which led to convictions of numerous MPs, local elected officials, civil servants, and so on. Their stake in recent years rather has been to change the categories of criminal law[22] concerning corruption. Increasingly vulnerable, political parties have to accept the obvious presence of intelligence services in politics, a situation that increases the scale of the regime's crisis.

The current structural crisis of Romanian political parties and their incapacity to fend off the onslaught of anti-corruption prosecutions demonstrate that these parties have a patrimonial understanding of the state, they behave as if they owned the state, they distribute its resources, and they use politics in a patrimonial way because they do not know what to do with politics itself. Hence, the absence of a clear left-right ideological commitment.

The fundamental limit of the current anti-corruption approach focused on the DNA is that, however many of their political personnel are tried and convicted, the parties themselves are not changing their *modus operandi.* The next mayor, minister, or local official will continue the same behavior, ask for more legal protection from his party, and press for even more insulation and consolidation of patronage networks. In recent years, the DNA has become the institution that focuses political passions and electoral programs, since anti-corruption prosecutors completed the investigation of some key characters, with resounding convictions: former Prime Minister Adrian Năstase and oligarchs like Sorin Ovidiu Vântu and Dan Voiculescu. The way parties operate makes them easy victims of the DNA: access to public resources is mediated almost exclusively through party networks. The DNA's intransigence has sparked numerous heated debates. The problem is that, barring a new paradigm structuring the parties, reform *via* the DNA is insufficient: prosecutors cannot reform the political class, the system of patronage and the relations between the parties and the state, and public resources. The DNA's future institutional role is unclear as of now, even if it benefits from the EU's entire support. In fact, the entire political model should be rethought, a regime that relies on a specific model of political party and a successful but eventually highly destructive formula – patronage.

NOTES

1. This is partially the case for the Anticorrp project (www.anticorrp.eu), designed to develop strategies to combat present-day corruption. This chapter does not consider corruption as a sign of backwardness as in Anechiarico and Jacobs 1996. On the limits of such a normative approach on corruption in Romania, see Zerilli (2013): 212–29.

2. In 1990s, the first contenders were the traditional parties with their prewar roots (the National Peasant Party, the National Liberal Party, and the Romanian Social Democratic Party).

3. *"Funcționar public," "funcții și demnități publice."*

4. "Prezență vot," http://prezenta.bec.ro/, accessed June 25, 2019. For the second round of the 2014 presidential elections, see "Rezultate," http://bec2014.roaep.ro/r ezultate-turul-ii-2/index.html, accessed June 25, 2019.

5. Indeed, recent street protests have had important electoral and political results – since 2011 such movements have toppled two governments (Emil Boc's in early 2012 and Victor Ponta's in late 2015) and blocked the special law designed for the *Roșia Montană* Gold Corporation.

6. The National Liberal Party, PNL, and the Liberal-Democrat Party, PDL, merged and formed the new PNL in 2014.

7. According to a study conducted by the Romanian NGO Institutul de Politici Publice in 2011, 61 percent of the government's strategic fund (*fondul de rezervă*) was directed to cities with mayors belonging to the then-governing Liberal Democrat Party (PDL), 18 percent went to PSD city halls (at that time with more parliamentary mandates than PDL), and 9 percent went to PNL city halls (*Adevărul*, April 14, 2011).

8. In 2004, president Băsescu nominated Călin Popescu Tăriceanu, from an alliance that did not yet have a parliamentary majority – having won less mandates than the PSD. Soon, however, a government was formed which lasted – after 2007 as a minority government – until 2008; the same president nominated then Emil Boc from the PDL – even if his party again had less seats in parliament than the PSD. A new government was formed – a grand coalition with the PSD, for a year, and after 2009 a coalition government led by the PDL.

9. Popescu, Chiru, and Toma (2014).

10. Parliamentary mandate is incompatible with local mandate.

11. Miat (2014); România Liberă (2013); Realitatea.net (2016); Roșca (2016). In August 2015, PP-DD was absorbed by UNPR; the latter remains an ally of PSD.

12. Formerly the Romanian Humanist Party (PUR), PSD's constant ally; in June 2015 it merged with the Liberal Reform Party and formed a new party, the Liberals and Democrats' Alliance Party (ALDE, with seats in parliament).

13. Revista 22 (2015).

14. Formed in February 2011 and composed of PSD, PNL, and PC, and joined by UNPR for the December 2012 parliamentary elections.

15. For instance, Presidential Commission for Analyzing Communist Dictatorship in Romania (2006); Presidential Commission for Analyzing and Creating Health Policies (2008); Presidential Commission on Education (2008); Presidential Commission on Agricultural Strategy (2013), and so on.

16. Ștefan and Grecu (2014), though from a different perspective, demonstrate the failed representative function of a parliament considered by MPs as a "transit station" on their way to (local or national) executive offices.

17. A significant number of MPs under prosecution or even convicted are re-elected in parliament (Negoiță 2014, 14–24).

18. See, for instance, the March 2014 speech on Hungary's national holiday (Orbán 2014a) and on July 2014 (Orbán 2014b).

19. Diacu (2016).

20. In contrast to the 1990s up to the early 2000s. After 2004, the Greater Romania Party (PRM) is in electoral decline, while the Romanian National Unity Party (PUNR) was absorbed in 2006 by the Conservative Party (PC), after its electoral success during the 1990s.

21. Originally a pop song.

22. For instance, in December 2013 when some MPs from practically all parliamentary parties proposed several bills (on amnesty of criminals and politicians, and a modification of the Criminal Law pertaining to the conflict of interest of MPs and civils servants) that caused public outrage (referred to as "Black Tuesday").

BIBLIOGRAPHY

Anechiarico, Frank, and James B. Jacobs. 1996. *The Pursuit of Absolute Integrity: How Corruption Makes Government Ineffective.* Chicago: University of Chicago Press.

Bojin, Lucian. 2010. "Câteva observații despre organizarea puterii executive." In *Comentarii la Constituția României,* edited by Gabriel Andreescu, Miklós Bakk, Lucian Bojin, and Valentin Constantin, 133–89. Iași: Polirom.

Briquet, Jean-Louis. 1997. *La tradition en mouvement. Clientélisme et politique en Corse.* Paris: Belin.

Constantin, Valentin. 2010. "Constituția României privită din perspectiva supremației dreptului (*rule of law*)." In *Comentarii la Constituția României,* edited by Gabriel Andreescu, Miklós Bakk, Lucian Bojin, and Valentin Constantin, 191–230. Iași: Polirom.

Crowther, William, and Oana-Valentina Suciu. 2013. "Romania." In *The Handbook of Political Change in Eastern Europe,* Third Edition, edited by Sten Berglund, Joakim Ekman, Kevin Deegan-Krause, and Terje Knutenin, 367–406. Cheltenham: Edward Elgar.

Diacu, Loredana. 2016. "Nicușor Dan, după retragerea lui Orban: A venit timpul să salvăm Bucureștiul de politicieni." http://epochtimes-romania.com/news/nicus or-dan-dupa-retragerea-lui-orban-a-venit-timpul-sa-salvam-bucurestiul-de-politic ieni---245998, accessed June 25, 2019.

Engels, Jens Ivo. 2008. "Corruption as a Political Issue in Modern Societies: France, Great Britain and the United States in the Long 19th Century." *Public Voices* X (2): 68–86.

———. 2014. "La modernisation du clientélisme politique dans l'Europe du XIXe et du XXe siècle. L'impact du capitalisme et des nouvelles formes d'organisation politique." In *Patronage et corruption politiques dans l'Europe contemporaine,* edited by Frédéric Monier, Olivier Dard, and Jens Ivo Engels, 33–50. Paris: Armand Colin.

Grabbe, Heather. 2006. *The EU's Transformative Power: Europeanization through Conditionality in Central and Eastern Europe*. New York: Palgrave Macmillan.

Gallagher, Tom. 2005. *Theft of a Nation: Romania since Communism*. London: Hurst & Co.

Grosescu, Raluca. 2007. "Traiectorii de conversie politică a nomenclaturii în România. Spre o taxonomie a partidelor create de fostele elite comuniste." In *Elitele comuniste înainte şi după 1989. Anuarul IICCR*, 199–231. Iaşi: Polirom.

Gussi, Alexandru. 2007. "L'anticommunisme en Roumanie (1996–2000)." *Studia Politica. Romanian Political Science Review* 7 (1): 117–32.

———. 2011. *La Roumanie face à son passé communiste. Mémoires et cultures politiques*. Paris: l'Harmattan.

Iancu, Alexandra. 2019. "Les présidents accusent: Moralité et (anti-)corruption en Roumanie contemporaine." In *Corruption et politique en Europe. Enjeux, réformes et controverses*, edited by Alexandra Iancu and Silvia Marton, 161–86. Paris: l'Harmattan.

Ionaşcu, Alexandra. 2006. "From Political to Party Patronage: The Case of the Romanian Post-Communism." *Sfera Politicii* 123–124: 62–77.

———. 2007. "Volatilité et stabilisation du personnel gouvernemental. Les cabinets roumains: 1919–1939 et 1989–2004." *Studia Politica. Romanian Political Science Review* 7 (1): 71–89.

Ionaşcu, Alexandra, and Sorina Soare. 2012a. "Le financement des partis politiques et leurs transformations organisationnelles. Un aperçu du cas roumain." *Transitions* 52 (1): 17–43.

———. 2012b. "În căutarea unui Mecena. Mecanisme şi procese de finanţare ale partidelor politice în România postcomunistă." *Sfera Politicii* 169: 56–64.

Ionescu, Alexandra. 2007. "Que font et que sont les partis politiques roumains?" *Studia Politica. Romanian Political Science Review* 7 (2): 257–66.

———. 2009. *Du Parti-Etat à l'Etat des partis. Changer de régime politique en Roumanie*. Bucharest: Editura Academiei Române.

Mair, Peter, and Richard S. Katz. 1995. "Changing Models of Party Organization and Party Democracy: The Emergence of the Cartel Party." *Party Politics* 1 (1): 5–28.

Mark, James. 2011. *The Unfinished Revolution: Making Sense of the Communist Past in Central-Eastern Europe*. New Haven, CT: Yale University Press.

Marton, Silvia. 2014. "Patronage, représentation et élections en Roumanie de 1875 à 1914." In *Patronage et corruption politiques dans l'Europe contemporaine*, edited by Frédéric Monier, Olivier Dard, and Jens Ivo Engels, 141–66. Paris: Armand Colin.

Miat, Sergiu. 2014. "Alţi doi parlamentari PP-DD trec la partidul lui Oprea." http://www.cotidianul.ro/alti-doi-parlamentari-pp-dd-trec-la-partidul-lui-oprea-238748/, accessed June 25, 2019.

Monier, Frédéric. 2014. "'Mais la véritable corruption n'existe plus.' Les patronages à l'ère de la critique." In *Patronage et corruption politiques dans l'Europe contemporaine*, edited by Frédéric Monier, Olivier Dard and Jens Ivo Engels, 13–50. Paris: Armand Colin.

Negoiță, Ciprian. 2014. "Imunitatea parlamentară. Limită a democrației în România postcomunistă." *Sfera Politicii* 177: 14–24.

O'Dwyer, Connor. 2006. *Runaway State Building. Patronage Politics and Democratic Development.* Baltimore: Johns Hopkins University Press.

Orbán, Viktor 2014a. "Orbán Viktor ünnepi beszéde." http://mno.hu/belfold/orban-viktor-unnepi-beszede-1216150, accessed June 25, 2019.

———. 2014b. "Full text of Viktor Orbán's speech at Băile Tuşnad (Tusnádfürdő) of 26 July 2014." https://budapestbeacon.com/full-text-of-viktor-orbans-speech-at-baile-tusnad-tusnadfurdo-of-26-july-2014/, accessed June 25, 2019.

Pârvu, Camil-Alexandru. 2015. "Populism and Democratic Malaise in Post-communist Romania." In *Thinking through Transition Liberal Democracy, Authoritarian Pasts, and Intellectual History in East Central Europe after 1989*, edited by Michal Kopeček and Piotr Wciślik, 259–74. Budapest: Central European University Press.

Popescu, Marina, Mihail Chiru, and Raluca Toma. 2014. "Parlamentarii migrează. Cauze, consecințe şi explicații comparative." http://www.openpolitics.ro/nou tati/homepage/parlamentarii-migreaza-cauze-consecinte-si-explicatii-comparative. html, accessed June 25, 2019.

Preda, Cristian, and Sorina Soare. 2008. *Regimul, partidele şi sistemul politic din România.* Bucureşti: Nemira.

Realitatea.net 2016. "Valeriu Zgonea: Parlamentarii UNPR care au trecut la PSD erau membri PP-DD, până recent." http://www.realitatea.net/valeriu-zgonea-parl amentarii-unpr-care-au-trecut-la-psd-erau-membri-pp-dd-pana-recent_1903541. html, accessed June 25, 2019.

Revista 22. 2015. "Deputații resping Ordonanța 55 privind migrația politică. Aleşii care au migrat NU îşi pierd mandatele." https://revista22.ro/actualitate-interna /deputatii-resping-ordonanta-55-privind-migratia-politica-alesii-care-au-migrat-nu-isi-pierd-mandatele, accessed June 25, 2019.

România Liberă. 2013. "Migrație în Parlament: Trei senatori PPDD au trecut la PSD, iar doi deputați independenți, la UNPR." http://www.romanialibera.ro/politica/ins titutii/migratie-in-parlament--trei-senatori-ppdd-au-trecut-la-psd--iar-doi-deputati-independenti--la-unpr-314596, accessed June 25, 2019.

Roşca, Iulia. 2016. "Şase deputați UNPR trec la PSD. Cinci dintre ei provin din PP-DD." http://www.hotnews.ro/stiri-politic-20854658-sase-deputati-unpr-trec-p sd.htm, accessed June 25, 2019.

Shefter, Martin. 1977. "Party and Patronage: Germany, England and Italy." *Politics and Society* 7: 403–51.

———. 1993. *Political Parties and the State: The American Historical Experience.* Princeton, NJ: Princeton University Press.

Siani-Davies, Peter. 2005. *The Romanian Revolution of December 1989.* Ithaca, NY: Cornell University Press.

Soare, Sorina. 2010. "Genul şi speciile populismului românesc. O incursiune pe tărâmul *Tinereții fără bătrânețe* şi al *Vieții fără de moarte.*" In *Partide şi personalități populiste în România postcomunistă*, edited by Sergiu Gherghina and Sergiu Mişcoiu, 87–118. Iaşi: Institutul European.

Ştefan, Laurentiu, and Răzvan Grecu. 2014. "'The Waiting Room': Romanian Parliament after 1989." In *Parliamentary Elites in Central and Eastern Europe:*

Recruitment and Representation, edited by Elena Semenova, Michael Edinger, and Heinrich Best, 194–215. London: Routledge.

Thompson, Dennis F. 2013. "Two Concepts of Corruption." Edmond J. Safra Research Lab Working Papers 16. Harvard University.

Tilly, Charles. 2005. *Trust and Rule*. Cambridge: Cambridge University Press.

Todorova, Maria. 1997. *Imagining the Balkans*. New York: Oxford University Press.

Zerilli, Filippo M. 2013. "Corruption and Anti-corruption. Local Discourses and International Practices in Post-Socialist Romania." *Human Affairs* 23: 212–29.

Conclusion

Hungary—Brave and New? Dissecting a Realistic Dystopia

János Mátyás Kovács and Balázs Trencsényi

Let us begin with a confession. Following the Weberian norm of revealing authors' value choices, we admit to harboring strong reservations about the System of National Cooperation (SNC). Otherwise, we would not speak of dystopia. There is no reason to conceal our liberal predisposition—even if the very fact that Fidesz was able to revitalize itself in the 2000s and the Orbán regime managed to thrive during the 2010s proves that the liberal consensus in Hungary has eroded during the past two decades (Kovács 2017; Trencsényi 2017).

As transpiring from the chapters of our volume, our research group has strong doubts about the democratic nature of Orbán's vision of illiberal (more exactly, anti-liberal[1]) democracy as well as about the uniqueness of his regime and its matureness as a system. Also, many of us challenged the truism concerning Orbán's exclusive role in designing and operating the SNC based on a long-cherished master plan. It was rather presumed that the regime is tamed by repeated compromises between the ruler and his adversaries, be they oligarchs, pressure groups, the European Union (EU), or citizens-at-large, and made popular by a variety of "carrots" instead of using just "sticks." As a consequence, a great many groups in Hungarian society may consider themselves winners of Orbanization today. We also supposed that the expansion of the SNC was grounded in a great deal of improvisation and exhibited the zigzags of *Realpolitik*. Orbán was often assisted by sheer luck or, alternatively, he made a virtue of necessity without any scruples.

Relying on these assumptions and our coauthors' insights, we will first rethink some concepts needed for a thorough understanding of the Fidesz universe and formulate a few hypotheses about its origins and modus operandi.

These concepts and assumptions then will be applied and tested in a review of the consecutive stages of the rise and partial consolidation of the Orbán regime and of its possible future evolution.

What do we mean by a *realistic* dystopia? Why is Aldous Huxley and his *Brave New World* invoked in the title of our volume? His vision in 1932 was a gloomy guess and a resolute warning, extrapolating frightening trends of social evolution at the time. In contrast, Orbán is a doer more than a thinker. He considers his own image of the future pleasing, and he has been working around the clock to put it in practice since the mid-1990s. Crucially, with remarkably little open violence and a creative talent for the use of law, corruption, intimidation, ideological mobilization, conversion of political power into economic assets, paralysis of constitutional checks and balances, and media capture, Fidesz has managed to attain a near-hegemonic position. Hence, the SNC has become a real-life dystopia *par excellence* in the eyes of liberals, and a possible future for many polities the world over.

The *Brave New World* imagined by Huxley is a depoliticized eugenic technocracy that was supposed to emerge in advanced countries; it is communist, liberal, and fascist at the same time, where rigid social hierarchies are nuanced by access to consumerist, psychedelic, and sexual satisfaction. In contrast, *Brave New Hungary* is a much less spectacular and rational regime, the components of which are glued together by the authoritarian and collectivist traditions including conformism, helplessness, inertia, and the like as well as by self-defense against the external, unknown Other.[2] However, social habituation described by Huxley, rooted in the rejection of mobility, openness, and indeterminacy, is common to both: "liking what you've *got* to do. All conditioning aims at that: making people like their unescapable social destiny" (Huxley 1932, 17). Yet, Huxley's new world projects a global end of history, an apocalypse of modernism, whereas Orbán's new world is located in a temporary suspense even if it promises an escape from the adversities of history through envisioning an everlasting pro-Fidesz *Gemeinschaft* that is premodern and postmodern at the same time.

We also twist John Rawls' term of "realistic utopia." Our aim is to emphasize the pragmatic nature of the construction process, in the course of which realism has overwritten idealism in the architects' mind time and again. Undoubtedly, as years passed, the initial vision of the brave new regime has radicalized a great deal but rarely crossed the boundaries of viability. Nevertheless, the Young Democrats never miss any chance to speed up the construction of SNC when new spaces open up for invasion. They do not wait passively until new possibilities arise to move ahead and often take huge risks to force the expansion of the regime's room to maneuver.

BENDING CONSERVATISM

Fidesz's doublespeak of "moving ahead" actually means moving backward, that is, rolling back time by laying the foundations of a "conservative revolution" that reaches back to the end of the nineteenth century and the interwar period for ideological ammunition. The SNC embodies a social engineering project that includes both the usual *desiderata* of old-school continental conservatism (respecting national tradition, Christian faith, law and order, paternalist state, patriarchal family values, etc.) and its *odiosa* (challenging cosmopolitanism, secularization, the rule of law, market rivalry, gender equality, etc.). Similar to the interwar "conservative revolutionaries," the engineers of the SNC are aware both of the constructed nature of tradition and of the task to actively recreate it rather than just to subscribe to its prescriptive power.

Therefore, the political style of the SNC can be described as re-sacralized mass politics combined with anti-modernism, which recently was baptized by Orbán as "Christian Democracy" to both normalize the SNC in the eyes of the European conservative public and reclaim the "real" conservative tradition from the mainstream of the European People's Party (EPP).[3] In reality, Orbán's regime jumps over the post-1945 Christian Democratic political doctrine that reconciled itself with the idea of economic liberalism and the rule of law within the doctrine of *Soziale Marktwirtschaft*. Since then, it also has endorsed the separation of state and church and recognized the merits of civil society. More recently, Christian Democrats in Western and Northern Europe weakened their ethnic and gender biases to a large degree, while retaining a commitment to the values of social solidarity and subscribing to a high-profile version of environmentalism as well as a lower-profile version of political correctness.

Loudly proclaiming a change of the guard between the "sixty-eighters" and his generation, Orbán declared a return to an allegedly authentic version of conservatism by reviving the norms of the *Kinder-Küche-Kirche/Travail-Famille-Patrie* triangles,[4] and using racist, homophobic, and chauvinistic language. At the same time, Fidesz denies the principle of social solidarity by promulgating a militant, almost libertarian critique of the welfare state and drawing on hate speech against the "undeserving poor" (often ethnicized as Roma or labeled as migrant). In order to fend off the accusation of neoliberalism, the architects of the SNC covered the introduction of the flat tax and other measures of an "inverse Robin Hood" income policy (supported by trickle-down economics) with anti-elitist rhetoric, pouring scorn on transnational companies, banks, and business tycoons and showering praise on "hardworking ordinary men." This *ouvrierist* discourse also serves to deflect attention from state-managed corruption deals made for the benefit of

Orbán's close circle of oligarchs/cronies and his own family, the replacement of social assistance with public work, the degrading of welfare services in general, and passing a new labor law that severely restricts workers' rights,[5] as well as the entanglement of the regime with a handful of foreign multinational companies.

Meanwhile, the regime borrowed the ideal of the paternalist/interventionist state from interwar radical conservatism along with disrespect for local self-government and civil society as such (e.g., upon the inception of the SNC local governments were deprived of the resources and right to manage schools and hospitals). Hierarchy, discipline, loyalty, and internal cohesion (*esprit de corps*) are advanced as core values of state administration. Civil servants are wooed with a series of status privileges while under close supervision by the ruling party. In this respect, the SNC might remind the observer of both Horthy's authoritarian regime and the communist party-state. The same applies to the preferential treatment of armed forces, the creeping militarization of state institutions and society at large, and the establishment of state-controlled corporatist structures (professional associations, chambers) and GONGOs.[6] Orbán's ideal regime is willing and able to nationalize, centralize, regulate, and micro-manage as energetically as possible, as well as to exercise discretionary power over all major fields of society ranging from dethroning a business magnate all the way down to appointing and dismissing the coach of the leader's favorite soccer team. The principal guarantee of the stability of the regime is a unitary, quasi-Leninist government party of strong discipline (with a cohesive group of its top leaders staunchly loyal to Orbán) that faces a weak and split opposition situated on the left and right edges of the so-called central field of force.

Orbán builds his regime on neo-feudal networks of personal dependency on each and every level of society, from the smallest village up to himself. In cultural terms, the SNC dives even farther into the past, combining the Christian traditions of Hungarians with their pre-Christian nomadic heritage.[7] While post-1945 European Christian Democracy was firmly Occidentalist, Orbán's worldview (just like that of interwar radical nationalists in Hungary) is emphatically anti-Western and finds the spiritual and ethnic kin of Hungarians in Nazarbaev's Kazakhstan, or Erdoğan's Turkey.

Despite the fact that Viktor Orbán champions *illiberal* democracy as a model to follow since delivering his 2014 speech at Băile Tușnad (Transylvania), we suggest to (a) apply the concept of *anti-liberalism* to portray the fundamental principle of his "Frankenstate" (Scheppele 2013); and (b) dispute the democratic nature of this creature.[8] In our opinion, Fidesz ideologues who contend that democracy must be cleansed from its liberal prerequisites are not committed democrats who happen to dislike liberalism or who try to find a comfortable ideological habitat for democracy to secure its survival, but rather devoted anti-liberals and—*nolens volens*—non-democrats or even anti-democrats. As militant purifiers, they seek to establish an allegedly democratic regime without firm constitutional checks and balances, emptying it of popular participation, and paving the way for authoritarian rule.

The concept of "illiberal democracy" usually is employed to describe governments that, to put it simply, play the democratic game without meeting requirements of the rule of law such as separation of powers or freedom of speech.[9] Reflecting upon the thought experiment by Fareed Zakaria (1997) who suggested "illiberal democracy" to denote such new hybrids, many of our authors pointed to the tension between the two components of the term.[10] In Zakaria's view, illiberal democracies may demolish liberal institutions restricting popular sovereignty without jeopardizing free and fair elections. One may challenge this proposition by asking simple questions: Why would those who decide to get rid of legal constraints be ready to remain under control by the *demos* that can eventually turn its back on them? Why would they refrain from election fraud if they can get away with it unpunished? Finally, provided that for some reason "illiberal democrats" opt for retaining a half-liberal constitution, why would they not interpret it by means of the other half and occupy the remaining institutions of checks and balances with the help of their parliamentary majority?

The reader finds the answers in the nine-year history of the SNC, curbing democracy by means of a purposeful deactivation of liberal constitutionalism. The scenery of a democratic game may have remained on stage, but why mistake simulated democracy for a real one? Furthermore, the concept of illiberal democracy is unduly narrow because it focuses almost exclusively on the political components of such regimes. What happens if a politically illiberal government does not reject some key elements of *economic* liberalism? If one insists on the paradigm of hybridization, the SNC may be regarded as a dual-hybrid mixing political anti-liberalism with *some* economic freedom and the dire straits of simulated (depleted) democracy. To be sure, the rule of law is not immune to simulation either. The determination of Fidesz to maintain a modicum of constitutionalism by writing a Fundamental Law and engaging in "lawfare," that is, packaging arbitrary/anti-constitutional government decisions in laws passed by "their" parliament, are telling examples of pseudo-liberal governance.

Reality or appearance? Reason or rhetoric? Sincere belief or cynical cover discourse? Words or deeds?—questions like these have been tormenting analysts at least since Orbán started to talk about his "peacock dance" in the EU and prompted observers to pay attention to his real moves rather than to what he was saying.[11] Be as it may, we do not consider these questions particularly productive in understanding the workings of the SNC. Rather than speculating whether Orbán and his close associates said something sincere or not, we regard their utterances as speech acts that may matter at certain points and have an "illocutionary force." At the same time, we have done our best to explore the key ideas, norms, values, etc., that transpire from the real world of the SNC, even if they are unintended consequences of the spur-of-the-moment decisions of Fidesz, especially its leader.

UNDER THE SPELL OF A ONE-MAN SHOW

Our research group sought to nuance the popular assumption of Orbán's dominant role played in designing and operating the System of National Cooperation. As our research (and the SNC) evolved, we could not help but ask how such a privileged position could be sustained after much of the economy as well as key fields of social and cultural life had been occupied by Fidesz, and Orbán became surrounded by an oversized ruling elite, the "SNC knights" as Hungarians call them sarcastically. Why does the "king" not fall victim to strife among the oligarchs? Or does he? Thus far, Orbán has succeeded in crowding out his rivals,[12] checking his own appointees, disrupting hostile conspiracies within his party, neutralizing dissenters, and producing very few dissidents. This was already the case during the eight years from 2002 to 2010 he spent in opposition when he possessed neither as much carrot to appease the potential rebels nor as much stick to compel them as today.[13]

The image of strong internal cohesion of the regime, however, tends to deceive observers. It obscures sharp conflicts among oligarchs, pressure groups, generations, industries, regions, and the like, and creates the impression that the supreme leader wins all fights if they nevertheless break out behind the scenes. In our view, the metaphor of a "one-man show" alluding to autocratic rule prevented the analysts from recognizing a series of cases in which Orbán had to accept compromises to ensure his own political survival. True, he proved able to turn defeats into victories by escaping ahead masterfully and painted a glorious picture of his own invulnerability. Much of current "Orbanology" inside and outside of Hungary accepts that picture and thereby tacitly contributes to the leader's self-celebration. His heroic story goes like this: yes, the SNC is me, I am the creative mind behind this authentic design that is bound to stay with Hungarians for decades, at least as long as Admiral Horthy and General Secretary Kádár governed the country.

Orbán's unsurpassable contribution to the SNC has prompted quite a few critical analysts to find literary analogies and describe the regime's process of construction as an *Entwicklungsroman* whose main character sells his soul for power, money, and prestige. In the Budapest circles of liberal-minded intellectuals, Stendhal's Julien Sorel in *The Red and the Black* or Jean-Paul Sartre's Lucien Fleurier in *The Childhood of a Leader* are often referred to in this respect, while Thomas Mann's *Mario and the Magician* is cited to stress Orbán's charismatic properties and William Shakespeare's *Richard III* to show his determination "to prove a villain." Similarly, statesmen of all kinds (from Nero to Napoleon to Hitler and Stalin) and political thinkers (from Machiavelli to Carl Schmitt) are evoked to demonstrate his instinctive ability to grab power and frantic insistence to hold on, not to mention his talent in defending dubious moves as an amateur philosopher who loves to meditate on the "decline of the West" or to brag about Hungarian "national character." His addiction to fighting with the enemy brings many of his political opponents to a lay diagnosis that Orbán balances on the edge of mental illnesses characteristic of dictators such as depression, megalomania, paranoia, and even schizophrenia.

On a similarly profane level of constructing Orbán's psychological profile, one encounters a plethora of character traits in the critical media, in recollections of fellow-politicians, or in popular jokes, which admit his diligence, willpower, intelligence, tactical finesse, intuition, etc., but reprimand his arrogance, cynicism, power hunger, disloyalty, sneakiness, and hypocrisy. In explaining that mix, even high-brow intellectuals on the liberal left go back to the village boy of short stature who was born into a communist middle-class family, oppressed by his father, and became a bully. According to this narrative, he wanted to become a world-class soccer player and cherished *macho* values (comfortable in men's company like his mates in the college dormitory who would become the bosses of Fidesz).

Switching from common-place psychology to elementary social anthropology, Orbán is often depicted as an instinctive politician who has an excellent ear for the *vox populi*; an ear that has been trained in the countryside, that is, "deep Hungary." He not only manipulates public opinion but also borrows from it. The scenarios of his major populist offensives could have been written in the stands of the soccer field or the pubs of his home village, Felcsút.[14] Hating the ex-communist rich, despising Roma, raising suspicion toward urban intellectuals, Eurocrats, bankers, lawyers, judges, students, feminists, foreigners, and Jews[15]; honoring physical (especially agricultural) work; respecting large families and the elderly; blaming the poor for their poverty; expecting free education and healthcare from the state; preferring personal/kinship relations to institutions; tolerating rule bending; paying lip service to religion but ignoring its moral values and opting for a nationalized version of denominational identity; longing for historical justice for Hungarians and the return of a strong paternalist leader; lumping together criminals, refugees, drug users, and homosexuals; demanding their exemplary punishment, etc.—these are just a selection of some motifs of the voices at the regulars' table.

Orbán's favorite themes were deeply rooted in the *Weltanschauung* of the Hungarian lower and middle classes (or, in another terminology, of the "post-peasant"[16] society) both under Horthy and Kádár. By the mid-1990s, Orbán realized that the allegedly "cold," rule-based project of the liberals could not win the hearts and minds of citizens, especially in the provinces. To put it simply, he supposed that Hungarian voters regard politicians as thieves, parliament as a hotbed of corruption, and expect their would-be leader to distance himself from representative democracy as such. The permission to distill their traditional fruit brandy *pálinka* at home, one of Orban's first government decrees in 2010, certainly made his own project warmer – a rare example of populist liberalization.

This blend of psychologizing, moralizing, and pathologizing offers juicy bits and pieces for an explanation of the emergence of the SNC, even if some of them rest on anecdotal evidence. They usually serve to substantiate why two formative turns took place in Orbán's political career. The first was a U-turn when he renounced his liberal conviction in the mid-1990s. The second was "only" a gradual shift from illiberalism to explicit anti-liberalism after his election defeat in 2002. To put it in moral terms, Orbán first betrayed liberalism to embrace moderate conservatism, then proved disloyal to the latter as well and started drifting to the populist right on his way to a hard authoritarian rule bordering on autocracy.[17] Certainly, in clarifying these turns one cannot help discovering personal motives such as the desire for upward mobility or the Freudian drive to "kill the liberal father figures" (former dissidents active in the Alliance of Free Democrats who were eventually compressed into the figure of George Soros, an erstwhile supporter of Fidesz). Moreover, some thorny questions arise about his political persona. Let us cite just three questions frequently asked by Orbán's critics: Was Orbán a "true" liberal back in 1989 or was his current authoritarian stance already apparent at that time? Are his *habitus* and ideological reflexes not quintessential products of socialization under Kádár (and, indirectly, Horthy), predestining him to become a leader who reminds observers of Don Corleone in the *Godfather* movies? Did the traditional cleavage in Hungarian political culture between the "urbanites" (Westernizers) and the "populists" (nativists), which does not tolerate go-betweens, push him out of the liberal camp, providing a sufficient explanation for Orbán's *volte face* and successive radicalization?

Why deny that we cannot always release ourselves from the cage of such quick-fix interpretations? However, we fear that, if glued together, they may offer an overarching narrative that reinforces the thesis of linear evolution spelled out by Orbán himself. When his critics use the image change from a slim, bearded and restless young rebel to a fat, middle-aged bureaucrat in suit and tie, they willy-nilly approve Orbán's tale. He would agree: yes, it was a long way, but we proceeded straight ahead and managed to leave our youthful peccadilloes of liberalism, atheism, and multiculturalism behind and became exemplary national conservatives.

To sum up, our research group wanted to understand the Orbán regime rather than Orbán himself and refused to detect "what Orbán *really* had in mind" at various stages of constructing his regime.[18] Instead of testing whether the high-sounding, almost messianic phrases about nation, religion, or family come from his heart or are well-selected elements of a pragmatic and/or cynical discourse, and rather than pointing to the discrepancy between the two with moral indignation, we studied what has been happening before our very eyes: the co-evolution of a regime and its language. Ironically, pragmatism is not incompatible with a strengthening conviction to having a mission. Pragmatic-minded authoritarian leaders begin to dig their own graves at the point when they fall in love with their decisions that brought success, and mistake *Realpolitik* for their calling. Orbán currently thinks he has secured sufficient control over Hungarian society to assume the role of a leader of the "Nationalist International" in Europe. In savoring his fortune "earned" while in government, he hopes to receive a few honorable pages in the future's history books as a hero of a regime named after him.

THE SNC: A SYSTEMATIC MOVE TOWARD THE SYSTEM?

In reflecting upon the Orbán regime, a great many analysts walk into a trap set by the regime's master narrative about its own authenticity as well as institutional and ideological consistency. Still, who could blame social scientists or journalists for being prone to discover, in addition to many dozen regime types, an allegedly brand-new one supported by a Grand Design; a type that did not emerge accidentally and seems sustainable, deserving the illustrious label of "system." In this way, a monument to the SNC and Orbán has been erected, either by praise or denigration.

The wish to elevate an ordinary change of government in 2010 to the level of a major systemic turn was underpinned by the simple rhetorical technique of calling it a revolution. Accordingly, regime building began with a "revolution in the polling booth," to use Orbán's pet neologism devised to prove the popular legitimacy of the SNC. Also, it makes no sense to waste time on discussing the terms "national" and "cooperation" in detail, knowing that these familiar speech acts aim to portray the regime, implementing extremely divisive policies and causing unprecedented ideological polarization, as an embodiment of an enormous joint effort and an unquestionable common cause.[19] Both are collectivist concepts cultivated by both national socialism and communism. "National" initially had been replaced by the adjectives "public," "social," or "socialist" in the communist discourse but was rehabilitated later in the form of "national specifics of building socialism." As regards "cooperation," it alludes to mutuality and social unity. Taken together, they draw on interwar terminology (cf., Mussolini's "national collaboration" and corporatism in general) without completely obliterating the memory of the Kádár era. The expression "national cooperation" crowded out the originally liberal-sounding catchphrase "civic Hungary" from the official rhetoric of Fidesz. The adjective "civic" (in Hungarian: *polgári*, invoking the German *Bürger* rather than the French *citoyen*) was added as a supplement to the name of Fidesz in 1995 to stress its anticommunist provenance. Today, it remains there but even steadfast Orbánites do not take it seriously.

Nevertheless, the new discourse is not empty in three crucial respects: it has managed to strengthen the feeling of *revolutionary* grandeur and *national* togetherness against *ethnic aliens*, which, in turn, contributes to a high level of voters' *cooperation* with the ruling party during elections. Between elections, cooperation is tantamount to a mix of passive acceptance, fear, and moderate satisfaction in large parts of society but Fidesz has been able to convert this "non-resistance" into massive electoral support. Does the well-oiled machinery of this conversion account for the "S" in SNC?

No doubt about it, an intricate mechanism of institutions and policies ranging from solemnly phrased anti-liberal constitutional provisions through repeated waves of a cultural revolution all the way down to gerrymandering and petty election fraud has been constructed by Fidesz to achieve the conversion. One might call it a kind of "electoral success generator." Probably, in 2010 Orbán did not recognize fully that such a mechanism only could promise success if it not only relativized and downgraded but also abandoned essential elements of liberal democracy. However, caught by the whirlpool of power politics, the Fidesz rhetoric of a "new conquest of Hungary" grew into a systematic institutional change that is still on the road to totalization. Bluntly put, the Orbán regime is systematically moving toward a System (with a capital "s"). To avoid misunderstanding, the SNC hopefully does not aim at a Big Brother-like total control of society, but "genetically" it can hardly stop expanding in the long run.[20] Therefore, it is exposed to institutional overstretch, blustering promises it may be unable to keep, and a glut of its cultural revolutionary mobilization.

Learning from the fall of his first government, Orbán's primary goal was to develop a political *perpetuum mobile* that would work, after the first push, as a coherent entity for a long time. While coining the term "national cooperation," he did not make great efforts to define the nature of the regime to be established and its place among the emerging varieties of capitalism in Central and Eastern Europe. (It was symptomatic that "capitalism" metamorphosed into a swear word in Fidesz discourse and was replaced by "social market economy" and later by "work-based society.") The Young Democrats saw one thing crystal clear: what is *not* to be done once in power to avoid repeating the suicide strategies of the preceding post-1989 governments (including their own) and make the new regime unshakable.

Prior to 2010, one heard a lot from the Fidesz ideologues about the corruption, incompetence, and chaotic governance of their opponents who were depicted as vicious agents of an international neoliberal conspiracy and, at the same time, as natural heirs of communism. They also were accused of maintaining close contacts to both Brussels and Moscow, and ignoring the cause of national independence and the religious traditions of Hungarians. The analysts could thus safely predict that Orbán's regime would be more state-, nation-, and church-oriented and less open to the West than its predecessor, at least in words. A constitutional *coup d'état* (Vörös 2014) was not in sight, but today, with the wisdom of hindsight, one can better understand the practical meaning of some of Orbán's pompous phrases formulated before the victory in 2010, invoking the spirit of the "tyranny of the majority": "we have to win only once but big," "the Parliament works also without an opposition," "there is life outside the European Union," and so on. One could detect the early symptoms of this attitude already under the first Fidesz government between 1998 and 2002.[21] Nevertheless, the possibility for the new regime to choose an openly anti-liberal course in 2010, and underpin it with a new constitution, could only be forecast if one projected the strengthening of Orbán's position within Fidesz upon the entire political system of the country. Yet, what he did was a sheer emulation of how other would-be authoritarian politicians used to seize power: to put it briefly, by conquering their party with the help of its apparatus and friendly oligarchs, then conquering the state with the help of the party, and finally conquering society with the help of the party-state.

Along these lines, we posit that Orbán and Fidesz focused on the seizure of power, the crafting of institutional guarantees of immunity to resistance thereafter, and relied on the classical approach of *on s'engage et puis on voit* as far as the substance of what they consider a "good society" (let alone "good capitalism") was concerned. Learning from the "mistake" of the first Orbán government, namely, that it did not demolish the opposition completely in terms of its financial and legal capabilities, and from the permissive stance of the socialist-liberal coalition that allowed Fidesz to prosper in opposition, Orbán entered his second term of government in 2010 with a meticulous plan to marginalize his opponents in order to bring about a TINA ("There Is No Alternative") situation. However, this plan was not limited to switching off the money taps of the opposition parties, making disloyal civil servants redundant, or occupying the public media. It was based on fundamental lessons learned since Fidesz left the liberal camp in the early 1990s.

Recognizing the enormous collectivist and nationalist potential within the popular frustration with post-communist liberalization, and discovering a market niche in the political playing field, which emerged due to the incompetence of the center- and far-right parties, Fidesz decided to enfranchise and modernize the constituencies of these parties, and thereby steal their show. Orbán and his colleagues framed Fidesz's discourse, like most postmodern populists,[22] by fabricating a blend of formerly leftist and rightist agendas. Accordingly, the Young Democrats combined civic and statist, nationalist and pro-European, social-liberal and conservative, secular and religious, etc., language depending on the daily requirements of *Realpolitik*, and, at least in the beginning, carefully avoided leaving the middle for the far-right. The "anything goes" approach—culminating in a double- or triple-faced (or amorphous) public identity, which, for example, allowed Fidesz leaders to be anti-communist and anti-liberal at the same time—offered the party enormous flexibility in its struggle for power.

Since 2010, the Young Democrats have built a huge propaganda machinery to assassinate the character of their opponents and spread conspiracy theories and "alternative facts" (often fabricated in Moscow) by the dozen. Meanwhile, they have never ceased to monitor the real norms and values of Hungarians. The rules of thumb emerging from the repeated surveys included: abandoning the increasingly unpopular "liberal" label, camouflaging elitism by a populist discourse, drawing on the collectivist legacy of communism and the popular demand for security versus freedom, hiding austerity measures, and rejecting the majoritarian position of foreign capital but making concessions to some of its powerful representatives. The nurturing of domestic capitalism was to be combined with a tight control of new oligarchs to prevent them from capturing the party and/or the state. The party and the state, in turn, were to be controlled closely (by severe punishments for dissidence), and political allies were forced into a subordinate position with no real power but the reception of symbolic compensation, making it impossible for them to create an alternative power center. A sharp dividing line was to be drawn between government and opposition in order to avoid fraternization between dissenters in the governing party and any oppositional group. In turn, the concept of the "central field of force" implied tolerating and even supporting weak opposition parties on both the left and the right, with the condition that they do not join forces against Fidesz.

Rather than addressing the whole population, Orbán realized that less than one-half of actual voters in the Hungarian electoral system is more than enough to win elections with a constitutional majority, provided that the other half is fragmented. To achieve this, the party had to stand on strong, independent financial pillars and possess its own media. The propaganda was to be focused on the *Lebenswelt* and value system of the countryside and to pay special attention to the Hungarian communities in neighboring countries. Rather than promoting good governance and pursuing a common good, the

Fidesz administration had to penetrate all levels of power: infiltrating local governments, public media, judiciary, and police, as well as creating its own informal paramilitary groups. Rule of law gradually gave way to "rule by the law," exploiting loopholes in the legal system as a means to the end of defeating the enemy and weakening checks and balances. This implied a reduction of democratic procedures to the electoral process and a number of symbolic but uncontrollable manifestations of popular sovereignty in the form of "national consultations."

Many of the above rules of thumb resulted from two large-sample, real-world experiments initiated by the Young Democrats in opposition. The first was a robust campaign to organize a broad network of so-called "civic circles", which protected Orbán from the revenge of his party colleagues for losing both the 2002 and 2006 elections. He checked, with success, whether he could launch and control a new social movement backing or perhaps replacing the party (and if need be, parliamentary democracy as such) and flirted with the idea of direct democracy connecting the strong leader with enthusiastic and/or obedient citizens without political mediation. The second initiative aimed at experimenting with extra-parliamentary (plebiscitarian) techniques in two steps: while in 2004 Fidesz lost the referendum on citizenship to be given to Hungarians beyond the border, in 2008 it won the so-called social referendum that helped block the partial marketization of higher education and healthcare and dealt a final blow to the reforms of socialist prime minister Ferenc Gyurcsány. The results of these experiments fed into two massive electoral campaigns in 2014 and 2018, promising the reduction of utility prices and fencing out refugees, respectively, bringing landslide victories to Fidesz. Orbán learned gradually that by cleverly mixing a reliance on acquisitive attitudes with primordial fear, as well as magnifying these with brand-new techniques of aggressive manipulation, his party could exert a vast influence on the citizenry. Nevertheless, Orbán's ruthless brain-washing and intimidation should not be mistaken for charisma. In our view, he has always been a sober political analyst, a stone-hearted commander, and a lucky gambler rather than a magician.

How would a program focusing on a comprehensive victory over the "evil forces" of "liberal-bolshevism" crystallize into a new social system? How do the above rules of thumb determine the logic of constructing the SNC? Observers tend to avoid asking these questions. Instead, they often compete to find the most adequate (and stunning) definition of the regime and suggest willy-nilly that it has achieved a level of completeness, which calls for a special designation. Most of them agree that the regime can no longer be characterized as liberal but think the time has yet to arrive to stop calling the SNC some sort of democracy. They are inclined to attach qualifiers to the words "democracy" and "authoritarianism" (e.g., populist democracy,

Führerdemokratie, electoral authoritarianism, externally constrained authoritarianism) in order to dull their edge, or they simply allude to the hybrid character of the regime.

Such adjectives have been mushrooming because analysts feel—reasonably so—that the Orbán regime cannot be classified by means of conventional ideal types of "liberal democracy" and "totalitarian dictatorship," which were widely used during the Cold War to express the opposition of two distinct polities and the victory of the former over the latter. They also are aware of the fact that in Hungary an agonizing authoritarian (rather than totalitarian) dictatorship was replaced by a nascent—and consequently ambiguous and rudimentary—version of liberal democracy after 1989, and the process of replacement suffered from repeated backlashes even before 2010. Hence, the assumption of hybridity did not come as a surprise to them. Furthermore, depending on how one defines the four main terms under scrutiny (i.e., liberalism, democracy, authoritarianism, and dictatorship), it has not been difficult to discover some traces of liberalism and democracy in the SNC and claim that the regime has not fulfilled all major criteria for authoritarian dictatorship. Those who sympathize with Fidesz refuse to think about the latter: for them even the assumption that Orbán is on the road to become an anti-democratic leader (let alone an autocrat or a tyrant) is tantamount to lese-majesty (Tellér 2014). Those, however, who are convinced that he had embarked on that road long ago are left with the thankless task of locating the SNC in a grey zone between the two ideal types.[23]

Thus, an impressive list of designations has arisen over the past couple of years. To limit ourselves to Hungarian authors, we enumerate here the most influential labels so far: autocracy, liberal autocracy, post-communist mafia state, post-communist neo-conservatism, mutant/soft fascism, neo-communism, neo-bolshevism, neo-feudalism, semi-feudalism, externally constrained hybrid regime, hybrid counter-revolutionary regime, managed democracy, semi-democracy, totalitarian democracy, plebiscitarian leader (Führer) democracy, competitive/electoral authoritarianism, informational autocracy, illiberal democracy, party-state regime, neoliberal authoritarianism, semi-authoritarianism, soft authoritarianism, tribalism, cleptocracy, right-wing populism, political capitalism, crony capitalism, managed national/state capitalism, neo-patrimonial/prebendial capitalism, rent-seeking capitalism, post-communist neo-conservatism, elitist/paternalist populism, patronage/clientelist democracy, etc.[24] The fact that many of these concepts are oxymoron-like constructions reminiscent of the old terms of *democradura* and *dictablanda* need not disappoint the reader. This stems from the logic of hybridization and results in many original discoveries from which historians may learn a great deal. Also, we would not blame some of the authors for ignoring consensual typologies (e.g., by confounding terms such as autocracy, authoritarianism, and dictatorship) or mixing principal dimensions of classification (e.g., by jumping back and forth between the analysis of the SNC's type of capitalism, the regime's political institutions, and their ideological pillars). These seem to be unavoidable side effects of the exciting venture of theorizing an unexpected turnaround in the current history of Hungary. It is also understandable that even those authors who are convinced that the regime left the stage of liberal democracy behind long ago do not prefer to call Orbán a dictator because they want to reserve the notion for leaders such as Putin and Erdoğan; moreover, they do not want to place him in the same rubric where communist autocrats from Lenin to Kádár used to reside. However, it would be a pity if the aforementioned inquiries got stuck in this assumptive phase of research even if the Hungarian authors here do not lag behind their foreign colleagues in inventing catchy designations and formulating inspiring working hypotheses.[25]

Having said that, a deeper insight into the evolutionary traits of the System of National Cooperation would be desirable.[26] It is not enough, we believe, to state that the regime has not (yet) turned to full-blown dictatorship, tyranny, despotism, or "totalitarian" rule, a notion carrying a heavy historical burden in Central and Eastern Europe.[27] Many observers think that there is a tipping point where the regime will eventually change (or has already changed) from liberal democracy to a kind of authoritarian rule. They make a scrupulous search for particular decisions of the Orbán government, which would serve as final evidence that a red line was crossed, beyond which the regime cannot be regarded as liberal and/or democratic any longer.[28] Deep down, they recognize that the SNC has followed an evolution from mere hybridity to softer or harder versions of authoritarianism, but they cannot cope with the problem that multiple red lines exist (some respected, some violated) and do not make significant efforts to identify the incentives driving the regime ahead.

The red lines are difficult to define at first. Although Orbán talks about a revolution, he portions out the anti-liberal measures flexibly, albeit incessantly, with only brief interruptions. His regime did not attempt to occupy society in one blow. Following a powerful first push to achieve irreversibility,[29] regime-building slowed down, and the Young Democrats occasionally decided to take a few steps back in order to move forward again. In a sense, the authoritarian attitudes of Fidesz have been frugal: the SNC unfolded as rapidly as its leaders deemed necessary *and* possible. For example, after having crossed a red line, say, by hampering democratic elections through a new law, the government postponed part of the *Gleichschaltung* of the judiciary; after conquering the lion's share of the media (another possible red line), no Chinese-style censorship has been introduced to control the remaining few independent media outlets; similarly, the legal criminalization of the NGO sector was not followed by wholesale police and judicial crackdown. Or, to list some other major holes in the tissue of a potential, full-fledged hard authoritarian system, capital punishment, the reintroduction of compulsory military service, a ban on abortion, exiting the EU, etc., are still legal taboos (despite careful preparation by propaganda campaigns touching on them), and the political opponents of the regime, including journalists, do not sit in prisons or mental hospitals quite yet. By and large, violence is quiet, non-physical, and mobilization is managed through indoctrination and intimidation rather than brute force. In other words, there are still a number of red lines that have not been crossed.[30]

Nonetheless, decisions to make "national cooperation" wider and deeper—which have not yet been taken due to internal or external resistance—were delayed rather than dropped for good. Today, experiencing a renewed attempt to tighten the screws of the regime after its third election victory, no sober observer would claim, as they did ten years ago, that it would be impossible even to imagine that show trials or political murders were organized by Orbán's party-state.[31] Similarly, more observers than before contemplate that Hungary eventually might leave the EU.[32] But why—against the hopes of the conservative supporters of the regime, who considered Fidesz's victory in 2010 a historical chance to return to "normalcy," and against the expectations of the remnants of the Kádárist middle class who saw Orbán as a champion of *étatist* welfare policies promising a kind of "goulash capitalism"—can the SNC not present its adherents with the joy of consolidation while bribing its opponents with the same?[33] We are afraid that, seen from a political science and legal perspective (and these are the disciplinary backgrounds of most analysts who strive to identify the regime),[34] it is not that easy to fathom its strong propensity for self-completion pointing toward autocracy.

However, if one resorts to an economic, historical, and sociological analysis, the reasons for the relentless perfecting of the SNC (i.e., creating a lasting and waterproof regime) will probably be less opaque. We have avoided constructing a "one-and-only" pigeon hole in which the Orbán regime can be placed and have not offered anything more concrete than a loose observation that in the long run the SNC aspires to move toward a hard authoritarian rule. Similarly, in a larger societal context, the regime was portrayed here as a sort of (interventionist) capitalism governed by a party-state and supported by an old-school conservative ideology.

In pondering on the possible destinations of the SNC, those approaches seem to us the most fruitful which rely on institutions and practices of societies in which personal dependence, reciprocity, kinship, gift, feudal hierarchy, loyalty, informality, etc., matter. To a large degree, these institutions and practices governed Hungarian semi-capitalism prior to state socialism and, having survived four decades of the latter (or even being reinforced during that period), appeared after 1989 as a fatal temptation for the new elites to adjust to the *longue durée* tradition.[35] Of course, certain pieces of this tradition can be combined with cutting-edge political techniques of mobilization and manipulation that may blur their true origin. Nevertheless, very little is known about the nature and process of re-feudalization (re-traditionalization) at various levels of Hungarian society.[36] Will it produce relatively stable *Stände* (estates) in the Weberian sense, an ongoing rivalry of oligarchs, or a combination of the two? Will the ruler be able to overpower them and develop a strong state following a patrimonial/prebendial scheme? If he will, is it likely that the state will operate that scheme through a mafia-like (or even tribal) organization led by the ruler's extended/adopted family that can substitute or employ the governing party? Would it still make sense to speak of a party-state in that case? As re-feudalization is contingent on a central redistribution of property, how peaceful can that process be after the "commons" and the "booty" have been allocated among the regime's supporters? How will such a neo-traditionalist regime be able to survive in a European or global capitalist environment?

In a sense, the initial plan to organize Fidesz around and by Orbán as a closed and disciplined group of a few selected professional politicians who are ready to engage in shady business deals and dubious political alliances was defensive. The Young Democrats were convinced that the only way to defeat what they considered (not entirely without foundation) the "liberal-bolshevik mafia"[37] in political competition was to emulate the behavior of the latter, but to make it more professional and less hesitant. This became a major determinant of the party's strategy in the subsequent decades. Below, we will recapitulate the main phases of establishing this organizational model and how its architects checked its feasibility. By 2010, the model proved extremely successful, and the election victory in that year, after two defeats in a row, silenced the few remaining skeptics within the party. However, even if the crash of the arch-enemy had not justified Orbán's strategy retroactively, he would not have had another model to offer. His "army"[38] was trained to conspire, fight, and invade, as well as introduce hierarchical rule and unconditional loyalty to the "occupied territories." This strategy was tested in all institutions in which Fidesz had a privileged position during the 1990s and 2000s—be it the administration of a city, a state-owned firm, the office of the president, the chief attorney, or the chairman of public television.

Following the first election victory in 1998—when Fidesz was far weaker than today—it had no other choice but to reconcile conquest with the rule of law, but it soon realized how vulnerable a regime becomes if it constantly must confront the power of an independent judiciary, central bank, media, and the like. Under such a system, Fidesz's former offenses (tax fraud, secret deals with the then-governing party in the early 1990s, etc.) and current corruption cases were exposed, and Fidesz's occupation of society was impeded. At this time, Orbán started dreaming of winning big, making a *tabula rasa*, and expanding the hierarchical structure of the party to a neo-feudal party-state to capture society. By 2010, he also learned that, in order to avoid anarchy caused by a rivalry among oligarchs close to Fidesz, he must retain the "single godfather" principle, display force, and go for some kind of an authoritarian solution.

A regime like this loses its meaning if it does not fill as much economic, political, and sociocultural space as possible. According to its internal logic, the ruler cannot stop moving: he'll lose his balance and fall from the saddle if he does not keep spurring his stallion forward. You need not necessarily regard him as paranoid, hysterical, or obsessed with the will to become a hegemonic leader. Given the SNC's prehistory, it is very likely that the regime also would have advanced systematically toward "perfection" and "eternity," with built-in incentives for totalization under a less ambitious ruler.

Why totalization? If applied in good harmony, the rules of thumb almost automatically result in a growing sovereignty of the supreme leader. In this sentence, the emphasis is on both sovereignty and its growth. The prerequisites of systematic escalation, ranging from the organization of a party of iron discipline and centralized (secret) financial operations to the absorption of smaller right-wing parties and the infiltration of high echelons of state administration prior to 2010 would not have urged Orbán to continue concentrating power thereafter if this endeavor had not been successful and accompanied by a whole series of populist promises. Success prompted Fidesz not to change course, whereas the promises made to its own elite and wider constituency accelerated its steps along that path. Maybe, if the party had not entered government right after the global financial crisis, it would not have felt such an urgent need and seen such a large window of opportunity to start dismantling the *Rechtsstaat*. However, Hungary's budget deficit and sovereign debt inherited from the previous government confronted the Young Democrats with a dilemma: either they accept tutelage by international organizations like the International Monetary Fund (IMF) for cheap loans along with austerity policies that would prevent them from keeping their election promises (e.g., "no more restriction"), or they avoid sovereign default through balancing the budget internally by means of interventionist (in Fidesz's language, "unorthodox") techniques of income redistribution, such as levying special taxes on transnational companies and banks, confiscating private pensions, as well as by taking more expensive loans on the free market. Orbán decided to choose the second option,[39] even if he knew it could not materialize without violating constitutional rights such as private ownership, nondiscrimination in economic regulation, and independence of the judiciary, not to mention the neutrality of public media.

The nature of the 2010 takeover thus predetermined the path of the SNC leading to its Fundamental Law and its numerous amendments as well as to new laws governing elections, labor, media, and more, all the way down to the introduction and prolongation of a partial *Ausnahmezustand* during and after the refugee crisis. It is particularly disturbing that all the ensuing limitations of human and citizenship rights were packaged in legal acts conveying the impression that the regime had not crossed the normal boundaries of the rule of law. In this sense, it was probably the parliamentary approval of the Fundamental Law in 2011 where the Young Democrats reached one of the most important points of no return away from liberal democracy, something barely noticed by Washington and Brussels as it was justified by a "constitutional majority" finally abrogating the "communist constitution."[40] (For example, the fact that the Fundamental Law does not contain the term "private property" did not alarm the Western observers.) Since then, the regime has rarely stopped marching on the "road to serfdom," no matter how one defines the consecutive stages and the potential destination of that road. In all probability, the top leaders of Fidesz long cherished the dream of crowning their anti-liberal turn with a new constitution in the future, and the coup-like enactment of the Fundamental Law promised a quick solution to the above dilemma. What had been just one of many instruments in their toolbox became *the* instrument of their choice, and it also proved successful.

They took a tremendous risk by opting for an "unorthodox" program of economic stabilization because it provoked much of their own constituency (cf., the seizure of private pensions or risking sovereign default). They could not have done so without paralyzing social resistance by radically constraining citizens' ability to organize strikes and initiate referenda, effectively stopping the Constitutional Court from rejecting government decisions, and reining in the media and its mission to inform citizens fairly and also present criticism. They could not have done so without playing on and reinforcing ideological cleavages within cultural and economic elites and gratifying their conservative and "nationally sensitive" supporters at the expense of their "cosmopolitan, liberal, leftist" opponents. Orbán trusted the lasting impact of the post-victory honeymoon. However, to play safe, Fidesz swiftly passed a new and extremely biased election law—another point of no return. The SNC was anticipated in the history of Young Democrats by twenty years of preparation including a repeated redesigning (and radicalization) of their project and accumulating organizational strength through piecemeal engineering,[41] learning by doing (and a bit of reading) as well as a good portion of improvisation and pure chance. In other words, Fidesz diligently did its homework for the course on "how to stage an anti-liberal revolution in a parliamentary democracy."

Beyond these points of no return, the process of totalization was animated to a large extent by populist pressures from below and by the vested interests of the emerging economic and political elites of the SNC. The supreme leader became prisoner of his own promises that brought him to power, because he had to fill the mouths of both the "foot soldiers" at large and the SNC knights (distributing money, jobs, prestige, or—if these were lacking—religious faith, historical justice, national dignity, or the illusion of security). Meanwhile, he had invested so much energy in the construction of the regime that he could not afford the risk of slipping on a banana peel. Thus, Orbán has done his best to cover even the smallest holes in the regime's armor. Repeated amendments of the Fundamental Law (which was said to be firm like granite by Orbán in 2012) over a few years are good examples.

GLOBAL DYNAMICS AND LOCAL PECULIARITIES

Originally, Orbán had little ambition beyond ruling Hungary. In a way, it was the disapproval by the European Parliament and the Commission of his emerging regime in the early 2010s that pushed him to place his agenda in a transnational frame but, even then, he was unable to position the SNC on the global map. The main ideological reference that he could present was anti-communism that earned him the sympathy of Western liberal and conservative politicians socialized during the Cold War. The situation changed around 2014 when Orbán started experimenting with a new theme, migration, as Hungary's main external threat. Initially, this was not taken seriously either in Hungary or in Europe since the country hardly was a target of immigration. However, the government had a long-term goal; it systematically heated the xenophobic mood of the public by creating its first propaganda campaign attacking foreigners who had allegedly come to crowd out Hungarians from the job market, rape women, and spread lethal diseases. The escalation of the refugee crisis in 2015 (Juhász, Hunyadi, and Zgut 2015) elevated Orbán's position dramatically.[42] The danger of a humanitarian catastrophe eventually triggered Angela Merkel's reaction to open Germany's borders. The spectacular nationalist performance by Orbán—in particular, erecting a fence on the Serbian border—earned him wide recognition on the right, including members of the EPP. Notably, he became a key reference in Germany as the Christian Social Union and the emerging radical right began to challenge Merkel's *Willkommenskultur*.

The anti-EU radicalization of Russian politics following sanctions leveled against the country in response to its occupation of Crimea in 2014 coincided with Orbán's growing conviction about the impotence of European political elites. As a consequence, he sought political and economic support from all geopolitical actors (especially China, Russia, and Turkey) who seemed to offer an alternative to the EU. In addition, he made efforts to be accepted among the Central Asian Turkic nations, overemphasizing family ties and stressing that Hungarians feel more at home among these peoples than in Europe. The "Eastern opening," as it was called by Fidesz, was inserted into a geopolitical master plan that evoked a late-nineteenth-century Hungarian imperialist narrative (see Kállay 1883). From this doctrine, Orbán borrowed the idea of promoting Hungary to Eastern partners as an outpost of their interests in Europe (i.e., as a Trojan horse) rather than acting as an emphatic Westernizer. The open identification with Russian geopolitical interests (most obviously in the case of blocking common EU and NATO policies toward Ukraine) is meant more as backup in Hungary's hardball with the EU.

For a long time, this strategy worked impeccably. With the help of his allies in the EPP, Orbán could counter political criticism about the SNC as nothing more than partisan attacks from the left-liberal corner—attacks that he began to describe as a conspiracy of pro-migration forces animated by George Soros. The first steps to demolish liberal democracy (through the Fundamental Law, the election law, the media law, the purging of the judiciary, etc.) were contested on a discursive level, but they did not provoke tangible reactions from Western partners. The Hungarian government's strategy of taking two steps forward and then backtracking a bit on minor issues proved very efficient.

While the report prepared by Rui Tavares on Hungary—which demanded the establishment of a new mechanism to ensure compliance by all Member States with the common values of the EU—was adopted by the European Parliament in July 2013,[43] its practical consequences were minimal. International reaction grew a little stronger when Orbán became an all-European symbol of breaking with the principles of liberal democracy, which brought him important allies (a motley crew including Steve Bannon, Nigel Farage, Janez Janša, Jarosław Kaczyński, Benjamin Netanyahu, Victor Ponta, Matteo Salvini, Horst Seehofer, Geert Wilders, and Miloš Zeman), but also exposed the danger of a populist chain reaction. It remains to be seen whether the recent decisions of the European Parliament (triggering Article 7 in September 2018, and the January 2019 endorsement of a draft law that makes it possible both to fund NGOs from EU sources in countries where civil society is under government attack and to block the transfer of EU funds to countries violating the basic values of the EU) will have a substantial impact in the future.

The growing fear of Orbanization also indicates that, while many of the regime's above-mentioned features seem idiosyncratic, only a few of them are actually unique. From Macedonia to Japan, many countries underwent a renationalization of their public and cultural spheres in the past two decades; there is endemic corruption targeting European funds, especially in East Central and Southern Europe; the independence of the media is increasingly threatened not only in China and Russia but also in Italy, Slovakia, and Slovenia; political leaders and parties rejecting liberal democratic traditions and practices emerged in countries ranging from Italy and Germany to Romania and Estonia; questions of migration and national homogeneity have become central to the political discourse from Denmark and Sweden to Bulgaria and Greece; and post-factual political propaganda—such as Orbán's anti-Soros campaign, which cost more than the whole Brexit campaign including the expenses of the Leave and Remain camps taken together[44]—is a pervasive political instrument from Russia to the United States.

We argue that the SNC could not have come into being and persisted without a complex transnational entanglement. The most spectacular example is offered by multinational companies that use their influence to attenuate political attacks against Orbán in exchange for preferential treatment in Hungary.[45] This matched the sympathy or inertia of European conservative politicians who considered Fidesz a pioneer in the opening of the center-right toward themes that have been taboo for a long time, such as ethnic purity, the return of religion to the public sphere, and the reinforcement of traditional family models and gender hierarchies. Rather than an instinctive country boor, as Orbán is often depicted in the Western media, he built his political persona carefully with the help of advisors such as the late Arthur J. Finkelstein, a master of negative campaigns.[46] There were many global factors that helped consolidate his power under profound ideological and socioeconomic insecurity when previously unquestionable norms of political behavior became much less consensual. A definitive shift toward chauvinistic discourse in Hungary followed Donald Trump's victory. Reacting to the "America First" slogan, Orbán happily stated that no universalist political projects, such as the vision of a "supranational Europe," are to be accepted in a new era of bilateral relationships.[47]

At the same time, the Orbánist *combination* of all these developments and features is less typical. For instance, although some analysts still tend to consider Poland the prototype of new authoritarianism, the dominance of PiS can barely be compared to that of Fidesz: most Polish local governments are controlled by the opposition, free media stand on solid ground, economic elites are less dependent on state power, cultural institutions have broader autonomy, and judges resist the subordination of the courts to politics much more openly and efficiently than their Hungarian colleagues.[48] Similarly, while in many post-communist countries, such as Romania, certain components of Orbánism are evidently present on both the left and the right, they have not crystallized into a comprehensive regime comparable to the SNC.[49]

HISTORICIZING THE SYSTEM OF NATIONAL COOPERATION: THE LONG MARCH AWAY FROM THE LIBERAL CONSENSUS

The Orbán regime can be better understood if put in a genealogical framework that traces its emergence from the early 1990s to the present as a series of challenges and responses. Historicizing the SNC, that is, examining both its consecutive phases of development and major historical sources by focusing on the interplay of ideas and practices, is meant to contribute to rethinking its dominant interpretations.[50]

By and large, the literature on Orbánism has been written from two—hardly compatible—historical perspectives. One of them links it to a *longue durée* liberal and democratic deficit that marks out Hungarian society as particularly predisposed to anti-Western resentment. The other perspective stems from a genuine surprise felt by many observers who expected such a backlash to occur not in Hungary but rather in the new democracies of Bulgaria, Croatia, Romania, or Slovakia (held to be much less "consolidated" in the 1990s and carrying a heavier burden of communism), or in Poland in the mid-2000s. In contrast, we consider the current Hungarian regime neither accidental nor fatefully predetermined, but the result of a cumulative process of trial and error with a strong dependence on the cultural and political codes and expectations of a large part of the elite and the middle class as well as some of the marginalized groups of society. Rather than indicating a Hungarian *Sonderweg*, these attitudes show remarkable regional parallels (Trencsényi et al. 2018). Thus, the national specifics of the SNC are not acutely predetermined by Hungarian cultural or political traditions.

Nevertheless, as opposed to interpretations that start telling the story of the SNC with the "revolution in the polling booth" in 2010, one can find the deeper roots of the Orbán regime—stretching to (a) interwar Hungary, (b) the Kádár era, and, more recently, to (c) the first two decades of post-communist liberalization. The Horthy regime offered part of the post-1989 elite a vision that integrated anti-communism, irredentism, the symbolism of the Holy Crown, paternalism, national capitalism, feudal hierarchy, the myth of a strong-handed leader, law and order (without the rule of law), limited parliamentarism, state interventionism, welfare chauvinism, the "Christian middle class," a "neo-baroque" political aesthetics, geopolitical reliance on Germany, and a nostalgia for great-power identity. While emerging as oppositional streams under Horthy, ethno-populism (both on the left and the right) and fascism (on the extreme right, but occasionally filling the niches of the radical left) also belong to his regime's legacy, preserved sub-culturally during the long decades of communist rule.

In its turn, Kádárism left behind a somewhat Faustian "social contract" (offering relative existential security in exchange for depoliticization) that was often depicted in terms of "goulash communism," "soft dictatorship," or the "happiest barrack." It provided a mixture of market socialism and informal economy with wide-scale corruption, bargaining, and rule bending, flavored by a rather inclusive cultural policy, a broad stratum of intelligentsia cooperating with the regime, and increasing social differentiation with little solidarity toward those who fell through the safety net of the communist "welfare state."

Importantly, both Horthysm and Kádárism were hybrid models (of capitalism and communism, respectively), including substantial post-feudal components and various ideas of finding a "Third Way." Although their *prima facie* ideological outlook may have diverged, there were many similarities between them in terms of governance cultures and popular attitudes embedded in social reflexes due to the long socialization/acculturation processes under the two regimes (lasting twenty-five and thirty-three years, respectively). Parallels notwithstanding, there is an obvious tension between the heritage of either Horthy or Kádár with regard to the status of nationalism and religion. The interwar authoritarian regime was outspokenly nationalist and focused on the revision of the Treaty of Trianon, whereas Kádárism was extremely cautious in raising national sentiment and reticent to instrumentalize the deteriorating conditions of Hungarians in neighboring states. At the same time, goulash communism had its own implicit national discourse combining the narratives of civilizational superiority and welfare chauvinism. Furthermore, with the public sphere opening up in the 1980s, many unprocessed national traumas, such as the cataclysm of Soviet occupation, the expulsion of Hungarians from Czechoslovakia, and the massacre of Hungarians in Vojvodina, just to mention three consequences of the Second World War, resurfaced. Thus, the anti-nationalist, technocratic, quasi-liberal attitude of the late communist political elite left a convenient space for anti-communist nationalism to emerge.

The politicization of religion and the sacralization of political rituals were central to the political culture of the Horthy regime. It called itself a "Christian-national course," drawing legitimacy from the anti-communist "counter-revolution" of 1919, which brought together Christian socialist, proto-fascist paramilitary, and traditional conservative forces. Kádárism obviously was unable to apply religion as a central point of reference, but from the 1960s onward it forged a tactical compromise with the "historical churches." In exchange for the political subservience of the clergy (including the cooperation of its leading members with the secret police), it offered them a relatively broad spiritual and institutional field of operation. Here, Fidesz combines the Horthyist and Kádárist legacies, turning, on the one hand, Christianity into a central instrument of justification and, on the other, subjecting the clergy to financial dependence and strong political control. By limiting the political autonomy of churches, the government also fights against any "leftist" influence coming from the Vatican after the election of Francis to the papal throne.

While the authoritarian legacies of the interwar right-wing and postwar communist regimes were challenged in 1989, there were heated debates about the nature of democratic and liberal values already during the 1990s. The conflicts were fueled by the incessant culture war between the "urbanites" and "populists." The symbolic cleavages between these camps were formative of the emerging political system due to close links between these subcultures and the new non-communist parties. Nevertheless, most conservatives, liberals, and socialists were involved (under the pressure of pragmatic considerations) with implementing economic liberalization, and the long years of the so-called transformational recession and subsequent stabilization in the 1990s questioned their main promise: namely, that political freedom would necessarily lead to welfare. This considerably weakened the prestige of economic liberalism, which was not too high anyway because it had been identified with the "reform economists" (communist technocrats and their academic advisors) before the collapse of the old regime. Also, the popular frustration with a persistent gap between Hungary and "the West" (abruptly starting at the western border of the country) gave a standing invitation to populist political and moral entrepreneurs, including Orbán and other less successful contenders (e.g., József Torgyán from the post-agrarian Smallholders' Party and István Csurka from the extreme-right MIÉP, the Party of Hungarian Justice and Life) who rejected the entire transition as a conspiracy of "alien" and "liberal-communist" elites to sell the country to the West.

While Fidesz was long hailed as a genuinely liberal party of the post-communist transition, it was not only cooperating but also competing with the Free Democrats (SZDSZ) that emerged from the "Democratic Opposition" born in the mid-1970s. The Free Democrats became a much more influential actor in the 1989 revolution than the Young Democrats, who were literally young and inexperienced at that time. Apart from the obvious generational difference, their sociocultural background also diverged—a fact often contributing to a simplistic explanation of why the two parties drifted away from each other.

SZDSZ leaders typically came from the urban intelligentsia (most of them from Budapest and many of them from families who had embraced communist ideology as Holocaust survivors), and despite their anti-communist thrust, they showed sympathy toward the reformist wing of the party-state. At the same time, most of the founders of Fidesz were born in the countryside, usually into middle class families, and moved to Budapest to complete their university studies. They became politicized under the wings of the "Democratic Opposition" during the mid-1980s, but surpassed their mentors in terms of anti-communist radicalism, activist fervor, and fresh political style.

Following the 1990 elections and the formation of the first non-communist government led by the national-conservative József Antall, Fidesz developed an ambiguous relationship with the two main political forces of the transition, namely, Antall's Hungarian Democratic Forum (MDF) and the Free Democrats. While cooperating with the latter in opposition—and disapproving the conservatism and clericalism of the government more harshly than the Free

Democrats—the leaders of Fidesz sought to distance themselves from both sides by stressing the futility of "culture wars." Thus, it was unsurprising that, in 1993, Fidesz came to reject any Popular Front-style cooperation between the liberals and the post-communist Hungarian Socialist Party (MSZP), both detecting in national conservatism the possibility of a radical right-wing turn. Orbán's move toward MDF through a dubious business deal,[51] and the fact that much of its revenue was transferred to the stone quarries of Orbán's father, came as an embarrassment for many. The deal marked the beginning of a merger of economic and political spheres (Ferenczi 2015) in the Fidesz world, already well-known among the ex-communist half of the political sphere. The shift to the right, combined with efforts to create an economic *Hinterland*, eventually led to a substantial transformation of Fidesz. The departure of a number of liberal-leaning members from party leadership made it easier for Orbán to adopt an even more intransigent anti-communist strategy.

The 1994 elections, at which Orbán placed his party between the disintegrating right-wing government and its left-liberal contenders, dealt a serious blow to Fidesz that barely received enough votes to enter parliament. Meanwhile, MSZP gained more than half of the seats, the liberals came second, and the populist Smallholders became the strongest opposition party. After some hesitation, and following the advice of leading businesspeople, the liberals joined the government of Gyula Horn (a former moderate reform-communist with a murky past due to his participation in repressions after 1956), led by the hope to steer the socialists toward further liberalization. This move to the left opened up a niche for the Young Democrats to integrate some of the former supporters of SZDSZ who were convinced that their party betrayed its anti-communist agenda. Fidesz's popularity grew steadily after the austerity package implemented in 1995 by Horn's minister of finance, Lajos Bokros, whose resolute measures were rejected by Orbán as an attack on the middle class, which would undermine the future of young generations. This was the moment when Orbán realized that a rational policy of macro-stabilization promising welfare gains in the long run can be discredited by emphasizing its contribution to short-run welfare losses (Bauer 2000).

In 1998, Fidesz managed to defeat the socialist-liberal coalition, gaining many voters of national-conservative persuasion, but also former liberals who saw the Young Democrats as an alternative to the MSZP-SZDSZ coalition government ravaged by corruption scandals. The nationalist (occasionally anti-Semitic) overtones of Orbán's election campaign were considered either as a tactical weapon to compete with the Smallholders or disregarded as accidental. The coalition government formed in 1998, which co-opted the Smallholders and was thus infected with the antics of violent ethnopopulist rhetoric, was usually credited with mainstream center-right policies capitalizing on the—otherwise condemned—"neoliberal" accomplishments of the Bokros package.

Nevertheless, in retrospect, one discovers a number of indications about the direction Fidesz would take ten years later. The party recruited a group of government-friendly entrepreneurs who rechanneled part of the money acquired from public tenders to support the aim of building a solid political infrastructure around Orbán. The *grosso modo* moderate socioeconomic policies of the government were increasingly combined with a populist rhetoric accusing the previous administration of serving foreign capital instead of fostering a domestic entrepreneurial class. Parts of the legislative and judicial spheres were subordinated to the executive,[52] the activities of the opposition were constrained, the "traditional" Christian churches enjoyed privileges, and the public media was hijacked with the help of the extreme right-wing party MIÉP.

While initially the Young Democrats experimented with a quasi-republican discourse focusing on the concept of *Bürger*, they gradually recognized how limited the mobilizing power of such a notion was against a strong nostalgia for goulash communism and the actual lack of historical models for civic identification. Therefore, around 2000, in the wake of commemorating the millennium of the Hungarian state, the Orbán government started drifting toward ethno-nationalism and immersing its supporters in the "politics of history." Ignoring the virtues of republicanism, the Holy Crown was moved from the National Museum to the Parliament, conferring an actual political function upon a relic. A similar symbolic investment was the establishment of the highly controversial House of Terror in 2002, a museum that was meant to justify the anti-communist zeal of the government,[53] targeting both the socialists and the former dissident liberals who allegedly conspired to steal the 1989 revolution. However, between 1998 and 2002, there was no talk about building a new "system." The self-professed agenda of the first Orbán government was to "complete the post-1989 regime change."

The year 2002 humiliated Orbán both politically and personally. He began the election campaign from a favorable position, at a moment of economic growth and with a country soon entering the EU, but he was defeated by a soft-spoken and colorless former communist technocrat, Péter Medgyessy, who was revealed, right after his victory, to have been a secret agent in the 1970s–1980s. Orbán refused to accept defeat and mobilized his supporters at mass rallies with fiery speeches against the "alien-hearted" socialists and liberals whose rule, he said, was illegitimate by default. At the same time, he reemerged as an organizer of "civic circles" supporting his own survival within Fidesz and reinforcing the infrastructure of the party while in opposition as well as creating preconditions for cultural hegemony (Greskovits 2017).[54]

Orbán wrote his MA thesis (1987) on Polish anti-communist social movements in the 1970s–1980s, and his main point of orientation was Antonio Gramsci and the then fashionable theories of civil society (e.g., by Alain Touraine and Jadwiga Staniszkis). The civic circles thus presented a fascinating instance of Orbán's ability to recycle political ideas rooted in liberal democratic dissident culture in a completely different context. Another example was the discourse of Central Europe of the 1980s, used after 2015 against what Orbán described as the decadent, multicultural West. He offered a travesty of Milan Kundera's *Occident kidnappé*, which also bore a certain resentment toward Western political elites for having abandoned their Central European brothers and sisters to the clutches of the Soviet empire. In this way, Orbán combined anti-Western and anti-communist codes in an ingenious way (hence his recurrent rhetorical *topos* equating the "Brusselites" of the EU with the "Muscovites" before 1989).

While the civic circles followed the logic of civil society theories in many ways (prompting voluntary activism, creating parallel structures ranging from visual arts and journalism to viticulture and sports, etc.), their main goal was to challenge the institutions of liberal democracy. They can be characterized as a postmodern version of *totale Mobilmachung*, dividing the society into authentic Hungarians (who support Orbán) and all others, whose unwillingness to follow the leader labels them as "unpatriotic." The ethno-nationalist reconfiguration of political discourse also triggered a preoccupation with Hungarians outside the country.[55] After 2002, the Young Democrats demanded the introduction of dual citizenship for all Hungarians living in neighboring countries.[56] When they forced a referendum on this issue in 2004, the socialists launched a populist counter-campaign warning that dual citizenship would open the Hungarian job market to "twenty-three million Romanians." Although the referendum failed because of the number of participants fell below the stipulated quorum, it mobilized and hystericized Hungarians inside and outside the country, particularly in Romania, providing Orbán with enthusiastic support among social strata who normally had little interest in or information about party politics in Hungary (and with about 200 thousand votes from abroad after 2010).

Examining the transformation of Hungarian political culture after 2002, especially the eventual collapse of the party system consisting of a strong socialist and a center-right party, with an influential liberal party and some outlier national-populist formations,[57] one must not forget that in Hungary the years around the European accession were far from successful in socioeconomic terms. In 2002, the socialist-led government introduced what it called a "welfare-oriented systemic change" that proved self-defeating as pay rises in education and healthcare severely burdened the budget while other measures of the administration did not provide long-term gains for most of the social groups that considered themselves losers of the post-communist transition. Similarly, the incentives (initiated by Fidesz but maintained by the socialist-liberal coalition) for the middle class to take credit and purchase flats, cars, computers, and the like, which they could not afford during the post-1989 recession, produced a huge budget deficit rather than triggering economic growth.

To make things even worse, the advantages of the Hungarian economy as the most advanced in terms of liberalization increasingly were reduced by neighboring countries, especially Slovakia. They reached a level of stability, implemented a series of (neo-)liberal reforms (such as cutting corporate taxes and introducing a flat income tax) and offered Western investors more attractive deals. Despite economic development in Hungary, the growing budget deficit and indebtedness of the middle class created an impression of stagnation and supported Orbán's claim of the government's incompetence and the need for an elite change. Such was the context of the electoral campaign of 2006 where Orbán clashed with Ferenc Gyurcsány, a young and dynamic socialist prime minister adhering to the ideas of the Blairian "Third Way." Struggling with the etatist/interventionist wing of his party, Gyurcsány and his circle focused on the mobile, pro-Western urban strata who demanded a more efficient government that stimulated entrepreneurship and, in general, a coherent program of modernization.

The results of the 2006 elections were very close: Fidesz lost mainly due to its failure to integrate the anti-government forces in one camp. (MDF was running on a separate ticket and got into parliament with the support of moderate conservative voters who disliked the socialist-liberal coalition but also sought to distance themselves from the populism of Orbán.) During a televised debate of the top candidates, an energetic Gyurcsány swept away the somewhat intimidated and incompetent Orbán. The latter concluded from the election defeat that in the future the Young Democrats must not allow a conservative but anti-Fidesz contender to run. Similarly, public debates before the election should be abandoned by claiming that competitors are morally unfit to join in fair dialogue. While Orbán faced post-election discontent within his party after the defeat, his nemesis came to his rescue as the socialist-liberal coalition created its biggest (self-induced) crisis. In order to persuade the leadership of MSZP to launch a comprehensive liberalization program, Gyurcsány gave a speech at a closed party conference in Őszöd at Lake Balaton, in which he admitted that the government lied "night and day" about the economic situation of the country. The speech, full of four-letter words, was leaked (by frustrated socialists or secret service agents working for Fidesz) and triggered mass protests. They culminated in October 2006 in violent clashes between the demonstrators and the police. The ensuing crisis reinforced the Orbánist discourse about the illegitimate nature of a government that commanded the police to beat up innocent citizens. It also extended the popular basis of the right, going way beyond the middle-class dominated civic circles and recruiting social groups (like football hooligans) who had hitherto been outside of party politics. The protests hindered the planned reforms, and although Gyurcsány pushed through a number of unpopular measures to balance the budget and managed to attain some economic growth by 2008, the global financial crisis erased the benefits of these reforms, forcing Hungary to turn to the IMF for help.

Meanwhile, the Young Democrats were steadily broadening their own power network. At the 2006 local elections that took place right after the Őszöd scandal, they won almost the entire countryside; their candidate László Sólyom became president of the republic in 2005; they managed to keep their representatives in various multi-party boards (Constitutional Court, public media, central bank, state-owned enterprises, etc.), and reactivated their former appointees in important ministries, the office of the chief attorney, the army, and the police. Whether on purpose or not, Orbán followed the Leninist pattern of *dvoevlastie* and looked forward to scoring the long-awaited Big Victory. As a matter of fact, he could sit back and relax, particularly after the government lost the "social referendum" urged by Fidesz in 2008. The liberals subsequently disintegrated, and—with the help of insiders in the state administration loyal to Orbán—corruption cases against socialist bosses were unveiled nearly every week in the media controlled by the Fidesz oligarch Lajos Simicska.

The reconfiguration of global politics also contributed to the delegitimization of the left-liberal government. While culturally pro-Western, Gyurcsány adjusted his policies to the growing weight of Russia in the mid-2000s, especially in view of the strong dependence of Hungary on Russian energy supply. In contrast, Orbán was busy assuring U.S. and EU diplomats of his Atlanticist commitment. That he combined his anti-communist talk with ethno-nationalist tropes was glossed over by his Western partners as mere rhetoric. They rather focused on the fundamental question of who would gain larger influence upon the new member states of the EU: the East or the West. This, together with Gyurcsány's loss of face due to his "lie speech," created an auspicious moment for Orbán to present himself as a representative of the European center-right. His election campaign in 2010 was boosted by the active participation of Western conservative politicians. Since there was little discussion about Fidesz's platform, most voters had no idea that they actually supported a party willing to initiate a comprehensive change in the constitutional arrangements of the Republic of Hungary, a change that was devised ultimately to delete even the term "republic" from the citizens' vocabulary.[58]

The 2010 elections—bringing 68 percent of the seats to Fidesz with 52 percent of the vote—humiliated the socialists, eliminated the liberals and the centrist MDF, and gave rise to two anti-systemic parties, the extreme-right Jobbik and the environmentalist LMP that located itself in the center as an economically anti-liberal movement respecting human and citizenship rights. The emerging political framework corresponded to Orbán's vision of the central field of force, placing Fidesz as a dominant actor between the discredited left and the deplorable extreme right. This strategy was coupled with an open shift to a decisionist understanding of politics, stressing that in the future the government must not be restrained by the fear that a strong opposition might turn the unpopular moves of the cabinet against it (like the Young Democrats had done for eight years). The planned configuration of power was expected to allow for more efficient governance and long-term planning. Whenever Orbán talked about the ideal of a "strong Hungary," he meant first and foremost a strong state. Rather than following a program of technocratic modernization, the concept of the central field of force was predicated upon historical examples, especially the Horthy regime, relegating its social democratic and fascist opposition to the background. One also can find analogies with the Kádár regime, in which sustaining hegemony implied a so-called two-front struggle against the nostalgic Stalinist and neo-Stalinist/Maoist ultra-left, on the one hand, and the national communist and revisionist/liberal "right", on the other.

The political transformation of the republic in 2010 was framed as an outcome of popular will (cf., "revolution in the polling booth") bringing forth a foundational moment for the new regime. Orbán decided to start his tenure by frontally attacking the inbuilt checks and balances of the liberal constitutional system that limited his government's power. In the beginning, the main battlefields were the judiciary, the media, and the financial sphere. The measures implemented (transforming the Constitutional Court by packing it with pro-Fidesz yes-men and severely constraining its competence, pensioning off leading judges, passing a new law limiting the independence of the non-government-supported media outlets, extending control over the banking system, eliminating the independence of the National Bank, etc.) led to an unheard of concentration of power. Each of these decisions were criticized by various EU bodies. However, Orbán's strategy of compartmentalizing the debate, focusing on minor technical details, pointing to the existing parallels of the contested measures in other European legal systems, and making a few tactical concessions, was successful. While his government did its best to find similar (in fact, usually insignificant) elements of not-quite-liberal regulation lurking in the constitutions of Western democracies to strengthen its position in a noisy international discussion, Orbán managed to silently but decidedly centralize, homogenize, and militarize the state apparatus as a whole without noteworthy resistance during the post-election state of grace.

INSTITUTING THE SYSTEM

Rhetorically, the Fundamental Law adopted in 2011 responded to the democratic deficit of the post-1989 order. The "Founding Fathers" of the post-communist transition amended the communist constitution of 1949 beyond recognition, but failed to exploit the symbolic opportunity of creating a new one. To be sure, the lack of a new constitution after 1989 was due to the consensualist policy of the socialist-liberal coalition that had a supermajority between 1994 and 1998 but, facing the resistance of the opposition, especially the Young Democrats, did not insist on writing a new constitution. The Fundamental Law broke with the activist interpretation of the constitution advocated by László Sólyom, former president of the Constitutional Court (and president of the republic between 2005 and 2010), who developed the concept of an "invisible constitution." This was a self-regulating set of basic constitutional principles underlying the practice of the Constitutional Court after 1989, which circumvented the challenge of not having a fully-fledged new constitution. In contrast, the professed intention of the authors of the Fundamental Law was to create a permanent order, a *novus ordo saeclorum*, as it were, preventing the constitutional review of major executive decisions, and above all those concerning economic policy. This quest for permanence, manifested also in such grandiose projects as exhibiting decorated copies of the Fundamental Law in all public offices to celebrate Orbán's "democratic *Machtergreifung*."

In 2010, Fidesz broke with the stabilization policy of the expert government led by the socialist Gordon Bajnai in 2009–2010, which cooperated closely with the IMF and the EU. Orbán applied an ingenious method of political attrition described by Kim Lane Scheppele (2014) as selective austerity. Seemingly fitting in the European patterns of crisis management, it targeted institutions (in healthcare and social assistance as well as in cultural and educational spheres), the impoverishment of which produced less conflict in the short run than say, freezing wages or raising income taxes, and in many cases hurt the critics of government in person. "Unorthodoxy" was sold to the local and international public as a new way of anti-neoliberal economic thinking promoted by György Matolcsy, the "right hand" of Orbán.[59] As minister for economic affairs (later president of the National Bank), he advocated Keynesian-style state interventionism to raise employment and consumption, as well as accelerate export-led growth based on the "re-industrialization" of the country, initiated a bundle of protectionist policies to shelter "national capital," prompted the renationalization of certain industries and banks, and promoted the establishment of corporatist institutions. Unorthodoxy was combined with measures that in other contexts would be described as expressly neoliberal, such as introducing a flat income tax,[60] cutting welfare expenditure, and extending workfare.[61]

Frustrated with the fact that the economic survival of the Orbán government basically depended on Western demand for products manufactured in Hungary as well as EU transfers and American hedge funds that bought plenty of Hungarian state bonds, Orbán and Matolcsy sought to balance the country's dependence by making use of the "Eastern wind." Turning toward the East, that is, a rapidly developing part of the world as compared to the "declining West," was also motivated by political sympathy *vis-à-vis* anti-liberal regimes. Orbán's new "Russophilia" is the best example. After 2010, he abandoned his suspicions about Vladimir Putin, developed close political and economic ties with Russia, and encouraged the freedom of movement that Russian oligarchs and spies enjoy in Hungary (constantly provoking its partners in the EU and NATO). In 2014, the new friendship culminated in a contract for a new nuclear power plant to be financed and built by Russia in Hungary, and later in the pathetically ambiguous approach taken by the Orbán government to Russian aggression against Ukraine.

Most observers considered these policies unsustainable and even self-destructive, but economic stabilization in Europe after 2012 and, primarily, the robust performance of German industry had a salutary impact upon the Hungarian economy that largely hinges on a number of German blue chip companies such as Audi, Bosch, Mercedes-Benz, and Siemens.[62] Fortunately for the Young Democrats, recovery also was promoted by three other—accidental—factors: an ample supply of credit on international money markets, falling energy and raw material prices, and an unexpected growth of remittances from Hungarians working abroad. Preferential deals (formal and informal) proved profitable for favored multinational companies, providing them with a promising economic environment, with the power of the trade unions broken and the protection of the workers' interests minimized.[63] In exchange, they were ready to intervene in Orbán's favor in the political arena.

Overcoming the crisis entailed a further invasion by the state into business life in strategic sectors,[64] which, in turn, contributed to the withdrawal of a number of foreign investors. After having suffered serious losses during the recession, they decided to clean their portfolios and were happy to sell their assets, accepting bids that were often well above the market price. This strategy was extremely successful in sectors like banking and media, where such transactions often were made by government-funded buyers.[65]

Simultaneously, the government developed a well-designed mechanism for channeling EU funds to government-friendly companies.[66] This is how Fidesz exponentially strengthened the network of its own oligarchs. With the intimidation of entrepreneurs close to the socialists and their exclusion from public investment projects by informal means, new vistas opened to create a "national bourgeoisie" that was planned to become a main pillar of the SNC. Nevertheless, while the procedures to funnel European money to Orbán's cronies (such as Lajos Simicska, István Garancsi, and Lőrinc Mészáros) have been obvious from the start, there has hardly been any intervention by European authorities to prosecute the private expropriation of funds. Sadly, Eurocrats closed their eyes over the paradoxical situation, in which a huge amount of EU money has been used to consolidate a regime that proudly rejects the principles of liberal democracy and challenges the Union as such day-by-day. What may explain the reticence to intervene is, besides the proverbial clumsiness of Brussels, that part of the funds coming from the EU is directly or indirectly channeled westward in the form of subsidies for foreign investors.

Another key sphere of selective austerity was social policy. Here again, the statist drive has phased out most non-governmental actors (for example, in homeless care) and established a strong hierarchy between "deserving" and "undeserving" citizens. Focusing on the middle class and trusting in trickle-down effects, the Young Democrats ignored the underclass (whose members do not vote in great numbers) or relegated them to workfare. This also has an ethnic subtext rooted in a demographic panic that animated Hungarian ethno-populism since the 1930s, exaggerating the danger of the extinction of ethnically pure Hungarians and the growth of non-Hungarian population. Segregation of Roma children in the school system—a process tolerated if not encouraged by the government—is a sad consequence of the panic.[67]

Both the economic and social policies of the Orbán regime are permeated by nationalist concerns. Supporting Hungarians who live outside the country is a key aspect of the self-legitimization of the SNC.[68] This is manifest in symbolic gestures such as replacing the EU flag with that of Transylvania's Szeklers on the parliament building in Budapest or the introduction of a "Trianon memorial day" to anchor the national identity of a new generation of Hungarians in the collective trauma of being "dismembered" by the neighboring states and their Western allies after the First World War. In some way, the Orbán governments accomplished the dream of the national conservatives of the 1990s: the "reunification of the Hungarian nation" without changing the Trianon frontiers. Hungarian communities in neighboring states are shaped to a large extent by Hungarian public media, and lavish subsidies coming from Budapest contributed to the subordination of the local elites to Fidesz.

While the SNC seeks to integrate Hungarians living in neighboring countries, it has been reluctant to offer political voice to domestic citizens who migrated to Western Europe and overseas from 1989 onward. The electoral law allows the former to cast postal ballots whereas the latter need to appear at the Hungarian embassies in person. Thus, many young, oppositional-minded émigrés end up not voting at all, while more than 90 percent of the votes of Hungarians in Romania or Serbia are harvested by Fidesz.

Moreover, the entire symbolic space is engineered in a way that any criticism addressed to Orbán can be interpreted as an attack on the Hungarian nation as a whole. Hence, national history is re-narrated in terms of a millennial struggle to preserve the independence and ethnic homogeneity of the country. A binary opposition occurs between ethnic Hungarians and "aliens," the latter constructed as the source of all evils (ranging from Habsburg imperial bureaucracy to fascists and communists). From here there is only a small step to reach the far-right. Since 2014, Fidesz has been pillorying indigenous NGOs, which, as "foreign agents," spread political correctness and other cosmopolitan values, not to mention the "caressing of migrants," to copy right-wing newspeak. Another aspect of identity politics is coming to terms with the totalitarian heritage of the twentieth century. In this field, the historical narrative of the SNC is also highly controversial.[69] The Young Democrats aim at reshaping remembrance through the memorialization of communist crimes by basically equating communism and fascism.[70] Adding that the former had more victims than the latter (cf., the notorious method of "blood algebra"), this narrative had two functions: to justify the struggle against socialists, the alleged heirs of communist rule, and to accuse their liberal allies of having totalitarian leanings.

The memory of the Holocaust posed a great challenge for the ideologists of the SNC. The internal logic of the Orbánist historical narrative (reflected by the Preamble of the Fundamental Law as well as by the highly contested "Occupation of Hungary" monument in downtown Budapest) exempts the Horthy regime of any responsibility, declaring that the Holocaust occurred after Hungary had lost its sovereignty due to German occupation in March 1944. Nevertheless, both obvious factual problems (e.g., heavy anti-Jewish legislation before the Second World War, the eager involvement of the Hungarian state in deportations, etc.) and external constraints (e.g., the similarity between Orbán's and Netanyahu's political agendas) made it hard for Fidesz to reject moral obligation. This led to a doublespeak that in everyday politics avoids making reference to the Holocaust but expresses some regret in internationally visible situations.

THE SYSTEM OF NATIONAL COOPERATION AS A SIMULACRUM

In sum, the apparent eclecticism of the ideological universe of "national cooperation" notwithstanding, its constituents have something in common. They point to real dilemmas and dysfunctions of the post-1989 order, ranging from the "historical compromise" between the old and new elites, insider privatization, the corruption of the socialist-liberal coalition and the ensuing discrediting of democratic and liberal virtues, to an unprecedented dependence of the economy as a whole on a number of transnational firms, growing social polarization, the precarious situation of Hungarians living in neighboring states, and the unprocessed traumas of the right- and left-wing dictatorships in the twentieth century. Yet, rather than discussing these issues by taking into account the different perspectives and interests of all sides involved, Fidesz took them out of their context and tweaked them beyond recognition in the framework of its cultural revolution in order to justify its own move toward authoritarianism.

Rather than featuring a "fearful symmetry" commonly attributed to authoritarian regimes, the one built by Orbán and Fidesz is characterized by many inconsistencies and compromises. The *bricolage* of logically often incompatible components can be a source of strength, and the relative resilience of the SNC is due not to the innovative nature of these components but precisely to the unique and seemingly irrational combination of them. This is, however, not just an eclectic blend of policies and institutions taken out from other contexts, which often prompted analysts to describe the SNC as a hybrid regime. In fact, the lack of an essential core (beyond insisting on power *per se*) and the capacity of turning different faces to different observers may well be *the* main characteristic trait of Orbán's regime. In our opinion, the SNC works as a simulacrum.

It shows different images to different viewers, and these images are often distorted deliberately (bordering on travesty) to meet the viewers' expectations. Thus, it offers neoliberal economic policies to foreign investors and state subsidies to domestic entrepreneurs; a springboard for undermining the unity of the EU and NATO to Russian *siloviki*; traditional norms to old-school conservatives; permanent mobilization to those craving communal solidarity; the harassment of civil society to those who look back to the Horthyst or Kádárist police state with nostalgia; the defense of Judeo-Christian heritage against Islam to neo-traditionalist Jewish splinter groups and charismatic neo-Protestants; a political religion with a hero cult and a quasi-eschatological narrative of collective sin and redemption for secularized post-Christians longing for some sort of transcendence; anti-cosmopolitan campaigns with racist overtones to avatars of the interwar radical right; an ethnicist "theme park" for Western adherents of white supremacy,[71] but also an attractive location for African and Asian students hoping to get a cheap European diploma; a tax paradise and a gateway to the EU for Chinese, Israeli, Russian, Syrian, or Turkish businesspeople; a wannabe regional power for the local and global adherents of anti-liberalism and national egoism; and a docile and cooperative economic subregion of German industrial space for technocrats who believe in non-ideological mutual economic dependence. The SNC treats apolitical social groups rather liberally, leaving most of their private choices, including lifestyle and sexual orientation, to them, while repeatedly provoking and humiliating their ideals through the regime's influencers. Even worse is the fate of the liberal or leftist (and lately also anti-government rightist) activists and their organizations: they are doomed to face the entire repertoire of smear campaigns in the government-controlled media and embarrassing institutional harassment.

Having said that, ordinary citizens may have the impression that the government (more exactly, the supreme leader) hears their voice and provides them with goods they want: the worker dismissed by a foreign owner gets a new job in the renationalized firm, the farmer receives a parcel of state-owned land, the small entrepreneur a preferential credit from the central bank, retired persons higher pensions, and families larger tax benefits. Public employees (from teachers to soldiers—amounting to a quarter of the labor force in Hungary!) have preferential treatment in terms of salaries and/or job security, prestige, etc. The jobs, assets, and benefits are distributed selectively as political goods with the hardly hidden aim of extending the Fidesz constituency,[72] even if a considerable part of the "presents" come from the EU. In this way, most citizens who vote can count on *some* beneficial service from the paternalist government, while it is the task of all-encompassing state brainwashing to make them forget which goods they did not get from the *pater familias*, which goods proved to be fake, and which goods were taken away from them in exchange. The simulacrum (including its electoral success generator) works well if the imperfections and shortage of political goods are counterbalanced by their clever marketing. Meanwhile, a large part of citizens may feel to be among the "chosen." What is more, the xenophobic campaigns targeting the alleged conspiracy of all-too-familiar "enemies of the people" (Soros, the NGOs, Juncker, etc.) create a compelling illusion that fits well into Hungarian political culture, traditionally tuned as oppositional to the external powers that be.[73]

It would be too easy, we believe, to consider all this hypocrisy,[74] a chameleon attitude, or an orgy of post-truth, and blame the myopic median voter. It seems more telling in this regard that, despite having been cheated by the regime more than once, Hungarians at large still feel ready to compartmentalize reality and focus on their own (immediate) personal or group benefits rather than (future) costs because "national cooperation" is capable of turning its compassionate and supportive face toward them. The main characteristic of the SNC is exactly this mix of segmentation, fragmentation, variability, and camouflage (i.e., not just hybridity) that make it extremely hard to level a coherent political criticism against it. Last but not least, the fragmentation of reality is also central to political mobilization under the SNC. What Orbán needs is a highly mobilized minority and a highly demotivated and divided majority. This explains also his focus on migration when it comes to European-level politics: he does not aim at convincing the majority of European citizens with his intransigent biopolitical rhetoric but seeks to fragment the political discussion in a way that he can carve out a strong minority focusing on migration as an explanation for all troubles, while relegating all other issues to the background.

Hannah Arendt memorably described totalitarian regimes in terms of an onion structure, where one can peel back the layers (of more and more exclusive and elitist organizations), which have an external facade of normality and an internal interface of radicalism, while in the center there is a void in which the leader dwells.[75] In contrast, the structure of Hungary's System of National Cooperation resembles a garlic rather than an onion. What from the outside looks like a bulb is actually the aggregate of bigger and smaller cloves covered by a very thin papery sheath (the Fundamental Law, as it were). Rather than constituting the very center (garlic does not have an internal void), the leader is the flower that grows out of the scape. As the bulb lies underground, one first sees the flower. The larger and fancier the flower grows, the less energy the cloves actually get. The bulb is fed by its roots going deep in the soil: in our metaphor these roots are many, including authoritarian traditions, mobilization, indoctrination, and—last but not least—popular support.

SHAKY FORECASTS: CONSOLIDATION, IMPLOSION, OR . . . ?

Observers whose take on the SNC is shaped by the memory of authoritarian rule in the twentieth century tend to consider the regime transitory. They expect it to be able to preserve its variability until some sort of crisis causes its collapse into a genuine autocracy. It is just a question of time, they believe, when exactly Orbán will show his true colors as a dictator.

Needless to say, we do not consider it a primary task of history-writing to formulate predictions. Yet, if we had wrapped up this volume in early 2018, before Fidesz's third landslide victory, our forecast would have been more optimistic than afterwards, when the regime was quickening its steps on the way to become a de facto one-party state. Neither pre-election hope nor post-election apathy result in reliable estimates. Witnessing, during the past two years, a series of corruption scandals, a few strikes and street demonstrations, the bitter fight between Orbán and Simicska, victories of opposition candidates in local elections, and strong warnings by the European Commission against the authoritarian turn in Hungary, a number of analysts thought wishfully that the consolidation of the SNC was interrupted and its decline has begun. And vice versa, often the same people are observing the current moves of the Young Democrats to complete what they call "national systemic change" with consternation mixed with lethargy.

Indeed, the regime is busy to demolish the remaining bastions of resistance by launching a new round of *Kulturkampf* to break the independence of academic institutions such as the Hungarian Academy of Sciences. The "rationalization" of the Academy of Sciences is one of the final organizational steps in Orbán's cultural revolution, taken after subordinating the National Scientific Research Fund to the Ministry of Innovation; bolstering the regime's own "counter-academy," the Hungarian Academy of Arts; disciplining universities by curtailing their budgets and deploying Fidesz-appointee "chancellors" next to the rectors; chasing away the Central European University;[76] cleansing the school curricula; occupying the National Cultural Fund, the largest public grant-giving institution in the cultural sphere; laying off "disloyal" directors of museums and theaters; not to speak of creating an atmosphere in which the publication of blacklists, denunciation, or encouraging students to report on the political views of their professors may become business as usual. The immediate consequences are exit and loyalty (or at least self-censorship) rather than strong and lasting voice.

Another move by Orbán to perfect his regime is to please his party's constituency by implementing a major goal of the conservative revolution: pronatalism combined with nativism, or—as one of the Fidesz bosses put it—"those who fill the world with children own the world."[77] By means of a new "family protection" program, the government wants to raise birthrates through lavish benefits to be given to women who live in "normal" (i.e., not same-sex) marriages, have taxable income, are eligible to take a bank loan, and are ready to give birth to more than one child. Should we conclude from this that the Young Democrats continue to hijack the middle class in order to totalize "national cooperation" and humiliate women as machines of procreation? Or had we better suggest that preferring the carrot to the stick, that is, refraining from hardening the rules of abortion, Orbán does *not* escalate authoritarian control even if the financial incentives of his current pronatalist campaign are packaged in old-school conservative rhetoric? Again, both explanations can be correct depending on the perspective of the observer. However, one cannot resist the impression that—despite the ambiguities of the System of National Cooperation displayed by such snapshots—the film of the regime portrays an unmistakable process of Hungary creeping toward hardball varieties of authoritarian rule. True, she may not arrive there, neither sooner nor later.

To finish, we briefly sketch out two scenarios of how the film of the SNC could roll on:

Consolidation

Many social groups in Hungary have made their peace with the SNC and loyally accept it as long as wages go up, income tax is low, welfare allowances are distributed generously among middle-class and upper-middle-class families whose members also feel protected by law and order. The fragmentation of society follows many lines: economic, rural-urban, generational, educational, informational, etc., and existing divisions are reinforced by a government that incites the different groups against each other. The outcome resembles the pattern of post-Stalinist atomization and social *anomie* of Hungarian society following 1956 or the post-1968 "normalization" period in Czechoslovakia. By combining consumerism for citizens-at-large with a selective oppression of dissidents, these regimes proved relatively resistant to change and successful in muddling-through.

It may well be a long way to go until the consolidation of the Orbán regime turns into decline as well as popular acceptance into fatigue and resilience due to the growing inability of the SNC to deliver and/or to mounting external pressure. In all probability, a simple binary evolutionary model of rise and fall will not match the actual course of events. Further consolidation will be less a triumphal march to heaven than a pathetic craving to preserve the main pillars of the regime. It may overlap with decline, show cyclical features of tightening versus loosening the regime's grip over society, radicalization versus moderation or, in other words, accelerating versus slowing down the conservative revolution. Maybe creeping toward dictatorship will manifest itself in certain fields of the SNC while in other fields the regime will stop moving ahead or—God forbid—move backward a little. One thing is certain: any attempt to discontinue the authoritarian muddling through in *all* important fields, even for a while, carries the risk of discrediting the revolution, ridiculing the "supreme revolutionary," and may result in the ex- or implosion of his regime.

Implosion

Collaboration with the SNC penetrated the formal and informal institutions and cultures of society too deeply to be dismantled rapidly by either external intervention or an outburst of home-grown resistance leading to explosion. At the same time, "national cooperation" is not immune to an implosion. Undoubtedly, the SNC knights have amassed large fortunes during the past decade, and the political system became sufficiently polarized for the Fidesz elite to fear a rapid political downturn. However, a combination of increasingly unfavorable external conditions (e.g., slowdown of German industry, and a growing reticence of the EU to subsidize anti-liberal elites) and internal developments (e.g., emigration of qualified workforce, growing discontent with the deterioration of public services, especially education and healthcare) may well destabilize the regime. This was shown by the local elections in October 2019, in which Fidesz lost Budapest and a number of large towns in the provinces. The elections also proved that the central field of force can be damaged by a tactical coalition of the opposition parties. Also, the desiccation of resources sustaining its underlying social contract may invalidate Orbán's strategy of regime-building. As the SNC has been allocating to its supporters what others possessed or earned rather than generating new revenue, at a certain point it will have to make a distinction between its "deserving" and "undeserving" supporters.

Orbán also may fall victim to Orbánism itself. He has built "national cooperation" precisely around himself, which only works smoothly if he is able to balance the different stakeholders. Without him, the SNC may collapse overnight. As mentioned earlier, the regime is exposed to other threats, too. It may suffer from institutional overstretch or from an overdose of revolutionary mobilization and hubris and prove unable to keep its promises (bluntly put, to feed its voters and oligarchs at the same time). The 2019 local elections also demonstrated that overconfidence in the mobilizing techniques of Fidesz can backfire. Furthermore, underperformance of the regime at lower levels of society certainly increases citizens' frustration with corruption at higher levels. As soon as the hierarchy within the SNC becomes shaken, the regime may fast-track toward its own collapse.[78]

In contrast, a different configuration of almost the very same internal and external factors mentioned earlier also could catalyze a more repressive regime, pushing Hungary onto a road leading to Ankara, Beijing, or Moscow. The growing determination of authoritarian leaders to stiffen their regimes in response to a dwindling of resources likely will transform a slow process of implosion to explosion before Orbán becomes a senile, octogenarian "grandfather of the nation." It is already close to impossible to force him to quit by means of democratic elections. Maybe we, as the proverbial generals who always prepare for the previous war, trust too much in the plausibility of reviving the 1989-style negotiated regime change that at a certain juncture put an end to the implosion of the then *ancien régime* and led to the construction of a new one. However, the System of National Cooperation is not "ancient" yet and still has huge reserves of indoctrination and terror to employ. Currently, as paradoxical as it may be, Orbán is too strong to use sheer force.

Even if the current Hungarian variety of authoritarianism described in our book will eventually prove less than bulletproof and collapse before becoming a straightforward autocracy, its emergence and successful self-perpetuation must be an important point of comparative reference. Studying the "peripheries" may offer insights into patterns of evolution that manifest themselves less sharply in the "central" zones. The post-communist region of Central and

Eastern Europe was praised widely for its bloodless and smooth exit from decaying communist authoritarianism in 1989. Now, it provides a number of painful examples for a bloodless and smooth introduction of authoritarian rule under emerging capitalism.[79] The SNC, as dystopias are wont to do, anticipates a possible future of humankind; therefore, it may serve as a powerful warning for those who are just about to switch from understanding the new authoritarian temptations to their toleration or even acceptance.

While opponents of liberal democracy are more than conscious of their transnational entanglements, its adherents tend to sink into self-complacency or self-pity, and fail to develop transnational solidarity as long as things seem to go reasonably well in their own countries. If, in turn, they were also swallowed by the vortex of authoritarianism, they would have little moral basis to appeal to such solidarity.

NOTES

1. The authors were free to decide which term they wanted to apply.

2. While eugenics is arguably not central to the ideology of the SNC, one should not disregard its obvious biopolitical components, such as the focus on demography. As Ivan Krastev and Stephen Holmes (2018) argue, the demographic panic caused by low birth rates and sizable out-migration is one of the possible triggers of populist mobilization in Central and Eastern Europe, while the rejection of immigration is rather the cover story. At the same time, in Hungary, the boom of ethnopopulist mobilization predated (and perhaps contributed to) mass out-migration.

3. At the inauguration of Jair Bolsonaro in Brazil in January 2019, Orbán went even further. According to him, the best model of European Christian Democracy is in Brazil, where the newly elected president's slogan is: "Brazil first and God above all." Initially Orbán's strategy has been surprisingly successful within the Christian Democratic party family, keen on preserving its relative majority in the European Parliament, and it also resonates with the current program of the alt-right in the United States and Europe. In March 2019, the EPP decided to suspend the membership of Fidesz. Although in Hungary the decision was preceded by a large-scale propaganda campaign against the European Commission (ridiculing George Soros and Jean-Claude Juncker), the Political Assembly of the EPP did not exclude Orbán's party, and even allowed him to make the impression that Fidesz suspended its own membership.

4. In the Hungarian context he refers mainly to "Isten, Haza, Család" (God, Fatherland, Family), previously the slogan of the anti-communist Smallholders' Party (and of the Portuguese clerico-fascist *Estado Novo*) or, recently, to "Munka, Család, Haza" (Work, Family, Fatherland), which is identical to the catchphrase of the Vichy regime.

5. See the chapter by Dorottya Szikra in this volume.

6. There are spectacular rites of symbiosis between church, state, and army, such as the inauguration of military officers with a church blessing, or the festive commencement at the newly created National University of Public Service, where future

public servants are surrounded by military and religious paraphernalia. As for new military organizations, colorful examples range from the generously equipped anti-terror security service (TEK), which is regarded by the public as Orbán's personal guard led by his former driver, a separate Parliamentary Guard, and the Guard of the Hungarian National Bank, to setting up shooting ranges all over the country and the reintroduction of military education in secondary schools.

7. This is also reflected by Orbán's rhetoric when he likes to talk about Hungarians as a "half-Asiatic people" who understand the language of force, as well as by cultivating the totemic bird of Hungarian myth of origin, the *Turul*, and by giving official aura to such events as the *Kurultáj*, a jamboree of Turkic nations, organized in Hungary. Stressing these Asiatic features, he inadvertently follows the logic of most recent value surveys evidencing the survival of authoritarian/paternalist/egalitarian values in Hungarian society after communism (see Tóth 2017).

8. See Orbán (2014).

9. For similar concepts, see the notions of quasi-democracy (Villalon and Von Doepp 2005), hybrid democracy (Karl 1995), electoral democracy (Diamond 2002), guided democracy (Brown 2001), managed democracy (Wolin 2008), defective democracy (Merkel 2004), and Potemkin democracy (King 2001). See also the concept of informational autocracy (Guriev and Treisman 2015), as well as the studies by Diamond (2003), Bunce and Wolchyk (2011), and Müller (2016a).

10. For critical approaches to Zakaria's concept in Hungarian political science literature, see, for example, Kis (2014) and Bozóki (2016).

11. "Peacock dance" is an allusion to Hungarian "swing politics" between Germany and Great Britain in the Horthy era. Orbán memorably warned U.S. diplomats before the 2010 elections to disregard his words in order to dispel their worries about his radical nationalist rhetoric.

12. The defeated competitors range from Gábor Fodor to Lajos Simicska (both long-time friends of Orbán). The former was the leading figure of the liberals within Fidesz in the early 1990s, whereas the latter worked as the "cashier" of the party and grew into a major oligarch before 2014 when he broke with Orbán. From the old guard, it is only the president of the parliament, László Kövér, president of state, János Áder, and head of Fidesz MEPs in Brussels, József Szájer, who have remained on top, albeit assuming rather empty power positions. Meanwhile, Orbán surrounds himself with younger yes-men like his former secretaries, cabinet chief Antal Rogán, and foreign minister Péter Szijjártó. While Fidesz ministers come and go, minister of interior Sándor Pintér (a leading police officer prior to 1989) has remained in office in each Orbán government until today.

13. It is well known that, by that time, Fidesz controlled a number of large local governments and relied on leading dignitaries—such as the state president, members of the constitutional court, or key managers of the public media—to put pressure on the socialist-liberal governments and prevent the formation of alternative power centers in conservative politics. However, there is a hitherto uncovered aspect of informal interference by Fidesz (with the help of the richest banker in the country, Sándor Csányi) in the elections within the Hungarian Democratic Forum (MDF) by means of using secret service methods in 2008. The operation eventually resulted in the collapse of the only serious contender to Orbán on the center-right. Those organizing the

conspiracy in technical terms had worked for the state security during the first Orbán government.

14. Felcsút became internationally known after a luxury stadium had been built literally next to Orbán's house, with a capacity far exceeding the population of the village. The stadium is owned by a football club under his supervision, which—lavishly subsidized from taxpayers' money—skyrocketed to the first league in the subsequent months.

15. Among all aspects of the propaganda campaigns after 2010, the question of anti-Semitic connotations has been the most controversial because of the intolerance of political anti-Semitism by two Western powers shaping Hungarian politics (the United States and Germany), and because of a complex political game the Orbán government plays with the local Jewish community and the Israeli government. Fidesz seeks to forge a common nationalist and anti-Muslim agenda with Benjamin Netanyahu and support the neo-traditionalist radicalism of fringe groups of Judaism (e.g., the Chabad community) against mainstream Jewish organizations dominated by the assimilated and liberal Budapest Jewish elite. This entanglement provided Orbán with tangible benefits when critics of the anti-Soros campaign, who revealed the similarities of the posters with the Nazi propaganda images of Jewish plutocrats, could be silenced by the Israeli prime minister. Netanyahu confirmed that inciting hatred toward Soros is not anti-Semitism but a legitimate assertion of national interest.

16. On the concept of "post-peasant society," see Buzalka (2008).

17. As will be explained later, we use this term to make a cautious distinction between authoritarian rule, on the one hand, and autocracy, dictatorship, tyranny, etc., on the other. In our opinion, the SNC has been moving toward hard authoritarianism, thereby approaching (and in certain fields satisfying the criteria for) autocracy. Of course, the two terms tend to overlap but in Orbán's case they do so in a peculiar way, causing some confusion. In certain respects, his regime is still relatively soft while his quasi-hegemonic position within the regime probably would allow him to opt for harder authoritarian solutions. (Cf. Kornai 2011 and Kis 2019.)

18. Many contributors to this volume met Orbán in person either as his teacher, political ally, or opponent, a panelist in a public debate, or just a participant in private gatherings years ago when he was still accessible to academics like ourselves.

19. Cf. Dénes (2012). Hurrying to include the adjective "national" in names of state institutions and companies, for example, *Nemzeti Dohánybolt* (National Tobacco Shop), it has lost its solemn meaning in Hungarian as a notion related to Fatherland.

20. Critical journalism in Hungary uses the metaphor of *kisgömböc* (pig stomach) from a folk tale, which grows by swallowing people until it finally cracks, to depict the insatiable appetite of Orbán for power.

21. As for Orbán's personal attitude to law, here is an episode from his life, a man who graduated at the Law Faculty of the Eötvös University in Budapest. In 2001, he employed various tricks to obtain a state subsidy to enlarge his wife's winery, and when the corruption case became public after his fall from power in 2002, Orbán downplayed it with obscure arguments in court, with success. This was the third big corruption scandal of Fidesz after surviving a tax fraud case concerning firms within the party's orbit and the so-called quarry case linked to Orbán's father during the

1990s. These instances must have convinced the Fidesz leaders of the need to put a leash on the judiciary once in government again.

22. See Kovács (1998).

23. For example, Greskovits (2015) wrote about the "hollowing and backsliding of democracy" and reverting to "semi-authoritarian practices," Csillag and Szelényi (2015) about "drifting to managed illiberal democracy," and Szelényi (2017) about the "road to Damascus," where Orbán turned to authoritarianism, without estimating the distance the SNC already covered. For a rare instance of the opposite approach, see János Kornai (2015 and 2016) who set up a long list of characteristics of what he calls autocracy to distinguish it from both democracy (the point of departure) and dictatorship (a potential destination) while describing the "U-turn of Hungary." See also the concept of "autocratic breakthrough" in Kis (2019).

24. See Heller (2010); Kornai (2011, 2015, 2016); Pataki (2013); Tölgyessy (2013); Halmai (2014); Kis (2014, 2019); Ladányi and Szelényi (2014); Ungváry (2014); Greskovits (2015); Körösényi (2015, 2017); Csillag and Szelényi (2015); Szilágyi (2015); Enyedi (2016); Magyar (2016); Bozóki (2016); Szalai (2016, 2018); Antal (2017); Magyar and Vásárhelyi (2017); Bozóki and Hegedüs (2017, 2018); Filippov (2018); Szűcs (2018).

25. See, for example, Bozóki and Hegedüs (2018), who pioneeringly put the SNC in a European framework to demonstrate the external constraints and stimuli of its move toward authoritarianism. Csillag and Szelényi (2015) excel by focusing on property rights and introducing the concepts of patrimonialism and prebendalism in examining Orbán's drift toward authoritarian rule.

26. For an original attempt at periodization, see Krekó and Enyedi (2018).

27. These comparisons are, however, accepted widely in daily politics and journalism. If, for example, the concept of fascism occurs in the analysis, then a qualifier (like "mutant" or "soft") is attached to it, or it is moderated to "fascistoid" (Ungváry 2014). Likewise, the term "national socialism" is changed to "nation-socialism" (Bokros 2018) to avoid full identification with Nazism. For a broader overview, see Stanley 2018. The possibility of reviving monarchic rule in Hungary appears—for the time being—only in the analogy of Bonapartism if one disregards popular jokes about Orbán's absurd instruction in 2000 to move the royal crown to parliament, where his office was also located.

28. Only a few analysts, such as Kornai (2011), took the risk to call the SNC an autocracy right after the regime's birth, realizing that Fidesz could not be removed from power by democratic means in the future.

29. Among the institutional guarantees of irreversibility, the substantial extension of the period of service of the chief attorney, chief justice, members of the Constitutional Court, etc., (all Fidesz appointees) was perhaps the most expedient for the new rule.

30. True, the government's heartless attitude to refugees (e.g., keeping them in prison camps in miserable conditions) and the poor (e.g., expelling homeless people from public spaces) as well as criminalizing political opponents or employing criminals and private security guards to terrorize them demonstrates that the regime does not have any scruples about taking harsh measures if those promise political gain.

31. Interestingly enough, it is still widely supposed that Fidesz steals, bullies, and lies as well as organizes smaller show trials, but it does not kill.

32. A good illustration of this is Manfred Weber's statement in February 2019 about the need for a dialogue with Orbán to avoid making him, as he says, a new Cameron who eventually would take his country out of the EU. See Weise (2019).

33. Consolidation managed by the counterrevolutionary regimes after both 1919 and 1956 is remembered clearly in the Hungarian historical mind.

34. Plausibly, these are the fields in which scholarship had to react rapidly to radical and spectacular changes in the constitution. See the chapters by Gábor Halmai and Renáta Uitz in this volume, as well as the studies by Kim Lane Scheppele (2013, 2018).

35. It is perhaps not by chance that the concept of mafia is so popular in Hungarian political sociology. Compared to other metaphors, it has been examined in empirical terms the most profoundly thus far by Magyar and his colleagues. This was an important reason for us to organize a discussion on the relevance of the concept on the pages of our volume (see the contributions by Bálint Magyar, Stephen Holmes, and Balázs Váradi). For "re-feudalization" and "semi-feudalism," see Szalai (2016, 2018); Ádám (2019); for "patronalism," see Hale (2019); for ownership of land and local hierarchies in the countryside, see Kovách (2016, 2017).

36. An interesting feature of the Fidesz elite is its attraction to landed property, castles, wineries, real estate at Lake Balaton, and so on—a phenomenon that cannot be explained only by business rationale or snobbery.

37. To use analytical language, both terms denote a thick layer of communist and liberal elites who preserved strong links to the ex-communist party and converted their pre-1989 political privileges into economic power. In Hungary they were called "clotted structures" (*megalvadt struktúrák*); in Poland, pact or system (*układ*).

38. In the subculture of Fidesz, including the civic circles, Orbán often has been referred to as the "commanding general" (*vezénylő tábornok*) of the party.

39. In addition, the government declared proudly that Hungary would postpone the date of her joining the Eurozone, eschewing all advantages of the common currency but preventing the EU from intervening in Orbán's major economic decisions.

40. Western European politicians—explaining their inaction *vis-à-vis* the Hungarian government after 2010 versus the determined opposition shown to less radical measures of the PiS government in Poland after 2015—have often pointed to the "constitutional" nature of the SNC.

41. Another nickname for Orbán among his followers is "chief engineer."

42. To be sure, his government substantially contributed to this escalation by disrupting the system of domestic refugee care, cramming the refugees in Budapest, transporting all those who got stuck in Hungary to Austria during the night, and passing inaccurate information to the Austrian and German authorities about the number of those brought to the Western border.

43. For the text of the Tavares report, see http://www.europarl.europa.eu/sides/getDoc.do?type=TA&language=EN&reference=P7-TA-2013-315, accessed June 25, 2019.

44. In 2017 alone, the government spent EUR 40 million on the campaign against George Soros (see atlatszo.hu 2018). The French-based multinational advertising

company JCDecaux displayed most of the anti-Soros posters and earned about EUR 13 million from this account in the same year.

45. A similar game is played by the government within NATO where it compensates for fraternization with China and Russia by importing military equipment from the West.

46. On Finkelstein's role, see Grassegger 2019, even though many critics argued that this article overstated the importance of the advisors and understated the local ingredients of the hate campaign.

47. See "Többpólusúvá kell tenni Európát," https://www.youtube.com/watch?v=Md4agRiiBH0. Earlier, Orbán borrowed Silvio Berlusconi's slogan "Forza Italia!", and he still finishes every speech with "Hajrá Magyarország!" (Let's go, Hungary!).

48. See the chapter by Radosław Markowski in this volume. For a comparative analysis of various aspects of the Hungarian and Polish anti-liberal regime-building projects, see the articles in the thematic issue of *Osteuropa*, edited by Sapper and Weichsel (2018).

49. See the chapter by Silvia Marton in this volume.

50. Although "Orbánism" has become a trope in the global literature on new forms of anti-liberal politics, there are not so many diachronic analyses of the SNC available for international readership. A good recent overview is Bos (2018). Our reservations about typologies based on "snapshots" freezing reality and ignoring change concurs with János Kis's interpretation (Kis 2019).

51. It was known in Hungary as the "quarry case" and meant accepting hidden state subsidies in the form of precious buildings (given to Fidesz by the government with the aim of hosting the offices of the party) that were subsequently sold and the money was reinvested into companies around the party.

52. In addition, government agencies (such as the tax authority managed by Fidesz's chief of party finance, Lajos Simicska) were used to blackmail political opponents and business rivals.

53. The same government was notorious for co-opting a series of former communist dignitaries (including a member of the Politburo, a secretary of the Central Committee, and a deputy minister) and ordinary party members in the Fidesz *nomenklatura*, providing them with high-level positions such as president of the republic, chairman of parliament, minister of finance, minister of the interior, foreign minister, and so on.

54. See also Virág Molnár's chapter in this volume.

55. The engagement of the Orbán government with this issue in 2000–2002 also had a pragmatic reason. The expectation that Hungary would join the EU soon but the neighboring countries only later (or maybe never) produced a legitimate fear about the hardening of borders, which might cut channels of mobility as well as cultural and economic transfer between the Hungarian communities beyond the borders and the Hungarian state.

56. See the analysis of the so-called Status Law of 2001 in the chapters by Gábor Egry and Attila Melegh.

57. The Hungarian party system had been previously considered by most observers particularly stable (see, e.g., Enyedi and Tóka 2007; Casal Bértoa 2011).

58. See Renáta Uitz's chapter in this volume.

59. See the chapters by János Mátyás Kovács and Péter Mihályi in this volume.

60. While reducing personal income tax, the government raised VAT to a record high of 27 percent and introduced a great many special taxes in order to balance the budget.

61. See the chapter by János Köllő in this volume.

62. Throughout the 2010s, Germany has been the source or destination of about one quarter of Hungarian foreign trade. See: https://atlas.media.mit.edu/en/profile/country/hun/.

63. For example, the government recently passed a law allowing employers to demand up to 400 hours of overtime work a year and defer payment for three years.

64. See the chapter by Péter Mihályi in this volume.

65. See the chapter by Miklós Haraszti in this volume.

66. Orbán's former classmate and friend, Lőrinc Mészáros, who in 2010 still worked as a village plumber, became the richest person in the country by 2018 (his wealth exceeds one billion euros). In 2017 alone, he was awarded contracts worth EUR 850 million at public tenders, with 93 percent of this exorbitant sum coming from the EU. See atlatszo.hu (2019).

67. For instance, the subsidization of church schools that typically teach non-Roma children who are taken out from state-run schools by their parents leads to gradual ghettoization within the public education system. Selective pronatalist policies (supporting higher-income families) yield a similar result. Likewise, the public work system, set up by the government to tackle unemployment, offers low incomes in exchange for unproductive work while preventing the unemployed (many of them Roma) from escaping from dependency and reentering the job market. (In 2015, 42 percent of all employed Roma took part in the public work program, in contrast to the 4 percent of non-Roma; see "Időszaki munkaerőhelyzet," http://www.ksh.hu/docs/hun/xftp/idoszaki/munkerohelyz/munkerohelyz15.pdf, accessed June 25, 2019.) Due to the lack of alternatives, workfare has seemed a viable and acceptable solution in the eyes of many Roma families living in the poorest regions of the country—and actually secured their votes for Fidesz in 2014 and 2018.

68. See the chapter by Gábor Egry in this volume.

69. The spin doctor of Orbán's memory politics is Mária Schmidt, director of the House of Terror, head of state-sponsored nationwide commemoration projects, and—last, but not least—a wealthy businesswoman.

70. See the chapter by Ferenc Laczó in this volume.

71. See Bayer (2017).

72. Perhaps the most revolting example of bribing voters is when Fidesz activists distribute election goodies (potatoes, canned food, firewood, etc.) in Roma communities.

73. This is how a political style based on anti-systemic mobilization can turn systemic. For a long time, this development was neglected by most external observers captivated by the anti-institutional and anti-systemic features of Western European populist politics. Jan-Werner Müller (2016b) was among the first to focus on the possibility of populist regime-building, taking Hungary as one of his central test cases.

74. See Anne Applebaum (2019) on the hypocrisy of populist leaders.

75. "In contradistinction to both tyrannical and authoritarian regimes, the proper image of totalitarian rule and organization seems to me to be the structure of the onion, in whose center, in a kind of empty space, the leader is located; whatever he does—whether he integrates the body politic as in an authoritarian hierarchy, or oppresses his subjects like a tyrant—he does it from within, and not from without or above. All the extraordinarily manifold parts of the movement: the front organizations, the various professional societies, the party membership, the party bureaucracy, the elite formations and police groups, are related in such a way that each forms the facade in one direction and the center in the other, that is, plays the role of normal outside world for one layer and the role of radical extremism for another." (Arendt 1961, 99)

76. See the chapter by Zsolt Enyedi in this volume.

77. See HVG (2017).

78. One of Orbán's fans argues that his "political career will either come with him walking away, or with the sad fate of even a successful politician in a democracy; eventually everyone gets tired of you" (Fischer 2016). Walking away? Currently, all opposition parties promise meticulous justice-making, and the SNC knights do their best to keep much of their "savings" abroad and make sure that Fidesz appointees will continue to occupy leading positions in law enforcement long after the possible collapse of "national cooperation."

79. Tellingly, a leading expert on the post-communist trajectory of the region, Jacques Rupnik, argued twelve years ago (Rupnik 2007) that the backlash was relative: "For all these reasons, Europe is less vulnerable than other regions facing democratic regression." In contrast, in a recent (2018) article, he detected crisis phenomena all over the continent: "The post-1989 liberal cycle is exhausted. In Central Europe, it represented a triple transition: democracy, the market economy, and Europe. These three objectives were successfully attained, but all three are now in crisis."

BIBLIOGRAPHY

Ádám, Zoltán. 2019. "Refeudalizing Democracy: An Approach to Authoritarian Populism Taken from Institutional Economics." *Journal of Institutional Economics*, 1–14. https://doi.org/10.1017/S1744137419000304.

Antal, Attila. 2017. *A populista demokrácia természete*. Budapest: Napvilág.

Applebaum, Anne. 2019. "It's not xenophobia that links the 'new populists.' It's hypocrisy." https://www.washingtonpost.com/opinions/2019/02/11/its-not-xenophobia-that-links-new-populists-its-hypocrisy/?noredirect=on&utm_term=.69968d92e37b, accessed June 25, 2019.

Arendt, Hannah. 1961. *Between Past and Future: Six Exercises in Political Thought*. London: Faber and Faber.

atlatszo.hu. 2018. "Tavaly 12 milliárdot költött sorosozós reklámkampányokra a kormány." https://atlatszo.hu/2018/02/02/tavaly-12-milliardot-koltott-sorosozos-reklamkampanyokra-a-kormany/, accessed July 25, 2019.

————. 2019. "2018-ban Mészáros Lőrinc érdekeltségei nyerték a nemzeti tőkésosztály közbeszerzési versenyét." https://atlatszo.hu/2019/01/17/2018-ban-meszaros-lorinc-erdekeltsegei-nyertek-a-nemzeti-tokesosztaly-kozbeszerzesi-versenyet/, accessed July 25, 2019.

Bauer, Tamás. 2000. "1995." *Beszélő* 6: 51–89. http://beszelo.c3.hu/cikkek/1995.

Bayer, Lili. 2017."European far-right flocks to Hungary." https://budapestbeacon.co m/european-far-right-flocks-hungary/, accessed June 25, 2019.

Bermeo, Nancy. 2016. "On Democratic Backsliding." *Journal of Democracy* 27 (1): 5–19.

Bokros, Lajos. 2018. "Szabadság és Szolidaritás." *Élet és Irodalom* 62 (51–52), December 19.

Bos, Ellen. 2018. "Das System Orbán. Antipluralismus in Aktion." In *Unterm Messer. Der illiberale Staat in Ungarn und Polen.* Thematic issue, edited by Manfred Sapper and Volker Weichsel, *Osteuropa* 3–5: 19–32.

Bozóki, András. 2016. "Liberális autokrácia?" *Élet és Irodalom* 60 (10), March 11.

Bozóki, András, and Dániel Hegedűs. 2017. "Így írunk mi: az Orbán-rezsim értelmezései." *Mozgó Világ* 43 (2): 1–13.

————. 2018. "An Externally Constrained Hybrid Regime: Hungary in the European Union." *Democratization* 25 (7): 1173–89.

Brown, Archie. 2001. "From Democratization to 'Guided Democracy.'" *Journal of Democracy* 12 (4): 35–41.

Bunce, Valerie, Kathryn Stoner-Weiss, and Michael McFaul, eds. 2009. *Democracy and Authoritarianism in the Postcommunist World.* Cambridge: Cambridge University Press.

Bunce, Valerie, and Sharon L. Wolchik. 2011. *Defeating Authoritarian Leaders in Postcommunist Countries.* Cambridge: Cambridge University Press.

Buzalka, Juraj. 2008. "Post-peasant Memories: Populist or Communist Nostalgia." *East European Politics and Societies and Cultures* 32 (4): 988–1006.

Cameron, David R., and Mitchell A. Orenstein. 2012. "Post-Soviet Authoritarianism: The Influence of Russia in Its 'Near Abroad.'" *Post-Soviet Affairs* 28 (1): 1–44.

Carothers, Thomas. 2002. "The End of the Transition Paradigm." *Journal of Democracy* 13 (1): 5–21.

Casal Bértoa, Fernando. 2011. *Sources of Party System Institutionalization in New Democracies. Lessons from East Central Europe.* EUI Working Paper Series, SPS 2011 (1).

Collier, David, and Steven Levitsky. 1997. "Democracy with Adjectives: Conceptual Innovation in Comparative Research." *World Politics* 49 (3): 430–51.

Csillag, Tamás, and Iván Szelényi. 2015. "Drifting from Liberal Democracy: Traditionalist/Neo-conservative Ideology of Managed Illiberal Democratic Capitalism in Post-communist Europe." *Intersections* 1 (1): 18–48.

Debreczeni, József. 2017. *Az Orbán-rezsim 2010–201?.* Budapest: DE.HUKÖNYV Kft.

Dénes, Iván Zoltán. 2012. "Overcoming European Civil War: Patterns of Consolidation in Divided Societies, 2010–1800." *European Review* 20 (4): 455–74.

Diamond, Larry. 2002. "Thinking about Hybrid Regimes." *Journal of Democracy* 13 (2): 21–35.

————. 2003. The Illusion of Liberal Autocracy. *Journal of Democracy* 14 (4): 167–71.

Enyedi, Zsolt. 2016. "Paternalist Populism and Illiberal Elitism in Central Europe." *Journal of Political Ideologies* 21 (1): 9–25.

Enyedi, Zsolt, and Gábor Tóka. 2007. "The Only Game in Town: Party Politics in Hungary." In *Party Politics in New Democracies*, edited by Paul Webb and Stephen White, 147–78. Oxford: Oxford University Press.

Ferenczi, Krisztina. 2015. *Szüret – Az Orbán vagyonok nyomában*. Budapest: Tény 2014 Kft.

Filippov, Gábor. 2018. "A hybrid ellenforradalom kora." https://24.hu/belfold/201 8/07/31/filippov-gabor-a-hibrid-ellenforradalom-kora/.

Fischer, Tibor. 2016. "Viktor Orbán Is No Fascist." https://www.telegraph.co.uk/ne ws/worldnews/europe/hungary/12086883/Viktor-Orban-is-no-fascist-hes-David-C amerons-best-chance-at-EU-reform.html, accessed June 25, 2019.

Fish, M. Steven. 2005. *Democracy Derailed in Russia: The Failure of Open Politics*. Cambridge: Cambridge University Press.

Grassegger, Hannes. 2019. "Die Finkelstein Formel." https://www.dasmagazin.ch/ aktuelles_heft/n1-2-2/, accessed June 25, 2019.

Greskovits, Béla. 2015. "The Hollowing and Backsliding of Democracy in East Central Europe." *Global Policy* 6: 28–37.

————. 2017. *Rebuilding the Hungarian Right through Civil Organization and Contention: The Civic Circles Movement*. EUI Working Paper, RSCAS 2017 (37).

Guriev, Sergei, and Daniel Treisman. 2015. "How Modern Dictators Survive: An Informational Theory of the New Authoritarianism." NBER Working Papers 21136. Washington, DC: National Bureau of Economic Research.

Hale, Henry E. 2019. "Freeing Post-Soviet Regimes from the Procrustean Bed of Democracy Theory." In *Stubborn Structures*, edited by Bálint Magyar, 5–20. Budapest: CEU Press.

Halmai, Gábor. 2014. "Az illiberális demokrácián is túl?" *Élet és Irodalom*, September 5.

Heller, Ágnes. 2010. "Politikai bűnök és hibák." *Népszabadság*, October 2, 2010. http://nol.hu/belfold/20101002-politikai_bunok_es_hibak-831361.

Huxley, Aldous. 1932. *Brave New World*. New York: Random House.

HVG. 2017. "Németh Szilárd teleszülné a világot." https://hvg.hu/itthon/20170525 _Nemeth_Szilard_teleszulne_a_vilagot, accessed July 25, 2019.

Innes, Abby. 2013. "The Political Economy of State Capture in Central Europe." *Journal of Common Market Studies* 52 (1): 88–104.

Jakab, András, and László Urbán, eds. 2017. *Hegymenet. Társadalmi és politikai kihívások Magyarországon*. Budapest: Osiris.

Juhász, Attila, Bulcsú Hunyadi, and Edit Zgut. 2015. *Focus on Hungary: Refugees, Asylum and Migration*. Prague: Heinrich Böll Stiftung.

Kállay, Béni. 1883. *Magyarország a Kelet és Nyugot határán*. Budapest: M. T. Akadémia Könyvkiadó-Hivatala.

Karl, Terry Lynn. 1995. "The Hybrid Regimes of Central America." *Journal of Democracy* 6: 72–86.

King, Charles. 2001. "Potemkin Democracy." *The National Interest*, Summer: 93–104.

Kirchick, James. 2017. *The End of Europe: Dictators, Demagogues, and the Coming Dark Age*. New Haven, CT: Yale University Press.

Kis, János. 2014. "Illiberális demokrácia nem létezik." *hvg.hu*, November 24. https://hvg.hu/velemeny/20141124_Kis_Janos_illiberalis_demokracia_nem.

———. 2019. "Demokráciából autokráciába. A rendszertipológia és az átmenet dinamikája." *Politikatudományi Szemle* 26 (4): 45–74.

Kornai, János. 2011. "Taking Stock." *Monthly Report of WIIW*, 2011/12: 1–12.

———. 2015. "Hungary's U-Turn." *Capitalism and Society* 10 (2): 1–24.

———. 2016. "The System Paradigm Revisited." *Acta Oeconomica* 66 (4): 547–96.

Kovách, Imre. 2016. *Földek és emberek*. Budapest: MTA TK – Dupress.

———, ed. 2017. *Társadalmi integráció. Az egyenlőtlenségek, az együttműködés, az újraelosztás és a hatalom szerkezete a magyar társadalomban*. Szeged: MTA Szociológia Intézet and Belvedere Meridionale Kiadó.

Kovács, János Mátyás. 1998. "Uncertain Ghosts. Populists and Urbans in Postcommunist Hungary." In *The Limits of Social Cohesion*, edited by Peter L. Berger, 113–45. Boulder, CO: Westview Press.

———. 2017. "Vom Zweifel zur Scham: sieben falsche Vorhersagen über das postkommunistische Ungarn." *Transit* 50: 145–57.

Körösényi, András. 2015. "A magyar demokrácia három szakasza és az Orbán-rezsim." In *A magyar politikai rendszer – negyedszázad után*, edited by András Körösényi, 401–22. Budapest: Osiris-MTA TK.

———. 2017. "Weber és az Orbán-rezsim: plebisziter vezérdemokrácia Magyarországon." *Politikatudományi Szemle* 26 (4): 7–28.

Krastev, Ivan, and Stephen Holmes. 2018. "Explaining Eastern Europe: Imitation and Its Discontents." *Journal of Democracy* 29 (3): 117–128.

Krasztev, Péter, and Jon Van Til, eds. 2015. *The Hungarian Patient: Social Opposition to an Illiberal Democracy*. Budapest: CEU Press.

Krekó, Péter, and Zsolt Enyedi. 2018. "Explaining Eastern Europe: Orbán's Laboratory of Illiberalism." *Journal of Democracy* 29 (3): 39–51.

Ladányi, János, and Iván Szelényi. 2014. "Posztkommunista neokonzervativizmus." *Élet és Irodalom*, February 21.

Lendvai, Paul. 2012. *Hungary: Between Democracy and Authoritarianism*. New York: Columbia University Press.

———. 2017. *Orbán: Hungary's Strongman*. Oxford: Oxford University Press.

Levitsky, Steven, and Lucan A. Way. 2010. *Competitive Authoritarianism: Hybrid Regimes after the Cold War*. Cambridge: Cambridge University Press.

Levitsky, Steven, and Daniel Ziblatt. 2018. *How Democracies Die: What History Tells Us about Our Future*. New York: Crown.

Levitz, Philip, and Grigore Pop-Eleches. 2010. "Why No Backsliding? The European Union's Impact on Democracy and Governance before and after Accession." *Comparative Political Studies* 43 (4): 457–85.

Linde, Jonas, and Joakim Ekman. 2011. "Patterns of Stability and Change in in Post-Communist Hybrid Regimes." In *20 Years Since the Fall of the Berlin Wall:*

Transitions, State Break-Up and Democratic Politics in Central Europe and Germany, edited by Elisabeth Bakke and Ingo Peters, 97–120. Berlin: Berliner Wissenschafts-Verlag.

Magyar, Bálint. 2016. *Post-Communist Mafia State. The Case of Hungary.* Budapest: CEU Press.

———. 2019, ed. *Stubborn Structures. Reconceptualizing Post-Communist Regimes.* Budapest: CEU Press.

———, and Júlia Vásárhelyi, eds. 2014 and 2015. *A magyar polip*, Volumes I and II. Budapest: Noran Libro.

———, and Júlia Vásárhelyi, eds. 2017. *Twenty-Five Sides of a Post-Communist Mafia State.* Budapest: Central European University Press.

Merkel, Wolfgang. 2004. "Embedded and Defective Democracies." *Democratization* 11 (5): 33–58.

Mihályi, Péter. 2017. "Hol élünk? Az Orbán-rendszer logikája." *Mozgó Világ* 43 (7–8): 3–16.

Müller, Jan-Werner. 2013. *Wo Europa endet. Ungarn, Brüssel und das Schicksal der liberalen Demokratie.* Berlin: Suhrkamp.

———. 2016a. "The Problem with 'Illiberal Democracy.'" *Project Syndicate*, January 21. https://www.socialeurope.eu/the-problem-with-illiberal-democracy.

———. 2016b. *What Is Populism?* Philadelphia: University of Pennsylvania Press.

———. 2018. "Homo Orbanicus." *The New York Review of Books*, April 5, 2018.

Orbán, Viktor. 1987. "Társadalmi önszerveződés és mozgalom a politikai rendszerben (A lengyel példa)." Budapest: ELTE ÁJTK. http://2010-2015.miniszterelno k.hu/attachment/0017/szakdolgozat.pdf.

———. 2014. "Full text of Viktor Orbán's speech at Băile Tuşnad (Tusnádfürdő) of 26 July 2014." https://budapestbeacon.com/full-text-of-viktor-orbans-speech-at-b aile-tusnad-tusnadfurdo-of-26-july-2014/, accessed June 25, 2019.

Pap, András László. 2017. *Democratic Decline in Hungary: Law and Society in an Illiberal Democracy.* Abingdon: Routledge.

Pataki, Ferenc. 2013. *Hosszú menetelés: a Fidesz-jelenség.* Budapest: Noran Libro.

Rupnik, Jacques. 2007. "From Democracy Fatigue to Populist Backlash." *Journal of Democracy* 18 (4): 17–25.

———. 2018. "Explaining Eastern Europe: The Crisis of Liberalism." *Journal of Democracy* 29 (3): 24–38.

Rupnik, Jacques, Martin Butora, Bela Greskovits, Ivan Krastev, Alina Mungiu-Pippidi, Krzysztof Jasiewicz, and Vladimir Tismaneanu. 2007. "Is East-Central Europe Backsliding?" *Journal of Democracy* 18 (4).

Sapper, Manfred, and Volker Weichsel, eds. 2018. *Unterm Messer. Der illiberale Staat in Ungarn und Polen.* Thematic issue. *Osteuropa* 3–5.

Scheppele, Kim Lane. 2013. "The Rule of Law and the Frankenstate: Why Governance Checklists Do Not Work." *Governance* 26 (4): 559–62.

———. 2014. "Hungary and the End of Politics." *The Nation.* May. https://www.the nation.com/article/hungary-and-end-politics/.

———. 2018. "Autocratic Legalism." *The University of Chicago Law Review* 85 (2): 545–83. https://lawreview.uchicago.edu/publication/autocratic-legalism.

Szalai, Erzsébet. 2016. "A refeudalizáció." *Replika* 1: 207–22.

———. 2018. "Félfeudális hatalmi rend Magyarországon." https://hvg.hu/itthon/201 80927_szalai_erzsebet_felfeudalis_hatalmi_rend_magyarorszagon.

Szelényi, Iván. 2017. "Utószó." In *Hegymenet. Társadalmi és politikai kihívások Magyarországon*, edited by András Jakab and László Urbán, 461–65. Budapest: Osiris.

Szilágyi, Ákos. 2015. "Vezérdemokrácia vagy Cezarizmus?" *2000* (5): 1–65.

Szűcs, Zoltán Gábor. 2018. "Ha nem demokráciában élünk, akkor . . . ?" *Élet és Irodalom*, August 3.

Tellér, Gyula. 2014. "Született-e Orbán-rendszer 2010 és 2014 között?" *Nagyvilág* 59 (3): 346–67.

Tóth, István György. 2017. "Turánbánya? Értékválasztások, beidegződések és az illiberalizmusra való fogadókészség Magyarországon." In *Hegymenet. Társadalmi és politikai kihívások Magyarországon*, edited by András Jakab and László Urbán, 37–51. Budapest: Osiris.

Tölgyessy, Péter. 2013. "Az Orbán-rendszer természete." *Komment.hu*, June 18, 19, 20, 21, 23.1–6.

Trencsényi, Balázs. 2014. "Beyond Liminality? The Kulturkampf of the Early 2000s in East Central Europe." *Boundary* 2 (41): 135–52.

———. 2017. "Transit wohin? Die Rückkehr der Geschichte, nachdem sie eine Weile als vermisst galt." *Transit* 50: 72–85.

Trencsényi, Balázs, Maciej Janowski, Mónika Baár, Maria Falina, Luka Lisjak-Gabrijelčič, and Michal Kopeček. 2018. *History of Modern Political Thought in East Central Europe*. Volume II/1: *Negotiating Modernity in the "Short Twentieth Century and Beyond" (1918–1968)*; and Volume II/2: *Negotiating Modernity in the "Short Twentieth Century and Beyond" (1968–2018)*. Oxford: Oxford University Press.

Ungváry, Rudolf. 2014. *A láthatatlan valóság: a fasisztoid mutáció Magyarországon*. Bratislava: Kalligram.

Villalon, Leonardo Alfonso, and Peter Von Doepp, eds. 2005. *The Fate of Africa's Democratic Experiments: Elites and Institutions*. Bloomington: Indiana University Press.

Vörös, Imre. 2014. "Alkotmányos puccs Magyarországon 2010–2014." In *Magyar Polip–A posztkommunista maffiaállam 2*, edited by Bálint Magyar and Júlia Vásárhelyi, 69–96. Budapest: Noran Libro.

Weise, Zia. 2019."Weber on Orban." https://www.politico.eu/article/munich-securi ty-conference-live-blog/#1254293, accessed June 25, 2019.

Wolin, Sheldon. 2008. *Democracy Incorporated: Managed Democracy and the Specter of Inverted Totalitarianism*. Princeton, NJ: Princeton University Press.

Zacsek, Gyula. 1992. "Termeszek rágják a nemzetet, avagy gondolatok a Soros-kurzusról és a Soros-birodalomról." *Magyar Fórum* 4 (36): 9–16.

Zakaria, Fareed. 1997. "The Rise of Illiberal Democracy." *Foreign Affairs* 76 (6): 22–43.

Index

abortion, 166, 169, 232, 234, 340, 350, 394, 417
acquis communautaire, 188, 319
Áder, János, 213, 250, 421
Antall, József, 13, 31, 44, 74, 75, 120, 213, 403
anti–communism, 30, 34, 35, 100, 119, 230, 354, 390, 401–6, 408, 420
anti–liberalism, 1, 3, 33, 216, 292–99, 379, 382–83, 388–90, 393, 397, 409, 414, 418, 425. *See also* liberalism
anti–Roma sentiment, 17–18, 66, 69, 84, 153, 169, 173, 222, 234, 236–38, 300, 371, 381, 385, 426
anti–Semitism, 38, 43, 69, 130, 207, 222, 295, 404, 422. *See also* Jews
Arendt, Hannah, 221, 416, 427
Arrow-Cross Party, 65, 122–23. *See also* fascism, national socialism
Article 7 (Treaty on European Union), 255, 312, 315–17, 319–20, 349, 399
austerity, 116,119, 153, 225–26, 230, 326, 390, 396, 404, 410, 412
Austria, 115, 118, 146, 149, 163–64, 177, 217, 255, 261, 315, 323–24, 424
authoritarianism, 2, 10, 11, 36, 38, 51, 55, 99, 100, 118, 178–79, 245, 269, 292, 294, 296, 299–300, 305, 309, 313, 318, 320, 325–27, 348, 362,

380, 382–83, 386–87, 389, 391–94, 396, 402, 414, 416–23, 427
autocracy, 2, 270, 295, 348, 386, 392–94, 416, 419, 421–23
autonomy: of national minorities, 75–79, 83, 84, 87–89; of academia and universities, 30, 126–27, 187, 243, 254, 257, 260, 264, 348

backsliding, 2, 298, 314, 319, 423
Balkans, 271, 372
banks, 10, 61, 111–12, 115, 117–18, 124, 126, 149, 169, 186, 188–89, 193–95, 199, 203–4, 207, 217, 221, 231, 237, 275, 298, 353, 381, 385, 395, 396, 408–11, 415, 417, 421; banking system, 10, 111–12, 117–18, 126–27, 130, 169, 186, 188, 203, 204, 207, 221, 353, 408–11, 415, 421
Bauer, Tamás, 78, 128
Bavaria, 115, 317
Bayerische Landesbank, 193, 204
Berlusconi, Silvio, 1, 324, 425
biopolitics, 170, 178, 416, 420
Bokros, Lajos, 128, 168, 404–5, 423
Bolshevism, Bolsheviks, 287, 391–92, 395. *See also* anti–communism and communism
Boross, Péter, 31, 44, 232

Brexit, 177, 294, 297, 400
bricolage, 2, 113, 227, 414
Brussels, 19–20, 25, 58–59, 89, 117,
	159, 221, 251, 258, 294, 297–300,
	311, 313–14, 316, 320, 323, 325,
	327, 389, 397, 412, 421
Budapest, 3, 20, 40–42, 55, 56, 64–66,
	69, 74–75, 85, 87, 97, 99, 187, 191,
	193, 204, 215, 233, 244–47, 250,
	252, 254–56, 258, 279, 284, 287,
	317, 322–23, 345, 384, 403, 412–13,
	419, 422, 424
bureaucracy, 53, 56, 58, 79, 212, 246,
	257–58, 316, 358–60, 366, 370, 386,
	413, 427

Calvinism, 75, 106, 108
Cameron, David, 177, 424
capitalism, 2, 113, 116–17, 119–20,
	122, 124, 127, 229, 270, 295,
	297–300, 352, 388–90, 392–95,
	401, 402, 419
Carpathian Basin, 64, 86, 88, 90
Catholicism, 83, 97–100, 106–8, 332,
	336, 340, 347, 349, 402
Ceauşescu, Nicolae, 74, 366
censorship (self-censorship), 57,
	211–12, 221, 301, 393, 417
Central Europe, 2, 3, 33–34, 36–37, 41,
	57, 61, 97, 124, 167, 176, 207, 217,
	226, 332, 346, 371, 406, 427
Central European University (CEU,
	KEE), 3, 17, 61, 69, 233, 243–66,
	417; Lex CEU, 69, 243–66; "Soros
	University," 247, 249, 260
central field of force, 382, 390, 409, 419
children, 41, 76, 83, 139, 142–45, 151,
	153, 155, 166–69, 222, 231–36,
	238–39, 261, 306, 308, 332, 333,
	353, 417, 426
China, 100, 129, 165, 166, 187, 295,
	297, 307, 398–99, 425
Christian Democracy, 9, 101, 233, 255,
	317, 323, 366, 381–82, 420
Christian Democratic People's Party
	(KDNP), 9, 219, 233

Christianity, Christians, 9, 14, 16, 23,
	63, 91, 96, 98–102, 105, 124, 176–
	77, 195, 218, 228, 233, 254–55, 299,
	307, 308, 317, 323, 366, 381–82,
	398, 401–2, 405, 414, 420
Church, 55, 83, 85, 95–109, 153, 219,
	227–28, 236–37, 243, 308, 332, 336,
	340, 347, 381, 389, 402, 405, 420,
	426. *See also* religion
civic circles, 53, 391, 405–6, 408, 424
civil society, uncivil society, 18, 20, 33,
	51–72, 105, 226, 228, 247, 273, 323,
	325, 349–50, 352, 370–71, 381–82,
	399, 406, 414
citizenship, 16, 51, 62, 73–74, 76–81,
	83–84, 86–89, 91, 172–73, 179, 320,
	391, 397, 406, 409
class: upper class, 125, 168, 204–5, 212,
	216–17, 234, 236, 295, 299, 301,
	307, 341, 385, 401, 421, 426; middle
	class, 83, 91, 117, 121, 124, 168–70,
	234–36, 264, 281, 297, 306, 341,
	385, 394, 401, 403–4, 407–8, 412,
	417–18; lower class, 18, 117, 121,
	124, 140, 149, 150, 154, 168, 170,
	175, 226, 234, 236–38, 281, 293,
	297, 300, 320, 341, 353, 381, 385,
	419, 423, 426
clientelism, 170, 194, 204–5, 270, 281,
	291, 300, 348, 357, 364, 392
Cold War, 33, 62, 68, 294, 392, 398
communism, communists, 14, 30–36,
	39, 41, 44, 66, 74, 81–82, 96, 100,
	108, 112–13, 116, 119–22, 125–27,
	159, 190, 206, 212–13, 221–22, 234,
	287, 295, 305–6, 340, 347, 354,
	358–59, 366, 368–69, 371, 380, 382,
	385, 387–90, 392–93, 397, 401–10,
	413, 419–21, 424–25
colonialism, 172, 294, 314
competition (economic, political), 74,
	84, 105, 120, 155, 162, 170, 178,
	194–95, 200, 206, 214, 218, 226,
	243, 260, 271, 276, 295, 297, 305,
	309, 326, 350, 357–58, 360, 362,
	366, 392, 395, 407, 421

conservatism, 9, 13, 16, 31, 34–35, 45,
56, 88, 99, 100, 107, 113, 116, 119,
122, 127, 169, 170, 176, 213, 218,
226–28, 231–32, 236–37, 255, 263–
64, 305, 308, 317, 323, 349, 363,
365, 368, 371, 375, 381–82, 386,
390, 392, 394, 397–98, 400, 402–4,
407–8, 412, 414, 417–18, 421
consolidation, 2, 21–22, 52–53, 76, 113,
118, 127, 177, 243–44, 293, 309,
314, 331, 352, 358, 361, 370, 373,
380, 394, 400–401, 412, 416, 418,
424
conspiracy theory, 125, 127, 176, 262,
309, 384, 389–90, 399, 403, 415, 422
Constitution: constitutional
amendments, 9, 10, 12, 14, 16, 20,
24–25, 56, 69, 98, 100, 102–4, 107,
222, 248–50, 252, 255–56, 260, 262,
277–79, 322, 397–98; constitutional
coup, 3, 10, 22, 389, 397. *See also*
Fundamental Law
Constitutional Court, 9, 10, 12–13, 16,
18–20, 22, 96–97, 101–3, 107–8,
220, 230, 251, 253–54, 258, 316,
321, 326, 350–51, 360, 364, 367,
397, 408–10, 421, 423
"Copenhagen Commission"
(Copenhagen criteria), 77, 311, 318–
20, 323–25, 349
corporatism, 74, 83–84, 88, 90, 124,
349, 382, 388, 410
corruption, 21, 34, 56, 58–59, 191, 214,
216, 218, 220, 245, 270–73, 275,
281–86, 292–93, 295, 301, 333–34,
349, 353, 357, 360–61, 367–75,
380–81, 386, 389, 396, 399, 401,
404, 408, 414, 416, 419, 422
courts, 9, 10, 12–14, 16–22, 59, 61,
66, 88, 96, 97, 101–4, 107–8, 192,
195–96, 198, 200–3, 215, 220, 230,
250–54, 258, 272–73, 276, 286,
313–14, 316, 320–21, 324, 326, 345,
350–51, 360, 364, 367, 397, 400,
408–10, 421–23. *See also* judges,
judiciary

Criminalization: of aid to refugees, 18,
61, 99, 222; of immigration, 19, 25,
66, 161, 174; of NGOs, 60–61, 222,
393
cronyism, cronies, 126–27, 211, 216,
270, 291, 306, 345, 382, 392
Croatia, 36–37, 174, 191, 255, 401
CSOK (family home-building benefit),
169, 235, 237
Csurka, István, 35, 74, 213, 403
culture war, *Kulturkampf*, 34, 323, 403,
404, 417

Declaration of National Cooperation,
9–28
democracy, democratization, 9, 11,
13–14, 19, 22–24, 33–34, 36, 51, 58,
62, 105–6, 109, 120, 185, 211, 215,
221–22, 225, 227, 245, 267, 269,
271, 273, 285–86, 291–301, 303–5,
309, 311–12, 314–15, 317, 323,
325–28, 332, 338, 346, 348–49, 351,
353, 357, 360, 379, 381–83, 386,
388, 391–93, 397, 399, 401, 406,
409, 412, 420–21, 423, 427. *See also*
illiberal democracy
Denmark, 106, 152, 399
deserving/undeserving poor/groups,
168–69, 228, 236–38, 381–412, 419
Deutsche Telekom, 217, 219
disability: disabled people 16–17,
231–32, 237, 282; disability pensions
16–17, 19, 141, 164, 227, 229–32,
237–38
discrimination, 16, 36, 61, 66–68, 77,
87, 101–4, 149, 173, 177, 194–95,
212, 235, 237–38, 245, 249, 259–60,
262, 277, 280, 316, 328, 396
dystopia, 1, 379–80, 420

Eastern Europe 2, 35, 43, 45, 51, 64, 89,
116, 163, 165, 172, 315, 321, 372,
388, 393, 419, 420
East Central Europe 33–37, 41, 97, 149,
167, 176, 315, 321, 371–72, 388,
393, 419–20

Eastern opening, 187, 307–8, 399
economy, 3, 15, 17, 32, 34, 36, 39,
    51, 75, 79–80, 83, 85–90, 111–36,
    142, 146–47, 150, 154–55, 162–65,
    168–71, 173, 176, 178, 186, 189–91,
    195–96, 198, 200, 202, 206, 211–12,
    225, 227–28, 234, 236, 238, 243,
    270–73, 275, 278–79, 286, 293–95,
    297–300, 304, 306–9, 313, 326, 332–
    34, 340–42, 348, 350–53, 370–72,
    380–84, 388, 394, 396–401, 403–12,
    414–15, 418, 424–25, 427
education, 40, 58, 68, 69, 78, 83, 88,
    90, 127, 139–46, 151–54, 165–66,
    168, 170, 173, 187, 200, 231, 236,
    243–66, 308, 342, 346–48, 385, 391,
    406, 410, 418–19, 421, 426
EEA (European Economic Area), 57–
    59, 248, 259
elections, 1, 9–14, 16, 18, 21–24, 29,
    52, 53, 55, 68, 73, 75, 80–81, 87,
    109, 125–26, 139–41, 185–88, 190,
    203, 206–7, 211, 213–15, 217–22,
    253–54, 264, 297, 304–5, 308,
    317–18, 327, 331–48, 352, 354,
    357, 359–72, 383, 385, 386, 388,
    390–91, 393–97, 402–5, 407–9, 416,
    419, 421, 426; election campaign,
    18, 23–24, 29, 38, 55–56, 77, 85,
    140, 172, 205, 213–14, 216–17, 220,
    233–34, 318, 333–34, 338–39, 341,
    344–46, 353–54, 361, 364, 371, 391,
    400, 404–8; election/electoral law,
    73, 338, 358, 367, 397, 399, 412;
    "electoral success generator," 388,
    415
employment, 84, 114–15, 117, 124–26,
    139–58, 165–66, 178, 200, 238,
    244–45, 364, 410, 415
Erdoğan, RecepTayyip, 105, 382, 393
ethnopopulism, 404, 420
European Commission, 9, 21, 61, 174,
    196, 198, 200, 202, 251–52, 259,
    314–15, 319–20, 326, 349, 367, 420

European Court of Human Rights
    (ECtHR), 9, 17, 21, 61, 102–4, 107,
    195–96, 198, 200, 202
European Court of Justice, 230, 252,
    254, 316, 320, 328
European Parliament, 9, 100, 160, 251,
    255, 261, 303, 317–18, 398–99, 420
European People's Party (EPP), 100,
    251, 255, 317, 318, 371, 381, 398,
    399, 420
European Union (EU), 2, 20, 36–38, 43,
    45, 54–55, 57, 61, 64, 84, 89,100,
    106, 117–18, 124, 127, 139–40,
    149, 155, 161–63, 166–67, 171–74,
    177–79, 185–88, 191 196, 198, 200,
    202–3, 206, 211–12, 215–17, 220,
    222, 230, 234, 249, 251, 262, 271,
    283, 287, 294, 299–300, 303, 305,
    308, 311–30, 332–33, 339–40, 346–
    47, 349–50, 353, 358–59, 372–73,
    379, 383, 389, 394, 398–99, 405–6,
    408–12, 414–15, 418, 424–26
Europeanization, 34, 37, 317–18, 359,
    366
Euroskepticism, 20, 100, 187, 299,
    326–27, 332, 345, 354, 372, 398

fake news, 217, 221
family, 16, 43, 81, 98, 115, 117, 121,
    123–24, 129, 153–54, 161, 167–70,
    198, 204–5, 212, 216, 226–28,
    232–39, 271–73, 276–78, 280–86,
    300–301, 303, 317, 323, 346, 353–
    54, 381–82, 385, 387, 395, 398, 400,
    417, 420; family policy, 161, 169,
    227, 232–38; family tax allowance,
    167–70, 234–36, 239, 346; "family
    values", 232–33, 381; political
    family, 271–73, 280–86, 300–301
fascism, 2, 38, 65, 114, 123, 126, 170,
    205, 221, 300, 321, 371, 380, 392,
    401–2, 409, 413, 420, 423. *See also*
    Nazism
Felcsút, 217, 385, 422

Fidesz (Alliance of Young Democrats), 1, 9–10, 12, 14, 21, 23, 29–30, 34, 38–39, 41–45, 52, 54–55, 57, 60, 64, 68, 73–80, 83–91, 100, 109, 112, 119, 139–43, 146–47, 149, 160, 173, 186, 188, 191–95, 205–7, 213–17, 219–20, 225, 228–31, 233, 235, 237–39, 245, 250–51, 254, 256–57, 259, 263, 281, 283, 285, 287, 297, 306–8, 316–17, 332, 339, 341, 349, 350, 364–65, 368–72, 379–86, 388–98, 400, 402–5, 407–18, 420–27

Finkelstein, Arthur, 217, 400, 425

First World War, 44, 82, 95, 99, 412

football (soccer), 63, 201, 203, 279, 300, 363, 382, 385, 408, 422

France, 37, 68, 106, 195, 321

"Frankenstate",10, 382

foreign agent, 51, 56–57, 61, 68, 212, 413

foreign minister, foreign ministry (of Hungary), 18, 252, 353, 421, 425

Fundamental Law, 3, 9–26, 31–32, 42, 81–82, 98, 100, 102–3, 107–8, 126, 186–87, 222, 225, 229–30, 232–33, 237–38, 322, 383, 397, 410, 413, 416

Garancsi, István, 283, 412

gender, 16, 58, 144, 166, 170, 227–28, 231–32, 233, 236–37, 245, 381, 400; gender roles, 227, 231, 233, 236–37, 400; gender studies, 232–33, 247, 256, 263; LGBT rights, 228, 232, 263, 299–300, 365, 385

Germany, Germans, 32–33, 35–38, 40, 42–45, 68, 81, 96–97, 106, 118–19, 122, 124, 126, 130, 142, 146, 149, 152, 163, 164, 177, 190, 193, 195, 204, 218–19, 255, 292–93, 295, 317, 333, 345–46, 352, 388, 398–99, 401, 411, 413–14, 418, 421–22, 424, 426

GONGOs, 54–56, 382

"good society", 51, 228, 389

goulash communism, 401, 402, 405

government, 10–11, 13–25, 29–30, 32, 36, 38–40, 42–43, 46, 51–61, 64, 67–69, 73, 75–76, 78–80, 83–90, 98–99, 102–5, 108–9, 112–13, 116–17, 119–20, 122, 125–29, 139–42, 146–47, 149–50, 152, 154, 159–60, 168–76, 179, 185–95, 203, 205–7, 211–22, 225, 227, 229–34, 236, 238–39, 243, 245–64, 271–73, 277–83, 285, 291, 297–98, 300–301, 303, 307–8, 312–25, 327–28, 332–34, 336, 338, 341, 344–52, 354, 358–60, 362–68, 370, 372 , 374, 382–83, 386–91, 393, 396–400, 402–12, 415, 417–18, 421–26, 438

Gramsci, Antonio, 52, 178, 406

GYED (parental leave system), 142–45, 235

Gyurcsány, Ferenc, 21, 30, 56, 89, 214, 391, 407, 408

Habsburg Empire, 33, 64, 100, 413

Haider, Jörg, 1, 323–24

half-Asian people, 99, 421

Helsinki Committee, 61, 245

Hernádi, Zsolt, 191, 287

higher education, 69, 126, 165,170, 187, 231, 243–44, 246, 248–49, 251–53, 255–56, 258, 260, 263–65, 391

historical memory, 29–44, 73, 163, 371, 388, 413, 416, 426

historicization, 1, 32–33, 400–401

Hitler, Adolf, 45, 205, 321, 385

homelessness, homeless people, 153, 412, 423

homophobia, 237, 381

Holocaust, 33, 37–46, 297, 346, 403, 413

Holy Crown, 81, 98, 401, 405, 423

Horn, Gyula, 404

Horthy, Miklós, 31, 44, 46, 95, 99, 100, 127, 205, 238, 382, 384, 386, 401–2, 409, 413–14, 421

House of Fates, 41–42

House of Terror, 29, 41, 405, 426
housing, 18, 168–69, 199, 202, 235
human rights, 9, 16–18, 21, 56, 58, 61,
    66, 68, 102, 107, 161, 175–76, 195–
    96, 198, 200, 202, 245, 295, 312, 321
Hungarian Academy of Sciences, 30,
    126, 258, 417
Hungarians living outside of the border,
    16, 24, 39, 73–80, 82–89, 172, 365
Huxley, Aldous, 218, 380

ideology, 3, 11, 14–15, 23, 33, 38, 45,
    74, 80, 82–83, 91, 96–98, 107, 112,
    122, 160, 168, 170, 175, 178, 185,
    203–5, 216, 225–28, 230–32, 235–
    38, 243, 245, 273, 282, 291–95, 297,
    300, 304, 306, 309, 323, 339–41,
    343–44, 354, 358, 361, 363–66,
    368–71, 373, 380–82, 386–87, 389,
    393–94, 397–98, 400, 402–3, 413,
    415, 420
Ignatieff, Michael, 246
illiberal democracy, 1, 2, 10, 23, 51,
    59, 101, 105, 230, 269, 292, 297,
    323, 348, 382–83, 392, 423. *See also*
    liberalism
immigrants, 17, 56, 60, 62, 160–66,
    171–74, 177, 246, 253, 259, 293, 299
implosion, 416, 418–19
indoctrination, 394, 416, 419
inequality, 253, 272, 293
Institute for Human Sciences (IWM),
    3, 433
International Monetary Fund (IMF),
    117, 221, 372, 396, 408, 410
Interventionism, state intervention,
    112–13, 115, 117, 119–20, 123, 125,
    130, 147, 149, 179, 195, 382, 394,
    396, 401, 407, 410
Iohannis, Klaus, 365, 367, 369
India, 129, 155, 207, 321
Islam, Muslims, 99, 101, 105, 108, 177,
    414, 422
Israel, 60, 164, 217, 346, 414, 422

Jews, 39–46, 61, 69, 95–96, 101, 106,
    122–23, 126, 298, 300, 346, 352,
    354, 385, 413–14, 422; Jews in
    Hungary, 39–46, 95–96, 101, 106,
    122–23, 126, 385, 413–14, 422
Jobbik, 17, 56, 64–65, 220, 339, 409
judges, 19, 103, 108, 129, 220, 230,
    238, 258, 305, 315–16, 320, 385,
    400, 409
judiciary, 10–11, 13–14, 19, 78, 220,
    253–54, 313, 318, 323–24, 345, 348,
    391, 393, 395–96, 399, 409, 423

Kaczyński, Jarosław, 22, 186, 228, 288,
    324, 333–34, 345, 347, 349–50,
    353–54, 399
Kádár, János, 36, 384, 386, 388, 393–
    94, 401–2, 409, 414
Kertész, Imre, 41, 108
Kis, János, 78–79, 306, 421–23, 425
Keynes, John Maynard, 113, 120, 125,
    128–29, 410
Kopátsy, Sándor, 121, 123, 125, 128–29
Kornai, János, 120, 128, 186, 205,
    422–23
Kovács, Imre, 122, 124
Kövér, László, 84, 88, 91, 160, 168,
    170, 233, 421

Labor Law/Code, 140, 229, 382
labor market, 115, 139–43, 147–53,
    162–63, 170, 172–73, 175, 179,
    230–31, 235
lawfare, 383
liberalism, 1, 2, 29, 33–35, 51, 61–62,
    67–69, 74–75, 77–79, 89, 96–100,
    105–7, 109, 113, 116, 119–20, 122–
    24,126–27, 130, 186, 206, 212–14,
    221, 226, 245–46, 262, 269, 273,
    285–86, 292–305, 307, 309, 311–12,
    314–15, 318–27, 334, 336, 339, 341,
    347–48, 351–52, 361, 363, 366, 370–
    71, 374, 379–93, 397–409, 411–16,
    420–22, 424, 427

LMP (Politics Can Be Different), 59, 409

Magyar, Bálint, 205, 212, 217, 291–310, 320, 424
Magyar Gárda (Hungarian Guard), 64
market, 21, 51, 62, 88, 113, 115, 118–23, 127, 129, 139–41, 143, 147–53, 162–63, 168–70, 172–73, 175, 179, 186, 188, 193–95, 199–203, 206–7, 212, 215, 217–19, 230–31, 235, 261–62, 271, 281–82, 284, 286, 298, 307, 320, 326, 334, 352, 372, 381, 388, 390–91, 396, 398, 401, 406, 411, 415, 426–27
marriage, 16, 169, 232–33, 237, 239, 323, 365
Matolcsy, Mátyás, 114, 122–24, 130
Matolcsy, György, 86, 111–30, 217, 410–11
MDF (Hungarian Democratic Forum), 74–75, 213, 403–4, 407, 409, 421
media, 3, 11, 17–18, 21, 23, 42, 45, 55, 58–60, 63, 104, 146, 185, 199, 201, 203, 205, 211–24, 227, 233–34, 243, 249, 258, 262, 264, 275, 284, 316, 323–24, 336, 345, 348–49, 353, 380, 385, 389–91, 393, 395–97, 399–400, 405, 408–9, 411–12, 415, 421, 434
memory politics, 31, 426
Mészáros, Lőrinc, 204, 217–18, 284, 412, 426
Merkel, Angela, 317, 398
migration, migrants, 17–19, 60–61, 64, 66–68, 76, 80, 91, 99, 159–67, 171–77, 207, 218, 222, 246, 253, 299, 301, 323, 398–99, 416, 419–20; migration crisis, 60, 64, 66–68, 99, 159–61, 164–65, 299, 398. *See also* refugees
militarization, 382, 409
mobilization, political, 33, 42, 55, 60, 74, 79, 113, 118, 203, 220, 254, 258, 263–64, 336, 360–61, 365, 368–69,

372, 380, 388, 394–95, 405–6, 414–16, 419–20, 426
MOL (Hungarian oil and gas company), 191, 193, 207, 287
Momentum (political party), 20
monopoly, 56, 66, 87, 115, 170, 194, 201, 206, 211–12, 215–17, 220–21, 243, 270–71, 280, 281, 300, 364
Most–Híd (Hungarian–Slovak party), 76, 80
Mussolini, Benito, 65, 124, 170–71, 205, 388
MSZP (Hungarian Socialist Party), 29–31, 34, 56, 307 369, 404, 407. *See also* socialism
MVM (Hungarian Electricity Company), 56, 190, 206, 283

Nagy, Imre, 23, 31
National Avowal, 14–16, 81, 107, 232
National Bank, 10, 111–12, 118, 126–27, 130, 186, 188, 204, 217, 409–10, 421
National Consultation on the "Soros Plan", 19–20, 25, 159, 221–22, 253
National Consultation "Stop Brussels", 19, 25, 222, 327
nationalism, 1, 3, 29, 32, 34, 36–38, 42–43, 62–64, 66–67, 69, 74–78, 80, 83–84, 89–91, 100, 162, 167, 170–71, 174–79, 213, 226, 228–29, 231, 245, 296–98, 300–301, 311–12, 323, 326–27, 339, 341, 345, 349–50, 352, 354, 359, 364–66, 368–69, 371–72, 382, 387, 389–90, 398, 402, 404–6, 408, 412, 421–22; demographic nationalism, 162, 167, 171, 174, 177–78
nationalization (renationalization), 3, 62, 117, 185–95, 203–7, 230, 232, 236–37, 264, 272, 282, 284, 300, 313, 347, 382, 399, 410, 415
national minorities, 62, 66, 76, 78, 153, 296

national religion (*nemzetvallás*), 100
national unification, 73, 80
NATO, 185, 188, 203, 346, 349, 372, 399, 411, 414, 425
nazism, national socialism, 33, 35–38, 40–41, 65, 69, 81, 96, 114, 119, 122–24, 295–97, 300, 324, 354, 387, 422–23. *See also* neo-nazism
Németh, Zsolt, 75, 85
neocommunism, 359, 392. *See also* communism
neoconservatism, 113, 227–28, 392
neoliberalism, 34, 112–13, 115–16, 119–20, 125, 163, 226, 230, 358, 371–72, 381, 389, 392, 405, 410–11, 414
neo–feudalism, 121, 382, 392, 396
neo–nazism, 69, 324, 354
Netanyahu, Benjamin, 399, 413, 422
new rich, 299, 341
newspapers, 128, 189, 192, 217–18, 281, 316; *Népszabadság*, 217–19, 279, 282
nomenklatura, 340, 425
non–governmental organizations (NGOs), 17–18, 25, 57–62, 67–68, 104, 174, 178, 222, 243, 262–63, 300, 345, 361, 368, 374, 393, 399, 413, 415
Norway, 57–59, 69, 106, 171
Norway Grants, 57–59, 68, 69
Nowoczesna (Modern), 334–36, 339, 342–43, 353

Ökotárs, 57–61, 68, 69
oligarchy, oligarchs, 205, 207, 216–19, 221, 270–72, 276–77, 280, 282–84, 297, 320, 373, 379, 382, 384, 389–90, 395–96, 408, 411, 419, 421
Olympic Games, 2024 Budapest bid, 20
Open Society Foundations, 57, 61, 68
opposition, 9, 12, 17, 21, 24, 29, 41–42, 52, 75, 77, 100, 104, 108, 112, 119, 171, 173, 188, 191, 212–14, 216, 218, 222, 227, 233, 245, 255, 262, 264, 301, 303, 317, 324, 333,

336, 347–48, 350, 359–63, 365–66, 369–71, 382, 384, 389–92, 400–401, 403–5, 409–10, 412–13, 415–16, 424, 427
Orbán, Viktor, 1–3, 9–13, 16–18, 21–25, 29, 38–39, 43, 52, 55, 59, 64, 73–76, 80–82, 84–87, 89, 98–100, 108, 111–18, 121, 124–29, 139, 141, 143, 145–47, 150–51, 153–54, 159–62, 168–72, 174–79, 185–91, 193, 195, 203–7, 211–22, 226–29, 232, 236, 246, 249–50, 255, 279, 283–84, 291–301, 303–9, 314, 317–18, 322–24, 327, 345, 348–49, 358, 365, 369, 372, 379–401, 403–27; Orbánism, 1, 216, 297, 358, 400–401, 407, 413, 419, 425
Organisation for Economic Cooperation and Development (OECD), 139–44, 153, 185–86, 226, 233, 248–49, 259
"organized upperworld", 271–72, 274–76
Origo.hu, 125, 217, 219, 247–48, 260
ORTT (National Radio and Television Authority), 214–15
ownership, property, 21, 83, 88, 96, 115, 119–21, 123–24, 128–29, 185, 187–89, 191, 203–4, 206–7, 212, 269–71, 275–78, 281–84, 286, 293, 307, 348–49, 395–97, 423–24
Őszöd scandal, 407, 408

Palermo Protocols, 275, 286, 287
Parliament, 9–14, 17–25, 32, 39, 40, 53, 55, 60, 68, 74–76, 84, 87–89, 91, 95, 97–98, 100–104, 108, 118, 123, 126, 128, 160, 174, 185–88, 192, 194, 206, 213, 215, 218, 220, 229, 230, 233, 237, 239, 244, 248–53, 255, 258, 261, 263–64, 272, 277–79, 281–82, 284, 303, 312, 317–18, 321, 331–36, 338, 340–42, 344–45, 349–50, 352–53, 359–60, 362–69, 374–75, 383, 386, 389, 391, 397–99, 401, 405, 407, 412, 420–21, 423, 425

parliamentary democracy, 185, 391, 397. *See also* democracy

Party of Hungarian Coalition (PHC, Slovakia), 76, 80

patronage, patron-client relationship, 11, 21, 270, 272, 282, 286, 348, 357–75, 392, 424

Peace March (*Békemenet*), 55

pension system, 17, 19, 115, 117, 121, 141, 143–45, 164, 185, 187, 190, 206–7, 226–33, 236–38, 264, 284, 341–42, 396–97, 409, 415; private pension funds, 117, 189–90, 206, 229–30, 237, 264, 284

PiS (Law and Justice), 316, 333–36, 338, 340–41, 344–50, 352–54, 400, 424

PO (Civic Platform), 333–36, 339, 341–45, 350, 352–53

Poland, Poles, 22, 36, 37, 52, 57, 64, 100, 139, 149, 154–55, 160, 230, 287–98, 303, 308, 311, 313–16, 319, 321, 323–24, 326–28, 331–54, 400–401, 406 424–25

police, 25, 30, 56, 59, 64–65, 95, 121, 128, 214, 314, 391, 393, 402, 407–8, 414, 421, 427

political cleavages, 344, 358–59, 362, 367–69, 371–72, 386, 397, 403

political culture, 121, 296, 323, 351, 370, 386, 402, 406, 415

political entrepreneurship, 296

politics of history (historical politics), 29, 33–34, 36–38, 43–44, 121, 346, 405

politics of nation-building (*nemzetpolitika*), 74, 87

population policy (population replacement), 159, 167, 169–70, 174–75

populism, populists, 1, 9–10, 15, 23, 31, 35, 51, 62, 64, 74, 91, 100, 113–14, 122, 124, 130, 168, 204, 212, 221, 255, 264, 294, 298–301, 307, 332, 336, 339, 341, 348–49, 352, 370,

385–86, 390–92, 396–97, 399, 401, 403–7, 412, 420, 426–27, 437

post–communism, post–communist, 2, 30–32, 34–35, 41, 44, 64, 185–86, 193, 207, 221, 225–28, 231, 234, 236, 269–71, 286, 291–93, 296, 303, 305–6, 320, 341, 351, 357–58, 389, 392, 400, 404, 407, 419, 427. *See also* communism

poverty, 151, 295, 371, 385

private property, 119, 121, 123–24, 185, 271, 284, 293

privatization, 112, 116, 120, 121, 125, 163, 185–86, 188–89, 193–94, 204–6, 229, 269–71, 293, 297, 300, 340, 414

pronatalism, 143, 162, 168, 170, 175, 177–78, 231, 235, 417, 426

propaganda, 17, 19, 20, 53, 61, 85, 159, 211–22, 252, 255, 258–60, 263, 292, 295–96, 345, 390, 394, 398, 400, 420, 422

Protestantism, Protestants, 99, 100, 106, 108, 121, 128, 414

PSD (Social Democratic Party, Romania), 358, 360–71, 374

public opinion, 38, 161–62, 167, 169, 173, 188, 203, 212, 220, 258, 297, 332, 341, 347, 385

public works, 16, 83, 117, 140–41, 143–44, 146–48, 150–51, 155, 170, 175, 231, 235–36, 361, 382, 426. *See also* workfare

Putin, Vladimir (Putinism), 1, 193, 205, 207, 216, 219, 221, 228, 296, 299, 348, 372, 393, 411

Rawls, John, 380

Realpolitik, 379, 387, 390

referendum, plebiscite, 19–21, 25, 76–77, 79, 85, 172, 174, 222, 294, 297, 308, 324, 360, 367, 391–92, 397, 406, 408. *See also* national consultation

reform economists, 114, 119–21, 125–26, 128, 403

refugees (asylum seekers), 1, 12, 17–18,
    20, 60, 64, 67, 85, 99, 163–64, 173–
    76, 203, 219, 246, 262, 317, 323,
    372, 385, 391, 397–98, 423–24
1989 regime change, 2, 12, 14, 16, 22,
    24, 30–31, 33–35, 37–38, 74, 81, 85,
    95–96, 112, 119–21, 125, 163–64,
    166, 171, 186, 189, 191, 222, 225,
    238, 271, 293–95, 297–98, 306, 321,
    338, 347, 350, 358–59, 364, 366,
    369, 386, 389, 392, 394, 401–3, 405–
    7, 410, 412, 419, 421, 424, 427
religion, religious, 55, 62–63, 95–108,
    227–28, 236, 243, 292, 308, 347,
    358, 365, 371, 387, 389–91, 398,
    400, 402, 414, 421, 438. *See also*
    church
republic, 1, 16, 19, 69, 405, 408–9
reindustralization, 117
restrictions (economic), 114–16, 122,
    212, 396. *See also* austerity
revolution in the polling booth, 13–14,
    21, 387, 401, 409
Revolution of 1956, 30–31, 44, 65, 121,
    159, 214, 404, 418, 424
RMDSZ (Democratic Association of
    Hungarians in Romania, UDMR),
    79, 87, 365–66, 368–69
Roma, Romany, Gypsies, 17–18, 58,
    66, 69, 84, 153, 169, 173, 222, 234,
    236–38, 300, 371, 381, 385, 426. *See
    also* anti-Roma sentiments
Romania, Romanians, 36, 37, 57, 74–
    76, 78–80, 84–88, 95, 154–55, 161,
    163, 165–66, 187, 255, 314–15, 324,
    326,357–75, 399–401, 406, 413
rule of law, 1, 9, 11, 22–24, 60, 68, 101,
    119, 212, 245, 254, 272, 298–99,
    305, 312–16, 318–20, 322–23, 325–
    26, 349, 352, 381, 383, 391, 395,
    397, 401
Russia, Russians, 1, 53, 57, 60, 68, 100,
    187, 190–91, 193, 205, 215–16, 219,
    271, 296, 308, 354, 372, 398–400,
    406, 408, 411, 414, 425

Sargentini, Judit, 255
Second World War, 36–38, 42, 83, 96,
    160, 295, 346, 354, 363, 402, 413
Scheppele, Kim Lane, 328, 410
Schmidt, Mária, 29, 33, 38, 41, 43–44,
    46, 426
Schmitt, Carl, 385
Schöpflin, George, 78
separation of church and state, 95, 97,
    105–7, 381
Serbia, 1, 75, 78, 80, 85–87, 89, 161,
    164–65, 174, 187, 398, 413
Simicska, Lajos, 205, 213–20, 284, 408,
    412, 416, 421, 425
simulacrum, 126, 413–15
slot machines, 195, 201, 278, 280,
    283–84
Slovakia, Slovaks, 36, 37, 57, 75–76,
    78–80, 86–87, 89, 149, 151, 154–55,
    160, 317, 327, 399, 401–2, 407
Slovenia, 45, 115, 154, 399
Smallholders Party, 75, 123, 213,
    403–4, 420
social contract, 13, 52, 371, 401, 419
socialism, socialists, 29, 51, 53, 55–57,
    62, 67, 74–77, 79, 81, 85, 89, 113–
    14, 116, 119, 120, 122–25, 141–42,
    154, 163–65, 167–72, 188, 190–91,
    195, 204, 214, 218, 229, 238, 281,
    307, 317, 341, 369, 371, 387, 389,
    391, 394, 401–8, 410–11, 413–14,
    421, 423
socialist-liberal coalition, 75–76, 89,
    113, 116, 125, 195, 214, 229, 389,
    404, 407, 410, 414, 421
social market economy (*Soziale
    Marktwirtschaft*), 113, 119, 127, 381,
    388
social (welfare) policy, 16, 19, 25, 83,
    113, 116–17, 124, 140, 145, 151,
    167–68, 170, 177, 225–41, 381–82,
    394, 401–4, 406, 411–12, 418,
    437–38
Solidarity (Solidarność), 52, 346, 347
Sólyom, László, 13, 408, 410

Sonderweg (special road), 124, 401
Soros, George, 17–21, 25, 60–61, 68,
  159, 174, 207, 216–17, 221–22, 233,
  244–47, 249, 253–55, 259–61, 263–
  64, 295, 370–71, 386, 399–400, 415,
  420, 422, 424; "Soros Plan," 19–20,
  25, 159, 221–22, 253; "Stop Soros,"
  18, 61, 174, 222, 263. *See also* CEU
Soviet Union, 33, 36, 37, 75, 82, 130,
  159, 163, 165, 173, 212, 244, 271,
  295, 306, 402, 406
Spéder, Zoltán, 204
Stalinism, Stalinist, 14, 35, 36, 45, 385,
  409, 418
state, 1–3, 10, 14, 23, 29–32, 36, 38–40,
  51, 53–59, 62–64, 66, 68, 74–76,
  78, 80–86, 88–91, 95–107, 109, 112,
  115–30, 139–40, 144, 149, 154–55,
  160–62, 164–65, 167–68, 172, 177–
  79, 185, 187–88, 190–94, 198, 201–
  7, 211–22, 225–27, 229–34, 236–38,
  245, 257–58, 260, 264, 269–288,
  291–92, 294, 296, 298–301, 303,
  305–8, 311–28, 331–32, 345–48,
  352–53, 357–61, 364, 367, 371,
  373, 381–82, 385, 389–90, 392–96,
  399–403, 405, 408–16, 420–22, 425–
  26, 434–37; caring state, 231, 237;
  criminal state, 269–310; mafia state,
  269–310; parasite state, 271
state of emergency (*Ausnahmezustand*),
  25, 364, 397
statist, étatist, 112, 119, 130, 226,
  228, 230–31, 237, 341, 390, 394,
  407, 412
Status Law, 76–78, 86, 91, 164, 172
strike, 31, 140, 218, 397, 416
students, 142, 145, 152–53, 155, 175,
  179, 243–45, 250, 254–56, 259–62,
  342, 385, 414, 417
Suez Environment Co., 192–93
supply side revolution, 331–54
Surgutneftegaz (Russian gas company),
  191, 193
Szájer, József, 421

SZDSZ (Alliance of Free Democrats,
  Hungary), 206, 222, 307, 386, 403–4
Szima, Gábor, 279, 280
System of National Cooperation (SNC),
  1–3, 13, 14, 24, 29, 52, 74, 82–84,
  87, 89, 99, 113, 153, 225–28, 232,
  236, 238, 305, 379–88, 391–401,
  412–27; SNC as garlic, 416; SNC
  knights, 384, 398, 418, 427

tax, 17–19, 21, 31, 59, 61, 69, 83, 101,
  104, 106–7, 113, 115, 117–18, 124,
  126, 140, 143–44, 149, 155, 167–69,
  193–94, 197–201, 203, 207, 211,
  218, 220–22, 229, 232, 234–35,
  238–39, 269, 272, 277–85, 307–8,
  320, 333, 340–41, 381, 395–96,
  407, 410–11, 414–15, 417–18, 422,
  425–26; income tax, 19, 69, 104,
  113, 117, 126, 140, 143, 207, 218,
  232, 235, 307–8, 333, 381, 407,
  410–11, 417–18, 426; tax on internet
  usage, 220
Tavares, Rui, 304, 328, 399, 424
technocracy, technocrats, 316, 323,
  325–26, 351, 358–59, 361, 366–68,
  370, 372, 380, 402–3, 405, 409, 414
terrorism, 60, 160–62, 177, 349
Third Way, 113, 122, 124, 402, 407
tobacco monopoly, 170, 194, 197, 199,
  201, 281–84, 307, 422
tolerance, toleration, 51, 95, 98–99,
  105–6, 293, 325, 327, 357, 420, 422
Torgyán, József, 213, 403
totalitarianism, 29–46, 88, 218, 221,
  243, 392–93, 413, 416, 427
trade union, 64, 113, 140, 149, 228,
  359, 411
tradition, traditionalism, 35, 39, 55, 63,
  65, 75, 82, 89, 98, 100–101, 106,
  125, 160–61, 169–70, 176, 226–28,
  231–33, 236–38, 272, 277, 291–92,
  295, 308, 340–41, 346–47, 361–62,
  374, 380–82, 386, 389, 395, 399–
  402, 405, 414–16, 422

traditional family, 227–28, 232–33, 237–38, 400

transition, to democracy and capitalism, 2, 13–14, 22, 34–35, 51, 95–96, 120, 222, 270, 294, 297–99, 314, 321, 352, 358, 403, 407, 410, 427

transitology, 269, 298

Transparency International, 58, 245

Transylvania, Transylvanism, 63–64, 75–76, 95, 292, 297, 382, 412

Trianon, treaty of, 32, 64, 73, 77, 296, 297, 402, 412

Trump, Donald, 1, 188, 251, 296–97, 400

Turkey, 1, 100, 105–6, 164, 382, 398, 414

Tusk, Donald, 333

two-thirds majority, 9–10, 12, 20, 25, 73, 96, 98, 101, 104, 109, 186–87, 206, 213, 215, 239, 364

Ukraine, 75, 80, 86, 87, 97, 161, 165, 187, 221, 399, 411

unemployment, 83, 129, 140–43, 146, 148, 150, 153–54, 163, 185, 187, 226, 231, 234–35, 238, 333

universities, 17, 40, 52, 61, 69, 111–12, 127, 129, 142, 144, 152, 179, 198, 233, 243–66, 348, 417, 420. *See also* CEU

unorthodox economic policy, 3, 80, 111–14, 116–17, 120, 126, 195, 396–97, 410

United States of America, 31, 45, 53, 56, 68, 101, 125, 151, 164, 176, 187–88, 194, 218, 227, 244–54, 256–63, 265, 282, 294–95, 299, 308, 318, 400, 411, 420, 422

urbanites and populists, 386, 403

Vajna, Andy, 217–18, 279–80

Venice Commission, 9, 18, 104, 251–52, 257–59, 319, 322, 345

Veritas Research Institute for History, 30, 31, 44

violence, 58, 62, 66, 160, 212, 272, 275, 277, 285, 295, 300–301, 364, 380, 394

Visegrad Group, 108, 160, 176, 178

Vona, Gábor, 65

vocational training, 85, 140, 142, 144–45, 152–53

Weber, Manfred, 424

welfare state, 1, 140, 225–26, 238, 381, 402

Westernization, 34, 297, 373, 386

Willkommenskultur, 160, 398

women, 58, 63, 139

work-based society, work-based state, 124, 139, 143, 145, 150, 155, 166, 229–35, 237, 319, 347, 350, 398, 417

workers, 83–84, 117, 142–43, 146, 150–51, 154, 164, 170, 176–77, 198, 235, 237, 293, 342, 382, 411, 415

workfare, 3, 54, 151, 153–54, 299, 411–12, 426

World Bank, 155, 229

xenophobia, 77, 172, 222, 245, 292, 294, 296, 299, 332, 336, 344, 372, 398, 415

youth, 34, 35, 45, 86, 139, 142–43, 153, 163, 194, 293, 334, 342, 359, 403–4, 412–13

Zeitgeist, 296, 299

About the Editors and Contributors

János Mátyás Kovács is senior member at RECET, Institute of East European History, University of Vienna; permanent fellow emeritus at the Institute for Human Sciences (IWM), Vienna; and senior lecturer at the Department of Economics, Eötvös Loránd University, Budapest. His research fields include history of economic thought in Eastern Europe, history of communist economies, political economy of postcommunist capitalism, economic cultures after communism, and institutional economics. Currently, he runs a long-term research project "Between Bukharin and Balcerowicz. A Comparative History of Economic Thought under Communism." He is the editor of *Reform and Transformation: Eastern European Economics on the Threshold of Change* (1992, with Márton Tardos); *Transition to Capitalism? The Communist Legacy in Eastern Europe* (1994); *Capitalism from Outside? Economic Cultures in Eastern Europe after 1989* (2012, with Violetta Zentai); and *Populating No Man's Land: Economic Concepts of Ownership Under Communism* (2018).

Balázs Trencsényi is professor in the History Department of Central European University, Budapest, and codirector of Pasts, Inc. Center for Historical Studies. His main field of interest is the history of modern political thought in East Central Europe. Between 2008 and 2013, he was principal investigator of the ERC project, *"Negotiating Modernity": History of Modern Political Thought in East Central Europe.* Among others, he is the author of the monograph *The Politics of "National Character": A Study in Interwar East European Thought* (2012), and coauthor of *A History of Modern Political Thought in East Central Europe*, Vols. I–II (2016, 2018).

Gábor Egry is director of the Institute of Political History, Budapest, and principal investigator of the ERC Consolidator Grant project, "Negotiating Post-imperial Transitions: From Remobilization to State Consolidation: A Comparative Study of Local Transition in Post-Habsburg East and Central Europe." His main interests are nationalism, everyday ethnicity, and the politics of memory in modern East Central Europe. He is, among others, the author of the article "Unholy Alliances? Language Exams, Loyalty, and Identification in Interwar Romania," *Slavic Review* 76:4 (2017), and the monograph *Etnicitás, identitás, politika. Magyar kisebbségek nacionaliz-mus és regionalizmus között Romániában és Csehszlovákiában 1918–1944* [Ethnicity, identity, politics. Hungarian minorities between nationalism and regionalism in Romania and Czechoslovakia 1918–1944] (2015).

Zsolt Enyedi is professor in the Political Science Department of Central European University. He (co)authored two and (co)edited eight volumes and published numerous articles and book chapters, mainly on party politics and political attitudes. His articles appeared in journals such as *European Journal of Political Research, Political Studies, Political Psychology, West European Politics, Party Politics, Europe-Asia Studies, Perspectives on Politics,* and *European Review.* He was the 2003 recipient of the Rudolf Wildenmann Prize and the 2004 winner of the Bibó Award. He held research fellowships at the Woodrow Wilson Center, Notre Dame University, NIAS, EUI, and Johns Hopkins University.

Gábor Halmai is professor and chair of comparative constitutional law at the European University Institute (EUI) in Florence. He is also director of graduate studies in the Law Department. His primary research interests are comparative constitutional law and international human rights. He has published several books and articles, as well as edited volumes in English, German, and Hungarian. He joined the EUI after a teaching and research career (at Eötvös Loránd University in Budapest and Princeton University), as well as years as chief advisor to the president of the Hungarian Constitu-tional Court, member of the EU Fundamental Rights Agency's Management Board, and numerous other civic activities. His latest book, *Perspectives on Global Constitutionalism,* deals with the use of foreign and international law by domestic courts.

Miklós Haraszti is a Hungarian author, professor, and human rights pro-moter. He was a founder of Hungary's human rights and free press movement in the 1970s, and member of Parliament in the 1990s. From 2004 to 2010, he served as the OSCE Representative on Freedom of the Media. From 2012 to

2018, he was UN Special Rapporteur on human rights in Belarus. Recently, he headed several OSCE/ODIHR international election observation missions. He has taught at several universities, including Columbia University and Central European University, Budapest. He is a fellow at the Center for Media, Data and Society in CEU's School of Public Policy, and director of research on human rights at CEU's Center for European Neighborhood Studies.

Stephen Holmes is professor of law at New York University School of Law. After receiving his PhD from Yale in 1976, Holmes taught briefly at Yale and Wesleyan universities before becoming a member of the Institute for Advanced Study at Princeton University in 1978. He later taught at Harvard University, the University of Chicago, and Princeton before joining the law faculty at NYU in 2000. He was named a Carnegie Scholar in 2003–2005 for his work on Russian legal reform. Besides numerous articles on the history of political thought, democratic and constitutional theory, state building in post-communist Russia, and the war on terror, Holmes has written several books including *The Cost of Rights: Why Liberty Depends on Taxes*, coauthored with Cass Sunstein (1998), *The Matador's Cape: America's Reckless Response to Terror* (2007), and *The Beginning of Politics*, coauthored with Moshe Halbertal (2017), and *The Light that Failed. A Reckoning*, coauthored with Ivan Krastev (2019).

János Köllő is an economist affiliated with the Institute of Economics of the Hungarian Academy of Sciences. Previously he held research scholarships at Collegium Budapest – Institute for Advanced Study and the University of Michigan, and a part-time research job at the CEU. His research is mostly focused on the labor market, education, and regional inequalities. Besides academic research, he was involved in several projects of the International Labour Organization, the World Bank, and United Nations Development Programme. He is fellow of IZA (Institute of Labor Economics, Bonn), and member of the Academia Europaea. He currently heads the Data Bank of the Institute of Economics, which provides access to the largest collection of data for social science research in Hungary.

Ferenc Laczó is assistant professor in modern and contemporary European history at Maastricht University. He is the author of three books, including *Hungarian Jews in the Age of Genocide: An Intellectual History, 1929–1948* (2016), as well as the editor of several volumes, most recently *Catastrophe and Utopia: Jewish Intellectuals in Central and Eastern Europe in the 1930s and 1940s* (2017, with Joachim von Puttkamer). His main research interests lie in political and intellectual history, Central and Eastern Europe in the twentieth century, and Holocaust and genocide studies.

Bálint Magyar is a sociologist and liberal politician. His book, *Post-Communist Mafia State*, was translated into English, Russian, Bulgarian, and Polish. Before the regime change, he was a human right activist of the anti-communist opposition movement. He was one of the founders and leaders of the Alliance of Free Democrats (SZDSZ). Between 1988 and 1990, he took part in the negotiations about the peaceful transition. He served as an MP (1990–2010), as a minister of education (1996–1998, 2002–2006), and as a board member of the European Institute of Innovation and Technology (2008–2012). Since 2010, he is senior researcher of the Financial Research Institute. Recently, he was senior fellow of the Institute of Advanced Studies at the CEU.

Radosław Markowski is professor of political science and director at the Center for the Study of Democracy, University of Social Sciences and Humanities Warsaw, PI of the Polish National Election Study, and recurrent visiting professor at CEU, Budapest. He specializes in comparative politics, democratization, party systems, and electoral studies. He has published many studies in, among others, *Electoral Studies*, *Party Politics*, *Political Studies*, and *West European Politics*. His books include *Post-Communist Party Systems* (1999, with Herbert Kitschelt), *Europeanising Party Politics?* (2011, coeditor with Paul G. Lewis), and *Democratic Audit of Poland* (2015, with M. Kotnarowski et al.). He is also an expert of the Varieties of Democracy (V-Dem), Bertelsmann SGI project, and Dahrendorf Forum at the Hertie School of Governance

Silvia Marton is assistant professor in the Faculty of Political Science, University of Bucharest, and associate researcher at the Centre Norbert Elias (France). Since 2009, she coorganizes the focus-group "Political and Social History of the 18th and 19th Century" at the New Europe College, Bucharest. Since 2012, she coordinates the research direction "Metamorphosis of Democracy" within the CeReFrEA-Villa Noel at the University of Bucharest. She is currently member of the CNRS-funded European GDRI-network "Politics and Corruption: History and Sociology." Her research is focused on the history and politics of corruption as well as the processes of nation- and state-building in Eastern Europe. Her recent publications include the coedited book *Moralité du pouvoir et corruption en France et en Roumanie, XVIIIe-XXe siècle* (2017, with F. Monier and O. Dard).

Attila Melegh is a sociologist, economist, and historian. He is associate professor at Corvinus University, Budapest, and senior researcher at the Demographic Research Institute. He has taught in the United States, Russia, Georgia, and Hungary. His research focuses on the global history of social change in the twentieth century, and international migration. He was the project leader of "Managing Migration and Its Effects in South-East Europe: Transnational Actions Towards Evidence-Based Strategies" in the EU program SEEMIG. He is author of the book *On the East/West Slope, Globalization, Nationalism, Racism and Discourses on Central and Eastern Europe* (2005). He is the founding director of Karl Polányi Research Center at Corvinus University.

Péter Mihályi is professor in the Macroeconomics Department of Corvinus University of Budapest and visiting professor in the Department of Economics and Business of Central European University. His main fields of research are linked to the economic aspects of the regime changes, such as privatization, healthcare reform, pension reform, and the introduction of the Euro. His scholarly works include a two-volume monograph on Hungarian privatization, *A magyar privatizáció enciklopédiája* [Encyclopedia of Hungarian Privatization] (2010).

Virág Molnár is associate professor of sociology at the New School for Social Research. Her research explores the intersections of culture, politics, social change, and knowledge production in Eastern Europe, with special focus on urban culture, the built environment, and material culture. She has written about the relationship between architecture and state formation in socialist and post-socialist Eastern Europe, post-1989 reconstruction of Berlin, and the new housing landscape of post-socialist cities. Her book *Building the State Architecture, Politics, and State Formation in Postwar Central Europe* (2013) received the 2014 Mary Douglas Prize from the American Sociological Association. Her current work examines the role of civil society and consumer culture in the rise of radical populism in contemporary Hungary.

Jan-Werner Müller is professor of politics at Princeton University where he also directs the project in the history of political thought. His previous books include *Another Country: German Intellectuals, Unification and National Identity* (2000); *A Dangerous Mind: Carl Schmitt in Post-War European Thought* (2003); *Constitutional Patriotism* (2007); *Contesting Democracy: Political Ideas in Twentieth-Century Europe* (2011); *What Is Populism?* (2016). He also writes for the *Guardian*, the *London Review of Books*, and *The New York Review of Books*.

Dorottya Szikra is head of the research department and senior researcher at the Hungarian Academy of Sciences, Centre for Social Sciences. Her main research field is welfare state development in Central and Eastern Europe.

She has recently accomplished a comparative monograph together with Tomasz Inglot and Cristina Raţ on family policy transformations since 1945 in Poland, Hungary, and Romania. Since 2016, she has acted as the cochair of the European Social Policy Analysis Network (ESPAnet). In 2016, she served as the Marie Jahoda Visiting Chair in International Gender Studies at Ruhr University, Bochum, Germany.

Renáta Uitz is professor of law and chair of the Comparative Constitutional Law Program in the Department of Legal Studies at the Central European University. Her research interests are in comparative constitutional law, with a focus on transition to and from constitutional government, questions of personal autonomy and equality, including religious liberty and sexual autonomy. Most recently she coauthored *The Constitution of Freedom: An Introduction to Legal Constitutionalism* (2017, with András Sajó), and edited *Arguments That Work: Strategies, Contexts and Limits in Constitutional Law* (2013); *Religion in the Public Square: Perspectives on Secularism* (2014); and *Freedom and Its Enemies: The Tragedy of Liberty* (2015).

Balázs Váradi is a Hungarian economist and public policy analyst. He was senior policy adviser to the prime minister of Hungary between 2007 and 2008. He teaches political economy and public economics at Eötvös Loránd University, Budapest, and, in 2008, he was one of the founders of the Budapest Institute for Policy Analysis, an independent think tank, where he has been in charge of policy design and evaluation efforts for international, European, and domestic clients in the fields of social, education, and health policy.